MAYA WORLDVIEWS AT CONQUEST

MAYA WORLDVIEWS AT CONQUEST

UNIVERSITY PRESS OF COLORADO

edited by
Leslie G. Cecil &
Timothy W. Pugh

Published by the University Press of Colorado
5589 Arapahoe Avenue, Suite 206C
Boulder, Colorado 80303

 The University Press of Colorado is a proud member of
the Association of American University Presses.

The University Press of Colorado is a cooperative publishing enterprise supported, in part, by Adams
State College, Colorado State University, Fort Lewis College, Mesa State College, Metropolitan State
College of Denver, University of Colorado, University of Northern Colorado, and Western State
College of Colorado.

∞ The paper used in this publication meets the minimum requirements of the American National
Standard for Information Sciences—Permanence of Paper for Printed Library Materials. ANSI
Z39.48-1992

Library of Congress Cataloging-in-Publication Data

Maya worldviews at conquest / Leslie G. Cecil and Timothy W. Pugh, Editors.
   p. cm. — (Mesoamerican worlds)
  Includes bibliographical references and index.
  ISBN 978-0-87081-945-2 (hardcover : alk. paper) 1. Maya philosophy. 2. Mayas—Religion. 3.
Mayas—Civilization. 4. Mayas—Antiquities. 5. Mayas—Rites and ceremonies. 6. Mayas—First
contact with Europeans. I. Cecil, Leslie G. II. Pugh, Timothy W.
  F1435.3.P5M39 2009
  972.81'02—dc22

                                                         2009013373

Design by Daniel Pratt

18 17 16 15 14 13 12 11 10 09   10 9 8 7 6 5 4 3 2 1

CONTENTS

vii   List of Figures

xi   List of Tables

xiii   Foreword by Florine Asselbergs

xvii   Preface

1   **CHAPTER 1**   *Leslie G. Cecil*
Introduction

17   **CHAPTER 2**   *Elizabeth Graham*
Close Encounters

39   **CHAPTER 3**   *William M. Ringle*
"In Recalling Things Past, I Strengthen My Heart":
Accommodating the Past in Early Colonial Yucatán

61   **CHAPTER 4**   *Prudence M. Rice*
Time, History, and Worldview

83   **CHAPTER 5**   *Gabrielle Vail*
Cosmology and Creation in Late Postclassic Maya
Literature and Art

111   **CHAPTER 6**   *Andrea Stone*
Colonial Cave Art in the Northern Maya Lowlands: The
Dark Side of the Maya Worldview after the Conquest

135   CHAPTER 7   *John F. Chuchiak IV*
De Descriptio Idolorum: An Ethnohistorical Examination of the
Production, Imagery, and Functions of Colonial Yucatec Maya Idols and
Effigy Censers, 1540–1700

159   CHAPTER 8   *Miguel Astor-Aguilera*
Mesoamerican Communicating Objects: Mayan Worldviews Before,
During, and After Spanish Contact

183   CHAPTER 9   *Susan Milbrath and Carlos Peraza Lope*
Clash of Worldviews in Late Mayapán

205   CHAPTER 10   *Shankari Patel*
Religious Resistance and Persistence on Cozumel Island

219   CHAPTER 11   *Diane Z. Chase and Arlen F. Chase*
Changes in Maya Religious Worldview: Liminality and the
Archaeological Record

239   CHAPTER 12   *Leslie G. Cecil*
Kowoj Worldview: A View from Tipu

261   CHAPTER 13   *Joel W. Palka*
Agency and Worldviews of the Unconquered Lacandon Maya

279   CHAPTER 14   *Mark Howell*
Music Syncretism in the Postclassic K'iche' Warrior Dance and the
Colonial Period Baile de los Moros y Cristianos

299   CHAPTER 15   *Robert S. Carlsen*
Footpath of the Dawn, Footpath of the Sun: Maya Worldviews at Lake
Atitlán

317   CHAPTER 16   *Timothy W. Pugh*
Maya Sacred Landscapes at Contact

335   References Cited
407   List of Contributors
413   Index

5	**1.1**	Map of major locations mentioned in volume
41	**3.1**	Map of the principal native provinces at the time of the conquest
42	**3.2**	Map of the Cehpech province
44	**3.3**	Genealogy of the principal figures in the Chac Xulub Ch'en chronicle
68	**4.1**	The Maya concept of time as a burden borne by gods
73	**4.2**	Calendars of the Maya area in the sixteenth century A.D.
88	**5.1**	Tun mural, east half of the north wall, Santa Rita Mound 1
90	**5.2**	Pages 34b–35b of the Dresden codex
91	**5.3**	Emergence of deities from serpents and other creatures from the Madrid codex
92	**5.4**	Page 61 of the Dresden codex serpent pages
95	**5.5**	Lower register of the Dresden year-bearer pages (Dresden 25c–28c)
97	**5.6**	K'atun 13 Ahaw illustrated on Paris 3
100	**5.7**	Flood scenes of the Dresden codex and the Temple of the Fisherman Mural
102	**5.8**	Page 46 of the Dresden Venus table
103	**5.9**	Page 22 of the Paris codex
106	**5.10**	Creation imagery associated with a quadripartite structure of the world

FIGURES

114 **6.1** Comparison of Colonial double- and single-headed eagles

118 **6.2** Cave drawings of Colonial personification heads

119 **6.3** Yucatecan Colonial manuscripts with personification heads

121 **6.4** Cave drawings of turtle-ajaws

123 **6.5** Cave drawings of horses and riders

125 **6.6** Cave drawings with Colonial-style traits

127 **6.7** Colonial figural drawings

128 **6.8** Illustration from folio 113 of the *Chilam Balam of Kaua*

138 **7.1** Ceramic Maya effigy censers

143 **7.2** Map showing major stone and clay "image cults" uncovered during the Colonial period, 1563–1813

145 **7.3** Details of possible tun or stone idol images from the Maya codices

146 **7.4** Maya figures cutting and carving wooden idols or masks

147 **7.5** Maya deity-priest making an offering to what may be a clay deity image or censer from the Madrid codex

148 **7.6** Clay "idols"/god images and typical clay effigy censers

149 **7.7** Map showing the distribution of censer forms at Maya sites

166 **8.1** Postclassic Yukatek Ah Muzencab

167 **8.2** K'axob Preclassic quadripartite-cross vessel

169 **8.3** Chipicuaro Preclassic cup

172 **8.4** Classic Palenque Temple 14 k'awil bundle

175 **8.5** Modern Yukatek-Mayan communicating skeletal bundle

177 **8.6** Modern Yukatek-Mayan communicating cross

185 **9.1** Map of Mayapán

188 **9.2** Mayapán's Q151, the Hall of Chac Masks

188 **9.3** Mayapán's Q162 pyramid

189 **9.4** Mayapán's Q152 Round Temple

191 **9.5** Chen Mul Modeled effigy censer from Mayapán representing Chac

197 **9.6** Temple of the Fisherman

199 **9.7** Hall of Sun Disks

211 **10.1** Seventeen-year-old Lord 8 Deer performing cave rituals

211 **10.2** Pilgrimage to the Sun Oracle

213 **10.3** Cenote adjacent to the oracle shrine of San Gervasio

214 **10.4** Chen Pita Cave

215 **10.5** Xcaret Cave Temple

222 **11.1** Carved wooden lintel from Temple 1 at Tikal

224 **11.2** Late Postclassic figurine cache set in the fill of Santa Rita Corozal Structure 213

228 **11.3** Late Classic stucco building frieze from Caracol Structure B16-2nd

229 **11.4** Carved stone vessel from Early Classic tomb at Santa Rita Corozal

231 **11.5** Late Classic carved stone Stela 7 from Machaquila, Guatemala

232 **11.6** Stela 18 from Caracol, Belize

233 **11.7** Altar 1 from Zacpetén, Guatemala

234 **11.8** Ceramic vessel from Uaxactún, Guatemala

235 **11.9** Late Postclassic cache from Santa Rita Corozal Structure 37

240 **12.1** Map of Postclassic archaeological sites in the central Petén lakes region and the possible corridor between Tipu and Nojpeten (Tah Itza)

243 **12.2** Complex I and Historic structures at Tipu, Belize

246 **12.3** Complex I, Tipu, Belize

253 **12.4** Kowoj technological style pottery

255 **12.5** Principal component plots of strong-acid digestion ICP-MS analysis of Postclassic slipped wares

256 **12.6** LA-ICP-MS elemental concentration bivariate plots of exterior slips

262 **13.1** Map of the Lacandon region with modern settlements and archaeological sites

270 **13.2** Lacandon trade goods from El Caobal, Petén, Guatemala

273 **13.3** Lacandon god pot, El Mangal, Petén, Guatemala

274 **13.4** Tlaloc iconography

276 **13.5** Lacandon god pots

285 **14.1** Dancing warrior at K'umarkaj

286 **14.2** Cobán *Moros* procession

288 **14.3** Distribution of conquest dance-plays in Guatemala

290 **14.4** Framed aperture shown on a four-holed tubular flute

292 **14.5** Goiter flute with bat-head goiter

294 **14.6** Drummer with other musicians, Lubaantún

302 **15.1** Maximón hung from a post adorned with willow branches

305 **15.2** Map of the Footpath of the Sun, Footpath of the Dawn

307 **15.3** Holy Week procession of Maximón

310 **15.4** *Nabeysil* dancing the Martín bundle

311 **15.5** Preconquest jaguar stone, Tigre, of the Cofradía Ch'eep San Juan

43 **3.1** Selected versions of the Pech chronicles

49 **3.2** Christian calendar correlations of k'atun cycles in the Books of Chilam Balam

70 **4.1** Comparison of Classic, Postclassic, and Colonial calendars used in the Maya lowlands

186 **9.1** Mayapán's history in relation to the k'atun cycle

250 **12.1** Petén Postclassic slipped wares: Groups, types, and varieties

281 **14.1** Highland Guatemalan music instrument and dance-play classification

Florine Asselbergs

People see and interact with the world based on their knowledge, ideas, and beliefs—their worldview. A worldview translates the world into an understandable model that explains why things are as they are, what is true and what is false, what one should do or not do, and how things can be achieved. It also includes ideas and beliefs about the world's origin and future and influences how one interacts and communicates with others and with one's surroundings. Worldviews may be adapted when knowledge, ideas, and beliefs change, but generally they are deep-rooted in the human mind.

In the 1520s, Spanish conquistadors started invading Maya lands. Preceded by stories of massacres and destruction and with the advantage of cavalry, better military technology, and the assistance of local allies, they defeated Maya armies effectively. As with many invading armies throughout history, they brought with them not only destruction but also new cultural traditions, which inspired the growth of a combination of European and indigenous cultures in Mesoamerica, transforming existing worldviews.

This book focuses on the effect of the Spaniards' arrival on a number of socio-political Maya groups in México, Belize, and Guatemala and illuminates how Maya worldviews were used and/or transformed as a result. For the Maya, the stories of massacres and destruction by Spanish hands had become reality, and their arrival brought about disorder and deprivation of riches, lands, and indigenous books containing ancient knowledge about calendars, genealogies, and sacred history. And it was not only the physical world that was affected: the

Spaniards forced the Maya to alter their rituals and daily practices by imposing on them a new socio-political, economic, and religious system. Although less effective than their military triumphs, the Spaniards' attempts to wipe out Maya religion and cosmology threatened Maya traditional knowledge, ideas, and beliefs that had thus far explained their world.

Throughout history, however, peoples have proven capable of recovering from periods of war and disequilibrium surprisingly rapidly, and the same applies to the Maya. The human mind is creative and flexible. Before the Spaniards' arrival, many Maya groups had already dealt with the arrival of other indigenous groups in their lands. Now they had to deal with the chaos caused by the Spanish conquistadors and their allies and create a new sense of order, certainty, and identity. Each Maya group dealt with these social crises differently. Some maintained their preconquest worldviews and emphasized their own traditions, whereas others adapted and started including European elements and new experiences into their stories and rituals. Yet others took over European elements or customs but encrypted in them preconquest moral, political, and/or religious messages. As Leslie Cecil states in Chapter 1, "each Maya social group had a unique solution to contact that resulted in as many different worldviews and different material cultures."

The editors of this book have brought together a wide group of scholars who have studied this process in general, and more specifically how Maya responses to Spanish-Maya contact are manifested in their material legacy. The authors use and analyze archaeological and epigraphic evidence from before, during, and after the conquest, some of which is presented here for the first time, and link preconquest customs and patterns to colonial practices and expression. They show us when ancient customs fused with European customs, when preconquest beliefs were kept alive through continuing patterns in indigenous communication and expression, and when new ideas and beliefs came into play. The result is a unique and rich overview of Maya responses to contact with the Spaniards.

The compilation of these data not only offers intriguing new perspectives about the Conquest period but more broadly it also provides new insights into the processes through which the Maya defined and redefined themselves when the world around them changed, whether through continuation or transformation or a combination thereof.

This book is therefore a valuable source of information for archaeologists, historians, anthropologists, and ethnographers who work in Maya territory, and especially for those interested in Spanish-Maya contact and the continuation of preconquest Maya customs, traditions, and beliefs. This book, however, is not only useful for specialists. Since it presents studies of a wide variety of aspects of Maya life, it provides useful introductions into each of these topics, from music and dances, religion, cosmology, and daily customs to cave art, ceramics, and writings.

Finally, the authors move the discourse forward on whether researchers are capable of defining an authentic worldview of another culture without projecting their own and introducing biases, and on how this problem can be addressed. This book teaches us not only about preconquest and colonial worldviews, the complexity of mental transformation when the world changes, and how the Maya dealt with this but also about how we deal with our own worldviews.

—Florine Asselbergs

Timothy W. Pugh

Most chapters of this volume emerged from papers presented in the session Maya Worldview at Conquest at the 69th Annual Meeting of the Society for American Archaeology in Montreal. Like many session organizers, Leslie Cecil and I had an axe to grind. Many conference papers, books, and journal articles posit that meaning is irrelevant and one should instead examine only practice. The essays of this volume clearly indicate the importance of practice, but they also demonstrate that practices occur in a meaningful world and impart significance into that world. Practice divorced from meaning is not a characteristic of practice theory—at least not that of Pierre Bourdieu, Michel Foucault, and Anthony Giddens. It is instead the latest manifestation of the eclipsing of the emic by the etic, a characteristic of cultural materialism. Hence, one of the contributions of this volume is to bring together the work of scholars who appreciate that meaning and practice are inseparable. The choice of the Maya at conquest as the focus of the volume has no remarkable explanation—it is the area of specialization of the two editors. Nevertheless, as the so-called World of Trade and Tribute, the Postclassic has been a favorite target of materialism. However, the Postclassic and particularly the Contact periods are the eras to which one can apply colonial Spanish and Maya descriptions of meaning as well as those of the codices with the greatest validity. A second contribution of this volume is to get beyond the overemphasis of the economy in studies of the Postclassic and Contact period Maya.

Most of the essays of this volume utilize the orthography of the Academia de Lenguas Mayas de Guatemala (ALMG) in the spelling of Maya words. Some authors diverge from ALMG as they wish to be consistent with colonial orthographies.

MAYA WORLDVIEWS AT CONQUEST

Introduction

CHAPTER ONE

Leslie G. Cecil

> It is not because thoughts are similar that we can evoke them; it is
> rather because the same group is interested in those memories, and
> is able to evoke them, that they are assembled together in our minds.
>
> CONNERTON 1989:37

As a result of research into Postclassic and Colonial Maya cultures, the
Maya area on the eve of Spanish contact/conquest can be described
as a series of dynamic socio-political alliances and dominance relations, changing religious cults, long-distance exchange, and migrations throughout the area rather than a region of "decline, decadence,
and depopulation" (A. Chase and D. Chase 1985:4). This holds true
for the Maya of the Yucatán peninsula and Chiapas of México, Belize,
and lowland and highland Guatemala. Many of these research programs have taken as their point of departure the various indigenous
"prophetic histories" known as the Books of Chilam Balam of multiple towns in northern Yucatán (Bricker and Miram 2002; Edmonson
1982, 1986; Roys 1933; among others) to reconstruct Postclassic,
Contact, and Colonial period (ca. A.D. 1200–1830) history in the
Maya lowlands.[1] In addition to these documents that record the histories of the diverse socio-political lineage groups, other important
sources of information are the records of early Spaniards in the area,
the best known of which is that of sixteenth-century Bishop Diego de
Landa (Tozzer 1941).

In the mid-sixteenth century, Bishop Diego de Landa identified
sixteen northern Yucatán states (Tozzer 1941:17–18), some headed

by different leaders (*cuchcabalob* or *kuchcabaloob'*). Each group is described as being a distinct social and/or political group (Roys 1957). During the Late Postclassic period (ca. A.D. 1200–1513), these provinces/territories were under the rule of the League of Mayapán, headed by the Xiws, the Kokoms, and the Canuls, although the Kokoms and Xiws dominated rule and are best documented in the ethnohistoric record (Ringle and Bey 2001; Roys 1972).

According to the *Chilam Balam of Maní*, in K'atun 2 Ajau (A.D. 751?), the Xiw (also Tutul-Xiw) arrived in the Pu'uc region from the west (the land of Tulapan) after stopping in Petén 500 years earlier; there they founded and governed Uxmal (Craine and Reindorp 1970:138–139; Restall 1998:141; however, see Kowalski 1987:56–68 for origins from Tabasco). They joined the Kokom/Itza as part of a *multepal* (joint rule) that ruled Mayapán. Munro Edmonson (1982:x, 24, 45–46) states that the Xiw controlled the western half of Yucatán and had a different ritual calendar from the Kokom/Itza.

The *Chilam Balam of Tizimin* states that the Kokom claimed to have come from Chich'en Itzá after two k'atuns of exile (Edmonson 1986; Roys 1962). The Itza lineage founded Mayapán and seated the *may* (a time period of thirteen twenty–year k'atuns or 260 *tuns* for which a capital city ruled over a given territory [Rice, this volume]) in K'atun 8 Ajau (ca. A.D. 1080–1104 or A.D. 1185–1204) (Milbrath and Peraza Lope 2003b). The Itza lineage of the Kokom ruled Mayapán for approximately 100 years and in A.D. 1362/82 a revolt brought a different Kokom lineage (the rival Itza) into power at Mayapán (Roys 1962:44–46; Tozzer 1941:26). However, problems soon arose for the Kokom as the Xiw revolted against them, resulting in the Kokom fleeing "by sea down the east coast, and . . . inland to Lake Petén Itzá" (Roys 1962:47). Edmonson (1986:58) also states that a migration occurred after the destruction of Mayapán and "they went to the heart of the forest—Chak'an Putun, Tan Xuluc Mul by name." Chak'an Putun is believed to be located in the territory of Chak'an Itza—the northwest quarter of Petén Itza territory (Jones 1998; Schele and Matthews 1998:204). As a result of the expulsions and revolts, Kokom rulership at Mayapán ended, Mayapán was destroyed, and nobles carried codices to, and built temples in, their homelands—the sixteen independent states (Roys 1962:47; Tozzer 1941:38, 98). Cultures at sites on the east coast and Belize had friendly ties with Mayapán (Kepecs and Masson 2003:43).

In the central Petén lowlands, ethnohistorical research has indicated that the Itza and Kowoj (as well as other sociopolitical groups) occupied territory in the region in the sixteenth and seventeenth centuries (Jones 1989, 1998). Spanish documents and Postclassic to Colonial period native histories of these groups (especially the Xiw and the Itza) record their presence, various alliances in Petén, as well as repeated movements to and from northern Yucatán. In the central Petén lakes region, the Itza controlled the southern and western basin of Lake Petén Itzá. Their Late Postclassic ruler, Kan Ek', claimed ancestry from Chich'en Itzá when it fell at approximately A.D. 1200 (Edmonson 1986; Jones 1998; Roys 1933). The Kowoj controlled the northeastern area of Lake Petén Itzá and the east-central Petén lakes (Jones 1998). They claimed to have migrated from Mayapán around A.D. 1530 (but see Cecil, this volume, for a discussion of earlier migrations) and were the guardians of the east gate of Mayapán (Roys 1933:79). To the west of the central Petén lakes region, the Lacandon escaped European contact until the nineteenth century. They lived in scattered settlements in Chiapas, México, but did have contact with other displaced (as a result of Spanish contact/conquest) Maya populations that included the Itza in Petén (Schwartz 1990). Additionally, the Cholan Maya lived in the Chiapas region before the Spanish Conquest. The Spaniards drove them out and the void was filled by the Lacandon Maya.

Other Maya socio-political groups (such as the K'iche' and the Kaqchikel) lived in the Guatemalan highlands to the south of the Maya lowlands. These groups, as well as others, established and maintained a number of independent states (Carmack 1981; Fox 1987). While maintaining regional capitals in the highlands, the K'iche' and Kaqchikel warred with each other until the Spanish Conquest. Highland Guatemala is still a stronghold for the Maya culture.

From this brief synopsis of the Maya at the time of Spanish contact, it is apparent that there were many different Maya ethnicities throughout México, Belize, and Guatemala. Not surprisingly, the ways that they constructed and understood their worlds was diverse. Consequently, how they dealt with and/or incorporated the contact/conquest experience(s) into their rituals, religions, and cosmologies was as varied.

Ritual, religion, and cosmology are essential components of Maya life and Maya worldviews that were affected by Postclassic (ca. A.D. 1200–1513) and Colonial (A.D. 1513–ca. 1830) period indigenous migrations and Spanish Conquest. Various Maya socio-political groups invented unique solutions to cope with "the other" resulting in the (re)shaping of cultural patterns that were established through and reinforced by daily practices and rituals. These modified or new traditions were chosen by the different Maya groups as "metonyms of identity" to which they could consciously attach material culture resulting in "authentic signs of true identity" (Upton 1996:5). Although there are pan-Mesoamerican characteristics describing "Mayaness" (Smith and Berdan 2003a; Robertson 1970; among others), responses to contact/conquest were quite varied, resulting in heterogeneous worldviews rather than a single Maya worldview. This volume presents a regional investigation of archaeological and epigraphic evidence of Maya ideology, landscape, historical consciousness, ritual practices, and religious symbolism before, during, and after the Spanish Conquest that illuminates aspects of Precolumbian Maya worldviews that survived the impact of the conquest as well as contact by other Mesoamerican cultures. The resulting "new" and varied worldviews were the product of processes of conversion, hybridization, resistance, and revitalization of their different social and political structures that were ultimately reinforced by daily and ritual practice.

The different social and political groups of the Maya and their worldviews described in this volume represent the Postclassic and Historic period Maya of México, Belize, and Guatemala (Figure 1.1). Each chapter presents a unique response to contact and conquest circumstances, their different ramifications on Maya worldviews, and the manner by which those responses were manifest in the material record. For example, some Maya incorporated aspects of the contact culture with their own, resulting in synchronism of multiple worldviews; whereas other Maya resisted the incorporation of the contact culture's worldviews into their own. What becomes apparent with each successive chapter is that each Maya social or political group had a unique solution to contact that resulted in as many different worldviews and different manifestations in the material record. Therefore, rather than attempting to present an all-encompassing Maya worldview, the authors present the different characteristics of Postclassic and Colonial Maya worldviews that resulted from the different responses to contact and conflict with other indigenous Maya groups and the Spanish.

As "culturally organized systems of knowledge" (Kearney 1975:248), worldviews provide people with a sense of place and confidence by taking ideas and beliefs from the past and (re)shaping the present and future (Heylighen 2000; Kearney 1984:5). Worldviews are culturally organized, typically by the elites (but see following), in that they are a collection of social memories and concepts that allow people (such as the various groups of Postclassic/Colonial Maya) to construct an image of the world that provides them with a basis to understand experiences (Heylighen 2000). Many of these accepted worldviews (re)created by the elite Maya (and other Maya) through practice also existed in an already-defined world in which they acted in a certain context (Friedman 1992). In order for that image to be reinforced, it must "depend on the expectations of the participants and the cultural values of the themes presented in these events as shaped in specific social and historical contexts" as well as be "generated and maintained through practice" (Inomata and Coben 2006:21, 25). Social rituals, one form of practice, (re)construct worldviews by creating and maintaining a community reality that "would be nothing without them, for it is impossible to have social relations without symbolic acts" because all performance is an interconnected series of actions across space and time (Douglas 1966:62; Gosden 1994). Through reenactment of the experiences with dances, rituals, the daily practice of making pottery, or providing offerings to personal deities, "remembering strengthens what has been recalled" because to (re)use or (re)enact involves (re)interpretation of the past instituting collective memories and frameworks of explanation—worldviews (Joyce 2003:107).

How people "see" the world in which they live and structure a meaning of that world largely depends on collective memories as well as what the individuals " 'know'

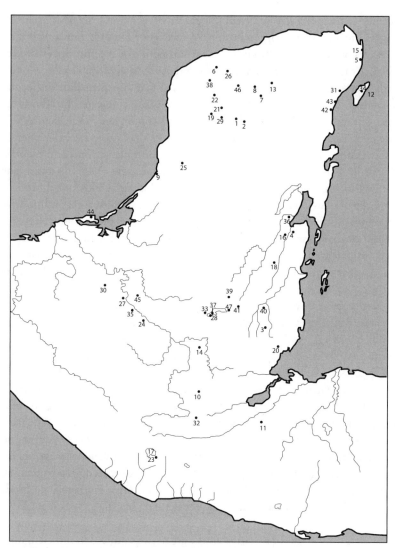

I.I. Map of major locations (archaeological and historic sites) discussed in the volume: (1) Actun Hom; (2) Actun Kaua; (3) Caracol; (4) Caye Coco; (5) Chacmool; (6) Chac Xulub Ch'en; (7) Chan Kom; (8) Chich'en Itzá; (9) Champoton; (10) Cobán; (11) Copán; (12) Cozumel; (13) Dzibichen; (14) El Caobal; (15) El Meco; (16) K'axob; (17) Lake Atitlán; (18) Lamanai; (19) Loltun; (20) Lubaantún; (21) Maní; (22) Mayapán; (23) Maya Santiago Atitlán; (24) Mensabak; (25) Mirimar; (26) Motul; (27) Najá; (28) Nojpeten; (29) Oxkutzcab; (30) Palenque; (31) Ppole; (32) Rabinal; (33) San Andres; (34) San Gervasio; (36) Santa Rita Corozal; (37) Tayasal; (38) Tihoo (TiHo); (39) Tikal; (40) Tipu; (41) Topoxté; (42) Tulum; (43) Xel-ha; (44) Xicalango; (45) Yaxchilán; (46) Yaxkukul; and (47) Zacpetén.

as 'reality' in their everyday . . . lives" (Berger and Luckmann 1967:15). Their reality is a dynamic interrelationship reflecting knowledge of the past that is replicated in the images of the past to legitimate a present ordering of the universe (Connerton 1989:3; Kearney 1984). When intergroup dynamics/worldviews shift, there is a "synthesis of imposed and adopted characteristics that [are] forged through contact and conflict. It is a role played for the benefit of others. Objects—buildings, dress, foods—are called on to prove that volatile and contingent social identities [and worldviews] are stable and intrinsic personal ones" (Upton 1996:4). Therefore, because people are constantly creating and recreating their world and their place in it, worldviews cannot be so rigid as to deteriorate with changing social, political, cosmological, and/or environmental milieus. Instead worldviews must be able to be altered, individually and collectively, as a result of historical conditions so as to serve their purpose—to provide a means by which people can understand their world in order to make decisions about the past, present, and future. Therefore, every worldview is a "temporary construction, a precipitation of a crystal from thoughts that from day to day are carried in the flowing solution of life's doings" (Redfield 1989:91).

Worldviews provide a sense of solidarity that results from collective performance, but they do not necessarily imply that all people are of a like mind (Durkheim 1933). As Takeshi Inomata (2006:210) aptly states, ritual events, or theatrical events, used for "ideological campaigns may have been an effective strategy for elites. This, however, does not deny the presence of those who were disinterested in, reluctant to, or opposed to participating in community events. Nor is it likely that all community members blindly subscribed to the elite version of ideology." Therefore, although the elites may have controlled the restructuring and practice of rituals, thus appearing to be the driving force of the dominant "new" worldviews and the recreating of a collective conscience, individuals have self interests and choices that may run up against the taken-for-granted, "ready-made standardized scheme of the cultural pattern" (Schutz 1964:95; Fischer 1999; Inomata and Coben 2006). The individual cannot be ignored, but the archaeological record often masks/misses these individual choices that may oppose the dominant ideologies because those items of material culture are not reproduced in sufficient quantities to appear to fit within the "accepted" worldviews.

An examination of Maya worldview(s) can provide insight into how they saw and structured their world, but when discussing the worldviews, researchers must ask whose worldview is being examined. Robert Redfield (1989), Michael Kearney (1984), and Elizabeth Graham (this volume) question that, although a worldview is an outlook on life that can have its own internal dynamics, are researchers capable of defining authentic worldviews or are the hypothesized worldviews merely reflections of the researchers' worldviews being imposed on the cultures being examined? The various authors of this volume present many different aspects of Maya worldviews (self, relationships, space, and time). The core similarities of how the Maya viewed their universe and their place within it allow the authors to present many different concepts of Maya life during the Postclassic and Colonial periods without introducing their own biases.

The Maya structured aspects of their world so as to allow them to understand how the world functioned and their place in it (Heylighen 2000). Faced with changing social, political, and environmental conditions, the Maya responded (overtly and subversively) by recalling their past histories and/or by creating new collective memories and histories. They then incorporated these events into their worldviews through performance (Meskell 2003). Through Maya ethnohistories (and other written records), idols and other forms of pottery, cave art, architecture, visual performances (such as dance and processions), and methods of recording time, researchers are better able to understand the various characteristics that were important to the Maya when constructing their worldviews during times of disequilibrium. These characteristics include how they defined themselves, their universe, and their past, present, and future.

Us versus Them: Setting Apart "the Other"

One place where adaptations/changes to Maya worldviews can be detected is in the need to securely situate a person with a given social or political group or elite status. This became important when the Spaniards imposed their social order (primarily through *reducciónes*) on the Maya communities, thus altering Maya social and political roles. Securing or reassigning social and/or political status was typically achieved by evoking ancestors, supernaturals, animals, architecture, history, and memories used to actively link individuals to a past, a powerful (or important) lineage, an apical ancestor of a kin group, or a significant built landscape.

Throughout Maya history, rulers ensured elite status through genealogical ties to various family lines and many times tied their ancestry to the founding lineage of an archaeological site. For example, Altar Q at Copán displays the unbroken link of ruler Yax Pasaj to the "founder" of Copán, K'inich Yax K'uk' Mo (Schele and Freidel 1990:figure 8.3). In the same vein, many of the Postclassic Books of Chilam Balam relate "genealogies" of Maya elites to various ancestral groups. William Ringle (this volume) demonstrates how the first generation of native leaders (such as Nakuk Pech) of the Cehpech province formulated a sense of self and place during social and political unrest and a time of identify loss. This was primarily accomplished through the incorporation of the Spanish Conquest into existing narratives of renewal; during the Conquest period, Maya agents walked with their ancestors, thus connecting the two events (past and present) as well as the two lineages. Miguel Astor-Aguilera (this volume) also demonstrates that Yukatek Maya called upon the ethos of their ancestors to establish social and political ties. This act was accomplished by "speaking" with their descendants through communicating bundles and talking crosses. These relationships and others were used to establish and continue political and religious connections to the ancestors as they were a classic means by which the Maya traced and established property, privilege, and authority (McAnany 1995:37).

Establishing and maintaining an identity also was important during the Postclassic and Colonial periods because of the constant social and political turmoil that existed as a result of migrating Maya socio-political groups and/or the presence of the Spanish. This was manifest in the style of architecture and pottery. Susan Milbrath and Carlos Peraza Lope (this volume) explain how Xiw (traditional, conservative Pu'uc) and Kokom (a more international flavor) worldviews clashed at Mayapán from the twelfth to the fifteenth centuries. As a result of the opposing worldviews, the Xiw modified and erected monuments and created mosaics in the Pu'uc style (e.g., the Cenote Ch'en Mul group), whereas the Kokom erected monuments similar to those at Chich'en Itzá (e.g., the Castillo) and introduced an effigy censer cult with Chaak and the long-nosed merchant god as central images. The revitalization of both styles served to evoke past memories through expressive acts, thus reestablishing worldviews that reflected differences in social and political identities. Differences in pottery styles that related to worldviews were also present at the archaeological site of Tipu (Cecil, this volume). The Kowoj (related to a lineage of the Xiw at Mayapán) erected monumental architecture and made and decorated their pottery (red-slipped plates and jars and effigy censers) to distinguish themselves from other, later occupants of the site—the Itza (a lineage of the Kokom) and the Spanish. These sets of symbols demonstrated that the reenactment of history, myths, and national identities were integral factors in establishing and maintaining the different Maya social and political groups, their histories, and their worldviews.

In addition to establishing and maintaining relationships of past and present familial lineages and social/political group affiliations, the Maya also participated in deity veneration to help cement relationships between the "participants and the roles they play" in the different earthly and celestial realms (Inomata and Coben 2006:32). The Maya and their deities interacted on a regular basis through a series of communal and individual social rituals. When performing rituals such as the New Year ceremony and bloodletting, the Maya called upon various deities to ensure rains and good harvests as well as the life and health of the elite and the community. The relationship of the Maya and the cosmos is most apparent in the Maya codices (Vail, this volume), the ideology of pilgrimage centers (Patel, this volume), and the deities that appear as idols or on effigy *incensarios* (Chuchiak, this volume). The Dresden and Madrid codices depict many human-deity relationships that are prominent and enduring (at least from the Late Classic to the Colonial period) features in the daily and ritual life of the Maya. The rituals, and their timing, ensured proper communication between human petitioners and the deities. One human-deity relationship that was prominent during the Postclassic and Contact periods was that with Ix Chel. Ix Chel (goddess of fertility, childbirth, and medicine) is the Moon Goddess in the codices and serves as the deity for the pilgrimage center at Cozumel (Patel, this volume). At Cozumel, Ix Chel's association with caves and water ties together the Maya primordial past with the present trade and pilgrimage routes, thus bolstering claims to traditional powers and memories of the past. To ensure safe passage, the Maya, and perhaps other traders, gave offerings to clay idols of Ix Chel. These idols and other deity idols are found throughout the Maya region (Chuchiak, this volume; Tozzer 1941), attesting to the human-deity relationship that was an integral feature in Postclassic and Colonial Maya worldviews.

Although many of the associations of the Maya to their past remained relatively unchanged throughout the Postclassic and Colonial eras, Colonial period Maya worldviews also demonstrated a degree of syncretism of Maya and Spanish world-views. Syncretism was possible because one of the features of worldviews is that a worldview can be changed by a culture in response to historical conditions (as well as possible future conditions) to fit with the present situation (Heylighen 2000; Kearney 1984). Because of this inherent flexibility, "the reformulation, accordingly, may be dramatically revitalizing, or simply sustaining," thus preserving a culture's integrity and ensuring the survival of worldview(s) (Kehoe 1989:123).

The flexibility of Colonial and post-Colonial Tz'utujil and K'iche' Maya worldviews after the Spanish Conquest is demonstrated by the blending of Maya *costumbre* with Catholic saints and events surrounding the conquest. Robert Carlsen (this volume) explains how the Tz'utujil Maya of Maya Santiago Atitlán transformed Judas into Maximón/Mam and used the resulting ideology to enter subversive elements into Maya costumbre, thus defining the Tz'utujil as separate from the Spanish/Catholic intruders. Similarly, the *Baile de los Moros y Cristianos* performed by the K'iche' Maya follows the conquest theme but with the addition of local instruments, such as drums and flutes (Howell, this volume). The inclusion of local (and pre-conquest in origin) instruments with embedded meaning (e.g., male versus female and cardinal directions) in the Spanish dances provided a level of meaning that was known to and reenacted by the Maya but went undetected by the Spanish, thus preserving Maya costumbre.

Lowland Maya also incorporated aspects of Spanish life into their traditional iconography and mythology without losing a sense of self and community. Various Maya social and political groups were able to "construct a shared understanding of the historical past that enable[d] them to understand their present conditions as a result of their own way of making history," thus creating worldviews that enabled the Maya to incorporate cultural aspects of Spanish worldviews (Hill 1996b:17). Andrea Stone (this volume) suggests that colonial imagery found in caves and in many of the Books of Chilam Balam were not entirely foreign constructions. The double-headed eagle was prominent in the Greek, Roman, and Persian art and iconography of kingship (and the Spanish coat of arms), but it was also associated with Kablikot, a highland Maya spirit being. Additionally, although circular faces are European in design (circular and frontal features), the Maya may have used them as ersatz hieroglyphs in lieu of Maya calendrical day signs and time periods such as *ajaw* and k'atun.

Many Maya groups restructured aspects of their worldviews to accommodate Spanish influence, but the Lacandon Maya of eastern Chiapas, México, and adjacent Petén, Guatemala, created mythologies related to contact and trade with the Europeans. The reason that the Lacandon state that the Ladinos controlled writing, metal tools, money, medicine, and other non-Lacandon goods was because the Lacandon originally had received these items from their gods but had lost them because of laziness (Palka, this volume). Although the Lacandon may have restructured some of their mythology to explain the presence of the Other, they continued to worship deities that had their origin with Precolumbian Maya deities such as Itsamna and Chaak. As these examples suggest, although the Maya were faced with the ever-present yoke of Spanish and Catholic culture, many different Maya social and political groups were able to incorporate their worldviews and practices to either subversively practice costumbre or to situate the Other in the Maya world.

Space

In addition to relationships with ancestors and various deities, Maya worldviews also established and reinforced relationships with space. Maya conceptions of space can be understood by examining how the Maya defined their universe, planned sites, and conveyed directionality through monuments, burials, caches, and dances. According to Dennis Cosgrove (1989:125–127), built landscapes embody the symbolic, verbal, and visual interconnections of history. The creation of the built landscape, or a social landscape that can last many generations, produces a medium through which customs and performances are (re)enacted and become internal to the social being (Gosden 1994:11, 16; Pugh, this volume). As such, the Maya environment (sacred and secular) may have served to recall the images and social order of the past through the physical construction of various structures, the directionality of those structures, and the rituals that took place within the structures (Connerton 1989; Joyce 2003). "The literal construction of built spaces[,] ... embedded with visual images, channeled the construction of memories over spans far longer than an individual human lifetime" (Joyce 2003:112), and those memories reinforced aspects of Maya worldviews.

The Maya conceived of their universe as divided into three realms: the celestial realm (upper world); the earth (the terrestrial world); and Xibalba (the underworld). Each part of the universe was associated with a direction relative to the terrestrial level (upper and under) as well as being associated with a series of gods and a number of layers: the celestial realm was composed of thirteen layers and was ruled by one of the thirteen Gods of the Upper World (Oxlahuntiku) and Xibalba had nine layers and was ruled by the nine Gods of the Lower World (B'olon ti' K'uh) (Thompson 1970). The upper world is associated with east and Xibalba with west (Hanks 1990:304–306). The terrestrial realm is typically shown as a turtle, an earth crocodile (Itzam Cab Ayin), a circle, or a rectangle (Sosa 1985; Taube 1988a). All three realms were linked together and Maya living on the terrestrial realm communicated with and were affected by the supernatural beings in the celestial realm and Xibalba.

The Maya displayed directionality through a number of media. The general structure and association of gods in the various realms was portrayed in many of the Maya codices (Vail, this volume). In addition to these pictorial and glyphic representations, migrations of groups of Maya (e.g., the Itza) and supernatural deities with human characteristics (e.g., Kukulcan) are associated with direction-specific journeys across the landscape (Ringle, this volume). *Costumbristas* state that Santiago Atitlán in highland Guatemala is the sacred center of the Maya universe and the surrounding peaks represent the four-cornered world (Carlsen, this volume). Finally, the layout of caches excavated at Caracol and Santa Rita Corozal, Belize, display directionality through the different layers of objects as well as the objects themselves in cache vessels (Chase and Chase, this volume). For example, Xibalba was represented by marine items or figurines of marine animals, and the upper world was represented by perishable items such as beehives. In addition to cache vessels, many caches were offerings of figurines arranged to emphasize the four cardinal directions and the center of the Maya universe.

Site planning and construction were conveyed and sustained by acts that relied heavily on past experiences and knowledge of the organization of the Maya universe and sacred landscapes. By constructing a city, the Maya put their worldviews and collective memories about the past and their identity into action. Built space results from ordered events of social practice (Gregory 1985:78–85). "Landscapes are social products, but are not first and foremost symbolic constructs or landscapes of the mind. Rather, they are spaces carved out by patterns of action, which then help to channel future action. The symbolic aspect of the landscape is derived from the actions carried out in it: a conscious gloss on unthought practice. It is thus the changing pattern of activity as a whole which should form the basis for understanding the human creation of space" (Gosden 1994:81). The typical focus (and/or center) of a Maya site is the ritual architecture (e.g., temples and oratorios). It is here where elites interacted with gods of the three realms of the Maya universe (Pugh, this volume). In addition to the focus of a site, Maya worldviews were reinforced through quadrilateral divisions. Structures that faced east typically were associated with the living or rituals involving "active" deities, and those that faced west were associated with the dead or dangerous characteristics of deities (Pugh 2001a).

In addition to the directionality of the structures at a city, the Maya displayed their affiliation to a specific social or political group through the types of buildings constructed at a site. There are many similarities in architecture among the Itza at Chich'en Itzá and the Kokom at Mayapán (Milbrath and Peraza Lope, this volume) and between the Kowoj of central Petén and the Xiw at Mayapán (Cecil, this volume; Pugh, this volume). The type of building and associated structures and their place on the landscape reinforces social and political identity and ultimately reflects differences in worldviews. "A familiar landscape is not nature in opposition to . . . culture, but a web of connections which people have become used to warping in special ways" (Gosden 1994:82).

Main structures at a site also were associated with nature. Many structures throughout the Maya region exhibit solar alignments. For example, the niches of the Round Temple and the radial pyramid (Q162) at Mayapán have solar alignments that reflect similar structures and alignments at Chich'en Itzá (Milbrath and Peraza Lope, this volume, 2003b). Milbrath and Peraza Lope (this volume, 2003b) believe that this reflects the commonality of knowledge, memory, and worldviews between the Terminal Classic Maya inhabitants of Chich'en Itzá and those of Postclassic Mayapán. In addition to solar alignments, structures were built near, around, or over cenotes and caves. This placement linked the structure and the social and political groups associated with that structure with the watery underworld and the mythic primordium (Pugh, this volume, 2001a).

Within these directionally oriented structures the Maya performed many of their rituals. Because rituals are commemorative ceremonies that act out a culture's mythology and are formalized and repetitive, they communicate and shape collective memories, making the spaces where they are performed also imbued with historical and mythical significance (Connerton 1989:43–48, 61; Smart 1995:79). Landa (Tozzer 1941:108, 161) stated that the Maya designated separate areas within a site for the manufacture of clay and wooden idols that were used for many of the commemorative rituals. The designation of sacred spaces for idol manufacture and worship continued throughout the Conquest and Colonial periods (Chuchiak, this volume; Pugh, this volume). For example, offerings to Ix Chel at the oracle shrine on Cozumel created that landscape and the act of the pilgrimage as a sacred part of the Maya universe (Patel, this volume). Additionally, Carlsen (this volume) explains that the Footpath of the Dawn, Footpath of the Sun *cofradía* ritual of highland Guatemala employed the sacred landscape and directionality to reinforce their ancestral past in the face of Spanish Conquest. This ritual used the reenactment of moving the sun to refer to prototypical events and persons, reminding the Maya community of their identity and various aspects of their worldviews.

Time

Marking of time through calendrical associations is a prevalent feature in worldviews of all Maya social and political groups. Time is fundamentally a result of habit and practice and is a means by which present acts create future events. Calendar systems are critical to identity and worldviews because they are linked to religion, claims to land, site planning, ritual, and genealogies (Connerton 1989; Gosden 1994; Kearney 1984; León-Portilla 1988; Milbrath and Peraza Lope, this volume; Rice, this volume). For the Maya, time recorded events (e.g., celestial events, reigns of rulers, and crop-planting times) and was used as a prophetic device to understand the future; it recorded the past, present, and future. "The sages conceived of time itself as the primordial reality, the deity of multiple countenances, periods, and cycles, which in alternating journeys and with the possibility of returns in an never-ending flow, communicates his burdens to all the places and quarters of the world" (León-Portilla 1988:96).

By situating events in the past, the Maya remembered their history, propagated ancestor and deity veneration, and continued a strong sense of costumbre. For example, k'atun circular faces that were an integral aspect of secret cave ceremonialism during the Colonial period preserved the history of k'atun counts and the calendrical system in the face of Spanish domination and survived over 1,000 years. The Maya calendar also located events in the future, which allowed the Maya to incorporate outside sources of change that became prominent during the Conquest and Colonial periods. In addition to past and future events, the Maya marking of time dealt with events and ritual in the present, and different calendar systems were used to highlight differences in social and political groups and worldviews. For example, during the Postclassic period (and perhaps as early as the Terminal Classic period), the Xiw and the Itza/Kokom used similar calendar systems based on the k'atun cycle, but differences occurred at major transition points of the calendar (Milbrath and Peraza Lope, this volume; Rice, this volume), thus reinforcing ethnically specific starts to k'atun cycles and ritual timings.

In addition to recording and understanding the past, present, and future, Maya time can be understood as linear and cyclical. Linear time "is rather like an arrow coming out of the past, passing by us here in the present, and traveling on into the future" (Kearney 1984:100; see Rice, this volume, for an alternate view). The Maya Long Count marked linear time as it recorded a succession of events that was essential for documenting divine kingship and daily activities and for timing the planting and harvesting of crops. On the other hand, cyclical time swings back and forth, rhythmically, between repeated events (Kearney 1984:98–99) and provides predictability in the life and history of a culture. A Kaqchikel religious specialist, Don Domingo (pseudonym), maintains the 260-day ritual calendar in Tecpán, and Fischer (1999:476) states that Don Domingo believes that "humans make sacrifices to propagate the god(s) in order to ensure agricultural and reproductive fertility. Sacrifices must be made for the covenant to continue in order to perpetuate the grand cycle of cosmic and terrestrial existence." As with Don Domingo and ancient Maya society, cyclical time was featured in the Short Count calendar and was under the purview of ritual specialists and used for ritual expression, thus reinforcing histories and worldviews. Linear and cyclical time are similar to public time (Gosden 1994; Heidegger 1996) in that they are not arbitrary creations but result from problem solving with habitual actions, thus creating power and habitual time with the manipulation of materials, space, and time. Continual ritual practices produce structures of time that connect activities and supply "orientation which does not have to be consciously thought out" and "over time becomes part of what people are, rather than something that they know" (Gosden 1994:124–125).

The connection of public time and Maya worldviews is displayed during the Postclassic period when various Maya social and political groups switched from recording time in both the Long Count and the Short Count to recording time in only the Short Count (Rice, this volume). At approximately the same time the concept of divine kingship was also replaced with multepal rulerships, suggesting a fundamental change in some characteristics of Maya political organization and possibly worldviews. The conquest was also incorporated into the cycles of Maya history, demonstrating the continuity of understanding present history in a similar fashion as did their ancestors (Rice, this volume; Ringle, this volume). As a coping mechanism for these social and political changes, a reinvented temporal cycle was introduced and eventually rose into the collective consciousness of public rituals and daily practice.

Similar to the syncretism seen with ancestor and deity veneration, the Maya also incorporated their indigenous concept of time with Spanish/Catholic time and rituals. Carlsen (this volume) explains that the Footpath of the Dawn, Footpath of the Sun cofradía rituals occur during Holy Week in the Catholic calendar, but the Maya saw the five days not related to Jesus but to the five days of *wayeb*. Additionally, the *Baile de los Moros y Cristianos* and the *Baile del Venado* (Howell, this volume) were referred to by local populations as "tun dances" ("tun" means twenty years in the Maya calendrical system), thus demonstrating that various dances reenacting Maya history and memories were tied to the indigenous calendar and reinforced Maya worldviews about time and history. As León-Portilla states:

> In adverse, or even in fatal moments, the *chronovision* of the wise men always permitted the discovery of meanings. Perhaps because of this, with the hope of receiving the ancient meaning of existence or finding a new one in its stead, some Maya groups surviving the Spanish Conquest continued or remade as best they could the wheels of the *katuns* and the books of the prophecies. Clinging to the theme of time in order to save themselves, they also bequeathed the word a last

testimony of the ancient *chronovision* which, with all its variants, was the soul of a culture that lived for almost two thousand years. (1988:111, emphasis his)

History, time, space, and self are all essential aspects of Maya worldviews. It is the interrelationships of these components that aided the Maya in understanding and interacting with their environment during socially and politically unstable times. "What exists today is a *sui generis* product constituted by elements of both origins (Maya and European) that have managed to accommodate themselves in a functional whole" (Villa Rojas 1988:114). How the Maya perceived reality, created and explained a model of their world and their place in it, understood their future and alternative paths to that future, defined values, verified their history, and acted in their environment are essential components to their construction of Maya worldviews. Although some aspects of Maya worldviews are shared by the various groups of Maya throughout México, Guatemala, and Belize, these social groups also demonstrate unique responses to contact and Spanish Conquest. Regardless of the situation, each Maya social group had a unique solution to contact that resulted in as many different worldviews and different material cultures. Therefore, the response of the Maya to the Spanish Conquest and contact with other indigenous cultures can no longer be generalized as one of domination by the contacting culture. Instead it must be viewed as a series of unique responses to the various types of contact.

Note

1. These documents record the histories of various ethno-political lineage groups but are difficult to interpret in Gregorian years because they use the ancient Maya convention of recording time by means of repeating twenty-year units called *k'atuns*. Additionally, they are written as competing histories and/or from the Spanish point of view. Therefore, caution needs to be taken when interpreting these writings.

CHAPTER TWO

Close Encounters

Elizabeth Graham

The contributions to this volume present a range of insights into Maya worldviews, from native engagement with history to time, cosmology, and creation. For the Late Postclassic and Colonial periods, varieties of expression are described from cave art to architecture and from ritual paths to dancing. My broad goal is articulated by Don Rice (1989:4), who reminds us that what is lacking in archaeological reconstructions of Maya society is the system of beliefs that mediated the decisions and activities that we propose took place on the basis of our interpretations of material culture. Most scholars would agree that our knowledge of ancient Maya thought pales in comparison to what we know about Maya physical lives (Burns 1983:4). This chapter is an effort to use what I know about the colonial encounter and late Maya history (Graham 1991, 1998, 2009; Graham et al. 1989) to bring aspects of Maya and Spanish worldviews into focus, not least because "[a] touchstone of understanding for an anthropology of a Maya history is Maya world view" (D. Rice 1989:4). In addition, I critically examine the encounter between the Maya (our subjects) and us.

My first step is to examine a range of concepts that we employ in describing Maya worldviews; my rationale is based on the idea that knowing ourselves better helps us to know the Maya. I also explore "what concepts do for us" by examining a range of terms that we commonly use in describing or referencing Maya beliefs, such as "religion," "science," "worship," "warfare," and "sacrifice." I hope to show that we must recognize that these concepts have histories or we will limit our depth of understanding. Finally, I experiment with different/same and inside/outside standpoints to introduce new takes on old ideas about Maya worldviews.

What I have termed "inside/outside standpoints" are not the same as objectivist versus subjectivist stances as articulated, for example, by Pierre Bourdieu (1995). In the objectivist construction, social phenomena are treated as having to be explained outside the conception of those who participate. But this "outside" way of explaining (in accordance with the Durkheim maxim) is supposed to be scientific and outside consciousness, whereas subjectivism reduces the social world to representations that agents make of it. In a sense, both my "inside" and "outside" perspectives are subjectivist or perhaps even phenomenological in that I try to imagine how it would feel to be part of a group, and what it would mean to stand outside the group. Standing outside, however, still involves an agent's representation of what it means to be "outside."

Examining Our Own Experience

Part of our desire to know about the past stems from wanting to understand ourselves and who we are (Smart 1995:75). Perhaps the depth of this desire blinds us to the ways in which who we are—or who we think we are—structures the past we seek to know. There is always the impulse to romanticize the past (Smart 1995:75), and I cannot guarantee that my desire to know about the Maya past is not partly a longing for the pristine or the innocent (Hacking 2002:7) or a quest for a long-lost way of doing things that would help our society in modern times. Such idealism is not inherently bad or unproductive as long as it is recognized for what it is, and as long as it serves as a source of motivation and inspiration and not as validation for truth.

Who we are is not an easy question to answer. We can seek to describe our own worldviews—their origins, expression, and links to contemporary social life—because our experiences, our rituals, our religions, our theism, our atheism, and our cosmologies all can provide windows on the Precolumbian world. Implicit or explicit in the contributions to this volume is the idea that our learning experiences—personal, social, cultural, historical, and philosophical—are relevant to understanding the Maya. Nonetheless, our concepts are outgrowths of our own experience and intellectual traditions, and it might be a useful heuristic exercise to ask where our concepts come from and how and why we use them to learn about the experience of others.

Concepts Have History

It has been said that concepts have memories and that some of the problems we encounter in using concepts are the result of their history (Hacking 2002:37).

According to Hacking, whose work I hope I paraphrase accurately, concepts come into being at a point in space and time and are made possible by arrangements of ideas that change or become irrevocably altered or fade away. Problems are then created by incoherencies between the earlier state of the concept and the later one. He observes that "[c]oncepts remember this, but we do not" (Hacking 2002:37). Consequently, we often find ourselves perplexed because we do not understand that the source of the problem is lack of coherence between the concept and the prior arrangement of ideas that made the concept possible.

If concepts have histories, how do we use this knowledge? Perhaps by not seeking meaning in concepts as words that stand immutably for something (that is, in "religion" or "worldview" as representative of a reality that is illuminated by having a name) but in how the words are and have been used provides the knowledge. This entails putting aside the idea that meanings are objects that are expressed by words and giving primacy instead to what we actually do with words (Hacking 2002:217–218; Reese-Taylor and Koontz 2001:3–4).

In the discussion that follows, I examine terms such as "worldview," "religion," and "science" (among others) and suggest that although their meanings are problematic, they have utility if we accept them as problematic and take their "memories" or history into account. In other words, the very things that make them problematic make them useful and informative because they tell us as much about ourselves as they tell us about the Maya. Put simply, we should not take concepts for granted.[1]

Metaphors and the Maya

Recognition of the use of metaphor—or, perhaps more broadly, tropes—is important in any approach to understanding Maya worldviews. Kathryn Reese-Taylor and Rex Koontz (2001:3–6) argue elegantly for the importance of aesthetic tropes as expressions of a sense of cultural cohesiveness; such tropes can therefore be said to be cultural and part of the fabric of a Maya worldview. I do not attempt here to bring new knowledge to our understanding of the Maya metaphorical vocabulary (as the contributions in Koontz et al. 2001 have done) so much as I attempt to point to ways in which recognition of this vocabulary has further potential.

A strong case has been made for the primacy of metaphorical understanding and for the fact that the way we think and act is fundamentally metaphorical in nature (Gibbs 1994; Lakoff and Johnson 1980; Tilley 1999:16). What we call literal statements can describe and explain the world simply because the words we label as "literal" have old roots as metaphors that, through time, have worked so efficiently and become so widely used that their origins as metaphors have been forgotten (Lakoff and Johnson 1980; Lakoff and Turner 1989; Tilley 1999:16–21). This kind of forgetting, unlike our forgetting that concepts have memories, is actually a good thing because it enriches our inventory of ideas and makes rapid thought processing possible. If someone yells, "Fire! Get out of the building!" we understand immediately what is at stake because whatever metaphorical mapping took place between the utterance that became "fire" in English and the phenomena of burning and danger occurred so far back in time that we make the connection instantaneously. If a poet living in the building instead gave voice to "Great red tongues arise! Let us flee!" we might burn to death.[2]

As in all human societies, the history of Maya thought is one in which metaphors can, through time, become what we call literal. Metaphors are continually created, and the way in which they become systematically linked in the functioning of the human mind—some have argued for embodied experiences—is universal (Lakoff and Johnson 1980; Lakoff and Turner 1989). However, metaphors take culturally specific forms (Reese-Taylor and Kuntz 2001; Tilley 1999:34). This factor is both a blessing and a curse; commonality of human thought means that insight can be afforded us by, for example, an exploration of the metaphorical aspects of material culture (Tilley 1999), but my exploration of Christian imagery and material culture during the colonial encounter suggests that the connections between imagery or revered objects and the histories they represent are not readily accessible to cultural outsiders (Graham 1992, 2009).

The recognition that we do not know enough about Maya stories, and especially ancient Maya stories, is ironically a kind of breakthrough. Otherwise we trivialize links between material and culture (as in "material culture"), whereas such links are neither trivial nor self-evident. Solving the problem of envisioning the links between stories or histories and material culture may therefore involve coming to terms with the metaphors and the figurative understandings that are part of *our* history and *our* material culture. Maya metaphors and literal meanings differ from ours, but the history of Maya knowledge-building will be the same because (if one accepts cognitive hypotheses at least as something to work with) the Maya constructed understanding in the same way that we do.

Much of the confusion that arose in the conversion process between Mayas and Spaniards occurred because the Spaniards read their own imagery metaphorically but read Maya imagery literally in the sense that they ignored or refused to consider the fact that Maya imagery, like Christian imagery, could not be "read" without knowledge of the stories represented (Graham 1992). Spanish priests and proselytizers therefore made simple associations between a figurine of a particular shape or color and the place where it was found. If a jaguar figure was found in a room, the Spaniards assumed that the person using the room worshipped either the figure itself or the jaguar that the figure represented. They gave no consideration to the possibility that the representation of a jaguar may have symbolized a set of complex ideas or stories or histories in the same way that a Christian lamb symbolizes a set of complex ideas, stories, and histories. The Maya, in turn, less prejudiced than the Spaniards as regards who should be made to think what, mapped their metaphors onto Christian objects and appropriated Christian symbolism and Christian thought.

What this tells us is that knowing or understanding Maya worldviews entails grappling with the implications of metaphorical understanding. A specific example might be Prudence Rice's (1989) examination of the prominent role that serpent and reptilian themes played in the political iconography of the lowland Maya Classic and Postclassic. She interprets central Petén Postclassic reptilian images within the context of rulership, cosmology, and historical cycling and suggests that pottery with reptilian imagery, sometimes associated with mats or twists, functioned in the realm of renewal ritual (P. Rice 1989:307, 317). This makes eminent good sense, and fortunately is amenable to further testing in the archaeological record. My aim here is to view Rice's conclusion from another angle, which is that changes in the pace of metaphorical mapping are very likely to have taken place through time, although essential meanings did not change. Essential meanings became nested within other meanings or became part of a complex of symbols as a process of becoming literal—in other words "read" more easily by more people.

Based on archaeological contexts, those entitled to use the imagery seem to have changed from Classic to Postclassic times (Kristan-Graham 2001). At Lamanai there is some indication of a broadening of the use of these symbols by the Late Postclassic (Graham 2004:226–227; John 2008; Pendergast 1991:343), which suggests that change occurred in the way people read and internalized symbols. It is possible that some changes represented a move from the metaphorical to the literal in the sense that symbolism once associated only with dynastic rulers and kingship came to stand for a property that was appropriated by a broader spectrum of people. This process would have facilitated the transformation suggested by P. Rice (1989:317), in which reptilian symbolism came to be read as a symbol of renewal that could be conceived broadly in secular or political terms.

Concepts with History

My theme combines two facets of analysis: examination of our own approaches and practices on the basis that concepts have histories; and exploration of the ways in which assuming sameness versus difference—or standing outside as opposed to inside—can produce different sorts of insights.

Worldview

Before I became an archaeologist, did I have a concept of a worldview, or did I lack such a concept until it became an object of inquiry (Hacking 2002:11)? According to Ninian Smart (1995:2), English does not have a term that encompasses both traditional religions and ideologies, which leaves "worldview" as a best option: the overall perspective from which one sees and interprets the world; or, a collection of beliefs about life and the universe held by an individual or a group; translation of the German *Weltanschauung*.[3]

Even if I did not have a concept of a worldview before I became an archaeologist, I have one now, and I feel comfortable using it. I feel less comfortable, however, with terms such as "religion" and "science," perhaps because they have deeper histories and problematic memories. Religion, magic,[4] and science—concepts used widely in anthropology—are currently being critically re-examined (Coleman 2004:8, 11), but the words are nonetheless often still used to stand for something divorced from positionality or history, despite the fact that they derive meaning entirely from positionality and history (Wilce and Silverstein 2004:9).

Religion

Although not often looked upon as having historical roots, the term "religion," like all words, obviously came into being at some place and time. Smart (1995:1) defines religions as "systems of belief that, through symbols and actions, mobilize the feelings and wills of human beings." According to the dictionary, the origins of the word "religion" are rooted in the Latin word *religare*, which means to tie or to bind fast. Hence, the word "religion," like "magic," has its origins *not* in an attempt to describe or to characterize a relationship with the natural or supernatural but instead in an attempt to label people. In the case of "magic," it was a label of exclusion, whereas "religion" refers to people held together, or said to be held together, by a belief. Like the term "ethnicity" (Graham 2006a), "religion" did not originate as a term of inclusion in that it was not an attempt to explain or to describe a relationship one shared with the natural/supernatural or with ancestors or the cosmos. Instead, it was an attempt to put people into categories in order to identify and differentiate them, which is closer to a process of exclusion. Unease at being excluded is what I first experienced when I was introduced to the concept of "worldview"; I never thought about a worldview until I became aware of people with views other than my own. As John Monaghan (2000:25) observes, the concept of a religion "is characteristically articulated only when one group is attempting to validate its truths according to the terms of another."

Archaeologists, myself included, have traditionally used terms such as "religion" or "worldview" to describe a reality believed to exist without being relative to anything else. In other words, describing Maya religion is supposed to provide an explanation for an aspect of Maya behavior that can be nothing else but religious. This leads me to the question, What is a religious experience? If the term "religion" arose to recognize a group of people on the basis of something that bound them together, such an attempt at categorization would only have arisen once a group or a society no longer held a single worldview. People who think alike do not categorize themselves as part of a larger set unless they seek to differentiate themselves from people who do not think in the same way. Does this mean that an isolated group of people without a term for "religion" would not have had what we call a religious experience? Pascal Boyer (1994:30–32) would say that this cannot be a serious argument, but his driving question is "Why do people have religious ideas?" (Boyer 1994:vii–viii), whereas mine is "What *is* a religious idea?" What do we mean when we use, as Smart (1995:33) does, the term "religious experience"? Can we substitute "worldview experience"? Perhaps we simply mean "experience," and what makes an experience religious is based on bias or culture or history, or at least on something that needs to be queried rather than taken for granted.

People who experience the insight that they have encountered some eternal truth generally do not qualify the experience (as "religious" or otherwise) because to do so would mean that their worldview was just one way of looking at the world among many that were equally valid. Normally, such occurrences are used to *validate* one's individual perspective or set of beliefs. This is as true of a scientist such as Richard Dawkins (2004) or a professed atheist such as Christopher Hitchens (2007) as it is of a Roman Catholic. The practicing Catholic who experienced a vision of the Virgin Mary would not greet fellow Catholics, saying "Wow, I had a religious experience this weekend!" Instead he would say ecstatically that he had been blessed with a visit by the Virgin Mary, just as the scientist experiences evolution as truth and does not qualify evolution as only "scientific" truth. Again, perhaps what we are talking about is simply "experience," and what makes those who have not had the experience describe it as religious or scientific is based on standpoint, society, and history (e.g., Bell 1992:222; Liljefors Persson 2000:123).

How do Mayanists conceptualize religion? Twenty years ago we distinguished religious knowledge from other knowledge. Our views were summarized by Allan Burns:

> Religious knowledge was highly valued, and an important function of religious specialists was divination. These specialists gave practical advice to peasants about meteorological changes in the wet and dry season and used their calendrical knowledge to predict which days would be auspicious for planting, harvesting, or preparing agricultural plots. In addition, more esoteric knowledge of how to interpret people's dreams, the supernatural winds and beings of the night, and the future of political intrigue gave the ancient Mayan philosopher-priests authority over the emotional and social lives of both the elite and the peasantry. (1983:3–4)

Today we might just say that knowledge was highly valued; that farmers knew very well how to plant and how to recognize the onset of the dry or wet seasons, but they would have taken account of information and advice from those specialists who kept long-term records. The term "philosopher-priest" is no longer widely used, but combining religion and philosophy is a Western way of describing a holistic universe.

More problematic are the five themes or symbolic clusters that are said to have spatial and temporal persistence in Mesoamerican thought (see D. Rice 1989:5). They are described as metaphysical premises underlying considerable diversity in the expression of Mesoamerican verbal and iconographic ideas (Gossen 1986b:5–6). They are:

1. The abiding theme of cyclical time as a sacred entity.

2. A consistent delimitation of sky, earth, and underworld in the spatial layout of the cosmos, with mediation among these realms as a key intellectual, political, and religious activity, for with successful mediation come power, wisdom, even personal health, and community survival.

3. Supernatural combat and secular conflict as creative and life-sustaining forces.

4. The principle of complementary dualism.

5. The extraordinary power of spoken and written language as a symbolic entity in itself, beyond its neutral role as a medium for routine communication.

These themes seem to describe truthfully the metaphysical premises underlying Mesoamerican thought, but how do the premises differ from those that could be said to be applicable to our own worldview? If there is no difference, what does this tell us about our approaches to illuminating Maya worldviews?

Cyclical time is no less sacred to us. Linear time is said to be the most familiar conception to Westerners (Rice, this volume), but our reckoning is both cyclical and linear. Like the Maya, we keep a count of days, which cycle as "years" that are reckoned from the date of the birth of a god; we have recurring named days of the week and named months composed of known numbers of days, to which we faithfully refer in order to keep track of what we are doing. My diary comprises a count of days with two pages per day, plus a five-year calendar, plus a calendar of months with all the days on one page so that I can keep track of what needs to be done in the near, slightly distant, and far distant future. The diary's style is important to me because it embodies a particular font, crisp margins, a colored image of the world laid flat, and neat tables of time zones. My days of the week and my months are named after deities or after rulers who were made into deities following their deaths.[5] I have calendars with pictures on my walls in places that allow me to see the picture associated with a particular month. My calendars and diary are among my most precious possessions. Even if we do not talk about our time-keeping as "sacred," our behavior speaks for itself. We are also under the illusion that we have more control than did the Maya in reckoning cyclical time, yet without calendars or astronomers, most of us could no more track the cyclical movements of the heavenly bodies than we could split an atom.

As regards the delimitation of the sky, earth, and underworld, what civilization has *not* made these or similar distinctions? (See Chase and Chase, this volume, for the idea that Maya watery otherworld symbolism was replaced by Christian-inspired hell and hence *under*world symbolism.) The mediation of these realms is everywhere a key intellectual, political, and religious activity and it is not just priests, monks, rabbis, and imams who involve themselves in mediation. Secular governments are intent on mastering space travel, and fishing rights as well as rights to undersea resources are numbered among the most contentious issues in modern times.

The view that supernatural combat and secular conflict are creative and life-sustaining forces is characteristic of the modern world. Supernatural combat is seen by many besides Christians as having given rise to good and evil, which are seen as part of life. Secular conflict has always been seen as a means of sustaining life; this is why wars are fought, or at least why it is said that wars should be fought.

Finally, complementary dualism is certainly not unique to Mesoamerica, and the power of spoken and written language as a symbolic entity is also characteristic of Western and many other bodies of thought. My point is not that these themes are inapplicable to Mesoamerica, but rather that their subsumption as a significant set—that is, their power as a set to inform us about Mesoamerican worldviews—should lie in their distinctiveness as metaphysical premises. Yet if we subject our own ways of thinking (or being) to similar analysis and generalization, such distinctiveness is difficult to uphold. Therefore the only way these themes can be seen to distinguish Mesoamerica is on the basis of an (unquestioned?) *assumption* of difference.

Science and the Maya

That the term "science" has problematic roots is evident in its multiple definitions (Lindberg 1992:1–4). When it is perceived as applying to beliefs characterized by rigor, precision, or objectivity, or to a set of procedures for exploring nature or the environment and confirming regularities in the natural world (Lindberg 1992:1–2), the Maya can be said to have practiced science. Nonetheless, despite advanced writing, a system for concisely representing and calculating large numbers that surpassed contemporaneous systems in Rome and the medieval West, and a method of predicting natural events (Aveni 1992:4–5; Frake 1992:275), the body of Maya knowledge to which these practices contributed is still often set apart as serving astrological and religious ends (Aveni 1992:17; Sharer 1994:515). Anthony Aveni (1992:17) observes that our own Western inquiry into nature possessed a foundation similar to that of the Maya in that religion is said to have been a stimulus to scientific enterprises in both cultures. This statement as it stands would generate little debate, but the boundary between religion and science is more often assumed than clarified, for us and for the Maya. Employment of the heading "Prehistoric attitudes toward nature" to cover eight pages in a 455-page modern history of science (Lindberg 1992) suggests that neither logic nor rigor but instead preconceived ideas about how and why "the past" should be segregated characterize those who write about science. Charles Frake (1992:287–288) observes that "Mayan science, in its mathematics, its representation of numbers, and its empirical base is in many respects superior to the science of their European contemporaries." Yet how many books about science recognize the Maya achievement?

I do not dispute the statement that "[t]here is no evidence that the ancient Maya understood [planetary] movements as Kepler and Copernicus did" (Sharer 1994:581), but Copernicus, in fact, did not understand planetary movements as Kepler did, and Kepler's advances were based in part on access to newly invented telescopic instruments. Very few people except for astronomers and mathematicians can claim even today to understand planetary movements as Kepler did. I certainly cannot make the claim, but does this mean that my thinking lies closer to astrology? Should we still maintain that the raison d'être of Maya astronomy was divinatory and ritualistic (Aveni 1980:17)? Any astronomy, including modern astronomy, involves detailed, repetitive observation and measurement; such activity would be classified as ritual no matter what the motivation. The deification of celestial bodies was said at one time to distinguish the Maya from us (Aveni 1980:3), despite the fact that our names for celestial bodies—sun, moon, Venus, Mars—are those of deities. Even the word "planet," which is now taken by us to be a literal description of a celestial body, derives from a Greek word that means "to wander," which is a verb that takes a living subject. "Divination" is supposed to denote prediction on the basis of supernatural agency, but if celestial bodies' identification with gods makes their movements supernatural, then our astronomy is divinatory as well.

Although "science" gives all appearances of describing a definitive set of approaches to problems, the term arose just as much to differentiate a "them" (superstitious primitives or ancients or women) from an "us" (rigorous-thinking moderns, mostly male) as it did to describe a (still rather elusive) method of arriving at better accounts of the world (e.g., Laudan 1996; Nola and Sankey 2000). Exclusion or inclusion regarding science need not be a problem, as long as we remain aware of the history of our use of the term and that the drive behind exclusion has been, and still often remains, cultural. At the same time, even the most radical historical contingency claims can be seen as part of the goal of producing better accounts of the world—that is, science (Haraway 1991:183–201). Thus, science, if it is meant to describe an effort at a better account of the world, is an understandable goal; but given the history of the term, our understanding of Maya worldviews may be hindered by our positioning of archaeology as science, and of archaeologists as scientists. We, and not just the concept, must retain the memory of its origins, for without making clear how we are using the term, "science" as an approach to understanding Maya worldviews is as problematic as religion.

Smart (1995:12–13) begins an analysis of religion and worldviews with a reference to Darwin's "new way of thinking about the origin of the human race [that] challenged earlier Western beliefs about the way humankind was created by God." Smart mentions Darwin because of the way in which evolution influenced thought (Johnson 1999:132–143), and particularly the idea that human society, including religion, developed in stages. My point about evolution is rather different. Darwin's thinking is widely described as revolutionary (Dawkins 1989:1), but Smart (1995:12–13) hit the nail on the head by situating Darwin's revolution clearly in terms of its impact on Western beliefs, and particularly Christianity (see also Bowler 1984). Consideration of the world before Christianity shows that many societies and cultures did not see humans as unique creations or decidedly separate from animals.

The Maya saw humans as the latest in a line of experiments in living (Christenson 2007; Graham 2006b; Taube 1993; see also Vail, this volume); there was more than one creation, and there were instances in which humans became animals and animals took on human characteristics. Scientists might say that such beliefs were not based on evidence, or that such beliefs were myths, but this is irrelevant. If people believed that humans had been or could be transformed into animals, their belief affected their everyday relationship with animals and the environment. If Darwin had lived at Copán in the eighth century and had proposed that the forms of all living things change very slowly through time under environmental influence, the idea would not have rocked the Maya world as it did the Christian one (Graham 2006b).

As far as we know, all Maya groups attributed human creation to the whims of deities or supernaturals; but Maya creation was more complex, drawn out, and fraught with problems than the creation envisioned by Christians. The setting, however, is the same as that of Western creation narratives, including Darwin's. Darwin's evolutionary idea did not involve an alternative explanation for the origins of the earth as the setting in which evolution took place; planets are neither naturally selected nor do they adapt or change allele frequencies. The import of Darwin's idea with regard to the earth was not its origins, but the nature and time depth of change. Christians had problems with evolution because they believed that God had created the earth in seven days, that the Bible told us how old the earth was, that God created people separately from animals, and that each type of animal had been continuously present since it was created by God. Maya beliefs on the other hand seem to have had little problem with huge time depth and seem not to have rejected the idea that human and animal forms were related. Thus becoming an animal was more of a transformation that would allow a different perception of the world than a step down from God's special shelf of creation.

My take on science, Darwin, and the Maya is an admittedly quirky route to an expansion of our understanding of Maya worldviews. My hope is that it will help to dispel the linear thinking that pervades scholarship in which Darwin's ideas are seen to be a turning point in world thought, and world thought is seen to owe it all—as one might expect—to the Greeks (Collingwood 1960; Lindberg 1992). Darwin's idea is revolutionary within the framework of Christianity owing to the particular way in which Christians came to position themselves with regard to the world around them; against the backdrop of Christianity, his ideas stood out sharply. Coming to terms with this historical condition might help us to dispel entrenched notions of "development" in which pre-Christian ("ancient") ways of thinking are characterized as inherently more religious or cosmological than ours. Gossen's themes are a good example of traits that might not have been identified if we did not see ourselves as modern, post-Enlightenment thinkers in a world changed irrevocably by science. If we can imagine "having never been modern" (Latour 1993), we can imagine Darwin at Copán. Even if such images elude us, we can gauge by European science's own standards that Maya thought was more highly developed and receptive to evolutionary ideas in the eighth century than was European thought in the nineteenth.

Inside and Outside

In the following paragraphs I employ the strategy of positioning or standpoint—sameness or difference, inside or outside—to arrive at new perspectives on Maya worldviews. Our approach to the use of concepts is still important, but in the cases that follow, positioning is the key to new perspectives.

Worship, Images, and Ancestors

Very few of us today, unlike the Spanish priests of the past (Chuchiak, this volume), would describe the ancient Maya as having *worshiped* images. Even the Maya themselves, according to Chuchiak's documentary evidence, resisted the idea and only used the concept because they were given no option. Yet images were clearly a focus of attention, and any society's relationships with their images are important in understanding its worldviews. We have been known to describe the Maya as having worshiped ancestors (Sharer 1994:86, 526) or the forces of nature (Chuchiak, this volume), although the term "veneration" is more noncommittal and encompasses a broader range of behaviors (McAnany 1995; Sharer 1994:125; Sharer 2006:97, 171). The difference is that worship generally involves a deity whereas veneration, defined as profound respect or reverence, is more subdued or even equivocal. In the Roman Catholic Church, the term "venerable" is a form of address for a dead person who has reached the first stage of canonization. So on a line from human to god, veneration is somewhere in the middle.

What is entailed in worshiping a deity? What feelings does the act of worship generate? Does worship feel different from veneration? Who counts as an ancestor? Can we appropriate ancestors? What is the place of an image in worship? How does the image function? What is the relationship between the material components of an image and its status as an object of worship? Is it a representation? And in the case of venerating ancestors (McAnany 1995), is the image of the ancestor in people's minds?

No one who has ever been part of a religion in which images are an important component of ritual behavior would say that the image itself is the object of veneration or worship. Yet it is interesting that the dictionary defines "worship" as reverent love and devotion accorded a deity, *an idol, or a sacred object* [emphasis mine]. An image is not considered "holy" in Roman Catholicism until it is blessed by a priest. If the image is a statue and it shatters, it can be discarded, although images on paper must be burned. The image is meant to stand for, or represent, something. Outsiders observe a person with his attention focused on a statue—for example, talking, or muttering, or acting in a particular way—and the assumption is that the person's energy is directed at the statue or the image *for its own sake*, or that the image is essential to the experience. The observer, as in the case of Spanish priests observing the Maya or an anthropologist observing a religious procession, does not ask the sorts of questions that might reveal the complexities of the interaction between the human and the image because the observer often has no basis for imagining what to ask. If he is *outside* the experience being observed, he will feel comfortable in describing (reducing?) the relationship to a single word: worship or veneration. Either undoubtedly serves to define a relationship—that is, draws our attention to the existence of a relationship—but how do we go from this to an explanation?

In any intellectual endeavor, we should pay heed to whether we are standing inside or outside when we ask a question.[6] An outsider's take on things makes definition and categorization possible, can serve as a fast track to particular kinds of information (see Graham 1987 on levels of analysis), and serves to focus our attention on something of possible significance. But staying outside can blind us to some of the critical details of people's worldviews or to the way people connect with the forces around them. Therefore we should consider exploring ways of being "inside."

For example, an anthropologist or archaeologist—let us identify the individual as a man, although it could equally well be a woman—studying the Maya probably does not include himself in a category of people who worship images or idols. Yet as a boy he played with action figures and with video games, and as an adult he goes to the cinema or to museums. An outsider—one who is not part of the same culture and does not share our archaeologist's imagery or image technology—could situate himself as an observer and record the researcher's behavior as a child at play or as an adult watching *Predator* or *The Bourne Ultimatum* or gazing at Rodin's sculptures; the outsider's conclusion might well be that the archaeologist worshiped or venerated the images to which he was riveted, sometimes for hours on end.

Let us accept, then, that both worship and veneration can encompass a variety of experiences. "To worship" and "to venerate" are verbs that take an object, but the nature of the object is not obvious. A relationship is implied between the subject—an individual—and either an actual image or one that the individual has *in his or her mind*. "Worship," perhaps more than "veneration," focuses on control of spiritual resources. But both "worship" and "veneration" can be about establishing material connections to a non-material world, about attempting to deal with the unknown, or about dealing with time and its devastating effects. They can be concerned with agency, with personal wants and desires, or with the constitution of personal and social identity. This last certainly applies to collecting and playing with action figures.

In the context of Roman Catholicism, I have found myself trying to recall if the word "worship" was used by the nuns and priests who taught me the catechism when I was a child. I do not remember that it was used very frequently, except when we were told that pagans were idol worshipers. God was supposed to be worshiped, but we were encouraged *not* to deal directly with God except on rare occasions. We did not pray to Jesus either. We got the distinct impression from the nuns that both God and Jesus were too important to be pestered with our mundane problems. We were encouraged, instead, to pray to the saints, who at one time were just ordinary people.

Praying can involve conversation, but its many forms invariably involve a request for something. If prayer can be a form of worship, then worship inevitably involves asking for things. If worship is asking for things, then perhaps saying that "the Maya worshiped Itsamna" or "Maya rulers worshiped the corn deity" is not particularly informative as a blanket statement. Perhaps we should be thinking about whom the Maya thought they could approach to ask for things (Patel, this volume), and how this kind of relationship might be manifested in imagery. If they felt about a deity as I was taught to think about God or Jesus, it is possible that the most powerful supernaturals would either not make their way into imagery, or their imagery would be distinct from the sort that enabled repeated prayer or supplication. Among the Maya, changes in imagery and in what might be called the expressive or decorative arts—how ceramics, for example, were decorated and elaborated (John 2008)—suggest strongly that the Postclassic period involved shifts in patterns of veneration and supplication, both in who could be asked for what and in the location and organization of space set aside for contemplative or communicative or ritual experience related to worship (Milbrath and Peraza Lope, this volume; Pugh, this volume).

In the world of Roman Catholics, the most popular saints occur most frequently in imagery. Because saints are people who lived in times past, their imagery—their visages, costume styles, and objects they hold—reflects their history. Mythical beings, however, who are known for having affected the future of the world and humankind before history, have trappings that tell the important story again and again. Their visages and styles of costume can change drastically, depending on how they are being appropriated and by whom, but their deeds will speak for them. Images of people known or thought to have existed will, on the other hand, reflect the individual's life story, or what is believed to be the life story, and perhaps his or her place in history. Such imagery will express an anchoring in time and place, whereas mythical imagery can take great liberties with both.

Might it be possible for us to detect such differences in the imagery of the Maya? Can we distinguish situations, such as that outlined for Quetzalcoatl/Kukulcan, in which a human draws on myth but nonetheless has a history of sufficient importance that we might expect some of the historical symbolism to surface when the human is the focus of attention (Miller and Taube 1993:142)? Do the shrines to which pilgrimages are directed (Patel, this volume) have roots in historical events in which individuals have become "deified"? To what extent were foreign or new deities or spirits appropriated as part of an age-old process, as Robert Carlsen (this volume) describes for the Colonial period in communities of Lake Atitlán?

Warfare and Sacrifice

Of all our beliefs about the Maya and their worldviews, perhaps the most entrenched is that they were committed to human sacrifice. Rather than contrasting an inside and an outside perspective, I approach the matter through ideas of "sameness" and "difference." Owing to their practice of "human sacrifice," which is rarely if ever defined, the Maya are generally agreed to have been different from us because they are said to have killed humans to appease or please their gods (Graham 2008). At least this is the story that has come down to us from conquest times, accompanied by accusations of "idolatry."

If instead the Maya were like us, they would have seen death as we do and would not have adduced their gods' appeasement as the sole reason for killing humans. How, then, would the Maya have accounted for those times when people were killed, sometimes in large numbers? Perhaps Maya men and women justified killing in the way that we do: it was sanctioned socially as *war*.

Maya warfare at the time of the conquest was part of Mesoamerican warfare. If Michael Smith (1986) is on target with his Aztec model, Mesoamerican warfare may well have permitted and indeed thrived on intra- and interregional and even multiethnic alliances among elites who shared interests, particularly economic ones, and who joined forces primarily to win access to resources both spiritual and economic. In the Terminal Classic and Postclassic, as in the Classic period, wars took the form of hand-to-hand combat and fights were won by individuals who were able to take their opponents captive. With the addition of the apparent presence of commoners in very restricted roles, these same rules applied to the Aztecs (Hassig 1988:116–117). Unlike European warfare, the Mesoamerican version conferred no honor on those killed on the battlefield (Clendinnen 1991b). When elite individuals died in Aztec battles (almost certainly not the result of the killer's intention?), their bodies were returned to their home cities (Hassig 1988:117). Only enemy *captives* served strategic purposes, which may well have involved the right of the captor to exact or to appropriate tribute based on the captive's resources. The struggle for control over resources was surely an impetus to warfare, and "territory" per se was not involved. It was not necessary that cities or towns be overrun, except symbolically as in the burning of a temple (Hassig 1988:95–121). Tribute was the name of the game, and being on the winning side brought with it the gods' favor and spiritual resources.

Where do these statements about control of resources lead? I assume that the Maya, like us, fought wars for economic and spiritual resources and not, as is often claimed, for the sheer religious ecstasy of capturing people and excising their hearts. Within the bounds of my hypothesis, the windshield of the Maya worldview was not any more bloodied than our own. The Maya worldview, in other words, did not sanction "human sacrifice" any more or less than does our own. We allow our warriors—in the past mostly men, but more recently both men and women—to die from being shot full of holes or blown to bits on the battlefield; the Maya captured their opponents in hand-to-hand struggles with the intention of having them die at a later time. Both are war; both involve killing that is socially sanctioned (otherwise it would be murder). If Maya warfare was human sacrifice, then so is ours. The bulk of "sacrificial" killing among the Aztecs was directed at prisoners captured in war. When women or children were involved, it is hard to know where they originated, but information from several sources (Clendinnen 1987, 1991a, 1991b; Díaz del Castillo 1963; Hassig 1988:95–121) suggests that they were drawn from outside the community. They may well have been taken on the rare occasions when cities were sacked (Hassig 1988:106–107) or in some other way as a consequence of raids or warfare. If war was responsible for the capture of individuals, some of whom were later killed in religious ceremonies, then the situation is clearly one of delayed killing. In the context of Western warfare it is justifiable to kill men, women, and children by raiding, bombing, or destroying a city as long as those killed are the enemy. If they turn out not to be the enemy but are accidentally killed, they are classified as collateral damage and no one is held accountable. But the Maya and Aztec practice of capturing individuals in warfare and killing them after capture is called "human sacrifice."

None of the foregoing is intended to condone having captives brought to priests, who carry out the killing and in some cases have to drag the captives to the sacrificial stone if they falter (Hassig 1988:121). However horrible delayed killing seems to us, what we do as war and what the Maya and Aztecs did are nevertheless both *socially sanctioned killing*, justified on the basis of social and religious ideals but aimed at acquiring or stabilizing economic resources, the winning of which is seen to reflect spiritual favor. Thus it is possible to imagine that a Maya man could wake up in the morning and, on the way to his *milpa*,[7] pass a ceremony in the temple in which someone was being killed and bow his head but continue on his way, just as Western civilization has become accustomed to getting through the day even though men and women and children are suffering and dying in wars. In war, whoever kills but keeps the resources clearly has the gods on his side.

The foregoing case positions us as *like*, rather than *different from*, the Maya in order to highlight potential contradictions in our characterizations of Maya worldview. I have proposed difference where others have assumed commonality in the idea that wars somehow resulted in territorial conquest, or that a Maya city, through its fighting force, had hegemony over another city (Graham 2006a; Martin and Grube 2000). If wars were waged and won by individuals who fought to bring back captives and thereby appropriate tribute, the aftermath of battle must have been a complex affair, owing to the political and economic implications of tribute negotiations. A ruler may well have captured another ruler, but what happened when he lost nobles to individuals from the rival city? How was tribute divided? How were lesser lords rewarded? In this sense, the Maya world in the Postclassic emerges as a patchwork of competing factions, with warfare only one of many ways to shift and redistribute resources in a complex social and political network, all members of which nonetheless shared common interests in maintaining economic control through tribute. The relationship of warfare in Mesoamerica to tribute appropriation and not to territory per se can also explain the behavior of the Maya toward the conquering Spaniards (e.g., the Montejos), who were continually perplexed that conquering a town and receiving pledges of fealty from its leaders did not give them permanent control (Chamberlain 1948).

From the Postclassic to the Conquest Worldview

Distinguishing Maya worldviews—and in the case of this volume, worldviews at conquest—will always be a problematic task because our understanding is colored by our own worldviews and our historical and cultural experience. Yet acknowledging that our worldviews are the lens through which we "see" the Maya is a first step in positioning any conclusions we may draw regarding Maya worldviews as only part of a larger picture that can be seen from many angles. Our information on how the Maya thought at the time of the conquest—for example, their use of "idols"—

comes from Spanish sources. Therefore our first step should be to examine Spanish worldviews of the time in order to understand how the Spaniards "familiarized" the Maya and what reactions this engendered (Chuchiak, this volume; also Bricker and Miram 2002; Chuchiak 2000, 2005; Graham 2009). In this vein, Jesper Nielsen and Toke Sellner Reunert (2008) note the influence of European worldviews and theology on what we have come to accept without question as the Mesoamerican multilayered universe.

Many of us have also uncritically adopted a range of terms common in Western scholarship as descriptive or even objectively neutral that in fact are problematic—terms such as "idols," "polytheism," "pantheism," "monotheism," "sacrifice," "gods," "cults," and "underworld." Because the colonial Maya adjusted so quickly to the terms that the Spaniards used to characterize them (because they had no choice) there is always the danger of mistaking the words for representative descriptions of Precolumbian ways of thinking. We need to subject the history and use of our own concepts and categories to exhaustive study, or at least be aware that we are weighed down by them before we consider them as windows onto Maya worldviews.

There is also the issue of whether Maya worldviews prior to the conquest were centered on the community, or whether communities comprised individuals with worldviews of different scales. Recent excavations at Lamanai focused on the Terminal Classic to Postclassic transition (Graham 2004) have suggested that incremental economic changes can lead to the kind of social change that allows for a variety of worldviews. I have in mind the development of a context in which cultural differences can become, in our terms, "ethnic" divisions (Milbrath and Peraza Lope, this volume; Ringle, this volume). "Ethnicity" is a concept with complex origins and usage (Sachse 2006); although "ethnic" is an adjective that is widely used, "ethnicity" is rooted in particular conditions in which otherness comes to be recognized (Graham 2006a).

Whether we can speak in terms of ethnic differences or merely cultural differences at Lamanai in the Postclassic and early Historic periods remains a subject for debate, but it is not surprising that a community focused on trade and exchange was inclusive of difference. For example, elites imported metal objects from as far away as West México and Oaxaca (Hosler 1994:145, 201, 209; see also Pendergast 1989). In addition, recent multifaceted analysis of skeletal remains suggests that some of Lamanai's inhabitants had foreign roots (White et al. 2009). Although the oxygen isotope ratios of a man, woman, and newborn in an unusual Postclassic burial are consistent with individuals assumed to be local to Lamanai, there are features that strongly suggest foreign connections (Pendergast 1989; White et al. 2009). They include the fact that the male had a type of cranial modification (lambdoidal flattening) that is uncommon at Lamanai (where the dominant style was fronto-occipital) but is reported in West México (White 1996). He was buried with West Mexican–style copper tweezers suspended around his neck. His young female companion had her hair formed into a braid, bound in cloth, and held in place by five copper-tin bronze rings; such a hairstyle was common in West México during the Postclassic and is still known in the area. Christine White and colleagues (2009) suggest that the individuals could have come to Lamanai as children and/or had family roots in West México.

In general, the people of Lamanai depended less on maize than other communities in the region, although they consumed large quantities of C4 sources. Significant quantities of marine foods were also a part of the diet (White and Schwarcz 1988). This orientation toward the coast, the evidence of foreign items, and the results of skeletal analysis all suggest that Lamanai was a cosmopolitan community of people who were exposed to, and may even have held, a range of worldviews.

Such a cosmopolitan orientation was probably not limited to the Postclassic and the time of European contact. Further evidence from Lamanai and other sites in Belize attests that the changes that were ultimately to manifest themselves in the Postclassic and even Colonial periods were in fact spread over many years and began deep in Classic times, if not earlier. If Lamanai was not unusual, then other Maya communities were also diverse in membership and cosmopolitan in flavor and embraced worldviews that were both rooted and fluid, perhaps in a kind of dynamic equilibrium. This was not least because the Maya in various communities were accustomed to a cultural and natural environment that exhibited both continuity and change.

For example, the patterns of coastal traffic and long-distance interaction and communication that were to serve so well in Postclassic commerce and in maintaining the connections that enabled colonial Maya to flee towns in Yucatán under Spanish control were well established by Early Classic times (Graham 1989, 2009). The extensive burning of wood for fuel that almost certainly accompanied the intensive salt processing up and down the Belize coast in the Late Classic probably contributed to environmental degradation but also ultimately contributed to favorable growth conditions that enabled expanded coastal settlement and cultivation in the Postclassic period and beyond (Graham 1998; McKillop 2002). Changes in architectural features of buildings at Lamanai in the Late Classic (seventh and early eighth centuries A.D.) (Graham 2004, 2007) already reflect the incorporation of cultural elements that are nonlocal in origin. Furthermore, the custom of burying individuals face down with their legs bent back at the knees that appears along the Belize coast in the Terminal Classic period (ninth century) (Pendergast and Graham 1990:3) and at Lamanai in the Early Postclassic (late tenth or eleventh century) reflects a new option in cultural or religious expression that was not dissimilar to the changes that took place during the early Spanish Colonial period when Christian burial practices were introduced. Thus one can draw a parallel between the Spanish Conquest and the Terminal Classic to Early Postclassic transition as regards the spread of new burial customs, which could be said to reflect the influx of new ideas about the relationship among humans, death, and the cosmos (Chase and Chase, this volume; Ringle et al. 1998).

Their history prepared the Maya of Conquest period communities well to deal with a new conceptual inventory. If the colonial experience is any guide (Carlsen, this volume; Howell, this volume), we can assume that the members of each community had as much influence over new ideas and non-Maya imagery and practices in the Postclassic as they had in the Colonial period.

There is an interesting twist to the comparison of earlier events with Conquest period Christianization. The Spanish priests called Maya images "idols," but some sources—for example, the *Relación de Citilcum y Cabiche*—state that Kukulcan, a Mexican captain, introduced "idolatry" to Yucatán when he came to Chich'en Itzá (Chuchiak, this volume; Garza 1983:182; Thompson 1990:187). The identification of Maya images as "idols" by Roman Catholic Spaniards, who were no strangers to churches filled with statues and a range of holy images, is indeed demonizing "the other" in a case in which practices were behaviorally very similar. Perhaps the Maya likewise demonized "the other" when they claimed that outsiders had brought idolatry into Yucatán, despite the fact that the practices involved may likewise have been similar. Nonetheless the Maya saw their own images as sacred and complex representations, whereas the images introduced by the outsider, Kukulcan, could be characterized as idols.

Close Encounters

To return to the theme of close encounters—between the Spaniards and the Maya, and between the Maya and us—there is room to explore the connections between approaches that assume difference and approaches that assume commonality and their outcomes. Both are productive, but only if we remain aware of our positioning. Does our terminology arise from being on the outside or on the inside? When we describe Maya worldviews, do the words we use stem from an assumption of sameness or of difference?

There is yet another issue, which is how we accord legitimacy to the insights that we propose. Acknowledging that concepts are the result of their histories and being open about standpoints and positioning can help us in the structuring of our expectations about Maya worldviews, as well as in the interpretation of data from Spanish documents, Maya texts, or archaeology. Whether our interpretations or hypotheses about worldviews are legitimate or even true is another matter. What I have focused on here is not the truth or predictive value of any given insight into worldview but instead the "strategic value" of the approaches we use in relation to the question raised (Lyotard 1984:7). According to Jean-François Lyotard (1984:7), what is required of a working hypothesis is "a fine capacity for discrimination." I hope that I have drawn attention to the need for fine-tuning our capacity to discriminate among the range of possible approaches we can use to learn about ancient Maya views of their world. Some approaches require considerable examination and criticism of the bases of our assumptions; some require us to envision Maya prehistory within an environment of fluid as well as periodic change; still others require us to envision the Maya in a variety of community contexts, exposed for centuries to cultural input and interaction both regionally and on an interregional scale.

Acknowledgments. The excavations that provided much of the information on which this chapter is based would not have been possible without the cooperation and support of the Institute of Archaeology in Belize, formerly the Department of Archaeology, and its directors and staff: Jaime Awe, John Morris, Allan Moore, the late Winnel Branche, and the late Harriot Topsey. Excavations at Tipu and Lamanai were funded by Social Sciences and Humanities Research Council of Canada; National Geographic Society; British Academy; Foundation for Mesoamerican Studies, Inc. (FAMSI); Institute of Archaeology, University College London; Royal Ontario Museum; and York University (Ontario). My thanks to Leslie Cecil and Tim Pugh for including me in the original symposium on Maya Worldviews, to the anonymous reviewers who read the manuscript and recommended improvements, and to David Pendergast, Miguel Astor-Aguilera, Christine White, and Allan Burns for their very useful feedback. I did not always heed advice, however, and remain solely responsible for the chapter's content.

Notes

1. Approaches that stand out as having outcomes that depend on taking concepts for granted are those of Girard (1977), who questions nothing, and Boyer (1994), who has doubts but writes them off.

2. One of the reviewers pointed out that "fire" (as we now use the term) does not seem to be a metaphor. It is not. That was my point, but I did not think that I could explain what I was trying to say any better without taking up a great deal more space. I refer interested readers to Lakoff and Johnson (1980) and Lakoff and Turner (1989) for in-depth discussions of the role of time and metaphor in the development of the literal.

3. Definitions of terms from this point onward are taken from Soukhanov (1992).

4. "Magic" derives from the Old Persian word *magus*, a member of the Zoroastrian priestly caste of the Medes and Persians (Soukhanov 1992) and also a sorcerer. The term "magic" is used to refer to the manipulation of supernatural forces, or today to the apparent manipulation of such unexplained forces. But the origins of the term lie in its application to the actions of those who operated outside the accepted religion or worldview (Wiener 2004). Surely the change from the magus as a priest of Persia to the magician as a wielder of the black arts can be seen as a reflection of the history of Christianity and of Christian efforts to suppress non-Christian views of the world. It is easy to see how Christians might have come to use "magic" to describe the activities of "pagan" priests, and how Western anthropologists came to use "magic" to describe the activities of so-called primitives (Lowie

1952:136–152). Although magicians have proudly appropriated the term, the meaning of "magic" originated in a process of exclusion.

5. Sunday and Monday were named after the Anglo-Saxon sun and moon deities; Thursday and Friday were named for Nordic deities. January was named after Janus and March after Mars; July after Julius Caesar and August after Augustus Caesar, both of whom were deified after their deaths.

6. Standing outside in this sense does not necessarily imply objectivism, although I thank the reviewer who read my words critically and suggested Bourdieu's (1995:514) writing on transcending the opposition between the objectivist position (treating social phenomena as things) and subjectivism (reducing the social world to representations that agents make of it). Being objective, in the sense discussed by Bourdieu and also characteristic of Western science, requires more than simply standing "outside," either literally or metaphorically, although standing "outside" is a good first step to objectivity. Being objective requires treating phenomena as things (a slippage of which outsiders are often guilty, but they need not be), but it also assumes that the outsider is somehow competent in a socially sanctioned way to comment on the insider's behavior. My example envisions a case in which the outsider is on equal footing with the insider and is simply "outside" because he/she does not share the worldview of the insider. This could be a Protestant commenting on Catholic worship or a Buddhist commenting on Islamic practice. It *could* be an anthropologist or archaeologist who is (as it happens) socially sanctioned to comment from the outside, but in this case I am attempting to position the anthropologist or archaeologist as "outside" without any more authority than the insider has in terms of the value or truth of worldview.

7. Field or farm plot.

"In Recalling Things Past, I Strengthen My Heart": Accommodating the Past in Early Colonial Yucatán

CHAPTER THREE

William M. Ringle

Memory—the specifics of name, place, time, and deed—is critical to the establishment of self and community, and it is thus not surprising that each of these aspects was systematically subverted by Spanish colonial policy. Most infamous are the *auto de fé*'s, which attempted to root out the religious underpinnings of collective identity, and the policies of relocating and reducing native communities, but also important were the wholesale renaming of the populace and the landscape, the replacement of the native system of timekeeping with that of the Christian, and the substitution of new conventions of formal discourse for old.

Without wishing to undervalue the devastation wrought by the conquest, cultural upheavals and the corresponding loss of social memory were not unfamiliar to many Maya communities. By the time of the Spanish Conquest, mechanisms were already in place to ameliorate the psychological trauma caused by the collapse of orientation and meaning. The rhythms of the calendrical cycle provided one method for accommodating the waxing and waning of various cultures, so that, for instance, the rise and fall of Chich'en Itzá and Mayapán could be explained as events that were like in kind, each tragic in their own right but part of larger cycles of history. A related mechanism was prophetic history, which, by "foretelling" calamities, could at the same time incorporate them within existing frameworks of explanation.

Over the past two or three decades, the ways in which native historians reused and refashioned the past to address current concerns have been eloquently explored by ethnohistorians such as Victoria Bricker (1981), Grant Jones (1989, 1998), and Matthew Restall (1997, 1998), among others. With respect to earlier ethnohistorical studies, these works have emphasized indigenous agency and engagement, especially regarding resistance to colonial rule. But these works have also fostered a more nuanced view of the colonial Maya that refuses to essentialize them as a single political or ideological group. Jones's (1998) study of the southern frontier zone presents a highly balkanized region in which neighboring groups often posed a more immediate threat than did the Spanish, whereas Bricker's study of colonial rebellions has demonstrated that we cannot ascribe the rhetoric of such conflicts to atavistic memories of the precolonial past. This emphasis on agency has also extended to indigenous historical traditions. We can no longer regard native historians as naive scribes content to recopy the old chronicles, perhaps introducing the odd error or two but unengaged in contemporary intellectual currents of the Ladino world. Restall (1998) has argued that Yucatec colonial documents strongly reflect genres from elsewhere in Mesoamerica, whereas the recent publication and study of the *Chilam Balam of Kaua* spectacularly documents the intellectual sophistication of some native scribes and their access to a surprising range of literary sources (Bricker and Miram 2002:33–36, 66–67).

This chapter will address native reaction to the process of identity loss as reflected in a group of less well-known documents from the Cehpech province of northern Yucatán (Figure 3.1), ostensibly among the earliest written by natives in Romanized Maya. The particular focus will be a short personal narrative written by Nakuk Pech, an early sixteenth-century *batab*[1] residing in the small town of Chac Xulub Ch'en (Figure 3.2). The author emerged during a particularly troubled period in Yucatecan history, the century between the fall of Mayapán and the finalization of the Spanish Conquest in 1546. On one level, the chronicle of Nakuk Pech and its associated documents are less history or legal documents than attempts to accommodate the events of the conquest within the loss of memory. In fact, this text might be called Nakuk Pech's memorial, not so much in testimony to his deeds but rather because of the way he uses the text to refashion and reassert his own identity and heritage. Thus, at the close of a lengthy list of the officials involved in the settlement of Chac Xulub Ch'en, he revealingly states, "And so it is that in recalling things past, I strengthen my heart" (§12).[2] This is an appealing sentiment, but, as will be seen, the gaps in the narrator's memory may ultimately lead us in a quite different direction, one in which the trustworthiness of his account and perhaps even his ultimate identity no longer appear quite so transparent.

Sometime during *katun* 8 Ahau (A.D. 1441–1461),[3] according to several native chronicles, the Maya suffered the last major political upheaval of the precolonial era, the civil war that rent the coalition of noble families ruling Mayapán. Several noble families, led by the Tutul Xiu, attacked and expelled the Cocom faction from Mayapán. The Cocom family were the legendary founders of Mayapán,

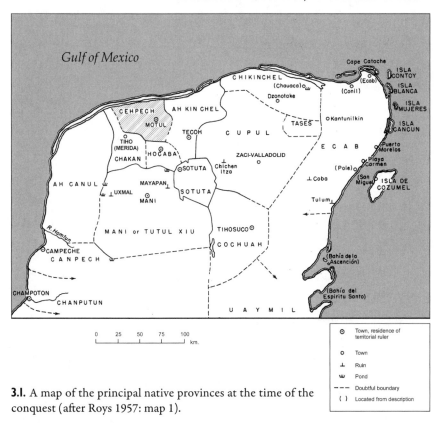

3.1. A map of the principal native provinces at the time of the conquest (after Roys 1957: map 1).

and several accounts indicate that the Xius and the Cocoms were first among equals in the confederacy or alternated as kings at various times.[4] The Xiu party had taken particular offense to the destruction of the city walls and the introduction of "Mexican" mercenaries to support Cocom tyranny. Supposedly this uprising resulted in the extermination of the entire Cocom family with the exception of a single son who was trading in Honduras at the time. Nevertheless, the ruined city continued to provide the material touchstones of rank and nobility long after its abandonment. In a famous statement, the early Maya scribe Gaspar Chi noted that "at the present day, lords and nobles in the land remember the sites of their former homes [in Mayapán]" (Tozzer 1941:230). The ruins of Chich'en Itzá and TiHo probably played a similar role for earlier generations of nobles.

We know little of the diaspora that followed. Some families apparently returned to their ancestral seats, such as the Tutul Xiu of Maní, but others were moved to settle new lands. Among the latter were members of the Pech patriline. Several Pech nobles traced their ancestry to Nohcabal Pech, a person of some importance

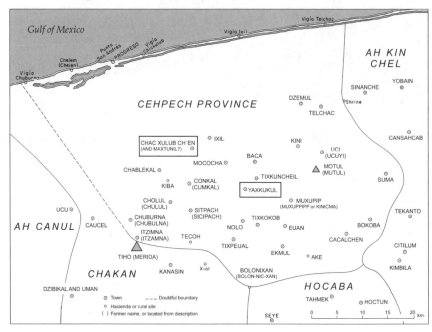

3.2. A map of the Cehpech province (from Roys 1957: map 5).

at Mayapán. The *Relación* from the capital town of Motul, for instance, indicates he was a close relative of the great lord of Mayapán who, after the fall of that city, organized what came to be known as the province of Cehpech (Garza 1983, 1:269).[5] Pech nobles obtained control of many of the leading towns of the province (Figure 3.2), including Motul, the capital, Maxtunil, Yaxkukul, Conkal, and Chac Xulub Ch'en. They appear to have replaced only the existing power structure; however, the *Relación de Motul*, among others, recounts its much earlier conquest by the legendary Kaku Pacal of Chich'en Itzá, whom hieroglyphic dates would place during the ninth century.

In addition to several *Relaciones*[6] concerning encomiendas in the Cehpech province, our knowledge of the Pech family derives from an important collection of native documents ostensibly dating to the mid-sixteenth century. This group includes the chronicle from Chac Xulub Ch'en, a very similar document from Yaxkukul (Table 3.1), and two boundary surveys of Yaxkukul that were carried out within a span of eight days.[7] The chronicles concern the actions of a small group of closely related figures, primarily Nakuk Pech of Chac Xulub Ch'en, his father Ah Kom Pech, his uncle Ah Macan Pech of Yaxkukul, another younger uncle Ixkil Itzam Pech of Conkal, and Ah Macan's father Ah Naum Pech (Figure 3.3). By the late fifteenth century the Cehpech province had been centralized under the ruler-

Table 3.1. Selected versions of the Pech chronicles

Crónica de Yaxkukul	Crónica de Chac Xulub Ch'en (Chicxulub)
lost original: Ah Macan Pech, narrator	lost original: Nakuk Pech, narrator (1882)
1769 ms. copy, LAL, Tulane University	nineteenth-century ms. copy, ex-Regil collection
Martínez Hernández 1926 (Maya and Spanish)	Pio Pérez—Códice Pérez
	Berendt Collection (copy of Pio Pérez)
	Brinton (1969)—Maya Chronicles (1882, Maya/English)
	Charency—Crestomatie Maya (from Brinton)
	Pérez Martínez (1936, Spanish, from Brinton)
Restall's (1998) synthetic version	

ship of a Pech *halach uinic*, with other town leaders serving as *batabob* in his court. The Chac Xulub chronicle suggests there may have been even smaller divisions, for Nakuk Pech seems to have recognized his father Ah Kom Pech and his uncle[8] Ah Macan Pech as his immediate superiors and makes no mention of acting with or for the halach uinic. He in turn was batab of two small districts (*cacab*) within the Chac Xulub polity, Chinchinicab and Chac Xulub Ch'en itself.

As most editors have noted, the texts that have come down to us are a pastiche of various documents from various periods that shift perspective without warning. For instance, in the Chac Xulub chronicle (§§9–10), after a section recording the transferal of office from Nakuk Pech to his son Pedro in 1552, the son himself begins a short first-person interjection recording this fact, only to have Nakuk Pech's narrative resume once again (§11). Also embedded within this chronicle are sections concerning Naum Pech (§§30–35), the halach uinic of Motul, and events in Valladolid. Nevertheless, there was clearly some attempt to cobble the whole together in a single, albeit dissonant, narrative.

The extraordinarily ordinary opening of this document reads *Ten cen yn Nakuk Pech yax hidalgos concixtadoren uay ti lum lae* ("I, who am Nakuk Pech, of the first lordly conquistadors here in this land"). When seen against the backdrop of pre-conquest Maya historical conventions, the passage is revolutionary. Not only does personal history reappear following the long lacuna of the Postclassic period, but more importantly this text appears to mark the emergence of autobiography. This reflects a radical change in perspective, since for hundreds of years the conventions of hieroglyphic history had demanded the near-exclusive use of the third person. Unlike the boasts of Old World monarchs, the deeds of Maya *ahauob* of the Classic period were invariably presented impersonally and often passively. Here, however, the reader is ostensibly privy to the thoughts and perspective of a Maya lord, albeit a rather minor one.

It is therefore with some surprise that we read in the associated chronicle from the nearby town of Yaxkukul the identical opening paragraph followed by "I, who

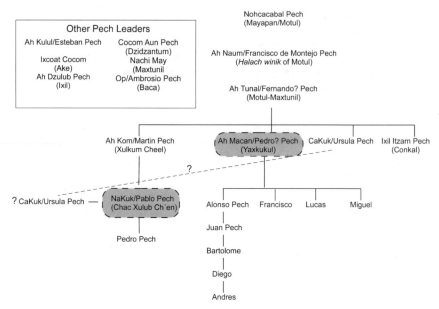

3.3. A genealogy of the principal figures in the Chac Xulub Ch'en chronicle.

am Ah Macan Pech, first conquistador here in this land." Both documents are in fact almost identical, except for the authorial voice and the towns concerned. Must these documents therefore be rejected out of hand? That was the conclusion of a Spanish magistrate who, when presented with the Yaxkukul chronicle and associated documents in a 1793 lawsuit, summarily dismissed them as evidence on the basis of their implausibly early date (Martínez Hernández 1926:3). There are other problems as well. For instance, Bishop Toral is mentioned as the first bishop of Yucatán and as having conducted baptisms in 1518 (§28), although in fact he was the fourth bishop and arrived only in 1562. Furthermore, there is considerable doubt whether the encomenderos named in the documents actually were so, since the Cehpech territory was part of Francisco de Montejo's personal estate.[9] Finally, Nakuk Pech identifies himself as a halach uinic (§3), a rather grandiose claim for the leader of what was a town of modest proportions at best.

Might this unusual group of texts reflect more interesting issues, however? Might we see in their rhetoric some trace of how this first generation of native leaders began to formulate an official self, or, if they are indeed later fabrications, how memory transformed the events of the conquest into new conventions of legitimacy and history? This analysis takes as its point of departure an observation made by the historian of religion Jonathan Z. Smith (1987:chapter 1), who noted that in studying myth and ritual in ancient states, we have most often interpreted them as mirroring or replicating cosmic myths or templates. The emphasis therefore is on examining the vertical links forged between the terrestrial world, the underworld, and the celestial realm. Such studies might be said to be "centro-centric" in that they emphasize the primacy of the center (omphalos, axis mundi) as a point of communication between the spheres. In Maya scholarship, the many studies of world trees, archaeoastronomy, directionality, and cosmologically ordered sacred architecture (especially cosmic temple-mountains) would clearly fall within this approach.

But Smith points out the importance of another broad class of myths whose concern is exclusively with the terrestrial realm. These myths have to do with the actions of earthly ancestral figures, human or quasi-human, whose actions usually determine the terrestrial realm either by naming places and objects or by leaving traces (that is, memorials) of their wanderings in the form of landscape features. Like the affairs of humans, these events are altogether untidy and cannot easily be fitted into neat cosmic templates. They also tend to multiply, often with little connection from one event to the next. Therefore, the forms most appropriate to such events are lists—lists of ancestors, lists of the places they visited, lists of their deeds—and, significantly, the map.

Smith notes that this terrestrial class of origin myths typically has been assumed to reflect a more "primitive" worldview, prior to the formation of agricultural states. Yet parallels can be seen with the ritual circuits of Egyptian *sed* festivals (Kemp 1989:59–62, 213–217), among others. It hardly needs stating that in Mesoamerica such stories and rituals are also of critical importance, *uayeb* rituals being an obvious example. As Elizabeth Boone (1991:122) contends, the many pictorial migration documents of Central México are dramatic in presentation and ritual in function: "[The migration story] can be thought of as a historical or narrative play, but it is too ideologically and culturally important to be merely a secular play. It has all the trappings and stylizations of a ceremony, and I think it most similar to a ritual performance." Such migrations ground a people in a place of origin but then provide both spatial and temporal links connecting them to a final destination. Along the way cities are laid out, cultivation begins, crafts are taught, and the calendar is initiated—in other words, the landscape is created and domesticated. In the Mesoamerican tradition such journeys have a strongly cyclic tendency. In some traditions, for instance, the Aztecs leave Aztlan and arrive in Tenochtitlan in 1 Flint years, and both share strong similarities as places (Gingerich 1986).

No such pictorial documents have survived in the Maya area, but a case could easily be made that many of the sections of the Books of Chilam Balam, especially those concerning the wanderings of the Itza, are written versions of now-lost pictorial originals. We also possess a number of stories about gods, or quasi-gods, who wander about the landscape constructing order. Perhaps the most famous is the man-god Quetzalcoatl, or Kukulcan as he was known in the Maya area, whose various journeys resulted in the founding of cities such as Chich'en Itzá, Mayapán, and Cozumel, at least according to legend. An alternative passage from Fray Diego López de Cogolludo (1957, IV:3:178, author's translation) concerns the settlement of Yucatán by a migration from the west:

> With those arrived from the west came one, who was like one of their priests, named Zamna, that they say . . . assigned the names of all the ports of the sea, points of land, estuaries, coasts, and all the regions, sites, hills, and places of all this land, the names which today they are called in their language—[it is] certainly a thing to be admired, if it is so, that such division as was made of everything, so that each could be known . . . , for there is hardly a spot for which they don't have a name in their language.

Zamna, probably a reference to the paramount god Itzam Na, is here described as "like one of their priests," in other words, another ancestral man-god who created the landscape by walking and naming it and whose memory is preserved in its toponyms.

It is also important to note that in the Mesoamerican tradition, such journeys can happen within history. For instance, the Mixtecan creation events displaced the existing "stone men" at the end of the Late Classic, whereas within the Maya area, the arrival of Kukulcan and the Itza in Yucatán took place in a landscape already well-populated. However, such arrivals or migrations frequently mark the boundary between historical epochs or wholesale cultural transformations, so in that sense they are in fact creation—or, better, recreation—events.

Time in the Chronicles

The histories recorded in the Chac Xulub Ch'en and Yaxkukul chronicles and the processions of the Yaxkukul land documents resemble in large measure these stories about the first events and orderings of the landscape, except that the point of transformation is the conquest.[10] Like the first events of myths, it is interesting that the period prior to the coming of Spanish is characterized as almost *in illo tempore* (in Eliade's sense). Again and again the narrator is at pains to mark off this period as a world that had not yet come into being: "When I was placed to govern in Chac Xulub Ch'en, the Spaniards had not yet come to this land of Yucatan" (§2). "And we were the principal leaders in this land when there still was no Holy Church in these lands, when these lands were not governed by the Spaniards, in the times when they did not congregate to worship. And before men became Christians, I, Nakuk Pech, was chief" (§9). This rhetorical pattern of layering formulaic statements of aboriginal legitimacy against events that have not yet happened sets the former apart as oddly inchoate and static. The latent state of the preconquest period is further reinforced by the almost complete absence of prehispanic events in these documents. Members of the Pech family are placed in office among the Cehpech towns, but abstractly and passively. Apart from these brief inaugurations, no one *does* anything: the chronicle is silent on visits, wars, tribute payments, rituals, and so forth—in short, all the sorts of events that figure so prominently after the arrival of Montejo.

This is true for the temporal framework as well since there is not a single date prior to the shipwreck of Geronimo de Aguilar in 1511 or 1517 (§§14–15). Significantly, this first appearance of foreigners in Yucatán is paired with the cessation of the practice of erecting katun stones: "This year [1517] they ceased to carry the katun, that is, ceased to erect the public memorial stone for each twenty *tuns*. The public stone was put in place before the arrival of the foreigners, the Spaniards, here on our boundaries. Since they have come it has never been done again" (§15).[11]

But the very first date, although chronologically later, *is* presented in the native system. "The fifth division of the seating of katun 11 Ahau was when the Spaniards came and settled at the great town of TiHo [i.e., 1541]. And then it was in 9 Ahau that Christianity began here. This was the year when the Spanish first came here to this land: 1511 years" (§1).[12] This 1541 event, which also marks the assignment of the Pech lords to encomenderos, is the only date so recorded, and 9 Ahau is the only other named katun. Somewhat later, 1541 is also associated with the single mention of a year-bearer, in this case 13 Kan (§18), and as discussed below, the sole *tzolkin* date in the chronicle begins katun 11 Ahau.

Although it is not uncommon for Maya documents to open with a date, no other official document from the sixteenth or seventeenth centuries even mentions the word "katun,"[13] perhaps because it was beyond the pale of official discourse. Yet we know from the Books of Chilam Balam that the katun count continued to be kept for centuries, and in fact this passage is a fairly close paraphrase of some of the Chumayel, Tizimin, and Maní katun records (Barrera Vásquez and Morley 1949:42, ll. 252–257). The inclusion of this passage may therefore have been a deliberate attempt to archaize the document and thus bolster the claims of its possessors. But I contend it was also in some measure a conscious strategy to depict the conquest in terms of cyclic regeneration and renewal, of renaming and recreating the world. The millenarian nature of these first events is brought home in a prophecy concerning the arrival of the Spanish in a section of the document called the "Chronicle of Ah Naum Pech" by Martínez Hernández (since it concerns the halach uinic of Motul). After a recitation of how leaders of the various provinces urged submission to the Spanish and the peaceful acceptance of Christianity, Ah Naum Pech is said to have addressed the young men thusly: "Know that One Imix is the name of the day when, at dawn, there will come from the eastern districts bearded men carrying the sign of one god to the province! Go and receive them with your white pendants" (§33, translation by Restall 1998:121).

This prophecy seems to have been borrowed from very similar utterances by the seer Chilam Balam, associated in the Books of Chilam Balam with katun 11 Ahau rather than a tzolkin date (e.g., Edmonson 1982:l. 3987, 1986:ll. 539, 1921). The depiction of the arriving Spaniards as bearded men coming from the east at dawn also strongly suggests a local recasting of the familiar legend concerning Cortés found in the *Anales de Cuahtitlan* and the *Leyendas de las Soles* (Bierhorst 1992), among others. These texts last place the arrival of the Spanish in the Aztec year 1 Reed, neatly repeating the birth date and departure or death date of Quetzalcoatl, and for the Aztecs, the departure from Chicomoztoc. The Chac Xulub passage seems to conflate Montejo and Cortés, whereas the mentions of bearded men coming from the east only strengthens the overtones of the Quetzalcoatl-Tlahuizcalpantecuhtli myth.

The date 1 Imix is *not* the cognate of highland 1 Reed (the former is a tzolkin date, the later the name of a year),[14] but it *is* the beginning of the 260-day tzolkin. The day was doubly significant, for as Ralph Roys (1949:7) noted, 1 Imix was also the first day of katun 11 Ahau. It thus marks the initiation (or better, restarting) of time, much as Quetzalcoatl is said to have introduced the calendar in certain highland sources, since in virtually all of the Chilam Balam chronicles, the Spaniards were said to have arrived in katun 11 Ahau, rather than 2 or 13 Ahau (Barrera Vásquez and Morley 1949:32, ll. 252–253; 52, ll. 60–64). In the *Chilam Balam of Chumayel*, 1 Imix is also associated in some murky fashion with the fall of Chich'en Itzá, perhaps the date when its leader was captured.[15] There is thus again a structural parallel with 1 Reed in that the latter also marked the abandonment of Tula by its leader Quetzalcoatl.

One final comment concerns the katun count in this document. As noted, the opening statement records the arrival of the Spanish in the fifth division of katun 11 Ahau and then the beginning of Christianity in katun 9 Ahau. Similar statements are made in three of the Books of Chilam Balam (Barrera Vásquez and Morley 1949:42). Elsewhere in the manuscript the first date clearly refers to the Spanish occupation of TiHo in 1541–1542. In the Mayapán calendar, katun 11 Ahau began in the year 1539 and 9 Ahau followed twenty years later (Table 3.2). Therefore, although 11 Ahau was the correct katun, 1541 was not its fifth division, and Christianity arrived well before katun 9 Ahau. Franciscans had arrived in Champoton in 1535 and then again in 1544–1546. By 1548 they were in Maní, and in Valladolid in 1552 (Edmonson 1982:n l. 1190; Barrera Vásquez and Morley 1949:43n70). Presumably some baptisms were carried out before the start of the Mayapán katun 9 Ahau in 1559.

But later in the Colonial period there was a calendrical reform involving a shift to a 24-solar-year (*haab*) katun, which Munro Edmonson (1988:137, 262–264) refers to as the Valladolid calendar (Table 3.2). Several calendrical tables in the Books of Chilam Balam back-calculate dates in the Colonial period according to this system. Victoria Bricker and Helga-Maria Miram (2002:73) date the reform to June 1, 1776, because of several propitious coincidences between the various cycles in that year. This does not exclude the possibility that the mathematics had been

Table 3.2. Christian calendar correlations of katun cycles in the Books of Chilam Balam

Katun[a]	Mayapán Calendar (Gregorian)	Valladolid Calendar[b]
6 Ahau	5 Jan 1461–21 Sep 1480	1416–1440
4 Ahau	22 Sep 1480–9 Jun 1500	1440–1464
2 Ahau	10 Jun 1500–25 Feb 1520	1464–1488
13 Ahau	26 Feb 1520–12 Nov 1539	1488–1512
11 Ahau	13 Nov 1539–30 Jul 1559	1512–1536
9 Ahau	31 Jul 1559–16 Apr 1579	1536–1560
7 Ahau	17 Apr 1579–1 Jan 1599	1560–1584
5 Ahau	2 Jan 1599–18 Sep 1618	1584–1608
3 Ahau	19 Sep 1618–5 Jun 1638	1608–1632
1 Ahau	6 Jun 1638–20 Feb 1658	1632–1656
12 Ahau	21 Feb 1658–7 Nov 1677	1656–1680
10 Ahau	8 Nov 1677–25 Jul 1697	1680–1704
8 Ahau	26 Jul 1697–12 Apr 1717	1704–1728
6 Ahau	13 Apr 1717–28 Dec 1736	1728–1752
4 Ahau	29 Dec 1736–14 Sep 1756	1752–1776
2 Ahau	15 Sep 1756–1 Jun 1776	1776–1800
13 Ahau	2 Jun 1776–17 Feb 1796	1800–1824
11 Ahau	18 Feb 1796–5 Nov 1815	1824–1848
9 Ahau	6 Nov 1815–23 Jul 1835	1848–1872
7 Ahau	24 Jul 1835–9 Apr 1855	1872–1896
5 Ahau	10 Apr 1855–24 Dec 1874	1896–1920

a. Data from Bricker and Miram (2002:table 20).
b. These are also the spans given in some of the *Codex Pérez* tables (Craine and Reindorp 1979:128–129, 157–171).

worked out at some other time, however. A table of Valladolid-style Ahau *katunob* in the *Codex Pérez* (Craine and Reindorp 1979:128–130) seems to have a composition date of 1752, although statements within it suggest a slightly later date of 1759–1763. Roys (1954:7) argued that a copyist date of 1689 associated with the cycle of 24-year katuns, also from the *Codex Pérez*, may place the origin of this calendar in the seventeenth century.

Some of the aberrant dates seem to have resulted from garbled attempts to translate from one katun count to the other. The 11 Ahau statement may have been an attempt to retain the katun name known from an earlier Mayapán-based chronicle. Knowing the Christian date from a Spanish source, the author may have used the katun limits from the Valladolid calendar to assign the tun/haab placement, since 1541 falls in Valladolid katun 9 Ahau in either its fifth or sixth division. As for the 9 Ahau statement involving the introduction of Christianity, it is difficult to argue for its placement in the Mayapán system (1559–1579).[16]

In a parallel statement, the *Codex Pérez* (Craine and Reindorp 1979:164) states that for tun 15 of katun 9 Ahau, "The priests began baptizing," with the notation that this happened in 1550.[17] Note, however, that this would be a back-calculated Valladolid calendar date. In short, the antiquity of these native calendrical statements in the Pech chronicles is strongly suspect. Although the exact date for the inception of the Valladolid calendar is not precisely known, its composition surely postdated the conquest by at least a century yet predated the 1793 lawsuit involving the Yaxkukul chronicle (see Restall 1997:290–291 for other reasons to believe the chronicle is late).

Other chronicle dates are impossibly early. For instance, it is claimed that Bishop Toral performed a mass baptism on October 13, 1518, in Maxtunil (§28), the year of Grijalva's voyage. In fact, Toral did not arrive until 1562. This is apparently another conversion error, since the third Chumayel chronicle indicates Toral arrived in the sixth tun of katun 11 Ahau, or 1545 (Roys 1967:143). Although this is also incorrect, 1518 falls in the sixth division of the Valladolid katun 11 Ahau, further support for the use of this calendar and the late composition date of the Pech chronicles. It is also claimed that Montejo the Adelantado visited Chich'en Itzá in 1519 (§16), well before his first *entrada*, and then again in 1528 (§16). This chronicle in fact seems to be the sole authority for these events (Chamberlain 1948:57–58); the documented entrada was only made in 1532–1534 under the command of Montejo the Younger. A map accompanying the first land document apparently carried a date of 1522, as does the Yaxkukul land survey (Barrera Vásquez 1984; Martínez Hernández 1926:37), although this date clearly conflicts with individuals and buildings mentioned in the text.

These errors are not easily explained. Although some may result from incorrect back-conversions of native dates, the errors do not seem to be consistently wrong. Rather, the facts that the conquest of México (mentioned in §17) was separated from the foundation of Mérida by a katun, that the latter was five katuns after the fall of Mayapán,[18] and that Aguilar and Guerrero had arrived a half-katun prior to 1521 were probably not lost on the authors. The intent seems to be to compress dates into two horizons, one focused on 1519–1521 and the other on the claiming of TiHo. In this manner, the misdated events become part of the two epochal acts marking the loss of native rule and thus partake of the prestige of origins. This is clearly seen in the annalistic section of the Chac Xulub chronicle (§§15–28), where the description of events in 1511, 1519, and 1521 is followed by a gap of twenty years, omitting the dates of the first two entradas entirely, after which events are narrated year by year until 1552. Termination of the annals in the year of López Medel's visit may also be significant in that this year of course marked a sweeping attempt to once and for all systematically undermine native social organization.

It is also interesting that naming too is disrupted at this crucial juncture between the two epochs. Nakuk Pech is unusual in favoring his birth, rather than baptismal, name.[19] This is surprising, since as a reward for his usefulness to the Spanish, he was granted hidalgo status and exemption from tribute, as well as the right to the honorific "Don" as a result of his baptism. Yet he consistently prefers to identify himself as Nakuk well after the conquest, except in three situations. The first is when he describes his baptism, where Pablo is unavoidable. The second is at the close of the document. The third and most interesting are two passages in which he anachronistically identifies himself as Pablo precisely at the first appearance of the Spanish in 1519 (§§13, 28). It is as if this watershed event magically had the power to transform names into the new system.

The Events of the Chronicles

The events of the conquest are presented in a variety of forms with little attempt to provide a sequential narrative. Rather, the repetition of the events of the conquest seems to be a rhetorical device heightening their dramatic effect. Several ordering schemes are used that parallel narrative devices used in pictorial codices. As mentioned, one large chunk is presented in annalistic format, recording the years from 1519–1552 (§§15–28; Restall 1998:115–121). Matthew Restall has dubbed this the *Title of Saci-Sisal* because it concerns events in the Valladolid region, but at least part of this section is narrated in the first person by Nakuk Pech, suggesting its interpolation into an independent document by some later copyist. In contrast, the border surveys strongly recall what Elizabeth Boone (1994, 2000:chapter 4) has called "cartographic histories," whereas much of the remainder of the chronicles fall within what she refers to as an event-driven format. This is especially true of the first subsection of the Nakuk Pech chronicle (§§1–9). It recounts the conquest in three acts, each punctuated by an "I, who am Nakuk Pech, was lord when" statement identifying the author, his ancestry, and the dynastic basis for his authority. These interjections, examples of what Hanks (1987:674) has called "cyclic description," help focus attention on the peak moments of each of the three scenes, while at the same time underscoring the narrator's connection to these primordial deeds and grounding them in preconquest authority structures.

The first act (§§2–5) encompasses events from the arrival of Montejo the Adelantado, here dated 1519, to the first rendering of tribute in Champoton, to which the author went attended by his father and uncles. Its central section recounts the abortive first entrada from Ecab, presented as a search for Chich'en Itzá by the Spaniards at which they supposedly arrived and stayed before returning to the coast. The second act (§§6–7) concerns the move by Montejo from Champoton into Yucatán, culminating in his arrival at TiHo in 1541 and a second tribute requisition. This is presented in similar fashion to the first, with Nakuk Pech being accompanied by the same individuals save for his father, paralleling a similar list of captains accompanying Montejo the Younger. The third act (§§7–9) was the repartimiento of the towns among the conquistadors, also in TiHo in 1542. The culmination of this section is also the most personal: "All those of my land, and myself, were given to Don Julian Doncel, encomendero and new lord of Chac Xulub Ch'en. The new encomendero took my hand, before the captain Don Francisco de Montejo. I thus was given to the hand of Don Julian Doncel, and the tribute began to be paid by me to the lords, the saintly men" (§8). The section concludes with another "I who am Nakuk Pech" refrain followed by a brief account his baptism and the coming of the *oidor* Tomas Lopez. Yet another coda recounts all this, beginning with his accession before the arrival of the Spanish and carrying the story forward to a new, later conclusion, the transfer of power to his son in 1552.

The overtones of this section are suggestive of a typical migration narrative. The first entrada records wandering visits to several towns but culminates in the arrival of the Adelantado at Chich'en Itzá (which apparently only his son ever visited). This entrada is rendered even more succinctly in a later passage, which states, "Thus, the first thing that the great Spaniard Don Francisco Montejo, *el Adelantado*, and his high captains, became familiar with was Chichén Itzá, where they settled"(§16). Given the identification of Montejo and the Spaniards with the return of Quetzalcoatl, this journey reflects the initial return to the mythical place of origin shared with other migration stories. Both passages place this event early, in 1519 in the latter case, and chronologically compressed it with the arrival of Cortés in Cozumel and thus, of course, with the 1 Reed date associated with the return of Quetzalcoatl. The second entrada is only touched upon in sections 17–18 but significantly is said to have happened exactly twenty years before the arrival in TiHo.[20] This entrada seems to be conflated with Montejo the Younger's entrada of 1531–1534.

Having returned to the ancestral place of origin, Montejo could now begin the second stage in his assumption of rulership by moving to TiHo from whence the new era would be ruled. Critical to rulership in Mesoamerican experience was the apportionment of tribute, which is here characterized as much as a badge of honor as it was an obligation. It is a scene with an ancient pedigree, reaching back to the reliefs of Chich'en Itzá, an action that once again restored a political charter to the land. Central to this second tribute request was the drawing up of the tribute list, for the repartimiento was in effect another creation event creating new divisions and replacing the first families of the old order with new ones. And it is interesting that it was presided over by the Adelantado himself, who in actuality was far removed during this entire campaign (Chamberlain 1948:185, 217). Although the credibility of this narrative as an eyewitness account is left in doubt, the substitution of the father for the son perhaps follows a higher logic in emphasizing the significance of this act for the future political structure of the peninsula. It also strongly echoes a passage in the Chumayel (Roys 1967:70–75), in which the Itza, after a long journey across Yucatán "setting in order," surveying, and naming the towns and wells, then finally settle at Chich'en Itzá. Here the first action was to requisition tribute, immediately after which "[t]hen began their reign; then began their rule" (Roys 1967:5).

In a later section (§18), this primordial act of submission and tribute is said to have occurred on a mound called Chuncaan ("base of the sky," "horizon"), the main mound and main deity of Mérida.[21] On the one hand, this grounds the scene in a (native) cosmological framework. In this respect, the closing rhetoric of the earlier scene, "and the tribute began to be paid by me to the lords, the saintly men," is interesting in its characterization of the Spaniards as *kul uinicob*. *Kul* ("sacred," "holy") of course had been applied to the highest lords of the Classic period: here the word probably refers to their Christianity, but the rhetorical pattern seems to be no accident. It is also noteworthy that this event is marked with a 13 Kan year-bearer, as mentioned above, one of the few uses of the native calendar.

But more importantly, this act of submission on top of the main mound of TiHo seems to be cast within the framework of a preconquest investiture ceremony, if what we know of Chich'en Itzá is any guide. As I argue elsewhere (Ringle 2004), the power of Chich'en Itzá, Uxmal, Mayapán, and probably TiHo derived in large measure from the ritual authority they claimed to legitimize rulers. TiHo at this historical moment was the proper place because it happened to be the seat of the calendrical *may* cycle precisely during this katun, according to the *Chilam Balam of Maní* (Craine and Reindorp 1979:77).[22] In fact, the parallels between the earlier visits to Chich'en Itzá and the final success at TiHo are made most succinctly and powerfully in this section (§18), where the two earlier visits to Chich'en Itzá are mentioned immediately afterward and framed as a prelude to this "final and permanent settling" of Yucatán. As noted above, it is noteworthy that the two are said to have been separated by twenty years, and so the impression of a mythical coming-into-being is hard to avoid, marked by a pilgrimage from the site initiating the last major stage of the preconquest history to the seat of the coming age of Spanish domination.

Conclusions

As Restall (1997:276; 1998) has argued, these documents are primordial titles, at least in spirit. The conclusion of the chronicle makes clear its concern with first things: "And this is the entire account of where the Spanish wandered and how the first friars were received. And the names of the first foreign lords I put in order so that they can be shown. This is put down so that the manner in which the conquest happened can be known, and how much anguish we suffered here, under the trees, under the vines, under the branches, at that time and in addition the principal men and the elders . . ." (§36). But in what sense are these documents ritual or mythic history rather than simply a record of deeds that were in fact first? These stories cannot really be said to encode or allegorize religious or mythic ideas except occasionally and obliquely. Given the absence of evidence to the contrary, we must take Nakuk Pech's professions of Christianity as sincere. It is unlikely that the identification of the Spaniards with Quetzalcoatl or the reference to them as kul uinicob reflects Maya credulity; by 1541, twenty years of armed conflict had probably dispelled any lingering illusions in this regard. If these are ritual or mythic accounts, they are concerned only incidentally with the transcendent.

But as mentioned at the beginning, ritual and myth may have other, no less powerful functions. Definitions of ritual are many, but Jonathan Smith (1987:103–111) points out that ritual functions first as a means to focus attention. This can be seen in the repetitions of names, events, and formulaic expressions in the documents. Second, ritual is a form of practice (Bradley 2005:34) by no means restricted to the "sacred" sphere in traditional societies, but one whose formal aspects may vary with the importance of the task at hand. Third, ritual acts direct attention to differences of state, as between sacred and profane space, then and now, human and divine, and foster exchanges between them. Ritual therefore does not have any independent substantive reality but depends wholly on context, causing its performers to have a heightened awareness of the categories being distinguished.

These characteristics may be seen in the temporal distortions of the chronicles and surveys. Victoria Bricker (1981) has noted similar tendencies in other colonial Maya documents, suggesting that temporal distortions bring certain "historical" events into conjunction, while at the same time distinguishing them from others. "The prophetic tradition of the Maya tends to blur the distinction between myth and history. In serving as a precedent, as a guide for human action, myth becomes just another event in history. But since the events in the corresponding parts of two cycles are never identical, the myth may acquire some new elements before it is eventually reintegrated into oral tradition. This is one source of syncretism in myth" (Bricker 1981:180).

These documents concern a particularly crucial time in Maya history, for political subjugation and oppression was accompanied by a wholesale turnover in personal and place-names, in the ordering of the landscape, and in political relations. Thus, the ritual elements in documents such as the boundary surveys do not make any transcendent reference but simply treat the division of land. But such actions must be seen against the backdrop of much earlier surveys and measurements, such as in the Chumayel, where they are associated with the new Itza order, or even as far afield as the Mixtec *Codex Vindobonensis*, where the foundation of new dynasties is consistently associated with measurements (e.g., ff. 13–21).

As for the events in the chronicles, the conquest likewise presented events wholly unforeseen. To be comprehended, some attempt was necessary to fit them within the existing historical framework. Here the effort was to inscribe the stories into previous stories or to invent those prior stories within which new events could be inscribed. Thus, the arrival of Montejo was likened to what was probably already a famous story concerning Cortés, which in turn was inscribed in early mythic cycles concerning the rise and fall of Chich'en Itzá and Quetzalcoatl, both associated with major cultural transformations. This gave the recent events precedent and weight in the sense that they were no longer contingent but partook of the order of creation. For a while at least, and in some limited fashion, the conquest was appropriated into Maya history not as an external event but as one of the several calamitous transitions between the evolutionary cycles of history. In this fashion the foreigners were somehow domesticated and the new order received and legitimized not as primarily political events but as events foreordained and mythical in their telling. The documents do not minimize the suffering caused therein, but suffering after all is an experience not necessarily alien to founding myths. It is in this sense that perhaps we can understand the opening statement in which Nakuk Pech identifies himself as one of the *yax hidalgos concixtadoren uay ti lum lae* ("the first lordly conquistadors here in this land"), as less a forced ally of the Spanish than one who recognized the coming epoch and willingly fostered its arrival.

Although suspect as contemporary historical narratives, these documents may preserve some elements of objective truth: they agree in many particulars with others from the period. But what is interesting is the way that they were edited, recopied, recompiled, and added to over time, at each stage adding a new telling of a slightly different story with slightly different protagonists, often rupturing the narrative boundaries of the documents. Thus, for instance, at the close of one of the land surveys supposedly written in 1544, we find not only the name of Ah Macan Pech but the names of five descending generations as well. What was important was the grounding of the actors in the primordial events of 1540–1546, the demonstration that these ancestors walked with the ancestors of the conquest, and that they marched across the peninsula and the boundaries of provinces, naming and placing the stones that became their memorials.

It is also impossible to know whether there is a truly personal narrative at the core of these documents. Transposition of these lives into the first person was perhaps ultimately a rhetorical attempt to enhance the text's authority, and ultimately we cannot decide whether the author was Nakuk or Ah Macan Pech, but it probably meant very little to the possessors. As Bricker (1981:150) has stated, "In the timelessness of oral tradition and ritual there is no place for individuality. The hero of one conflict is the hero of all conflicts." Of more concern was the demonstration of a prehispanic genealogical charter for rulership. Here the *ch'ibal* is of central importance (see also Restall 1997). Often translated as *linaje* in Spanish dictionaries and somewhat uncritically rendered as "lineage" in English, it seems to have a much more restricted meaning in these documents, to short lines of direct dynastic descent—in other words, to the genealogy or pedigree of a particular actor. So, again, the substitution of Ah Macan Pech for Nakuk Pech was perhaps ultimately irrelevant to all but the Spanish magistrates. As members of the same ch'ibal, Nakuk and Ah Macan Pech were both ultimately ancestral rather than historical figures. Since the primary purpose of these documents was to demonstrate legitimacy, the process of transmission necessarily involved the suppression of differences and the winnowing of detail. By suppressing individualism, these figures became something far more important, founding ancestors present at the creation.

And yet, although such an interpretation may reflect current emphases and perhaps provide a better fit for a volume on worldview, to see these documents as the products of an impersonal mythologizing folk process is only a partial explanation ultimately at odds with the points made earlier regarding agency and the need to avoid essentializing the "Maya." The author(s) of these documents was not a Maya everyman. He or she apparently had access to at least one version of the Chilam Balam chronicles and probably Spanish-language accounts of the conquest of both Yucatán and México (see note 20). The writer also had knowledge of the native calendar, but an imperfect one. Most likely the author was therefore a community leader of some stature and perhaps a ritual specialist, one intelligent enough to have known what authorities might expect the form of an aboriginal title to be, yet not quite sophisticated enough to avoid some rather egregious errors of fact. The first-person narrative adopted may well have been modeled more on Spanish testimonials than any native precedents, and the lack of prehispanic events may simply reflect the absence of any documentation available to the author(s) when the chronicle was composed.

But most importantly, these documents were almost certainly produced for a purpose; they were not the reminiscences of an old man looking back on an eventful life but arguments prepared for the legal arena. Thus, they are unlikely to be in any sense examples of a "pristine" Maya worldview, written in isolation from the Ladino world, but rather examples of a Maya engaged in the full workings of colonial society, as Restall has also argued. Their composition shows a complex marshaling of texts from various genres with full knowledge that they would be read by more than one audience. And if the texts do reflect mythologizing, it may well have be the mythologizing of an author who felt some compunction to do so. That does not negate their value, however, but instead shifts our focus to the concerns of a later historical period. We can see in these documents dialogues with other documents and genres, and they serve to show that the accommodation of the conquest was an ongoing problem. If there is more art than artlessness in the chronicles, this may, if anything, increase our fascination with the circumstances responsible for their creation.

Acknowledgements. I wish to thank the editors of this volume for the opportunity to participate in both this volume and the preceding SAA symposium, and Robert Sharer and Loa Traxler for an invitation to the 2000 Maya Weekend at the University of Pennsylvania, where an earlier version of this chapter was presented. I also wish to thank Victoria Bricker and the anonymous volume reviewers for providing critical readings of this manuscript.

Notes

1. To avoid confusion, I have retained colonial Maya orthography throughout this chapter.

2. The symbol § refers to the divisions of the Chac Xulub Ch'en manuscript in the edition of Pérez Martínez (1936).

3. This event is specifically dated in the *Codex Perez* (Craine and Reindorp 1979:153) to the seventh *tun* of katun 8 Ahau, or perhaps A.D. 1448. As a translation of a translation, this version must be used with caution. I have endeavored to cross-check my citations with the original Maya and other translations of those same passages.

4. See Roys (1962) for a summary of the ethnohistorical evidence. Ringle and Bey (2001:273–27) marshal the evidence for monarchical rule at Mayapán. Milbrath and Peraza (this volume and earlier publications) offer detailed commentary on the correlations between the recent archaeology of Mayapán and related ethnohistorical texts.

5. Roys (1967:141, 1957:50) suggests that the lord with whom he was allied was a Tutul-Xiu, since the Pech later warred against the Cocoms at the time of conquest, but other sources indicate generally close relations with the lords of Chich'en Itzá and Sotuta.

6. The relevant documents are the *Relaciones de Motul, Cacalchen, Yaxa, Sihunchen, Chubulna, Hunucma, Tixkokob, Nolo, Mococha, Buctzotz, Muxuppipp, Sinanche*, and *Egum* (Garza 1983).

7. The first land document and the Yaxkukul chronicle were published by Martínez Hernández (1926). The second land survey, together with a reprint of the first, was edited by Barrera Vásquez (1984). See Table 3.1 for the publication history of the chronicles from Chac Xulub Ch'en and Yaxkukul. I am grateful to Victoria Bricker for a transcription of the Chac Xulub Ch'en manuscript.

8. Martínez Hernández (1926:3) wrongly states that they were brothers; in fact, they were of different generations. The father of Nakuk Pech was Ah Kom Pech, who in turn was the son of Ah Tunal Pech, also the father of Ah Macan Pech (Figure 3.3).

9. Barrera Vásquez (1984:82, note to lines 333–335). He further notes the two land surveys, although dated only eight days apart, list different encomenderos: the first lists Gonzalo Mendez, the second Julian Doncel (otherwise associated with Chac Xulub Ch'en).

10. For discussion of the rhetoric and ritual language of the Yaxkukul boundary surveys, see Hanks (1987). Restall (1997:281–292) provides an excellent analysis of the narrative forms present in the document and a nuanced view of the possible circumstances of its production. With regard to authenticity, Restall (1997:290) states: "This is not to say that the Deslinde [the boundary survey] lacks all authenticity: it is an authentic contrivance, a late-colonial title that was spawned by necessity and purposefully misdated"; yet he accepts that it may have incorporated now-lost earlier surveys, possibly of sixteenth-century date. The pattern of errors in many ways parallels those of the chronicles.

11. In the *Chumayel*, stones ceased to be erected in katun 9 Ahau (Barrera Vásquez and Morley 1949:52, ll. 68). Immediately before is a statement recording the coming of Christianity in 1519. Perhaps the Pech author misunderstood this statement or had access to a defective copy lacking the intervening 9 Ahau.

12. This was the shipwreck of Gonzalo Guerrero and Geronimo de Aguilar.

13. This statement is based on a concordance of sixteenth-century texts transcribed in large part by Victoria Bricker, who has kindly given permission to refer to these results. Concordance software was written by the author.

14. In the *Anales de Cuahtitlan*, 1 Cipactli (the cognate of 1 Imix) is mentioned as a day associated with Quetzalcoatl as Venus (Bierhorst 1992:36), evidently one of the days he could reappear as the morning star. Caso (1961:80) notes that 1 Cipactli is associated with a person entitled Ce Acatl (1 Reed) in the *Codex Borbonicus* 18 and may also be found in the headdress of an image of Xolotl, another figure closely associated with Quetzalcoatl.

15. Edmonson (1986:ll. 5965–5974); Roys (1967:115). The two translations differ significantly.

16. In the third Chumayel chronicle, which generally follows the Mayapán system, it is the stated that Christianity was introduced in the seventh tun of the katun 11 Ahau (rather than 9 Ahau). This would make it in 1545–1546, possibly referring to the second group of Franciscans to arrive in Champoton (Roys 1967:143), except that 1519 is explicitly noted in the next line. This is a valid placement in the Valladolid system, possibly referring to the introduction of Christianity by Cortés. But more importantly it shows the type of look-up errors that occurred during later recompilations of native documents and may also be an illustration of attempting to compress events near the 1519–1521 horizon. The following lines state that the arrival of Bishop Toral happened during the sixth tun of katun 9 Ahau (Edmonson 1986:365–372), or 1565 in the Mayapán calendar.

17. This perhaps refers to the commencement of baptisms in Zaci-Valladolid, dated in the Chac Xulub chronicle to 1551 (§26). Alternatively, the friars first arrived in Maní in the year 1550, according to the *Chilam Balams of Maní* and *Tizimin* (Barrera Vásquez and Morley 1949:42, ll. 267–268).

18. See Tozzer (1941:57n279), who quotes Roys as suggesting that this might be what was meant by the "fifth division" of katun 11 Ahau in the first section.

19. Aside from passages dealing specifically with his baptism (supposedly in 1518, a year before Grijalva's expedition), he uses his Christian name only at the conclusion of the document where he records the triumph of Christianity in his town.

20. In the parallel Yaxkukul text, a date of 1528 is assigned to this "second" visit to Chich'en Itzá and the foundation of a city there (Martínez Hernández 1926:17). This would actually place it during the Adelantado's entrance from Ecab during the first entrada, for which no other record mentions his passing through Chichén Itzá. The Ciudad Real de Chich'en Itzá was in fact founded in 1532–1533 by his son, Montejo the Younger, during the second entrada (Chamberlain 1948:134–139). The errors committed in this section, particularly the conflation of the first (1527–1529) entrada with the second (1531–1535) and the identification of the Adelantado as the leader of both, further support the late date of the chronicle. As Chamberlain (1948:132n2; 347–348) has noted, these mistakes were common to several earlier chroniclers, including López de Cogolludo (Book 2:VI), Landa (Tozzer 1941:50–51), and Herrera, among others, but only López de Cogolludo placed the Spanish there in 1528 (Tozzer 1941:51n246). Since López de Cogolludo's history was printed in 1688, it seems likely that the 1528 date in the Yaxkukul version may well have been borrowed from that source. Since Cogolludo does not mention these documents, the reverse is unlikely.

21. For gloss, see entry at http://www.famsi.org/reports/96072/ch/chulu_chuna.htm (accessed January 31, 2005). It is a primordial act because in §18 this is described as the first offering of tribute, omitting the two earlier episodes mentioned in this chronicle. The mound is also mentioned in the *Codex Pérez* (Craine and Reindorp 1979:71, 75–76) as the place where an important book of prophecy was kept and from whence it was taken by the prophets Chilam Balam and Xupan Nauat.

22. The mention is in the prophecies of the 13 Ahau katun series. The katun is said to end in 1548, part of a 24-year series but not the one of the Valladolid calendar. See Rice (this volume) for discussion of the may cycle.

Time, History, and Worldview

CHAPTER FOUR

Prudence M. Rice

The concept of time—perhaps better, for present purposes, writ large as Time—is a complex abstraction related to Western scholarly notions such as history, worldview, cosmology, ideology, and spatiality, among other things. Michael Kearney (1984:94–106), in his treatise on worldview, identified time as one of its universal components. But such universality does not extend to content: concepts of time, and the cognitive systems of which they are a part, are socially constructed; perceptions and representations of time vary from society to society, Western and non-Western (see Gell 1996; Munn 1992). Conceptions of time may be linear or cyclical, and different cultures have different degrees of orientation to the past, present, and future, but nonetheless all known cultures manifest some sense of time or history. And how a given society conceptualizes time is embodied in its calendar (Hassig 2001:4).

Within the range of societal emphases on time, the lowland Maya of the Classic period (A.D. 200–900) are frequently said to have been "obsessed" with time, as evidenced by their reckoning of time's passage by means of numerous calendars and painstakingly carved hieroglyphic dates on stone monuments. The role of time among the Maya has played center stage for many scholars as reflected in publication titles: "The Shape of Time," referring to certain glyphs (Coggins 1980), and *Maya Rulers of Time*, referring to Maya kings (Miller 1986). What is intriguing, however, is that key components of Maya concepts of time and worldviews endured from the Formative period (Rice 2007) through the wrenching Spanish Conquest and into the twentieth century.

Here I review some general concepts of time highlighted in recent anthropological and archaeological discussions of time, history, and ritual. I then summarize what is known about time reckoning and calendars among the Classic Maya. This sets the stage for an examination of Maya concepts of time and worldviews at conquest and in the Colonial period,[1] especially as they pertain to geopolitical relations.

Concepts and Components of Time

Modern anthropological, historical, scientific, and philosophical analyses of time have explored its construction in terms of various dimensions, some closely intertwined and others related more distantly. Time is often conceived in terms of dichotomies, such as linear versus cyclical or process versus representation, and contrasted (or conflated) with space. But as is usually the case, strict dichotomies oversimplify the situation and are often false.

Linear Time and Cyclical Time

Maurice Bloch (1977:282), discussing the relativism of concepts of time, points out that the variability largely "boils down to only two notions of time," linear and cyclical, whereas others (see, e.g., Howe 1981) note that time can be conceived in both ways but operate in different domains. Linear time is the most familiar conception of time to Westerners and might be thought of as secular, historical, or chronological time. In this view, time is envisioned as a line, an arrow, or a continuous, unidimensional flow from past to present to future. Time is asymmetrical and irreversible (Greene 2004:13)[2]; until time travel becomes a reality, we cannot return to the past to correct mistakes, relive pleasant events, or eliminate hurtful words, and the future consequences of today's acts remain unknown. Experiences of linear time, as well as written representations of it, are formulated in terms of three fundamental features: the succession or sequencing of events, the apparent simultaneity of events, and the duration of events and intervals between them (Bailey 1983:167). "Duration" is an interesting notion in such discussions: Bloch (1977:282) conceives of linear time as "durational" time, because the perception of duration, or ongoingness, provides the sense of time's directional flow.

"Cyclical" time resides in awareness of the rhythms of recurring events, particularly those of nature, such as the rising and setting of the sun and moon or the changing of the seasons. The predictable repetition of these events seems to be critical, especially in agrarian societies: as E. E. Evans-Pritchard commented (1961:49, quoted in Bailey 1983:172), "events lose much, even all, of their meaning if they are not seen as having some degree of regularity." Perhaps this is why so-called cyclical time is a common construct in non-Western and non-literate societies (Eliade 1954).

The notion of time being "cyclical" is somewhat misleading, however, and perhaps rather disingenuous. In the societies reputed to conceptualize cyclical time, technologies of circular or rotary motion are absent (Kearney 1984:98) and time does not spin around a pivot point like a wheel about its axis (although the sun might be thought to revolve around the earth). During the course of a cycle, time proceeds in linear fashion (Farriss 1987:572; cf. Bloch 1977, who refers to cyclical time as "static"). Kearney (1984:98–99) refers to this view of time as "oscillating" time, quoting Edmund Leach's (1966a:126) notion of a "zig-zag" motion: time experienced "as something discontinuous, a repetition of repeated reversal, a sequence of oscillations between polar opposites: night and day, winter and summer, drought and flood. . . . In such a scheme the past has no 'depth' to it, all past is equally past."

This notion of oscillation also seems misleading as it suggests a back-and-forth motion between extremes or about a point, with the emphasis on those extremes rather than on the movement or gradations between them. This would imply that humans recognize only day and night but not dawn and dusk, or youth and age but not the life changes that have occurred in between. As Ross Hassig (2001:61) points out in his study of time and history among the Aztecs, part of the difficulty is that scholars treat time as an abstraction rather than time as humanly lived (but cf. Shanks and Tilley 1987:chapter 5) and, with respect to the latter, virtually everyone recognizes both cyclical time (the repetition of days and seasons) and linear time (birth through death). A preferable descriptor or representation of cyclical time might be that of a Slinky™ toy (Farriss 1987:572): a spiral that combines cyclical and linear time (Hassig 2001:3). Regardless of the term used, cyclical or oscillating or spiraling time has a signal characteristic: it is everywhere closely identified with ritual expression.

Time as Representation and Time as Process

The "time as representation" notion returns us to the position that concepts of time are social constructs. Humans create mental representations—constructs, concepts, images, metaphors—in reference to time: not only can time be linear or cyclical but it can be an arrow or a river or sand; times can be good or bad, hard or high; and there can be "quality time" with loved ones. For North Americans, time has been commodified: it can be spent, wasted, or killed; time is money (but being two-timed is not twice as much). Time may also be personified into an aged Father Time. These kinds of representations say much about a society's attitudes, values, and worldviews.

G. N. Bailey (1983) discusses the similarities and differences between the notions of time as process and time as representation. The "time as process" view is at least partially related to the idea of time as linear, with events occurring along a continuum. These event series or processes may be short-term or long-term, the latter, obviously, making major contributions to concepts of linear time. Short-term processes, particularly if recurring—for example, the movement of the sun across the sky and the changes in size and shape of the moon—contribute to "cyclical" views of time. Ultimately, however, there is an "interplay between processes and our conceptual representations of those processes, and that interplay is itself a process which forms part of the continuum of events" (Bailey 1983:170). In other words, for those of the time-as-process school, "processes do not 'occur over time,' [they] *are* time" (Bailey 1983:168, quoting Parkes and Thrift 1980:37).

An example comes from the Nuer, a semi-pastoral society in Sudan. Evans-Pritchard (1940) claimed that "the Nuer have no expression equivalent to 'time' in our language, and they cannot . . . speak of time" (quoted by Aveni 2002:147). But although they may lack a word for time, they certainly have means for representing the present as distinct from the past. Evans-Pritchard distinguished concepts of "eco-time" and "structural time" in analyzing how the Nuer interrelate time and society. Eco-time is based on the activities governed by nature's basic rhythms, rainy and dry seasons, which determine their seasonally alternating settlement and subsistence patterns; it is cyclical time. Structural time is linear time; it crosses the seasons and moves progressively, as in the Nuer age-grade or age-set system that initiates males into the successive categories boy, warrior, and elder. This system also governs social relations among Nuer males, as well as the women with whom they might marry. History, for the Nuer, is measured in units of these age-sets, rather than in years, as well as by the distance from their clan founders; as such, structural time is particular to particular territorial groups, and history, time—as representation and as process—and space are interrelated.

Bailey (1983:181) points out that "environmental, biological, and social phenomena are each characterized by a series or hierarchy of different processes, representing different time scales of organization and operating over different time spans." In the case of biological processes, he cites J.B.S. Haldane (1956), who defined five categories by the time depths over which they occur, from molecular (on the order of a second) to evolutionary (hundreds of thousands of years). Socially, Anthony Giddens (1981:19, quoted in Bailey 1983:181) posits "'three intersecting planes of temporality involved in every moment of social reproduction': the flow of day-to-day life; the life cycle of the individual; and the development or persistence of social institutions which outlive the individual." One caution might be offered here: if taken to an extreme, the notion of time as process might be seen as deterministic—the past determines the present—and a denial of individual agency (Bailey 1983:172).

Human Time and Ritual Time

Richard Bradley (1991) summarizes the views of many "time theorists" in ways that illuminate the Maya experience. For example, time might be distinguished, following Michael Shanks and Christopher Tilley (1987:chapter 5), as human or "substantial" time versus abstract or chronological time (Bradley 1991:209). In human or substantial time, there are many "recurrent moments" of human experience, and people understand their world in reference to the past and to tradition. In abstract or chronological time, time is measured and managed in equal segments that repeat endlessly, and that can be used to plan the future. Related to this, Fernand Braudel (e.g., 1972; see Bradley 1991:210) conceptualized time in three layers: *événements* (individual time, the history of events), *conjonctures* (social time, or the history of certain groups of peoples), and *longue durée* (the scale of environmental change; see also Bailey 1983:181).

Ritual time is typically cyclical time. Bloch (1977:284–285), in dismissing Clifford Geertz's (1973) assertion that time among the Balinese is "non-durational," notes that different notions of time, linear or cyclical, relate to different forms of communication. Linear or durational time is human time and reflects praxis; it is essential to the experience of and communication about practical activities, especially agriculture. Cyclical or static time is ritual time; it is invoked in various situations of formal, public, social behavior and especially ritual performance in order to interweave "the past in the present":

> For Bloch, public rituals communicate through very specialized media. They follow a set pattern, and their contents are formalized to an extent that allows little modification. That is why they may communicate through song or dance, or employ forms of language which are not in everyday use. The texts may be accompanied by prescribed postures, gestures and movements, and they can be characterized by a restricted vocabulary. There may be further rules that determine how the texts are to be performed, and these may include specialized kinds of utterance. These are all features by which rituals come to be memorized so that they are transmitted from one generation to the next. . . . The effect is to protect the contents of such performances from evaluation or challenge." (Bradley 1991:211)

Similarly, ritual or cyclical time is Eliade's "cosmic time" (Hassig 2001:61–62), making it primarily the purview of religious specialists. Such individuals—shamans, daykeepers, calendar priests—sacralize time as the sphere in which the affairs of the gods and the fates are replayed and reinterpreted and through which the endlessly repetitive commemoration of salient events such as societal origins stand as sacred moments. Hassig (2001:62) observes that cyclical, cosmic, or ritual time makes "ritual practitioners the perfect keepers of the calendars, especially after religions have become bureaucratized and dogmatized," whereas secular "political" authorities are more likely to focus on linear time because of the unpredictability of events in the political realm.

Time, Space, and Social Relationships

Notions of time and worldviews are also closely related to concepts of space. In advanced physics and cosmological studies, the concepts of space and time are now thought of as "spacetime," almost a single but multidimensional entity (Monastersky 2002; Osborne et al. 2002). In a more prosaic example of the conflation of time and space, most people today are aware of the existence of the international date line and worldwide time zones, in which the planet is divided by longitude into sectors, all keeping time with respect to "Coordinated Universal Time" (formerly Greenwich mean time) based on the radioactive decay of Cesium-133 (Aveni 2002:85–86; Whitrow 1988:3–4, 167–169).

In traditional societies, concepts of time take on social meanings, further indications of time as a cultural construct. Again referring to the Nuer, "time reckoning [beyond the annual cycle] is a conceptualization of the social structure, and the points of reference are a projection into the past of actual relations between groups of persons. It is less a means of coordinating events than of coordinating relationships, and is therefore mainly a looking backwards" to trace genealogical relations (Evans-Pritchard 1940:108). Bloch interjects the role of public ritual, suggesting a direct relationship between concepts of time and social distinctions protected by ritual: "[R]ituals maintain social divisions by making them part of a timeless natural order" (Bradley 1991:211). Many societies, such as those in Mesoamerica (and also the Catholic Church), structure rituals around the calendar, but Hassig (2001:50) calls calendars "weak ideological constructs" onto which other social concerns are mapped for various purposes.

Worldviews conflating concepts of space, time, and society frequently track claims to power and rulership, as well as land ownership under the principle of "first-comers" (Kopytoff 1987:43, 51; Farriss 1987:577). As C. R. Hallpike (1979:361, quoted in Bailey 1983:169–170) comments, "[I]n primitive society ... temporal concepts are inherently socio-spatial concepts." Rituals celebrating time, with their prescribed and highly repetitive content, contribute to maintaining social order and stability, but as many writers point out, ritual and time can also be manipulated to serve social and geopolitical ends: "At an everyday level, days and nights varied in length, as did seasons, and even the heavenly bodies wandered across the horizon. Is it any wonder that time would be viewed as flexible and even manipulable" (Hassig 2001:36).

Maya Concepts of Time

The most basic unit of time among the Maya, as among all Mesoamerican peoples, was the day, or *k'in*; this same word also means "time" and "sun" (see Earle 1986; León-Portilla 1988; Watanabe 1983:716). Counts of days were the basis for all

Mesoamerican calendars, but the Maya recorded periodicities in the cycles of other celestial bodies besides the sun: the moon, Venus, and Mars, and other intervals not clearly understood. As discussed below, counts of days were grouped into named bundles or units of time.

The most important Mesoamerican calendars were those of 260 days (the so-called Maya *tzolk'in*, or "count of days"; *tonalpohualli* among the Aztec) and of 360+5 days (the Maya *ja'ab'*; Aztec *xihuitl*). The 260-day permutative calendar was composed of a series of numerals 1 through 13 plus twenty day-names; 260 days had to pass before the same number and name would reoccur. The 365-day calendar is distinguished by grouping days into eighteen twenty-day *winals* ("months"); each day was identified with a numeral from 0 to 19 followed by the month name. Eighteen months of twenty days equals 360 days, a period the Maya called a *tun*. The tun roughly approximated the solar year but was 5.2422 days short, a discrepancy Mesoamericans compensated for by adding a short month of five unlucky days, which the Maya named Wayeb' (*nemontemi* among the Aztec). The resultant 365-day calendar was the ja'ab'/xihuitl.[3] These calendars distinguished their days by both numbers and day-names, and the two ran concurrently such that any individual day had a four-part designation, for example, 8 Ajaw 4 Kumk'u: 8 Ajaw is the number and day in the Maya tzolk'in, and 4 Kumk'u is the number of the "month" in the ja'ab'.

The simultaneous cycling of these two calendars, 260- and 365-days long, meant that 94,900 days, roughly fifty-two of our years, passed before the same day-names and numbers—such as 8 Ajaw 4 Kumk'u—occurred again. This cycle is called the Calendar Round by scholars of Mesoamerica; the Aztec called it *xiuh-molpilli*. The cycling of the xiuhmolpilli was of great importance to the Aztecs and they celebrated its ending (which of course coincided with the five unlucky nemontemi days) through the New Fire ceremony. During this period, all fires were extinguished, houses were swept clean of all their goods, people went into hiding, and on the last night the priests sacrificed a captive and kindled a new fire in his chest, the fire subsequently being passed to all the temples and homes to start the new year (Hassig 2001:16–17).

Little is formally known about how or if the Maya celebrated 52-year cycles.[4] Better known are the longer periods of time they commemorated, as recorded by glyphs inscribed on Classic period stelae, and these are based on ever-larger bundles of "years" in the 360-day tun. The most common are the *k'atun* consisting of twenty tuns (7,200 days) and what archaeologists call the *b'ak'tun* of 400 tuns (144,000 days, or 394 of our years). K'atuns are divided into four units of five tuns each, known as the *jotun* (five years), *lajuntun* (ten years), and *jolajuntun* (fifteen years). Possibly b'ak'tuns were similarly divided, but there is no clear evidence for this.

Each of these bundles of time was personified as a god. The duty of these deities was to bear their burden of time through the cosmos; they are sometimes shown

4.1. The Maya concept of time as a burden borne by gods (redrawn from Thompson 1960:fig. 28.3). This example, from Copán Stela D, dated 9.15.5.0.0 10 Ajaw 8 Ch'en, shows the god of number 9 carrying the b'ak'tun on his back by a tumpline; the b'ak'tun is represented by a large bird, whose head is the usual b'ak'tun glyph. As Thompson (1960:59) interprets it, the god is resting briefly but will momentarily have to take up his burden again, as the B'ak'tun 9 must continue another five k'atuns until it ends with the beginning of B'ak'tun 10.

as anthropomorphic figures carrying the glyph for a unit of time in a tumpline or removing this burden to rest at the end of the period (Figure 4.1). For the Maya, then, "cosmic forces dominate not only by imposing their cyclical pattern according to the calendar but also by intervening directly as sacred personages whose identity merges with that of the human actors" (Farriss 1987:577). In the complex cycling of the calendars, only four of the twenty named days in the 365-day ja'ab' can begin the year, and these are known as year-bearers; in the Colonial period, they had directional associations and were also known as Fathers of the Land (Edmonson 1986:6). Time is thus a journey for the gods and has spatial implications: a beginning, resting spots, a destination, and land tenure.

The several units of tuns are the basic constituents of the Long Count utilized by the Maya, also used by the earlier Epi-Olmec, and constitute a distinctive difference between Maya thinking about time (and Maya worldviews) from that of peoples living in Central México. The Long Count represents a distinctly linear or durational concept of time, as it is a tally of elapsed days since a zero or starting point beginning on August 13, 3114 B.C.[5] There were no culturally or ethno-linguistically known "Maya" in Mesoamerica in 3114 B.C., of course, so this origin date is clearly a retrodiction. But the later Maya used this date as the beginning of their count of days, through which time was recorded hieroglyphically in terms of numbers of completed b'ak'tuns, completed k'atuns, completed tuns, completed months, and days since this origin date . . . definitely longue durée! Archaeologists' conventional notation of such dates follows this order, recording a specific date in the Long Count as, for example, 9.15.8.3.2 (nine b'ak'tuns completed, fifteen k'atuns completed, eight tuns, and so on).

When the Classic Maya recorded the Long Count dates of royal events on their carved stone monuments, they signaled the start of the date with an oversize glyph called the Initial Series Introducing Glyph, followed in order by the glyphs for the b'ak'tun, k'atun, tun, and so forth in a two-column top-to-bottom format. After the glyph announcing the number of k'ins that had passed, the day number and name of the event in the 260-day calendar was given. Then a series of glyphs recorded the Lords of the Night and the date in the lunar cycles, after which appeared the day number and month in the 365-day calendar. More than a dozen glyphs might have been carved to specify the precise intersection of a dynastic event in the many flows of time recorded by the Maya.

Within the Long Count, then, numerous temporal cycles were in operation and had been (in theory, at least) since 3114 B.C. For ritual purposes during the Classic period, one of the most important of these was the cycling of k'atuns, which were celebrated at the completion of their cycle ("turning" or "folding" is the meta-phor used) rather than at the beginning. As a consequence, k'atuns were named by their ending day, always a day Ajaw. In the calendar in operation during the Classic period, variously dubbed the Classic or Tikal calendar (Edmonson 1988:246–250), that ending date was always a K'atun 8 Ajaw (Table 4.1).

Beginning in the mid-fourth century A.D., k'atun endings in central Petén were celebrated by the erection of carved, dated monuments; the earliest of these are Uaxactún Stelae 18 and 19, dated 8.16.0.0.0 3 Ajaw (A.D. 357), which were set in front (west) of the eastern structure of that site's early E-Group "observatory" com-plex (Aimers and Rice 2006). In the Late Classic period, the commemoration of k'atun endings is best known through Tikal's twin-pyramid complexes, distinctive architectural arrangements with carved stelae bearing k'atun-ending dates erected in their northern stelae enclosures (Jones 1969; Rice 2004:121–144).

The date and place of origin of the Long Count is unknown: conventional wisdom dates it to the Gulf Coast in the last centuries before the Common Era, although I am inclined to favor a date about a millennium earlier (Rice 2007). The first attestation of the Long Count in the Maya lowlands is on Tikal Stela 29, which features a date corresponding to A.D. 292, the conventional starting point of the Maya Classic period for archaeologists. The latest carved Long Count dates

Table 4.I. Comparison of Classic, Postclassic, and Colonial calendars used in the Maya lowlands

Calendar	Year-bearers[a]	Ja'ab' start day	Naming	Numbering	K'atun start	End	Naming
Tikal/Classic	II	0 Pop	Initial	0–19	6 Ajaw	8 Ajaw	Terminal
Palenque	III	?[b]	Terminal	1–20	6 Ajaw	8 Ajaw	Terminal
Campeche	IV	?[b]	Terminal	?	?	?	Terminal?
Xiw[c]	II	1 Pop	Initial	0–19?	6 Ajaw	8 Ajaw	Terminal
Itza[c]	IV	1 Pop?	Terminal?	1–20	11 Ajaw	13 Ajaw	Initial
Mayapán[c]	IV	1 Pop[d]	Initial	1–20	11 Ajaw	13 Ajaw	Initial
Valladolid[c]	IV	2 Pop	2nd day	1–20	11 Ajaw	13 Ajaw	2nd day

Source: Edmonson 1988.

a. Year-bearers: Type II—Ik', Manik', Eb', Kab'an; Type III—Ak'b'al, Lamat, B'en, Etz'nab'; Type IV—Kan, Muluk, Ix, Kawak (Edmonson 1986:10).

b. The Palenque and Campeche calendars are not known in detail. It appears that the starting date of each was moved one day forward, essentially a leap-year correction, so that the Palenque calendar began one day after Tikal's and the Campeche calendar began one day after the Palenque calendar (Edmonson 1988:106).

c. The Xiw numbered and named k'atun cycles in the same way as did the Classic Maya, running from 6 Ajaw through 4 Ajaw, 2 Ajaw, 13 Ajaw, 11 Ajaw, 9 Ajaw, 7 Ajaw, 5 Ajaw, 3 Ajaw, 1 Ajaw, 12 Ajaw, and 10 Ajaw, and recording them with the name of the last day of the last k'atun, 8 Ajaw. The Itza, on the other hand, registered k'atuns by the first day of their first k'atun, a k'atun 11 Ajaw, and then the cycle continued through 9 Ajaw, 7 Ajaw, 5 Ajaw, 3 Ajaw, 1 Ajaw, 12 Ajaw, 10 Ajaw, 8 Ajaw, 6 Ajaw, 4 Ajaw, and 2 Ajaw, ending on a 13 Ajaw.

d. This is actually an adjustment of two days later than the 1 Pop beginning day of the Tikal calendar, as an adjustment of one day from the Campeche calendar.

e. In the Valladolid calendar, developed by the Itza and adopted in 1752, tun periods were no longer counted, the Long Count ceased to be used, and the k'atun was lengthened to twenty-four ja'ab's rather than twenty tuns. Munro Edmonson (1988:262) says this calendar had Type IV year-bearers, but earlier (1976a:713) he claimed it had Type I year-bearers (Imix, Kimi, Chuwen, and Kib').

correspond to A.D. 909, and they appear at only a very few widely separated sites far from the Classic lowland heartland.

The Long Count was used by the Maya throughout the Classic period—indeed, it essentially bounds the beginning and ending of the Classic period for archaeologists. What did the Long Count mean in terms of the "worldview" of the Classic Maya? It is generally agreed that the Long Count was closely identified with divine kingship, although the development of the two did not precisely coincide: the Long Count was initiated sometime in the Formative period (between ca. 1200 B.C. and 200 B.C.), whereas divine kingship is thought to have begun later around A.D. 100 (Freidel and Schele 1988). Anthony Aveni (2002:187) suggests that the increasing length of durational time recorded by the Classic Maya was intended "by a person or class of persons" to promulgate "the notion that the present can be stabilized by projecting it much further back into the past than anyone had ever contemplated." This certainly would have been a salient desideratum of kingly dynasties. Elsewhere (Rice 2007), I have argued that even earlier, sometime during the Preclassic, the ideas about (or the ideology of) leadership became identified with solar movements and are manifest in a distinct east-west (as opposed to the earlier north-south) orientation of site and structure layouts. As part of this transformation, Maya kings were identified with the sun and with the various deities bearing solar aspects (e.g., GI, GIII, Jaguar Sun God) and initiated the institution of divine kingship (*k'ul ajaw*).

Time and Worldview among the Postclassic and Contact Period Maya

The Classic period drew to a close in the ninth and tenth centuries, an interval commonly referred to as the Terminal Classic and generally characterized as the time of the so-called collapse of Classic civilization of the southern lowlands (Demarest et al. 2004). This "collapse" is identified archaeologically by the cessation of traits and activities characterizing the Classic period: carved, dated stelae, polychrome painted pottery, and sumptuous royal tombs. Their absence marks the apparent disappearance of far more salient and deeply related traits of the Classic Maya, at least in terms of time and worldviews: divine kingship and use of the Long Count.

The lowland Maya had begun to change their methods of recording time in the middle of the Late Classic period, ceasing to record the b'ak'tun and instead registering dates only by the k'atun ending day (a tzolk'in day) and day in the ja'ab'. By the Late Postclassic period they had further abbreviated formal timekeeping to the so-called Short Count in which events were dated only by reference to the ending day of the k'atun in which they occurred, that day always being a day Ajaw. This latter practice reflects continuation of use of the 260-day "cyclical" or ritual calendar, but the day-name and number in the ja'ab' were no longer recorded. This system, still in use at the time of contact and Conquest and evident in indigenous histories, makes it difficult to determine the actual year of the event, however, because k'atuns of the same name, for example, a K'atun 8 Ajaw, occurred every 260 tuns, or roughly every 256 solar years.

At the same time that Long Count dates ceased to be recorded, the concept of divine kingship disappeared, replaced by some form(s) of more secular shared governance and, eventually, by the concept of *multepal*, generally translated as "council rule." The apparent disappearance of linear timekeeping among the Maya reflects the opinions mentioned above that linear time tends to be a record of "événements" in individual histories, in the Maya case the salient events of royal dynastic rule.

It is not at all clear how or why these changes took place. It is tempting to link them to the entry of new calendars in the western Maya lowlands, the so-called Campeche and Palenque calendars. The Campeche calendar appeared in the Pu'uc area and the Usumacinta region (e.g., Bonampak, Yaxchilán) in the seventh century and suggests Zapotec or Mixtec influence (Edmonson 1988:148); the Palenque calendar is closely related to the Campeche calendar (Edmonson 1988:233). These differed from the Tikal calendar in naming the year not by its initial day (its year-bearer) but by its terminal day, a characteristic of cultures of western Mesoamerica

(Edmonson 1988:10). It is also tempting to link these new calendars with increasing contacts between the Maya and Gulf Coastal peoples, variously identified as Chontal Maya, Mexicanized Maya, Mayanized Mexicans, or Putun (Thompson 1970:3–47). Although these outside groups are not well known archaeologically, they apparently did not embrace the Long Count (nor did Mexican cultures in general)[6] and the idea of divine kingship.

Edmonson (1988:103–107) notes that the Postclassic period was one of considerable differentiation of calendars throughout Mesoamerica, partly a consequence of Mixtec and Nahuatl (Aztec, Pipil) expansions. I suggest that another factor might be identity maintenance: the many calendars in existence at the time of Spanish Conquest—Edmonson (1988:106) estimates that there were thirty-eight, although there were only two in the Maya lowlands (Figure 4.2)—do not map precisely onto the territories of the region's varied ethno-linguistic groups, but it is evident that calendars were critical to the identity, religion, ritual, and worldview of Mesoamericans everywhere (Marcus 1992:118).

Time, Space, and Geopolitics

In an article provocatively titled "Remembering the Future, Anticipating the Past," the eminent Maya historian Nancy Farriss (1987) discussed the concepts of linear and cyclical time among the Conquest period Yucatán Maya. Although her emphasis is on cyclical time and indigenous histories, she also notes that linear time was registered in Colonial period documents, especially in the common New World post-contact genre in which indigenous families asserted their claims to land by virtue of the length of their occupancy. Indigenous Maya histories of the Colonial period (variously called *crónicas* or *relaciones* in Spanish) are "not only of relatively short duration but also decidedly this-worldly in subject matter, devoted primarily to genealogical succession within the ruling families and to sequences of migration and conquest. In other words, they encode information about political power: who wields it, when, where, and, most especially, by what authority" (Farriss 1987:576–577).

The Books of Chilam Balam

The Books of Chilam Balam ("spokesman" [*chilam*] of the jaguar priest [*b'alam*], the official k'atun prophet[7]) are indigenous histories, originally recorded in hieroglyphic or oral form or both. It is important to remember that these were probably initially committed to writing by the sons of high-ranking Maya who knew or would have known of these traditions, or by native priests/shamans, who were sent to Spanish (Franciscan) religious schools for inculcation in reading, writing, and catechism. The books begin with events of the tenth century but were written

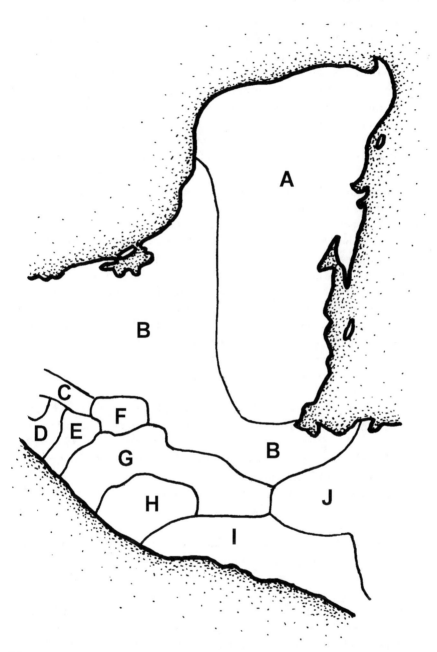

4.2. The calendars of the Maya area in the sixteenth century A.D. (redrawn from Edmonson 1988:106, fig. 12). (A) Mayapán; (B) Tikal; (C) Guitiapa; (D) Tz'otz'il; (E) Tzeltal; (F) Q'anjob'al; (G) K'iche'; (H) Kaqchikel; (I) Teotitlan; (J) Jicaque.

in final form in Yukateko Mayan using Spanish orthography, probably in the nineteenth century. They are named for the towns in Yucatán where they were discovered by scholars and presumably were written, as, for example, the *Chilam Balam of Chumayel, of Tizimin, of Maní*, and so forth. The two best known, the *Chumayel* (Edmonson 1986; Roys 1967) and the *Tizimin* (Edmonson 1982), are the interpretive records of two rival elite lineage alliances in the region, the Xiw in the western peninsula and the Itza in the east.

The books recorded events in the Short Count, that is, their occurrence in the repetitive cycling of k'atuns. The cycling of these k'atuns and the events characterizing them in the past—famine, drought, disease, warfare, and so forth—were believed to reveal what would happen in the upcoming recurrence of the K'atun Ajaw with the same number. These books thus are referred to as "prophetic histories," which combined syntheses of past k'atuns with the b'alams' prophecies for the future. Robert Sharer (1994:573) notes that the Short Count "was a kind of historical synopsis presented in a succession of approximately twenty-year periods," but it failed to provide a more precise dating by year other than this twenty-year period within the 256-year cycles. As a result of this ambiguity, various debates ensued among archaeologists over how to correlate the Maya calendar with the Christian ones, Julian and Gregorian (see note 5). Also, the degree to which scholars regard these books as actual event histories in our sense of the term has varied over time: Sylvanus Morley (1911), for example, believed they were historical chronicles because of their close agreement with one another regarding what occurred when.

The content of the Books of Chilam Balam exhibits many of the characteristics of cyclical and ritual time already discussed. One of the most specific characteristics is that of ritual language (see Bradley quote above). Farriss (1987:577, emphasis added) notes that the style of writing in these books is not prose but poetry, "a highly charged and allusive language that stresses *the quality of time over its factual content.*" The events that are recorded are not only generalized by virtue of their recursive and prophetic nature, but also, apparently, contrived through metaphors and images to obfuscate and confound the Maya's Spanish oppressors. One component of this symbolic overlay is the use of the "Language of Zuyua" in a series of esoteric questions asked of candidates for office. Ralph Roys (1967:192) dubbed this "a sort of civil service examination conducted by the *jalach winik* [ruler] with the object of weeding out from the ranks of legitimate chieftainship the upstarts, pretenders, and those who had obtained office under false pretences." Inga Clendinnen (1980:387; also Edmonson 1986:171–172) cites as a (post-conquest) example the situation in which a candidate is ordered to "bring the sun . . . a lance is planted, a lofty cross, in the middle of its heart. A green jaguar is seated over the sun to drink its blood," but in actuality this refers to a fried egg "over which the sign of the cross has been made, with a green chile pepper sitting beside it."

Time and Space

Besides strong senses of linear and cyclical time, the Maya also possessed strong beliefs about the spatial dimensions of their cosmos, both vertically and horizontally. Vertical space was divided into thirteen levels of the heavens and nine levels of the underworld, with the earth's surface being the shared first level in both systems. Horizontal space was fundamentally quadripartite, although scholars disagree as to whether the emphasis was on the cardinal or the intercardinal directions. The cardinal points, of course, are north, south, east, and west; the intercardinal directions emphasize the extremes in the seasonal movements of the rising and setting sun along the horizon from solstice to solstice, and the other directions are "up" (zenith; north) and "down" (night; south).

Many of the Maya gods associated with nature were also typically quadripartite,[8] each having a direction and color association. Color-direction associations are common in the western hemisphere and vary from culture to culture, but among the Maya north is white, east red, south yellow, and west black. "Center" is a "world tree," a *Ceiba pentandra*, and has the color green or blue-green. Quadripartition is also evident in the built environment: household compounds and civic-ceremonial architecture were oriented to the four directions.

Among twentieth-century speakers of Mam, a Mayan language spoken in the western highlands of Guatemala, time and space are "mapped onto" the daily and annual paths of the sun (Watanabe 1983:716; see also Earle 1986; Sosa 1986). For example, the day is divided into four periods: morning, when the sun is between its rising point on the horizon and zenith; noon, when the sun is at its highest point in the sky; afternoon, when the sun is between its apogee and the point of sunset; and night, when the sun travels below the surface of the earth from west to east to rise again.

For the Maya, then, the all-pervasive quadripartite or quadrilateral structuring of their cosmology and religion extended to time itself, as time was endowed with form (a spatial quality): the Classic Maya conceived the "shape of time" (Coggins 1980) as a four- or five-part glyph marking the four corners and center. This glyph was used to mark the completion of units of time, as periods' endings were more significant than their beginnings.

Geopolitical Organization

The conflation of space and time is nowhere so apparent in the Maya region as in the geopolitico-ritual organization of the northern Maya lowlands during the Late Postclassic and Contact periods, which was based on calendrical cycles. As elucidated by Edmonson (1986:5), the Maya of Yucatán recognized a series of "capital" cities that "ruled" over a given territory for a period of thirteen twenty-year k'atuns, or 260 tuns, or 256.25 of our years. This interval was known as a cycle or *may* (pronounced "my"). The capital city was held to be sacred or "heaven born" during its period of rule, with a sacred temple, cenote, ceiba tree, and so on. At the end of the may cycle, the city was abandoned and symbolically destroyed in ritual termination of its sacrality, and another city took its place.[9]

During the 260-tun period of governance, various subsidiary towns and cities within a may realm held the prestigious position of seating one or more of the thirteen constituent k'atuns in the cycle. Seats of the k'atun held considerable real power, as they controlled land rights, tribute, and appointments to public office for the twenty-year duration. Because of this power, cities vied for the position of k'atun seat and wars were frequently fought for this privilege. In fact the word "k'atun" means not only a period of twenty tuns but also "war(rior)," "fight(er)," "combat," and "conquest" (*Diccionario maya*).

The best exemplar of a may seat is the Late Postclassic city of Mayapán, southeast of Mérida. Although the city has evidence of Terminal Classic Pu'uc-style architecture, its primary period of eminence was from the early thirteenth to the mid-fifteenth century, or roughly A.D. 1204–1461—a 256-year may cycle bound at both ends by K'atuns 8 Ajaw. According to the prophetic histories and the information given to Landa (Tozzer 1941:25), this walled city was occupied by the elites of as many as sixteen provinces in the northern Yucatán peninsula and represented a governing alliance between the powerful rival elite lineages, the Xiw and the Kokom. The history of these two groups is unclear both documentarily and archaeologically, although the Xiw are said to have controlled the western peninsula after having established a capital at Uxmal in the Terminal Classic period. The Kokom are more generally identified as the Itza, who established their first capital at Chich'en Itzá and dominated the eastern part of the peninsula.

One aspect of the rivalry between the Xiw and Kokom/Itza is that they maintained different calendars (see Table 4.1). Their calendrical differences are apparent in the Books of the Chilam Balam, for the *Chumayel* is a Xiw document whereas the *Tizimin* is Itza. The Xiw observed the same Classic or Tikal calendar as did the Classic Maya in Petén, identifying may cycles by their completion on the last day of a K'atun 8 Ajaw. The Kokom or Itza, on the other hand, counted k'atuns from their initial dates and began them with K'atun 11 Ajaw. Initial dating, as mentioned above, is largely associated with Mexican rather than Maya calendrical conventions, and this practice suggests that the Itza/Kokom maintained some aspects of the introduced Campeche calendar through the Postclassic period.

Mayapán's end as cycle seat came in a K'atun 8 Ajaw, A.D. 1441–1461, when the Xiw overthrew the Itza and the site was abandoned, all lineage heads returning to their respective provinces. This "collapse" of Mayapán sounds like the ritual termination of a may seat at the end of its cycle and its end in a K'atun 8 Ajaw suggests that this was part of a larger Xiw plot to upend their rivals in a (to them) cosmically significant calendrical interval. Another explanation comes from Susan

Milbrath (2005, and personal communication 2005), who suggests the Xiw uprising occurred because the Kokom invited Aztec mercenaries to live in the city to encourage trade with Central México. She also notes late-dating architectural features at Mayapán that might be evidence of Aztec influence.[10]

After Mayapán's end as may seat, the Xiw established TiHo (modern Mérida) as the seat of both the may and the k'atun (Edmonson 1982:xvii). Calendrical conflicts continued between the Xiw and the Kokom, however, until 1539, when these rivals reached a compromise between their two calendars. This compromise, the Mayapán calendar, used the day and month names and glyphs of the Classic or Tikal calendar, but abandoned zero counting (instead starting units with 1 rather than 0), and counted the k'atuns and may by initial rather than terminal naming.

The Duration of Durational Time

Maya concepts of time, space, history, and worldview perdured throughout the centuries of the Classic, the Postclassic, and the Contact and Conquest periods. Most discussions of time among the Maya after the Classic period have focused on cyclical time and the persistence of the 260-day calendar and its rituals, assuming the permanent abandonment of the Long Count and linear time. But as the preceding discussion has revealed, such was not the case at all. The Long Count and concepts of linear time persisted through the Postclassic and well into the Colonial period, albeit with a great deal of subterfuge.

The *Chilam Balam of Chumayel*, for example, incorporates a few apparent references to the Long Count, including a phrase that mentions a K'atun 6 Ajaw as the fourteenth k'atun of B'ak'tun 11 (A.D. 1480) (Edmonson 1986:173–174; 1988:56–58). In the mid-sixteenth century, Bishop Diego de Landa noted carved, dated stelae at then-abandoned Mayapán and was told that it was customary to erect one of these stones every twenty years (Tozzer 1941:38–39), obviously in celebration of k'atuns. And in 1539 the Xiw and the Kokom, still preoccupied by their conflicting calendars, met to effect a compromise. This particular year was one of the turning of the may: it was the ending of a K'atun 13 Ajaw and the beginning of the k'atun that would end on a day, and thus be named for, 11 Ajaw at 11.16.0.0.0. This date was well after first contact with Spaniards but just before the conquest was beginning its violent phase (Edmonson 1976a). The resulting "Mayapán calendar" was used for a little more than two centuries. As a result of this change, as in our references to "B.C. and A.D. centuries, Mayan dates for the may and the k'atun before 1539 are counted backward from their endings, and those afterward are counted forward from their beginnings" (Edmonson 1986:11).

In 1618, well after conquest and the establishment of Colonial rule, a celebration of the turning of the b'ak'tun, from B'ak'tun 11 to B'ak'tun 12, was held in Mérida (Edmonson 1985).[11] Apparently some confusion or competition still reigned about the starting and ending of k'atuns and b'ak'tuns well after the establishment of the Mayapán calendar, because this ceremony, which would have ended a K'atun 5 Ajaw (in the Tikal calendar), was actually held eighty days after the beginning of the succeeding k'atun, a K'atun 3 Ajaw (Mayapán) (Edmonson 1988:203).[12] As described in Edmonson's introduction to the *Chilam Balam of Chumayel*, these ceremonies of the turning of cycles of time were "ritually structured, historico-mythological 'dramas' of multiple 'acts' that included processions, feasting, speeches and recitations, sacrifice, recognition of ranks and titles, and other activities" (Rice 2004:79). The fact that the 1618 b'ak'tun ceremony was held in Mérida indicates that its celebration was organized by the Xiw, and the content bears this out. The ceremony occurred in twenty acts (twenty k'atuns in a b'ak'tun) and consisted of the following (Edmonson 1985; 1986:25–27, 152–168; 1988:262):

Act 1: Ceremonial drinking of *b'alche* (a type of mead or beer).

Act 2: The bee gods tie masks onto impersonators of the thirteen Gods of the Heavens.

Act 3: Impersonators of the nine Gods of the Underworld battled, defeated, and sacrificed the thirteen Gods of the Heavens, symbolizing the end of the cycle of thirteen k'atuns.

Act 4: The four year-bearers, or *b'akab's*, appearing as Burner gods, held a fire ceremony.

Act 5: The gods Quetzal and Hummingbird, symbolic ancestors of the Itza and Xiw as well as symbols of Venus, presented offerings.

Act 6: A procession was made to the temple for heart sacrifice (plant hearts were used).

Act 7: The four b'akab's reappeared as Chaaks (rain gods) and created a rainstorm, perhaps symbolizing baptism.

Act 8: A ritual circuit, probably counterclockwise, was made in homage to the four directions. The b'akab's carried alligator or "Imix trees" of the appropriate directional color, and the "Center Priest" carried his tree (green; a symbolic ceiba?) to the center of the plaza.

Act 9: The retiring b'alam, or jaguar priest, of the ending k'atun removed his regalia—mask, robe, staff, crown, fan, cask, cup, bowl, plate, and so forth—and the new priest for the upcoming k'atun was seated on his mat.

Act 10: The four year-bearers, or b'akab's, were seated.

Act 11: The seven Pacers, along with Itzam Cab Ayin wearing a surveying stick on his back, ritually renewed land titles, which were canceled at the end of a k'atun.

Act 12: The nine Gods of the Heavens sacrificed the seven Pacers and "counted the mats" (renewing the seats [*pop*; "mat"] or titles to ritual office). This might have taken place at dawn.

Act 13: The b'akab's reappeared as death gods, apparently to perform sacrifices.

Act 14: There was a feast and ritual interrogation, in the Language of Zuyua, of the aspirants to office.

Act 15: The nine Gods of the Heavens announced the prophecy (*mut*, "news") for the k'atun.

Act 16: The b'akab's performed penance through autosacrifice.

Act 17: In ancient times, this was the point of erecting a stelae as a commemoration of the ancestors. In the 1618 celebration, there was a performance of the Xiw (Flower) lineages' origin myth: the birth of the eighteen Flowers, which symbolize the eighteen twenty-day intervals (winals) of the tun. Nicte (Flower) is the mother of the Flowers.

Act 18: Flower (Nicte) was seated and "counted" the flowers and the calendrical structure.

Act 19: Comic relief was provided in the form of a "morality play" involving Envy, Spite, their wives, and the nine Gods of the Heavens (for a total of thirteen actors).

Act 20: The Chilam Balam, the spokesman for the jaguar priest, spoke the "sermon" or prophecy for the next k'atun, "predicting the conversion of the Itzá," whom the heavily converted Xiw regarded as stupid pagans and who strongly resisted capitulation to the Spaniards.

This ceremony featured hundreds of masked and costumed actors, probably involved thousands of spectators, and lasted day and night for 24 to 48 hours (Edmonson 1985:261). Obviously such an event held in the new colonial capital hardly could have escaped the attention of the Spanish overlords. The Catholic priests must have been deeply offended by the display of ancient "pagan" elements on the part of their new allies and converts, the Xiw, such as bloodletting and heart sacrifice, even though the hearts were plants and despite the fact that Christian concepts were clearly in evidence (e.g., the "morality play").[13]

In 1752 the Mayapán calendar ended and the Valladolid calendar was adopted, clearly an indication of the Maya, especially the Itza, calendar priests' response to a felt need for correlation with Spanish time-recording. The Valladolid calendar changed the period of the k'atun from twenty 360-day tuns to twenty-four 365-day ja'ab's, altered the beginning date of the k'atun, lengthened the duration of the may, and abandoned the b'ak'tun (Edmonson 1988:262–264; 1985:265). These calendrical modifications distorted the enduring integrity of fundamental units of ritual time for the Maya and clearly illustrate how time is a cultural construct manipulated—indeed mangled—for social and political ends. Although the last incidence of glyphic writing occurred about this same time, in the mid-eighteenth century, ceremonies of the may and k'atun continued at least until 1824 (Edmonson 1985:265).

All of this underscores the fact that, despite the horrors and abuses of the Spanish Conquest, a century and more after that debacle the lowland Maya were still "reading the world much as they had a hundred years before," according to Clendinnen (1980:381). She attributes much of this persistence to their conceptualizations of time and their own history (Clendinnen 1980:375).[14] Similarly, Philip C. Thompson (1999:311–312), who studied colonial documents in the Yucatán town of Tekanto, concluded that "fundamental preconquest concepts about the relationship between time and space and political power, concepts ultimately based in Maya calendrics," had survived into the eighteenth century. Indeed, many of these concepts, such as the 260-day calendar and year-bearers, and the practices of traditional daykeepers who maintain the calendars and appropriate ritual, have continued into the twentieth century (see, e.g., Bricker 1989; Tedlock 1992; Watanabe 1983); the calendar of highland Maya Kaqchikel speakers may even reflect some continued rudimentary remembrance of the Long Count (Edmonson 1988:105); and may-based geopolitical organization was still in operation in the nineteenth century in Yucatán (Edmonson 1986:5).

Rather than suffering a cultural breakdown in response to subjugation, the loss of native elites, and the extirpation of indigenous ritual practices and beliefs, the Maya displayed remarkable resilience, tenacity, and conservatism in retaining their traditions and worldview. Over two millennia the Maya constructed and reconstructed their histories and calendars to adapt to changing social and political circumstances but nevertheless were able to retain their fundamental concepts of time, space, and worldviews.

Notes

1. I acknowledge at the outset the possible perceptions of some circularity in this essay. That is, most of what is relatively certainly known about lowland Maya concepts of time and worldviews comes from indigenous and Spanish writings in the sixteenth and later centuries (e.g., Avendaño y Loyola 1987; Edmonson 1982, 1986; Jones 1998; Landa in Tozzer 1941; Roys 1967; Scholes and Roys 1968). These have been retrodicted into the Classic period to help scholars understand Classic period inscriptions, beliefs, and rituals (e.g., Coe 1965; Rice 2004; Schele and Freidel 1990; Schele and Mathews 1998; Thompson 1970). Our thus-enhanced knowledge of the Classic period, augmented by the accelerating glyphic decipherments of the last 25 to 30 years, can then be used to further illuminate our knowledge of the Postclassic, Conquest, and Colonial periods. I prefer to view what might be seen as circularity in such methods as a recursive exercise in building layers of comprehension of the past—much as the Maya built their own understanding of the past.

2. Greene (2004:13) notes that this asymmetry of time is contrary to laws of physics and suggests that "special physical conditions at the universe's inception—may have imprinted a direction on time" in the same way that the now rather archaic practice of winding up an analog clock tightens a spring that then ticks steadily forward.

3. The issue of how Mesoamericans corrected for the additional 0.2422 days beyond the five "nameless" days, which we accommodate through a "leap year," is complicated and beyond the scope of this essay.

4. Edmonson (1986:6–7) believes the Yukateko phrase *k'in tun y abil* ("day stone year period"), which appears in the *Chumayel* and *Tizimin* texts, refers to the Calendar Round and that its observance was a part of both the Mayapán and Tikal calendars. A Calendar Round ended/began in 1581 on a day/year 1 Kan. Among the Aztecs, the completion of the Calendar Round was the occasion for New Fire ceremonies; among the Postclassic Maya of Yucatán, the celebrations may have involved sacrifices.

5. The date of this creation varies depending on which of many different correlations with modern calendars, Gregorian or Julian, is used. I use the Goodman-Martínez-Thompson correlation of 584,283 days for a date of 11.16.0.0.0. See Sharer 1994:chapter 12; 755–758, for more information.

6. Gordon Brotherston (1983), however, claimed the Aztecs maintained linear time and recognized the same 3113 (3114) origination date of present time as did the Maya.

7. Victoria Bricker (Bricker and Miram 2002:1) asserts that the Books of Chilam Balam refers to a famous Maya prophet, or chilam, whose surname was Balam, "who lived during the years leading up to the coming of the Spaniards and supposedly foretold their arrival."

8. The quadripartite gods—which are also gods of the days—include those of Death, Wind, Sun, Rain, and Fire. Skybearers (*pawajtuns*) are also quadripartite, standing at the four corners of the world and holding up the sky.

9. I have recently (Rice 2004) argued that the Postclassic and Contact period may-based geopolitico-ritual organization also structured political organization during the Classic period, at least in the southern lowlands, and, further, that the calendrical and ideological basis for this structuring originated in the Preclassic or Formative period (Rice 2007).

10. It might also be significant in this regard that a severe famine in the valley of México in 1454, which was also the end of a 52-year cycle (Hassig 2001:59–60), coincided approximately with the collapse of Mayapán.

11. Previous turnings of the b'ak'tun had occurred in 435 (end of B'ak'tun 8 and beginning of B'ak'tun 9), 830 (end of B'ak'tun 9 and beginning of B'ak'tun 10), and 1224 (end of B'ak'tun 10 and beginning of B'ak'tun 11).

12. An eighty-day interval also occurred in regard to the inauguration of the Mayapán calendar in 1539. In this case, the explanation is that a K'atun 13 Ajaw was ending on a day 13 Ajaw (11.16.0.0.0) and the succeeding k'atun would be a K'atun 11 Ajaw. However, with the newly reformed calendar the day 11 Ajaw in the tzolk'in actually fell eighty days earlier than the day 13 Ajaw. It seems that the new k'atun, K'atun 11 Ajaw, was actually initiated on this date before the K'atun 13 Ajaw was officially retired (Edmonson 1976a:716). It is likely that this was an Itza decision to inaugurate the calendar on their ritually significant day or on a k'atun named 11 Ajaw (Edmonson 1986:11), as opposed to a day 13 Ajaw in the Classic/Tikal calendar observed by the Xiw.

13. Shortly after this b'ak'tun ceremonial, after the K'atun 1 Ajaw of 1638–1658, the Xiw ceased to seat the k'atun. This might have been because they were sufficiently catechized to forswear these pagan rituals, or because they were so closely under the watch of the Spaniards that they were unable to, or both.

14. She goes on (Clendinnen 1980:383–384) to talk about the Maya having a history of foreign conquests, for example, by the Itza: "It was this conviction of the endless repetition of history which enabled the Maya to grasp and to render intelligible, in their own terms, their defeat and subjugation by the Spaniards."

Cosmology and Creation in
Late Postclassic Maya Literature and Art

CHAPTER FIVE

Gabrielle Vail

The focus of this chapter is on creation stories recorded in Late Postclassic Maya painted media, including screenfold books (codices) and murals, believed to date from the mid-fourteenth to the early sixteenth centuries and to have been painted in the northern Maya area where Yucatec Maya was spoken (Vail 2006; Vail and Aveni 2004a). Maya stories of creation are focused not on one specific place but rather involve a complex movement between the earth, the underworld, and the celestial realm. What we know of this mythology comes from sources as distant geographically as Yucatán, the Guatemalan highlands, and the Petén and from narratives recorded in diverse media that are separated temporally by more than 1,500 years (e.g., the San Bartolo murals, Quirigua Stela C, Palenque Temple XIX, and the Books of Chilam Balam). This chapter looks specifically at primordial creation events, that is, those described as taking place many millennia before the creation of humans, and at the events of the more recent mythic past in order to explore the relationship between humans and their deity creators. Painted imagery and texts from the Late Postclassic northern Maya lowlands offer an unparalleled opportunity to examine these themes and contemplate what these data sets reveal about the worldviews of the Yucatec Maya on the eve of the Spanish Conquest. Despite considerable advances in our understanding of creation mythology in the Classic and even Late Preclassic time periods, there has been much less emphasis on these topics in codical studies (with certain exceptions noted below) until quite recently.

Central to prehispanic Maya cosmology, and indeed to that of many Meso-american cultures, was the belief in a number of cataclysmic destructions and re-creations of the world order (e.g., Taube 1988a:35–143). The threat of another such event was constantly present but was especially salient at times of transition focusing on either human or deity actors (accessions, period endings, etc.). Recent reinterpretations of Late Postclassic almanacs from the Maya codices and of murals that once adorned structures at Mayapán and Santa Rita Corozal in present-day Belize suggest that much of their painted imagery and texts revolve around ideas of mythic destructions and re-creations of the world and, moreover, that these form the metaphor by which all temporal and celestial events were understood.[1] This metaphor, as we currently understand it, is also reflected in the earlier (Late Preclassic and Classic period) tradition, as well as in Colonial period alphabetic texts, as will be discussed below.

Diego de Landa and the other Colonial chroniclers tell us that the Yucatec Maya recorded their history, rituals, prophecies, calendars, and science in screen-fold books (Thompson 1971:23). Although it is believed that each town had its own codices, housed with the *ah k'in* or daykeeper, only four survive to the present day—the Dresden, Madrid, Paris, and Grolier codices.[2] They consist of almanacs and tables of a ritual and astronomical nature.[3] No texts naming historical personages have been found. Instead, the extant codices are concerned with linking the activities of deities to the *tzolk'in*, *haab'*, and Long Count calendars (discussion follows). Dates internal to the manuscripts suggest that they represent a compilation of information gathered and recorded over many centuries (see V. Bricker and H. Bricker [1992] for a discussion of the Dresden codex and V. Bricker and Vail [1997] with regard to the Madrid codex). The physical documents themselves, however, were probably painted shortly before the Spanish Conquest (Grube 2001; Love 1994:8; Vail 2006).

In the codices, anthropomorphic beings identified explicitly as deities (*k'uh*) in the hieroglyphic texts are shown performing various activities that are believed to provide a model for the performance of similar activities and rituals by human actors, set within a calendrical framework. The codices picture deities related to rain, maize, creation, flowers and fertility, sustenance, warfare, the underworld, death, and destruction (Taube 1992; Vail 1996, 2000). These same deities represent the protagonists of much of the mural art associated with the Late Postclassic period. For the Maya and other ancient Mesoamericans, periods of time, as well as celestial bodies, were conceptualized as anthropomorphic deities; for example, the Maya sun god personified the number four, the maize god the number eight, and Venus had a number of different deity manifestations, depending on where and when it appeared in the sky (Thompson 1971:88–89, 219).[4]

Time and Maya Principles of Temporal Organization

The importance of time in our understanding of Maya worldview(s) cannot be overstated. This results from the belief, fundamental to prehispanic Maya cosmology, that time and the events underlying both human and mythic history are cyclical. Because of this, past occurrences, including the primordial events of destruction and creation, are bound to repeat. In order to know when, and thereby gain some measure of control over them when they recurred, calendrical specialists kept a close watch on seasonal cycles, changing patterns in the sky, and other natural phenomena and recorded this information for their own and future reference (Vail and Hernández 2009b).

To accurately make predictions, the Maya ah k'in had to understand various natural and numerological cycles on which prehispanic Maya culture depended, which included both solar and lunar calendars (to allow for the prediction of eclipses), the cycles of Venus, and seasonal cycles used to track the solstices and equinoxes, primarily to determine their relationship to the key events of the agricultural year (Aveni 2001:chapter 5; V. Bricker and H. Bricker 1992). As we know from Maya hieroglyphic inscriptions, these natural phenomena were tracked based on a number of different (and overlapping) calendars. Perhaps the most important of these was the tzolk'in of 260 days, which combined two numerical cycles—one consisting of thirteen deified numbers and the other of twenty named days. The numbers and the days each had their own series of associations that, when combined, determined the fate or character of the tzolk'in day. Etz'nab', for example, was associated with flint and therefore with bloodletting and sacrifice, whereas Kab'an days were especially appropriate for ceremonies associated with the bees, or *kaab'*.

Also of importance was the solar calendar (haab') consisting of eighteen months of twenty days, followed by a final month of five "nameless" days, or *wayeb'*. This calendar ran concurrently with the tzolk'in so that a day could be named for its position in both the 260-day calendar (e.g., 1 Ajaw) and in the haab' (e.g., 2 Pop). At the time of the Conquest, the years were named for their first day (1 Pop). Year-bearer days in the tzolk'in (i.e., those that could be paired with 1 Pop) included K'an, Muluk, Ix, and Kawak.[5] A year beginning on 1 K'an 1 Pop was followed 365 days later by one beginning on 2 Muluk 1 Pop, and then by 3 Ix 1 Pop, 4 Kawak 1 Pop, 5 K'an 1 Pop, and so forth until the cycle returned to 1 K'an 1 Pop in the fifty-third year.

The cycle of fifty-two year-bearers, dubbed the Calendar Round, was another important calendar used by Late Postclassic Maya cultures, where it seems to have assumed the significance previously held by the Long Count. The latter calendar, in use for hundreds of years beginning in the Late Preclassic period, fixed dates in absolute time by counting the number of *k'ins* (days), *winals* (20 days), *tuns* (18 winals), *k'atuns* (20 tuns), and *b'ak'tuns* (20 k'atuns) elapsed from an initial date in

August 3114 B.C., corresponding to 4 Ajaw 8 Kumk'u in the Calendar Round. The Long Count emphasized the endings of certain periods of time (specifically k'atuns, half k'atuns, and quarter k'atuns), which were marked by special ritual celebrations that included the erection of carved monuments such as stelae and sometimes altars (Morley 1920:577; Rice, this volume; Stuart 1996:150).

Although the Long Count forms the basis of several of the astronomical tables in the Dresden Codex, this can be attributed to the fact that they were created when Long Count dating was still in widespread use (i.e., during the Classic period; see previous discussion about codices representing a compilation of almanacs and tables from various time periods). An almanac in the Paris codex (on pages 2–14) refers to k'atun endings, but only within a cycle of thirteen repeating k'atuns named for the Ajaw date on which they end. A similar convention is used in the "histories" related in the colonial Yucatec Books of Chilam Balam (Edmonson 1982; Roys 1967), as Prudence Rice discusses in detail in her chapter. The Paris codex also includes an almanac focused on tun endings, which likewise forms the basis for one of the murals documented by Thomas Gann (1900) at Santa Rita (see Love 1994:chapter 4; Vail and Hernández 2009c).

More commonly, however, almanacs believed to be contemporary with the painting of the three codices focus not on the Long Count or one of its components (such as the tun or k'atun) but rather on the tzolk'in and the Calendar Round. This may be related to a proposed increase in interaction between members of the literate classes from throughout Mesoamerica during the time period immediately prior to the Spanish Conquest (Vail and Aveni 2004a; Vail et al. 2003; Vail and Hernández 2009a). Ethnohistoric documents highlight the importance of the cycle of fifty-two years in central Mexican Nahuatl culture (Sahagún 1953, 8:25). There is little textual evidence to suggest that the Calendar Round played a similarly important role in lowland Maya culture prior to the Postclassic period, although that evidence may once have been found in codices that are no longer extant. Nevertheless, very few references to haab' or Calendar Round ceremonies have been documented in the Classic period glyphic corpus, in contrast to the situation in the codices.

Maya Gods and the Establishment of the Cosmos

A surprising number of events described in hieroglyphic texts and represented iconographically concern the actions and lives of the deities and supernatural ancestors in the time before humans existed. These mythological events form the subject of various Classic period texts and of iconographic programs dating from both the Late Preclassic and Classic periods. As such, they provide a basis for understanding Maya conceptions of mythic time. We learn from Quirigua Stela C, for example, about a foundation event performed by the gods that allowed the establishment of the present universe. We are told that three stones were set in place—the first, in the form of a jaguar, was erected at Na Ho' Ka'an ("First Five Sky") by two entities called Jaguar Paddler and Stingray Paddler; the second, in the form of a snake, was set up at the "earth place"; and the third—said to be in the form of a crocodile or shark monster—was placed in the sea by the creator deity Itsamna (Freidel et al. 1993:66–67; Looper 1995; Schele 1992:122–125; Schele and Mathews 1998:36–37). Linda Schele (in Freidel et al. 1993:66–67) interprets this event as the establishment of a "cosmic hearth," comparable in all respects to that seen in the homes of traditional Maya families to this day. As many researchers have noted, a Maya house represents a microcosm of the universe itself (Freidel et al. 1993:130; Vogt 1993:58–59).

In both prehispanic and colonial Maya texts and imagery, the earth is represented in the form of a crocodile, which goes by the name of Itzam Kab' Ayin (primordial earth crocodile) in the Books of Chilam Balam (Taube 1989; Thompson 1970:216–217). Caves and other entrances into the earth are commonly portrayed as a crocodilian's maw. This region can be identified as a portal and was believed to be the home of the ancestors and of the earth and rain gods; it also provided a pathway to the underworld region, called Metnal by the Yucatec Maya (Tozzer 1941:132) and Xib'alb'a by the highland K'iche'. Moreover, caves are believed to represent the birthplaces of humans and of certain deities, including the sun and the moon (Nielsen and Brady 2006; Pugh 2005:50–51; Villa Rojas 1945:155).

The Quirigua text, and the worldviews that it embodies, is relevant to our understanding of several hieroglyphic and pictorial sources represented in Late Postclassic painted media. The first example that I will consider involves the murals that were once painted on the outside walls of Structure 1 at Santa Rita (they were destroyed very shortly after their discovery, and our only information concerning them comes from the description and paintings made by Thomas Gann [1900] at the turn of the last century). Of particular interest to this discussion is the mural from the east side of the structure's north wall (Figure 5.1), which is believed to date to the fifteenth century on the basis of archaeological as well as stylistic evidence (Chase and Chase 1988:78–81; Gann 1900:676; Masson 2003:194; Quirarte 1982; Robertson 1970; Sidrys 1983:147). It depicts a series of deities with bound wrists associated with tun dates and toponyms (place glyphs) that seem to be references primarily to mythic locales. As indicated by the dates, the mural should be read from right to left, unlike the more traditional left to right reading order. It is of interest in this regard that several pages from the Paris codex that are also believed to relate to creation events are likewise read in this fashion (Taube 1988a:266).

A recent reanalysis of the mural program (Vail 2008; Vail and Hernández 2009c) suggests that its ten frames record various pivotal moments from the story of creation, rather than being concerned primarily with human affairs as previous scholars have suggested (Masson 2000:245, 247; 2003:198; Quirarte 1975, 1982). What first led to the recognition of this possibility was the reference to Na Ho' Ka'an above a figure wearing a jaguar headdress, suggesting that this section of the

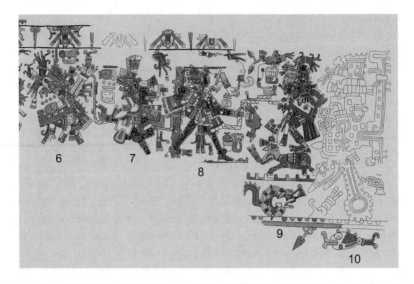

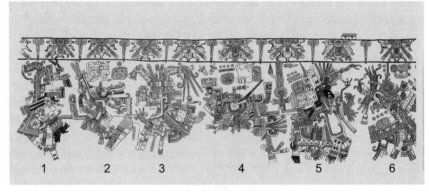

5.I. Tun mural, east half of the north wall, Santa Rita Mound 1 (after Gann 1900:pl. 29). Note that it was originally composed of one long segment, which has been divided into two here for the purposes of illustration.

mural (associated with an 8 Ajaw tun ending) portrays the Jaguar Paddler and is meant to convey the moment of creation when he and Stingray Paddler set the first of the three stones (the jaguar stone) in place. From here, it became possible to construct a narrative sequence involving the events of mythic time from when the world was in darkness to the first dawning of the sun. The events referenced in the text are paralleled by creation stories known to us from Colonial period contexts, those recorded not only in the Yucatec Maya area but also in the Maya highlands, as related in the *Popol Vuj* and in central Mexican mythology from various sources (Bierhorst 1992; Garibay 1979). Of particular interest are the inclusion of Itzam

Kab' Ayin, representing the earth (section 10); the birth of time and the scribal arts (section 8), with its parallels to the story of the Hero Twins' brothers in the *Popol Vuj*; a reference to Wuk Ha' Nal ("7 Water Place"), which we identify with the mythic cave from which humans emerged from the underworld to the surface of the earth (section 6); and the presence of a Nahuatl deity who appears to represent Nanahuatzin, who sacrificed himself in order to become the sun to light and warm the earth (Boone 2007:197). Following this in frames 4–1 are various Maya deities who likewise play an important role in the story of creation—the maize god and K'awil, who provided the sustenance required by the first people; and the sun god K'inich Ajaw and a Venus deity (God L), who here appear to symbolize the first dawn witnessed by the newly created humans (see Vail and Hernández 2009c). The latter event is described in the *Popol Vuj*, where we are told: "Greatly they rejoiced . . . when they saw the Morning Star. It came forth glittering before the face of the sun. And when the sun came forth, all the small animals and great animals rejoiced" (Christenson 2007:228).

Like the Santa Rita mural, several scenes from the Maya codices can be understood by reference to the text from Quirigua Stela C, as I have only recently proposed (Vail 2009). In each of the relevant examples, a deity (usually Chaak) emerges from the open mouth of a serpent figure, which is occasionally associated with water, or we see Chaak's head attached to a serpent's body. The associated hieroglyphic captions may include the expression *kaab'-ch'e'en/nal* ("earth cave/place"), or the serpents in question may be associated with earth (kaab') glyphs in some other way.

The almanac on Dresden 31b–35b contains eight frames, three of which picture Chaak emerging from an open-mouthed serpent cenote, holding his upraised lightning axe (Figure 5.2). The hieroglyphic captions to all three frames are parallel, reading *och-chi-ya tu-tuun-ni chaak-ki b'olon-k'ik'-il u siih? (ta) kaab'-b'a-ch'e'en?/nal?-na*. The resultant clauses can be read as *och-i chi' tu tuun chaak* ("Chaak entered from the mouth of the stone"), *b'olon k'ik'il* ("nine rubber [offerings]"), *u siih? ta kaab' ch'e'en/nal* ("he [Chaak] is born from the earth cave/place"). Reference to Quirigua Stela C suggests that the serpent pictured in this almanac, which is associated explicitly with tuun ("stone") in the Dresden text, can be identified with the serpent stone set on 4 Ajaw 8 Kumk'u at a location named in the Quirigua text as "earth place." Rather than representing the actual setting of the "stone," the three pictures in the Dresden almanac instead show the birth of the rain gods from this serpent cenote/foundation stone.

A series of almanacs in the Madrid codex spanning the upper register of pages 18, 19, and 20 may also be related (Figure 5.3). Chaak and a death god are shown emerging from open-mouthed deity (*k'uh*) heads on page 18a (Figure 5.3a), holding vessels with plumeria flowers (*nikte'*). The text includes the verb *u lok'* ("to leave, escape") and here appears to signify the birth of the gods, as is also suggested by the plumeria (in contemporary Lacandon Maya mythology, the gods were born

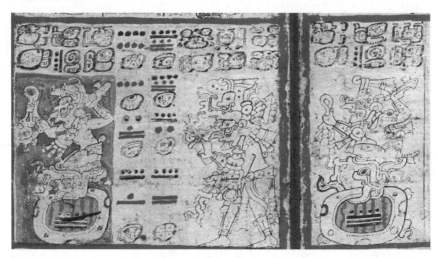

5.2. Pages 34b–35b of the Dresden codex, showing three of the eight frames of the almanac on Dresden 31b–35b (after Förstemann 1880).

from the plumeria flower; McGee [1990:60]). On the following page, the same verb appears, and in this instance the deities are shown emerging from serpents with gaping jaws (Figure 5.3b). The creator Itsamna is pictured holding glyphs representing food and drink, whereas the death god raises his hand to his face in a gesture signifying imminent death. These, then, appear to be the gifts that they bring to the world (food and drink, on the one hand, and death on the other) when they emerge upon its surface.

The almanac on Madrid 20a likewise shows a deity figure, who can be identified with the wind and flower god Nik, emerging from a serpent in the first frame (Figure 5.3c). Nik is painted blue, symbolic of rain and fertility, and holds a maize seed (the material from which humans were formed) in his outstretched hand. What is especially interesting about this example is the reference in the text to the serpent pictured (at B2), where it is associated very explicitly with kaab' glyphs, indicating that it is an earth serpent, possibly the serpent "stone" set upon the earth to establish the cosmos. Similar kaab' markings are found on representations of caves in the Dresden codex (e.g., Dresden 29a, frame 2, and Dresden 67b, frame 2). Additionally, they are likewise seen on two composite creatures in the Madrid codex (on page 64a) that appear to combine the characteristics of serpents, jaguars, and possibly bats. In this almanac, the space defined as within the earth appears to be a kiln used for firing pottery vessels (Graff 1997:152).

Textual links between the Dresden almanac on pages 31b–35b, the Madrid almanacs on pages 18a–20a, and a series of pages referred to as the "serpent series"

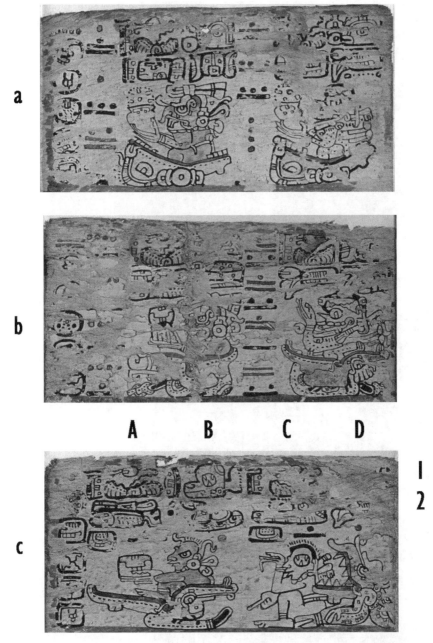

5.3. Emergence of deities from serpents and other creatures: (a) Madrid 18a; (b) Madrid 19a; (c) Madrid 20a (after Anders 1967; courtesy of the Museo de América, Madrid).

5.4. Page 61 of the Dresden codex serpent pages (after Förstemann 1880).

on Dresden 61–63 and 69–70 (Figure 5.4) suggest that the figures pictured emerging from serpents on those pages are parallel to those described above and signify the birth of these deities from serpent "stones" in the mythic time before the creation of humans (see additional discussion in Vail 2009). Calendrical references in the almanacs in question, which refer to dates many millennia before historical time (Beyer 1933; Grofe 2007; V. Bricker and H. Bricker 1988), provide support for this interpretation.

Another Classic period text relevant to the mythic time before the creation of humans that is of interest for its parallels to Late Postclassic and Colonial period sources involves a passage from Temple XIX at Palenque as follows.

Period-Ending Ceremonies and Metaphors of World Destruction and Creation

In the discussion that follows, I offer examples from the Maya codices and murals of scenes that appear to reference creation events but can be related to historical time, including several that have only recently been identified. Ongoing research suggests that certain elements found in Late Postclassic Maya iconography and texts, such as a crocodilian associated with the sky, eclipses paired with downpours, and references to the world trees raised at the time of creation, are symbolic of world destruction and renewal events. The fact that they occur in texts dating to the historic period rather than in those associated with mythic time indicates that they were probably meant to remind the reader, by alluding to like in kind events, of the (mythological) past and its continuing influence on the present and the future. References to these events are common in both astronomical tables and almanacs highlighting calendrical period endings, that is, at times of transition including celestial events such as eclipses and Venus's heliacal rise. They can be viewed as metaphors of the destruction and renewal that such periods of time embody and as reminders of the ritual actions that are required to keep these metaphorical events from becoming real (Vail and Hernández 2009b).

Period-ending almanacs in the codices have been previously interpreted within the metaphor of world destruction and creation events. Karl Taube (1988a:chapter 7), for example, has suggested that the ceremonies pictured in the lower register of Dresden 25–28 (Figure 5.5) correspond to the setting up of the world trees that occurred following a flood that destroyed the previous creation. A passage from the *Chilam Balam of Chumayel* describes the re-creation as follows (Knowlton n.d.):

Valic can tul ti ku	Four stand as gods
Can tul ti bacab	Four as Bacabs
Lay hayesob	They caused their [the core-less people] destruction
Tuchij tun ca dzoci hay cabil	And then when the destruction of the world was finished

Lay cahcunah uchebal ca tzolic kan xib yui	They settled this [land] so that Kan Xib Yui puts it in order
Ca ualhi sac imix che ti xaman	Then the White Imix Tree stands in the North
Ca ix ualhi y ocmal caan	And stood as the pillar of the sky
V chicul hay cabal	The sign of the destruction of the world
Lay sac imix che valic cuchic	This White Imix Tree stands there supporting it
Ca yx ualhi ek ymix che	Then the Black Imix Tree stood
Cu [lic] ek tan pidzoy	where the Black Bellied Pidzoy resides
Ca yx ualhij kan ymix che	Then stood the Yellow Imix Tree
V chicul hay cabal	The sign of the destruction of the world
Culic kan tan pidzoy	The Yellow Bellied Pidzoy resides
Cumlic ix kan xib yui	And Kan Xib Yui sits
Yx kan oyal mut	The Yellow Caller Bird
Ca ix ualhij yax imix che t u chumuc	Then the Blue-Green Imix Tree stood in the center
U kahlay hay cabal	The History of the destruction of the world
Cumtal u cah u lac canah ual katun	The ceramic idol sits down above the page [relating the] katun (Chumayel 43:16–28)

In the Dresden almanac, the world trees are set in place at yearly (haab') intervals, within the context of a ritual described by Landa as involving the sacrifice of a hen and the scattering of incense at the entrance to the community (Tozzer 1941:136–149). These rituals were overseen by deities who represented patrons of the new year—the sun god K'inich Ajaw, the god of sustenance K'awil, the death god Kimil, and the creator deity Itsamna (seen in the lower register of Dresden pages 25–28). The ceremony began in the east in a B'en year and continued through each of the four world directions, progressing from one page to the next at 365-day intervals.[6] The year-bearer system reflected in this almanac is the Classic period Tikal system (see Rice, this volume) rather than the later Mayapán calendar that is highlighted in several almanacs in the Madrid codex.

The captions to the four Dresden year-bearer scenes refer to the trees pictured on each page as the *yax itzamna te'*, or the "first tree of creation," with the exception of the tree on Dresden 25, which is called the *chak itzamna te'*, the "red [or "great"] tree of creation."[7] The first three glyph blocks on each page refer to the setting up of trees at one of the four world directions (east, south, west, and north). The captions then conclude with (optionally) the name of the deity patron and a series of auguries for the year. Dresden 25c, for example, reads *chak tan yah? nal k'in tuun haab'*, meaning "great presence" (probably a reference to the sun deity), "damage? to the maize; drought." The sun god, who is the patron of the year, is frequently associated

D. 25c   **D. 26c**

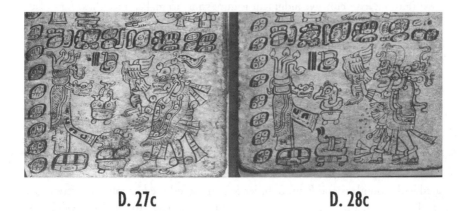

D. 27c   **D. 28c**

5.5. Lower register of the Dresden year-bearer pages (Dresden 25c–28c) (after Förstemann 1880).

with too much heat and not enough rain, a condition that causes the maize crop to wither and die. Kimil on Dresden 27c is likewise linked to death and drought. The remaining years, those associated with K'awil and Itsamna, include prognostications for fertile and/or abundant years.

As Karl Taube (1988a:265–266) notes, the dedication of world trees shown in the Dresden codex, a ceremony believed to be analogous to erecting a monument in Classic period-ending ceremonies (see Rice, this volume), is performed at the start of the new year to symbolize a new beginning comparable to that which occurred after the flood. This connection is further emphasized by the placement of the Dresden year-bearer pages directly following page 74, where a scene that can be interpreted within the context of world destruction appears (see following discussion).[8]

Period-ending ceremonies in the Paris codex likewise make use of metaphors of world destruction and creation, although in this instance the period of time is not the 365-day haab' but rather the k'atun of approximately twenty years. Each page refers to a particular k'atun (e.g., 4 Ajaw), named for the day on which it ends, within a series of thirteen repeating k'atuns (2 Ajaw, 13 Ajaw, 11 Ajaw, etc.). Although the figures vary from page to page, the format is the same (Figure 5.6): a deity stands on the left of the page, holding a K'awil headdress in his outstretched hand toward a figure seated on a skyband throne associated with a bound crocodilian. Offerings in a tripod vase appear between the two figures, and a bird hovers in the air above the K'awil headdress (Love 1994:17).[9] By analogy with Classic period monuments associated with k'atun endings, the figures on the throne can be identified as the ruling patrons of the k'atun. Because they appear to change from one k'atun to the next (although a definitive judgment is impossible to make, since these figures are substantially eroded and therefore difficult to identify), their assumption of the skyband throne likely represents their "accession."

During the Classic period, accession is symbolized by the presentation of a particular symbol of office, very frequently a scepter in the form of K'awil. In the case of the Paris k'atun pages, the scepter has been replaced by an effigy of K'awil's head, perhaps representing a headdress (Love 1994:18). By accepting the accoutrements of K'awil, the person in question was assuming his role as the god of lightning (i.e., associated with the life-giving rains) and the giver of sustenance (k'aa "surplus" plus wi'il "food"; see discussion in Martin 2006:182–183n28).

Also of particular interest in the Paris scenes are the skyband thrones associated with bound crocodilians. In order to understand the metaphoric references in the Paris k'atun almanac, it is necessary to turn once again to the Books of Chilam Balam. In section 117.5–15 of the Códice Pérez, we read:

Ca ix liki noh Itzam Cab Ain cuchi	And then great Itzam Cab Ain ascended, back then
Dzocebal u than u vudz katun heklai hun ye ciil	That this deluge may complete the word of the katun series
Bin dzocebal u than katun	That the word of the katun might be complete
Uaxaclahun tuc bak u habil	Eighteen piles of four hundred is the the era
Ca tac uuclahun pis i	When there's already seventeen counts there
Dzocebal u than katun	That it may complete the word of the katun
Ma ix y oltah bolon ti ku	But Bolon Ti Ku did not desire it
Ca ix xoti u cal Itzam Cab Ain	So then Itzam Cab Ain's throat was cut
Ca ix u ch'aah u petenil u pach	And then he sprinkled the island of its back

5.6. K'atun 13 Ahaw illustrated on Paris 3 (after Rosny 1888).

Heklay ah vuoh puc u kabae	This is its name: Calligrapher Hill
Ma ix u toh pultah u kaba tiobi	Neither did he really confess to them its name
Ti ti xan [kaxan?] tun u uich ti ualac y ahaulil hele lae	He had (bound?) the eyes then of this current reign (translated by Knowlton n.d.)

This passage makes reference to Itzam Kab' Ayin (Colonial *Itzam Cab Ain*), who can be identified as a crocodilian figure whose body forms the surface of the earth (Taube 1989; Thompson 1970:218–219).[10] Depictions of the crocodilian earth are quite common in Late Postclassic Maya and Mexican art (see Codex Borgia, page 27, for the latter region), and earlier examples are also known from the Maya region (see Thompson 1970:220), suggesting that this was an important aspect of Maya cosmology predating the Postclassic period.

Although Itzam Kab' Ayin is described as representing the earth, in the Pérez passage (which has cognates in the Chumayel and Tizimin manuscripts; see Knowlton [n.d.]) the earth crocodilian ascends to the sky and is sacrificed. This occurs just prior to the flood that destroyed a previous creation of the world in k'atun 11 Ajaw (Knowlton n.d.). Flood imagery is linked very explicitly to a bound and/or sacrificed crocodilian in several scenes from the Late Postclassic corpus, including Dresden 74 and a mural from Mayapán's Temple of the Fisherman (discussion follows).

Christine Hernández and I have proposed that the Paris k'atun almanac symbolizes the transition inherent in period endings through a visual metaphor referring to world destruction (the bound sky crocodilian) and consequent renewal through the assumption of the K'awil headdress (Vail and Hernández 2009c). Texts and imagery referencing a bound crocodilian are also associated with accession rituals on Classic period monuments (Love 1994:26; Stuart 2005:89), where we believe they serve the same purpose.

The Chilam Balam text is paralleled by a passage from Temple XIX at Palenque dating from the early eighth century but pertaining to events that occurred in mythological time. David Stuart (2005:68–76) translates the relevant text as follows: "On 1 Etz'nab' 6 Yaxk'in its head was chopped off, the Hole-Backed 'Starry Deer Crocodile,' the Painted-Back 'Starry Deer Crocodile.' Thrice the blood flowed(?)." The Palenque text clearly indicates that the Chilam Balam narrative had early antecedents in the Maya region and that this particular mythic episode was found in a wide geographic region. We know that it had a pan-Mesoamerican distribution by the Colonial period, based on parallels between the Chilam Balam narrative and references to the binding and killing of a crocodilian earth monster in the K'iche'an *Popol Vuj*. Moreover, a Mexican myth, related in the *Histoyre du Mechique*, also contains a similar account. It describes the dismemberment of the earth monster by the deities Quetzalcoatl and Tezcatlipoca, with one portion of its body becoming the earth, and the other the heavens (Garibay 1979:108).

In the Books of Chilam Balam, the flooding of the earth is associated with a battle between the Oxlahun ti' K'uh (thirteen gods) and the B'olon ti' K'uh (nine gods) (Roys 1967:99; Taube 1988a:139–141). Late Postclassic imagery makes no explicit reference to these deities but instead suggests that various celestial phenomena were involved, including an eclipse (seen on Dresden 74) and a heliacal Venus event. Venus is portrayed as an agent of this event on Dresden 74, in the Temple of the Fisherman mural at Mayapán, and, as I have recently proposed, in the Dresden Venus table (Vail 2008).

Creation Imagery and Venus Events

Dresden 74 (Figure 5.7a) pictures the ascent of a crocodilian into the sky (as suggested by the band of glyphs referring to celestial elements on its body), its dismemberment, and the resulting flood event. Water gushes not only from the crocodilian's mouth but also from a paired solar and lunar eclipse glyph dangling from its body and from the *olla* being overturned by the female creator deity Chak Chel. At the bottom of the page, a black deity known as God L appears carrying weapons and in a pose similar to the deities depicted in the Venus table on pages 46–50 of the Dresden codex (Hernández and Vail 2007; Vail and Hernández 2009b).[11] In his warrior aspect, God L was a deity to be feared. Lore associated with Venus suggests that *chak eek'*, the "great star," was considered especially dangerous when it reappeared in the celestial sphere following its sojourn in the underworld realm (equated with its disappearance during inferior and superior conjunction; see Aveni 2001:186; Thompson 1972:67).

Christine Hernández (in Vail and Hernández 2009b) notes that, during the sixty-five days referenced on Dresden 74, the following events occurred. Five days into the interval, corresponding to January 29, A.D. 536, Venus made its first appearance as an evening star in the western sky, which accounts for the presence of God L in his role as Venus at the bottom of the scene. Twenty-five days later, an eclipse season opened on February 23, A.D. 536, and a solar eclipse occurred on the penultimate day of the interval on 3 Kib' 9 Kumk'u, or March 10, A.D. 536. In addition to the dangers associated with Venus's reappearance, eclipses were likewise considered especially perilous; indeed, contemporary Maya groups link the end of the current world era with a solar eclipse (see Closs 1989; Milbrath 1999:25–27). Having two such inauspicious events fall within such a short span of time appears to have given rise to considerable concern on the part of the daykeeper/scribe responsible for drafting the almanac, leading him to caution others regarding a possible flood comparable to that believed to have destroyed the previous creation (Vail and Hernández 2009b).

a   b

5.7. Flood scenes: (a) from page 74 of the Dresden codex (after Förstemann 1880); (b) the Temple of the Fisherman Mural, Mayapán (photograph by author).

Another scene featuring a crocodile, occurring in a mural painted on the floor of the Temple of the Fisherman at Mayapán (Figure 5.7b), has been linked very explicitly to the central Mexican myth referenced above of the destruction of the crocodilian earth by Quetzalcoatl and Tezcatlipoca (Masson and Peraza Lope 2007; Stuart 2005:179). The mural depicts a figure identified as Quetzalcoatl, partially eroded but wearing a shell pectoral associated with this deity in other contexts, in a watery environment where we also see a bound and speared crocodilian and several fish. The spearing of the crocodilian, rather than its being torn apart, has clear associations with Venus events, specifically those occurring during the heliacal rise of the planet. As we read in the *Anales de Cuahtitlan* (Bierhorst 1992:36):

> What they said is that when he [Quetzalcoatl] died he disappeared for four days. They said he went to the dead land then. And he spent four more days making darts for himself. So it was after eight days that the morning star came out, which

they said was Quetzalcoatl. . . . And so, when he goes forth, they know on what day sign he casts light on certain people, venting his anger against them and shooting them with darts.

This passage suggests that the Temple of the Fisherman mural portrays the heliacal rise of Venus, as represented by Quetzalcoatl and his speared crocodilian victim. I find this especially interesting in light of the scene on Dresden 74, which likewise depicts a crocodilian in association with a Venus deity carrying darts.

The belief that Venus represents a destructive agent may have had a Mexican origin, as originally suggested by J. Eric S. Thompson (1970:249). Scenes from the Maya codices (e.g., Dresden 46–50), as well as the Borgia group manuscripts (e.g., Borgia 53–54), depict the heliacal rise of the planet in terms of its emergence in deity form from the underworld, where it has been fashioning darts to vent its anger against certain groups of people (Aveni 1999; V. Bricker 2001; Seler 1898; Thompson 1972:67–71). The Temple of the Fisherman mural appears to represent a Mexican myth imported to the Maya area, as suggested by the presence of Quetzalcoatl rather than a Maya deity, and the fact that the crocodilian has been speared, rather than decapitated, as occurs in both the Palenque and Chilam Balam texts.

The metaphor of world destruction and creation detailed in these sources forms the basis of a number of almanacs and tables in the Maya codices, particularly those with an astronomical focus. The Dresden Venus table offers a case in point. Its five pages depict a succession of events related to the heliacal rise of Venus along the right side of the page (each page refers to a different M-first event, separated by intervals of 584 days). On Dresden 46 (Figure 5.8), the upper picture features a Pawahtun figure wearing a crocodilian headdress who is seated on a skyband marked with the head of K'awil, a deity associated with the power of lightning and also the personification of sustenance (see previous discussion). The Pawahtun figure is named in the text as Pawahtun Ayin, the crocodile Pawahtun. This calls to mind the ascent of Itzam Kab' Ayin (the earth crocodilian) into the sky just prior to the deluge that destroyed the previous world, as described in the passage from the Códice Pérez cited above. The same event is also described in the Chilam Balam manuscripts from Chumayel and Tizimin (Knowlton n.d.).

As Timothy Knowlton (n.d.) notes, the above-referenced event takes place on the day 1 Ajaw within k'atun 13 Ajaw. This is of interest in light of the calendrical structure of the Venus table, as 1 Ajaw marks the starting date of the Dresden scene on page 46 mentioned above.[12] The passage from the Chilam Balam manuscripts appears just prior to the 11 Ajaw myth of the flood, which concerns the destruction and re-creation of the world. The flood itself is described as "one fetching of rain, one lancing of rain" (Chumayel 43.14; translated by Knowlton n.d.). As Knowlton has recently suggested, this parallels the scene on Dresden 74, where rain is shown

5.8. Page 46, right, of the Dresden Venus table: (a) upper register; (b) middle register; (c) lower register (after Förstemann 1880).

being poured from an olla (its "fetching"), whereas its "lancing" can be linked to the darts and spear wielded by God L.

This event—the destruction of the world by water—is followed by its re-creation in the Books of Chilam Balam (see text referencing the Bak'ab's [*Bacabs*] above). The Bak'ab's mentioned in this passage correspond to the deities known in other contexts as Pawahtuns (Taube 1992). They are described in Landa's *Relacion de las cosas de Yucatan* as "four brothers whom God placed, when he created the world, at the four points of it, holding up the sky so that it should not fall. They also said of these Bacabs that they escaped when the world was destroyed by the deluge" (Tozzer 1941:135–136). The figure seated on the skyband on Dresden 46, therefore, embodies the events discussed in the Chilam Balam texts referenced above—in this case, the ascent to the sky of Itzam Kab' Ayin, in the form of a Pawahtun, prior to the flooding of the earth. Another scene, that on Paris 22 (Figure 5.9), shows the four Pawahtuns in the sky.[13] They, and the skyband on which they are seated, are surrounded by a blue cord that appears to be filled with water rather than with blood like the *kuxan su'um* cord described by Alfred Tozzer (1907:153–154) that was a conduit for sustaining the deities (see discussion of Madrid 19b below). It was presumably as the result of the cutting or severing of the water-filled cord depicted in the Paris

5.9. Page 22 of the Paris codex (after Rosny 1888).

codex that the great flood was precipitated (Vail and Hernández 2009c).[14] Whether there is a connection between this mythological event and the sacrifice of Itzam Kab' Ayin remains to be established.

The middle register of Dresden 46 (Figure 5.8b), which is the first page of the Venus table proper (as opposed to the preface on page 24), contains additional connections to the scene on Dresden 74. Both feature a black-painted deity with weapons, who is identified textually as "God L" on Dresden 46 and linked to the eastern appearance of Venus (i.e., its heliacal rise as morning star). The figure on Dresden 74 has likewise been identified as God L (see previous), and he, too, carries weapons associated with Venus in its role as a warrior (a spear and atlatl darts). On Dresden 46b, God L holds a shield in one hand and an *atlatl* in the other. His dart is apparently aimed at K'awil, who is described in the caption as being speared (A7–B7 of text in Figure 5.8b). Indeed, we see K'awil with a dart emerging from his chest in the bottom register of the page (Figure 5.8c).

The spearing of K'awil, we are told, causes "damage to" (*yah?*) the people, the maize, and the food (C5–D5 and C7–D7 of text in Figure 5.8b). The text continues with another negative passage: *u muk ka' yax-k'an* ("it is an evil omen for the green and yellow [maize]," or alternately, "the green and yellow [i.e., ripe and unripe] [maize] are buried"; at C6–D6 in Figure 5.8b). This may refer to the time when maize was not available on the surface of the earth but was buried within a mountain. We learn of this from the *Popol Vuj*; similarly, it is a common theme in the mythology of highland México (Bierhorst 1992, cited in Taube 1993:39–40; Christenson 2003:193). In the Yucatecan Books of Chilam Balam, the seed corn was stolen and was taken not to the Underworld but rather to the sky, where it remained out of reach of those residing on the earth (Knowlton n.d.).[15] The theft of the maize is the event preceding the flood itself (previously described). Once the maize goes missing, life on earth cannot be sustained. This state of affairs seems to be reflected in the hieroglyphic caption to the scene depicting the wounded K'awil on Dresden 46c (Figure 5.8c), which refers to *u muk* ("evil omens for") the mats and thrones (a couplet referring to "rulership"; at B8–A9 of text), followed by negative auguries for the rulers (*ajaw*) and the "sprouts," or *ch'ok* (sons of rulers; at C8–D9).

Although not previously interpreted in this light, Dresden 46 appears to embody references to the mythological destruction of the world that occurred when Itzam Kab' Ayin ascended into the sky and the maize seed was stolen, incidents recorded not only in the codex but also by the scribes who compiled the texts contained in the Chilam Balam manuscripts.[16] In the Dresden Codex, this event is framed within the context of the heliacal rise of Venus as God L, who is responsible for wounding the embodiment of maize and abundance on the earth.[17] The prehispanic Maya who drafted this table as a warning of Venus's might have framed it within a powerful metaphor known to all Maya—the destruction of the earth, which was believed to be the fate of humanity should the appropriate rituals not be enacted.

The remaining four pages of the Dresden Venus table may likewise have connections to Maya creation mythology, specifically that relating to maize, as each page includes glyphic references to evil omens for (and/or the burial of) maize and sustenance. The figures depicted do not all relate as clearly as those on Dresden 46 to known mythology involving the theft of the maize (or the death of the maize god, as recounted in the *Popol Vuj*), although the maize god is indeed one of the figures shown as speared (on Dresden 48). The role of the other "victims" remains to be determined (but see Milbrath 1999:176–177 for her interpretation of these figures).

It is of interest that each of the figures depicted in the upper register can be associated with well-known Maya deities (the death god on page 47, Pawahtun on page 48, the moon goddess on page 49, and the maize god and Jun Ajaw on page 50), whereas those symbolizing Venus as a warrior, with the exception of God L on page 46, derive from outside of the Yucatec-speaking lowlands. Included are Lahun Chan, "10 Sky," on Dresden 47 (note that *chan* is the Ch'olan word for "sky"), a Chontal deity who is also referenced in the Books of Chilam Balam, and three Nahuatl deities—Tawisikal (Dresden 48), Chak Xiwitel (Dresden 49), and Kakatunal (Dresden 50) (Riese 1982; Taube and Bade 1991; Whittaker 1986). In interpreting these pages, we may expect to find that the cosmology being referenced likewise derives from "foreign" (i.e., non-Yucatec) sources.

Connections between Dresden 46 and Dresden 74 suggest the importance of reexamining the latter in light of the thesis that world destruction and creation provide a template for modeling events in the past that inform on the present and the future, such as are commonly seen in Maya astronomical tables. The disconnect that has always existed between those who view the scene in question as the destruction of the world by flood (see Freidel et al. 1993:106–107; Taube 1988a:143–147) and those who see it instead as a historical event that can be linked to Long Count dates in the table (see V. Bricker and H. Bricker 2005) can be easily resolved if one takes into account the framing of historical episodes within metaphors of world destruction and renewal. Astronomical events in the form of eclipses and the heliacal rise of Venus, among others, appear to have been linked very explicitly with the mythology of world destruction described in detail in Colonial sources like the Books of Chilam Balam or the *Popol Vuj*. Such events would have been followed by a restoration of the world order, such as occurs, for example, on Dresden 25–28 (the pages immediately following Dresden 74), as previously discussed.

Creation Events in the Madrid Codex

Several almanacs in the Madrid codex are cognate with Dresden 74, as previous scholars have noted (Taube 1988a:150–151; Zimmermann 1956:164; see Vail and Hernández 2009c for a recent discussion). Various other almanacs in the Madrid

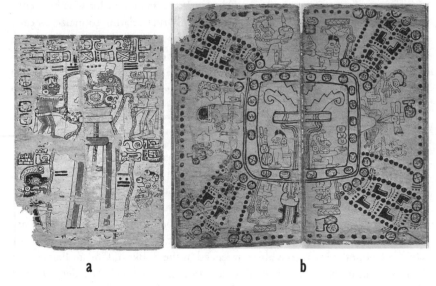

a   b

5.10. Creation imagery associated with a quadripartite structure of the world: (a) Madrid 19b; (b) Madrid 75–76 (after Anders 1967; courtesy of the Museo de América, Madrid).

codex, like the New Year's almanac on pages 34–37, can be interpreted as signifying the creation of the present world, or foundation rituals to sustain it, comparable to those discussed previously in relation to the Dresden year-bearer pages. Two additional almanacs featuring creation imagery may be found on Madrid 19b and 75–76. The first of these shows five deities linked by a rope, who are performing genital sacrifice within the courtyard of a temple; a k'in glyph representing the sun appears on the rope, and a turtle is perched on the temple's summit (Figure 5.10a). The almanac begins with the tzolk'in date 4 Ajaw, the same tzolk'in date associated with the start of the Long Count and the present era in 3114 B.C. (Vail 2005).

The scene on Madrid 19b recalls the *kuxan su'um* myth—the flowing of blood through a rope that was like an umbilical cord (Tozzer 1907:153)—and also echoes two Aztec myths associated with the time of creation. In one, the gods must sacrifice themselves to set the sun on its path across the sky (here represented by the k'in glyph; see Milbrath 1999:76–77). In another, the gods shed their blood so that it can be mixed with the ground bones of the previous race in order for humans to be created (Taube 1993:39, 43–44). In light of possible ties to the time of creation suggested by the 4 Ajaw date, it is of interest that the five deities pictured on Madrid 19b include the creator Itsamna, a merchant deity—who is here named as one of the Pawahtuns (or B'akab's), the rain god Chaak, and two underworld or death gods.

Like the examples discussed by Timothy Pugh (this volume), Madrid 19b encapsulates the quadripartite view of space at the core of prehispanic and contemporary Maya cultures, which is defined in relation to a central point of reference that marks the focal point of ritual action. A related scene, which I believe may also be associated with the creation of the present world and its inhabitants, appears on Madrid 75–76 (Figure 5.10b). Both almanacs emphasize blood sacrifice in relation to a quadripartite structured universe, with the central space being associated specifically with creation events. Like Madrid 19b, pages 75–76 also include an admixture of Mexican and Maya elements, suggesting some of the ways in which the two cultures influenced each other. As previous scholars have noted, Madrid 75–76 has a structure that is in many ways cognate to that of Fejérváry-Mayer page 1 (see Boone 2003; Hernández and Vail 2009; Thomas 1884; Vail and Hernández 2006). The two reference 260-day and 52-year cycles in their calendrics and iconography (Hernández and Vail 2009; Paxton 2001; Vail 2004; Vail and Hernández 2006).

Madrid 75–76 also, I suggest, portrays the creation of humans in its central frame, where Itsamna and his female counterpart Chak Chel are pictured seated beneath a stylized world tree. The three glyphs in front of Itsamna's outstretched hands may signify both *ik'* ("wind, breath, life") and also the maize seeds out of which humans were formed. The four quadrants represented at the perimeter of the almanac, which can be tied to dates in the 52-year calendar, portray the charter for the relationship between deities and humans (Vail and Hernández 2006)—the giving of human life (right and left frames) and blood (as indicated by the bloodletters in the top and bottom frames) in exchange for maize (represented by the T506 glyphs in the upper and lower frames).

Through its iconography and symbolism, the almanac also serves to link the calendar to the moment of creation. Various calendrical cycles are represented—the ritual cycle beginning with 1 Imix (bottom frame) and counting through all 260 days, represented either by explicit dates or by dots similar to the spacers seen in highland Mexican codices; a cycle of haab's (365-day years), encoded within the day glyphs surrounding the creator couple;[18] and a cycle of year-bearer dates linked to the quadrants and arms of the almanac, separated from each other by thirteen haab' intervals (Hernández and Vail 2006; Vail 2004:242–243).

Mexican conventions represented in the almanac include an emphasis on a 1 Imix starting date (in place of 4 Ajaw) and a focus on the Calendar Round rather than on the k'atun count emphasized in Colonial Yucatec texts. A further link to the Mexican tradition involves the extraction of the heart of a sacrificial victim (see Figure 5.10b, right quadrant), much as Fray Bernardino de Sahagún (1953:25–26) described in reference to the Aztec New Fire ceremony performed at midnight at the end of the 52-year cycle: "And when they drew the new fire . . . at midnight . . . they drew it upon the breast of a captive. . . . Then speedily [the priest] slashed open the breast of the captive, seized his heart, and quickly cast it there into the fire." Like the ritual described by Sahagún, that on Madrid 75–76 can be shown to take place at fifty-two-year intervals (Vail 2004:242).

Discussion

Metaphors of world destruction and creation form the central organizing principle of painted texts and imagery from Late Postclassic Yucatán. That this is the case should not be especially surprising, given the importance of creation episodes in colonial texts from throughout the Maya area and, indeed, in neighboring Mesoamerican cultures. Nevertheless, references to these events in the Maya codices have remained largely unrecognized prior to now, despite their identification in certain contexts (e.g., Dresden 74 and the Dresden year-bearer pages by Karl Taube and Linda Schele's work with almanacs in the Paris codex).

The creation stories referenced in Late Postclassic sources have a long time depth in the Maya area and among other Mesoamerican cultures. Nevertheless, it is of considerable interest that Nahuatl deities and versions of these stories played such a key role in the iconographic programs at sites such as Mayapán and Santa Rita, as well as in certain almanacs contained within the surviving Maya codices. Our understanding of the worldviews of the Yucatec Maya in the century or so preceding the Spanish Conquest must be broadened, therefore, to encompass a number of highland Mexican beliefs. Evidence from earlier time periods indicates that interchange between the two regions was of a long-standing nature (Braswell 2003; Smith and Berdan 2003a; Stone 1989), but it appears to be especially prevalent in the texts and images that form the subject of this chapter. As others have previously noted, the content of the Maya codices and Late Postclassic murals from the northern lowlands suggests that an active exchange existed among calendrical specialists and scribes/artists working in the central Mexican and Maya traditions during the fifteenth century (Boone 2003; Hernández and V. Bricker 2004; Just 2004; Vail et al. 2003). Late Postclassic Yukatek worldviews, therefore, can be seen as a blending of indigenous Maya beliefs (i.e., those with a long time depth in the Maya region, as previously described) with those introduced during contact with highland Mexican cultures.

Acknowledgments. The research discussed in this chapter was undertaken with the financial assistance of the National Endowment for the Humanities (Collaborative Research Grant RZ-50311, held from July 2004 to April 2007). I thank Leslie Cecil and Timothy Pugh for inviting me to participate in the 2004 SAA symposium "Maya Worldview at Conquest," which prompted the research for the present undertaking and resulted in a lively exchange among the participants, and I am grateful to the two anonymous reviewers for their comments on a previous draft of my chapter. I am especially indebted to Tony Aveni, Liz Graham, Christine

Hernández, Timothy Knowlton, and Susan Milbrath for discussions over the past several years relating to the ideas considered in my chapter.

Notes

1. See Elizabeth Graham, this volume, for a discussion of how metaphors reflect a group's or culture's worldviews. I am using spellings preferred by researchers in Yucatán rather than AMGL orthography.

2. For a discussion of their discovery and history, see Chuchiak (2004b), Coe (1989), Glass with Robertson (1975:125–126, 153–155, 179–180), and Vail (2006:503–506). The authenticity of the Grolier codex remains in question (Baudez 2002; Milbrath 2002; but see Carlson 1983). Until it is definitively proven not to be a prehispanic codex, however, I continue to group it with the others.

3. Tables include dates in the absolute (Long Count) calendar, whereas almanacs generally only contain dates in the 260-day ritual calendar (the tzolk'in) and occasionally in the haab' (365-day calendar).

4. Venus has two periods of visibility (as Morning Star and Evening Star), paired with two periods of invisibility (superior conjunction, following its Morning Star phase, and inferior conjunction, following the Evening Star phase). Its first appearance in the dawn or evening sky following conjunction (called M-first or E-first, respectively) was considered especially significant by the prehispanic Maya and other Mesoamerican cultures, and M-first, or its heliacal rise, is highlighted in the Dresden Venus table (Aveni 2001:184–186).

5. In the Classic period, a different system was used, based on a 0 Pop year-bearer paired with the days Ik', Manik', Eb', and Kab'an (see Rice, this volume).

6. Much has been written about the unusual order of the directional glyphs on Dresden 25c–28c (east, south, west, and north instead of east, north, west, and south). I agree with Thompson (1934), who first suggested that the scenes pictured on pages 26c and 28c were mistakenly transposed by the scribe. If the two are reversed, this results in the correct ordering of deities such that the incoming patron of the year appears in the lower register of one page and is pictured on the following page as the outgoing patron in the middle register.

7. Dresden 25c is associated with the east (mentioned at C1 in the caption) and, by extension, with the color red. This may be the association intended by the *chak* glyph at B1.

8. The pages of the Dresden codex were initially misnumbered (see Thompson 1972). It is now known that (misnumbered) page 25 should follow directly after page 74.

9. Birds are known to represent auguries for different periods of time, as may be seen, for example, in a series of almanacs on pages 16–18 of the Dresden codex. As various commentators have previously noted, the word *mut* appearing in the texts of these almanacs refers to "bird" but also to "omen" (see discussion in Houston et al. 2006:230–232).

10. I have italicized proper names spelled using the Colonial orthography (e.g., *Itzam Cab Ain*) to distinguish them from the spellings used by epigraphers today (e.g., Itzam Kab' Ayin).

11. The identification of this deity as God L was made by various scholars, including Susan Milbrath (1999:277) and Gunter Zimmermann (1956:164); but see Karl Taube (1988a:144), who identifies him as a black version of the rain god Chaak.

12. See Thompson (1972:62–67) and H. Bricker and V. Bricker (2007) for a discussion of the calendrical structure of the Venus table.

13. Like the Chaaks, the Pawahtuns had directional aspects associated with the four world quarters.

14. Water and blood were closely connected in prehispanic Maya thought, however, as we learn from the *Popol Vuj* (Christenson 2003:195), where the creator deities form humans from ground maize (representing their flesh) and water (representing their blood).

15. Recall that K'awil's head is found on the end of the skyband upon which the Pawahtun Ayin is seated in the upper register of Dresden 46. In the Chilam Balam manuscripts, *Bolon Dzacab* plays the role assumed by K'awil in the Dresden codex. The two are believed to be aspects of the same deity (Taube 1992:73, 78).

16. It is important to bear in mind that the Dresden Venus table is a copy of a table originally composed in the ninth century and later updated to be relevant through the thirteenth century (H. Bricker and V. Bricker 2007). It is not clear when during this process the content of the table that we see today was included, but it is possible that the references to mythology involving Itzam Kab' Ayin, Venus, and K'awil predate by many centuries the painting of the physical codex itself.

17. It is of interest in this regard that in the Chumayel version of the 11 Ajaw myth, *Bolon Dzacab* only returns after the appearance of Venus, here called *Lahun Chan*, and the sun (Timothy Knowlton, personal communication, February 12, 2008).

18. V. Bricker (2009) shows how this set of day glyphs can also be used to represent successive dates of Venus's heliacal rise at 584-day intervals.

Colonial Cave Art in the Northern Maya Lowlands: The Dark Side of the Maya Worldview after the Conquest

CHAPTER SIX

Andrea Stone

Defining Colonial Cave Art

Prior to the publication of my book, in 1995, *Images from the Underworld*, little was known about Maya cave art apart from Strecker's work of the 1970s and 1980s in the Puuc area (see bibliography in Strecker and Künne 2003) and J. Eric S. Thompson's (1975) reference to several cave art sites in Chiapas. What has emerged is a clearer picture of the Maya's cave art legacy, which is among the richest in the world and can be traced back at least to the Late Preclassic period. In addition, we know that the preponderance of this cave art is prehispanic; however, some portion, the extent of which is presently unclear, appears to be colonial. Although this is hardly earth-shaking news, not much thought has been given to its significance. It is the aim of this chapter to take a first step toward understanding colonial Maya cave art, despite the fact that our knowledge of the corpus is just coming into focus. Colonial cave art deserves our consideration as it offers a unique perspective on the evolving nature of Maya culture in the aftermath of the Spanish Conquest. It also sheds light on the continued practice of cave ceremonialism in the Maya area after and, in some sense, in defiance of this conquest, indeed, during what must have been a dangerous period for the practice of cave ritual. In light of post-conquest demography in the Maya area, it is not surprising to find colonial cave art concentrated in northern Yucatán and Campeche, which had relatively vibrant colonial cultures compared with the sparsely populated southern lowlands. Yet, we must also keep in mind that cave art in Yucatán, hardly a late phenomenon, was as prolific during the Classic period as it was in the southern lowlands (for an overview of this topic see Strecker and Stone 2003). Cave ritual, and concomitantly cave art, merely persisted in the northern lowlands.

Problems inevitably arise in suggesting colonial facture for a drawing or painting—no carved colonial cave art has yet been identified—found in a Maya cave. It is now possible to date pigments used in cave art by AMS radiocarbon analysis (Rowe 2001); however, to date no such testing has been attempted in Yucatán (see Rowe 2004 for a recent summary of where AMS testing has been carried out on Maya rock art). The best approach for identifying colonial cave art still rests on the more subjective style dating supplemented by contextual evidence when available. Fortunately, certain stylistic traits and subject matter are clearly diagnostic of the Colonial period. In other cases, the placement, style, and reoccurrences of an image may offer enough circumstantial evidence to suggest contemporaneity with depictions that are obviously colonial. Sticking to these conservative criteria, which admittedly are biased toward more Europeanized images, yields a limited, albeit secure, colonial corpus. Without doubt this corpus is much larger and includes a variety of schematic animals and figures and enigmatic geometric designs that may look Precolumbian but are in fact colonial. I have suspicions about a number of cave drawings of this type from Dzibichen, Actun Kaua, Miramar, and Loltun, to be discussed below, that probably date to the Colonial era; however, corroborating these suspicions would require more extensive archaeological investigation. For the purposes of this chapter, then, colonial cave art is narrowly defined by the most salient examples in order to establish a baseline inventory.

Among cave art sites with definitive colonial drawings and paintings, three stand out in importance. One is Dzibichen, a cave near the village of Yokdzonot Presentado, in the municipio of Tizimin, east of Yalcoba (Casado López et al. 1990; Stone 1995:74–86). This is a small single-chamber cave that lacks a true dark zone, but it does contain a pool of water (for plan see Stone 1995:figure 4-65). The back wall is covered in charcoal drawings that appear to be pre- and post-conquest. Conversations with local residents and the presence of a wooden cross at the entrance (Stone 1995:figure 4-66) indicate that the cave still serves a ritual function. Dzibichen is the most important colonial cave art site known in the Maya area and will be discussed in more detail below. Another notable colonial cave art site is Miramar (Breuil 1986), in the vicinity of Bolonchen, Campeche, whose own cave, accessed by an enormous ladder, was immortalized in Frederick Catherwood's famous lithograph. According to a description by James Reddel (1977:246), the nearby cave of Miramar, which he calls Actun Huachap, has hundreds of meters of passage. On the walls are dozens of schematic drawings, which I have only had the opportunity to observe in photographs. Some of these drawings are indisputably colonial. Probably many more are as well but lack the kind of Europeanized diagnostic features that make such an identification certain. A third interesting cave is Santa Cruz, described as a "collapsed dome with a vertical entrance shaft" (Normark 2003:73). The description recalls the collapsed dome caves common in northern Quintana Roo that have "voluminous dome-shaped chambers, the ceilings of which are sometimes breached in the center by narrow shafts leading up to the surface" (Rissolo 2005:352). The Santa Cruz collapsed dome has a collection of colonial drawings, crudely executed but telling in their iconography. Santa Cruz is in the Cochuah zone straddling eastern Yucatán and central-western Quintana Roo, a region that has been under archaeological investigation by Justine Shaw. Several cave art sites in the Puuc zone also contain colonial drawings. A single example has been published from the cave of Actun Hom in the vicinity of Tekax (Uc González 1999:134). The presence of other colonial drawings in this cave has not been verified. Tixcuytun (Barrera Rubio and Peraza Lope 1999; Stone 1995:69–71), also near Tekax, has a few images that appear to be colonial. One likely colonial drawing is detectable at Actun Kaua (Sayther et al. 1998:figure 5); probably many more of the dozens of drawings in this cave are as well but again lack definitive traits. Finally, some drawings from the Puuc cave of Loltun appear to be colonial. Although modest, this group of seven caves provides a starting point to identify recurrent types of imagery that can be reliably dated to the Colonial period. Following is a summary of major categories of colonial cave art derived from this corpus.

The Double-Headed Eagle

Within the corpus of colonial cave art thus far identified, the double-headed eagle—and its single headed variant—provides the most reliable iconographic marker of a Colonial date (Figure 6.1). The double-headed eagle is a fascinating case study in the devolution and dissemination of a symbol in time and space. We might pause briefly to consider the extraordinary longevity and widespread distribution of the double-headed eagle in world art (Wittkower 1938/39). According to my sketchy understanding of this complex subject (Stone 2003), the double-headed eagle is of Near Eastern origin, with examples dating back to ancient Mesopotamia (Gerola 1934). From this precocious start the double-headed eagle persisted over millennia and can be detected in Persian art from where it probably spread to Byzantium. It was especially in vogue during the late Byzantine period (Kazhdan 1991). The eagle of Greek and Roman art, although having only one head and appearing more lifelike, nevertheless has roots in the same Near Eastern traditions that spawned the double-headed eagle. For the Greeks, the eagle was Zeus's avian counterpart, as it was Jupiter's in ancient Rome. The Romans gave a political spin to the eagle by deploying it as an imperial logo, especially linked with the imperial family.

Although the double-headed eagle circulated primarily in the art of the non-Classical world, this heraldic-looking bird seems to have merged with the more

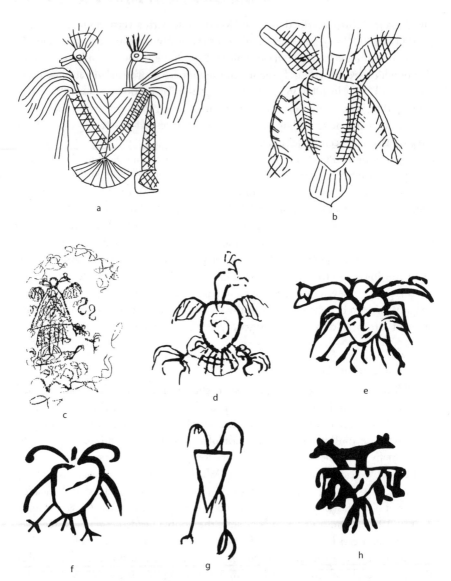

6.1. Comparison of Colonial double- and single-headed eagles from Yucatán and Campeche based on the Hapsburg crest: (a–b) Graffitti from the Palacio Principal, Hochob, Campeche (redrawn after de Robina 1956:fig. 19a); (c) Cave drawing Dzibichen 37, Yucatán (drawing by A. Stone); (d) Cave drawing Dzibichen 38, Yucatán (drawing by A. Stone); (e–f) Cave drawings Miramar, Campeche (drawing by A. Stone); (g) Cave drawing Actun Hom, Yucatán (redrawn after Uc 1999:134); (h) Cave drawing, Santa Cruz Cave, Yucatán (redrawn after Normack 2003:fig. 38).

naturalistic single-headed Roman eagle during the Middle Ages. By the thirteenth century the double-headed eagle, now crowned in an unfettered display of imperial authority, was incorporated into the heraldry of the Holy Roman Empire and later that of dozens of noble families, petty states, and religious institutions affiliated with either the Holy Roman or Byzantine Empire throughout central Europe, Russia, and beyond. Often a shield containing heraldry was placed on the bird's chest or the image of the bird was emblazoned on a heraldic shield. Since between 1453 and 1700 the Holy Roman emperor was a Hapsburg, the double-headed eagle, a token of international esteem and political legitimacy linked to the Roman Empire, served as the Hapsburg crest. The Hapsburg king, Charles V of Spain, grandson of the Holy Roman emperor Maximilian I and himself a Holy Roman emperor, incorporated the double-headed eagle into the Spanish coat of arms. As the Conquest occurred during the reign of Charles V, the double-headed eagle made its way to the New World where it embellished church façades, government buildings, documents, and religious paraphernalia, ascribing patronage or official sanction from the Spanish crown.

Native exposure to the double-headed eagle in the Maya area produced some interesting local responses to this most venerable Old World symbol of institutional authority. In highland Guatemala the double-headed eagle became a standard design woven into colonial huipils (Schevill 1985), a practice that has gone unabated. Among the Mam, this design is seen as a wholly indigenous expression of a spirit being called Kablikot (Looper 2001:286), or "two eagles." This spirit bird seems to be a counterpart of Kalkoj, a protective two-headed bird spirit found among the Tz'utujil of Santiago Atitlán (Christenson 2001:138, figure 5.18). Several Colonial K'iche' chronicles depict double-headed eagles serving as a crest of K'iche' elite and lending these native documents an official imprimatur (Christenson 2001:138–141, figure 5.19). The absorption of the double-headed eagle into native iconographies during the Colonial period in Mesoamerica seems to have been widespread. For instance, the motif appears in modern Huichol yarn paintings, likely a borrowing from earlier colonial textile designs. One catalog description of a Huichol yarn painting identifies a double-headed eagle, clearly derived from the Hapsburg crest, as "Our Mother Eagle Girl" (Berrin and Seligman 1978:no. 17). Obviously, the Huichol absorbed the double-headed eagle into the local culture just as the highland Maya did.

No comparable survivals of the double-headed eagle with ethnographically attested meanings have been reported in the northern Maya lowlands. However, my colleague Miguel Astor-Aguilera showed drawings of double-headed eagles from northern lowland caves, which I supplied, to some Maya informants living in Quintana Roo. Astor-Aguilera (personal communication, 2004) observed that the more traditional individuals, who seem to have had no previous experience with this kind of imagery, related the bird figures to the winds, the *iik'o'ob*. Caves, especially "breathing" caves, emit winds, and birds fly in and out of cave entrances and are generally related to the winds, which they use for flight. Interestingly, Maya more assimilated into Spanish culture identified the eagle with liberty and freedom, this view likely deriving from exposure to the eagle on the Mexican flag and other modern-day political uses of the eagle logo, including in the United States, all of which descend from the Old World eagle tradition.

Although the double-headed eagle did not survive in the recent folk culture of the northern lowlands, it filtered into the colonial indigenous imagination. A line in the *Chilam Balam of Tizimin, yemel ahau ka p'el u poli,* "the descent of the lord with two heads," is thought by Ralph Roys (1954:18) to refer to Charles V in the guise of the Hapsburg crest. In Yucatán and Campeche, the Hapsburg eagle is found in official public contexts, such as church façades—I have seen one crudely scratched into the stucco surrounding the window of a small colonial church exterior near Valladolid, the window forming the bird's shield-like body. Double-headed eagles also occur as graffiti—as many as four are scratched into the stucco walls of prehispanic buildings at Hochob, Campeche (Figures 6.1a–b). Two are found in Structure V along with a cross (de Robina 1956:47), and two in Structure II, one overlapping a scene depicting a ritual centering on a prehispanic pyramid (de Robina 1956:figure 19a).

Examples of double-headed eagles from northern lowland caves are fairly distinct (Figures 6.1c–h). The two heads are quite stylized, sometimes reduced to two out-curving lines or two projections sprouting from a central hump. The bird's chest is usually an inverted triangle or somewhat more rounded. This conforms to the heraldic shield placed on the bird's chest. The wings tend to be narrow, small, or not even present. Generally, there are clawed stick legs and some allusion to the tail feathers between them. Interesting variations on this formula occur. At Dzibichen, the bird's triangular chest has the pointed end at the top, perhaps a garbled version of the shield (Figure 6.1c). In this example, each projecting "head" has a circle drawn above, probably stemming from the crown worn by the bird in standard representations. At Miramar, a face is rendered on the heart-shaped shield-chest of one bird (Figure 6.1e). Dzibichen also has a single-headed eagle, an alternate form of the Hapsburg crest (Figure 6.1d). Here an *S* is emblazoned on the shield-like chest area. Both the bird from Actun Hom (Figure 6.1g) and the Santa Cruz Cave (Figure 6.1h) have typical inverted triangles forming the chest.

No historical records have survived to put into context what the double-headed eagle meant to a colonial Maya of the northern lowlands. Yet, their repeated occurrences in caves suggest that on a local level the bird's meaning became divorced from a direct association with the Spanish crown. Caves were religious sanctuaries beyond church and state control except in unfortunate cases where cave ritual inadvertently came to the attention of Spanish authorities who considered this idolatrous behavior a punishable crime. Nancy Farriss (1984:291) notes that the lightest sentence for idolatry was a hundred lashes. Given the consequences of detection, forcing cave ritual to be more clandestine than even during the prehispanic period, the performance of cave ritual can be viewed as an act of native resistance. In caves, the indigenous culture in its hybrid European-prehispanic form could be given relatively free expression. It seems unlikely that the Maya would have deployed the image of a Hapsburg eagle to link themselves to the Spanish hierarchy who disapproved of this very behavior. European symbols of this sort were likely assimilated into a colonial native iconography. The eagle may have been appropriated as a power symbol by native elite, as it was among the K'iche', or it may have embodied a wholly indigenous spirit being as it did in other regions of Mesoamerica. Given that no ethnographic evidence for such a spirit being has come to light, the former is more likely.

Circular Faces

A seemingly innocuous but fascinating colonial cave art motif consists of circular frontal faces (Figure 6.2). The basic form is a circle enclosing eyes, nose, and mouth; some are also rayed. Although circular faces are present in prehispanic cave art, colonial examples are in many respects distinct. For instance, they are always drawn in pigment, whereas prehispanic ones tend to be carved. In addition, the colonial faces are quite round and use specific conventions for the facial features, such as a continuous line for the eyebrows and nose. The eyes are generally dots or small circles and the mouth, when present, a line forming a "smiley face." One circular face with these features, located directly under a double-headed eagle, is present at Miramar but has suggestions of a neck (Figure 6.2a). The best collection of these faces is at Dzibichen where there are about six examples of the basic and rayed type (Figures 6.2b–e). In an analysis of these faces, I pointed out their similarity to illustrations in the *Chilam Balam of Chumayel* (Stone 1995:85), as had been earlier noted by Maria Pilar Casado López and colleagues (1990). In the *Chumayel*, both plain and elaborated circular faces of this type stand for the Lords of the K'atun in the k'atun histories (Figure 6.3a) and for astronomical bodies, such as the sun and moon, in eclipse diagrams and other astronomical charts (Figure 6.3c). These heads are even more prolific in the *Chilam Balam of Ixil*, where, like the *Chumayel*, they stand for both k'atuns, seen in the *Ixil's* k'atun wheel (Figure 6.3b, left), and the sun and moon, seen in the *Ixil's* astronomical illustrations (Figure 6.3d); in the *Ixil*, however, the same simple round heads additionally stand for the twenty days of the *veintena*.[1] In the *Ixil's* list of the twenty days, a cross marks the year-bearers (Figure 6.3b, middle) and a crown adorns the *ajaw* glyph (Figure 6.3b, right), both rendered as circular faces.

I had earlier assumed that these round faces evolved out of Europeanized versions of prehispanic symbols, particularly the ajaw glyph, which is also a frontal

6.2. Cave drawings of Colonial personification heads: (a) Miramar, Campeche (drawing by A. Stone); (b) Dzibichen 48, Yucatán (drawing by A. Stone); (c) Dzibichen 4, Yucatán (drawing by A. Stone); (d) Dzibichen 35, Yucatán (drawing by A. Stone); (e) Dzibichen 34, Yucatán (drawing A. Stone).

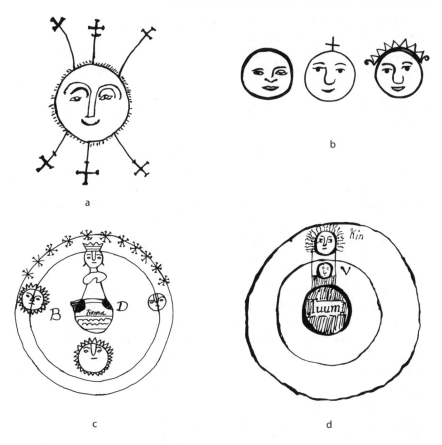

6.3. Colonial manuscripts from Yucatán with personification heads: (a) Lord of Katun 13 Ahau, *Chilam Balam of Chumayel* (redrawn after Roys 1954:fig. 43); (b) *Chilam Balam of Ixil*, left; k'atun personification, middle and right, year-bearer with cross and ahaw glyph with crown from veintena list (redrawn after Bricker and Miram 2002:fig. 39; drawn from photographic copy in the Library of Congress); (c) Representation of solar and lunar eclipses, *Chilam Balam of Chumayel* (redrawn after Roys 1954:fig. 9); (d) Representation of an eclipse, *Chilam Balam of Ixil* (drawn from photographic copy in the Library of Congress).

face standing for the k'atun. It is not hard to imagine an ajaw glyph evolving into a circular face with European features. However, a study by Helga-Maria Miram and Victoria Bricker (1996) has shown that these heads are wholly European, at least in design. They relate broadly to the use of disembodied heads as personifications of the winds, planets, sun, moon, and other astronomical bodies seen in European astrological diagrams, maps, and an assortment of scientific illustrations. European personification heads are usually placed around a circular structure representing cosmic or world space. As Miram and Bricker (2002:34) demonstrate, these circular diagrams, seen by the Maya in illustrated books sent from Europe, many dating from the late sixteenth century, are the direct antecedent of colonial k'atun wheels.

Yet, conceptually, European personification heads do not represent a wholly foreign idea intrusive to the Maya frame of reference since personification by head forms was a mainstay of the prehispanic visual vocabulary, commonly serving as a synecdoche for an entire figure (Houston et al. 2006:68). In extending the deployment of colonial circular heads from astronomical to calendrical contexts, the Maya used them as ersatz hieroglyphs in lieu of prehispanic day signs, memory of which had rapidly faded. The ready deployment of crowned and bearded disembodied heads to symbolize k'atuns as early as the sixteenth century, as seen in the illustration known as the *Xiu Coat of Arms* (Miram and Bricker 1996:figure 9), also stems from an indigenous impulse, even though the heads are of Spanish type. European-style personification heads thus reflect a mixture of European form and indigenous modes of signification.

I previously argued that the Dzibichen circular faces represent Lords of the K'atun, such as those seen in the *Chilam Balams of Chumayel* and *Ixil* (Stone 1995). This argument was supported by the fact that on a lower section of the cave wall are depicted curious four-legged creatures with pointed heads and ajaw glyphs on their backs (Figure 6.4). Karl Taube (1988b) noted that a stone censer from Mayapán in the form of a turtle has an arrangement of thirteen ajaw glyphs around the rim of the shell, an obvious reference to the k'atun cycle. He suggested that the Dzibichen "turtle-ajaws" therefore be construed as references to the k'atun but each in the guise of a separate turtle, of which there are nine in the cave. This k'atun-turtle iconography, which seems to be Late Postclassic, suggested that k'atun imagery was important at Dzibichen and that the circular heads are also k'atun personifications. One of the rayed solar heads even resembles the personification head for k'atun 13 Ajaw in the *Chumayel* (cf. Figures 6.2d and 6.3a).

However, Miram and Bricker's work reminds us that these heads were iconographically flexible and could have various symbolic references, especially of an astronomical nature. The basic form of the circular personification head seems to derive from the European personifications of the sun and moon. Bricker and Miram (2002:272, figure 75) have tracked down the source for one astronomical diagram in the *Chilam Balam of Kaua* that uses personification heads, a Spanish *reportorio* dating to 1585. The European sources they have uncovered point generally to dates no earlier than the seventeenth century for this class of colonial iconography, making it unlikely that the Dzibichen personification heads are sixteenth century; they could even date as late as the eighteenth century.

Drawing 35 from Dzibichen portrays the sun with projecting lines ending in asterisks, a Colonial convention for stars and planets (Figure 6.2d). On one level

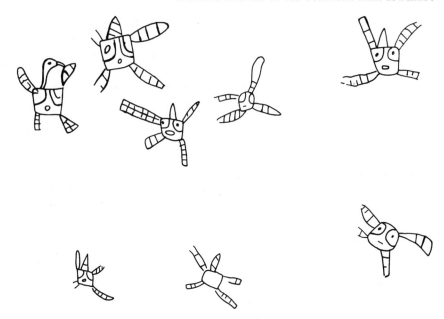

6.4. Cave drawings of turtle-ajaws, Dzibichen 20 (drawing by A. Stone).

this cave image is a kind of astronomical diagram recalling those seen in the *Chilam Balams of Chumayel* (Figure 6.3c), *Ixil* (Figure 6.3d), and *Kaua* (Bricker and Miram 2002:271). It is also significant that the two solar heads at Dzibichen have juxtaposed, emphatically smaller non-rayed personification heads (Figures 6.2d–e). Since they occur twice, these pairings seem deliberate and especially recall eclipse diagrams in the above-mentioned Books of Chilam Balam (Figures 6.3c–d). These diagrams juxtapose a large rayed sun with a small plain head standing for the moon. The exaggerated difference in scale between the paired heads at Dzibichen may mark a similar distinction between the sun and moon or other astronomical body. The elaboration and size of solar images at Dzibichen also points to the fact that Maya exposure to European scientific thought gave the sun a newfound dominant role in their cosmological constructs. Rayed solar images are a regular part of the inventory of colonial cave art and are also present at Miramar and Santa Cruz.

Although the astronomical implications are intriguing, a case can also be made for the Dzibichen personification heads representing k'atuns. The 13 Ajaw K'atun Lord from the Chumayel (Figure 6.3a) is a solar image with projecting lines ending in crosses. Dzibichen's different size personification heads could simply reflect the fact that solar representations tend to be larger, a sign of the sun's status. The presence of two eagles, one double- and one single-headed (Figures 6.1c–d) is also intriguing in the context of a k'atun interpretation. In the prehispanic period, k'atun prophecies were represented by birds, this being the case in the k'atun pages of the Paris codex (Love 1994:17). Is it possible that the eagle emblems, although clearly derived from the Hapsburg crest, allude to the prophetic associations of birds?

Thus, the Dzibichen personification heads could refer to k'atuns or astrological lore. In either case, it is intriguing to find this kind of imagery, a striking correlate of colonial manuscript illustrations of indigenous calendrical and astronomical concepts, in a cave. Its presence provides further evidence of the perpetuation of esoteric knowledge and historical traditions by the indigenous priesthood and also reveals the survival, or more likely colonial invention, of ritual practices pertaining to this sacred knowledge, safely hidden away in caves. Just as one sees in the Books of Chilam Balam a record of native history along with cosmological conceptualizations formulated in diagrams and descriptions, one may well witness in caves with comparable illustrations the ritual practices associated with these new religious and scientific ideas embraced by colonial Yukatek Maya.

Horse and Rider

The motif of the horse and rider is clearly post-conquest but could conceivably date to any later time. However, evidence suggests that this type of figure was in vogue during the Colonial period. The mounted horse is found in painted rock art in other parts of Mesoamerica. Guy Stresser-Péan (1990) published examples from the Huasteca that he dates from the sixteenth to the eighteenth centuries based on the region's indigenous occupation. Nor does it not seem coincidental that three caves in the northern Maya lowlands with images of horses and riders have other examples of colonial cave art: Dzibichen, Miramar, and Santa Cruz. This circumstantial evidence further suggests a colonial date for the horse and rider, as will be assumed in the present study. Miramar is the most interesting site displaying the horse-and-rider theme since figures of this type are exceptionally abundant (Figure 6.5a–d). In one section of the cave wall this imagery was hastily and repeatedly painted by the same individual. There appear to be well over a dozen examples; however, many are so sketchy that they blend into a confusing tangle of lines and cannot be accurately counted. Is the multitude of mounted horses here the record of a cavalry invasion? The Miramar horses and riders are stick figures with a single line forming the horse's body and a line forming each leg with hardly a suggestion of the beast's head. The rider resembles a cross in that one arm goes forward and one back. This stylization is similar to Huastec examples (Stresser-Péan 1990:594). Dzibichen has one mounted horse in a rudimentary stick-figure style. The animal has a single line for the body and four descending stick legs (Figure 6.5e), the rider reduced to a mere vertical line. In a second example at Dzibichen both the horse's and rider's bodies are outlined and the rider's arms go forward and back as at Miramar (Figure 6.5f). This figure rests on a groundline and may date to a later period since two

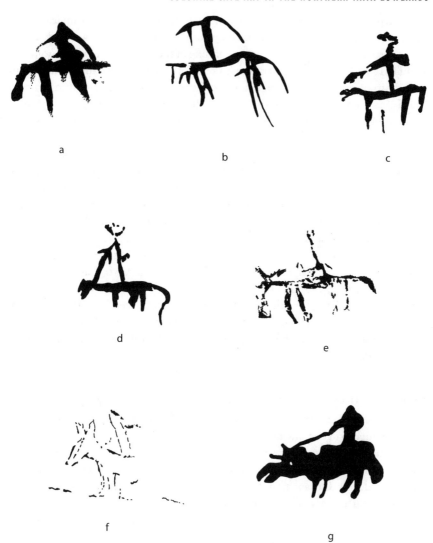

6.5. Cave drawings of horses and riders: (a–d) Miramar, Campeche (drawing by A. Stone); (e) Dzibichen 31, Yucatán (drawing by A. Stone); (f) Dzibichen 46, Yucatán (drawing by A. Stone); (g) Santa Cruz, Yucatán (redrawn after Normark 2003:fig. 42).

drawings of bicycles also sit over groundlines (Stone 1995:figures 4-73d and 4-74c). The horse and rider from Santa Cruz are painted in solid infill (Figure 6.5g). The rider's right arm appears to hold onto the reins. The horse is rather misshapen (possibly being a mule), but the quality of the drawings here is generally crude.

Farriss (1984:178) states that in colonial Yucatán, horses and mules were a rarity only accessible to the elite or those who could afford such a luxury. If this were the case, it would color our understanding of these figures. However, Matthew Restall (1997:180) notes that although the Spanish imposed a ban on indigenous ownership of horses for anyone below the rank of *indio hidalgo*, seeming to confirm Farriss's assertion, the ban had little effect and perhaps was not even known in the countryside. Based on the contents of wills, he concludes that horses were regularly kept by rural villagers and were a common form of transportation. We are then left to wonder if these cave drawings of horses and riders should be viewed as a quaint reflection of daily life or as images of status, power, and economic success. In historic Plains Indian rock art of North America, depictions of mounted horses do reflect status and power, figuring into the pictorial record of "accomplishments of individual warriors" (Sundstrom 2004:chapter 9). Admittedly, the horse did not play a role in colonial Yucatán comparable to that in the American Plains, but it was still tied to economic success and must have been seen as a privileged form of transportation. As earlier noted, Dzibichen also contains two drawings of riderless bicycles (Stone 1995:figures 4-73d and 4-74c) dating from sometime during the post-Colonial era. Like the horse, the bicycle can be seen as a privileged form of transportation, emblematic of status and economic success. One lesson to be learned from this is that even what appears to be crude, folksy rock art may concern issues of power and status.

Crosses, Interlaces, and Ornamental Details

The linear elaboration of European illustrations that likely influenced indigenous colonial art generally exhibits a curvilinear, ornamental style. Book illustrations, which were important sources for indigenous artists, frequently have ornamental borders filled with arabesques, swags, interlaces, and other classically derived decorative details. Ornamental flourishes occur in some examples of colonial cave art. This is particularly clear in one of the double-headed eagles from Dzibichen. Surrounding it are scribbly interlaces, reverse *S*'s, loops, and various hooked shapes that seem to form an ornamental frame (Figure 6.6a). To the left of this is a straight line with loops on the end (see Figure 6.7a), and further left a vertical interlace. In another area is an interlace with crosses projecting top and bottom and a surrounding curved line (Figure 6.6b). Loltun houses a linear frontal figure with a box-shaped body, characteristic of colonial schematic figures, as discussed below (Figure 6.7d). The tight, stiff scrolls projecting from the shoulders are in keeping with the ornamental tendencies seen in these other examples of colonial cave art. In the cave of Tixcuytun in the Puuc area are three drawings that contain crosses that may be colonial. One is a cross with hooked lines (Figure 6.6c) and another is a stick figure with cross-like elements forming the hand and head and projecting from the

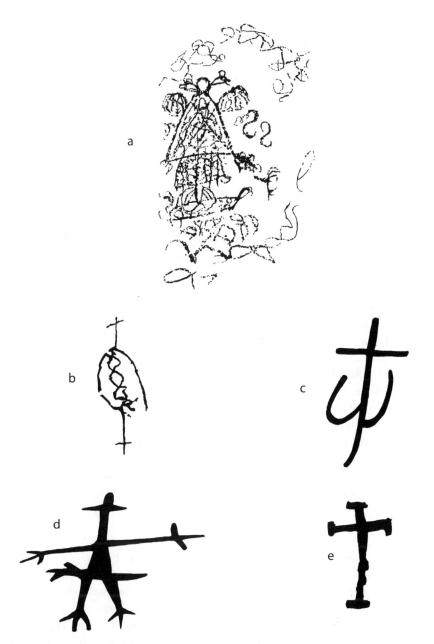

6.6. Cave drawings with Colonial-style traits: (a) Cave drawing Dzibichen 37, Yucatán (drawing by A. Stone); (b) Dzibichen 40, Yucatán (drawing by A. Stone); (c) Tixcuytun, Yucatán (drawing by A. Stone); (d) Tixcuytun, Yucatán (redrawn after Barrera Rubio and Peraza Lope 1999:foto 13); (e) Actun Kaua (redrawn after Sayther et al. 1998:fig. 5).

legs (Barrera Rubio and Peraza Lope 1999:foto 13) (Figure 6.6d). A blue cross is painted nearby on the ceiling. At Santa Cruz, a cave with colonial art has a figure in the shape of a cross (Normark 2003:figure 37). A painted cross with short bars at the ends, a type common in colonial manuscripts, is found at Actun Kaua (Figure 6.6e).

Boxy Frontal Figures

Schematic linear figures are very hard to date. However, evidence suggests that some figures of this type are colonial, perhaps even the majority of them. In terms of confidence in style dating, this category of colonial cave art is less certain than, say, the double-headed eagle, given that conventions for drawing schematic figures can be highly idiosyncratic. Thus, the following identifications of colonial schematic figures should be treated as proposals to be tested against future evidence. Typically, figures, as well as depictions of heads, seen in prehispanic Maya painted or drawn cave art are represented in profile, which affords better opportunity for the inclusion of iconographic details and indications of bodily movement. I believe many schematic frontal figures, on the other hand, are colonial, or perhaps later. Proving this is difficult given that dated comparative material is impossible to find and it is not clear if this style extended into the modern era. However, the frequent association of frontal figures having round heads and box-shaped bodies with identifiable colonial cave art leads to this conclusion. For instance, at Dzibichen the entire row of drawings at the highest level, over three meters above the cave floor, consists of colonial images, including personification heads and double-headed eagles. Among them is a partial frontal figure with outlined box-like body sitting next to a line ending in loops (Figure 6.7a). At Miramar is an unusually detailed frontal figure with round head and carefully outlined body (Figure 6.7b). The figure wears headgear that flares out at the sides, likely representing the brim of a hat. In fact, this kind of awkward frontal depiction of a Spanish helmet is seen in early colonial manuscripts. The costume is a knee-length robe that seems to have long sleeves, perhaps the vestments of a priest. This large figure is located directly beneath a horse and rider. At Santa Cruz is a frontal figure wearing a European-style hat (Figure 6.7c). The arms and legs are stick-like, but the body and face are outlined. As noted above, a frontal figure from Loltun has a round face, box-like body, and curved lines projecting from the shoulders, details that suggest a Colonial date (Figure 6.7d). Miramar has dozens of simple figures that conform to this type: with round heads, boxy bodies, and linear arms and legs (Figure 6.7e). The circular head seems more likely to be a colonial convention than a prehispanic one. Many of the round-headed figures at Miramar have one hand on the hip and one raised. The raised hand may be a convention for dancing. Another possibility is that it imitates the raised hand gesture common in colonial illustrations (Figure

6.7. Colonial figural drawings: (a) Dzibichen 49, Yucatán (drawing by A. Stone); (b) Miramar, Campeche (drawing by A. Stone); (c) Santa Cruz, Yucatán (redrawn after Normark 2003:37); (d) Loltun, Yucatán (drawing by A. Stone; (e) Miramar, Campeche (drawing by A. Stone).

6.8. Illustration from folio 113 of the *Chilam Balam of Kaua* (redrawn after Bricker and Miram 2002).

6.8). Although the colonial dating of the cave drawings seems likely, their thematic intent is uncertain.

The Implications of Colonial Cave Art

The existence of Colonial cave art speaks to a number of issues. One is the view that colonial Yukatekans lived under the shadow of Spanish rule while still maintaining autonomous political and religious systems through which their native traditions were preserved. These autonomous indigenous systems were strengthened by the survival of a native nobility and hierarchical priesthood who lent resources, leadership, and knowledge of the collective past to the preservation of a Maya identity. Regarding the nature of the indigenous religion, Farriss (1984:288–289) draws a useful distinction between a private sphere of household and milpa rituals (see Chuchiak, this volume, for comments on the private nature of colonial Maya ritual) and a public sphere or "community cult," the latter an outgrowth of prehispanic state religion. It is within the community cult that *ah k'ino'ob'*, leaders of the hierarchical priesthood (discussed by John Chuchiak [2001]), operated. Patronized by the native elite and integrated with the system of civil-religious officeholders, this priesthood was responsible for the continued production of hieroglyphic bark-paper books during the Colonial period and the preservation of native history and lore in its syncretic guise, as recorded in the Books of Chilam Balam.

Farriss (1984:288) argues that the Spanish clergy was most bent on abolishing the community cult, that is, the residue of the state religion, which posed the greatest threat to the Spanish power structure. The private sphere household and milpa rituals, conducted by local *hmeeno'ob*, although an embarrassing reminder of paganism's tenacity, were harder to detect and were considered less serious infringements of church doctrine. Data presented by Chuchiak (2001:136) seem to corroborate this as he notes the harsh punishment meted out to members of the hierarchical priesthood for being caught merely in possession of ritual vestments and paraphernalia, this being a capital offense. His documentary evidence for the persecution of *ah k'ino'ob* across the peninsula (Chuchiak 2001:map 1) speaks to the Spanish clergy's determination to eliminate them.

Historians thus paint a picture of a "traditional" Maya society negotiating its existence under the pressure of Spanish domination. The native system is often described as "underground" or "clandestine," and caves are assumed to have been refuges for the enactment of the pagan rites that so infuriated religious authorities (Clendinnen 1987:161; Farriss 1984:290). That they actually were is attested in some colonial documents (Stone 1995:255n1), most famously Pedro Sánchez de Aguilar's (1937) 1613 investigative report on the extirpation of idolatry that had been exposed in a number of caves.

Cave art of the Colonial period confirms this anecdotal evidence and adds further insights into the role of caves as theaters of a colonial clandestine religion. We recall Farriss's distinction between the private sphere and the community cult or public sphere. It can be assumed that private sphere cave rituals, perhaps supervised by hmeeno'ob to address healing, hunting, and agricultural concerns, were conducted in caves throughout the Colonial period, as they currently are in some areas of Yucatán. At the same time, the cave art suggests that community cult rites were also sequestered in caves for at least part of the Colonial period. Likewise, in the prehispanic past, elite religion found expression in cave ceremonialism, as attested archaeologically, but the motivation surrounding this residual practice in the Colonial period had certainly changed from one of custom to necessity.

The case for community cult rites in caves is strongest at Dzibichen with its imagery corresponding to illustrations found in the Books of Chilam Balam, these being a distillation of a community's sacred history and cosmic lore, guarded and passed down by members of the educated priesthood. The hierarchical nature of the community cult, with its ties to prominent families and the status attached to the sacred knowledge under the watchful eyes of the priesthood, is perhaps reflected in the double- and single-headed eagles found in this cave, indeed, drawn at such a height that they literally preside over all other cave drawings. That this bird emblem is found in at least five other caves that we know of, spanning the width of the peninsula, can be cited as evidence to further this argument. It suggests a formal association of the bird logo with the cave cult during the Colonial period. This kind of formal linkage is likely to have evolved through activities of the hierarchical priesthood rather than in the private sphere.

K'atun Rituals in Caves

If the Dzibichen circular heads personify k'atuns, something, however, that is not certain, it would suggest a heretofore unrecognized performance of k'atun ceremonies during the Colonial period. K'atun wheels and k'atun prophecies in the Books of Chilam Balam provide unequivocal evidence that colonial Maya preserved their historical traditions by means of a k'atun count. We know something about the performative aspect of Late Postclassic k'atun ceremonialism since it is described retrospectively in colonial documents. K'atuns were celebrated publicly with processions involving the transportation of a stone to be set up in the town designated as the seat of the k'atun for that twenty-year period. Ceremonies were overseen by priests and rulers from the great cities, such as Mayapán. Archaeological evidence suggests that a new plaza floor was laid at Mayapán for each successive k'atun (Milbrath and Peraza Lope 2003b:38). As Bruce Love (1994:25) notes, public rituals associated with k'atun celebrations ceased in the wake of the conquest; certainly the Spanish would not have tolerated such public displays of pagan belief led by powerful community leaders. Colonial cave art raises the possibility that caves provided a sequestered arena for some type of performance of k'atun ceremonies. We can imagine in the shadows of Dzibichen a small gathering of religious and civic leaders and the echo of recitations of k'atun histories accompanying the production of the drawings.

The European Style of Colonial Cave Art

The European pictorial vocabulary of the colonial Maya cave art examined in this chapter reflects a process of acculturation that was ongoing in other regions of the Americas. The similarity of these foreign intrusions on native populations resulted in a number of cross-cultural convergences of rock art imagery. In some measure, then, the iconography of colonial Maya cave art fits into a pan-American pattern of colonial rock art production. For instance, in cases where horses figured into the lives of indigenous people and rock art continued to be made, the horse-and-rider theme is likely to be found in rock art. This is as true in the American Plains (Sundstrom 2004) and Southwest (Schaafsma 1980:328–332) as in the South American Andes. A volume dedicated to Colonial rock art in Bolivia and neighboring countries illustrates numerous sites with this imagery (Querejazu Lewis 1992). Yet, the images' details vary: sometimes the Spanish are the horsemen, at other times indigenous people are. Although roughly drawn, Bolivian examples include narrative scenes with mounted horsemen holding weapons. Indeed, the thematic context of both Bolivian and North American horse-and-rider compositions generally revolves around hostility and conflict; sometimes the actual historical event is known (Schaafsma 1980:figures 273, 275). The Maya and Huastec versions of this theme are in comparison nondescript and seem merely repetitive, making it difficult to understand their import. The double-headed eagle is also present in Bolivian rock art; one example occurs on a painted panel from Chiripaca, Bolivia, that includes many horses and riders (Taboada 1992:figure 54). In Bolivia the motif of the Latin cross is also very common. Crosses are often free-floating or they are set upon structures representing sanctuaries and altars. In Maya caves free-floating painted crosses are found at Tixcuytun and Actun Kaua. A painting of a cross set upon what looks like a building is found at Santa Cruz Cave (Normack 2003:figure 39). It would not be surprising to find more of these church-like structures in Maya cave art.

What about the survival of the indigenous graphic system in Maya cave art? First, we must recall that colonial survivals of the northern lowland Late Postclassic graphic system are rare. In Yucatán, they are limited to hieroglyphic signs, mainly seen in Landa and the Books of Chilam Balam, and a few details found in sixteenth-century manuscript illustrations, such as the *Xiu Family Tree* and the *Xiu Coat of Arms* (Cortez 2002:figures 12.1, 12.4). One wonders to what extent colonial hiero-glyphic books, purported to have existed in great numbers, also included pictures. Seeing what they looked like would help enormously to identify more colonial cave art apart from the most blatantly European in inspiration. The loss of this evidence and the paucity of illustrated native manuscripts of Colonial date from anywhere in the Maya lowlands have limited our ability to analyze colonial pictorial production in general. Similarly, we know that "idols" decried by Spanish priests were every-where to be found during the colonial period, but these too are a rare survival. It is my belief, although as yet unconfirmed, that many schematic depictions of animals, humans, and abstract symbols seen in Maya caves are colonial drawings retaining a measure of prehispanic influence. However, more work needs to be done on this material before anything definitive can be said about it.

Multiple pressures acted on the Maya to encourage the adoption of European pictorial conventions, no less the obvious effect of sheer exposure to new ideas conveyed in European books, something that would have increased with the passage of time. It is also possible that native identity in its newly forged colonial guise was not as invested in the indigenous pictorial system as it was in social and religious practices, making the former expendable. This echoes George Kubler's (1961:32) remark that in terms of Precolumbian survivals, "symbolic forms are perishable." However, Kubler, who took an extreme position on the "death" of prehispanic culture, believed that only practical and utilitarian traits could have much longevity, seeing religion as susceptible to extinction as art. Yet, the cave cult witnesses the survival of prehispanic religion throughout the Colonial period.

Another pressure to adopt new visual forms is the appeal of foreign symbols as status markers, a long-standing Mesoamerican tradition (Stone 1989). In considering this, it is significant that a much-diminished native nobility that had held the reins of power during the Late Postclassic period both in the northern lowlands and Guatemala highlands survived into the Colonial period. Several authors have commented that these colonial native elites continued to deploy strategies of social distancing that had worked successfully for them during the Late Postclassic. Geoffrey Braswell (2001) makes this point regarding K'iche' elite, who cloaked themselves in central Mexican cultural trappings, a process he believes intensified during the immediate preconquest era, owing to the looming Aztec presence in nearby Soconusco, and in the post-conquest era, through a desire to maintain social distinction in the eyes of the masses and the Spanish who were most responsive to Nahua ways. Similarly, Restall (2001a:18) observes that Yukatek noble families continued to claim origins in mythic foreign places during the Colonial period, just as Postclassic elites from across the Maya realm claimed origins in a mythic Tollan. The *Xiu Family Tree*, with its extensive use of central Mexican iconography, is a pictorial instantiation of this process (Cortez 2002).

As might be expected, in the Colonial period social distancing was accomplished by adopting Spanish manners and material culture (Farriss 1984:228). Farriss (1984:97) states that Maya elite had a proclivity to adopt Spanish-style dress and other conspicuous status symbols, especially in the first century after the conquest. This can help explain the appearance of the double-headed eagle in caves, which, although arenas of resistance, provided a rare venue to display elite status symbols. The double-headed eagle is a consummate example of a symbol conferring legitimate authority on those who used it because it is was not just foreign but derived from something so inextricably associated with the powerful that it had a kind of built-in pedigree, this in itself a passport to privilege. A final consideration of the Europeanized style of colonial cave art is, as earlier noted, that some of it may date as late as the eighteenth century. It would be interesting to find more obviously hybrid or transitional examples from an earlier period; yet, these may be difficult to isolate given the dearth of evidence. Colonial cave art helps us to understand Maya society as it engaged a foreign culture violently thrust upon it. The continuity of cave art and cave ceremonialism witnesses the Maya's spirit of resistance and determination to hang on to many of the old ways while their culture and society underwent inevitable transformations.

Note

1. Illustrations for the *Chilam Balam of Ixil* were consulted in a photographic copy held in the Wilkinson Collection at the Library of Congress, Acc. No. 4056.

CHAPTER SEVEN

De Descriptio Idolorum: An Ethnohistorical Examination of the Production, Imagery, and Functions of Colonial Yucatec Maya Idols and Effigy Censers, 1540–1700

John F. Chuchiak IV

> Do not believe in what the friars say because they lie to us ... and their images [of saints] that are here on this retable of the altar where they say mass are nothing because they lie to us. These idols that we have here before us are the true gods.
>
> (AH KIN GASPAR CHIM [AGI, ESCRIBANÍA DE CÁMARA 1562:1009A])

On April 2, 1674, in the Maya town of Sital, an ecclesiastical judge, Don Joseph Montalvo y Vera summoned Maya prisoner Antonio Chable before him and through the interpreter Pedro Martin, he began to interrogate him concerning a ritual he had been caught conducting several days before.

> "Is it true that these instruments that you see here, these hanging pots, these clay idols and the food and drink offerings are yours?" sternly asked the ecclesiastical judge.
> "Yes, they are mine," Chable replied honestly.
> "What are they for and why did you worship them?" the judge continued the interrogation.
> "They were placed there where you found them not so that I can worship them, but rather so that I can ask for the coming of the rains and the good weather for my crops," Chable responded.[1]

Chable and a large group of Maya had been apprehended in flagrante delicto in the act of offering food and drink and other sacrifices to various images and aspects of the Maya rain god Chac. When asked to explain why he had offered these exact objects, Chable appeared perplexed. It was not his idea to "worship" these objects, but according to Chable and other witnesses and participants, these objects were necessary for the petitioning of the rain and good crop seasons.

A month later, after incessant questioning, Antonio Chable finally confessed that he did indeed worship the images and that

> [t]he first four images are of the gods of the four corners of the world, to whom they make their petitions for rain, and requests for abundant crops in their fields, and that the other two images are the gods who conserve and protect them, who also ensure very thick stocks of maize, and that the last of the images was a stone which served as the god of beans, squash seeds, and other vegetables that they harvest . . . and all of these idols and images are the ones that give them what is necessary for Human life . . . and when they knew that it would be a bad harvest, they judged that these gods were angry, so they went to their fields and to caves where these idols sit and these and other Indians bleed themselves and offer their blood to these said idols so that their gods will become pleased.[2]

The testimony of Chable and many other Maya in similar ecclesiastical trials for "idolatry" gave evidence to the continued later Colonial use of ceramic "idols"[3] (or what archaeologists have come to call "effigy censers") (Russell 2000). Moreover, the information gathered during these idolatry trials serves as an invaluable, previously unused source to aid scholars (ethnohistorians and archaeologists alike) in the identification of the forms, functions, and deity associations of Postclassic Maya effigy censers (Chuchiak 2000, 2001, 2002, 2004a).

Many colonial clergy examined in great detail a number of the clay, wooden, and stone idols that they confiscated in order to understand the connection between these ceramic images and Maya ritual and religion. Their examination of these confiscated Maya ritual implements, especially the ceramic effigy censers, often culminated in a legal document, trial, or descriptive inventory that several friars called *Descriptio Idolorum*. They referred to their forms, shapes, and images as demonic and saw their native deities as devils. The first bishop of Yucatán, Fray Francisco Toral, warned his parish priests to "abominate the things of the Devil and exhort all of them [the Indians] not to believe in the idols nor place hope in their promises, but rather to know them for stones, wood and clay in which there are demons who trick and deceive men."[4] Toral did not deny the power of the Maya's god images nor insist that they were merely inanimate objects of stone, wood, and clay, but rather he attributed their powers, promises, and other interactions with the Indians as the work of the Devil and demonic trickery to lure them away from the Church and the "True God." The fact that the friars used the direct translation of the Spanish term "devil" (Maya *cizin*) to describe all of the Maya's prehispanic deities, religious images, and rituals shows the impact of this concept of diabolism in the minds of the first Franciscan friars.[5] Their colonial dictionaries contain many verbs like *pay cizin* ("to call the devil"), *tanlah cizin* ("to serve the devil"), and *u uin bal cizin* ("the figure of the devil, idol, or image") (Alvarez 1980:592–593). For the Maya, however, what the clergy viewed as "idolatry" actually served as a focus of religious expression for their traditional religion.

Maya God Images: Maya Concepts of the Use of Effigy Censers

To the Maya, "idolatry" was nothing more than the outward practice of piety to images that in their conception contained the spirits of their ancient gods and the supernatural forces that moved the world. Unlike the Christian concept that sharply divided good from evil, God from the Devil, the prehispanic Maya pantheon could not be so easily divided. Maya gods could be both benevolent and malevolent. The very nature of the gods, their almost human propensity for changing their minds and the violence of their desires, made it imperative that the Maya propitiate them and offer them gifts and sacrifices in order to sway their opinions, appease their anger, or "bribe" them when asking for some benefit such as rain for the *milpas*, sun for the crops, or health in times of epidemics.

Polytheistic religions do not demand exclusivity nor do they covet the faith of their followers but rather only demand the outward show of piety through offerings and sacrifices. Moreover, polytheistic religions constantly change for they permit the adoption of many and newer gods and spiritual intercessors. The Maya in the *relaciones* of Citilcum and Cabiche told the Spaniards that "the first people at Chich'en Itza were not idolaters until Kukulkan, a Mexican Captain, came to these parts and taught them to commit idolatry, or by necessity, as they said, he taught them to worship idols" (Garza 1983:82). Archaeological excavations at the Postclassic site of Mayapán, where the fragments of effigy censers number in the hundreds of thousands, illustrate that the Maya who inherited this "tradition of idolatry" began to mass-produce ceramic images of their gods during the Postclassic period (Shook and Irving 1955; Winters 1955a).

Maya religion was and is animistic in that the forces of nature themselves are worshipped (Garza 1996:197–220; Nájera Coronado 1996:221–257; Thompson 1997:234–239). Every living thing is seen as having potential spiritual power. In order to harness this spiritual power, the Maya made images and idols in the form of these spirits or divinities so that the spirit or deity would come into and inhabit the idol.

The Judeo-Christian religion and its emphasis on a faceless god is more the exception than the rule. Nevertheless, the images of the Maya gods did take on the fanciful and elaborate images of the deities whose aspects had been created and continue to dwell in the collective consciousness of the Maya of today. These god images, often attached to incense braziers, served them just as the modern Lacandons' "god pots" continue to serve today (Palka, this volume) as material receptacles for the

7.1. Ceramic Maya effigy censers: *u uich ku*, "the face of god" (redrawn and adapted from Thompson 1957a:fig. 1; all drawings by Argelia Segovia Liga).

offerings of the gods and images before which the pious Maya attempted to appease or propitiate the gods they believed were contained within.[6] For the Maya of the prehispanic and Colonial periods there was no separation between the image and the deity. The Maya called these god images *u uich ku*, or "the face of god" (Figure 7.1).[7] Fray Juan de Santamaria, writing in 1610, stated that "the natives hold these idols and images in great reverence.... They call the idols *u uich ku*, or the "face of god"[,] and they hold them to be receptacles where their gods dwell after their creation."[8]

According to the Maya worldviews at conquest, not only could the Maya's deities intercede in the daily life and affairs of the Maya but also they were believed to have the power to affect the general well-being of individuals as well as that of entire communities. Since the daily life and economy of the Maya revolved around agriculture and the procurement of food, Maya deities and their images were primarily agricultural and hunting divinities, concerned with all aspects of the crop cycle (sowing, growing, and harvesting) and the procurement of food from the hunt. In the words of Colonial Maya priest, or *ah kin*, Francisco Pech, the gods were "those who give us life and bring the rains and provide us with food and all things that are necessary."[9] These deities in their aspect of controllers of fertility, water sources, and weather were seen as providers and protectors of the Maya in good times and their persecutors in times of drought and famine. Similarly, violations of the norms, on the part of an individual Maya or an entire community, might anger the gods, who in retribution sent a pestilence, crop failure, or drought to punish their wayward Maya worshippers.

The Maya, in turn, also grew angered over the whims of the gods and idols. In some cases, the Maya even destroyed their god's image if he/she failed to grant a petition that was presented correctly. In some instances, according to the Maya *relación* of Tekit, if the god (idol) did not grant the wish, an Indian "would go to his house ... and break the idol, smashing it and saying that it was not a good god" (Garza 1983:286). The most notable aspect of Maya religion and Maya worldviews after the conquest was that it was an "interactive" religion in which the individual played a very active part in the petitioning, propitiating, and honoring of the gods. Every individual Maya could petition directly to the gods through the worship of his image in stone, clay, or wood.

Maya Idols and Effigy Censers: Their Images, Offerings, and Illicit Trade

Who or what did the colonial Maya worship? What exactly did these clay, wood, and stone images represent? How were they worshipped by the Maya and why? The answers to these questions are central to a better understanding of the uses, functions, and forms of colonial Maya effigy censers and their use in Maya religion and ritual. The Maya themselves answered these questions when they faced the ecclesiastical extirpators. During their interrogations, in their confessions and in their testimony, many Maya throughout the Colonial period provided valuable insights into the nature of colonial Maya religion (Bricker 1984, 1989, 1991; Chuchiak 2004a; Pohl 1981). In many instances, the Maya were caught openly worshipping clay, stone, and wooden images of their deities. In these cases, caught without the hope for escape, the Maya proved to be very willing to discuss the nature and aspects of their gods with the inquisitive ecclesiastical judges. For instance, a detailed 1674 account of a rain ceremony dedicated to idols and images of the rain god Chac survived. The testimony of witnesses in this trial helped to elaborate the contexts and ritual formularies used in the adoration of Maya gods in the form of stone and clay effigy censers. One witness to the ritual testified that

> [t]hey placed several idols on an altar made out of the branches of certain trees and they covered the altar with a canopy of green branches and they placed in front of this altar several piles of corn tortillas and several small gourds, and being shown the confiscated instruments, this witness said that they were the same placed before the altar, which had been filled with the intoxicating beverage called *balché* and this witness saw that the Indians were in the process of worshipping these idols and incensarios, and Antonio Chable, Esteban Dzul, and several other Indians this witness did not know were offering them copal incense.[10]

A second witness and participant in the ritual, Miguel Noh, another Maya prisoner from the town of Teya, completed the ritual scene in greater detail:

> What they do is take out the idols and incensarios that the Priest, or the ceremonies patron[,] brings and they place them on the ground and in front of these images they place four gourds filled with pozole and another stone that serves as a candle holder and incense burner where they burn the copal incense, and all of this is governed and controlled by the said patron of the ceremony, and the owner of the house divides and shares the ritual drink balché with the invited guests and in this manner they sing and dance until they grow tired or they become drunk, and then the person who brought the idols goes about guarding and putting the idols away.[11]

Nevertheless, it was Marcos Uc, the young son of the Maya alcalde of the village of Santa Catalina, who gave the most important details of the ceremony and its significance. Marcos confessed in reference to the confiscated idols:

> [The idols] are placed on a wooden board, attached by and covered with copal incense and these are the idols that they worship as their gods and that the man who officiated at the ceremony and who made the sacrifices was Bonifacio Ku, who raised the father of this witness and who took him as his own son, who served as the Priest, and the way in which they conducted their worship was to create a bench as an altar and around it several arches made from the branches and sticks of the *Habin* tree, and on top of the said bench which served as an altar, they placed the table or board with the images of the gods on them . . . in front of these images they placed several gourds full of balché . . . with a small branch and the leaves of the Habin tree the priest anointed and sprinkled the idols with balché . . . then he offered and sprinkled balché using this branch to the four directions and parts of the world which are called in their native language *Tilkin, Chikin, Nohol, Ixaman*, and after lighting a brazier with copal the

priest drew blood from the Indians who attended the said worship, sometimes having the blood drawn by the hand of Esteban Dzul, and other times by the hand of Juan Uc, the father of this witness, and others by the hand of Bonifacio Ku, and the blood that they took from these people who attended the ceremony, they placed on a large leaf of the Habin tree and they burned it in the brazier with the copal.[12]

The singing, dancing, burning of copal incense, and offerings described in this idolatry trial are reminiscent of mural painting scenes and images in the Maya codices showing Maya priests or god impersonators offering sacrifices and incense to Maya deity images or ceremonial effigy censers. Many of the same directional, color, and other aspects in this colonial ceremony also closely parallel ethnographically documented Maya ceremonies (Hanks 1990:335–339).

The Private Nature of Maya Religion in the Colonial Period

In the Postclassic and post-conquest Maya worldviews, Maya gods were not so easily defined in terms of good and evil. They shared both qualities. A benevolent sun god could also wreck havoc on the Maya by sending a drought that would destroy the all-important corn crop. This dualistic nature of Maya deities necessitated the single most important act of worship: the private or public propitiation of the gods with offerings and sacrifices. In return, the gods, if they were pleased with the offering, granted the request on behalf of the individual or community.

Maya god images came in many shapes and forms. The images that the Maya worshipped could be as simple as a deformed or colored stone or as elaborate as a large sculpted image of a particular deity carved in stone or made out of clay. Many god images were housed within secret *templos o adoratorios*, which they still managed to keep hidden well into the Colonial period. The Maya also kept other god images in sacred places like underground *cenotes* (caves) or even ensconced deep within the forest (*monte* as the Spaniards termed it) or in cornfields (milpas) of the local Maya (Chuchiak 2000, 2001). The Maya kept many other smaller wooden or clay images in the homes of the caciques and principal Indians, as Diego de Landa stated: "[B]esides the community temples, the lords and priests and leading men also had oratories and idols in their houses; where they made their prayers and offerings in private"(Tozzer 1941:108).[13]

Both earlier and more recent archaeological excavations at Mayapán have revealed the existence of many shrines and oratories in the context of elite homes and structures (Masson and Peraza Lope 2007; Shook and Irving 1955; Thompson 1957b; Winters 1955a). However, common Maya families also kept smaller god images in their own homes. Spaniards attested to in the *Relación de Mérida*, that the common Maya family "also had their own particular idols, to whom they sacrificed, each one according to his office and the occupation that he had, and they were so ceremonial that for whatever thing they had to do, they offered first to their idols"(Garza 1983:73).

This private nature of Postclassic and colonial Maya religion is very clearly illustrated in the nature of religion and ritual among the modern Lacandon Maya, as previous scholars have shown and as Palka in his own contribution in this volume argues (McGee 1990; Tozzer 1941:109n497; Villa Rojas 1995). Scholars such as Ralph L. Roys and Nancy Farriss may have overemphasized the rapid disappearance of public temple cults and their use after the conquest as evidence of the eradication of traditional prehispanic Maya religion and ritual shortly after the conquest. In the archaeological record, god images or effigy censers were found mostly in house and palace mounds, with few censers being discovered in the temple complexes (Ruppert and Smith 1954; Thompson 1957b). Thus, when Nancy Farriss (1984) states that what continued after the conquest was more "private agricultural rituals" rather than "public idol cults," she supports the arguments in favor of the continuation of private Maya image worship.[14] It was exactly this private worship of god images and ancestral deities that composed the basis of Maya religion and worldviews during and after the conquest and long into the eighteenth century.

A Typology of Colonial Maya Idols and Effigy Censers

In order to understand what was actually referred to when the clergy lamented the continuation of Maya "idolatry" we must briefly examine what and how the Maya worshipped. It is the description of these god images, or the *Descriptio Idolorum*, that is the subject of this chapter. Each Maya male had his own god images that he brought to public ceremonies (Scholes and Adams 1938:88). These wooden and clay deity images were owned privately, unlike the larger stone idols, or *tunes*, which were owned by the community. Wooden and clay images were prized personal possessions during the Colonial period.

Idolos de Piedra, Cul tunichob

The rarest and the most venerated of Maya god images continued to be those carved in stone. Called properly *tun*[15] or *tunich* ("stone") in Maya, these images were the most difficult to elaborate and often very large in form. It was not uncommon for a stone god image to reach more than two meters in height (*dos varas*). Unfortunately, the Spanish clergy destroyed most of these large stone idols during the many campaigns against idolatry conducted during the sixteenth through the nineteenth centuries. Surprisingly, Catholic clergymen discovered several larger stone deity images and destroyed them in Yaxcaba in 1686 and another one near the village of Oxkutzcab in 1791 (Figure 7.2). The larger of these stone images was

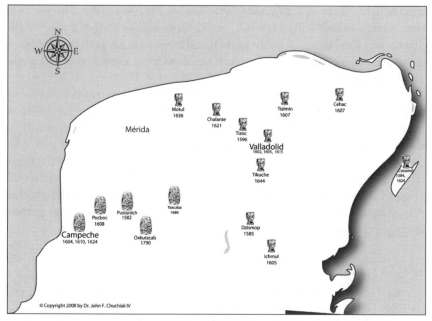

Major Maya Public Idol Cults Uncovered During the Colonial Period, 1550-1813

Major Public Stone Idol Cult Uncovered   Major Public Ceramic Idol Cult Uncovered

7.2. Map showing major stone and clay "image cults" uncovered during the Colonial period, 1563–1813.

very rare indeed. Even the famous idol of Ix Chel at the shrine on Cozumel apparently consisted of only a partial stone base, the rest was described as "a great ceramic figure attached to the wall of the sanctuary with mortar" (Thompson 1970:189).

The types of stone used in the construction of these religious icons varied, but limestone (the most readily available stone found in the peninsula) and occasionally even carved basalt images, mostly imported into the peninsula, are found. The most common form of stone idols described in the colonial documents were smaller stone idols made of limestone or other soft stone with the sculpted form of the deity on the front side of the stone and the rest of the stone remaining without carving or containing perforated holes in one or several places.

For instance, in 1721, Br. Don Diego Marcos Novelo, the parish priest of the village of Dzonotchel, described eleven similar smaller stone god images that he confiscated from a group of Maya idolaters. He described them, stating that he took from the Indians "eleven medium and small stone idols, all perforated with holes and smeared with copal incense."[16] In a previous *memoria* or *Descriptio Idolorum* he described them in more detail, stating that "the one has a face sculpted on the front side . . . one is rounded, like a crystal . . . another one is like a sheaf of feathers in the manner of a coral design. . . . One white round stone with a hole in the middle . . . four other rounded and squared stone images and three smaller stones all perforated with holes in them."[17]

The *caratula*, "sculpted face," described by the priest contained an image or sculpted mask of a Maya deity. Many stone idols of this type are currently found in museums throughout the world. They usually have the form of human, animal, or deity faces and images sculpted roughly in limestone.

The Maya codices may represent these stone god images as seen by the figure of a Maya deity seated on the hieroglyphic symbol for the word "tun," or "stone" (Figure 7.3). The ethnohistorical documentation and iconography tends to bolster this interpretation, for other standing figures offer sacrifices and offerings to these stone god images, or tunes.

Idolos de Madera, Cul Cheob

God images carved of wood remained more common than those of stone and probably belonged primarily to the Precolumbian Maya nobility and colonial cacique clans. According to Fr. Diego de Landa, and many other early chroniclers, these idols carved in wood were typically very small (usually somewhat larger than ten centimeters at most). Some of these wooden deity images were much larger and often hollowed out. These hollow wooden idols apparently served as receptacles for the ashes of dead ancestors (Tozzer 1941:110n504). Landa stated that "the wood used for these idols was always cedar" (Tozzer 1941:160). Unfortunately, wooden god images rarely survived the harsh elements in the Yucatán peninsula so very few examples survive to the present day.

Another type of wooden idol involved the carving and use of wooden masks by the priests who performed functions as god impersonators. The masks also served as idols or images of adoration. Maya made these wooden god masks almost exclusively out of cedar wood (Figure 7.4). The cedar tree was called *ku che*, meaning "god tree."[18]

Idolos de barro, Cul Lacob

By far the most common and most widely used form of god image remained those made of clay. The various descriptions of the confiscation of these clay idols in the numbers of tens of thousands are common in the colonial documents. For instance, in 1618 alone, Bishop Gonzalo de Salazar assembled the incredible quantity of 20,000 clay deity images that had been confiscated during province-wide campaigns of extirpation.[19]

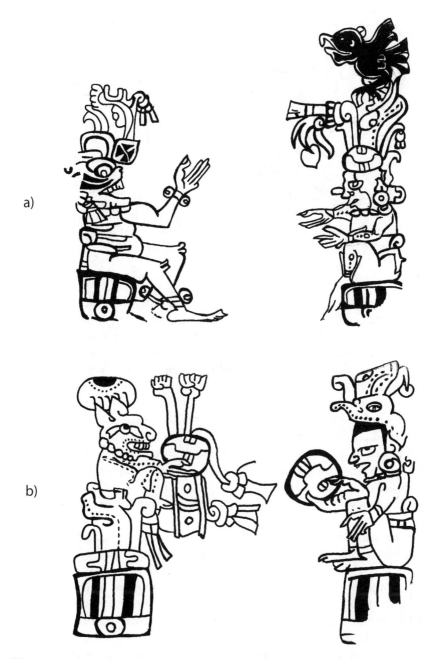

7.3. Details of possible tun or stone idol images from the Maya codices (redrawn from Vail 1996:figs. 1.4a, 1.7a–b, 1.8a–b; Madrid codex; all drawings by Argelia Segovia Liga).

7.4. Maya figures cutting and carving wooden idols or masks (redrawn from Villacorta and Villacorta 1976:354–416; drawing by Argelia Segovia Liga).

The clay used to fashion these god images often came from sacred places such as the cave at Loltun and other clay mines throughout the Maya lowlands (Arnold and Bohor 1977:575–582). The sacredness of the clay involved in the making of idols was also evidenced by the Maya's desire to make new god images out of the ashes and dust of older ones. Clay idol makers attempted to use the ground powders of older god images in the fashioning of their new clay creations. In 1588 Capitan Martin Ruiz de Arze, with a commission from the bishop and the governor, discovered a great quantity of these *idolos de barro*, which he presented before the bishop during his Episcopal visit in the village of Sacalca. Ruiz de Arze wrote that "the idols were broken by Your Lordships *fiscal* and their dust and ashes were thrown into a near-by cenote so that the Indians could not make new ones out of their dust and leaven like they used to do in the past."[20]

The most common forms of clay god images remained those with the faces of the deity attached or coming out from the body of a clay incense brazier, or *incensario*. One Spaniard described these common idols, or incensarios, in the *Relación de Valladolid*, stating, "They worshipped idols made out of clay in the form of jars or terra-cotta pots, and placed on the outside of these, unseemly faces and images; they burned inside of these idols, a resin called copal, of a great odor. . . . There were idols of the fields, idols of water and many other types of idols for everything else, each idol being differentiated by the different figures on the outside of the jar" (Garza 1983:39). The connections between idols and incense burners was further exemplified in 1590 when Juan Malah, the cacique of the village of Ppole, periodically went to the island of Cozumel with his own "idols and vases in which he performed his rites and ceremonies, burning copal incense inside of them."[21]

7.5. Maya deity-priest making an offering to what may be a clay deity image or censer detail of Madrid codex 35 (rawing by Argelia Segovia Liga).

The average size of these idolos de barro ranged from twenty-one to forty-three centimeters high. We know this from comparing the clay "idols" described in the colonial sources to the archaeological remains of effigy censers (Figures 7.5 and 7.6). Colonial documents often gave approximate sizes of these effigy censers. For instance, one witness in the turbulent idolatry trials in 1562 at Maní testified that "this witness saw what could have been more than one hundred idols of clay, the size of two *palmos* some of them, and others measuring a *palmo y medio* and others still smaller than that" (Scholes and Adams 1938:25). The measurement dos palmos, or "two spans," was approximately 43.2 centimeters in height (one palmo is approximately 21.6 cm [Hemming 1970:518]). This rough estimate of the average height

7.6. Clay "idols"/god images and typical clay effigy censers (illustrations from Thompson 1957a).

of many of the idolos de barro is in close approximation to many of the effigy censers discovered in the archaeological excavations at Mayapán (Ruppert and Smith 1954; Thompson 1957a). More recently, Bradley Russell (2000:1–45) has composed perhaps the most complete comparative typology of information concerning Maya effigy censers from site reports and archaeological information from several Maya sites, all of which with similar types of effigy censers. In his analysis of effigy censer vessels from excavations from Burial 20 at Caye Coco, he shows that the average height of the vessels was forty-eight centimeters. Russell's map showing the distribution of ceramic remains from several selected Maya lowland sites also illustrates that at no site are these ceramic clay "effigy censers" absent from Postclassic contexts (Figure 7.7) (Russell 2000:figure 13).

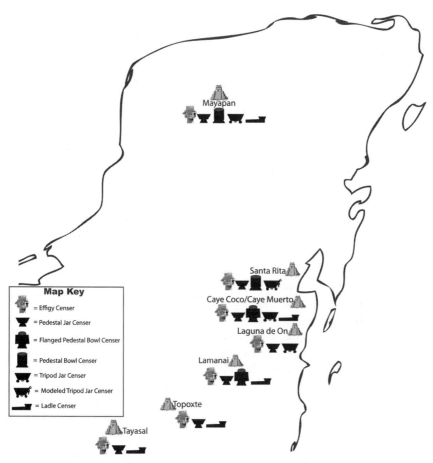

7.7. Map showing the distribution of censer forms at Maya sites (redrawn from Russell 2000:13; adapted from Chase 1985a).

The Making of an "Idol" / Effigy Censer

The Maya performed one of several complete rituals, depending on what type of god image was to be fashioned (Tozzer 1941:160n823). Certain pages in several of the codices describe rituals associated with the making of wooden and ceramic god images. Moreover, Landa described the rituals involved in the manufacture of the wooden god images and masks of their gods. Some of them were destined to be used in ancestor worship, whereas others would be images of the deities. The process and ceremony involved in making idols of wood "they called making gods. And so they had fixed a particular time for this and it was in the month of Mol.... Therefore those who wished to make some consulted the priest first, having taken his advice,

149

JOHN F. CHUCHIAK IV

they went to the workmen who engaged in this work" (Tozzer 1941:159). Landa
remarked that the idol makers and others "chosen for this purpose, as well as the
priest and the workman, began their fastings. . . . While they were fasting, the man
to whom the idols belonged went in person or else sent someone into the forests for
the wood for them, and this was always cedar" (Tozzer 1941:159–160).

Maya craftsmen who fashioned the god images made of wood went into a
trance-like state of euphoria. They painted themselves black with soot as a symbol of their penitence and their sacred occupation. They bled themselves, obviously
adding to their trance, and offered the blood to the god images. When the "idols"
were finished, the owner "made the best present he could of birds, game and their
money, in payment of the work of those who had made them" (Tozzer 1941:160).
The Maya priests then blessed the new god images and they were placed in a special
building, an oratory, in the family's yard. After the priest spoke several prayers of
blessing to the new images, the craftsmen, the idols' owner, and the priest partook
of the ritual intoxicant balché until they became drunk in celebration.

The renewal and making of the god images of clay and their ceremonial clay
braziers occurred in the Maya month Yax. Landa wrote that they used the same
huts in which to make these "idols and in the month Yax . . . they renewed the
idols of clay and their braziers, for it was the custom that each idol should have its
brazier in which they should burn their incense to it; and if it was necessary they
would rebuild the house [where they were manufactured] or renovate it" (Tozzer
1941:161). Even modern Lacandon Maya construct their own clay god pots in
a similar "small shelter of palm leaves . . . built some distance from their regular
encampment" (Tozzer 1907:108). The use of this enclosed sacred space for making god images shows the continuity in the use of sacred space in Maya worldviews
after the Conquest.

In ceremonies for the making of both wooden and clay god images, the Maya
craftsmen worked within a sacred ritual space that was bounded on the four cardinal
directions by stone images of the gods called Acantunes. The four Acantunes served
as the spiritual guardians of the Maya idol makers during the long and dangerous
process of making gods. The sacred space within the hut symbolized the Maya universe with its quadrilateral divisions into the cardinal directions. The blood offerings of the craftsmen were a necessary part of the life-giving force required to bring
the gods to life. At the end, the Maya priest invoked the gods to come and reside
within these images. The secrecy involved in covering the god images and placing
them in ceramic pots until they were finished is portrayed in the codices and still
maintained by the Lacandon Maya, who continue to use low sloping roofs in their
god houses (*yatoch k'uh*) to hide their god pot images from view (Palka, this volume). No one could see the god's image until it was finished. These ceremonial huts
were constructed, as Landa notes, far away from their own dwellings to protect the
images and their own families from any possible spiritual harm.

Considering the cost in time and ceremony involved in the creation of god images, it was no surprise that the Maya went to great measures to guard and protect their images from the colonial extirpators. As Friar Juan de Benavides later lamented in 1615, the Maya refused, even after their punishment, to cease from making new ceramic effigy censers: "While I was their minister I discovered them committing terrible idolatries with horrible idols of clay. . . . Even though I have taken the idols from them and smashed them, reprehending them for this sin, my efforts have not been sufficient enough to uproot from them this evil . . . even today they continue to make and fashion in secret new idols with horrible images of their demons . . . nothing has been able to stop them from this."[22]

Many Maya would later suffer from tortures at the hands of the extirpators and resist them in order to save the sacred images of their gods from the bonfires of the *Provisorato de Indios*. By the end of the sixteenth century, the Catholic clergy began to target and issue harsher punishments to "especially those who serve as *Ah Kines* and those who serve as master artisans in the making of their infernal idols and those who bless them."[23]

Guarding and Keeping an Idol in a Dangerous Colonial World

With the increase in extirpation, having and protecting a Maya god image became a risky prospect. The Maya realized that if their gods' images were to survive, they had to adopt more clandestine hiding places; thus, they became increasingly adept at hiding their idols in diverse locations. Some idols and other ritual instruments were hidden in hollowed-out canoes that were overturned and left in their fields. Still others hid their god images away in distant caves and cenotes. They even conducted their rituals under the dark of night and in those distant places in order to avoid detection. Other Maya chose to hide their images and other religious paraphernalia in the forests or under rocks. Still other Maya, especially caciques and noblemen, hid their idols among their clothing and other valuables in wooden trunks under lock and key.[24] For instance, in 1590, the parish priest of the town of San Miguel on the island of Cozumel received word that a native of the village, Martin Cab, continued to offer sacrifices to idols he kept in a wooden trunk. When the priest confronted Martin Cab with the accusations, he denied them, stating that instead of "idols" he "had several figures of Christian saints in his trunk."[25] When the priest asked him to open the trunk so that he could see what was in it, Martin Cab refused to give him the key. The priest left in order to summon the cacique and ordered him to disassemble the trunk. During the priest's absence, Martin Cab quickly opened the trunk and secreted the idols he had inside, transferring them to his friend Pedro Chi.

In 1598, Ah Kin Francisco Pech was discovered to have a large clay idol of Ix Ahau Caan in his milpa, hidden in the hollow part of the cedar tree (ku che) in the middle of his field. Two Indian officials sent to investigate the idol asked Pech, "Whose idol is it?" Pech replied that it was an idol left there by their ancestors. Because a fresh offering had been placed there, one of the men asked Pech, "Well, how is it that fresh copal and all of the signs of recent offerings and sacrifices are here?" And then Francisco Che, one of the two officials, asked him, "If you knew it was there why didn't you destroy it instead of offering sacrifices to it?"[26] Angered by their questions, Pech replied, "By what reason do I have to throw her out of her house that she has had in her possession for such a long time?"

Unsatisfied the two men picked up the idol. Francisco Pech screamed at them and yelled, "Give me back my goddess!" The two men quickly took the image with them to the town and gave it to the local *vicario*. They reported that Pech became belligerent and threatened to shoot them with arrows if they did not leave his milpa and the god image alone. During subsequent investigations, the vicario discovered that a great number of Maya from Calotmul and Peto committed "idolatry and hid idols in their own cornfields and even in their own houses within the town."[27]

Regardless of the dangers, countless numbers of Maya continued to hide images of their gods and other ritual instruments in various places throughout the Colonial period. So great was the number of these images and idols that even as late as 1813, the parish priests reported that they constantly took from the Maya "idols, ceremonial trappings and other instruments of their barbarous religion."[28]

Inheritance of an "Idol" / God Image

Each Maya god image became the property and legacy of a specific Maya and his family to be passed on from father to son or uncle to nephew.[29] In some cases, when a Maya man had no sons or nephews, inheritance of an idol passed on to his son-in-law, who then became the guardian of the family's sacred images (Chuchiak 2000:336–341). It fell upon the oldest male member of each family to inherit the sacred images of their fathers and uncles. Landa commented that especially the wooden idols were inherited. He said that "the wooden idols were so much esteemed that they were considered as heirlooms and the most important part of one's inherited property" (Tozzer 1941:111).

Maya women, the wives and daughters of the men, were not permitted to inherit property or idols directly from their husbands and fathers. However, it was the responsibility of Maya women to help their husbands hide and protect the images of their gods. Women were also responsible for the ritual preparation of food and drink offerings to be sacrificed to the gods. Females, however, were left out of the actual rituals and ceremonies in most cases, and they were not considered for the direct stewardship of the idols themselves.

Illicit Trade in Idols, Effigy Censers, and Idolatrous Goods

An entire informal and underground economy of idolatrous goods apparently flourished in colonial Yucatán. The small colored stones, called *cuzcas*, that Landa once said "served as money for these Indians" continued to be honored and used in rituals and in the purchase of ritual accoutrements and other offerings (Peniche Rivero 1990). As a testament to the persistence of the Maya worldviews, these stones maintained their value in a changing colonial world. Juan Pablo Dominguez de Sepúlveda stated that many of his commissary judges uncovered rituals and offerings of "several stones called cuzcas that are the money and treasure of their idols."[30] With these cuzcas, the extirpators uncovered an entire network of illicit trade. Apparently, as late as 1636 the Maya continued to use these stone cuzcas as a means of exchange.

These stone beads were used by the Maya and traded in order to obtain balché bark and even ceramic clay god images and offering dishes, called *zuhuy lac*. As the extirpators discovered more and more cases of idolatry during the seventeenth century, they also uncovered a complete underground trade in idolatrous goods that had continued unbeknownst to the Spaniards and the clergy. Older principal residents of Maya towns, Ah Chun Than, continued to carry out an illicit underground trade in god images, balché bark, copal, and other idolatrous goods that were exchanged for turkeys, cuzcas, and other indigenous products such as honey and wax.[31] Maya from the coastal cities traded the dried bones of certain fish and the spines of stingrays throughout the peninsula in a regular system of trade (Scholes and Adams 1938).[32] Similarly, from 1542 and at least until the decade of the 1570s, the Maya secretly engaged in the slave trade, either purchasing young children as sacrificial victims or kidnapping them from unsuspecting mothers from distant towns (Scholes and Adams 1938, 1:101). The Maya often purchased slaves and even animals for sacrificial offerings with cuzcas (Freidel et al. 1993).

Cacao and cedar wood was harvested and traded throughout the peninsula, and pagan Itza Maya traded ritual specialists and sacred cuzcas with the Yucatec Maya. There was constant contact and trade across the colonial frontier. From Oxkutzcab, Hecelchakan, Campeche, and Champoton, Maya traders followed trails southward and eastward to the interior to trade with the apostate fugitives and the pagan Maya. This illicit trade not only continued in the face of Spanish attempts to stop it, but by 1610 it actually increased as the size and numbers of fugitive Mayas living in the jungle increased (Scholes and Roys 1968:245).

Fray Diego de Landa mentioned that the trade in clay and wooden god images was one of the major items of commerce for the Maya before the conquest. Both archaeological and ethnohistorical evidence show that ceramic effigy censers were made in the areas in and around the towns of Chancenote and Cehac as well as to the south near Oxkutzcab and the rich clay deposits of the caves near Loltun (Graff

1997:162–167). So famous and numerous were the ceramic braziers and idols that archaeologists have named a major Postclassic pottery style and type Cehac Style (Graff 1997; Kepecs 1998:121–135). Local Maya craftsmen, called *ah men cul lac* ("makers of clay images"), manufactured and traded ceramic braziers and idols from the region around the town of Cehac well into the Colonial period (Alvarez 1980:606).

Because they were conducting illicit trade, Maya who exchanged idols and sacred images and implements had to hide their wares. They could not openly carry them throughout the peninsula. Colonial evidence points to cases of idols hidden in bushels of corn, in the hollow trunks of trees, in wooden boxes or chests, in bundles of cotton cloth, and in many other ingenious places. Pedro Sanchez de Aguilar discovered a group of Maya fugitives living outside of the town of Chancenote in 1608. One of them, a Maya priest named Ah Kin Na Chi Pot, made god images and exchanged them with other Maya from the region.[33] Several more *reducciónes* of fugitive idolaters yielded even larger caches of manufactured clay idols.

Later in 1618, the local vicario Gregorio de Aguilar discovered a group of Maya from the region around Bacalar transporting several heavy cloth "bundles." When questioned about these bundles, the Maya tried to run away but they were apprehended. Within these tightly wrapped bundles, the vicario discovered a large number of clay god images that had apparently been recently fashioned. A few years later, in 1621, the extirpator Nicolas de Tapia discovered a great number of Maya making idols near the town of Ppole.[34] The Maya of the island of Cozumel actively traded god images and balché bark with the Maya of the mainland. The cacique of the town of Ppole, Don Diego Malah, was even caught bringing balché bark and other balché instruments to trade with the Maya of the island of Cozumel (Chuchiak 2004a). During his campaign of extirpation from 1619 until 1623 in the region around Ppole and Zama, Br. Tapia discovered and destroyed a reported quantity of 20,000 god images of clay and wood.[35] Br. Juan Pablo Dominguez de Sepúlveda, while serving as *juez provisor* of the Diocese of Yucatán, in 1637 complained to the Crown, arguing for permission to pass harsher sentences on Maya priests and the makers and traders of idols. He lamented, "[D]uring this year of 1637 alone, as Judge Provisor, I punished more than 3,000 idolaters myself along with a greater number of others punished by my Commissaries, and among them many Indian priests, dogmatizers and the makers and fashioners of their idols, and the guardians of their idols and their rites and ceremonies.... And even though I have given them harsher penalties than those given on other occasions, they continue to persist in their idolatries."[36] No matter how many of the idols the extirpators confiscated, they could not stop the creation of new ones. As long as the Maya demanded clay and wooden images of their gods, their manufacture would continue.

Conclusion

Colonial Maya religion has been one of the most neglected aspects in the study of the colonial Yucatec Maya. Aside from brief mentions of Landa's inquisition, scant attention is given to colonial Maya religion, its relationship to the Precolumbian past, and its interaction, persistence, and accommodations to colonial Catholicism. Little discussion or description exists of the religious worldviews of the Maya or the actual religion practiced by the Yucatec Maya during the 300 years of colonial domination. Authors such as Nancy Farriss commented on the disappearance of the major idol cults and the continuation of the peasants' agricultural rituals, but no more is said about one of the most important aspects of the daily life of the Yucatec Maya from 1542 to 1820. The sheer number of idols confiscated and destroyed by the extirpators of idolatry during the Colonial period and the similarities and descriptions of the Maya god images confiscated in comparison with the surviving examples of ceramic and stone effigy censers from the archaeological record serve as our only lens through which we can examine the nature, form, function, and deity images represented by these censers. As other scholars have shown through their own analyses of the imagery and iconography of ritual censers and ceramic Maya implements, the cautious use of ethnohistorical materials is essential in any future reconstruction or interpretation of Maya religion both pre- and post-conquest (Rice 1999).

As we have seen, it was the use and worship of these material objects of Maya divinity that the Catholic clergy called "idols" that became the focus of their campaigns of extirpation. The Catholic clergy perceived Maya idols as the hated enemy that they faced in their battle to convert the Maya to their exclusive religion. The countless numbers of ceramic effigy censers and wooden and stone god images discovered by the early friars and secular priests, and the demons that they believed influenced their creation, became the focus of their godly wrath and the objects of their destruction.

Notes

1. *Declaración de Antonio Chable, reo del crimen de ydolatria, en el proceso del Santo Oficio contra unos mulatos*, May 17, 1674, AGN, Inquisición, Vol. 629, Exp. 4.

2. Ibid.

3. Although the terms "idol" and "idolatry" are problematical and evidently part of the colonial discourse, I have chosen not to abandon the terms. Instead, I have chosen to respect the original terminology in the colonial documentation in order to contrast the opposing worldviews of the Maya and Spaniards in terms of the use of effigy censer images. I have also retained colonial Maya orthography throughout this chapter in order to avoid confusion.

4. *Instrucciones del Obispo Fr. Francisco de Toral a los padres curas y vicarios de Yucatán, 1562*. Quote translated by the author.

5. See *Calepino de Motul* and its many definitions of "cizin" for "devil," "idol," "idolatry," "Maya deities," "Maya spirits," and so forth. The friars in Yucatán, not interested like Fray Bernardino de Sahagún before them in the preservation of native religious information and customs, were content to use the generic term "cizin" to describe all aspects of prehispanic Maya religion and the continued worship of idols into the Colonial period.

6. Similarly, besides Lacandon evidence, John Monaghan's (2000) ethnographic survey of Mesoamerican ritual tends to also point out that the Maya believed that their deities were very much present in their images and during their ritual acts. Similarly, Houston and Stuart (1998) both point to this central idea that the carving or god image was not a representation but rather a manifestation of the deity itself.

7. See the term that means "el rostro de Dios" in Cristiana Alvarez (1980:608); this was one of the many names that the Maya gave to "idolos, estatua que se adora." And, in fact, most of the idols discovered, especially the clay ones, were no more than the face of a deity attached to an incense brazier. It is interesting to note that among the Lacandon (a Maya group descended from the Yucatec Maya who fled into the jungle during the Colonial period) these incensarios *"cumplen la doble función de servir de ídolos y a la vez de recipientes para quemar el copal o incienso nativo. Cada rostro lleva el nombre del dios que representa."* See Alfonso Villa Rojas, "Los Lacandones: Sus Dioses, Ritos y Creencias Religiosas," in *Estudios Etnologicos: Los Mayas* (México: UNAM, 1995), 314.

8. *Carta de Fr. Juan de Santamaría*, 1610, AGI, Indiferente General, 3167.

9. *Prision y Confesion de los acusados idolatras de Petu, con la confession de Juan Tun,* July 7, 1598, AGI, Audiencia de México, 292, 4 folios.

10. *Auto del testimonio de los yndios ydolatras contra los mulatos enculpados por el crimen de ydolatria*, July 18, 1674, AGN, Inquisición, Vol. 629, Exp. 4, folios 336r–337r.

11. *Testimonio de Miguel Noh, yndio ydolatra preso en el pueblo de Teya, contra los mulatos enculpados por el crimen de ydolatria*, July 18, 1674, AGN, Inquisición, Vol. 629, Exp. 4, folios 336r–337r.

12. *Testimonio de Marcos Uc en el proceso de idolatria*, July 18, 1674, AGN, Inquisición, Vol. 629, Exp. 4.

13. The continued existence of these "private oratories" and idols in the houses and cornfields of the caciques and principales during the Colonial period are attested to in innumerable cases within the archives. For a few examples, see *Testimonio contra Cristobal May, Pablo Chable y Mateo Mocul, principales del pueblo de Yobain por ydolatras*, 1606, AGI, Audiencia de México, 3048, folio 215; also see *Sumaria información contra don Gaspar Chan, cacique del pueblo de Chunhuhub, por ydolatra*, 1596, AGI, Audiencia de México, 294; similarly, also see *Denuncia contra Francisco Pech, indio principal del pueblo de Peto, por idolatra Ah Kin*, 1597, AGI, Audiencia de México, 292. See table of "Provisorato cases" in Chuchiak (2000, 2002). Also, there is overwhelming archaeological evidence for the existence of these private "altars and oratories" in the houses of the elites in the Postclassic Maya city of Mayapán. See Karl Ruppert and A. L. Smith (1954:45–67); also see J. E. Thompson (1957b:71–89). Archaeologists discovered many of these idols or "incensarios" in-situ on small altars or platforms within what have been termed "nobles' residences."

14. Nancy Farriss (1984) does compellingly show that during the eighteenth century (where the bulk of her documentation lies) domestic and community rituals regarding

Catholic saint cults grew in importance, but these cults of saints are markedly absent from sixteenth- and seventeenth-century documentation.

15. The Maya word *tun* was used for all idols, even those not made out of stone in some cases. In the codices, deity figures seated on a tun symbol I believe represent idols or stone images of the deity. Thus, the tun sign may be a form of "marked" description for the deities in their "idol" representation; whereas when the deities appear without the tun symbol, they may refer to the gods or god impersonators. Thus the word "tun," as Marcos Uc testified in 1674, meant "idol" or was used to refer to one of their gods. He testified, "Son unas piedras que llaman Tunes, y sabe que dichas piedras son tres pequeñas . . . y son los ydolos que adoraban por dioses." See *Confesión de Marcos Uc, hijo de Juan Uc, Alcalde del pueblo de Santa Catalina, extramuros de Mérida, en los autos de Ydolatria*, April 26, 1674, AGN, Ramo de Inquisición, Vol. 629, Exp. 4, folios 352r–356r.

16. *Certificación del recibo de los ydolos hecho por el secretario del Obispo*, May 20, 1721, AGN, Ramo de Inquisición, Vol. 789, Exp. 31, folio 559v.

17. *Auto de remisión de la sumaria ynformación contra Don Pedro Coyi, al Obispo Dr. Juan Gomez de Parada, con el reo y los ydolos*, April 30, 1721, AGN, Ramo de Inquisición, Vol. 789, Exp. 31, folios 557r–v.

18. Ralph Roys believed that the necessity of making these idols from cedar wood may stem from this fact (Tozzer 1941:160n824). Interestingly enough, even today the Maya of the village of Muna carve and sell to tourists the images of their ancient gods made in cedar wood.

19. Many prominent citizens of Mérida testified that during the period from 1611 to 1618 more than 20,000 idols of stone, wood, and clay were displayed within the Episcopal palace in Mérida; see *Testimonio del canonigo Fernando de Aldana y Maldonado en la probanza de méritos y servicios de clerigo Nicolas de Tapia*, April 28, 1618, AGI, Audiencia de México, 301, 4 folios; also see *Testimonio del Arcediano, Lic. Andres Fernandez de Castro, en la probanza de méritos y servicios de clerigo Nicolas de Tapia*, April 6, 1618, AGI, Audiencia de México, 301, 4 folios; similarly, see *Testimonio del Dr. Don Gaspar Nuñez de Leon, Chantre, en la probanza de méritos y servicios de clerigo Nicolas de Tapia*, April 6, 1618, AGI, Audiencia de México, 301, 4 folios.

20. *Carta de Martin de Arze al Obispo de Yucatán contra Juan de Loria y sobre sus méritos y servicios en la reducción de los ydolatras y apostatas en la región de la Bahia de Ascención*, 1588, AGN, Ramo de Inquisición, Vol. 213, Exp. 10, folios 48–49. In 1582, Pedro Sánchez de Aguilar, under the order of the same bishop, also threw the broken and smashed pieces of clay idols from the village of Tixmeuac into a nearby lake. See Dr. Pedro Sánchez de Aguilar, *Informe contra idolorum cultores del obispado del Yucatán* (Mérida: Editorial G. Triay e Hijos, 1937), 32.

21. See *Denuncia contra el cacique de Ppole, Juan Malah, por parte del cura beneficiado Hernando de Salinas por ydolatrias*, 1590, AGI, Audiencia de México, 292.

22. See *Paracer y testimonio del padre Fr. Juan de Benavides, Guardian del convento de San Antonio de Ichbalche en las Montañas*, February 1, 1615, AGI, Audiencia de México, 138, 8 folios.

23. *Comisión para el conocimiento y castigo de la ydolatria al Br. Andres Fernandez de Castro*, March 5, 1590, AGI, Audiencia de México, 294, 2 folios.

24. *Autos sobre la ydolatria de los yndios de la isla de Cozumel*, 1598, AGI, Audiencia de México, 292, 6 folios.

25. *Denuncia del cura de Cozumel, Hernando de Salinas, contra Martin Cab, vecino del pueblo de San Miguel, por sospechos de ydolatra,* 1590, AGI, Audiencia de México, 292, 4 folios.

26. *Testimonio de Francisco Che, alcalde del Pueblo de Calotmul,* March 16, 1598, AGI, Audiencia de México, 292, 4 folios.

27. *Testimonio de Melchor Xiu, gobernador del pueblo de Calotmul,* March 14, 1598, AGI, Audiencia de México, 292, 4 folios.

28. *Relación del cura y vicario del pueblo de Tihosuco y sus asistentes sobre los costumbres de los yndios de su partido,* 1813, AGI, Audiencia de México, 3168, 8 folios.

29. Earlier studies of the Classic Maya (Fox and Juteson 1986) focused on the possible hereditary of Maya lordship from uncle to nephew among the Classic Maya. Instances of the inheritance of colonial Maya idols from uncle to nephew appear to lend support and credulity to their hypothesis. Apparently, nephews were considered relatives equal to one's sons.

30. *Carta sobre las ydolatrias de los yndios de este obispado de Yucatán,* 1636, AGI, Indiferente General, 192, 10 folios.

31. Evidence on this illicit underground trading network of idolatrous goods is found in numerous colonial documents and official reports. The fear of this continued illicit trading network with the Itza Maya of the Petén jungles led to the final military conquest of the Itza capital at Tayasal in 1697. For a good discussion of some aspects of this illicit trade and the final conquest of the Itza Maya see Grant Jones (1998).

32. A regular coastal-inland trade of licit and illicit goods continued throughout the Colonial period. Many of the documents from the early governor's *residencias* discuss this coastal trade. For a few examples see *Residencia del alcalde Mayor de Yucatán, Don Diego Quijada,* 1567, AGI, Justicia 300; also see *Residencia del gobernador de Yucatán Don Diego de Santillán,* AGI, Justicia 300.

33. *Testimonio del gobernador del pueblo de Cehac, Don Francisco Chan,* December 5, 1608, AGI, Audiencia de México, 299, 8 folios.

34. *Carta y parecer del gobernador de Yucatán sobre los meritos y servicios del cura beneficiado y vicario de Cozumel, Nicolas de Tapia,* June 17, 1627, AGI, Audiencia de México, 305, 4 folios.

35. *Memorial y petición del cura beneficiado de Cozumel, Nicolas de Tapia, sobre sus meritos y servicios en la extirpación de la ydolatria,* June 21, 1627, AGI, Audiencia de México, 305, 3 folios.

36. See *Información sobre los autos y procesos de ydolatria hechas por el Juez Provisor y Vicario General Br. Pablo Dominguez de Sepúlveda,* June 19, 1637, AGI, Indiferente General, 192, 5 folios.

Mesoamerican Communicating Objects: Mayan Worldviews Before, During, and After Spanish Contact

CHAPTER EIGHT

Miguel Astor-Aguilera

In our Western View, religion is a kind of ideology, one based on belief in the supernatural, the use of ritual to communicate with the supernatural, and an explanation of the world and the universe that includes the supernatural, all of which tends to reinforce human values and guide human behavior. But these categorical distinctions are not so clear-cut when we begin to consider the ideology of the ancient Maya. The Maya of today continue to maintain vestiges of an ancient ideology quite unlike our Western concepts of life and the universe. We conceive of our world as being composed of two discrete components, the natural realm and the supernatural realm. [To us] the natural world corresponds to that which is observable ... [and] we reserve the unobservable realm to something we call the supernatural.... [Yet] the world of the ancient Maya, so different from our own, was governed by a cosmological order that transcended our distinction between the natural and supernatural realms.

(SHARER 1994:513–514)

Precolumbian Mesoamericans understood their world within much different worldviews than do Western Europeans and Euro-Americans. In this chapter, concentrating on politico-religious communicating objects, I suggest that although the Western scientific notion of separating the natural and supernatural worlds applies in our worldviews, such a dichotomy distorts Native American cosmologies. I further suggest that our continued application of the sacred and profane dichotomy has also hindered our progress in better understanding

Precolumbian, colonial, and contemporary Mesoamerican cosmologies. I begin by briefly summarizing our Western theoretical separation of the natural and supernatural, followed by contextualizing Precolumbian to contemporary Mesoamerican worldviews, and conclude by suggesting that the ancient Maya had, and some of their descendants continuing to have, a personal relationship with their living ancestors via communicating objects.

Universal Binary Religious Categories

Most studies concerning archaic religions tend to center on Western dichotomies (Garwood et al. 1991:v–ix; Hodder 1995:92–97), such as natural and supernatural, sacred and profane, and life and death, that are not typically present in non-Western peoples' worldviews (Bonfil Batalla 1996:27–28; Goody 1962:36–37). Much social theory concerning binary categories of human thought largely stems from Durkheim's (1965 [1912]) assumed elementary religious forms. Émile Durkheim (1982 [1895]:50–59) never clearly stated the foundation for his universal categories and provided little direct evidence to back up his claims (see Bell 1992:vii; Goldenweiser 1917; Pals 2006:111–114; Spiro 1971); however, this fact has not stopped many researchers from uncritically applying his theory. I (Astor-Aguilera 1998, 2000, 2004), to variable degrees, uncritically reified universalistic religious notions, but now my anthropological scholarship (focused on religious studies) doubts whether universal categories can be applied to all peoples.

The archaeological study of "religion" has been steadily shifting to concentrate on using less Western loaded concepts and was likely influenced by Ian Hodder's (1982) scholarship. This still-developing research stresses individual practice, such as "worldview," per this volume, as well as "personhood" and "embodiment" to better comprehend how life was experienced by ancient non-Cartesian-minded peoples such as Neolithic Europeans, Egyptians, Andeans, and the Maya (see Buikstra and Nystrom 2003:44–45; A. Jones 2005; Meskell and Joyce 2003:67–78). Non-Western peoples are obviously engaged within worldviews that have complex cosmologies; however, our attempts that seek to understand the symbolic behavior of those we study, via assumed religious universals, although perhaps containing degrees of fact, inevitably miss much indigenous meaning (Brody 1997; Scarre 1994:81; Thomas 2007).

Durkheim's (1965:52, 62 [1912]) sociological theory of religion can be a useful analytical tool when used with extreme caution; however, there is much evidence that Native Americans tend not to have worldview philosophies that readily fit his elementary forms. Additionally, there is a lack of evidence to support universal theories of religion, as most religious studies scholars cannot even agree on a simple definition for the term "religion," except to admit that it is an unusually highly loaded Judeo-Christian-Muslim concept that often has no self-referential term in other worldviews (see Graham, this volume; Monaghan 2000; Pharo 2007:29; Renfrew 1994:47–48; Spiro 1971:87). Despite many problems, the reification of the concept religion, as founded on binary categories, has been, and remains to be, widely applied (see Frazer 1911–1915; Freud 1950 [1913]; Hertz 1973 [1909]; Lévi-Strauss 1969 [1949]; Malinowski 1922; Mauss 1967 [1925]; Otto 1958 [1923]; Radcliffe-Brown 1964 [1922]; Tylor 1903 [1871]). The most indiscriminate application of universal binary concepts of religion, in an especially highly idealized and dramatized manner, is credited to Mircea Eliade (1959, 1974, 1976, 1990) because of his fixation on what he called sacred myths, sacred time, sacred space, sacred symbols, *sacred everything*, whereupon all human behavior is focused on divine manifestations (see Kehoe 2000:1–6, 37–40, 45, 48). Worldviews, however, are not as simple to schematize, especially through decontextualized cross-global, temporal as well as spatial, cultural "cherry-picking," as Eliade typically does for what appears to be his own personal mystical quest (see Gill 1998:3–19; Leach 1966b; Saliba 1976:110–118).

Societies should be studied within their specific historicities (Boas 1896) as humans are not single-minded in their cultural logic. Cultural philosophies are affected by both environment and specific socio-historical evolution. Rather than relying on general and universalistic concepts of religion that homogenize, distort, and ultimately fail as tools to understand (Beattie 1964:203: Bell 1992:13–17, 69–72; Goody 1977:27–29, 32–35; Klass 1995), we should allow that non-Western societies often have philosophical concepts we may consider scientifically illogical as well as very different from our own (see Renfrew 1972:496; Garwood et al. 1991:v–ix; Hodder 1995:98). In the following I suggest that Native American, in this case Maya, worldviews are not typically patterned on universal binaries. As I develop my argument for applying more indigenous epistemologies to our scholarship I thread in, and admittedly indulge in, pertinent quotations in order to get across that Native American studies has often been at a loss to explain why we have yet to get a firm grasp on these peoples' worldviews (see Rice 2004:xviii).

Our knowledge concerning ancient Mayan writing has been growing steadily (Houston et al. 2001:3–23) and the ultimate goal of reading the glyphs and their associated iconography should be a holistic understanding of Maya social processes (see Proskouriakoff 1978:113; Thompson 1950:295). Researchers' differential worldviews and mind-sets condition how they will interpret and accept or reject data and decide which of many meanings to apply over others in their decipherments of past scripts and ancient language translations (Houston et al. 2001:3, 7; López Austin 1980:50–51; Schele 2002:21). Indigenous epistemologies, I suggest, need to be a crucial component in our analysis of Maya worldviews because forcing Western understandings can be not only inaccurate but also misleading.

Alfredo Barrera Vásquez's (1980) Spanish-Mayan dictionary translates "sacred" in Yukatek Mayan as *kich*, *k'ul*, and *k'uyen*; however, these are loose linguistical glosses given as last options. Kich, for example, is foremost translated as meaning "something good," "pleasant," "well-behaved," and "of good character" in personality and humility. K'ul is translated as "to adore," "revere," or "venerate"; however, examples for the usage of k'ul are those for addressing a variety of Maya nobles, including, but not limited to, diplomats, administrators, and judges—only until the seventh terminological definition of k'ul is "something divine" given—and then in brackets and in Catholic contexts. K'uyen is glossed as "something divine," in referring to objects, humans, and processions, and in root is associated with the movement of the sun and therefore ritual. However, Christian elements are applied here in order to gloss k'uyen into the making of something sacred, like Catholic blessings and consecrations, such as rituals surrounding the Eucharist host. Additionally, the root *k'uy* refers not to sacrality but to the sun "shifting down" on its westward incline after passing zenith.

Despite the obvious problems in the above glossings of Mayan words, the same occurred with the Mixtec *nuhu* (Alvarado 1962 [1953]), the Zapotec *pitáo* (Córdova 1578), the Tarascan *hangua* (Gilberti 1962 [1559]), and most conspicuously with the Nahuatl *teotl* (Molina 1977 [1571]). Indeed, the term teotl, as concept and root found in indigenous ontologies and epistemologies and often meaning "true" or "authentic," was exploited by colonial friars into forced neologisms of "divine" and "god" (see Burkhart 1989:85, 102, 208, 208–214; Haly 1992; Read 1998:145–146, 206, 271n41). The above indigenous terms are also habitually glossed into Rudolf Otto's (1958 [1923]) Judeo-Christian-based concept of "holy" (see Spiro 1971:89) through metonymy and metaphoric modifications. They refer to "godly," but in actuality pertain to a powerful earth as seen through life, centrality, and manner of daily living as applied to administrators, patrons, objects, structures, and place. The authors of colonial dictionaries often painstakingly pegged indigenous concepts into their own understanding of religion. Therefore, all of their entries regarding this subject often have rather general meanings regarding indigenous concepts Catholic judged not being "secular" as they strived to distinguish and separate. Our reconstructions of pre-European-contact Native American philosophies cannot ignore as irrelevant the strong impact of the colonial lens and inherent Judeo-Christian biases in the Spanish chronicles (see Marcus 1978; Proskouriakoff 1978:113, 116–117; 1980). Much European domination, besides relying on brutal force, used language translation, rhetoric, and ideology as a tool to aid spiritual conquest and conversion (see Battiste and Henderson 2000:80–81; Brandt 1996:52; Means 1973).

The Ancient Maya, Sacredness, and the Living Ancestors

The Classic Maya use of k'ul when addressing rulers might have referred not to supposedly sacred individuals but to the seat they held (Rice 2004:286). As noted by Gillian Feeley-Harnik (1985:276–278), it is often the ruler's office that is highly respected and not the individual, therefore allowing easy transfer of revered title from one ruler to the next. Applying the above practice to the Classic Maya makes individual rulers acknowledged custodians of their particular city-state (see Rice 2004:289) with each city organized around lineage-based rule (see Houston 2000:173; Rice 2004:283). Much indigenous information points to a historically unstable system of Maya rulership whose claim to legitimacy was based on cosmologically charged ideological justifications (Rice 2004:285; Webster 1976:813–815). This explains why each Maya city-state ruler could claim cosmological right to rule and why revered royal lineages did not die out with the death of individual rulers. Royal deaths were not always of natural causes and, I suggest, people do not tend to kill those they believe godly, divine, holy, or sacred unless they are skeptical of such claims or do not have those theological constructs.

For the ancient Maya "ideologically and physically, the boundary between the living and the ancestors was a permeable one" (McAnany 1998:292). Evidence that an individual's life continued after our Western notion of physical death abounds in Maya monumental art (McAnany 1995:27–47), in burials (Houston et al. 2006:123), and in the K'iche' Mayan *Popol Vuj* (Tedlock 1985:113–115, 143–147, 153). The ancient Maya boundary between life and death was so porous that the previous was not distinguished from the latter. As noted by Lynn Meskell and Rosemary Joyce (2003:143), "death was no bar to the continuity of Classic Maya personhood." There is an abundance of Mesoamerican nonhumans interacting with humans, and it therefore follows, elaborating from Prudence Rice (2004:284), that "among the Maya, the 'sacred' and the 'secular' are so deeply intertwined as to be inseparable." Stephen Houston and David Stuart (1996:289–290) assess the primary problem concerning humans claiming themselves as divine as stemming in large part from a paradox created by scholars as to what constitutes "godhood." The larger question, however, is not one of supposed "divinity" but of universalistic and reified notions of "religion."

Maya rulers were much too human and this obvious fact would not have been lost on their surrounding circle or other subjects (see Houston and Stuart 1996:289). Maya worldviews should be analyzed not in terms of idealized generalities but in line with documented human practices composed of hegemonies, counter-hegemonies, and ideological distinctions regarding political claims (see Escobedo 2004:279; Houston 2004:271–275). Proclaiming to be kin of the sun, as is apparently stated by Maya rulers in their commissioned hieroglyphic inscriptions, and actually being worshipped as a divine god are not one and the same. We need to resist the temptation to over-mystify the politico-religious practices portrayed in Classic Maya art (Demarest 2004:176) by labeling every ruler and every city, glyphic text, cave, tree, spring, mountain, monument, mural, and so forth as sacred.

One of the major problems with a general assumption concerning ancient "Maya religion" is the supposition that all Maya responded to their rulers, objects, locations, and spaces in the same manner and for the same reasons. A similar but multivocal cosmological framework, interjected with a certain percentage of non-adherents, would have led to unstable and often short-lived rule—a trend that is quite evident in the hieroglyphic inscriptions where elite right to rule was so tenuous that rulers sometimes ended up as humiliated and tortured captives (see Miller and Martin 2004:65; Schele and Freidel 1990). The above is not meant to diminish the importance cosmology plays in ancient worldviews but instead to contextualize it (see Demarest 1992a:2; Demarest and Conrad 1992; Sharer and Ashmore 1987:406). Mayan inscriptions imply that rulers sought, in linking themselves to history, ancestors, and mythic nonhumans, to aggrandize themselves in seeking politico-religious legitimacy through the construction of monumental group architecture (Demarest 2004:176) and the rituals that took place within and around them (Houston 1996). My attempt here is to better integrate Maya cosmology with politics and economy rather than mystify and reify archaeologically or iconographically "witnessed" religiosity.

Maya Rulers, Politico-Religious Kinship, and Communicating with Ancestors

Maya cosmology, like that of other Native Americans, is not composed of the congregational religious activity one does at holy churches or sacred temples in a Judeo-Christian and Durkheimian (1965 [1912]:59) sense. Cosmological philosophies in non-Western societies are often central and internal to production, trade, and daily life (Godelier 1978); and within these societies it is often politico-religious "kinship," blood related or not, that forms the bond between the dominant and the dominated (Maurice Godelier, personal communication, 2005). I suggest that for Mesoamericans extended blood relatives could be secondary in importance and that strong relationships were formed along armatures based on politico-religious kinship. These political, economic, and cosmological kinships could be extended mytho-historically and linked to foreigners and their respective ancestors.

Classic Maya noble and non-noble worldviews were not much different in spite of large-scale material culture differences (Demarest 1992b, 2004:176; Freidel et al. 1993; McAnany 1995; Schele and Miller 1986); and ancient Maya families, elite and non-elite, centered their religious practices on the veneration of prominent ancestors. Particular ancestors, selected for unclear but perhaps variable reasons, were sometimes buried under house floors or housed in miniature shrines within household plaza compounds and thus, being buried within or directly outside the home, remained ever present (Freidel et al. 1993:204–207, 445–447; McAnany 1995; Schele and Freidel 1990; Tozzer 1941:113–121). The onset of the Postclassic saw large-scale political reorganizing in Mesoamerica as a whole concerning the right to rule (Byland and Pohl 1994; Carmack 1981; Chase 1986; Fox 1987; Masson

1999, 2000; Pohl 1994); however, until and after Spanish contact, Mesoamerican ancestors continued to maintain a communicative relationship with their descendants. These ancient worldviews, which the Spanish interpreted as being composed of a Medieval European–style pantheon of gods and demons (see Garza 1983: II; Lizana 1893 [1633]; López de Cogolludo 1867 [1688]; Martínez-Hernández 1929; Scholes and Adams 1938; Tozzer 1941), were not only misunderstood but also distorted.

Iberian-Catholic and Maya Hybrid Worldviews: Syncretism Meets Syncretism

> Spanish accounts were strongly partisan, so driven by subjectivity by their format and purpose, that they virtually count as secondary. Conversely, the published histories are so overwhelmingly Hispanocentric, so incestuous in their use of each other and of the Spanish sources, that they can be taken as primary—that is, primary sources on the European perspective. (Restall 1998:16)

Much reconstruction regarding ancient Maya cosmology depends on four surviving Mayan codices (Coe 1973; Love 1994; Paxton 2001; Taube 1987, 1988a, 1992; Taube and Bade 1991), the K'iche' Mayan *Popol Vuj* (Recinos 1972; Tedlock 1985), the Mayan Books of Chilam Balam (Edmonson 1982, 1986), and colonial writings like those of Fray Diego de Landa (Tozzer 1941) and his Maya informant Gaspar Xiu (Chi) (Restall 1997:4, 234; 1998:43, 152). Although Spanish chronicles are invaluable in aiding our comprehension of Mesoamerican worldviews, caution should be taken when mining their information (López Austin 1980:198). For example, Landa's *relación* (Tozzer 1941) contains many biases; and Gaspar Xiu, although a Maya, became so acculturated to the Iberian-Catholic faith that he adopted Christian terminologies (Gann and Thompson 1931:118; Karttunen 1994:84–114, 165–169, 308; Restall 1997:4; 1998:144–150, 172). Although we need to use Spanish chronicles to better our understanding of indigenous Native American worldviews, these should be used as supplements rather than primary sources of information.

The "conquest" of the Mayas was a centuries-long incomplete protracted process (Blom 1936; Bricker 1977, 1981; Chamberlain 1966; Clendinnen 1987; Dumond 1977, 1985, 1997; Farriss 1984; Gosner 1992; Jones 1974, 1989, 1992, 1998; Patch 1993, 2002; Reed 1964; Restall 1997, 1998; Rugeley 1996, 2001; Scholes and Adams 1991; Sullivan 1989; Villagutierre Soto-Mayor 1983); and during the initial Conquest period, many Spanish noticed that the Maya had structures containing objects with cross-like icons (Figure 8.1). For example, Bernal Díaz del Castillo (1956 [1632]:9–10) describes entering a Maya building during a 1514 Yucatán expedition and "on the walls were figured the bodies of many great serpents and other pictures of evil-looking idols. These walls surrounded a sort of altar

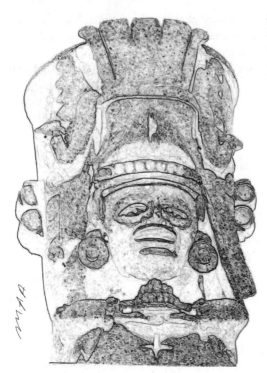

8.1. Postclassic Yukatek Ah Muzencab (line art generated by author; Museo de Antropolgía e Historia Palacio Cantón, Mérida, Yucatán).

covered with clotted blood. On the other side of the idols were symbols like crosses, and all were colored." Two such structures at Cozumel held such objects (Freidel 1975:108–110), and according to Francisco López de Gómara (1964 [1881]:35), one of these held an image of a Precolumbian "cross" that the Maya venerated.

Landa (Tozzer 1941:109–110, 154) mentions "talking" objects at both Cozumel and Chich'en Itzá, and according to Ralph Roys (1962:42), the side structure along Chich'en Itzá's "great well" probably housed one of these objects. Fray Diego López de Cogolludo (1867 [1688]:ix, 4) claims that one of the Cozumel objects was large and hollow and had a rear entry, enabling a Maya priest to enter and supposedly deceive the gullible into believing the object literally spoke. Attributing the voice of so-called talking idols to deceptive ventriloquism, however, is perhaps too cynical since Native Americans often cared for "effigies," communicated with nonhuman beings through these objects, and produced their emanating voices (Astor-Aguilera 2004:160–162; Freidel et al. 1993:177). So widespread, in fact, was the use of communicating objects throughout the indigenous Americas that the Spanish believed the Devil himself deceived the Native Americans through their "oracles" (see Durán 1967, 1:237; Marzal 1993:152; Motolinía 1971:88–89; Sahagún 1980 [1564]:82–90, 152).

8.2. K'axob Preclassic quadripartite-cross vessel (courtesy of Patricia McAnany).

The caretaking, communicating, and feeding of ancestral beings, in the form of objects, by Maya rulers has been noted for the cross group shrines at Palenque as well as being a pan-Mesoamerican-wide practice (Houston and Stuart 1996:292–294). Burials containing vessels with quadripartite cross motifs (Figure 8.2) appear early in Mesoamerica's archaeological record (McAnany 1995:57–58, 85–86) and appear related to elite accumulation of power through the practice of evocation (Headrick 2004). Andrea Stone (1988) has suggested that ancestors were evoked by elite females in metaphysical sexual encounters, and I have documented (Astor-Aguilera 2004:91) that contemporary Maya women believe that they can be impregnated by sentient invisible entities associated with communicating crosses. Significantly, as related to lineage and kinship, the Palenque cross group structures exhibit fertility overtones identifying them as symbolic birthing places (Houston 1996).

Spanish friars tended to impose so many Iberian-Catholic categories onto Mesoamerican worldviews (Gann and Thompson 1931:129) that this makes our ability to make distinctions between the two somewhat difficult (see Palka, this volume). Yet, it is unlikely that two worldviews like Catholicism and Maya, having historically evolved separately over millennia and each being its own historical syncretic-hybrid product, are practically now indistinguishable (Astor-Aguilera 2000, 2004; Frost 1993; Furst 1996:31). The term "syncretism" continues to be applied uncritically, its use implying the existence of pure culture and thus ultimately failing to describe actual human and historical processes (Comaroff and Comaroff 1997:59; Dening 1980:39; Gossen 1993:19–20; Kamstra 1989; Restall 1998:170; Stewart and Shaw 1994); however, "hybridity" then best describes the mutual transforming colonial–Native American encounters.

Key differences between Iberian-Catholicism and Native American cosmologies become evident if their worldviews are analyzed within historical depth (Astor-Aguilera 2004; Frost 1993; Marzal 1993; Rice 2004). J. Eric S. Thompson (1970:xxiii–xxiv) states that the Maya tended to adapt Spanish secular objects into their indigenous frameworks, and the Itza Maya of Nojpeten (modern-day Flores Island, Petén), for example, are known to have transformed Cortés's dead horse's bones into a communicating object—the bones of which they subsequently named Tzimin Chaak, "horse of thunder and lightning," and kept as a bundle until approximately 1697 (Jones 1998:xxiii, 36–37, 44, 72, 197–198, 301, 437n29; Means 1974 [1917]:35–36, 71–72). The Itza Maya caring for Cortés's horse's bones follows a Maya emphasis on using "talking idols" (see Bricker 1981:175–176; Reed 1964:134) and exemplifies the presence of communicating objects for these peoples (see Villagutierre Soto-Mayor 1983:387).

Communications by Itza Maya "oracular" objects appear related to the governance of Nojpeten-Tayasal and its quadripartitioned provinces by Ajaw Kan Ek' (Jones 1998:60); and curiously, the imagery on Mesoamerican material objects with quad motifs sometimes depicts a mouth as if the communicating object in question was actually talking (Figure 8.3). The keeping of vessels with quadripartite motifs, in apparent allusion to a quad sense of place, for the use of communication with ancestors is an archaic Maya tradition. For the colonial Maya, as noted by Matthew Restall (1998:29), ancestors retained vital connections with their living descendants and "the head played an important iconographic role . . . as carved or drawn images of heads represented the ongoing significance and presence of revered ancestors." The above practice was reciprocally based on debt and merit relationships that the Spanish apparently never understood in their campaign against assumed Maya "idolatry" (see Chuchiak, this volume).

Although not all Spaniards agreed with Franciscan coercive tactics against the Maya, many considered it justified (Restall 1998:151). Indeed, the Maya's fear of Catholic inquisitorial practices was so great that some would run off upon knowing that friars were visiting their communities (Clendinnen 1987:107; Restall 1998:152–153; Scholes and Adams 1938:2, 68–73). The "Holy Inquisition" in the Iberian Peninsula, as a horrific interrogation practice used against Jews and Muslims, has received much scholarly attention (Anderson 2002; Bennassar 1981; Netanyahu 2001), but the same cannot be said about the inquisitional practices in "New Spain" (Chuchiak 2005; Greenleaf 1969, 1978; Perry and Cruz 1991; Scholes 1935). The use of torture as an interrogation practice, contrary to popular notions, can be highly ineffective (DeClue 2005; Lassiter 2004) and there is a

8.3. Chipicuaro Preclassic cup (line art generated by author; Museo Nacional de Antropología, INAH, México).

great divide between free-will confessions and evidence collected under coercive tactics (Silverman 2001). Torture by Catholic inquisitors was often not utilized in efforts seeking actual answers and in investigations about supposed heresy but as punishment based on political justifications (Perez 2005; Roth 1996). According to Restall (1998:17), Spanish friars went through great "mental gymnastics . . . to justify to themselves the entire brutal endeavor."

Friars often accused the Maya, and other Native Americans, as knowingly participating in the practice of idol worship (see Chuchiak, this volume) and these accusations have often been accepted uncritically as Spanish political motivation (Bricker 1981:20; Farriss 1984:291; Means 1973; Scholes and Roys 1938; Thompson 1977:29; Tozzer 1941:80–81). Inga Clendinnen (1987:121–126, 161–189), however, points to the many political biases in the Spanish chronicles, and she as well as Dennis Tedlock (1993) have argued against our uncritical acceptance of Mayan statements extracted by physical and psychological torture. Restall (1998:165–166), contextualizing inquisitorial coercion and confession, cites explicit examples of Franciscan torture methods:

> They began to torture us, hanging us by the hands and flogging us cruelly, hanging weights of stone on our feet, torturing many of us on the rack [*en burros*], pouring a great quantity of water into our bodies, from which tortures many of us died or were maimed . . . [this due to us being accused] that we were idolaters . . . and other things far from all truth . . . we saw ourselves maimed by cruel tortures . . . [there were] many dead of them [us], and robbed of our property . . . they seized and imprisoned us in chains, like slaves, in the monastery at Merida, where many of us died; and there they told us that we were to be burned, without our knowing why.

Restall (1998:230n17), despite the cruelty described above, states that inquisitional torture "was actually worse than this account suggests," and therefore, some Mesoamericans preferred death to subjecting to Spanish interrogation (see Las Casas 1992:79–87; Restall 1998:31).

Information extraction under threat does not result in accurate statements reflecting actual actions or beliefs (Gates 1978b [1937]:115–117; Restall 1997:4; 1998:17, 31–33, 151–154, 162, 165–168, 171, 230n17). Additionally, the Maya most likely did not understand what their interrogators specifically asked because their worldviews were strikingly different. Native American cosmologies are based on relational experience, reflecting their daily practical world knowledge founded upon discrete and metaphorical observations of their environment (see Taube 1992:9) and not per a Christian-Catholic theological sense or on classifications and subdivisions per our Cartesian scientific categories (see McKeever Furst 1995:173–184). As Timothy Knab (2004:23) admits, "It is we, as Westerners, who seek neat schemes with traditional labels for these esoteric concepts . . . [for] at the time of the conquest, the friars—though sophisticated in theology—were burdened with the views of the Spanish renaissance humanism, [and] the Reformation . . . completely lacked the techniques necessary to analyze . . . Mesoamerican concepts."

Native American worldviews are not homogenous; however, being in "conversation" for millennia, through trade and other forms of social contact before their conquest by Europeans, these populations share much in common (see Coe and Van Stone 2005:123; Sugiyama 1993:105–106) and can be categorized within one broad "New World" philosophical system identifiable by similar core elements (see Pharo 2007:31; Schaafsma 1999:192). Native American philosophies express what Kenneth Morrison (2002:6) calls "negotiated agreements about the pluralistic nature of reality," and here I suggest that Mesoamericans tend to view their place in the world as relational to other beings, visible and invisible, with which they are in frequent communication. Per David Freidel and colleagues (1993:177–178), "the old [ancient Maya] statues also spoke through the written word. The old word for the human agent was chilan, 'translator,' . . . the tradition of talking statues certainly goes back to Pre-Columbian times." These communications are not always in verbal form and can take the shape of decorations, requests, song, dance, and offerings that are often focused on what we would classify as inanimate objects (see Lumholtz 1902:15). For the ancient Maya this practice is visible in their relational interaction with ceramic vessels, staffs, bones, and a variety of bundled objects like that of K'awil (Figure 8.4).

Perhaps the best-known examples of Mesoamerican communicating objects are the Quintana Roo Mayan "talking crosses." These crosses, associated with the so-called Caste War of Yucatán, are not only extant but remain guarded in eastern Yucatán villages (Astor-Aguilera 1998, 2000, 2004; Sullivan 1989; Villa-Rojas 1945, 1978). Although Maya crosses are often misinterpreted as being Catholic (Bricker 1981:108; Farriss 1984:315), the colonial Maya referred to their crosses as *che*, "tree" (Restall 1998:132). Trees for the ancient Maya symbolized rulers and vice-versa (Schele and Freidel 1990) and *che* could refer to trees, to "solid" individuals, or to both (Restall 1997:253, 413; 1998:224n33). The quadripartite-cross symbol, highly conspicuous in relation to trees, stelae, and rulers (Newsome 2001), has been dated in the Maya area to at least the Formative period (McAnany 1995:57–58, 85–86). At K'axob, Belize, quadripartite icons appear on burial-context ceramic vessels (Berry et al. 2004:240–241, 244–245); and Annabeth Headrick (2004) has argued that these bowls (Figure 8.2) were blood receptacles used during evocation rituals by Maya ruler-priests. Counter to Eliade's (1990:55) over-the-top claim that "originally all art was 'sacred' . . . [representing] an encounter between man and the divine," there is no evidence that the art on these bowls was categorized as sacred by the Maya. Concurring with Headrick, as noted above, ruler-priests probably manipulated the bowls and symbols in seeking to acquire or sustain politico-religious power. These quadripartite icons, as communicating and evocational foci, continued through the Postclassic and Colonial periods; and contemporary Mayan communicating crosses have similar meaning, albeit now transformed, as their ancient predecessors (Astor-Aguilera 2000, 2004).

8.4. Classic Palenque Temple 14 k'awil bundle (courtesy Linda Schele / FAMSI).

Cajoling the Ancestors: Contemporary Mayan Communicating Objects

Contemporary Mesoamerican cosmology centers on reciprocation with invisible beings associated with agricultural cycles dependent on the annual seasons (Broda 2004); the Yukatek Maya refer to their countryside-dwelling agricultural patrons as the *yuumil k'aaxo'ob* ("forest lords"). These forest lords, including the "maize god" and the "rain god Chaak," were some of the most important Precolumbian Maya nonhuman patrons (see Taube 1985, 1992). The high reciprocal importance placed on invisible forest lords is evident by their association with the cornfield, which gives life to the Maya. Pointing to the importance of the composite concepts represented by these sky and forest beings is their transformed survival despite the Spanish Conquest (Gann and Thompson 1931:126, 250). Many Maya continue the reciprocal veneration of some of these beings and often use clay images, incense burners, ancient artifacts, and speleothems during agricultural rituals (Astor-Aguilera 2004; Love 1989; Redfield and Villa Rojas 1962 [1934]; Sosa 1985). Thomas Gann and J. Eric S. Thompson (1931:249), in apparently describing the activation and communication with *kuxa'an*, "live," objects by *jmeeno'ob*, "Maya ritual production specialists," reported that the Maya believed their ritual objects were at times "endowed with life, and live and move, dance, eat, and drink just like mortals."

During activation Maya priests are not literally making an inanimate object animate; rather, they are summoning and "tethering" particular non-corporal beings to specific objects (Astor-Aguilera 2004:180, 194). Alfredo López Austin (1997:24–25, 30) describes similar actions in central Mexican indigenous practice as "the agency of individuals creates and sustains others . . . power is acknowledged to be in all beings and transformation is a fundamental component of being." Significantly, June Nash (1970:198) mentions that many "Pre-contact Maya 'deities' were literally called 'elder brother,' 'second brother,' and 'our grandmother.'" Fray Bernardino de Sahagún (1932:26, 39) similarly documented the Mexica speaking of nonhuman entities, that he categorized as "gods," as if human, in kinship terms, and as multidimensional; indeed, he mentions (Sahagún 1950–1982 [1578–1580], 7:20) how difficult it was to understand and peg the "identity" of composite beings such as Tlaloc.

Little differentiation appears throughout Mesoamerica in the conceptualizing and calling forth of ancestral-likened nonhuman beings, be it from grand structures, symbolic birthing places, or the simpler commoner ritual objects. Maya cosmology is concerned with two community objectives: protection and prosperity (Nash 1970:197). Harm to individuals in traditional Mesoamerican communities is often seen as caused by wind-like persons (see Kearney 1986; Morayta Mendoza 1997; Sandstrom 1991:269–273, 301–322). Air movement is caused, according to some Yukatek Maya, by the *pixano'ob* ("soul-like personhood") of the dead who take the form of wind after the physical death of the body vessel. These "wind-persons" are thought to freely roam the earth, upperworld, and underworld and can be friendly, unfriendly, or inimical, depending on their mood (Gann and Thompson 1931:248–250). Similar expressions, as the above, by the Classic Maya regarding their dead have been mentioned by Susan Gillespie (2002) as though the "spirit-being" of those deceased roamed about the world at will. Some traditional Yukatek Maya state that these wind-like persons are anchored in skeletal remains (Astor-Aguilera 2004:178), and the essence of these personalized and sentient "wind" entities, being ejaculated through a male's sexual organs, is at once linked to fertility as well as the bony-death state (Astor-Aguilera 2008). Furthermore, this ejaculated "skeletal matter," that is semen, is symbolically linked to corn gruel consumed during ancient and contemporary Maya rituals (Astor-Aguilera 2008; Freidel et al. 1993:181; Gossen 1986a:243). Additionally, Mesoamerican ritual communication can emphasize entreating, beseeching, cajoling, instructing, as well as threats toward ancestors (Knab 2004:9).

Crania, long bones, and ancestral objects have long been associated with Native American "oracular" bundles (Bullchild 1985:286; Byland and Pohl 1994:193–202, 206–208; Carlsen 1997:80–81; Carmack and Mondloch 1983:185; del Chamberlain 1982; Freidel et al. 1993:416; Furst 1986:62; Headrick 1999:75–79; López Austin 1980:78; McClintock 1935:6, 14; Mendelson 1956, 1958; Múnera Bermudez 1991:335–339; Pohl 1994:26–41, 70–77, 81–82; Reeves 1993; Schele and Miller 1986:72; Séjourné 1966:219; Stenzel 1972:348, 351; Tedlock 1985:198; Wissler 1912, 1920). Catharine Eshelman (2001:274–276) documents that Nahuas link "talking" bones to stones and cross icons. Furthermore, I have noted (Astor-Aguilera 2004:172–182) that some contemporary Yukatek Maya continue making skeletal bundles. Mayan communicating bundles often comprise exhumed partial or complete skeletons wrapped in a *sujuy sak nook'* ("white unused cloth") and are often associated with blue-green crosses (Figure 8.5).

Maya bundles are kept in home shrines where they are ritually "fed" and communicated with before being stored in the village cemetery. After cemetery placement, these bundles can then be fed and communicated with through surrogate objects, such as stones or crosses that are kept in the home, shrine, or elsewhere (Astor-Aguilera 2004:177–179). Communicating bundles and associated objects are apparently no longer reburied; however, they were in the recent past (Astor-Aguilera 2008). Ancient Maya deposits containing pieces of human bone may have functioned much like caches (see Becker 1992; Chase and Chase 1998) in structures. Thus, every aspect of domestic life, including production and construction, is in some respect indicative of Maya interrelated worldviews (see Harrison-Buck 2004:65–67; Thompson 1954:258).

Communication art through chants, dance, dreams, trance, and offerings is a Native American–wide practice seeking "kinship solidarity" with other humans and personalized nonhumans (Morrison 1992, 2002:6). Native American ritual production emphasizes transformative and generative performance, stressing the actions of a motivated sponsor or sponsors, for and with nonhumans, evoked in order to create meaning-making activities that build and strengthen bonds (Gill 1982:11; Monaghan 1998). Stacy Schaefer and Peter Furst (1996:12), for example, mention that for the Wixárika-Huichols, all beings are called forth "by kinship terms ... religion permeates all aspects of life. Most Huichols do not distinguish between the sacred and what we would regard as 'secular.' In truth nothing is really

8.5. Modern Yukatek-Mayan communicating skeletal bundle (photograph by author).

'profane.'" A critical assessment of Native American ontologies reveals, then, that these worldviews are *not* typically based on binaries.

The makeup of Mesoamerican nonhumans does not fit our Western concepts of gods, deities, demons, and ghosts existing in other worlds or dimensions, passing through supernatural portals into the natural world. Although the act of worshipping requires respect, the reverse is not true; that is, respectful veneration of some person or thing does *not* in and of itself equal worship. Although some ancestors gain more respect generation after generation (Holland 1964:303–304), as do other personalized and powerful nonhumans, this does not mean that these beings are worshipped as supernatural gods. According to Schaefer and Furst (1996:24), "we call these powers 'supernatural,' literally, something outside of, above, and greater than, nature. But for the Huichols, as for other native peoples, they are *in* nature. Indeed, they *are* nature." Knab (2004:109) similarly states that Mesoamerican cosmovisions are "based on a natural philosophy integrating the natural world with the supernatural." For many indigenous Mesoamericans, their interactive cosmos is replete with nonhuman persons that can be variably present in inanimate objects, and like humans, these sentient beings have volition. "Active" objects, however, are *not* literally considered animate since it is the invisible nonhuman persons in and surrounding the material vessel that are sentient (Astor-Aguilera 2004; Sosa 1985). Indeed, per Schaefer and Furst (1996:12), non-Western indigenous cosmologies "are often called 'animistic,' if not 'nature worship.' It would be more accurate to call them 'ecological,' " that is, not supernatural.

Mayan Communicating Objects and Ecological Beings

Some traditional Maya in Quintana Roo, México, utilize tree-like communicating objects in agricultural rituals focused on debt and merit reciprocation with ecological beings (Astor-Aguilera 2004:147–152). These objects, quadripartite in form, sometimes have tree-branch upswinging arms (Figure 8.6) and are often colored in blue to green hues, "shrouded" in *sujuy nook'* ("unused cloth"), adorned with pendants and necklaces, and communicated with through dreams and various rituals. The Yukatek Maya do not tend to associate their crosses with the suffering Christ and often address them as if they were trees (Astor-Aguilera 2004:145–151; Sosa 1985). Communicating objects are as often made of wood as they are of stone, and during 1867, in the Chamula Maya highlands of Chiapas, Pedro Diaz Cuscat created a shrine for three green communicating stones that supposedly fell from the sky (Gossen and Leventhal 1993:197; Marcos 1995:8). The three green stones appear related to the three-stone earth, symbolically linked to the upperworld, found in many Maya homes (Freidel et al. 1993:178). The Maya are known to house other types of communicating stones (Sullivan 1989) as well as communicating speleothems taken from caves (Astor-Aguilera 2008). Various other materials are also used by Mesoamericans for their communicating with nonhuman persons, for example, feathers by the Wixárika-Huichols (Schaefer and Furst 1996:25), ceramic bowls by the Yukatek Maya (Astor-Aguilera 2008), and blood by the Momostenango Maya (Tedlock 1982).

The Zinacanteco Maya are known to communicate with blood via the *ch'ulel* ("soul-like being") inside of people (Vogt 1993 [1976]:62); however, it is this blood-

8.6. Modern Yukatek-Mayan communicating cross (photograph by author).

being that "speaks" and not the blood itself. As Evon Vogt (1969:371) notes, to the Maya "the most important interaction going on in the universe is not between persons and material objects, but rather between souls inside these persons and material objects." The contemporary Maya concept of ch'ulel, which refers to "beings within blood," as unseen but felt "soul-like" persons, may have been depicted in ancient bloodletting and blood burned as incense imagery (Freidel et al. 1993:201–202; Houston and Stuart 1996:292). Freidel and colleagues (1993:202) state that blood was daubed on objects by the Maya in order to *p'a chi'* ("offer and open the mouth"). The contemporary Maya practice of making live blood offerings, such as throwing pigs onto their backs and ritually killing them, although now rare, is sometimes done in honor of communicating objects (Astor-Aguilera 2004:191–194; Gann 1918:4; Konrad 1991:133).

Mesoamerican ritual specialists, although following patterns and conventions, do not have a strictly codified religious practice in a Western sense (Astor-Aguilera 2004; Sandstrom 1991:300). Ancient Maya hieroglyphic inscriptions also lack theological rules, codes, and guidelines (see Houston and Stuart 1996:302), as well as any codified rules for burial rites or cadaver treatment (Meskell and Joyce 2003:138), and the presence of any centralized religious prophet (Miller and Martin 2004:20). Nevertheless, cosmological practices of the ancient Maya appear to pivot around composite beings, composed of foreign and local hybrid attributes, often wrapped in bundles and sheltered in order to be cared for and tended (see Houston and Stuart 1996:302–307). Not surprisingly, Morrison (2002:6) argues that Native Americans did not have Western-equivalent theological concepts before European contact and that to a certain extent, depending on degrees of acculturation, many still do not.

Discussion: Personal Being, Volition, Transformation, and the Invisible World

> As in many cultures other than our own, there is no Maya word for "religion,"
> … to the pre-Conquest Maya, the supernatural world was as real and tangible
> as the everyday world that our senses can perceive, and all of their behavior was
> oriented towards it. (Coe and Van Stone 2005:108)

Despite our increasing knowledge concerning much of ancient Maya politics and economics, we still lack a cohesive comprehension of Maya worldviews. Rice (2004: xviii) has admitted, what few Mayanists have dared and what this chapter tries to address, her struggle "to interrelate Maya ideology and cosmology with what we eth-nocentrically call 'the real world,' the normal, pragmatic, temporal interactions and concerns of humans and Western civilizations: politics, government, social organi-zation, materiality, and so on." This chapter, although focused to some degree on communicating objects, has been more about problematizing our interpretations of what we often reify as "Maya religion." The problem, I suggest, is that we often address questions regarding Mesoamerican worldviews through our Western categories— uncritically applied onto these peoples—while at once speaking authoritatively as if *witnessing* their "religious beliefs" through our assumed notions of recognizing "ritual" when we "see" it (see Goody 1961; Graham, this volume). Understanding foreign worldviews is difficult enough without making them even more complex by force fitting them onto our templates and therefore losing them in translation. As Arthur Demarest (2004:175) states, "religions, politics, and worldviews of other cultures are difficult for historians and anthropologists to analyze . . . they move us away from the common ground of humanity in the areas of biological needs and into the realm of thought, cultural values, and philosophy. The latter respond to psychological and emotional needs which are still poorly understood for even our own Western culture." McAnany (1995), furthermore, has argued that the ancient Maya did not practice "ancestor worship" but rather maintained active communication with their "living ancestors"; her hypothesis being that many Precolumbian Mesoamericans maintained dynamic social relations with select deceased kin.

I began this chapter exploring our assumptions that ancient Mesoamericans held beliefs concerning supernatural realms imbued with sacredness. Inherent to notions of supernatural sacredness is an awe-filling mysterious great power (see Berger 1990:25–26) that I argue tends to over-mystify and distort if applied to indigenous Mesoamerican worldviews. I suggest, elaborating from Harold McGee (1985:286), that although the practices and social concerns of a people, including politics, games, names, titles, and so on, "may reflect the worldview of a people [, this] should not be interpreted to mean that the worldview is inherent" within every activity as a mystical endeavor. Our current analyses of archaic religions may come close in our studies of their iconographic forms; however, our studies often lack indigenous contextual meaning, as applied in social theory and practice, in order to better grasp particular native subjectivities (Garwood et al. 1991:vii). There has been excellent work recognizing Maya nonhuman composite entities (see Coe and Kerr 1997; Ringle 1988; Schellhas 1904; Taube 1992); however, in providing a template for understanding Maya "deities" as overlapping composites, Gabrielle Vail (2000:123; this volume) notes that "our view of the Maya pantheon as consisting of a series of discrete entities . . . is a Western construct rather than a valid representation of pre-Hispanic Maya ideology" (see also Kubler 1969:32; Marcus 1978:180; Miller and Martin 2004:51, 118, 145; Proskouriakoff 1965:470–471). Indeed, Houston and Stuart (1996:295), in qualifying the term "god" as applied to Maya rulers, admit that the inscriptions provide little information on how, why, and what was actually meant by their associations with nonhumans, that is, our supposed "pantheon" of "deities."

Reluctant though we may be to relinquish applying our Western theological preconceptions onto other peoples, it is clear that by doing so we force fit our worldview onto radically differing systems (see Berrin 2004:14). Schaefer and Furst (1996:12–13), for example, mention that the Wixárika-Huichols have no word for "deity," the closest analogy meaning "our sandal straps," which reflects their environment and those beings "which tie [them] to the earth." The contemporary Yukatek

Maya similarly touch pebbles to their sandals when leaving offerings at stone pilings and crosses for the non-visible beings that likewise tie them to the earth (Astor-Aguilera 2008; Sosa 1985, 1990). Mesoamerican worldviews, despite their variability, are founded on relations with composite nonhuman sentient entities that are often addressed in kinship metaphors. Nonhumans not only need to interrelate with humans but are also dependent on reciprocal interactions with them in order to survive and prosper (Ingold 2000:90–92).

Ancestral beings, personalized in different composite guises, depend on humans because as "persons" they have needs such as hunger, thirst, and sexual desire and therefore react based on their emotions and reason. Mesoamericans provide ancestral beings with sustenance, as set forth in primordial arrangements whereby reciprocal interrelations were established, through the essence of offerings that maintain the original pact (Heyden 1991:192, 200). It is within these interrelations, between humans and variable nonhumans, which need to be maintained, that Native American social relations are constituted (Hallowell 1976 [1960]:361, 381). Redfield and Villa Rojas (1962 [1934]:107–126) dedicated a chapter in their classic ethnography to what they called the Maya "invisible world." This invisible world, despite its supernatural-sounding name, was the Chan Kom Maya's daily world conceived as being active with all sorts of sentient entities, human and nonhuman, where all things interacted in seen and unseen forms. Implicit in interacting with a world composed of that visible and invisible is that the Chan Kom Maya had no concept of a natural and supernatural dichotomy.

The confusion that appears present to us in cosmological ontologies of Native American worldviews likely stems from an unconscious interpretation of indigenous views as superstition and our tendency to impose Western categories upon non-Western peoples (Chidester 1996; Klass 1995; Lampe 2003). Many contemporary traditional Maya in the state of Quintana Roo, México, although they know the difference, do not distinguish them into binaries—what we define as human and nonhuman, awakened state and dreaming, life and death, and history and myth. That the Maya have what we classify as "talking stones," "talking trees," and "talking crosses" exemplifies their non-separation of natural and supernatural realms. Furthermore, that Native Americans communicate with, and attribute volition to, beings or objects with which we scientifically consider it impossible to relate and categorize as supernatural and therefore unreal and unverifiable, demonstrating that categories of impersonal and distant beings in a Judeo-Christian sense do not apply to these peoples (Hallowell 1976 [1960]:359; Morrison 2002:37–58). Houston and colleagues (2001a:506) have noted that Maya relationships with "supernaturals" are "still very poorly understood." Thus, as I have emphasized throughout this chapter, it is *not* whether we believe Maya "supernaturals" *are* supernatural, but whether the ancient Maya did. Rice (2004:283), in coming to terms that our Western secular understandings force the Maya onto foreign political templates, calls for more indigenous frameworks in analyzing the Maya not to completely discard all our previous models but to better comprehend Maya concepts. Indeed, indigenous epistemologies are all-important if we wish to get an approximate understanding of other peoples' worldview elements that cannot be scientifically verified (McGee 1985:264).

Robert Redfield and Alfonso Villa Rojas (1962 [1934]:112) stated that Maya invisibles, what I call nonhuman persons, were hard for them to categorize and therefore concluded that "the writers feel that there is much they do not yet understand about how the people of Chan Kom look upon the various gods and spirits." Unfortunately, having admitted this, their misunderstandings were placed on the Maya rather than themselves: "[B]ut it is plain that part of the confusion is in the minds of the natives . . . there is blurring in the attributes of deities; one deity is confounded with another" (Redfield and Villa Rojas 1962 [1934]:107). As previously explained, however, Maya cosmology is not strictly codified in a Western theological sense and their conception of the world is composed of interactions with that seen and unseen—made visible by "unexplainable actions" that take place in both community and forest—and attributed to often conflated composite entities. The assumed confused blurring of deity attributes is not confusion solely on the part of the contemporary Maya because ancient Mesoamericans, as noted previously, also intentionally conflated the attributes and identity of one "god" with others.

There is no solid indigenous evidence, colonial friars' assumptions not withstanding, for either the ancient or contemporary traditional Maya peoples' composite entities being supernatural gods. As noted by Mary Miller and Simon Martin (2004:51), "scholars have spilled a great deal of ink in their attempts to discern the 'real' from the 'supernatural' among the ancient Maya . . . scholars use the terms god and deity to describe the subjects of Maya worship, impersonation, and emulation, but these beings were not discrete, separate entities in the way we think of Greek or Roman gods." I suggest that these sentient entities, that are often lineage-associated, are personalized nonhumans conceptualized as found within these people's ecological surroundings, be it the "upperworld," "middleworld," and/or "underworld." Redfield and Villa Rojas (1962 [1934]:119, 209) documented that the deceased Maya took on a form of wind that was related to human biological breathing. Breath symbolism is highly important throughout the indigenous Americas as air is perceived as flowing in and out of all things (Taube 2001); humans, like mythic and invisible beings, are capable of transformation into wind, clouds, butterflies (López Austin 1980), and "non-material essences" as ancestors (Meskell and Joyce 2003:138, 142). Indeed, some Yukatek Maya consider the pixano'ob as residing within bones and blood and it is they that cause pulsing as air is circulated within and released from bodies. Similarly, Meskell and Joyce (2003:137) describe that Maya "deceased individuals are depicted in monumental sculpture engaged in interactions with their living successors and descendants, and their agency continued to be acknowledged in texts long after their death. . . . [F]or people who identified invisible substances as fundamental parts of the materiality of the self, the disappearance of the flesh appears not to have held the horror that characterized the Egyptian attitude towards the partibility and putrefaction of the dead body."

Implicit in Native American worldviews is that humans and nonhumans, be they visible or invisible, are not different in category of self (Hallowell 1967:172–182; Morrison 2002:26–28). Death equals life itself for the Maya (Carlsen and Prechtel 1991:26) and this concept is also exhibited in the central Mexican "cult of the dead" that in reality is a more like a "cult of life" (Astor-Aguilera 2004:253; Matos Moctezuma 1987:12; Paz 1985:54–55, 59–60). Death in ancient Mesoamerica was not in categorical opposition to life and vice versa because all things are eventually transformed. It was not the end of a person's life on earth but a continuum in a different phase with which communication was possible through ritual objects in continuous relational cosmological cycles. Mesoamerican invisible composite beings may reside in particular areas of the world, but they are free to roam about the entire cosmos. It is this cognitive orientation, based on communicating with interrelating ancestors and a great variety of other nonhumans, that gives Maya worldviews order, reason, and meaning and transformed continuity.

Acknowledgments. My sincere thanks to Timothy Pugh and Leslie Cecil for I was not an original participant in their symposium leading to this book; I greatly appreciate their thinking my research would strengthen the volume. A special nod to the suggestions made by anonymous reviewers of two drafts, both hurriedly pieced together to meet deadlines, which led to what I still consider a work in progress. I am grateful to each of my colleagues at Arizona State University's Religious Studies Department, who have further developed my thinking regarding the human cultural rubric we lump, delimit, and often reify under the label "religion." My deep respect to Linda Schele, who generously allowed her artwork to be reproduced through the Foundation for the Advancement of Mesoamerican Studies, Incorporated. I also extend much gratitude to Jane Buikstra, Patricia McAnany, and Kay Read for their scholarly support.

A scholar grows intellectually only as much as his students ask, challenge, and suggest. I am grateful to those who have come seeking my conversation as if I had the answers: Jason Barham, Rebecca Betts, Matt Correa, Janel Fairchild, Bradley Graupner, Brett Hendrickson, Robert Holguin, Patrick Kaup, Crystal Kennison, Brandon Lee, Ryan Leyba, Martha Málaga, Anna Novotny, Margarita Pignataro, Karrie Porter Brace, Scott Ortman, Ryan Reidel, Michael Sanders, Andrew Somerville, Nawa Sugiyama, and Deborah Williams. The end all be all for this work, however, are the Maya, and I take full responsibility for any misunderstandings contained herein.

Clash of Worldviews in Late Mayapán

Susan Milbrath and Carlos Peraza Lope

Mayapán played a dominant role in the lowland Maya area as both a political and religious center shortly following its foundation in the twelfth century.[1] Friar Diego de Landa recounts that the Cocom family was chosen to rule at Mayapán after the city was founded by Kukulcan, a culture hero associated with worship of the feathered serpent (Tozzer 1941:26). The Cocom were secular rulers apparently linked with the cult of Kukulcan (Milbrath and Peraza Lope 2003b:31–33). Among the twelve priests of Mayapán, the most powerful priests seem to be affiliated with the Xiu faction or lineage. Indeed, a Xiu priest took a leading role in politics by predicting the downfall of the Cocom (Tozzer 1941:40n194). The rivalry between the Xiu and Cocom documented by Landa may have been a power struggle between secular and religious factions, a partnership of priests and politicians that formed a strong government but was prone to instability (Masson et al. 2006:195; Tozzer 1941:35–37, 40).

Spanish chronicles note that the Xiu were known as fine architects who had constructed cities nearby (in the Puuc hills), and their architecture was so admired that they had been invited to build structures at Mayapán (Tozzer 1941:31, 215). Relationships between the Xiu and Cocom were apparently harmonious during this early period for the Xiu intermarried and accepted the Cocom as rulers. Late in Mayapán's history, after the Cocom invited foreign mercenaries to live in the city to support their reign, the two factions became increasingly hostile, and eventually the Xiu revolted against the Cocom in the mid-fifteenth century (Tozzer 1941:31–32, 35–

37). The animosity between the two factions continued into the Colonial period, as documented in the Cocom massacre of Xiu pilgrims on route to the Sacred Cenote of Chich'en Itzá to pray for rain during a major drought in 1536 (Restall 2001b:388n26; Tozzer 1941:40n197).

The Xiu and Cocom had different worldviews reflected in conflicting calendars and religious cults. The fact that these two groups used different calendars is not a minor disagreement in light of the fact that major calendar ceremonies involved large-scale rituals and architectural constructions. As Prudence Rice (this volume) shows, calendars are an expression of the Maya worldview. Both the Xiu and Cocom shared the cyclical *k'atun* calendar (*may*), but they disagreed on the transition point in the calendar and whether the k'atun had a terminal or initial dating. The Xiu cycle ran from k'atun 6 Ahau to k'atun 8 Ahau, and they identified the cycle by the completion on the last day (8 Ahau), whereas the Cocom followed the Itza traditions by counting the cycle from the initial dates and beginning the k'atun cycle with k'atun 11 Ahau (see Rice, this volume).[2] Study of the multiple founding events associated with Mayapán in the chronicles suggests that there was an initial founding event associated with the transition point in the Xiu calendar at the end of k'atun 8 Ahau, but some decades later the Cocom "refounded" Mayapán when the k'atun 13 Ahau came to a close, thereby initiating a new Itza k'atun cycle at the beginning of k'atun 11 Ahau (Table 9.1; Milbrath and Peraza Lope 2003b:37).

When any of key k'atun dates recurred during the period of Mayapán's occupation, there was smoldering discord that could ignite a new round of conflict reflecting incompatible worldviews. The materialized aspect of these conflicts over who controlled the calendar and which k'atun dates were to be celebrated may be seen in the architectural programs at the city. Initially, the Xiu and Cocom seemed to share control of the city, as evidenced by the fact that they shared ritual space in the central plaza in the twelfth century (Milbrath and Peraza Lope 2003b:38, 41). The Xiu probably initiated their calendar cycle at the end of k'atun 8 Ahau in 1204. Later, after the Cocom initiated the Itza k'atun cycle in 1283, the Xiu were increasingly marginalized, as is evident from the fact that no stelae are dated after this date. By the early fifteenth century, the Xiu compound with the Hall of Chac Masks associated with the Cenote Ch'en Mul was largely hidden from view by new construction around the Central Plaza that featured foreign artistic programs, especially those inspired by Central México.

Representing a conservative religious worldview, Xiu traditions were rooted in the local landscape of cenotes and Terminal Classic Puuc cities in what was later known as the Xiu province. The aborted Xiu pilgrimage of 1536 clearly links the Xiu with the worship of cenotes and the associated cult of Chac, the rain god. Many centuries earlier, Terminal Classic Uxmal had been the Xiu capital of the Puuc area, a site that prominently features Chac masks on a number of structures (Kowalski

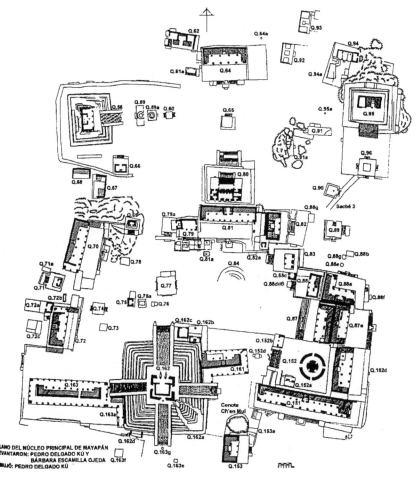

9.1. Map of Mayapán (map by Pedro Delgado Kú, courtesy of Carlos Peraza Lope, INAH).

2003). During the Postclassic, the Xiu priests apparently brought Terminal Classic masks from a Puuc city to Mayapán (Figures 9.1, 9.2; Milbrath and Peraza Lope 2003b:11, 39).

A contrasting worldview is evident in the Cocom tradition, reflected in an Itza worldview linked with long-distance trade and the cult of the feathered serpent imported from Central México (Ringle et al. 1998). The Colonial period Cocom claimed to be descendants of a ruling line from Chich'en Itzá (Farris 1984:245). At Mayapán, they apparently constructed a number of serpent temples and round temples modeled on those of Chich'en Itzá (Figures 9.3, 9.4; Table 9.1; Milbrath

Table 9.1 Mayapán's history in relation to the k'atun cycle

Events in Chronicles[a]	24-Year and 20-Tun K'atun		Art and Architecture[b]	Ceramics[c]
8 Ahau: Mayapán founded by Itzá from Chich'en Itzá and Mayapán's Hunac Ceel attacks Chich'en Itzá (Chumayel). Mayapán becomes seat of Xiu may at end of 8 Ahau?	1080–1104 8 Ahau	1185–1204 Bedrock	Stela 1: 10 Ahau (A.D. 1185). Round stela platform (Q84). Substructures: Q81(Floor 1), Q151, Q153, Q153a, H18.	Hocaba phase: Peto Cream ware mixed with Cehpech and small percentage of Sotuta. Early lots: C35c,d, C42, C43, C64, C70, C84, C85, C36, C37, C104.
	1104–1128 6 Ahau	1204–1224 Plaza Floor 1	Q77a, Q77 platforms. Q162a (Castillo-sub). Substructure of Q97. Q81 Phase I (Floor 2). Stela 5: 4 Ahau (A.D. 1244).	
4 Ahau: Chich'en Itzá invades Mayapán to avenge Hunac Ceel's attack (Chumayel).	1128–1152 4 Ahau	1224–1244 Plaza Floor 2		
2 Ahau: another founding of Mayapán by Itza refugees from Champoton (Tizimin).	1152–1176 2 Ahau	1244–1263 Plaza Floor 3	Q84 completed? Q58 Phase I? Q80 temple Phase I?	Cehac-Hunacti composite censers typical of Hocaba-Tases Transition.
13 Ahau: another founding of Mayapán by Itza of Chich'en Itzá (Chumayel). Mayapán becomes seat of Itza may at end of 13 Ahau?	1176–1200 13 Ahau	1263–1283 Plaza Floor 4	Stela 6: 13 Ahau (A.D. 1283). Q218 Phase I serpent temple? Round temples: Q214, H18. Q80 Phase II. Q81 Phase II.	Earliest Chen Mul Modeled censers. Middle lots: C40, C41, C62, C63, C71, C73, C88, C89, C90, C105, C106.
	1200–1224 11 Ahau	1293–1303 Plaza Floor 5		
K'atun 11 Ahau through 5 Ahau, relatively peaceful Mayapán?	1224–1248 9 Ahau	1303–1323 Plaza Floor 6	Serpent temples: Q58, Q143, Q159, Q218 Phase II, Castillo (Q162) built with Plaza Floor 6. Q80 Phase III? Q81 Phase III. Q152 Round Temple, Q126 Phase I: Q163a niche Level 8.	Middle Lot C63 sealed between Plaza Floors 4 and 8.
	1248–1272 7 Ahau	1323–1342 Plaza Floor 7		Tases phase Chen Mul Modeled censers abundant by Plaza Floor 8.
	1272–1296 5 Ahau	1342–1362 Plaza Floor 8	Q153 Cenote Temple Phase II. Q151 Hall of Chac Masks. Q81 Phase IV. Q126 Phase II. Jaguar Altar with 3 Ahau.	

Chronicle events[a]	K'atun	Plaza Floor date[b]	Art and architecture[b]	Ceramic lots / occupation[c]
3 Ahau: Zuyua questionnaire (Chumayel).	1296–1320 3 Ahau			Increased use of San Joaquin Bluff. Middle Lot C62 scaled between Plaza Floors 8 and 9.
1 Ahau: departure of Xiu faction and "Mexican" Canul "afflict" people of Mayapán (Chumayel). Cocom faction takes complete control of Mayapán, bringing more "Mexicans" into capital (Landa).	1320–1344 1 Ahau	1362–1382 Plaza Floor 9		
	1344–1368 12 Ahau	1382–1401 Plaza Floor 10	Mixteca-Puebla murals added to Q95 and Q80 Phase IV. Q81 Phase V shrine. Shrines added to Q162, Q162d, stucco jaguar with Plaza Floor 11.	Tases phase Late lots: C39, C61, C74, C92, C107.
	1368–1392 10 Ahau	1401–1421 Plaza Floor 11		
8 Ahau revolt at Mayapán (Chumayel). Xiu revolt against Cocom dates to 1420 (Gaspar Antonio Chi). Landa gives no date but says by 1566 the city had been abandoned for 120 years.	1392–1416 8 Ahau	1421–1441 Plaza Floor 12	Q163 colonnade figures. "Mexican" figures on H18a altar. "Mexican" solar murals on Q161.	
	1416–1440 6 Ahau	1441–1461 Plaza Floor 13	Xiu destroy altars and colonnade atlantid figures in Q163.	Small post-Tases phase occupation.
4 Ahau pestilence drives away remaining Xiu residents (Chumayel). Landa says Xiu had occupied city for 500 years when they finally left.	1440–1464 4 Ahau	1461–1480	Xiu reset fallen stelae in central plaza and covered "foreign" paintings with stucco.	
	1464–1488 2 Ahau	1480–1500		Complete abandonment.
	1488–1512 13 Ahau	1500–1520	Scattered offerings by pilgrims.	
11 Ahau men came from the east in 1513 and Maya were called Christians in 1519 (Chumayel).	1512–1536 11 Ahau	1520–1539		
		1539–1559		

[a] Chronicle events may refer to either 24-year k'atun or 20-tun k'atun.
[b] Art and architecture dates refer to or 20-tun k'atun; [c] Ceramic lots listed in Smith 1971.

9.2. Mayapán's Q151, the Hall of Chac Masks, a Xiu-Puuc revival-style building using masks (photograph by Susan Milbrath, courtesy of INAH).

9.3. Sunset on the winter solstice creates a diamondback rattler design on the staircase of Mayapán's Q162 pyramid (courtesy of Carlos Peraza Lope, INAH).

9.4. Mayapán's Q152 Round Temple, a Cocom-Itza revival-style building modeled on Chich'en Itzá's Caracol (photograph by Susan Milbrath, courtesy of INAH).

and Peraza Lope 2003b:16). During the last century of Mayapán's history (1350–1450), the Cocom worldview became increasingly mercantile and they looked far beyond Yucatán and their Itza heritage for ideological inspiration. By inviting mercenaries and traders from Central México, the Cocom introduced a foreign presence at Mayapán, resulting in profound changes in the predominant worldview at Mayapán.

Ceramics Reflecting Changes in Worldviews

In the early occupation of Mayapán, around the time of the K'atun 8 Ahau founding date, the predominant ceramics were localized ceramics types drawn from traditions in Yucatán (Table 9.1). Ceramics of the Hocaba component, including Peto Cream ware and composite non-effigy censers of the Navula group, apparently developed out of Terminal Classic types prominent at Chich'en Itzá (Milbrath and Peraza Lope 2003b:7–8; Smith 1971:204). A small percentage of Hoal Modeled effigy censers in the Hocaba component seem to represent a new form (Smith 1971:255, figure 6a). Some Cehpech ceramics types, representing a survival of the Puuc traditions, also occur during this early period (Milbrath and Peraza Lope 2003b:7, 38). Architecture associated with Hocaba ceramics is largely known from dismantled buildings that survive only in their foundations and platforms that continued in use in later times, most notably a stela platform (Q64) linked with Puuc traditions and a platform with radial stairways (Q77), like the dance platforms at Chich'en Itzá (Table 9.1; Milbrath and Peraza Lope 2003b:12–13, 18).

A major transition tied to K'atun 11 Ahau is seen in the introduction of the earliest Chen Mul Modeled effigy censers and serpent temples reflecting self-conscious revival of the architecture of Chich'en Itzá (Table 9.1). The Cocom introduced revival-style architecture inspired by the Itza heritage of Chich'en Itzá and effigy censers diagnostic of the Tases ceramic component (Figure 9.5). The introduction of Chen Mul Modeled effigy censers, considered a marker for the transition to the Tases phase, is a sign of an important religious change. At this time, the Cocom dismantled earlier buildings and conducted extensive renovations of the city. Over the course of several decades, Hocaba ceramics were replaced by new ceramic types, leading to a new phase, according to the Carnegie archaeologists (Smith 1971:242–243). There is no sharp division between the Hocaba and Tases components but rather a gradual transition. Some see Hocaba as a subcomplex associated with the early Tases phase (Ringle et al. 1998). Regardless of whether we can distinguish Hocaba as a distinct ceramic phase, an important religious change is evident in the introduction of Tases effigy censers that served as "idols" associated with altars. It seems that initially the Tases phase effigy censers were used only in certain types of buildings, those associated with Cocom-Itza rituals, and later the censers came into more generalized use in concert with the rising power of the Cocom.[3] Incense burners have a long tradition in the lowland Maya area (Rice 1999), but full-figure effigy incense burners are largely a Postclassic tradition in the northern Maya lowlands (Milbrath and Peraza Lope 2003b:7, 24). Tases effigy censers reflect a major change in Mayapán's religious practices associated with Cocom-Itza revival-style architecture.

No longer simple containers for burning copal, Tases phase effigy incense burners served as icons or idols. They were often associated with altars and can be related to Landa's account of Postclassic braziers that were idols used in New Year ceremonies celebrating the year-bearer cycle (Milbrath and Peraza Lope 2007; Tozzer 1941:140). Tases phase incense burners depict Maya deities resembling those in the Postclassic Maya codices, including Chac and the long-nosed merchant god (Figure 9.5; Thompson 1957a:figures 1e, 3f). Central Mexican deities are also fairly common (Taube 1992; Thompson 1957a). One extraordinary censer combines attributes of the Classic Maya monkey scribe and Postclassic monkey gods, who are patrons of the arts, such as the Aztec deity Xochipilli (Milbrath and Peraza Lope 2003a). Study of Chen Mul Modeled effigy censers indicates that some deities are apparently concentrated in specific buildings (Peraza Lope and Masson 2005). Nonetheless, it is clear that Maya and central Mexican deities appear together in a number of contexts, as in Lot C72 in Structure Q81, where altar figures include Chac and Itzamna alongside a Venus warrior and Quetzalcoatl/Kukulcan, the god of the feathered serpent (Milbrath and Peraza Lope 2007; Smith 1971:figure 67).

Merchants from the area of Central México may have introduced the cult of the feathered serpent at both Terminal Classic Chich'en Itzá and Postclassic Mayapán

9.5. Chen Mul Modeled effigy censer from Mayapán representing Chac (after Smith 1971:fig. 32n).

(Ringle et al. 1998). The earlier manifestation of the feathered serpent cult at Chich'en Itzá is not associated with effigy censers. Although effigy censers have not been included in the ceramic complex characterizing a later variant of the feathered serpent cult at Mayapán (Ringle et al. 1998:216–218), they do seem to be associated with the Itza revival-style and feathered serpent imagery at that site. Serpent images appear fairly frequently on Tases phase censer figures and several censer figures bear the spiral wind shell characteristic of Quetzalcoatl in central Mexican iconography (Smith 1971, 1:figures 67a, 71b; Peraza Lope and Masson 2005). Long ago, Tatiana Proskouriakoff (1955:98, 101–102) suggested that the effigy censers represent a new religion associated with the cult of Quetzalcoatl/Kukulcan.[4]

Quetzalcoatl's Cult in Cocom-Itza Architecture

Landa links the feathered serpent cult of Kukulcan to round structures at both Chich'en Itzá and Mayapán (Tozzer 1941:25). Feathered serpents appear on an altar associated with an earlier round temple (H18), a type of building probably linked with the Cocom contingent at Mayapán (Table 9.1; Milbrath and Peraza Lope 2003b:13–14, 26, figure 20a). Imagery of feathered serpents at Mayapán is most prominent in serpent temple groups that William Ringle and George Bey (2001:284–286) link to the Cocom. Architectural programs inspired by buildings at Chich'en Itzá, such as the first serpent temple (Q218, Phase I) and the early round temples, date to around the time of the transition to K'atun 11 Ahau, the first k'atun of the Cocom-Itza may (Table 9.1). Itza "founding" events at the end K'atun 13 Ahau, mentioned in the chronicles, may be linked to the first revival-style temples (Table 9.1). The subsequent k'atun, 9 Ahau (1303–1323), may be when the largest serpent temple, the Castillo (Q162), was constructed (Figure 9.3; Table 9.1). This pyramid was built at the time of Plaza Floor 6, midway through the sequence of thirteen floors in the Central Plaza (Milbrath and Peraza Lope 2003b:18). The Q162 pyramid is contemporary with a ceramic lot (C63) that had the earliest effigy censers in the stratigraphic cut of the plaza floors, sealed between Plaza Floors 4 and 8 (Table 9.1).

Archaeological evidence indicates a relatively late date for Mayapán's Round Temple (Q152) and the Castillo (Q162), a serpent temple with a radial pyramid, both close copies of structures built centuries earlier at Chich'en Itzá (Table 9.1; Figures 9.3, 9.4; Milbrath and Peraza Lope 2003b:16, 23). Based on its "pure" Tases phase deposits and the abundance of effigy censers excavated in the temple's rectangular platform, we estimate that the Round Temple was constructed around the epoch of Plaza Floor 8, ca. 1342–1362 (Table 9.1; Milbrath and Peraza Lope 2003b:12, 39; Peraza Lope et al. 1999:65). The apogee for Mayapán's Cocom-Itza revival-style dates between 1300 and 1350, and the earliest revival-style structures (H18, Q214, and Q218) probably date to the mid-thirteenth century (Table 9.1; Milbrath and Peraza Lope 2003b).

Dates for the five serpent-column temples (Q58, Q143, Q159, Q162, Q218) distributed around the Central Plaza are not certain, but clearly they were not all built at one time.[5] The earliest Cocom-Itza serpent temple, located to the south of the Cenote Ch'en Mul plaza, seems to be the substructure of Q218, a temple with serpent balustrades designated as Phase I in Table 9.1. The associated ceramics represent a middle lot with Hocaba and some effigy censers (Milbrath and Peraza Lope 2003b:16; Winters 1955b). Other feathered serpent temples (Q58, Q143, Q159, Q162) linked with the Cocom and their Itza heritage were built over temples of a different design, indicating that the Itza revival-style is not the earliest component at Mayapán (Proskouriakoff 1962b:100, 118; Winters 1955b:398, 409). The Round Temple, constructed over a colonnade that was partially dismantled, provides further evidence that the Itza revival architecture was introduced later at Mayapán (Milbrath and Peraza Lope 2003b:12). The Itza revival-style seems to last about a century and represents a conscious attempt by the Cocom to assert their Itza heritage and worldviews.

Mayapán's Q162 pyramid most closely replicates its namesake, the Castillo at Chich'en Itzá. Both are radial pyramids with four staircases, nine levels, and a north-facing temple with serpent columns accessed by a stairway with a serpent balustrade. Dating around 1300, the Q162 pyramid may have been built thirteen k'atuns (256 years) after Chich'en Itzá's Castillo (Milbrath and Peraza Lope 2003b:39). Mayapán's pyramid incorporates specific astronomical alignments that show clear parallels with Chich'en Itzá's Castillo (Aveni et al. 2004). The builders of Mayapán's revival-style pyramid understood the solar orientations at Chich'en Itzá and repeated them with creative modifications.

Round temples are also found at a number of Postclassic Maya sites, but the greatest elaboration of this architectural form is found at Mayapán, especially the Round Temple (Q152). This temple, clearly a direct copy of Chich'en Itzá's Caracol, reflects links with Chich'en Itzá and the Terminal Classic Cocom heritage (Figure 9.4). Solar alignments like those of Chich'en Itzá are evident in the positioning of niches in Mayapán's Round Temple, indicating a transfer of knowledge between the two cities and a link with the heritage of Terminal Classic Chich'en Itzá (Aveni et al. 2004). The western stairway of the Round Temple has virtually the same orientation as the midline of Window 1 of the Caracol, which functioned as an astronomical observatory from ca. 800 to 1100/1200 (Milbrath 1999:figure 3.1b; Milbrath and Peraza Lope 2003b:12). Mayapán's Q152 observatory may have been constructed as a revival-style structure one k'atun cycle or may after the Caracol (Milbrath and Peraza Lope 2003b:39). The worldview expressed by such purposeful revival of Itza structures at intervals timed by the k'atun cycle is certainly linked to the Cocom, who reasserted their Itza heritage by reviving architectural forms seen at Chich'en Itzá.

Mayapán's Xiu-Puuc Revivals

The Xiu probably had considerable power early in Mayapán's history (Milbrath and Peraza Lope 2003b:33, 41). They are linked with the stelae cult and the earliest known k'atun-ending inscription on Stela 1, dating to 1185, at the transition point between K'atun 10 Ahau and K'atun 8 Ahau, the final k'atun in the Xiu calendar cycle (Milbrath and Peraza Lope 2003b:39). All known stelae bear k'atun inscriptions that date the revival of the Classic stela cult dates between 1150 and 1300 (Table 9.1). Mayapán stelae seem to reflect a Puuc-Maya tradition linked with the Xiu (Milbrath and Peraza Lope 2003b:33). This conservative worldview was eventually suppressed when Mayapán's stelae were destroyed and removed from the stelae platform (Q84). Subsequently, the stelae platform became obsolete and was covered by Plaza Floor 8 during K'atun 5 Ahau (1342–1362) (Table 9.1; Milbrath and Peraza Lope 2003b:33, 39).

The Xiu also evoked their more glorious past in revival-style architecture, and they may have gone one step further by actually transporting Chac masks from Terminal Classic Puuc sites. The Hall of Chac Masks (Q151), a colonnaded hall in the Cenote Ch'en Mul compound, is one of a number of architectural groups with a colonnaded hall, shrine, and oratory, but no temple. Ringle and Bey (2001:284–286) identify this form of complex as Mayapán's Basic Ceremonial Group, which they suggest is linked with Xiu and Puuc traditions of the western *cuchcabalob* ("polities"). The Hall of Chac Masks (Q151) was probably commissioned by priests of Chac representing the cenote cult (Figure 9.2). The Puuc-style Chac masks on Q151 are part of a Xiu-Puuc revival-style, although the masks themselves were apparently salvaged from a Terminal Classic Puuc structure (Milbrath and Peraza Lope 2003b:10–11). In our proposed k'atun chronology, Structure Q151 dates to K'atun 3 Ahau (1362–1382), contemporary with Plaza Floor 9 (Table 9.1). It is not certain whether a razed substructure beneath the Q151 colonnade was also decorated with Chac masks (Shook and Irving 1955). This substructure was part of an early Xiu complex grouped alongside the Cenote Ch'en Mul with the substructures of Q153 and Q153a, which are among the earliest buildings at the site (Table 9.1).

The fact that so many substructures at Mayapán were completely razed could indicate a deliberate "obliteration" act reflecting a political upheaval when the Cocom began ambitious renovations honoring their patron deity, Quetzalcoatl/ Kukulcan. It is possible that some of the reused Puuc stones came from these razed structures. There are so many Puuc stones used as construction material that the source of the carved stones must have been a Puuc site at Mayapán or very nearby (Milbrath and Peraza Lope 2003b:21; Shook 1954a:90). With the exception of a few structures like Q151, the reuse of Puuc stones at Mayapán reflects a lack of interest in preserving Puuc forms. Ornate stones are randomly placed and used mainly as a foundation for a plain surface of stucco (Milbrath and Peraza Lope 2003b:figure 4).

During the Tases phase, Xiu-Puuc-style ceremonial architecture in the central area was apparently confined to the Cenote Ch'en Mul group (Q148, Q151, Q153, Q153a; Figures 9.1, 9.2). At this time, Puuc masks were prominent only in the Hall of Chac Masks, largely hidden from view to those in the Central Plaza. The conservative worldview of the Xiu priests was increasingly marginalized as non-Maya cults gained greater influence at Mayapán. Even though the Xiu were apparently under Cocom control by the time the Hall of Chac Masks (Q151) was constructed in ca. 1350, they probably retained some power through an ancient link with the Cenote Ch'en Mul, a focal point for early architectural construction at Mayapán. A severe drought around 1350 (Brenner et al. 2003:figure 4.9) may be one reason the Xiu priests sought to appease the rain god by displaying archaistic Chac masks on Structure Q151.

Proskouriakoff (1962b:113) identified a terraced structure (Q148) facing the Hall of Chac Masks as a late shrine. This recently restored structure displays columns carved with ring-shaped designs reminiscent of Puuc motifs (Peraza Lope et al. 2005). A large circular column (Q150) alongside resembles columnar altars at Sayil and Kabah (Pollock 1980:135, 201, figures 278b, 278h, 382). Similar columns were found in a compound (R86–R90) that has two residences with altars bearing Chac masks (Proskouriakoff and Temple 1955). Aside from Structure Q151 and two residences with shrines bearing Chac masks over the altars (R86, R87), there is little evidence of a Puuc revival during the Tases phase.

A large house in the residential compound (R86) is an austere structure that may reflect conservative tastes or religious temperament, according to Tatiana Proskouriakoff and Charles Temple (1955:304). Possibly the entire compound was occupied by Xiu priests. The Carnegie archaeologists interpreted a large deposit (Burial Cist 2) with broken effigy censers in Structure R86 as objects used in ceremonies just before the compound was burned and abandoned (Proskouriakoff and Temple 1955:327, 303–307). The profusion of central Mexican deities in this deposit is puzzling. The excavators noted that they were incomplete pieces that had been moved from their original locations. They suggested departing inhabitants probably dumped them there just before the buildings were burned. If so, it may be that the Xiu wanted to get the foreign idols out of sight for the same reasons that they plastered over central Mexican deities represented in late murals at Mayapán after their revolt (see below).

Foreign Worldviews at Mayapán

The Cocom worldviews evolved through contact with foreign ideas, becoming less focused on the heritage of Chich'en Itzá and turning to more distant sources of inspiration. Landa notes that the Cocom invited "Mexicans" (Canul) to live at Mayapán as a means of increasing trade and subjugating rival factions (Tozzer 1941:32). The Canul probably came from the Chontalpa, homeland of the Putun traders who traveled along the coasts of Yucatán from the Terminal Classic through the Postclassic. Landa notes that traders of Yucatán exchanged salt, cotton, and slaves for cacao and stone (jade) beads (Tozzer 1941:94–95). They probably also traded for honey from bee gardens in Cozumel (Batun-Alpuche 2005).

By 1400, Mayapán was a major center situated at the crossroads of international contact, and trade contacts extended in many different directions. Matillas Fine Orange, a Gulf Coast type most probably from Veracruz, may have come to the city via Champoton in Campeche, where effigy censers inspired by Mayapán attest to contact with Mayapán (Forsyth 2004:33–34).[6] Guatemala, Oaxaca, and México's central highlands supplied Mayapán with copper bells and obsidian (Escamilla Ojeda et al. 2004; Milbrath and Peraza Lope 2003b:29). Close ties with the Petén are evident in parallels between Mayapán's architecture and structures at Zacpetén and Topoxté, where provincial Mayapán-style effigy censers have been found in relatively late contexts (Bullard 1970:281–285; Pugh and Rice 1996). East coast sites, such as Tulum and San Gervasio, also share ceramic parallels with Mayapán, including similar effigy censers (Milbrath and Peraza Lope 2003b:25; Peraza Lope 1996). Murals from Tulum are also stylistically similar to some of Mayapán's murals and share a similarly lavish use of Maya Blue (Milbrath and Peraza Lope 2003b:27–28; Miller 1982:37).

The Cocom developed widespread trade contacts, bringing an influx of new ideas documented in murals related to the Mixteca-Puebla style, a Postclassic symbol set that spread across Mesoamerica (Masson 2003; Milbrath and Peraza Lope 2003b:26, figures 23–25; Nicholson and Quiñones Keber 1994; Robertson 1970; Smith and Heath-Smith 1980). This "international style" is seen in murals at Mayapán that reflect an interchange of ideas from places as far away as Oaxaca in western Mesoamerica—one of the principal sources for copper bells found at Mayapán (Milbrath and Peraza Lope 2003b:29).

The International style murals are clearly late additions to an eclectic style of architecture. The last phase of Mayapán's Temple of the Five Niches (Q80) displays paintings depicting Mixteca-Puebla style serpents positioned at the base of temple stairs, evoking the serpent balustrades of the Cocom-Itza revival-style architecture (Milbrath and Peraza Lope 2003b:figure 23; Pugh 2001b:figure 6; Winters 1955c). Nonetheless, the temples depicted in the murals are more closely linked with architecture represented in Mixtec codices, such as Quetzalcoatl's temple in Acatalán, Puebla, depicted on page 15 of the *Codex Nuttall* (Milbrath and Peraza Lope 2003b:26–27, figure 25). The sea snake in the Temple of the Fisherman (Q95) closely resembles the Chicchan Serpent of the *Codex Madrid* 11–18, a codex that seems to reflect Mixteca-Puebla parallels (Figure 9.6; Milbrath and Peraza Lope

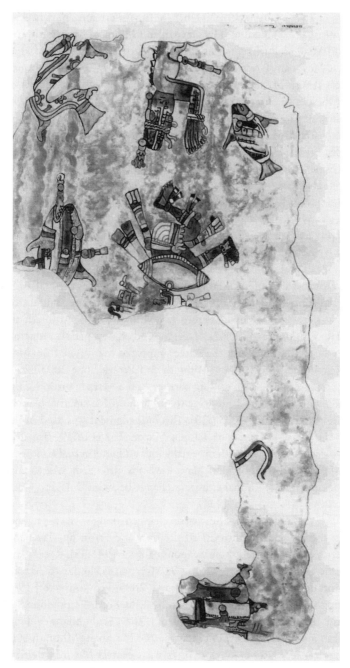

9.6. Temple of the Fisherman (Q95; painting by Anne Deane, courtesy of Marilyn Masson).

2003b:figure 28; Vail and Aveni 2004b:19). The fisherman's "pinwheel" pose, also seen in an east coast mural at Tancah (Miller 1982:plate 8), is fairly common in Mixtec and Mixteca-Puebla codices, providing further evidence of Mixteca-Puebla elements at Mayapán (Codex Nuttall 65–68, Miller 1975; Codex Borgia 26, Díaz and Rogers 1993). Mixteca-Puebla art at Mayapán reflects the impact of foreign trade and the desire of its rulers to show their cosmopolitan contacts by displaying the latest art style. This initial wave of foreign influence may be linked with the first appearance of Canul traders at Mayapán.[7] Whereas the Cocom-Itza revival had focused on the legacy of the most powerful Terminal Classic city in Yucatán, the changes in art forms resulting from Mixteca-Puebla influences reflect a foreign artistic style that was imported from Central México, perhaps via trade contact at east coast sites like Tulum.

A second wave of foreign influence seems to be linked with the latter part of the Tases phase when the Cocom power was bolstered by central Mexican trade.[8] Intrigued by non-Maya religious cults, Cocom rulers apparently commissioned Mexican murals and sculptures depicting central Mexican deities. Aztec influence is seen in portable art and late Mayapán architecture, such as the Hall of Sun Disks (Q161), depicting standard-bearers that closely resemble Aztec murals from Phase II murals at the Templo Mayor (Figure 9.7; Milbrath 2005; Milbrath and Peraza Lope 2003b; Proskouriakoff 1962a). Near the end of Mayapán's occupation, archaeological evidence indicates that the Aztecs imported Maya Blue from Mayapán for mural programs at Tenochtitlan (Milbrath and Peraza Lope 2003b:29–30). The Aztec *pochteca* or their Canul trading partners came to trade for Maya Blue, a pigment made with indigo and rare clay found around Mayapán (Folan 1969:182; Milbrath and Peraza Lope 2003b:30). This blue pigment was used in the Mexica capital in the Phase II murals of Templo Mayor (1375–1427). Broad trade networks involved exchange of both material goods and intellectual concepts between Central México and the northern Maya lowlands. This form of exchange echoes the well-documented Terminal Classic exchange between Tula and Chich'en Itzá (Kowalski 2007).

Ideology and technology also were exchanged along with trade goods. Landa notes that the "Mexicans" introduced the bow and arrow at Mayapán, and the Maya warriors soon adopted these weapons (Tozzer 1941:35). Recent studies suggest that the assemblage of stone tools at Mayapán is similar to Aztec forms of arrow points and sacrificial knives (C. Brown 2005; Proskouriakoff 1962a:figure 30). Foreign religious cults more profoundly influenced the predominant worldviews in the last decades of Mayapán's history. There is abundant evidence of central Mexican influence in late monumental art at Mayapán (Milbrath 2005). Tases phase effigy censers also show clear links with central Mexican deities, such as the Old Fire God and Tlahuizcalpantecuhtli (Taube 1992:125–127; Thompson 1957a).

9.7. Hall of Sun Disks, Q161 (courtesy of Carlos Peraza Lope, INAH).

The late transformation in Cocom religious cults is clearly evident in a stucco altar (H18a) constructed alongside an early round temple (H18). Rattlesnakes, originally created for the Cocom-Itza revival of the feathered serpent cult, were covered over by a monstrous figure resembling Aztec images of Tlaltecuhtli (Milbrath and Peraza Lope 2003b:26, figure 20; Pasztory 1983:figure 130). The stucco earth monster on this altar evokes forms developed in the Aztec capital, rarely seen beyond the confines of Central México.

Artists may have come from Central México or Aztec territories in Veracruz to create an atlantid colonnade (Q163) that was added to the Q162 pyramid (Milbrath and Peraza Lope 2003b:26). Carnegie archaeologists were not able to study the iconography because the life-sized stucco figures all had their heads lopped off. The heads, recovered in recent Instituto Nacional de Antropología e Historia (INAH) excavations, depict deities popular in Central México and coastal Veracruz, such as Xipe Totec (Peraza Lope 1999:51). Structures Q161 and Q163, both late additions to the Castillo, are positioned facing Mayapán's Central Plaza with foreign deities serving as signage of the profound changes in worldviews.

Just before the end of the Cocom reign, the ruler "introduced more Mexicans into the city" (Tozzer 1941:36, 39). This certainly angered the conservative Xiu priests, but they waited to destroy the Cocom until the K'atun 8 Ahau at the end of the Xiu k'atun cycle.[9] Munro Edmonson (1982:xvi) noted that the end of the may involved destruction of power symbols associated with one city and the transfer of power to a new city. Archaeological evidence confirms the destruction of Cocom monuments (Milbrath and Peraza Lope 2003b:29; Shook 1954a:96–97). During their revolt, the Xiu smashed Cocom censers and destroyed the Mexican deities in the Q163 colonnade. Subsequently, they attempted to obliterate all foreign presence by plastering over the International style murals in Q80 and Q161 (Barrera and Peraza Lope 2001:437, 439; Milbrath and Peraza Lope 2003b:29). In front of the Round Temple, the Xiu apparently reset stelae that had been mutilated by the Cocom at an earlier time (Milbrath and Peraza Lope 2003b:39). Most of the population returned to their original provinces, but the majority of the Xiu probably moved to Maní, which became the Xiu capital after the fall of Mayapán (Masson et al. 2006:196). The Xiu population that stayed on at Mayapán was probably quite small, but they continued to perform ceremonies in their main religious compound alongside the Cenote Ch'en Mul (Shook and Irving 1955:144). Finally, this group was forced to leave when an epidemic drove them away in K'atun 4 Ahau (Roys 1967:138).[10]

Calendar Conflicts Reflecting a Clash of Worldviews

The clash of worldviews at Mayapán probably has its roots back in the Terminal Classic period of Chich'en Itzá. Tun-ahau dates used predominantly at this site reflect a calendar reform that detached the historical records from the Classic Maya k'atun cycle, which was still in use at some Terminal Classic Puuc sites such as Uxmal (Milbrath and Peraza Lope 2003b:33, 39). The Xiu of Mayapán seem to have modeled their stela cult on Classic period traditions that involved erecting a k'atun monument at the period ending (20 × 360 days). Indeed, Landa tells us that Mayapán erected a stela every twenty years (Tozzer 1941:38). The Xiu followed the Classic period tradition of terminal dating, whereas the Itza k'atun cycle employed initial dating, apparently influenced by central Mexican patterns (Rice, this volume).

Monumental architecture at Mayapán was surely used as a stage for calendar ceremonies involving the k'atun cycle, recalling the role of the k'atun calendar in the construction of twin pyramid groups at Tikal during the Classic period (Milbrath 2004). The k'atun cycle determined the dates when the Xiu priests erected k'atun monuments at Mayapán and probably also when the Itza revival-style temples were constructed. A major period of renovation with Itza revival-style architecture was initiated at the beginning of the Itza k'atun cycle, in K'atun 11 Ahau. The most ambitious structures may have been built one k'atun cycle after their prototypes were completed at Chich'en Itzá, and the sequence of thirteen plaza floors may also be linked with intervals in the k'atun cycle (Milbrath and Peraza Lope 2003b:38). The k'atun calendar determined a number of other events at Mayapán, most notably the founding dates and the final rebellion. K'atun 8 Ahau, marking the beginning of

Mayapán's rise as an important city, is also the k'atun of the Xiu revolt, indicating the city was preeminent for one full k'atun cycle or may (Table 9.1; Milbrath and Peraza Lope 2003b:37).

The most interesting historical information on the k'atun cycle comes from the Books of Chilam Balam. These chronicles, written in the eighteenth century, sometimes use a variant k'atun of twenty-four years (Edmonson 1988:262–264; Rice, this volume). Known as the Ahau K'atun, this cycle of 13 × 24 years (312 years) was integrated with the Spanish colonial calendar by employing a year of 365 days rather than a tun of 360 days (Craine and Reindorp 1979:126). Using the Colonial period Books of Chilam Balam to interpret Mayapán's history requires caution because these texts sometimes mix the two different k'atun systems (Miram 1994). Table 9.1 records archaeological events at the site in relation to the k'atun chronology using both systems to provide alternative dates for events.

The Ahau K'atun recorded the first ahau date at the beginning of the k'atun and counted the *uinal* from 1–19, rather than 0–19. The new year invariably began on the uinal day 1 Pop, and the k'atun always began on a year-bearer day named Cauac (24 years being divisible by 4). It is possible that this system first developed around 1400 at Mayapán, after the traditional k'atun cycle was no longer recorded on stelae (Bolles 1990; Milbrath and Peraza Lope 2003b:36). If so, it represents an adaptation to the central Mexican focus on the solar year, providing another piece of evidence that the worldviews of Mayapán were strongly influenced by Central México.

Transforming the Worldviews at Mayapán

The Itza revival-style pays homage to the ancestral city of Chich'en Itzá at a time when the Itza k'atun cycle was inaugurated at Mayapán in K'atun 11 Ahau. Calendric renewal ceremonies probably took place amid Mayapán's newly constructed revival-style temples, modeled on architectural forms that date centuries earlier at Chich'en Itzá. Mayapán's round temples and serpent-column temples are directly inspired by Terminal Classic architecture dating centuries earlier at Chich'en Itzá. Revival styles express an aspect of worldviews because the art forms are designed to evoke a form of parallel with the past, claiming a present world that is as glorious as the past. Mayapán's stela cult and revival-style architecture have been seen as a sign of revival or revitalization by a number of scholars (Masson 2000:250–253; Masson et al. 2006:188–194; Milbrath and Peraza Lope 2003b). Marilyn Masson and her colleagues (2006:206–207) note that Mayapán emulated Chich'en Itzá in some aspects but distinguished itself by "reinstating the Classic institution of stela erection; creating an elaborate effigy censer tradition; inventing a sacrificial burial shaft temple tradition unique to Mesoamerica . . . and establishing a highly nucleated city that contrasts with Chichén's sprawl." Mayapán's Postclassic art and architecture successfully obscures the identities of individual rulers, as they note, but we believe it is possible to discern links to different political or religious factions in the architectural programs.

When the Cocom took control of the city at the transition point of the Itza may at the end of K'atun 13 Ahau, they began a massive reconstruction of the architecture using dismantled Puuc stones that were reused and covered with stucco (Milbrath and Peraza Lope 2003b:21). They effectively suppressed Xiu traditions and paved the way for a dramatic renovation of the city. The Cocom constructed serpent temples and round temples modeled on those at Chich'en Itzá to inaugurate the K'atun 11 Ahau (1283), the beginning of Itza k'atun cycle or may. This trend gained momentum in K'atun 9 Ahau (1303–1323), when the Cocom faction remodeled Mayapán's principle pyramid as a replica of Chich'en Itzá's Castillo. By 1350, the Cocom had constructed a number of serpent temples and they also invoked Chich'en Itzá's legacy by constructing an observatory modeled on one at Chich'en Itzá. This observatory not only copied architectural forms at Chich'en Itzá but also recreated the cosmic context by repeating many important astronomical alignments. Cocom-Itza revival-style architecture at Mayapán reflects a direct transfer of knowledge and an allusion to the past glory of Chich'en Itzá, a city that had extensive contacts with Central México. The homage to the Itza ancestors reflects a worldview that is quite different from the conservative Puuc traditions of the Xiu, so closely linked with the cult of Chac and cenotes.

By the fifteenth century, Mayapán's trade spanned from Central México south to Belize, signaling their pivotal position in Mesoamerican exchange systems. The Cocom began to transform the city into an international trading center that incorporated foreign artistic styles. Long-distance trade brought an influx of new ideas, but these outside influences had a destabilizing effect. The Xiu revolt against the Cocom and their Canul allies was not only a revolt against the imposition of foreign worldviews but it was also an assertion of the primacy of the Xiu calendar, which proclaimed a power shift at the end of the K'atun 8 Ahau. The Xiu killed virtually all the Cocom nobles and obliterated the religious imagery of the Cocom and their foreign allies by plastering over foreign murals and smashing altars. The Xiu stayed at Mayapán after the revolt, erecting fallen stelae and continuing to make offerings in the Hall of Chac Masks in an effort to reassert the conservative Yucatec Maya worldview.

Discussing the character of revival movements, Masson (2000:250–251) points out that in some cases the precondition is cultural depression or stress, as in the case of the Ghost Dance religion of the Plains Indians. She notes that other forms of revivalism reflect the vitality of the culture, as in the case of the Postclassic province of Chetumal, where local and long-distance trade engendered an affluent and growing settlement. A similar situation appears to be the case in the Cocom revival of earlier Itza traditions, which was conducted from a position of strength, reflecting a true revitalization. In contrast, the Xiu revivals represent a more complex situation. The initial revival of the stela cult probably reflected the power of the Xiu contingent and a revitalization of the Puuc stelae cult, for k'atun monuments were positioned prominently in the Central Plaza. After the stelae were removed, the Xiu power apparently waned. Later, the Xiu revival of the Chac cult in the Cenote Ch'en Mul complex in the mid-fourteenth century seems to coordinate with a time of environmental stress during a major drought. The isolated nature of this construction does not seem to express signs of a true Xiu revitalization. Similarly, after the revolt, the Xiu's efforts to efface the foreign presence and reposition the damaged stelae around the plaza seem to be actions taken under stress, expressing a rather weak attempt to revive Puuc traditions just prior to the complete collapse of the city.

Notes

1. We thank Jeff Karl Kowalski and Travis Stanton for their comments on this chapter. In addition, we thank Pedro Delago Kú and Bárbara Escamilla Ojeda, whose work at Mayapán has been instrumental in developing our interpretations. Colonial orthography has been maintained throughout this chapter.

2. The traditional k'atun cycle used at Mayapán is composed of thirteen numbered k'atuns forming a 256-year cycle. A k'atun-ending date repeats once every 256 years as part of the thirteen-k'atun cycle, or may. The *tun* of 360 days is the basic unit in a k'atun, which consists of twenty tuns, or approximately twenty years.

3. The introduction of Tases phase censers was initially gradual, involving low percentages of Ch'en Mul Modeled effigy censers in middle lots (Milbrath and Peraza Lope 2003b; Smith 1971, 2:table 24). Some middle lots had relatively high percentages, such as Lots C35a, b in the Q97 colonnade (26 percent) and the middle lots associated with the Q77 dance platform (14 percent in Lots C40 and C41; Table 9.1). The dance platform (Q77), representing an early attempt to copy forms developed at Chich'en Itzá, continued to be used during the Tases phase when effigy censers were introduced in ritual activity on the platform (Milbrath and Peraza Lope 2003b).

4. Kukulcan introduced idolatry at Chich'en Itzá, according to the *relaciones* of Yucatán (Garza 1983, 1:182, 306). Masson (2003:197) proposes that effigy censers may have been inspired by a style that spread from earlier traditions from the Gulf Coast or Zapotec areas. On the other hand, the inspiration could have been from Chontal populations in neighboring Tabasco, which produced Terminal Classic braziers with attached modeled figures. Other possible early prototypes include the Terminal Classic Xantile braziers with standing figures found at Cholula, a center for the worship of Quetzalcoatl (McCafferty 2007:222, figure 8.3).

5. Mayapán's serpent-column temples (Q58, Q143, Q159, Q162, Q218) employ Mayapán-style construction techniques, substituting modeled stucco for the carved architectural relief seen in Chich'en Itzá's serpent temples. They all were built on pyramid bases, distinguishing them from temples built on platform bases, such as Q81 and Q95 (Delgado

Kú 2004:143). Serpent columns form the entry to the temple and some also originally had serpent balustrades at the base of the pyramid; all had a statue platform in front and a facing shrine (Proskouriakoff 1962b:100, 111–112, 117–118, 123). A Mayapán oratory (Q82), dating to the epoch of Tases phase effigy censers, also has a serpent balustrade with carved serpent heads (Shook 1954b:265–267).

6. A Postclassic trade ware, Matillas Fine Orange (V Fine Orange), was connected to the spread of Quetzalcoatl's cult at Mayapán, just as Silho Fine Orange and Plumbate were linked with this cult in earlier times (Ringle et al. 1998:216–218). Matillas Fine Orange probably came from the Gulf Coast of Veracruz via the coastal route in the Chontalpa area of eastern Tabasco and western Campeche. It seems likely that Canul traders from Tabasco first introduced Matillas Fine Orange, the only trade ware of any significance in the Postclassic Yucatán (Ringle et al. 1998:218).

7. More than fifty years before the Xiu revolt in K'atun 8 Ahau, the rivalry between Cocom and Xiu erupted in a political upheaval during the K'atun 1 Ahau (1382–1401). The departure of a contingent of Xiu in K'atun 1 Ahau is probably linked to the initial arrival of Canul mercenaries at Mayapán (Roys 1967:141–142n3). This is when the Canuls "afflicted" the people for seven years, eating their food and destroying their crops (Roys 1967:89, 92, 106). There is evidence from mass burials dated by radiocarbon that some violent events took place at Mayapán just prior to 1400 (Peraza Lope et al. 2006). These could be related to the initial influx of Canul mercenaries.

8. The archaeological record in the Mixtequilla area of Veracruz, on the Lower Papaloapan drainage, indicates changes in settlement patterns and material culture associated with two waves of foreign influence, not unlike Mayapán. One is a Mixteca-Puebla component, dating to around 1200–1350, and a second is attributed to the expanding Aztec Triple Alliance, dating from 1350 to 1521 (Curet et al. 1994).

9. Chronicles in the *Chilam Balam of Chumayel* mention the revolt and the abandonment of Mayapán in K'atun 8 Ahau, but they do not specify who led the revolt (Roys 1967:137, 140). Landa and Herrera do not give us a k'atun date for the uprising, but they both tell us that it was the Xiu who destroyed the city (Tozzer 1941:36–37, 216). Although comparative data from Spanish sources and those of the native chronicles do not provide a definitive date for Mayapán's fall, the revolt took place sometime between 1441 and 1461, based on the 8 Ahau date in the traditional k'atun chronology (Edmonson 1982:10; Roys 1967:140; Tozzer 1941:3, 7–38, 230n180). Gaspar Antonio Xiu records that the Tutul-Xiu ruler of Mayapán destroyed the city 260 years after its foundation (Tozzer 1941:230). This suggests that the city was occupied for one k'atun cycle (about 256 years). With thirteen sequential plaza floors, it seems likely that a new floor was paved each k'atun over a period of around 260 years (Milbrath and Peraza Lope 2003b:38; Pugh 2001b). The sequential plaza floors can be related to the sequence of archaeological construction at Mayapán (Table 9.1).

10. The ceramic component associated with this period could be the scattered Post-Tases deposits described by Smith (1971:246–249). K'atun 4 Ahau dates to 1440–1464 in the Ahau-K'atun cycle or 1480–1500 in the traditional k'atun cycle. These dates approximately coincide with a major drought in Yucatán around 1450 (Brenner et al. 2003:figure 4.9). Since droughts often lead to pestilence (Gill 2000:372), the 1450 drought may have triggered the epidemic that finally left the city abandoned.

Religious Resistance and Persistence on Cozumel Island

CHAPTER TEN

Shankari Patel

From the first contact, Spanish explorers compared Maya pilgrimage to Cozumel as similar to what drew pilgrims to Jerusalem, Mecca, and Rome (Tozzer 1941). These ritual procession routes and their end points, oracular shrines, acted as conduits for trade, social and political interaction, and flow of pan-Mesoamerican beliefs and traditions. Within religious studies and geography, pilgrimage is understood as an innately religious process tied to the physical and ideological landscapes of its practitioners. Yet for anthropology and archaeology, pilgrimage continues to be explained in terms of functional models of trade, political domination, and cultural diffusion. Within ancient Maya society, iconographic and archaeological examinations identify pilgrimage constituents as elite men (Kubler 1985) or associates in the militaristic exploits of the cult of Quetzalcoatl (Ringle et al. 1998). What is often overlooked, however, is how pilgrimage was a vehicle for Mesoamerican worldviews embodied by shared artistic traditions of the International style, and one that created spaces of resistance for people of all classes and genders. In this chapter, I examine how pilgrimage practices to Cozumel Island were both a political and religious process responsible for shaping Postclassic and Colonial Maya society.

Pilgrimage Practice and Landscape

Pilgrimage involves traveling to culturally significant locations for an assortment of goals and experiences. Its importance to cultural studies is evident in that pilgrimage draws some of the largest assemblies of humans on earth (Morinis 1992). As a physical, cultural, and religious act, pilgrimage has untold economic, political, and social ramifications for the local community and for a region. Pilgrims embark from known personal space and join with strangers to take part in events that are outside their normal daily routine. According to Jill Dubisch (1995:38–39), aside from the works of Victor Turner, past anthropologists avoided examining pilgrimage because of the challenges involved in studying a phenomenon that violated ideas of a bounded field site. By the mid-1990s, however, postmodern anthropologists began reincorporating it into their work, recognizing the study of pilgrimage as a fertile field for understanding the ever-changing boundaries of a transnational and global world.

Pilgrimage encompasses both the destination and the journey and yet involves an interaction between place and faith. As such, pilgrimage is intricately tied to the landscape and the cultural and social meanings imbued in those landscapes. The association of deities with landscape features characterized the rituals of many polytheistic religions (Green 1996). For example, during the first millennium B.C.E., water ritual directed at healing deities was quite prevalent in ancient Europe. Watery places were numinous locales with rivers serving as the foci for many ritual activities directed toward female deities. Water represented a liminal space and gateway between the earth and the spirit realm. The connection between water and healing was thought to derive from a belief that water represented the life force, with warm springs holding particular curative powers because its self-generated heat resembled the life-giving heat of the sun. Many Romano-Celtic water healing sanctuaries attracted pilgrims who dropped offerings into wells (Green 1996).

Mesoamerican oracles and pilgrimage practices were also tied to the landscape, most commonly caves and cenotes, which received offerings in propitiation of the rain or water deities (Martínez Marín 1972; Turner 1973). The offerings recovered from the Cenote of Sacrifice at Chich'en Itzá provide the best evidence for the ritual importance of cenotes in northern Yucatán (Coggins 1992). In addition to their primacy as water sources for much of Yucatán, cenotes were politically and ritually important to settlement (Ashmore 2004:184). Rulers received their legitimacy and authority from public observances that displayed their connection to mountains, caves, and cenotes (Brady and Ashmore 1999:139). Dominique Rissolo (2003:139) notes that even when water sources found in caves were not critical to maintaining life in the Yalahau region of Quintana Roo, they were still the focus of ritual activity. The Maya of northern Yucatán named their cities after their cenotes. According to Ralph Roys (1935:2), "It was the watering places that were named first and that when towns grew up beside them, they usually retained the original name of the site on which they were founded." Chich'en Itzá corroborates this point for its name translates to "at the mouth of the cave of the Itza." Channing Arnold and Fredrick J. Tabor Frost (1909) witnessed the significance of cenotes in site names on Cozumel.

Intent of finding Precolumbian ruins, they employed a number of resident Maya guides in 1908 to lead them into the interior of the island. When stumbling upon a large group of ruins in the forest, they questioned the Maya as to the name of the site. The explorers remarked that the Maya remembered only the name of the site's cenote (Arnold and Frost 1909:174).

Postclassic Maya Pilgrimage and Oracular Ritual

Although Maya pilgrimage has been recognized as an important component in cultural diffusion, few studies have focused on it as an innately religious experience that was open to all segments of society. William Ringle and colleagues (1998) have argued that pilgrimage's importance was in the spread of the Quetzalcoatl or feathered serpent cult along a pan-Mesoamerican corridor that linked sites from Central México and Oaxaca to the Gulf Coast and Yucatán. "Pilgrimage was also an important activity at these centers. This cult axis apparently continued into the Postclassic period and was responsible for the distribution of the Mixteca-Puebla art style. . . . [W]e suggest that the suppression of personality cults, the prestige use of certain art styles, the de-emphasis of text, and the use of certain common symbols was an intentional strategy used to sustain the 'international' appearance of shrine centers and to facilitate communication with foreign pilgrims" (Ringle et al. 1998:183, 227).

The authors contend that conquest and pilgrimage was responsible for the distribution of the Mixteca-Puebla (International style) art style. Although their model recognizes the importance of pilgrimage in cultural and ideological diffusion, they define it as a militaristic process rather than a religious one. This ignores the experiential components of pilgrimage, particularly as a conduit for the sharing of Mesoamerican worldviews regarding the east, concepts of birth, renewal, and ancestor veneration. Additionally, the authors create a "top-down" model that situates authority and power among the elite. This ignores how pilgrimage and oracular ritual created spaces in which women and non-elites could voice their opinions and overtly resist the state.

To understand the importance of pilgrimage and religious practice in Yucatán, we need to view the region through the experiential lens of cosmological worldviews. For the Maya, east symbolized the direction of birth, renewal, and ancestors. Written accounts of cosmogonies such as the *Popol Vuj* and iconographic evidence from funerary pottery equate the east with rebirth (Miller and Taube 1993). Many cultures including Egyptians thought as the Maya did—each night the sun dies and descends into the west and must travel through the underworld to be reborn the following morning in the east. Similarly, the subsurface waters of Postclassic coastal centers poured into the Caribbean Sea, replicating the sun's passage through the underworld, from death (symbolized by being underground in the west) to rebirth (symbolized by the resurfacing in the east) (Miller 1982:5). This hydraulic process linked the eastern coastal landscape to a pan-Mesoamerican cosmology establishing these sites as both geographical and spiritual outposts (Andrews 1990). As Karl Taube (2006, 2007) notes, murals from Tulum, Tancah, and Santa Rita depict the region as the eastern paradisal realm of the sun and ancestors.

During the Postclassic period, eastern coastal and island sites utilized a pan-Mesoamerican art style originally known as Mixteca-Puebla but later defined as the International style. This art style can be found at many other religious sites in Mesoamerica during the Epiclassic and Postclassic periods. The International style influenced the artistic and religious traditions of the Aztecs. Codices and murals from Puebla, Tlaxcala, and the Mixtec region utilized the style to convey political, genealogical, and religious information (Vaillant 1940). Elements of this style were thought to have originated in Central México or northeastern Oaxaca and then spread to the rest of Mesoamerica through processes of migration (Ekholm 1942:128), diffusion (Nicholson 1960), religious exchange of codices (Robertson 1970; von Winning 1977), deliberate imperial promotion of Aztec traits (Miller 1982; Navarrete 1976, 1996), and the exchange of products and information (Smith and Berdan 2003a). Although labeled a "style" (how images are represented), it is actually an iconography (what images are represented). The common pictorial symbols of this tradition included lunar disks, celestial and terrestrial bands, the Venus or bright star symbol, skulls and skeletons, jade (*chalchihuitl*), water, fire and flame, heart, the war shield (*atl-tlachinolli*), mountain or place, flower, stylized eyes as stars, stepped frets (*xicalcoliuhqui*), sliced spiral shells, and the twenty day signs (*tonalpohualli*) (Nicholson 1982:229).

According to Taube (2007:9), many of the elements depicted in International style art relate to the eastern realm of the Maya. International style representations of solar imagery, plumed serpents, butterflies, and flowers frequently depict the Flower World complex. Jane Hill (1992) described the Flower World complex as a widespread spiritual belief in a solar paradise where the honored dead exist as birds and butterflies. Plumed serpents are also a major component of this complex, not as gods themselves but as conduits for communicating with the ancestors (Taube 2006, 2007:32). This eastern floral paradise was also a solar region inhabited by quetzals and other precious birds. Additionally, the fragrant blossoms of the Flower World symbolized souls as well as the life force of the breath. Flowers are not passive in this art style but rather dynamic passages or vehicles for gods and ancestors who emerge from flower cave-like portals.

Although recent models have alluded to the importance of pilgrimage as the medium by which the International style spread throughout Mesoamerica, they have privileged depictions of Quetzalcoatl/Kukulkan and overlooked iconographic depictions and ethnohistoric descriptions of female deities and rituals. As Anne Pyburn (2004:33) argues, "as with many early states, the visibility of women in ceremonial contexts is not considered evidence of genuine authority, economic control, or political autonomy." There is a great deal of female imagery depicted in the International style from religious codices and from sites in other regions of Mesoamerica to suggest a connection among women, feathered serpents, and the east.

Oracles of the Mixtec and Postclassic Maya of Quintana Roo

But who were the participants and petitioners along these pilgrimage routes? As noted above, previous interpretations of the International style and pilgrimage have argued for an elite point of view. Without question, elites participated in pilgrimage as these were potent sources of political and social legitimacy. Evidence throughout Mesoamerica and South America demonstrates, however, that pilgrimage and oracular shrines were patronized by diverse groups of people. Just as religion has been used to maintain and justify political authority, it also can serve as a medium to express criticism of social injustices. When the Spaniards arrived in the Andes they were not met by what seemed to be a peaceful and tranquil society. To the contrary, competition, rivalries, and factions made up the Andean world (Patterson 1985). No human was allowed to criticize the ruler directly, but objections to his policies could be expressed by his ancestors, speaking through oracle priests, and at temples found throughout the kingdom (Gose 1996). Oracle shrines provided pronouncements that both influenced and contested state politics. Peter Gose (1996:2) states, "The oracular mode was prominent in Inka politics because it allowed the dissemination of information, advice, and dissident opinions without challenging the ruler's supreme authority." Andean oracles were simultaneously linked to the state, but also separate from it. By consulting these oracles, the king in effect sounded the opinions of his subjects, which helped him decide which proposed policies would succeed (Trigger 2003). Evidence suggests that oracles in Mesoamerica may have operated in much the same manner as their Andean counterparts.

John Pohl's analysis of the Mixtec codices provides further evidence of oracle shrines as focal points for the negotiation of factional and political disputes. According to John Pohl (1994:2), the Codex Zouche-Nuttal and Egerton, Codices Bodley and Selden, Codex Vindobonensis, Codex Colombino, and Codices Becker I and II were written for the Postclassic ruling Mixtec class and the practice of documenting the myths, histories, and genealogies of the elite in pictorial manuscripts continued into the Colonial period. The codices portray the histories of how the ruling families came to rule their respective polities and how rulership was passed down to subsequent generations (Boone 2000:87). Despite the preoccupation with depicting lineage and kinship relations, the codices also contained references to the institutionalization of non-kin power groups in the form of the oracular priests associated with the temples at Chalcatongo and Mitla (Pohl 1994:10). In

Puebla and Oaxaca the dissolution of authority at the Classic sites of Teotihuacán and Monte Alban led to fissions within large-scale communities, prompting the creation of political factions (Pohl 1994:109). The Mixtec codices, the Mapas de Cuauhtinchan, and the lienzos of the Coixtlahuaca group document the evidence for the development of "factional alliance corridors" in the early Postclassic that united areas of Puebla and Oaxaca as the elites from one area married the elites from other groups. The oracle shrines of Oaxaca mediated disputes, sanctioned marriages, and answered questions regarding lineage during a period marked by an increase in political factions.

Although Landa contended women did not participate in religious rituals of Maya society, old women were an exception and attended rites on several occasions. In a ceremony that took place during the month of Yaxk'in, a drunken feast commenced where "the devout old woman took with her the means to get drunk at her own house so that she might not lose the feather of her office" (Tozzer 1941:155). Alfred Tozzer (1941:155n820) suspected that the feathers referred to in this passage represented a badge or title of religious office in ancient Maya society. Munro Edmonson (1993:78) found additional evidence for women's religious authority in several colonial texts that mentioned their exclusive participation in both lunar and Venus cult activities.

At the site of Xochitecatl in Tlaxcala, México, archaeologists uncovered a ritual center dedicated to a feminine cult located at the summit of an ancient volcano. This pilgrimage center displayed distinctive International style characteristics. The largest and most imposing pyramid at Xochitecatl is the Pyramid of Flowers located at the eastern end of the ceremonial plaza. This building yielded thirty-two female and infant interments accompanied by offerings and stone figurines of the female form in various stages of the life cycle. Stone monuments depicting skeletal and serpent women were found in the rubble of this pyramid's staircase. At the southern end of the central plaza is a structure known as the Building of the Serpent because of the serpent imagery on top of the platform. Both the Pyramid of Flowers and the Building of the Serpent had large monolithic vats or water holders in front of their main façades, suggesting the importance of water ritual (Serra Puche 2001).

According to the ethnohistoric records, prior to the conquest three important Yucatecan pilgrimage centers—Izamal, Chich'en Itzá, and Cozumel—each housed oracles near prominent landscape features. Chich'en Itzá's oracular power originated from its cenote. Tozzer (1941:182n949) indicated the oracle at Chich'en Itzá's Cenote of Sacrifice prophesized the triumphant reign of Hunac Ceel in the thirteenth century. According to Spanish accounts from the 1520s, old female priestesses residing on eastern islands acted as oracular intermediaries specifically in issues relating to war by delivering favorable or unfavorable pronouncements regarding its outcome (Antochiw and Dachary 1991:205). This gives some indica-

10.1. Seventeen-year-old Lord 8 Deer on pilgrimage performing cave rituals (Bodley, page 9) (courtesy of FAMSI).

10.2. Pilgrimage to the Sun Oracle (Nuttal-Zoche, page 80) (courtesy of FAMSI).

tion that oracle priestesses in the Maya area may have also mediated lineage disputes and received war consultations in much the same way as they did in Oaxaca.

Oracles occupied an important place in the religious and political life of the Mixtecs and Zapotecs. Pilgrimage to cave oracles received attention in several of the Mixtec codices painted in the International style (Figures 10.1 and 10.2). As the cave oracle of Chalcatongo, the elderly priestess Lady 9 Grass (who is depicted with both serpent and skeletal elements) presided over important alliance-building marriages between the kingdoms of the Mixtec. In the Selden, Zouche-Nuttal, Bodley, and Colombino codices she oversaw the ascension of Lord 8 Deer during a time of political turmoil and was regularly consulted regarding issues of war. Although the ethnohistoric records for the Maya area contain references to the importance of pilgrimage and oracles, they lack the rich pictorial record of these shrines that were available for Central México, Puebla, and Oaxaca and have added so much to the understanding of oracles in those regions.

Oracular Resistance at Cozumel

Cozumel, as the easternmost point of the Maya realm, was a significant focus of pilgrimage and oracular practice. Because it is the direction from which the rains and winds originate (Miller and Taube 1993), the east is associated with the paramount concerns of birth and regeneration (Miller 1977:105; Paxton 2001:23). Additionally, it is the direction of the rising sun and moon (Taube 1992) whose prominence is marked in Maya maps that normally place east at the top rather than north (Antochiw 1994:16). Arthur Miller (1977:107) felt that "[b]ecause Ix Chel is goddess of the moon, it makes sense that this astronomical association should be most important on the east coast where the moon rises and appears to be born out of the eastern sea." Cozumel's location within Maya geography established it as an important ideological and religious center. As Merideth Paxton (2001:124) notes, "The geographic position of Cozumel, almost due east of Chich'en Itzá[,] is nearly an exact earthly counterpart to the main locus of east in the Madrid diagram. The focus of the religious pilgrimages from 'all of this kingdom' on the Cozumel shrine of Ix Chel further supports recognition of the island as the primary regional symbol of east." The pilgrimage center in the east at Cozumel was so important that Spanish sources suggest that the *sakbe* system on the mainland was constructed expressly to accommodate religious traffic to the island (Tozzer 1941:109).

Although the Spanish explorers described an oracle shrine on the west coast of Cozumel, the Harvard-Arizona Archaeological Project identified an additional one at San Gervasio (Freidel 1975). Located directly adjacent to this oracle was a significant cenote temple (Freidel and Sabloff 1984:154) (Figure 10.3). Considerable evidence supports the utilization of caves and cenotes for religious activity on Cozumel. For instance, several of the early explorers described altars and structures that were built in, over, or next to caves (Arnold and Frost 1909; Mason 1927). William Davidson (1967) recorded a number of small cave shrines that seem to be situated in relation to water found deeper within the cave. Wyllys Andrews IV (1955–1956:8) also documented a cave/cenote temple at Chen Pita, in the southern portion of the island. The site consisted of two caves, each containing large pools of water. Within the sheltered overhang of the caves a number of fire opals, sourced

10.3. Cenote adjacent to the oracle shrine of San Gervasio (photograph by S. Patel).

to an area hundreds of kilometers away from the island (Phillips 1979:290), were cached under an altar (Figure 10.4).

Several archaeological surveys and projects have recovered religious artifacts from the island's cenotes (Luna Erreguerena 1989) and the Instituto Nacional de Antropología e Historia (INAH) has identified several of the island's caves as serving a ceremonial function (Velázquez Morlet et al. 1988). An underwater archaeological project in the 1980s discovered ceramics and a jade axe dating to the Late Classic period (Delgado 1998:276) within the cenote at Chankanaab (Luna Erreguerena 1989:150), and divers exploring the cenote of Chu-Ha near the airport in 1996 found several intact ceramic vessels. This pattern of building miniature temples and platforms in caves and cenotes on Cozumel also has counterparts at other sites along the east coast (Figure 10.5). The Island Caves Research Center (ICRC) has spent the past twenty years mapping an underwater cave system on Cozumel known as Cueva Quebrada. At a surface opening in this system, approximately 5,000 meters from the west coast entrance, divers discovered pottery, human bones, and a number of other artifacts. As they exited this cave entrance they were surprised to discover a previously unrecorded surface site (Bozanic 1991).

10.4. Chen Pita Cave, Cozumel (Loren M. Hewen Photographic Collection, Middle American Research Institute).

These sites also reference the moon goddess, Ix Chel, who was said to reside in caves and cenotes. As Susan Milbrath (1999:119) explains, "The Yucatec Maya say that the moon disappears into a well during conjunction, implying that it disappears into a watery underworld." Given its eastern position and connection to the goddess Ix Chel, Cozumel was the very embodiment of this underworld, particularly as a venue for women's religious participation. Ethnohistoric sources note that Maya women traveled to Ix Chel's shrine at Cozumel at least once in their lifetimes (Miller 1982; Miller and Taube 1993). Birth imagery adorns the architecture of a number of temples in the region. Sculptures of women kneeling in a birthing position accompanied shrines at Miramar and San Gervasio at Cozumel Island. The abundance of female representations (in the form of sculptures and figurines) found by the Spanish on the island north of Cozumel led them to name it Isla de las Mujeres, or Island of Women. Sculptural, iconographic, and ethnohistoric evidence suggest that women played significant roles both as officiates and participants in the ritual activity of this area. Yet archaeological discussions of pilgrimage and political authority in this region often downplay women's participation. During the Colonial period in particular, women's participation in these practices would have acted as outright resistance to Spanish colonial and patriarchal authority.

10.5. Xcaret Cave Temple (Loren M. Hewen Photographic Collection, Middle American Research Institute).

The colonial literature of Cozumel is dominated by one theme—that the Maya of Cozumel had not, despite the conquistadors' reassurances, adopted Christianity. Although the early conquistadors may have made a display of casting down idols and replacing them with the icons of the Christian faith, the Maya clearly did not see this action as an end to traditional beliefs. A relative of a high-ranking island nobleman had been caught in 1545 worshipping idols and was whipped by Juan de Contreras, the first encomendero of Cozumel. In response to his punishment, the Maya Indian reportedly stated, "I received the baptism, señor, but you did not order me to abandon my old faith; therefore, your punishment is unjust" (Rosado Iturralde 1949:42). The sixteenth-century colonial correspondences to Spain all mention the continuation of indigenous religion on the island. Idols could still be seen in Maya buildings and rumors abounded of ceremonies and sacrifices occurring in the interior of the island under the protection of the dense forest.

Piratical raids for goods and logwood by the British and French on both Cozumel and east coast settlements north of Chetumal Bay made this region a dangerous place to govern at the beginning of the seventeenth century. French pirates attacked Cozumel in 1571, and English pirates raided the island in 1598, 1600, and 1601 (Lothrop 1924:22). In response to the frequent raids many Maya left the island to settle on the mainland in the 1650s (Connors 1983:10). Yet records indicate two villages in existence on Cozumel in 1673 when the villages of Santa Maria and San Miguel acknowledged the *residencia* of interim governor Frutos de Delgado (Roys et al. 1940:10). The island was listed as abandoned at the close of the seventeenth century because maps from the area in 1766 and 1801 register the island as uninhabited (Roys et al. 1940:10). However, there is evidence that the Maya may have continued to utilize Cozumel as a site of resistance since ceramics and artifacts uncovered from a restoration project of several east coast structures in 1979 recovered offerings deposited at these shrines dating from the sixteenth through the eighteenth centuries (Peraza Lope 1996:67).

Religious activity may have persisted on Cozumel even after the Maya resettled on the island in the 1850s. A female statue situated at a cenote in the ruins of the island's Classic period center received offerings up until it was taken in the 1940s to be displayed at the museum in San Miguel. The idol, described as La Xnuc, La Vieja, and La Virgen de Santa Rita, held a special place of veneration among the people of Cozumel and local informants attested the cenote had received patrons for at least fifty years prior to the idol's removal from the site (Escalona Ramos 1946:559–560).

Landscape, oracles, and politics appear to be linked during the Colonial era. If oracles were consulted in times of conflict for their prophecies, then they may have dealt increasingly with Maya resistance to Spanish rule during the Colonial era. Although a number of Maya rebellions were fueled by revelations imparted by charismatic leaders (Bricker 1981; Patch 2002:18), the most successful Maya uprising of Yucatán involved an oracle and the religious revitalization movement that sprung up around it. The Speaking Cross, which played an important role in the Caste War, was initially discovered at a cenote on the mainland (Reed 2001:148).

Discussion and Conclusion

How did pan-Mesoamerican pilgrimage facilitate the diffusion of International style motifs? According to Ringle and colleagues (1998), the International art style transcended political boundaries by spreading into the Maya area during the Epiclassic through the imposition of a messianic and military cult centered on Quetzalcoatl. Although this argument might work for rectifying J. Eric S. Thompson's (1970) ethnohistoric models concerning the conquest of Chich'en Itzá, particularly when the authors (Ringle et al. 1998:226) state that the "Itza is a religious identity," it fails to account for the proliferation of the International art style along the east coast of Yucatán where evidence for military conquest is lacking. In addition, Bruce Love's (2004) examination of the ethnohistoric documents for the gods of Yucatán demonstrates Quetzalcoatl/Kulkukan to be a minor player in the religion of the Maya during the Contact and early Colonial periods. Also recent work with the

San Bartolo murals suggests that the feathered serpent was already established in the Maya area during the Preclassic period and was not the exclusive domain of Quetzalcoatl. Their discussion of pilgrimage is a welcome addition to the Mixteca-Puebla-International art style debate, but it does not correspond to known examples of Mesoamerican pilgrimage, which emphasize political neutrality and base religious authority on landscape associations rather than military might (Morinis 1992).

Pilgrimage to oracle shrines in Postclassic Oaxaca focused on ancestral and earth deities that could be accessed through caves. Yucatecan centers, particularly those along the east coast, had a similar oracular system based on cave/cenote associations that would have seemed familiar to pilgrims from Central México and the Oaxaca region. Andrews (1990:162) notes that coastal sites were associated with themes of birth, death, and the underworld, serving as the edge of geographical and spiritual frontiers. Pilgrimage from the Mixteca-Puebla region to the edge of the eastern Maya realm may have been important enough to the Oaxacan elite to have brought their scribes to record their journeys and to have also brought these shrines gifts of labor, which might explain the presence of Mixteca-Puebla motifs in Yucatán. This ultimately fits into a model of diffusion, so to speak, but it is a diffusion based on pilgrimage and the political significance of oracular ritual rather than one based solely on economics or trade.

Oracular prophesies made up the mechanism through which change was introduced, accepted, and implemented into Postclassic Maya society (Edmonson 1993:73). The Mixtecs and Zapotecs traveling to the Maya area would have found common ground in regards to the utilization of oracular shrines. During the politically fragmented Postclassic period, pilgrimage to these shrines provided a forum for elites to sound alternate political policies and one in which commoners could contest state ideologies. Prophesies linked to sacred sites such as Cozumel gave privileged significance to its pronouncements by linking them to the ancestors residing in an eastern flowery paradise. Pilgrimage and the spread of the International style allowed a greater number of adherents across Mesoamerica access to the ancestral realm. Gender ideologies may have also been one of the many topics contested through oracular channels. If women were the medium through whom protests were formed at Cozumel, then they may have played a central role in the legitimization of kingly power and a prominent role in Postclassic Maya politics and social order.

In this chapter, I have looked at spread of the International style and the consensus that its main motifs refer to religious symbols, specifically motifs belonging to the Flower World complex. I have also examined the political importance of Oaxacan and Yukatekan oracles in the context of pilgrimage during the Postclassic. Although more research is needed to document the nature of pan-Mesoamerican pilgrimage, I hope that I have laid the foundations for future forays into the nature of religious and artistic exchange in Postclassic Mesoamerica.

Changes in Maya Religious Worldview: Liminality and the Archaeological Record

CHAPTER ELEVEN

Diane Z. Chase and Arlen F. Chase

By focusing on Maya ritual symbolism found in the iconography and archaeology of the pre-contact New World, it is possible to isolate elements that significantly changed following the advent of the Spaniards. Among the aspects of Maya religion to be modified following contact were several key components of Maya worldviews—specifically, the symbolism and beliefs relating to life and death. Maya concepts of death were at odds with those stressed by the Catholic Church in the New World, and these indigenous belief systems were affected almost immediately upon contact—so much so that standard ethnohistoric references appear to reflect changes within a generation following the conquest of the Maya by the Spanish. However, other aspects of Maya religion remained or were transformed with less modification.

The changes that occurred in Maya religion are most readily visible when iconographic and archaeological data are compared with historic and ethnographic information. Although both Maya and Spanish cultures believed in some form of upper and lower realms, the implementation of these concepts was quite different in each society. A Maya underworld existed beneath the ground surface and within or beneath bodies of water (especially the sea); Maya underworld symbolism related to watery creatures is common in Preclassic (900 B.C.–A.D. 250), Classic (A.D. 250–A.D.900), and Postclassic (A.D. 900–A.D. 1542) period iconography, as well as in archaeologically recovered caches and burials. However, such watery underworld symbolism is not common in historic or contemporary Maya death ritual, which is instead dominated by considerations and descriptions of Christian-inspired heaven and hell, polar opposites that were at odds with traditional considerations of the Maya afterlife.

The rapidity of the change involved in Maya religious concepts of death contrasts greatly with Maya symbols and belief systems that could be more easily incorporated into Western models. Indeed, certain aspects of contemporary and historic Maya ritual and worldviews appear to have closer ties with an ancient Maya past and can be related to the archaeological and iconographic data. This includes symbolism relating to four directions and the conjoined concept of center (e.g., Coe 1965; Freidel et al. 1993; Pugh 2001b; Rice 2004). The nuanced nature of this syncretism is apparent in considerations of continuity as well as disjunction (Watanabe 1990). Similar functions may also be achieved by different actions and symbols, as is the case with materially distinct Classic and Postclassic period caching practices (D. Chase 1988).

Although religion is generally thought to be a conservative aspect of culture, changes and replacements in Maya concepts of death make sense in the context of the forced religious conversion of the Maya by sixteenth- and seventeenth-century Catholic priests (see also D. Chase and A. Chase 2001). Yet, it makes uncritical consideration of many historic texts, be they written in Spanish or Maya, problematic for two reasons: first, the Maya themselves were sometimes coerced into conforming (at least outwardly) to a new religious paradigm on pain of torture (Clendinnen 1982, 1987; Greenleaf 1994; Tedlock 1993); and, second, priests were actively attempting to identify evidence for prehispanic Christianity (Tozzer 1941:207) and, thus, misrepresented or misunderstood Maya religious symbols, instead translating them into their own frame of reference. Of further concern is the authenticity of Landa's *Relacion de las cosas de Yucatan* (Restall and Chuckiak 2002). Similarly, it is evident that Maya culture and religion also changed from the Contact period to the present day (Chance 1996; Chance and Taylor 1985); at no time were the Maya completely uniform in all aspects of culture. These findings underscore the difficulty in the simple application of analogies derived from contemporary or historic ritual practices to the interpretation of past behavior.

Liminality

Van Gennep employed the concept of liminality in 1907 in order to emphasize the tripartite nature of ritual transitions involved in various rites of passage during an individual's life cycle. Following Arnold Van Gennep (1960), an individual symbolically progressed from one role into a transitional or liminal period until the next role or status was attained. This tripartite division of ritual, specifically as related to mortuary activities, has also been referred to as "rites of separation," "rites of transition," and "rites of re-incorporation" (Metcalf and Huntington 1991; Meyerhoff 1982:116). According to Van Gennep (1960:146), the rites of transition are far more focal and important in funeral customs that either the rites of separation or re-incorporation.

Victor Turner (1969, 1974) expanded van Gennep's concept of liminality from a transitory stage to something more—particularly existing in either people or phenomenon charged with mystery, sacrality, and power. Barbara Meyerhoff (1982:117) points out that this enduring "liminal" category can include "tricksters, clowns, poets, shamans, court jesters, monks, 'dharma bums,' holy mendicants," and even "social movements" or "social principles"; symbols associated with liminality emphasize "innocence, rebirth, vulnerability, fertility, change, emotion, paradox, disorder, anomaly, opposition, and the like." The liminal person stands for "equality, undifferentiated humanness, androgyny, and humility" and exists in stark contrast to "social structure with its emphasis on differentiation, hierarchy, and separation" (Meyerhoff 1982:117).

It is argued here that pre-contact Maya ritual incorporated liminality—not solely as a stage in rites of passage but also as a transcendent state of being—and that this liminality was a critical feature in the ritual integration of community and cosmos. As will be described below, formal Maya iconographic portrayals of the Classic and Postclassic period depict transcendent subjects and events; this focus on liminality helps explicate Maya worldviews. We have expanded on Turner's (1969, 1974) concepts of liminality rather than focusing on "border" individuals and concepts (e.g., Weber 1995) because most of the Maya images present figures central to their society and, presumably, not the multi-cultural, imperialist, and post-colonial situations that are so applicable to modern "border" analysis.

Pre-Contact and Post-Contact Maya Worldview

There were basic differences between most Contact period Maya and Catholic worldviews related to life and death. Ancient Maya belief systems focused on transitions, liminality, and co-essences, as well as on portals or thresholds for movement among existences. Thus, a jaguar *way* could have a coeval existence and provide support to mortal Maya rulers, as can be seen in a wooden lintel from Late Classic Tikal, Guatemala (Figure 11.1). Caves located on the surface of the earth allowed passage to an underworld (Bassie-Sweet 1996). Chol myth had the sun—itself transcendent—descending into and rising out of the underworld through a cave that was protected by the jaguar at night and the deer during the day; a ceramic vessel from Early Classic Santa Rita Corozal, Belize, portrays this exact dyad in a mortuary context (D. Chase and A. Chase 2005:124). Catholicism, in contrast, maintained more clear-cut polarity and oppositions. This is most apparent in the disjunctions between heaven and hell—reachable only after death—and their associations with good and evil. Thus, conversion to Catholicism took place in conjunction with modification of traditional Maya concepts relating to life, death, and

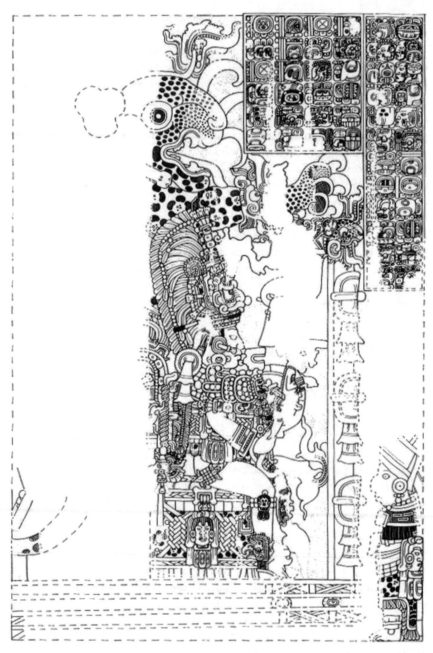

II.I. Carved wooden lintel from Temple 1 at Tikal portraying a jaguar protector or way above and behind a Late Classic ruler (after Jones and Satterthwaite 1982; used with permission from author).

afterlife. However, some aspects of Catholicism—particularly those that more easily were incorporated into Maya worldviews—were readily adopted and modified by the Maya to fit their own concepts. Specific examples include the Holy Trinity, with its co-essences, and the liminal All Souls' Day, now transformed into the popular Day of the Dead (Garciagodoy 1998). Other aspects of the Maya worldviews that were on the surface more similar to the European worldviews were retained with less modification. Thus, the Maya focus on four directions and a center was easily reconciled with European directionality and with the standard Spanish town plan focused on a central plaza (Lowe 1995), regardless of whether or not the Maya directional symbolism equated with cardinal directions (Coe and Van Stone 2001:123–124; Mathews and Garber 2004; Watanabe 1990).

Our conception of ancient Maya religion and beliefs derives from many different sources: history, archaeology, ethnography, hieroglyphs, iconography, and comparisons to other Mesoamerican cultures—especially the Aztec. Although J. Eric S. Thompson (1970:336–337) commented that "archaeological evidence for the cosmological beliefs of the Maya is not plentiful," within the last two decades these varying threads of data have been woven into conceptions of a Maya otherworld that is both watery and beneath the world of living humans (D. Chase and A. Chase 1989; Freidel et al. 1993; Miller and Taube 1993). Aspects of the pre-contact Maya underworld may be confused due to the use of imagery found on many forged and repainted vases (e.g., Robicsek and Hales 1981) and/or to the use of historic highland Maya texts to describe pre-contact lowland Maya beliefs and iconography. Although some unprovenienced materials present imagery of a Maya underworld that is found in post-contact texts like the *Popul Vuj*, these same images are unusual in materials recovered from the actual archaeological record. For example, Linda Schele and Mary Miller (1986:267) note that the underworld or "Xibalba of the Classic period . . . was a watery world that could be entered by sinking beneath water or by passing through a maw in the surface of the earth," but they also followed the ethnohistoric description of Xibalba found in the *Popul Vuj* in seeing the underworld's "primary characteristic" as "the stench of decaying corpses and rotting blood," a description potentially attributable to post-conquest influences.

As reconstructed, the ancient Maya view of the world contained three planes of existence: the earth's surface on which humans interacted; an underworld ruled by nine lords and possibly represented by five levels; and an upperworld with thirteen deities and seven levels. It is assumed that the levels corresponded with the daily stages in the passage of the sun (Thompson 1970:280–282). Four *bacabs* held up the sky (Thompson 1970:276–277), potentially escaping the last world destruction on the back of sea turtles (Figure 11.2; D. Chase and A. Chase 1998). The world on the earth's surface was one where at least some individuals had companion spirits; in ethnographic literature (Carlsen and Prechtel 1991) these souls could also regenerate. In spite of a sometimes rich and varied portraiture

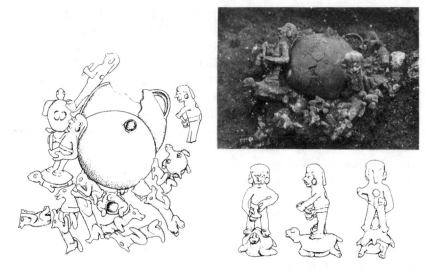

II.2. Late Postclassic ceramic figurine cache set in the fill of Santa Rita Corozal Structure 213 (see D. Chase and A. Chase 1988:48–51 for further information). Cache consists of three sets each of four animals plus four bacabs performing automutilation astride sea turtles. Another two sets each of four animals plus a human figure seated on a stool blowing a conch shell was located within the urn surrounded by the bacabs. The interior stool covered a quincunx arrangement of four shells with a central piece of jadeite. This figurine cache represents a Maya world creation myth and also demonstrates how the bacabs, who hold up the Maya sky, escaped the flood that destroyed the last world.

of the ancient Maya, it is difficult to pin down more specific Maya beliefs about life and death because detailed information about Contact period Maya religion and worldviews and its subsequent modifications, such as that documented for the Aztec by Fray Bernardino de Sahagún (1950–1982) and other writers, does not exist. Some academic interpretations of Maya belief systems are based on Aztec data (see Thompson 1970), whereas other interpretations are based on ethnohistoric documents that may already have been influenced by religious conversion (Clendinnen 1982, 1987; Greenleaf 1994; Tedlock 1993) or whose authorship is in question (Restall and Chuckiak 2002). Thus, although the nine lords of the night (or underworld) may have confirmation in glyphic texts naming the *B'olon ti' K'uh* (Montgomery 2002:89–93), in architectural complexes like the "twin-temple" complexes of Tikal (Harrison 1999; Jones 1969), and in physical sculptures that were once set in buildings at Palenque and Yaxchilán (Tate 1992:234), the thirteen levels of the above-world are assumed rather than proved by Maya data. Indeed, some researchers record the existence of only seven upper levels for the Yukatek

Maya (Tozzer 1941:132). That the Maya world existed in three planes, however, can be inferred from iconography, such as the registers in the Postclassic murals of Tulum (Miller 1982) and Santa Rita Corozal (Gann 1900), where the lowest plane always contains watery images.

Classic period stelae often depict three registers. A ruler generally occupies the middle register. He frequently stands on an earth (or *cauac*) monster, representing a portal to the underworld. A cosmic serpent often defines an upper level. Such a tripartite division is also in evidence on Postclassic murals where sea creatures are represented in the lower register and in the upper register celestial serpents can be represented either by a symbolic eye or presented in full body form (see Miller 1982:plates 28 and 40). In the Santa Rita Corozal murals (Gann 1900), darts and knives penetrate the surface, represented by the body of a serpent, perhaps indicative of the warrior's heaven described in Aztec documents (e.g., Thompson 1970)—for such knives are found in the upper register of other Postclassic murals at Tulum (Miller 1982:plate 39). In the middle register of the Santa Rita and Tulum murals, human agents mingled with deities on the surface of the earth. Miller (1982:91) notes that these scenes "are neither the world of the living nor the world of the dead, but is rather a liminal condition in between." Entrance into the underworld is pictured by intertwined snakes and by representations of caves (Miller 1982:plate 37). Postclassic mural iconography thus defines the three major layers of the Maya universe and implies that entry into the different levels is possible through portals (such as cauac monsters) and through sacrifice (as indicated by spears and flint knifes).

It is apparent from iconographic representations in murals, stucco friezes, other architectural embellishment, and archaeologically excavated materials that there were ways to penetrate the underworld using portals during both the Classic and Postclassic periods. These portals could be large or small; some were more symbolic than actual. Cauac or earth monsters symbolized the entry into the underworld during the Classic period. Rulers stood on these figures. Complete buildings were decorated as these entities. The gaping mouths of cauac monsters permitted individuals to symbolically enter this level, but it is also evident that cauac monsters literally swallowed the dead, thus bringing them into the underworld. This is physically evident in human skeletal remains encountered within a basal stair mask in Structure B20 at Caracol (D. Chase and A. Chase 1998) and in iconographic representations at Tikal (Miller 1986:41). Doorways framed by open-mouthed creatures indicate that temples could serve a similar purpose. Burials and tombs were carved into the underworld to place the dead, similarly penetrating the underworld; Stephen Houston (1998) has suggested that painted rectangles on tomb walls represented symbolic doors. Formal entranceways to tombs at sites like Caracol and Palenque provided the means to enter and re-enter tombs and the underworld (D. Chase and A. Chase 2003), a phenomenon also noted for Copán (Sharer and Traxler 2003).

Caches served a similar purpose in connecting levels. They could include the simple remains of sacrifice and offerings, sometimes including obsidian or chert blades, but also the physical depiction of deity images often occurred. Maya caches can be extremely complex and exhibit multiple components, providing great insight into Maya cosmology and to changes within their worldviews (D. Chase and A. Chase 1998). Key symbolic aspects of these caches are directionality, layering, and regeneration.

Caches from Classic period contexts at Caracol and Santa Rita Corozal, Belize, have been the subject of substantial previous analysis (D. Chase 1988; D. Chase and A. Chase 1998). Caches have been interpreted as community-centering mechanisms for both the Preclassic and Classic period Maya, largely because they frequently incorporate four examples of a particular object located toward four different sides or directions. Contents include natural objects such as shells or jadeite as well as organic remains like seeds and pine needles (if preserved). Human creations placed in caches include pyrite mirrors and mosaic figures in the Classic period; in the Postclassic period, gold and modeled ceramic figures and figurines were added to the repertoire. Frequently, a central object representing zenith and/or nadir was added to a cache. In the Preclassic and Classic periods, this could be a single green jadeite earflare (D. Chase 1988; A. Chase and D. Chase 1985; D. Chase and A. Chase 1998) or a jadeite mosaic figure (Moholy-Nagy 2006). In the Postclassic period, this could be a central figurine or a diving figure, clearly transitional from an upper level into a lower level (D. Chase 1985b), as is indicated on one of the Tulum murals (Miller 1982:plate 28).

Significantly, items included in Preclassic and Classic period caches at both Caracol and Santa Rita Corozal include underwater symbolism represented by stingray spines, sharks' teeth, coral, and seashells. The Postclassic period caches at Santa Rita Corozal are iconographically clearer as to meaning than their Classic era counterparts. Many of these Postclassic caches likewise contain explicit underworld symbolism represented by modeled ceramic figures of turtles, sharks, crocodiles, and cauac or earth monsters. However, items incorporated may also include a mixture of all three basic world levels, further supporting the role of caches as portals.

Lowland Maya cache contents can be extremely complex. Many caches are in fact layered (D. Chase 1988; Mathews and Garber 2004). A lower level generally consists of pyrite mirrors, green malachite pebbles, and even liquid mercury. The middle level generally consists of a fairly standard set of artifacts, such as "Charlie Chaplins," sea shells, and jadeite or obsidian (e.g., A. Chase and D. Chase 2005). These artifacts are often spatially arranged to emphasize four directions and a center; this arrangement sometimes is even found in termination rites on the floor of an abandoned building (Taschek and Ball 1999). An upper level may have consisted of perishable items. In one case at Caracol, this upper level was represented by a beehive (D. Chase 1988); in another, above-world and underworld deities are counterposed on the interior lid and interior base of a barrel cache (A. Chase and D. Chase 1987b:47).

Similar layering and directionality is sometimes in evidence in tombs. Painted red lines define doors and also break tomb space into multiple levels (e.g., Houston 1998). At Rio Azul, a painted deity figure and earth monster portrait extend from a tomb's ceiling (Adams 1986:438). In one Rio Azul tomb, hieroglyphs, interpreted as representing the four directions, are correctly painted on the four walls of the chamber (Graham 1986:456), further linking the sun with east, darkness with west, Venus with "south," and the moon with "north." Also present in this chamber are four glyphs painted in the corners representing interstitial directions and perhaps suggesting that the Maya utilized geomancy (e.g., Carlson 1981).

Some scholars do not see the Maya as having used true directionality, preferring to see the four directional glyphs as representing quadrants of the sun's position relative to the earth (e.g., Mathews and Garber 2004; Wantanabe 1990) or solstices (Coe and Van Stone 2001:123–124), but the repetition and standardization of four elements in caches and their overt association with directionality makes a strong case for the significance of geographic directions in Maya worldviews.

Although Postclassic period cache contents and placement may include four-part symbolism, much like their Classic period counterparts, Postclassic caches were likely related to calendric ritual, as has been established by comparing contents and contexts with ethnohistoric descriptions and Contact period codices (D. Chase 1985a, 1985b). An emphasis on the four corners and the center of a community is found in Postclassic rituals (Coe 1965). Many Postclassic caches exhibit a similar directionality tied to quadrants and a center. Four figures can be arranged around a central figure; in one case at Santa Rita Corozal, the central figure was seated on a bench, under which was a small jadeite piece with four small shells forming a quadrant about it (D. Chase and A. Chase 1988:51). This quincunx pattern shows great antiquity and significance in Maya cosmology (e.g., Mathews and Garber 2004). There is also a Postclassic focus on caches associated with the five *wayeb'* days at Santa Rita Corozal. These ritual deposits show some indications of distinct spatial locations at the site and may further be correlated with rituals that are described in Landa (Tozzer 1941) and are painted in Maya codices, linking archaeology to ethnohistory (D. Chase 1985a).

Besides archaeologically recovered caches, Classic period iconography, such as that found on stucco building friezes at Caracol (Figure 11.3), contains "underworld" and potentially transitional symbolism in fish nibbling on water lilies (something that can only physically occur at the transition between water and air) and in ancestral figures resting atop earth monsters, as opposed to being within the underworld itself. Classic period Maya burials, especially those of the elite, frequently incorporate symbols that are often interpreted as underworld or underwater metaphors explicitly through the inclusion of seashells, crocodile or turtle

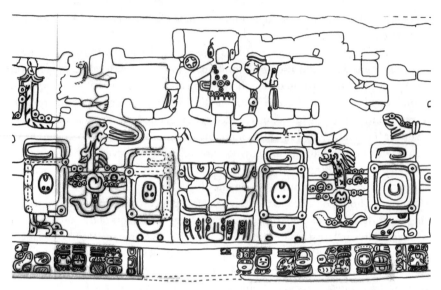

II.3. Late Classic stucco building frieze from Caracol Structure B16-2nd. Frieze is approximately two meters in height. Liminal Caracol personages are portrayed seated on earth monsters amongst fish nibbling on water lilies. The hieroglyphic text records information relative to at least two Caracol rulers and dates to after A.D. 680.

bones, and stingray spines, as well as metaphorically through painted portals and "planes" in chambers (Houston 1998). Rebirth symbolism may also be present in depictions on offerings; this specifically occurs in the inclusion of the potentially liminal old God N emerging from a seashell on some Maya burial vessels (Figure 11.4). The presence of sky creatures, such as birds, along with underworld or underwater creatures and green jadeite (representing the zenith) in many elite burials (e.g., Teeter and Chase 2004) also is consistent with the tomb as a portal and liminal arena.

In contrast to archaeological and iconographic data, historic and contemporary rituals infrequently mention underwater creatures as aspects of the underworld (see Gossen 2002). In Chan Kom and other Maya communities, ceremonies are conducted related to the four corners of town and the four corners of fields (Redfield and Villa Rojas 1962; Vogt 1993 [1976]). However, the actual offerings and timing for these offerings are different from their preceding counterparts. Early historic descriptions, such as those by Landa, rarely mention underworld sea creatures—already suggesting the blurring between Christian and Maya symbols and conceptions of heaven and hell, at least in the minds of Spanish priests (Tozzer 1941:132n616, 207n1154). But, these descriptions do mention other symbols or

II.4. A carved stone vessel included within an Early Classic tomb from Santa Rita Corozal with two representations of the old God N emerging from a seashell, symbolizing rebirth (see D. Chase and A. Chase 2005:119 for more detail; height = 8 cm).

metaphors related to rain and agricultural fertility that may appear to have been less directly affected by conversion. It is evident that the Maya were active participants in their own acculturation—they accepted, rejected, and modified Catholic symbols and provided their own interpretation of Christianity (Carmack et al. 1996:162–172; Chance 1996; Madsen 1967:384). However, conversion to Catholicism was not possible with traditional beliefs regarding life and death intact.

The Liminal Maya

As noted above, a number of scholars (such as Metcalf and Huntington [1991], Turner [1969], and Van Gennep [1960]) have focused on the liminal aspects of beliefs and rituals surrounding human lifespan transitions—and especially the liminal aspects of death and funerary ritual. Liminality, although inclusive of thresholds, entrances, and portals, specifically focuses on the transition of humans with regard to important life events. Death ritual provides perhaps the clearest example of liminality. In many cultures, an individual's existence continues beyond physiological death. They may no longer breathe and their hearts may not pump blood through their bodies, but they are not yet gone. Their souls or essences survive. Sometimes these liminal beings continue both to inhabit the world of the living for a substantial period of time and to have an impact on the day-to-day lives of their family members. Conversely, living beings could also occupy liminal realms, as may happen in near-death situations. It has been argued that liminality was an important aspect of at least some ancient Maya funerary rituals allowing transition from the world of the living to the underworld (Freidel et al. 1993). Multiple individual interments with disarticulated human remains at Caracol have been used to suggest the existence of double funerals that reflected a period of liminal existence before final interment (D. Chase and A. Chase 2004b).

The use of underworld and above-world symbolic metaphor by the ancient Maya is consistent with worldviews that join the worlds of the living and the dead in a constant cycle of rebirth. Whether pre-contact Maya religion was "world-rejecting" or whether it was "world-maintaining" (Bellah 1964) is an important, but difficult and potentially unanswerable, question. The Catholicism of the Spanish explorers maintained that the next world was a different and better place (thus termed as a "world-rejecting" religion), but it is not clear that the same can be said for that of the pre-contact Maya. The Maya, instead, conceived of a world that was a conjoined multiple-level cosmos.

Thompson (1970:300–304) combined ethnographic and ethnohistoric sources from highland and lowland Maya peoples to reconstruct an ancient Maya view of death, suggesting that the lowest level of the underworld was called Metnal or Xibalba and that access to the underworld was gained by a long journey that included crossing a body of water with the aid of dogs. It appears from these descriptions that the dead also passed through a cycle of rebirth much like that of the daily path of the sun, first moving into the underworld and then ending up in the heavens. Parts of this reconstruction are obviously influenced by post-conquest Christianity, but some of this scenario is likely to be pre-contact in origin.

There are potentially world-rejecting aspects of other Western Hemisphere religious systems in the "willing" sacrifices of Mesoamerican peoples, especially as described for the Aztec (Evans 2004:503–506). Whether this attribution is appropriate for the Maya is unknown. However, even in Central México, archaeological evidence indicates that earlier sacrificial victims at Teotihuacán were bound, indicating that they did not go to death "willingly" (Cabrera et al. 1991). Maya sacrifice was likely tied to both worldly and otherworldly ends (e.g., Demarest 1984; Schele 1984) and can be particularly tied to warfare and politics (A. Chase et al. 1991; Webster 2000). Perhaps supporting the idea of a single-cosmos, as opposed to world-rejecting, philosophy is the potential of certain liminal creatures—such as celestial serpents, cauac monsters, dwarfs, and even the sun itself—to exist in more than one plane and the ability of non-liminal beings to use portals, actions, or implements to accomplish a similar transgression. If Maya worldview is this-worldly or world-maintaining and focused on a single, yet multi-level, cosmos, the focus on liminal metaphor and the distinction with world-rejecting Christian views of life and death is further amplified.

Maya iconography contains numerous examples of the comingling of upper, middle, and lower world creatures and images. Individuals carved on stone monuments openly employed symbols that indicated their existence betwixt two worlds (such as fish nibbling on water lilies or snakes that operate both in and out of the earth [see Figure 11.5]). Other examples of liminality include birds, like herons, that

II.5. Late Classic carved stone Stela 7 from Machaquila, Guatemala (Graham 1967:fig. 57; courtesy MARI, Tulane University). The ruler's headdress exhibits both a sky serpent and a fish nibbling on a water lily. The ruler also stands on a watery cave (Bassie-Sweet 1996:71).

are comfortable in both air and water and dwarfs who are capable of going from the world of the living to the world of the dead (A. Chase and D. Chase 1994). The images and hieroglyphs are also ripe with fertility symbols related to both corn and to scattering (e.g., Schele and Miller 1986; Thompson 1970). Thus, Classic Maya worldviews appear to have centered on rulers, who apparently could exist in multiple levels, margins, and worlds. The androgyny of some of the carved portrayals of these rulers has led to extended discussion over whether or not the individuals portrayed were male or female (e.g., Joyce 2000). Much of the existing portraiture of these rulers depicts them in a transitional state.

It has long been known that the Maya used metaphor to draw connections among things. The ceiba was seen as a world tree—with its roots in the ground but yet having branches in the sky. Thus, it has been viewed as a portal between the upper and lower worlds (e.g., Freidel et al. 1993). It is

11.6. Stela 18 from Caracol, Belize, depicting a larger-than-life serpent rearing above a bound captive (from A. Chase and D. Chase 1987a:8).

also evident that the Maya symbolically represented transitional thresholds—caves were portals to the underworld and temple doorways represented entrances into symbolic earth monster (or *witz*) entities rising through the ground surface. That the individuals carved on stone stelae and altars were transitional is sometimes explicitly shown. One stela at Caracol directly substitutes an up-ended vision serpent rearing above a bound captive for what should have been a human (Figure 11.6). An altar from Guatemala (Figure 11.7), which would have been paired with a stela depicting an individual, portrays the conjunction of rulership (in the form of mat symbols) with the underworld (referenced in the central image of the "7 black-yellow place"; Freidel et al. 1993) and with centrality (in the form of the quadripartite organization of the image). Recognizing this intentional Maya focus on liminal, or transitional, metaphors provides an even greater perspective to their ancient worldviews.

Many Maya symbols, such as world trees, maize, jaguars, and caves, exist in more than one place or "plane" at the same time. They not only connect the underworld, the world of living humans, and the above-world but they are themselves transitional co-essences, existing not in one place but in two or more at the same time (Figure 11.8). Thus, the jaguar is not only guardian of the night and entrances to caves (portals to the underworld) but also is an animal

II.7. Altar 1 from Zacpetén, Guatemala, illustrating a quincunx pattern of hieroglyphs interspersed with elite mat symbols; the central element portrays a mythological place in the Maya underworld (after Rice 2004:161; used with permission from author). The altar, which probably once was paired with a stela, would have served to reaffirm the liminal aspects of Maya rulership.

that is usually seen at twilight and in the early morning hours—physically times of transition between day and night. The way—often jaguars themselves (Grube and Nahm 1994)—may be creatures from the world of the ancestors (Calvin 1997) or contemporary animal souls existing apart from their human companions but with fates intimately conjoined (Gossen 1975). The known Classic period depictions of way on lintels located in the thresholds or doorways of major temples at Tikal (Coe and Shook 1961; Figure 11.1) and on pottery included as funerary offerings (Adams 1963) reinforce their metaphorical coexistence in the Maya world. Other common symbols include crocodiles and turtles. Both may be found in the water and on land, but in addition, both are often seen at the surface of the water—above and below at the same time. At Tikal, the exact center of the Classic period site is

II.8. Ceramic vessel from Uaxactún, Guatemala, showing a dead individual descending into the underworld (from Smith 1934). A serpent forms the transitory earth surface, and two liminal jaguars and a liminal human are also portrayed. It is suspected that the imagery relates to lost mythology.

ritually delineated through the physical caching of crocodiles on the four sides of a sacred space (D. Chase and A. Chase 1998:326).

Other symbols that may initially be assumed to indicate single contexts only also may metaphorically refer to transitions. Sharks, for example, are represented in their entirety as ceramic cache figures in the Postclassic period and symbolically by teeth only in Preclassic and Classic period caches. Although sharks require water to survive, they also are liminal or transitional figures. Their single back fins break the surface of the water, extending into the air. Snakes exist on the ground yet also crawl into the earth or onto trees in the sky; their existence in three planes is explicitly

11.9. A ceramic diving figure placed in a Late Postclassic cache from Santa Rita Corozal Structure 37; the stuccoed and post-fire painted figure exhibits a combination of maize and earth monster attributes (see also D. Chase and A. Chase 1988:39).

acknowledged through the iconographic portrayal of the Maya "vision serpent" (Schele 1989; see also Figure 11.6). Fish nibbling on water lilies are often assumed to be a symbol of rulership; however, the action itself only takes place at the surface of the water—the transitional location between water and air. Deceased rulers are depicted in canoes at Tikal, at one point floating on the surface of the water but ultimately sinking below it (Coggins 1975; Schele and Miller 1986). Some caches may be liminal in exhibiting symbols of more than one realm (underworld, above-world, and human level) or in portraying figures that combine the imagery of humans and deities (Figure 11.9). Analyzing Maya deities is difficult because they did not have single discrete identities; Eva Hunt (1977:55–56) defines Maya religion as pantheistic, "neither polytheistic nor monotheistic," with multiple and fluidly changing aspects of deities that could be combined and merged.

If one views ancient Maya worldviews with regard to death and afterlife from the perspective of liminality, other aspects of ancient Maya culture become clearer. Interment of ancestors within still-functional residential plazuela groups (and contrary to Landa's [Tozzer 1941] assertions relating to household abandonment at the time of death, statements possibly formulated in conformance with Christian thought relative to cemeteries) reinforces the coexistence of the deceased and the living. Tombs with entranceways or psychoducts are necessary thresholds for the deceased, providing both access to the world of the living and passage to the underworld. Interments containing multiple individuals and disarticulated human remains in interments belie the unity of the family group in life and death—as well as the possibility of second funerals to signal the disjunction between biological and spiritual death (D. Chase and A. Chase 2003). Reentry into chambers by either descendants or liminal creatures like dwarfs to gain relics or disinter ancestors reflects the ability of the living to interact with the dead (A. Chase and D. Chase 1994) or with other transcendent and/or liminal beings.

Conclusion

Certain aspects of Classic and Postclassic Maya beliefs and practices continued into early historic and contemporary ritual; however, others changed dramatically after Spanish contact. Continuity is perhaps most apparent in those aspects of Maya belief that were compatible with or adaptable to European thought and Catholicism. Threads of continuity are apparent in the use of four directions conjoined with centering and a focus on contemporary agricultural and community rituals (Madsen 1967). As has been aptly noted, syncretism also occurred; because of this, continuities and discontinuities are often difficult to discern (Watanabe 1990). All Souls' Day took on a new significance in the New World context where ancestors are liminal creatures who can impact the lives of their descendants and who must be supplicated to avoid calamity (Garciagodoy 1998). Community-focused ritual is a key element of both pre- and post-contact Maya society; however, contexts varied. Caching and burial practices conjoined the community in shared identity and family-centered ritual in Classic period Caracol (D. Chase and A. Chase 2004a). Late Postclassic Santa Rita Corozal community integration was achieved through a ritual cycle that involved cache and censer deposition (D. Chase 1985a). Contemporary Maya communities achieve similar integration through *cofradías* (Cancian 1965; Chance and Taylor 1985; Watanabe 1995).

Key elements of ancient Maya worldviews were changed dramatically with Spanish contact and conversion to Catholicism. Specifically, conceptions of death and the afterlife became markedly altered. Many metaphors—such as those focusing on a watery underworld—appear to have dropped out of the symbolic repertoire shortly after contact. Once key portals to the Maya underworld, earth monsters became equated with Ladino Earth Lord plantation owners (Watanabe 1990). However, conjoined concepts of co-essences and companion souls were retained, as was the conception of the cyclical nature of life and death.

Archaeological data provide clear clues to the continuity and discontinuity of Maya culture—beyond simple changes in artifact or architectural styles. These data draw into sharp focus the changes in Maya ritual symbolism that accompanied sixteenth- and seventeenth-century culture contact, as well as the varied acceptance of Christian beliefs and symbolism. This analysis indicates the importance of considering pre-contact metaphor as inherently focused on transitions, liminality, thresholds, and co-essences. For the most part, the ancient Maya maintained a "this-worldly" religious tradition. Maya cosmology was based on a conception of regenerative cycles that ranged from daily passage of the sun to human life and death to the long-term passage of time. Liminal metaphor was used as a means to integrate the living and the dead, the community, and the cosmos within an interconnected and constantly cycling reality. Contextual analysis underscores the difficulty both in analyzing ancient Maya ritual and in assuming that analogies derived from contemporary or even historically recorded ritual practices can be used directly to interpret past behavior without cautious review and testing with pre-contact archaeological data.

Acknowledgements. Investigations at Santa Rita Corozal and Caracol, Belize, have been supported by a series of grants from the National Science Foundation, the Ahau Foundation, the Stans Foundation, the Harry Frank Guggenheim Foundation, FAMSI, U.S. AID, the government of Belize, and donations from private sources. Work at these sites has been greatly aided by thirty years of collaboration with the Belize Department of Archaeology (now the Institute of Archaeology). Sincere thanks are given to John Watanabe, who provided a detailed critique of an earlier draft of this chapter. Any errors in interpretation, however, are the sole responsibilities of the authors.

CHAPTER TWELVE

Leslie G. Cecil

> With worldview analysis comes symbolic analysis, for ideas need
> symbols to gain a grip on the world, and so stimulate action. It is no
> coincidence that between doctrine and ethical practice lies myth;
> for the stories which give us identity and a sense of direction also
> contain a strong infusion of symbolic elements.
>
> (SMART 1995:30)

Tipu is the easternmost Postclassic archaeological site associated with
the central Petén lakes region and was occupied from the Preclassic to
the Historic period (Figure 12.1). Ethnohistorical and archaeological
data suggest that Tipu is located within Kowoj territory; however,
individuals at Tipu may also have had ties to the Itza socio-political
group and/or the Dzuluinicob region in Belize (a province in Belize
that ran from the Northern River Lagoon to the Macal River including the towns of Lamanai and Tipu) throughout the Postclassic
period (Jones 1989, 1998). Many Spanish documents produced from
the period of conquest and conversion concerning Tipu note the
presence of the Itza. For example, Pérez's 1655 *matricula* noted that
some citizens at Tipu had compound names that were associated with
those of the Itza Kan royal matronyms as well as surnames, relating
themselves to descendants from Cozumel (Jones 1998:54–55; 2005).
Although Spanish documents indicate the presence of Itza at Tipu
during the mid-seventeenth century, the ritual architecture and pottery at Postclassic Complex I suggest a different interpretation—the
presence of the Kowoj.

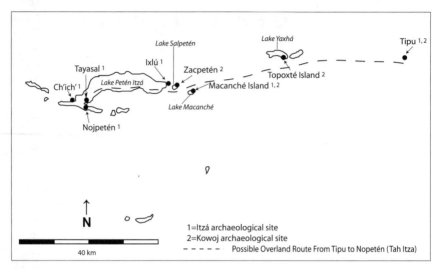

I2.I. Map of Postclassic archaeological sites in the central Petén lakes region and the possible corridor between Tipu and Nojpeten (Tah Itza) (redrawn from Jones 1989: map 2).

In order to better understand the competing worldviews at Tipu, one must look to the indigenous culture's material remains because it is here that social/political groups could consciously attach "authentic signs of true identity" (Upton 1996:5), such as their ancestral history, especially during times of socio-political instability (Cecil 2001; Smart 1995). Material culture can be viewed as a manifestation of a group's worldviews because a set of symbols (viewed by the archaeologists as technological patterns and/or iconography) demonstrates the practice and understanding of myths, histories, and national identities through ritual (Connerton 1989; Smart 1995:78–90). Rituals can include sacrifices to gods, the construction of buildings for ritual activities, the termination of ceramic vessels (such as effigy *incensarios*), as well as the manufacture of pottery used in ritual activities. By examining the stylistic and technological/behavioral attributes of pottery manufacture, one can elucidate different patterns that may be embedded in the culture that are a result of myth, history, and worldview. Therefore, a study of technological style based on pottery found at Tipu and other archaeological sites in the Kowoj territory of the central Petén lakes region provides a means to understand Kowoj traditions and worldviews at a place where multiple worldviews and identities clashed.

Pottery manufacture is a social activity that involves choices at many levels (resource procurement, formation, and decoration), and at some point in the potter's personal history, the manufacturing processes may become an established set of "rules" that result from subconscious knowledge (Glassie 1975; Leone 1984).

Therefore, when creating material culture, such as pottery, the producer may have many choices (operational sequences) to make that reflect the sociological and cultural constructs that underlie and direct his/her actions, and subtle differences in a choice can influence the social representation of the product (Cecil 2001; Dietler and Herbich 1998; Lechtman 1977, 1993, 1994; Lemonnier 1992, 1993; Wright 1985). As a result, both the material and the process of manufacture contribute to an object's style as much as does the surface decoration because technological acts are embedded in a symbolic system that reflects the social reality and indigenous knowledge.

Different technological styles may be developed and operate throughout a culture's history, but they will not be perpetuated unless the technological style is compatible with the ways in which a culture functions, perceives reality, and verifies and reenacts its history. Selective pressures at the individual and community levels decide what will represent social structures such as power, ancestry, and identity (Lemonnier 1993:15). The integration of behavior events, choices, and "selective pressures" at each step of manufacture defines technological style and it is recognizable in the archaeological record in the central Petén lakes region by the virtue that its pattern is repeated on different types of material culture (e.g., pottery and painting on a structure's walls and floors). It is the persistence of these patterns embodying Kowoj identity and worldviews, which were "generated and maintained through practice" (Inomata and Coben 2006:25) during the Late Postclassic period, and also the fact that "Tipuans were never to give up their previous identity or to join completely the pagan opposition at Tah Itza" (Jones 1989:239) that suggest the Kowoj were at Tipu and actively defined themselves as different from the Itza.

Kowoj and Tipu Ethnohistory

According to Spanish documents and Itza ethnohistorical records, numerous sociopolitical groups may have coexisted in the Petén lakes region in the Late Postclassic period, but at the time of Spanish contact two dominated, the Kowoj and the Itza. The Kowoj occupied the northern and eastern part of Lake Petén Itzá and Lake Salpetén. They claimed to have migrated from Mayapán around A.D. 1530 as a result of Spanish contact and political turmoil (Jones 1998:27–28). However, it is possible that they had a series of migrations to and from Mayapán throughout the Postclassic period, of which one occurred after the fall of Mayapán at around A.D. 1450 and the last may have been around A.D. 1530 (Rice et al. 1996). Migrations from northern Yucatán may have been much earlier, ca. A.D. 1100–1200, because architecture associated with the Kowoj and the Xiw at Mayapán occurs at Topoxté Island during this time period (Hermes 2000). A Kowoj relationship to Mayapán is strengthened with the linkage of Petén Kowoj kinship patronyms and matronyms to prestigious individuals at Mayapán. For example, Ralph Roys (1967:79) noted that in the *Chilam Balam of Chumayel* the name Kowoj was associated with an individual listed as the "guardian of the east gate" at Mayapán. Grant Jones (1998: table 1.1) also has shown that Kowoj surnames occur in the Petén lakes region during the seventeenth century. In the central Petén lakes region, the Kowoj were centered at Zacpetén and Topoxté Island.

The Itza controlled the southern and western basin of Lake Petén Itzá, an area stretching from Lake Quexil west to Lake Sacpuy, with their capital, Nojpeten (or Tah Itza), on modern Flores Island (Jones 1998; Jones et al. 1981). Their Late Postclassic ruler, Kan Ek', claimed ancestry from Chich'en Itzá in the northern Yucatán peninsula, and he stated that the Itza migrated from Chich'en Itzá when it fell at approximately A.D. 1200 (Edmonson 1986; Jones 1998; Roys 1933). In A.D. 1695, AjChan, Kan Ek's nephew, also claimed that his deceased mother was from Chich'en Itzá and that "members of the Itza nobility were still living there in the seventeenth century and successfully avoiding Spanish recognition" (Jones 1998:11). Many scholars (Boot 1997, 2005; Rice et al. 1996; Schele and Grube 1995; Schele et al. 1998; Schele and Mathews 1998) state that epigraphic and archaeological materials suggest that Itza origins might have been in central Petén in the Classic period, and portions of the Itza may have begun migrations to and from the northern Yucatán as early as A.D. 900. Regardless of their migration history, the Itza were present at Lake Petén Itzá when Cortés traveled through Petén on his way to Honduras in A.D. 1525 (Cortés 1976:219–285).

Upon, and possibly from the beginning of, the two groups' occupation in the central Petén lakes region, there was much conflict between the Kowoj and the Itza. For example, the overland route from Belize (Tipu) to the central Petén lakes during the Late Postclassic[1] period may have been controlled by the Itza and/or the Kowoj, depending on which socio-political group occupied/controlled Tipu (Figure 12.1). As a result, social and political boundaries may have been created to enhance and enforce social and political differences. It is possible that there were also dialect differences between the two groups (Hofling, personal communication, 1997). Finally, Itza and Kowoj architecture also differs. Zacpetén and Topoxté Island, archaeological sites in Kowoj territory, have architecture that is very similar to Mayapán's Cenote Ch'en Mul group dual hall temple assemblages that were constructed by the Xiw (Milbrath and Peraza Lope, this volume; Proskouriakoff 1962b; Pugh, this volume, 2001a, 2001b, 2003a). On the other hand, Itza architecture in the Petén lakes region consists of small ceremonial groups composed of C-shaped structures (D. Rice 1986:326) and has some correlates to Chich'en Itzá.

Tipu may have been the easternmost Kowoj site in the central Petén lakes region, but it was also described in the historic accounts of Fray Bartolomé de Fuensalida and Fray Juan de Orbita (1618) and Fray Andrés de Avendaño y Loyola (1696) as the southernmost point in Yucatán under Spanish control (Jones 1989). The church/mission at Tipu was located 200 kilometers from Salamanca de Bacalar

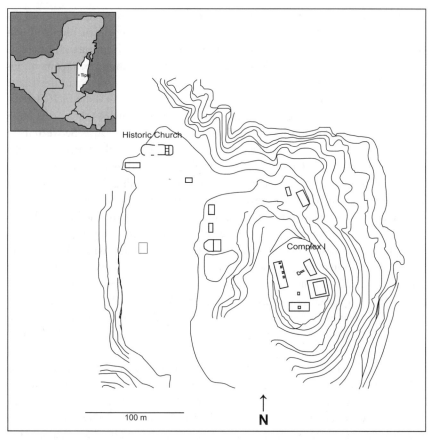

12.2. Complex I and Historic period structures at Tipu, Belize (redrawn from Graham et al. 1985:fig. 1).

and 100 kilometers from central Petén (Jones 1989:13–14). The construction of the church to the northwest of the largest Postclassic complex (hereafter Complex I) marked the inclusion of Tipu in the Spanish encomienda and mission system (Figure 12.2). It is from here that Fuensalida, Orbita, and Avendaño began their efforts to conquer and convert the Petén Itza. Although Tipu was under Spanish control, there was no permanent ecclesiastical presence, which led to several Maya uprisings and desecration of the Tipu church (Graham et al. 1985:210). In spite of the process of conversion, the inhabitants of Tipu retained their Maya rituals and methods of displaying identity.

Although Tipu was under Spanish authority from 1544 to 1707 (Jones 1989:14), previously it had been occupied almost continuously beginning in the Preclassic period (Cecil 1999; Graham et al. 1985, 1989; Rice 1984, 1985).

Therefore, it had a long Maya tradition that did not end with the appearance of the Spanish. This is seen most prominently in the material culture (structures and pottery) of Complex I as well as the burial patterns at the church. During the Postclassic period, the Spanish conquistadors invaded northern Yucatán, spurring migrations of Maya from northern Yucatán to the central Petén lakes region. According to the accounts of Fuensalida and Orbita, many of the inhabitants at Tipu in 1619 were from northern Yucatán and came as a result of Spanish presence in the north (Jones 1989; Scholes and Thompson 1977). Therefore, Tipu was a location between three socio-political spheres: the indigenous inhabitants of Tipu, the Spanish, and the Itza. The Mayas used Tipu to "hide both people and ideas and to maintain an underground of spirited resistance, even while transforming their own society to incorporate aspects of Spanish government and religion" (Jones 1989:16).

According to Spanish records, the inhabitants of Tipu defined themselves as ethnically different from the Itza and the Spanish. Avendaño (Bowditch and Rivera 1987:47) distinguishes between the Itza and the "men of Tipu to the east" and makes no mention of the presence of other socio-political groups in the Petén lakes region during his visit in the seventeenth century. He also states that the enemies of the "King of Petén [Kan Ek] are the Covoh [Kowoj]" (Bowditch and Rivera 1987:52). Additionally, Jones (2005) notes that the occupying forces of Tipu in 1638 were the Itza, suggesting that the previous occupants (perhaps the Kowoj) were not Itza.

In addition to the above distinctions made about the Itza and the inhabitants of Tipu, the personal appearances of the Itza and the inhabitants of Tipu were also different during battle. Avendaño (Bowditch and Rivera 1987:48) notes that Petén men (Itza) were scarred and painted black. The Chakan Itza (enemies of the Itza who lived to the north of the central area controlled by the Itza) were painted red (Bowditch and Rivera 1987:51). In 1641, Fuensalida returned to Belize with Fray Juan de Estada and noted that the Maya from Tipu appeared at their huts in war regalia with their faces painted red (Scholes and Thompson 1977:50).

Between 1544 and 1638, the Itza (re)gained control of Tipu and imposed their ideology, making the dominate ideology at Tipu during the earlier Colonial period that of the Itza. As a result of their control of Tipu, the Itza also appear to have controlled the corridor between the New and Belize rivers to Nojpeten in central Petén. This corridor ran from Nojpeten to Tipu and went south of Zacpetén and Topoxté Island (Kowoj territory) (Figure 12.1). Although this may be the case, Complex I was built and remodeled during the Terminal Classic and the earlier Postclassic periods and may reflect a different socio-political base that had closer ties to the eastern Petén lakes region and northern Yucatán (Cecil 1999; Jones 1998; Rice 1984, 1985). The Maya at Tipu did not choose to wholeheartedly adopt Spanish or Itza ideologies but instead "made the conscious choice to remain true people of the dual world in which they lived—neither Itzas nor Spanish Indians, but Mayas who negotiated with all the spiritual powers and temporal powers that surrounded them" (Jones 1989:154).

Postclassic and Contact Period Architecture at Tipu

There are two different zones of Postclassic and Contact period occupation that have been excavated at Tipu: Complex I and the Christian church (Graham et al. 1985, 1989; Jones et al. 1986). Architectural patterns are one method by which social/political groups can externalize collective identities (Cecil and Pugh 2004; Connerton 1989). Therefore, by tracing similarities and differences in ceremonial architecture across space and relating them to a group's history and worldviews, it is possible to better understand how a people define themselves as different from the "other."

Archaeological excavations at Tipu have investigated its place in the Maya social and political spheres at the time of Spanish contact and conquest (Graham et al. 1985, 1989; Jones et al. 1986; Thompson 1977). Archaeologically, Kautz and Graham excavated prehistoric and historic architecture from 1980 to 1987 in fieldwork aimed at locating the ethnohistorically known site (Graham 1991; Graham et al 1985). Excavations suggest that during the Postclassic period, Tipu had an increase in new house platforms that were either newly created or constructed over older archaeological remains (Graham et al. 1985:209). Although the basic residential construction techniques remained similar to earlier phases, platforms were more elaborate and new temple types (temple assemblages) were constructed.

Complex I at Tipu is an example of Postclassic civic-ceremonial architecture in that it is a combination of a basic ceremonial group and a temple assemblage (Figure 12.3) (Cecil and Pugh 2004; Pugh 2001a). Both patterns of architecture were first defined by Tatiana Proskouriakoff (1962b) at Mayapán in northern Yucatán. Typical ceremonial groups consist of open halls, shrines, and oratorios, and typical dual hall temple assemblages are represented by temples and a raised shrine (Cecil and Pugh 2004; Proskouriakoff 1962b:90; Pugh 2001a, 2001b). These ceremonial groups appear at Mayapán in northern Yucatán (Proskouriakoff 1962b), Isla Cilvituk in Campeche (Alexander 1998), Cozumel (Freidel and Sabloff 1984), Tipu (Cecil and Pugh 2004), and Topoxté Island, Zacpetén, Ixlú, and Muralla de Leon (Pugh 2001b)—the eastern portion of the Postclassic Maya territory.

Four structures with different ritual functions compose the architectural group at Tipu that sits atop a natural plateau. Structure 1 is an oratorio. This oratorio faces the same direction as the temple, Structure 2. Oratorios were "used by male members of the family for retirement before important ceremonies" (Proskouriakoff 1962b:90). Additionally, inside many of the oratorios in the central Petén lakes region are numerous deity effigy censers (Pugh 2001b).

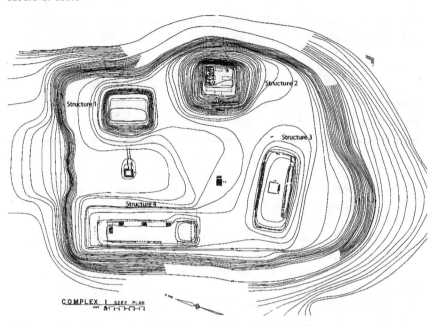

12.3. Complex I, Tipu, Belize (map drawn by Claude Belanger).

The temple in Complex I, Structure 2, faces west and has a platform and non-balustrade staircase (Jones et al. 1986). Within the structure is an upright uncarved stela that marks a narrow doorway inside of which is another plain stela bordered by thirteen facing stones that are above a lower chamber (Jones et al. 1986:47). Burning of offerings is evidenced by smoke-stained walls in the westernmost antechamber (Jones et al. 1986:47). In the rear chamber of Structure 2 is an altar, a bench, and a pedestal. This structure most closely resembles those at Topoxté Island (Cecil and Pugh 2004).

Structures 3 and 4 are open halls. Structure 3 is at a right angle to the temple and faces north. In front of this structure is a small shrine. Structure 4 is the westernmost building and faces into the oratorio and the temple. These open halls are C-shaped structures with benches running along the ends and the back wall. Open halls may have been used for lodging purposes rather than public or administrative purposes. They may also have served as council houses for different lineages or nobles (Pugh 2001a).

At Tipu, the basic ceremonial group is defined as the oratorio (Str. 1), the western open hall (Str. 4), and their associated platforms and shrine (Cecil and Pugh 2004). The temple assemblage is formed by the temple (Str. 2), the southern open hall (Str. 3), and the oratorio (Str. 1) and the small shrine in front of Structure 3. Since the two groups share an oratorio and surround a single plaza, they unite as a single group. Nevertheless, the space of this group was dualistic and this dualism was primarily manifest in its two (dual) open halls (Pugh 2001a). The association of one open hall with a basic ceremonial group and the other hall with a temple assemblage indicates some sort of ceremonial specialization for each group. One might speculate that the social group associated with the temple assemblage controlled the position of *ajk'in*, the high priest, and the group associated with the basic ceremonial group, the position of *jalach winik*, or the secular ruler (Cecil and Pugh 2004). Regardless of its function, this basic pattern is seen at Mayapán (the Kowoj ancestral homeland) and Topoxté Island and Zacpetén (archaeological sites defined as occupied by the Kowoj). Therefore, the architectural pattern at Complex I suggests the presence of the Kowoj or, at the very least, the Kowoj concept of construction of ritual architecture.

To the north of Complex I at Tipu is the Christian church built at the edge of a bluff. The ramada-style church faces west and was constructed of limestone, river stone, poles, and thatch (Graham et al. 1985:211). Its construction was also non-Maya in that the colonial church did not sit upon a platform, but it and other colonial structures were arranged around a cobblestone courtyard (Graham 1991:321). The church first may have been constructed in the mid-sixteenth century (Tipu became a mission site in 1544), and Spanish records and archaeological research indicate that it may have been remodeled in 1567/68 and 1608 as the Spanish portion of Tipu expanded (Jacobi 2000:1; Graham et al. 1985:212).

Associated with the church are the burials of more than 500 Maya (presumably inhabitants of Tipu). Wrobel (2002) compared long bone robusticity of these burials and concluded that there were no statistically significant morphological differences in the Maya burials. The individuals with more grave goods were buried inside of the walls of the church and those with fewer, if any, grave goods were placed outside the church walls (Jacobi 2000:26; Jones et al.1986). Twice as many males were buried inside of the church as females and 35 percent of the interred juveniles were buried within church walls (Jacobi 2000:table 6.1). It also appears that the burials inside the church were earlier in time (interred first), had dental modifications (a Maya practice), and may represent the first converts (Danforth et al. 1985:175). In addition to these practices, the burials were placed with their heads to the west and feet to the east (a European practice) but were accompanied with copal, Maya beads, incensarios, and the spreading of pine needles over the grave area (a Maya practice) (Vogt 1998:29; but also see Jacobi 2000:26, 56–58; Herndon 1994:49). These burial practices indicated that the Maya "managed to retain a way of life that acknowledged the presence of the Spanish and Catholicism, while at the same time silently and subtly followed their traditional Maya customs" (Jacobi 2000:17). Thus, the Maya of Tipu demonstrated through their burial customs the needs of the dead in their afterlife as well as the inhabitants' understanding of the differences between Christian and Maya ritual practices, identity, and histories.

As is indicated through ethnohistory and architectural patterns, the identities of the inhabitants of Tipu were deeply rooted in their worldviews and (re)enacted in the external world as material culture (Smart 1995:83). Therefore, the creation of temple assemblages and burial practices reflect ritual, myth, history, and identity. The remainder of this chapter demonstrates how the manufacture and trade of pottery was as symbolically loaded as other types of material culture and was used by the inhabitants of Tipu to actively signal their identity.

Postclassic Slipped Pottery at Tipu

In addition to the structures within Complex I displaying the collective identity of the Kowoj in Petén, the slipped pottery excavated from within those structures also indicates patterns of technological and stylistic characteristics that are distinctly Kowoj. Most of the completed ceramic studies are based on pottery excavated during the 1984 season (Aimers 2002; Cecil 2001, 2004; Cecil and Neff 2006; Foor 1994; Rice 1984, 1985; Weber-Wilson 1991). Rice (1984, 1985) synthesized the collection according to ceramic complexes from the Preclassic period to the Historic period and provided comparisons of Tipu pottery to central Petén pottery. She also defined the ceramic complexes at Tipu. Charles Foor (1994) analyzed Late Postclassic censer material from Structure 2 of Complex I to suggest how censers formed a stylistic, functional, and behavioral unit that reflected ritual events. Eden Weber-Wilson (1991) examined Johnny Walker Red pottery to determine its temporal significance. James Aimers (2002) conducted a stylistic analysis of Tipu's Terminal Classic to Early Postclassic pottery. He discussed the pottery production continuity in the Belize Valley and how Tipu may have been affected by the Maya "collapse." I (2001, 2004) discussed the possibility of Kowoj and/or Itza technological styles of pottery at Tipu. The following analysis builds on these previous works to associate Kowoj technological styles defined at Zacpetén and Topoxté Island with those at Tipu. In order to accomplish this goal, multiple analytical methods were used.[2] The pottery used in this analysis can be dated from the Late Postclassic to the early Colonial periods because it was found in association with Spanish olive jars, Sevilla Blue-on-White, and Columbia Plain pottery that occurred in Belize as a result of the presence of the Spanish and their attempts to establish a mission at Tipu (Rice 1984, 1985).

The first level of analysis used to develop a technological style for this pottery sample was a typological analysis using the type-variety system (Smith et al. 1960). All Postclassic slipped pottery from Tipu was classified as to ware, group, type, and variety (when possible) so as to facilitate comparison to other pottery in the central Petén lakes region. In this case, it was particularly useful to classify and compare pottery at the ware level because this category describes pottery based on paste attributes and surface finish and provides information about geographical location, time period, and decoration (Rice 1982:50)—all essential in the definition of technological styles. Differences with regard to clay pastes, surface finish, decoration, and overall technology are not numerous in the sample, but it was these small differences in wares that proved to be important when identifying technological styles in relation to social identity.

As a result of the type-variety analysis, I determined that three Postclassic pottery wares were represented at Tipu: Vitzil Orange-Red ware, Snail-Inclusion Paste ware, and Clemencia Cream Paste ware (see Table 12.1 for the Postclassic slipped pottery classifications). Vitzil Orange-Red ware pottery is the most prevalent Postclassic slipped ware at Tipu. The majority of sherds from this group have reddish-brown (2.5YR 4/4) to orange (2.5YR 5/8) pastes, but variation in paste color and degree of coring exists. Some sherds have a tan-colored (7.5YR 6/8) paste with black, gray, or orange cores. The sherd paste has a coarse texture that results from a variety of sizes, shapes, and frequencies of calcite, quartz, ferruginous lumps, feldspar, and biotite mineral inclusions.

In addition to paste variety in the Vitzil Orange-Red ware, there are differences in the slips (red and tan) and decorative modes (black and red-and-black painting and fine-line and deep-groove incising). The exterior red slip color ranges from dark red (7.5YR 4/8) to light red (2.5YR 5/8). The quality of the slips ranges from smoothed and/or polished (similar to the finish of Late Classic period polychromes) to a matte finish that is easily scratched. Most of the tripod dishes have a dark red slip (10R 4/6) and are polished. Although fireclouding is not prevalent on red-slipped pottery at Tipu, those that do occur are brown or tan (not black). Coexisting with the red slips of the Vitzil Orange-Red ware are sherds with a tan slip. Tan slip colors range from tan (10YR 8/2) to light tan-orange (2.5YR 5/8).

Vitzil Orange-Red ware decorative methods include painting and incising. Designs in black or red-and-black are painted on a lighter red slip (2.5YR 5/8). Decoration predominantly appears on the interior of tripod dishes and is banded. Although the majority of the motifs are eroded, two commonly occurring motifs in the Petén lakes region that also occur at Tipu are hook and mat motifs. Incising is either characterized by pre-fire deep, wide incisions that appear on grater bowls and drums or by post-fire, fine-line incising. Vitzil Orange-Red ware vessels with fine-line incising typically depict the *ilhuitl* (day, festival, or sky) glyph or feathers. The ilhuitl glyph is common on Postclassic pottery at Tulum and Tancah (Sanders 1960) and Lamanai (Graham, personal communication, 2000) and occurs less frequently at Topoxté Island, Mayapán, and Zacpetén (Cecil 2001).

The Snail-Inclusion Paste ware represents the second highest frequency of Postclassic ceramic sherds from Complex I. This ceramic ware also demonstrates some paste and slip variability, but the variability is less when compared to similar pottery from other archaeological sites in the Petén lakes region. Dark cores are uncommon at Tipu. When broken, some of these sherds emit a sulfur smell. Similar

Table 12.1. Petén Postclassic slipped wares: Groups, types, and varieties

Ceramic Ware	Snail Inclusion Paste	Snail Inclusion Paste	Snail Inclusion Paste	Vitzil Orange-Red	Clemencia Cream Paste
Ceramic Group	Paxcamán	Fulano	Trapeche	Augustine	Topoxté
Monochrome Slip	**Paxcamán Red**	**Fulano Black**	Trapeche Pink	**Augustine Red**	**Topoxté Red**
Black Painting	**Ixpop Polychrome**	Mul Polychrome	Picté Red-on-Paste	**Pek Polychrome**	Pastel Polychrome
Red Painting	**Macanché Red-on-Paste**	Sotano Red-on-Paste			**Chompoxté Red-on-Cream**
Banded design	**Macanché variety**	Sotano variety	Picté variety		Akalché variety
Curvilinear design	Ivo variety				Chompoxté variety
Geometric design					Kayukos variety
Red-and-black Painting	**Sacá Polychrome**			**Graciela Polychrome**	**Canté Polychrome**
Pre-fire, deep-line incising	**Picú Incised: Thub variety**	Mengano Incised: Bobo variety	Xuluc Incised: Tzalam variety	**Hobonmo Incised: Hobonmo variety**	Dulces Incised: Bebeto variety
Post-fire, fine-line incising	**Picú Incised: Picú variety**	Mengano Incised: Mengano variety	Xuluc Incised: Xuluc variety	**Hobonmo Incised: Ramsey variety**	Dulces Incised: Dulces variety

Note: Pottery excavated from Tipu's Complex I are in boldface.

sherds appear at Macanché Island (discussion follows) (Cecil 2004, 2001; Rice 1987). Snail-Inclusion Paste ware sherds from Tipu are characterized by a compact gray (10YR 5/2) to pinkish-gray (7.5YR 6/2) paste color. The most common inclusions in the sherd paste are snail shells and calcite.

Snail Inclusion-Paste ware red slips are similar to those of the Vitzil Orange-Red ware with regard to color and finish and range from red (10R 4/6) to red-orange (2.5YR 4/6), with the majority of slips occurring in the 10R 4/6 range. In general, Snail-Inclusion Paste ware slips are well smoothed. Only two decorative modes in this ware category exist at Tipu—black or red painting. Black circumferential bands define the decorative panels. Although the majority of the motifs have been eroded, possible twisted mat motifs occur. In addition to the black painted decoration, one sherd has red painted decoration, but it is too eroded to identify motifs.

Similar to the Vitzil Orange-Red ware, the Snail-Inclusion Paste ware at Tipu has pre-fire and post-fire incising. Deep-line, pre-fire incising occurs on grater bowls and post-fire, fine-line incising occurs on plates and narrow-neck jars. Fine-line incised motifs include the ilhuitl glyph, twisted mats, birds, and feathers.

The third most prevalent Postclassic slipped ware at Tipu is the Clemencia Cream Paste ware. A cream-colored marly paste characterizes this pottery. At Tipu, these pastes fall into three main color categories: tan/buff (10YR 8/2), off-white to gray (10YR 8/3), and greenish-gray (2.5YR 6/3). The difference in paste colors is most likely due to the differences in firing temperatures and manufacturing techniques/locales (Cecil 2004, 2007). Sherd pastes include calcite, quartz, biotite, feldspar, and ferruginous lumps. Two sherds with a tan/buff-colored paste have an almost total lack of typical Clemencia Cream Paste ware inclusions but instead are dominated by volcanic ash inclusions. This may represent the earliest (Late Terminal Classic / Early Postclassic) attempts at pottery manufacture with this type of clay (Cecil 2001, 2004, 2006).

Clemencia Cream Paste ware slips range from dark red (5YR 5/6) to a light orangish-red (2.5YR 6/8). These slips have a matte finish and are friable. Decorative modes on Topoxté ceramic group pottery excavated at Tipu exist only as red or red-and-black painted decoration. Again, two circumferential bands delimit the decorated area and all motifs within the bands are badly eroded. The red painted decoration is darker in color than the exterior red slip color. In addition to the red painted decoration, red-and-black painted bands (and presumably motifs) occur on Clemencia Cream Paste ware sherds.

The next category of analysis that was conducted to determine the presence of a Kowoj technological style at Tipu was a mineralogical analysis of the clay pastes and slips. Thin sections representing all Postclassic slipped wares (and types) at Tipu were examined using a petrographic microscope. Petrographic analysis allows for the identification of minerals by means of their unique optical properties and provides qualitative (sorting and shape) and quantitative (size and frequency) data for comparison at the ware level (Middlestone et al. 1985). The identification of the nonplastic inclusions, minerals, and rock fragments in the clay matrix as well as the slipped surfaces provided valuable information as to differences in resources and manufacturing "recipes" (Cecil 2001, 2004).

Inductively coupled plasma spectroscopy (ICPS) analysis (both strong-acid digestions and laser-ablation) was the final level of analysis performed on the Postclassic slipped pottery pastes, slips, and decorative paints from Tipu. ICPS is a chemical compositional characterization technique that can detect a variety of elements (major to rare earth elements) (Burton and Simon 1993, 1996; Neff 2003). This chemical characterization technique is a bulk method of analysis that has the potential to provide information about behavioral practices through testing the clay matrix (clays and inclusions) and slips. Because different technologies and pottery groups display different technological characteristicsm such as clay and temper, variability in chemical signatures can indicate differences in technological choices.

When data from the different kinds of analyses were combined, it was possible to identify technological styles that reflected differences in social identity at Tipu.

Kowoj Technological Styles at Tipu

Previous research that correlates technological styles of pottery with the various socio-political groups in the Petén lakes region suggests that the Kowoj had a distinct repertoire with three specific characteristics (Figure 12.4): (1) a cream-colored, marly sherd paste characteristic of the Clemencia Cream Paste ware; (2) red-on-paste painted decoration; and (3) red-and-black painted decoration (Cecil 2001, 2009). The Petén Kowoj decorative modes and use of a cream-colored clay paste also occur most predominantly at Mayapán and other Postclassic archaeological sites on the eastern coast of the Yucatán peninsula and Belize, but with local raw materials.

The cream-colored, marly clay used to manufacture Clemencia Cream Paste ware pottery comes from the Topoxté Island area (within the Kowoj territory). Mineralogical and chemical examinations of cream-colored clays from the Yaxhá area[3] and cream-colored pottery from Zacpetén, Ixlú, Nixtun Ch'ich' and Tipu suggest that the sherds were made from the Yaxhá clays (Cecil 2001, 2007; Cecil and Neff 2006). The majority of pottery is Clemencia Cream Paste ware pottery at Topoxté Island, almost to the exclusion of the occurrence of other Postclassic slipped wares (a low frequency of Snail-Inclusion ware pottery has recently been excavated at Topoxté) (Bullard 1960, 1970; Hermes 2000; Johnson 1985; Rice 1979). Outside of Topoxté Island, pottery of this ware is found almost exclusively at archaeological sites in the eastern portion of the central Petén lakes region (Kowoj territory)—Zacpetén, Macanché Island, and Tipu. I have also noted the presence of a Clemencia Cream Paste ware vessel with red-on-paste painted decoration in the excavated material from Mayapán. Therefore, if Topoxté Island is within the Kowoj

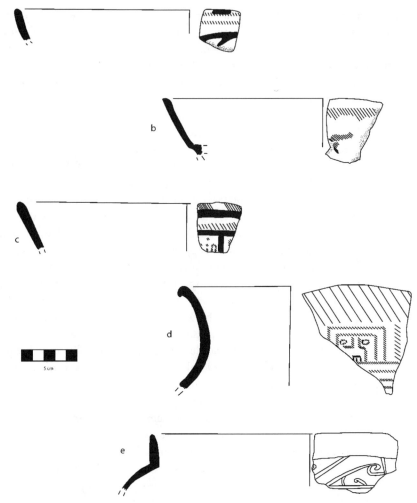

12.4. Kowoj technological style pottery: (a) Pastel Polychrome from Tipu; (b) Chompoxté Red-on-Paste: Akalché variety from Tipu; (c) Sacá Polychrome from Zacpetén; (d) Chompoxté Red-on-Paste: Alkaché variety from Zacpetén; (e) Picú Incised: Picú variety (ilhuitl glyph) from Tipu.

territory and controls the manufacture and trade of Clemencia Cream Paste ware pottery, inhabitants of Topoxté Island (presumably Kowoj) are trading within the Kowoj territory of which Tipu is a part.

In addition to cream-colored pottery originating at Topoxté Island, two decorative programs of the Kowoj technological style are present at Complex I: red-on-paste and red-and-black line decoration. These types of decoration on ceramic pastes that are specific to the pottery manufactured and traded within the eastern central Petén lakes region (Kowoj territory) appear almost exclusively on Clemencia Cream Paste ware pottery manufactured at Topoxté Island (Cecil 2001, 2004, 2007). They are also the main decorative program of Late Postclassic pottery at Mayapán in northern Yucatán (Smith 1971). Sometime during the Late Postclassic period, the red-on-paste and red-and-black painted decorative modes were transferred to the more local (but still eastern central Petén lakes region) lacustrine clays of the Snail-Inclusion Paste ware (Cecil 2001, 2004, 2007). As a result, gray-paste pottery was now being decorated with red-on-paste and red-and-black line decoration and the majority of these sherds exist at Zacpetén. It is hypothesized that during the Late Postclassic period, Zacpetén became the dominant Kowoj site in the central Petén lakes region (Jones 2009; Pugh 2001a). Complex I at Tipu does not have any red-and-black decorated gray-paste pottery (later Late Postclassic period), but a small number of the red-on-paste decorated sherds on cream-colored pastes (earlier Late Postclassic period) do exist. Therefore, slipped pottery that represents the earlier Late Postclassic period and Kowoj socio-political identity occurs at Tipu.

In addition to the presence of Kowoj-specific pottery at Tipu, when one examines the three Postclassic wares present at Tipu and elsewhere in the Petén lakes region, possible Kowoj trade patterns between Tipu and Zacpetén and Topoxté Island become apparent. This further suggests that Tipu is within the Kowoj cultural sphere. Only the Paxcamán and Topoxté ceramic groups will be discussed because the Augustine ceramic group may be a local product of Tipu as its ceramic pastes are distinguished from those of other Kowoj sites and because it occurs throughout the Postclassic period without any as yet definite patterns.

Clemencia Cream Paste ware pottery was manufactured at Topoxté Island or one of the other smaller islands, of which Topoxté Island is the largest, and traded to other communities in the Petén lakes region (Cecil 1997, 2002, 2009; Rice 1979). The majority of Clemencia Cream Paste ware sherds have been excavated from archaeological sites in the eastern lakes region—the ethnohistorically defined Kowoj territory. The majority of the Topoxté ceramic group sherds excavated from Tipu are chemically associated with half of the Topoxté ceramic group sherds excavated from Zacpetén (Figure 12.5a). Thus, Topoxté ceramic group pottery with a similar clay recipe is being traded from Topoxté to Zacpetén and Tipu—all Kowoj sites. Interestingly, the quality of the pottery being traded to Tipu is inferior to that at Topoxté Island and Zacpetén. Although there are three different "recipes" and two of them are being traded to Tipu and Zacpetén, the pottery that exists at Zacpetén (excavated from its temple assemblages) is fired at a higher temperature, resulting in a clearer cream paste color (almost white and without a gray core) and the decorative motifs are more complicated (mats, hooks, and *ajaw* motifs) and are executed more expertly. To put it another way, Zacpetén was receiving Wedgwood fine china whereas Tipu was receiving Corelle dinnerware.

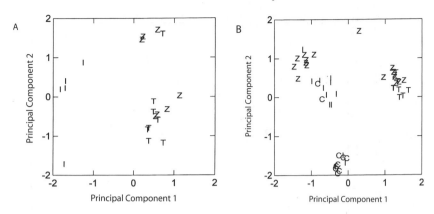

12.5. Principal component plots of strong-acid digestion ICP-MS analysis of Postclassic slipped wares: (a) Clemencia Cream Paste ware; and (b) Snail Inclusion Paste ware; C = Ch'ich, I = Ixlú, T = Tipu, Z = Zacpetén.

A similar pattern occurs with the pastes of the Snail-Inclusion Paste ware (Figure 12.5b). This association suggests that Snail-Inclusion Paste ware pottery may have been manufactured at Zacpetén and traded to Tipu. In order to suggest this direction of trade, versus trade from Tipu to Zacpetén, two observations can be made. First, the sherd pastes are mineralogically and chemically similar to the clays and sherd pastes from Zacpetén and other lacustrine areas in the central Petén lakes region. Second, there are sherd pastes with a sulfur smell when freshly broken that have been excavated from Tipu, Zacpetén, and Macanché Island. The raw clay most likely originated from Lake Macanché or Salpetén because of its high sulfur content (Deevey et al. 1980) and was traded either as a raw material or a finished product. Thus, it appears that trade of this pottery only occurred between various Kowoj sites in the eastern lakes region of central Petén and was not consistently traded with all of the archaeological sites in central Petén lakes region.

In addition to clay paste elemental analysis, the elemental analysis of the Clemencia Cream Paste ware exterior slips[4] on pottery excavated from Complex I also provides some interesting observations as to the technological and stylistic choices made by the Kowoj at Topoxté Island and their relationship to those Kowoj at Tipu (Cecil and Neff 2006). Exterior slips of monochromatically slipped and undecorated pottery and the paint used for red painted decoration are chemically distinct (Figure 12.6a). The undecorated, red-slipped pottery at Tipu tends to group chemically with those from Zacpetén (decorated and undecorated), but the red line decorative paint on sherds from Tipu is a distinct group from those found at Zacpetén. In thin section, the red line decorative paint on pottery from Zacpetén has biotite and calcite inclusions.

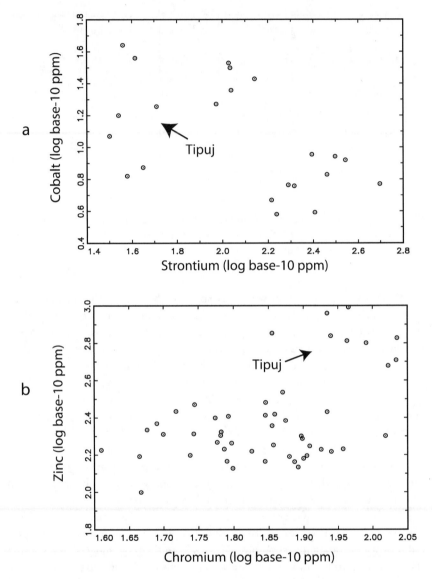

12.6. LA-ICP-MS elemental concentration bivariate plots of exterior slips: (a) Clemencia Cream Paste ware; (b) Snail Inclusion Paste ware.

This decorated pottery is also of poorer quality (darker cream with light gray cores). When comparing the slip information about the Tipu decorated pottery to its technological style data, it appears that the manufacturers of this pottery (presumably Kowoj at Topoxté Island) are trading "inferior" decorated pottery to Tipu. Tipu may be a secondary trading partner with Topoxté Island, but it is still within the Kowoj trading sphere.

Snail-Inclusion Paste ware exterior slips from Tipu are also chemically and visually distinct from those at other central Petén lake region sites (Figure 12.6b) (Cecil and Neff 2006). For the most part, monochromatically slipped and undecorated sherds have a richer and darker (10R 4/6) color and are well smoothed with a glossy surface. In thin section, the slips appear thin and very compact. Decorated sherds tend to have a lighter red-colored slip (2.5YR 4/6) with a matte finish and are petrographically distinct because of the possible inclusion of biotite. Again, it seems that decorated pottery with motifs specific to the Kowoj area[5] was being traded from the Zacpetén / Topoxté Island core area to Tipu.

Kowoj technological styles are distinct from those of the Itza. Although more analyses of Itza pottery need to be conducted, I can provisionally define some elements of Itza technological styles. Itza socio-political identity may be represented by orange paste pottery (Vitzil Orange-Red ware) with the presence of black painted reptilian (*kan*) motifs that may reflect the ruling Kan Ek' lineage of the Petén Itza. Although Kowoj pottery does occur in Complex I at Tipu, it occurs in lower frequencies than Itza pottery. To better understand the differences in pottery technological styles and socio-political groups at Tipu (specifically those of the Itza), further analysis of the historic structures needs to be conducted.

Kowoj at Tipu

The material culture of the Maya at Tipu demonstrates the strength and tenacity of a social/political group's ideology to survive the effects of Spanish contact and attempts at Christian conversion. One of the ways that the Kowoj at Tipu were able to maintain their worldviews was to actively manipulate it so that it served to verify their identity through their history and customs. The end result—Kowoj temple assemblages, Christian/Maya burials, and Kowoj technological styles of pottery—displayed who they were, what they believed to be their origins, and how they understood their future. The inhabitants of Tipu had many alternative worldviews from which to choose (e.g., Spanish, Itza, and Kowoj), but they acted in a manner that demonstrated their perception of reality—that of being Kowoj.

Tipu (and Kowoj) perceptions of reality were best exemplified in their ritual performances in social places where their identity was emphasized through their reenactment of myth and history. As a result, pottery displaying that identity should also be present and it is most likely to be decorated in order to display social identity (Hodder 1977, among others). An examination of ceramic wares and decorative modes at Complex I yields such results. In general, decorated pottery (representing Kowoj-specific clay recipes) associated with Kowoj identity occurs most frequently in the oratorio and the temple (Structures 1 and 2). On the other hand, undecorated slipped pottery occurs most commonly in the open halls (Structures 3 and 4) and less frequently in the temple and oratorio (Structures 1 and 2). This difference reflects the importance of decorated pottery communicating a message of history, myth, and identity through ritual—rituals typically occurring in the temples and oratorios. A similar pattern is also seen at other Kowoj sites and especially at Zacpetén's temple assemblage groups (Cecil 2009; Pugh 2001a; Rice and Cecil 2009).

Although all of the structures in Complex I represent a dual hall temple assemblage, two structures—the oratorio and the temple—are distinguished by the presence of pottery representing Kowoj identity. Structure 1, the oratorio, is a specialized temple for lineage deities that are distinguished/separated from other deities (Pugh 2001b) and as such represents one of the two highly ritualized structures within Complex I. The majority of Clemencia Cream Paste ware pottery as well as other red-on-paste and red-and-black decorated pottery from the Clemencia Cream Paste and Snail-Inclusion Paste wares were excavated from this structure. In addition, decorated pottery of the Vitzil Orange-Red ware also occurs within this structure.

Structure 2, the temple, is the location for ritual activities where the Kowoj elites interacted with the supernatural realm. Thus, one might also expect that slipped pottery associated with identity would be found within and around the structure. This is indeed the case; however, the decorative mode present on pottery from Structure 2 is distinct from the other structures within the complex. The decorated pottery from the Clemencia Cream Paste and Snail-Inclusion Paste wares only represents the red-on-paste painting and post-fire incising on a red slip—in essence a red-on-paste decorative mode with Kowoj-specific clays. The red-on-paste painted decoration is the most frequent decorative mode at Topoxté Island and is also very common at Zacpetén.

In contrast to Structures 1 and 2, the majority of excavated pottery representing the three Postclassic slipped ceramic groups from Structures 3 and 4 are undecorated with a red slip and a few sherds representing the Paxcamán ceramic group have black painted decoration. This distinction should be expected given that the open halls in Complex I may not have been the main loci of ritual activities.

Therefore, as a result of an examination of civic-ceremonial architecture and pottery excavated from the structures in Complex I and the ethnohistorical record, it is possible to suggest that the Postclassic inhabitants at Tipu constructed and reinforced their Kowoj identity through ritual space and ethnically specific pottery. Temple assemblages are found in many areas of the Maya lowlands, but the dual hall assemblage pattern represents a Kowoj-specific construction template. The Kowoj at Tipu, and at other Kowoj sites in the central Petén lakes region, had distinct migrations, histories, and material cultures that reflected their understanding of the changing world in which they lived. The creation of civic-ceremonial architecture, pottery, trade with Kowoj at other Kowoj archaeological sites, synchretization of Maya and Christian burial practices, distinguishing themselves from the Itza in the Spanish record, and painting themselves red in battle reinforced their identity at Tipu as well as connections to people with a similar Kowoj ideology. Therefore, given these data sets, the previous suggestions that Tipu was *always* controlled by the Itza may need to be revised.

Tipu may have functioned as the eastern outpost site for the Kowoj during their initial occupation (ca. A.D. 1100) in the Postclassic period. Kowoj, or "a generalized population of northern Yucatecans and their decendants" with Mayapán affiliations (Jones, personal communication, 2005), may have relocated to central Petén via the east coast of the Yucatán peninsula, down the New and Mopan rivers to Tipu. During their journey, the Kowoj could have rested at "friendly" (similarities in architecture and pottery, as well as the ilhuitl glyph, suggest a similar social and/or political ideology) sites such as Tulum, Tancah, Cozumel, and Lamanai before stopping at Tipu. Cozumel can be added at this point because of the similarities to Petén Postclassic slipped pottery (Connor 1975:126–129) and architecture (Pugh 2003a), and Fernando Cumux of Tipu stated that he was a descendant of the Contact period "lord" of Cozumel (Jones 1989:108). From Tipu, the Kowoj could have traveled west to Topoxté Island and Zacpetén as did the Spanish 500 years later.

As a result of these lines of ethnohistorical and archaeological data, it is apparent that the Kowoj at Tipu during the Postclassic period created material culture used for ritual purposes (Structures 1 and 2 and associated decorated pottery) to reinforce the collective Kowoj conscious and worldviews during the Postclassic period. Technological styles of pottery, especially those of the Kowoj, exemplify what is acceptable within their social milieu and how their culture was perceived by others—most specifically the Itza. It also demonstrates their understanding of their past, present, and future in the face of other competing worldviews.

Acknowledgments. This research was supported by funding by the National Science Foundation grants BCS-0228187 and SBR-9816325 (Dissertation Improvement Grant), Proyecto Maya Colonial of Southern Illinois University Carbondale, and Sigma Xi Grants-in-Aid of Research. The first author thanks Prudence M. Rice, Timothy W. Pugh, and Elizabeth Graham for their guidance and suggestions, as well as Sachiko Sakai for her laboratory assistance and Robert J. Speakman for his statistical assistance.

Notes

1. In central Petén, the Late Postclassic period dates from ca. A.D. 1300–1525 (Rice 2004). Unfortunately, a fine-grained chronology of the Postclassic period at Tipu based

on artifacts and stratigraphy has not been completed. Therefore, I am adopting the central Petén chronology for this chapter and understand that differences between Tipu and central Petén do exist.

2. The methods used to determine the technological style groups at Tipu are the same as those used for other sites in the central Petén lakes region. Please see Cecil (2001) for a complete description of each method.

3. The clay samples were collected by the Central Petén Historical Ecology Project (CPHEP) during the 1973–1974 field seasons. Four clay samples were tested: (1) from Brecha 4 at a depth of 100–110 centimeters near Mound 12, west of the Late/Terminal Classic site of Yaxhá; (2) from a roadcut near the intersection of the road to Yaxhá and Melchor de Mencos at kilometer marker 64–65; (3) from a roadcut at the Lake Yaxhá cruce at kilometer marker 62; and (4) from Pit 3 in Brecha 2 at Yaxhá (no depth given).

4. Although LA-ICP-MS data was collected on interior red paints of the Clemencia Cream Paste ware pottery excavated from Tipu, the sample size was three. Therefore, these data will not be discussed.

5. For a discussion of Kowoj decorative motifs, please see Rice and Cecil (2009).

Agency and Worldviews of the Unconquered Lacandon Maya

CHAPTER THIRTEEN

Joel W. Palka

Explorers trekking through the rainforests of the southern Maya lowlands during the Colonial and Republican periods encountered large numbers of Maya who they described as unconquered, non-Christian people. Many of these Maya were Lacandon,[1] who lived in scattered settlements throughout lowland eastern Chiapas, México, and adjacent Petén, Guatemala (Figure 13.1). They were Yukatek-speaking Lacandon and not the Ch'olti-Lacandon from the time of the initial conquest of the lowlands in the sixteenth century. The explorers' accounts of the lifeways of these free Maya closely match the ethnographic descriptions of the Lacandon from the nineteenth and early twentieth centuries. The ancestors of the contemporary Lacandon had largely escaped Spanish Conquest and colonization, but outside contact had shaped their lives since the Colonial period. More than likely, Lacandon culture formed during a period of intensified inter-indigenous interaction in the lowlands following the conquest. Contact between displaced Maya populations, intermarriage between Maya groups, and inter-indigenous trade for European goods in free Maya territory led to inter-ethnic Maya acculturation and the ethnogenesis of Lacandon culture.

A large part of the southern Maya lowlands remained in Maya hands until the nineteenth and early twentieth centuries. At this time, settlers, explorers, loggers, and missionaries entered the remote lowlands in unprecedented numbers and came in contact with the Lacandon. Subsequent to this culture contact, the waves of conflict, disease, and missionary activity affected Lacandon society. However,

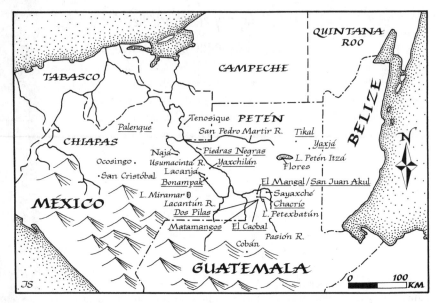

I3.I. Map of the Lacandon region with modern settlements and archaeological sites (drawing by Jack Scott).

since they lived in autonomous Maya territory, the Lacandon reacted to their changing world within their cultural milieu and for indigenous interests. Epidemics, acculturation, displacement, and fighting affected the Lacandon at this time, but they survived this "Second Conquest" by escaping further into the forest, resisting contact and change, and regulating outside trade to acquire items of cultural and economic importance. Specifically, some settlements were wiped out, other Lacandon joined missions, and many avoided outside contact except briefly to trade goods.

Despite the uneven effects of culture contact and native responses on different Lacandon settlements, some generalizations regarding Lacandon society and beliefs during the late conquest of their territory can be made. The advantage in this case study is that comparative information from history, archaeology, and ethnography is available for the study of Lacandon Maya worldviews. Because of the rich comparative data sets, native worldviews are a common theme in historical anthropology and archaeology (Dowson 1998; Kirch and Sahlins 1992; Rogers 1990). According to Christopher DeCorse's (1998:364) discussion of culture contact and social change in West Africa, the "noneconomic factors such as shared beliefs, cosmology, religion—in short, worldview—in delineating the form, character, and import of African-European relations" have not been sufficiently considered. DeCorse later demonstrates that economic, social, and religious factors are combined to form an evolved or adjusted worldview on the heels of contact and culture change.

These beliefs are the central themes and interpretations regarding worldviews addressed in this chapter. Lacandon views of their natural and supernatural realms and their place in them following the conquest are examined. Specifically, I will cover Lacandon perceptions of outsiders, beliefs concerning foreign trade goods, sacred landscapes, and religious survivalisms, all of which were shaped by culture contact and forged through indigenous agency. Continuities and changes in Lacandon worldviews followed indigenous norms that were maintained in autonomous native territory that remained a colonial frontier.

Indigenous Agency in the Frontier

Several important factors make the Lacandon distinctive with regard to culture contact and indigenous worldviews in the Maya area. For one, they lived beyond the frontier of colonial powers and, hence, were not directly subjugated by the Spanish. Because of their geographical and social realities, the Lacandon managed a significant amount of contact with outsiders on their terms. The examination of Lacandon agency is clear in the archaeological and historic records: they maintained culture continuity even in times of great change in their remote, autonomous settlements and they were frequently free to make choices as to who they contacted and why. For understanding Lacandon agency and culture contact, the concept of the middle ground in archaeological studies of colonialism is useful (Gosden 2004; White 1991). Culture change, ethnogenesis, and new perceptions of the world and a native people's place in it arise from culture contact in the middle ground. In the frontiers of expanding states, settlers and aboriginal groups find a common ground for interaction and trade. For instance, the cross-cultural contact without domination is often advantageous to all parties involved: mutual dependency evolves, and the actors are able to function within their value systems and retain autonomy (Gosden 2004:30–31, 82). This symmetrical interaction allows indigenous groups to have control over their lives and helps them make sense of the encounter with foreign peoples and goods according to native values.

Agency in frontier indigenous societies is readily apparent in the archaeology and ethnohistory of contact, culture change, and worldviews in different regions (see also Perttula 2002; Weisman 1999). For the Arikara, after the first century of European contact in the frontier of expanding European states in North America, cross-cultural interaction did not bring foreign domination to their distant lands and they did not wholeheartedly accept foreign goods (Rogers 1990:214). The interaction was largely governed by Arikara cultural values regarding the fur trade and by indigenous perceptions of Europeans and their material culture. The Arikara maintained native residential and ritual practices in their autonomous villages during the contact period, and they accepted or rejected foreign material culture according to native norms. Also, Arikara ceremonial earth lodges continued to be built and native burial practices predominated (Rogers 1990:176, 180). Furthermore, the Arikara did not always seek trade with Euro-Americans and they did not view foreign items as superior to native ones. Metal tools became important for Arikara quotidian life and they viewed guns as magical objects for spirit-like beings, like the Europeans who owned them (Rogers 1990:215).

In the remote Xingu region of Brazil, native societies maintained indigenous lifeways in the wake of contact, disease, and culture change from the 1500s to the present through native resistance and accommodation to distant colonial powers (Heckenberger 2005). Native ring villages continued to be the norm, the acceptance and rejection of foreign material culture were undertaken according to indigenous values, and perceptions of white foreigners followed native ideas of supernatural "others." Xingu peoples also maintained many sacred sites of natural and cultural origin that they associated with supernatural entities, ancestors, and native histories (Heckenberber 2005:227).

Similarly, through native agency in the unconquered frontier, Lacandon Maya reacted to conquest and colonialism according to native values in the middle ground. Centuries of contact and native perceptions of their changing world created contemporary Lacandon culture in an area that was not subjugated yet was affected by foreign colonizers. Here we will consider Lacandon agency with regard to ethnic labeling, foreign trade, sacred landscapes, and culture change and continuity to better comprehend Lacandon worldviews following European conquest and colonization of the southern Maya lowlands from the Colonial period to the present.

The Historic Lacandon

I will examine Lacandon Maya culture before 1980, after which they experienced extensive interaction with outsiders and dramatic culture change (McGee 2002). At this time, settlers constructed roads throughout Lacandon territory, leading to increased logging, tourism, and visits by priests and officials. Previously, many Lacandon followed indigenous lifeways, practiced native religion, and had minimal interaction with foreigners. However, the exposure to Western culture and foreign goods transformed Lacandon society in every way. The recent period of heightened social transformations in the late twentieth century, including the loss of native religion and the increase of the tourist economy, and the perception of the Lacandon as being the direct descendants of the ancient Maya, help explain why the Lacandon are one of the more intensely studied indigenous groups in Mesoamerica. Early missionaries, explorers, and government officials began recording Lacandon lifeways beginning in the late 1700s, and anthropologists and archaeologists have written about them and their "ancient ways" since the latter part of the nineteenth century (De Vos 1988b).

Historically, the Lacandon were recognized by their long hair, white tunics made of cotton or bark paper, and dialect of Yukatek Mayan. Their recent use of native bows and arrows and the preservation of indigenous rituals, which involved the use of ceramic incense burners with modeled faces and painted designs, also gained attention from anthropologists. The Lacandon worshiped native deities that have been intensively studied by numerous anthropologists over the last century (McGee 1990; G. Soustelle 1961; Tozzer 1907). The Lacandon typically lived in small, scattered settlements in the rainforest; some villages are still found at Lacanjá, Najá, and Mensabak (see Figure 13.1; Mensabak is adjacent to Najá). Their clearings contained the houses of nuclear or extended families, a ritual structure, gardens, and their cornfields. The Lacandon also relied on foraging in the forest, hunting, and fishing to make a living. They typically acquired foreign goods that became necessities, such as high-quality salt, cloth, and metal tools, by trading cacao, tobacco, and forest products in nearby towns. Informal political and religious leaders who acquired status and power through ritual and politics were the norm. Today only about 500 Lacandon live in settlement clusters in limited parts of lowland Chiapas; they have lost land and numbers to the encroachment of outsiders, particularly to the nearby Ch'ol and Tzeltal Maya and to Ladinos.[2]

Although many aspects of Lacandon culture did not change from the nineteenth to the early twentieth century, there were significant transformations, particularly in the early nineteenth century. Based on evidence from historic sources, it appears that Lacandon populations were much higher around 1850 (Palka 1998, 2005b). Settlements were encountered throughout Petén and the adjacent lands in lowland Chiapas, and overall population estimates run into the few thousands compared to the several hundreds today. Some documents mention large Lacandon villages, some with defensive perimeters of spiny plants, but their existence has yet to be confirmed through archaeology. Village life was part of the Lacandon reaction to encroachment, but defensible settlements are not common after the mid-nineteenth century in the written records. Lacandon leaders who may have had authority over a wide region and passed their status on to their sons are also described in the documents, but these roles are no longer present. Lacandon rituals including feasts, dances, and pilgrimages described in the nineteenth century also have disappeared.

The period from the mid- to the late nineteenth century was a time of extensive culture change for the Lacandon. This was the time of renewed conquest of the lowlands, which was encouraged by the Republics of México and Guatemala after independence from Spain. There were many lands and resources in the lowlands ready for the taking and transportation routes had to be established through the jungle to connect towns. Settlers and others who lost their land following economic reforms and privatization headed for the "uninhabited" rainforests of Chiapas and Petén. There they interacted with the Lacandon and subsequently brought news of the unconquered, "pagan" Maya—the Lacandon—to the Catholic Church. Priests traveled to Lacandon territory and missions were founded. Culture contact at this time led to increased trade, conflict, acculturation, and exposure to diseases. Many Lacandon died, were assimilated into Ladino society, or escaped further into the wilderness. The net result was that the Lacandon now had direct contact with foreigners, which had a profound effect on native culture and worldviews.

Conquest of the Maya Lowlands and Lacandon Origins

The regions occupied by the Lacandon Maya in the nineteenth century were never completely conquered and colonized by the Spanish or Ladinos. Southern and western Petén and eastern Chiapas remained in indigenous hands and the Lacandon lived in complete autonomy. Free Maya in this zone had minimal contact with outsiders, managed their local economies, maintained trade networks with outsiders and other Maya, and observed native religion and customs. All around them, however, other lowland Maya were subjugated by the Spanish and affected by this direct influence. Parts of Yucatán to the north were conquered in the 1540s with some free Maya populations present in the southern and eastern portions of the peninsula (Scholes and Roys 1968). Additionally, the Chontal Maya in southern Tabasco and Campeche were under the yoke of Spanish rule by the 1550s.

Thus, the Lacandon area contained some of the last independent Maya kingdoms. The Ch'ol-Lacandon, for instance, were located in the southern lands of the Chiapas lowlands near Lake Miramar (De Vos 1988a). After several attempts at conquest in the sixteenth and seventeenth centuries, the Spanish were finally successful around 1695, when they conquered and occupied a major Ch'ol-Lacandon center, called Sac Bahlan, for about two decades. It was abandoned around 1715 and the indigenous people either scattered to the forests or moved to colonial towns in Guatemala. Also during the seventeenth century, Spanish communication routes and missions were set up in the territory of the Manche-Ch'ol Maya in southern Petén, which led to their conquest and dispersal. Finally, the Itzaj Maya and other related Yukatek-speaking Maya groups in the central Petén lakes district suffered defeat by the Spanish military in 1697 (Jones 1998). These Maya were the last independent Maya kingdoms to fall to the Spanish; after their conquest, colonial towns and missions were created in the area. Nonetheless, many of the Itzaj Maya fled into the wilderness to maintain cultural autonomy by avoiding Spanish colonial rule.

Relatively little is known about the autonomous Maya in the rainforests of eastern Chiapas and much of Petén during the eighteenth century. A few written reports mention the presence of many free Maya who traded cacao, beeswax, honey, tobacco, and incense to outsiders—Spanish and indigenous alike—for metal tools, salt, and cloth (AGG 1936 [1754]; Orozco y Jimenez 1911). Little effort was made by the Spanish to subjugate or even contact the autonomous Maya in the southern lowlands at this time. By the late eighteenth century, the determined Spanish clergy attempted to establish contact and missions among these free, pagan Maya. It is at this time that we have the earliest cultural descriptions of the Lacandon. Beginning around 1785 in lowland Chiapas, contact was maintained between people in Palenque, Chiapas, and Maya who can be identified as Lacandon living in the forests nearby (Boremanse 1998a:4–6; De Vos 1988a, 1988b). A mission was established just south of the town where the Lacandon were visited by priests, townspersons, and officials for about twenty years. Here a church was built, the Lacandon maintained cornfields nearby, and they were given metal tools, cloth, and other goods by the missionaries. Similar attempts at establishing provisional mission centers in Petén near the Pasión and Usumacinta rivers were undertaken by Guatemalan authorities around 1815 (AGCA 1817).

Several scholars have suggested that the Lacandon were relatively recent migrants to the southern Maya lowlands (Duby and Blom 1962; Perera and Bruce 1985; Thompson 1977). They state that the Lacandon were probably descendants of Maya refugees from Yucatán escaping Spanish colonial rule. According to this scenario, these migrants pushed into the relatively uninhabited regions of lowland Chiapas and Petén to avoid contact, labor drafts, taxation, and religious conversion. Others indicate that perhaps the Kehach Maya of the upper Usumacinta River region near northern Petén and southern Campeche were the ancestors of the Lacandon (Villa Rojas 1985). After the conquest of the Kehach, it is possible that their remnant populations headed south to reside in the area today occupied by the Lacandon. Recently, it has been hypothesized that the Lacandon are descendants from Yukatek speakers from southern and eastern Petén who fled to the Usumacinta River region to avoid the renewed Spanish Conquest of the lowlands (Feldman 2000).

More than likely, the Lacandon had multiple ethnic origins from different interacting Maya groups occupying the free lowland Maya territories. The Lacandon probably descended from several indigenous peoples in the area, including Yukatek, Ch'olti-Lacandon, Ch'ol, Itzaj, and Cehach Maya, among others, including refugee highland Maya (Palka 2005b). Lacandon settlement patterns, religious beliefs, material culture, and lifeways are similar to other historic Mayas (see De Vos 1988a; Feldman 2000; Pugh, this volume; Villa Rojas 1985). In support of this is the fact that there were actually several Lacandon subgroups united by basic cultural elements but divided by particular social and linguistic differences, such as the Northern and Southern Lacandon (Boremanse 1998a). Therefore, the descendants of lowland and highland Mayas escaping conquest interacted heavily, eventually forming Lacandon society. Similar processes of ethnogenesis, or cultural formation and maintenance, in indigenous-controlled territories following conquest and foreign intrusion are documented for Amazonia (Hill 1996a).

Lacandon Identity and Viewing Others

Because of the long-term interaction between different groups in the southern Maya lowlands, the Lacandon created cultural categories pertaining to indigenous and foreign people. Their ethnic terms reflect indigenous values and control of interaction following culture contact in the colonial middle ground. The Lacandon refer to themselves as Hach Winik ("real people") or Winik ("people") and outsiders are seen as other kinds of people or beings (Nations 1984:32; Soustelle 1970:56). Typically, the Lacandon divide themselves into different ethnic groups with the Northern and Southern groups being the largest today. For example, the Northern Lacandon call the Southern Lacandon Chukuch Nok ("long tunics") (McGee 1990:1), and they indicate that other ethnic Lacandon existed until the mid-twentieth century. Lacandon from outside any particular group are sometimes called *kanakachi* ("they of the forest") by some Lacandon (Cline 1944:110; Nations 1984:33). When referring to themselves in Spanish, the Lacandon use the word *caribe*, which was a general term for "cannibal" borrowed during the Colonial period. This term may have been applied to the Lacandon by early Spanish explorers with the Lacandon hence adopting it as a self-identifier in the company of foreigners. Some Lacandon may have referred to themselves as *masewal*, which is a Nahuatl loan word for "peasant" or "commoner" commonly used as a self-identifying term in Yucatán (Farriss 1984; Tozzer 1907:3).

Other Maya people, such as the nearby Tzeltal and Ch'ol, are referred to as the somewhat derogatory term *kah*, "town" or something like "townspeople" or "city slicker," by the Lacandon, whereas foreigners, particularly light-skinned ones, are called *tsul*, which may be glossed as "foreigner." Women of European descent are known as *xunaan* (McGee 2002:30). Some Lacandon refer to people of European descent generally as *rayos*, which is a Spanish term used for "people who use lightning/guns," and familiar outsiders are called *la gente*, or "the [Spanish] people" (Duby and Blom 1962:296). According to the Lacandon, their indigenous language is *hach t'an* ("real language") and all outsiders have *putun t'an* ("outsider/foreign language"). Besides the differences in appearance and language, the Lacandon recognize the religious and behavioral divides that separate them from outsiders.

The ethnic categorization where indigenous peoples refer to themselves as superior or real humans and to others as lesser peoples or other beings occurs after periods of intensified contact (Barth 1969; Spicer 1980). The Lacandon attempted to maintain indigenous lifeways and autonomy in the face of colonial domination over many centuries, which is reflected in their ethnic categories. Thus, indigenous groups impacted by foreign contact maintain the ideal that they, and not the others, have real language and culture. Thus, Lacandon beliefs were reinforced by the use of ethnic terms when faced with culture contact and outside influences. Lacandon ethnic categories also explain their world, their place in it, and the indigenous histories regarding culture contact and its subsequent effects on society.

Western Goods and Shifts in Worldviews

The acquisition of foreign trade goods became an important impetus for interaction with outsiders for the Lacandon. When they came across outsiders in the forest, the Lacandon frequently attempted to initiate trade. Additionally, they periodically traveled to Ladino logging camps to barter for desired foreign items (Maler 1901). They also trekked to distant towns, such as Palenque in Chiapas, Tenosique in Tabasco, and La Libertad in Petén, for trade. Moreover, the Lacandon resided in missions to receive Western goods and to open trade networks with townspeople (Boremanse 1998a). The Lacandon learned the names of goods in Spanish, Tzeltal, and Ch'ol; they understood the value of certain materials for foreigners; and they actively acquired or produced what outsiders desired in trade. The written records state that the Lacandon exchanged cacao, tobacco, beeswax, honey, incense, and bows and arrows for machetes, axes, knives, salt, cloth, and jewelry (De Vos 1988b). Both sides benefited from the trade and interaction. Outsiders highly valued Lacandon products, and Western items became highly sought after by the Lacandon. The Lacandon received European-manufactured necessities and the colonizers received high-quality products from the unconquered territory for consumption or to pay taxes (cacao and tobacco, for instance).

Many scholars have felt that intensified cross-cultural interaction and trade in the Lacandon area did not occur until the second half of the twentieth century (Duby and Blom 1962; Perera and Bruce 1985). However, with the appearance of loggers, missionaries, explorers, and settlers in the lowlands in greater numbers during the nineteenth century, Western goods became more accessible in Lacandon settlements than in the Colonial period. The Lacandon had much control in trade and interaction, and they accepted some goods and rejected others, such as firearms and Western clothing, according to their norms and values. The importance of Western trade goods and the evidence for continuous contact with outsiders is obvious in the archaeology of nineteenth-century Lacandon sites.

Common trade items excavated at Lacandon sites, like El Caobal, Petén, consisted of axes, machetes, knives, medicine bottles, and foreign painted pottery (Figure 13.2; see Palka 1998, 2005b). The decorated pottery included hand-painted or transfer-print wares, such as Blue Willow pottery, the majority of which were cups, bowls, and platters. These types of foreign pottery indicate the importance of acquiring fine ceramics for serving food and the increasing importance of individual

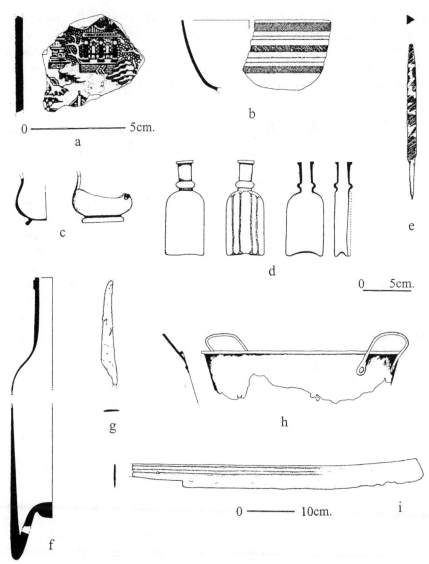

13.2. Lacandon trade goods from El Caobal, Petén, Guatemala: (a) Blue Willow ware; (b) painted white earthenware bowl; (c) white teacup; (d) medicine bottle; (e) metal file; (f) wine bottle; (g) scissor; (h) metal pot; and (i) machete (drawings by Luis F. Luin).

versus communal tableware resulting from the increase in foreign influence. Foreign clothing, Christian items (crosses, rosary beads), and firearms were notable in their absence at Lacandon sites. These goods were not often culturally acceptable and generally had no value for the Lacandon. The Lacandon maintained native dress, they often eschewed foreign religion and associated material culture, and they were frequently fearful of guns.

However, with trade came additional effects of culture contact. One result of interaction with foreigners was disease, especially influenza, yellow fever, malaria, measles, and smallpox. The reduction in the number of Lacandon sites and populations in the nineteenth century indicates that they experienced a substantial demographic decline from the mid-nineteenth century to the beginning of the twentieth century (Baer and Merrifield 1971; Palka 2005b). Additionally, many Lacandon chose to reside in Ladino towns and assimilate, as the following quote illustrates: "Sometimes in one of the *monterías* [logging camps] there is found a Lacandone who has adopted the life and customs of the Mexicans. His hair is short, and he is not readily to be distinguished from his fellow-Mexican" (Tozzer 1907:34). Furthermore, from the cross-cultural interaction came native culture change, such as the reliance on machine-made cloth over native cotton or bark cloth and the belief in Christ (*jesuclisto*) as an aspect of the sun (Bruce et al. 1971:170–171). Metal tools eventually replaced Lacandon stone axes and chert cutting tools.

Interestingly, the Lacandon developed folktales and mythology related to contact, foreign goods, and the effects on native lifeways. According to the Lacandon, Ladinos and outsiders controlled the production of writing, metal tools, domestic animals, money, medicine, and other modern necessities. Originally, the gods gave these things to the Lacandon, but the Lacandon subsequently lost them because they did not care for them. For example, their domesticated animals escaped while they slept. The deities punished them for their laziness and the Lacandon were then forced to scavenge for stone for tools, hunt for meat, and extract salt from palm ash (Bruce 1974:137–145; Cline 1944; McGee 1990:19–22).

On the other hand, the gods rewarded foreigners for their hard work and ingenuity. It is interesting to note that the Lacandon god of foreigners, Akyantho', rose in importance following increased contact with outsiders over the last 150 years. Akyantho' is a light-skinned deity who dresses in Western clothing and wears a cowboy hat and pistol. This god is associated with disease, Western goods, commerce, and lands belonging to foreigners (which are sometimes referred to as territories to the north) (Bruce et al. 1971:11, 17; Perera and Bruce 1985:290; Tozzer 1907:94). This deity subsequently became elevated in the Lacandon pantheon; some Lacandon even suggest that Akyantho' is older than their principal deity, Hachakyum ("Our True Lord"). They also suggest that Akyantho' will replace Hachakyum in the near future since more foreigners are migrating to the lowlands and are becoming increasingly more powerful economically and politically. The increased importance of the foreign god of commerce may indicate the presence of a Lacandon cargo cult during the contact era whereby natives could gain influence or control over foreign trade goods.

Lacandon Ceremonial Landscapes

It has been demonstrated in other parts of the world that people, especially agricultural societies, inhabiting a new area attempt to explain their surroundings and claim territory through the creation of sacred places (McAnany 1995:97–99). These ceremonial landscapes may include hills, springs, caves, and ruins of past civilizations. At these locales, rituals are often undertaken to communicate with rain and agricultural deities, earth and fertility beings, and ancestors. Although the religious importance of these sacred places is undeniable, newly arrived groups or recently formed ethnic groups create ties with deities and ancestors associated with their land to legitimize ownership of territory. The ties to ceremonial landscapes are also important in contested ground where outsiders have invaded indigenous regions. In this case, through indigenous agency the Lacandon observed their native religion and by extension enacted their sovereignty over the landscape.

Ancient Maya ruins, caves, hills, and cliffs, especially those with rock art, were important ceremonial landscapes for the Lacandon (McGee 1990). The earliest archaeologists exploring the forests of Chiapas and Petén mention the presence of Lacandon incense burners and signs of newly completed rituals in standing structures in ancient Maya ruins (Maler 1901). Explorers also found Lacandon incense burners on low ancient residential platforms. Additionally, excavations uncovered Lacandon *incensarios* near a rock outcrop in Petén, Guatemala (see Figure 13.3; Palka 2005b). Pilgrimages to sacred places and burning incense in brazers while giving offerings to deities is widely documented for other Postclassic and Historic period Mayas (see Chuchiak, this volume). The first ethnographers living with the Lacandon also recorded the sacred nature of caves and hills (Soustelle 1935). The Lacandon stated that these ceremonial landscapes were the homes of specific deities who had to be placated with offerings and rituals. The ancient Maya ruin of Yaxchilán, for instance, was a major pilgrimage site for the Lacandon, who traveled there to burn incense, leave offerings, and perform rituals to ensure agricultural fertility and human health (McGee 1990). Lacandon graves and god houses were actually oriented toward this important archaeological site. Lacandon settlements were located near, but rarely in, Classic Maya sites, and we know little about the specific cosmological importance of Maya ruins to the Lacandon (but see McGee 2005).

The same holds true for cliff shrines near lakes that exhibit painted rock art. These sites were sacred places and homes of the gods and had to be visited by the Lacandon to maintain balance in their world. One instance clearly demonstrating a Lacandon worldview of sacred cliffs following outside influences was recorded by an explorer examining rock art on a sacred cliff on Lake Itsanokuh (Petha) in Chiapas. A Lacandon religious leader rapidly approached in a canoe and said, "No *hombre*, get away from there, that is my *santo* [saint/god], it is our Christ-Mary, careful hom-

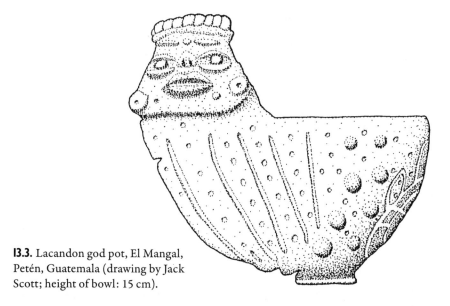

13.3. Lacandon god pot, El Mangal, Petén, Guatemala (drawing by Jack Scott; height of bowl: 15 cm).

bre, the *tigre* [jaguar] will eat you, let's go hombre, that is why there is so much water [flooding] from the bad heart of my santo" (Maler 1901:32). One painted design with crocodilian features on this cliff was said by a Lacandon headman to be the god Itsanokuh and it curiously resembles Postclassic images of Itsamna, a deity associated with crocodiles and water, which is probably more than coincidence (Palka 2005a). The Lacandon believe that another sacred cliff painting at Lake Mensabak (found close to the community of Najá) was the god called Mensabak, who lived in the cliff. Mensabak was the deity of rain, storms, and gunpowder (related to both thunder and war) and this entity received Lacandon offerings at the base of his cliff residence. What is particularly interesting is that one of the larger polychrome paintings and associated geometric designs on the rock face at Mensabak (Figure 13.4), which probably dates to late pre-conquest or early Colonial times (see Stone, this volume) may depict Tlaloc, the Precolumbian god associated with rain, storms, lightning, and military conflict throughout ancient Mesoamerica (Palka 2005a; Pasztory 1974). This god is shown as having round goggle eyes, large fangs, and holding jars with water pouring out. Could Mensabak actually be directly related to Tlaloc? If this is the case, then perhaps the Lacandon have specific knowledge of cultural practices of previous local inhabitants of the Protohistoric period that was passed down to them over many generations. Perhaps the Lacandon are actual descendants of earlier pilgrims to or residents of Lake Mensabak.

Regardless of the origin of the paintings and their creators, the Lacandon preserved aspects of an ancient worldview linked to sacred landscapes in their

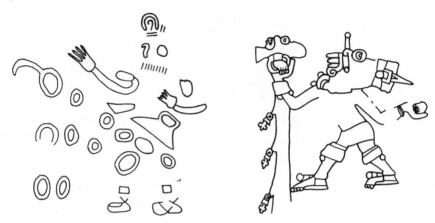

I3.4. Tlaloc iconography: left, Lake Mensabak, Chiapas, México; and right, Codex Borgia (drawings by author).

territory. In the final chapter in this volume, Pugh provides additional information and insights on Maya sacred landscapes and specific examples of Lacandon ceremonial importance of sacred places. The Lacandon and their ancestors, like the Yukatek Maya at Cozumel (Patel, this volume), made pilgrimages to sacred places to reaffirm ties to the supernatural, ancestors, and territory. The Lacandon maintain ties to important ritual places in their land where deities live and receive offerings from people. Obviously, the cliff sites are important for Lacandon beliefs regarding rain and water. The Lacandon inherited these sacred landscapes and attachments to territory. They may have focused certain rituals here following the migration of outsiders into the lowlands to reaffirm their ties to the land and resident gods in the face of outside threat and foreign influence.

Caves were equally important ritual places and ties to the landscape for the Lacandon. In this volume, Stone discusses Maya communal cave rites and the continued importance of native rites in their historical sacred places into the Colonial period. Caves were the doorways to the homes of the gods where Lacandon religious specialists could communicate with the supernatural beings and ancestors. One settlement in Chiapas was located near a cave believed to be the abode of the sun god (Duby and Blom 1962). The inhabitants refused to move from the area despite the fact that the ground there was not as fertile as other areas. Some Lacandon formerly buried their dead in caves, not to enter the underworld but to join the sun god, who traveled through the underground passages (Soustelle 1937). It was also recorded that other Lacandon explored caves, although reluctantly since they were the houses of gods. They also collected ancient Maya pottery from them to be used as ritual vessels at Lacandon shrines (Soustelle 1937).

Continuities in Worldviews

Because many historic Lacandon retained their autonomy into the twentieth century, much of their native religion was preserved, albeit modified by internal and external forces. Hence, a large number of Lacandon were not influenced greatly by Christianity like other Mesoamerican groups. Without fear of reprisal from foreign authorities and well beyond the gaze of foreigners, the Lacandon worshiped native deities and carried out traditional rituals in special buildings in their settlements into the late twentieth century. In fact, the Lacandon can be singled out from other lowland Maya in the historic records from the Late Colonial period to the twentieth century because of their distinctive ceremonial pottery and their ritual structures, or "god houses." The god house was often the physical and social center of Lacandon settlements, and men's activities were undertaken within this structure. Lacandon ritual behaviors have roots in Precolumbian times, and their indigenous beliefs survived until modern times because of indigenous agency. Their rituals and worldviews have been shaped by centuries of contact and indigenous social and religious transformations, but they reflect the needs, values, and cultural milieu of the Lacandon.

The Lacandon worshiped and contacted deities through their god pots (*u lakih k'uh*), or ceramic incense burners (Figure 13.5). John Chuchiak (this volume) explores parallel rites of the Yukatek Maya, who used similar incense burners, that were important from ancient to historic times. The Lacandon god pots had very distinctive forms and decorations, and each one represented a specific god. The bowls of these incensarios were shaped like traditional Lacandon hemispherical vessels and modeled anthropomorphic heads decorated the rims. The vessels were typically painted entirely white and then symbols and animal designs were done in red and black pigments. Earlier god pots had carved and modeled designs on the exterior walls of the vessels, as in an example excavated from El Mangal, Petén (Figure 13.3). Some of these incense burners had spikes, like their Precolumbian counterparts; had incised rather than painted designs; and had appendages, including arms, hands, legs, and handles. Some ethnographic incense burners and archaeological examples have zoomorphic features modeled onto them. The Lacandon manufactured the god pots to be proper ritual vessels to house deities through the native incense burner renewal ceremony, which included the placing of sacred objects, such as cacao beans, stones, and artifacts found in Maya ruins, in the pot to represent the deity's organs.

The Lacandon communicated with their gods by giving offerings to and chanting in front of the god pots. The Lacandon believed that the god pots were living embodiments of the deities they represented when they were utilized in rituals (McGee 2002). The Lacandon worshipped many deities related to nature, the underworld, and the cosmos, thus the quantities of god pots needed for different

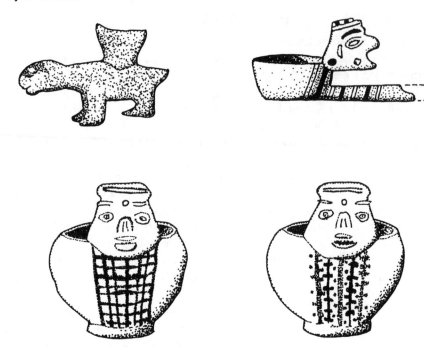

13.5. Lacandon god pots (top, after Tozzer 1907; bottom, after Bruce 1968; drawings by Jack Scott, not to scale).

ceremonies were great. Incense in the form of nodules and human or animal rubber figurines were burned in the bowl. Spoonfuls of *balché* (a mildly alcoholic drink made from tree bark and honey or sugarcane), various types of foods (especially ritual tamales), and cigars were placed in the mouths of the modeled heads on the god pots so the deities could consume them. A common request of the gods was good health and a bountiful harvest, each demanding constant offerings and prayer by the Lacandon religious specialists.

The ceremonial god house in each Lacandon settlement contained large numbers of god pots. These buildings were packed with ritual items, such as offering bowls, incense nodule boards, carved gourds, fire drills, bow and arrow sets, ceramic and turtle shell drums, rattles, and balché drinking pots. The god house (*yatoch k'uh*) was constructed similarly to the Lacandon residences, but it was often larger. They also contained roofs that nearly touched the ground so that the ritual items and ceremonies were completely hidden from outsiders. The Lacandon anointed the beams of this structure with red achiote dye that included painted designs, and they conceived of the dye as a blood offering to deities. The god house was also oriented to the cardinal directions to which offerings were spilled and a conch-shell trumpet blown to initiate the rites. Trails leading from the settlement were also placed along the cardinal points. These practices effectively "centered" the Lacandon settlement and god house in the universe and defined social and sacred space.

If rituals in the god house or at sacred places failed, deities could claim the lives of Lacandon or they would not act to cure the sick. The interments of the dead were placed near the god house or in a cemetery near the settlement. In the past, the Lacandon maintained some of these burial grounds and they visited sacred places to honor ancestors. During the burial ceremonies, the deceased undertook a journey to the underworld called *metlan* (from Nahuatl *mictlan*). The Lacandon placed their dead in a grave with their possessions and some food items. A mound of earth and a thatched roof were placed over the grave, and some offerings, such as food, candles, and palm-leaf effigies of dogs, sat near the grave for the deceased to take to the underworld.

Conclusions

We are fortunate to have much information on Lacandon Maya worldviews and how their perceptions of their surroundings, the cosmos, and their place in the world changed following the conquest of their territory. Corroborating evidence regarding Lacandon worldviews can be obtained from archaeology, historic documents, museum collections, and a century of ethnographies, enriching our knowledge of native religion and society in the lowlands after the Colonial period. Lacandon worldviews were shaped through interactions between various indigenous and foreign peoples over a long period. Therefore, Lacandon cosmology has elements related to Precolumbian cultures in addition to transformed religious beliefs that were formed following native ethnogenesis and cross-cultural interaction. They devised new perceptions of themselves and others and accepted into their lives or rejected certain kinds of foreign material culture. The Lacandon also modified ancient beliefs in sacred places and incorporated new religious sites to mark their identity and autonomous territory following colonialism.

Importantly, the Lacandon were able to preserve their worldviews, or alternatively shape them according to their needs and experiences. As this chapter has demonstrated, Lacandon religion and worldviews are not holdovers from ancient Maya times, as suggested in previous discussions (Boremanse 1998b; McGee 1984; Perera and Bruce 1985). They were successful at cultural preservation since they were largely unconquered and resided in a zone of indigenous refuge far from colonial powers, but their lives changed considerably nonetheless. It is the maintenance of indigenous culture and the observable native innovations that make the investigation of autonomous Lacandon society important for the study of native responses to European contact. The Lacandon are an example of an indigenous people that negotiated and constructed their identity, economic exchanges, autonomy, and territory in a colonial middle ground, like other unconquered peoples in other areas around the world. Thus, Lacandon agency and the maintenance of their values led to the formation of their worldviews following the conquest, combining change and continuity to form a new culture when others were being destroyed, heavily influenced by foreign powers, or assimilated.

Notes

1. In using the term Lacandon, rather than the lesser used Lakandon or Hach Winik, I follow the spelling from the literature on indigenous people of México.

2. Ladinos are defined as those people who speak Spanish, follow Christian beliefs, and have Western material culture.

Music Syncretism in the Postclassic K'iche' Warrior Dance and the Colonial Period Baile de los Moros y Cristianos

Mark Howell

CHAPTER FOURTEEN

Cultural Aesthetics and Dance-Plays and Their Music in Highland Guatemala

Having knowledge of a Precolumbian Maya cultural aesthetic of music would be valuable in revealing socially agreed-upon favored sounds and in helping fill in the blanks of a pre-conquest Maya gestalt. But as with the musics of most vanished cultures (the Harappan and Natchez come to mind), the music of the prehispanic Maya has proved elusive to modern ears. Luckily, the syncretism of Maya and Spanish music elements in a place apparently conducive to their joining, the Guatemalan highlands, has presented us a unique opportunity to discern vanished musics of the Precolumbian highland Maya through the abstraction of its hybridization with one whose makeup is rather well known, the Colonial and post-Colonial period music of the Spanish. One of the best preserved of such syncretic musics was that used to accompany dance-plays, Maya communal performance events involving dance and theatre, as well as music (Howell 2004).

There are several types of highland Guatemalan dance-plays, defined by their principle theme (e.g., conquest, hunting, and sacrifice), most of which apparently emerged during the Postclassic or the Colonial period. Today these performance events are called *bailes* and as in the colonial past are typically performed at a town's central church, *calvaria*, and/or *cofradía* houses during saint-day festivals. (For more on cofradías, see Carlsen, this volume.) The bailes of concern here, the K'iche' warrior dance, the *Baile de los Moros y*

Cristianos, and to a lesser extent the *Baile de la Conquista*, are three of the oldest known dance-plays in Guatemala. The latter two are still performed.

One unique highland Guatemalan baile characteristic revealed through ethnomusicology and music archaeology is the standardized pairing of a play's theme to accompanying music instruments, an association that in many cases can be traced to colonial times, if not earlier (Gage 1929; Goetz 1953; Howell 2004; Tedlock 2003). For instance, a baile type with a sacrificial theme, locally referred to as *tun*, has been documented since the Colonial period as accompanied by valveless trumpet(s) and/or a slit-drum, a short section of log made to produce pitches (sounds of specific frequency) (Howell 2004). Although both the theme and the instrumentation of tun bailes are indigenous (and likely Precolumbian), other Guatemalan Maya dance-plays combine local and foreign elements. For example, the deer dance, *Baile del Venado*, pairs an indigenous theme—hunting or wife procurement—with Western-introduced instrument types, typically the marimba (a xylophone variant), whereas the *Baile de los Moros y Cristianos* (often shortened here to *Moros*) pairs an introduced theme—Spanish Conquest—with local instrument types, the duct flute and skin drum. Table 14.1 lists theme-to-instrument pairings in a sampling of highland Guatemalan bailes documented by me (Howell 2004).

Although it is my belief that some Precolumbian meta-cultural concerns, such as duality and cardinal directions, are embedded in highland Guatemalan instruments and baile-instrument associations, the principle thesis of this chapter concerns syncretism: more specifically, the theorized transformation of the European-derived dance-play, *Moros*, introduced into Central America in the seventeenth century, through its absorption of a now-extinct Postclassic K'iche' performance event known as the warrior dance (Carmack 1973, 1981; Howell 2004). I argue that this merging is not only revealed in shared thematic elements of the two dances, such as war and preparation for war, but also—and more significantly—in shared instrumentation, flute and drum. This theory will be advanced by archaeological, anthropological, and ethnomusicological methods applied to the Postclassic K'iche' warrior dance and the *Baile de los Moros y Cristianos*, as performed in Europe and the Americas, and to the instrumentation of the former in Guatemala and the latter in Spain and Guatemala.

Su and *K'ojom:* Two K'iche' Music Instruments and the Postclassic K'iche' Warrior Dance

Etymological evidence for a K'iche' tradition of instrument-baile association includes su, the K'iche' term for either a duct flute (a flute with a narrow opening at its mouthpiece end that channels air to an aperture) or the European-introduced double-reed chirimia (an instrument similar in shape and tone, or sound quality, to an oboe) (Edmonson 1976b; Horspool 1982:32). Thematic context determines

Table 14.1 Highland Guatemala Music Instrument Dance-Play Classification Table

Type	Name	Theme	Instrumentation
Sacrifice (*Tun*)			
Xaioi tun	Song of Tolgom	Sacrifice	Unknown
	Lotzo Tun		Trumpet
	Rab'inal Achi		Slit-Drum, Trumpet
Tz'unum	*Tzunun*	Hunting to Agriculture Transition	Slit-Drum, Trumpet, Tortoise Shell
	Baile de las Canastas		Slit-Drum, Trumpet, Tortoise Shell
Dee	*Baile del Venada*	Hunting/Wife Procurement	Marimba
Warrior	Unknown	Celebration of War Heroes (Precolumbian)	Skin Drum, Flute
Conquest	*Baile de los Moros y Cristianos*	Christian Conversion (Postcolumbian)	Skin Drum, Flute
	Baile de la Conauista		Skin Drum, *Chirimia*

From Howell, 2004.

which of the two instruments are being desribed when the word is used. Although for the conquest-themed dance-play *Baile de la Conquista* (sometimes called *La Conquista*), a su is a chirimia paired with a tambor (skin drum), and for the conquest-and-religious-conversion-themed baile, *Moros*, a su is a flute paired with a tambor. The fact that the flute and chirimia share the same name may reflect a K'iche' belief that the sounds of the two instruments are largely analogous and that dance-plays that are thematically related require similar instrumentation. In other words, any melodic instrument that plays for a baile concerned with the theme of conquest may be referred to as a su. Such use of shared names for dance-plays and their accompanying instruments is not unique in highland Guatemala; for instance, sacrifice-themed bailes use valveless trumpets and/or slit-drums, with the baile and both accompanying instruments referred to as "tun" (Table 14.1). (For additional definitions of tun, see Chuchiak, this volume.)

At least two indigenous texts written in the early Colonial period, the *Título C'oyoi* and the *Annals of the Cakchiquels*, and one play recorded later, the *Rab'inal Achi*,[1] describe the K'iche' warrior dance and its use of flute(s) and drum(s).

According to Robert Carmack (1973:267–268), the *Título C'oyoi* is a lineage-migration tale that was most likely written at Q'umarkaj between 1550 and 1570 by members of the K'oyoi ruling lineage (its principal author being Juan de Penonias de Putanza). The *Annals of the Cakchiquels*, another such account, was written in two sections, the first authored by Hernández Arana, of the elite Kakchikel Xajil family, who like Putanza was a witness to the conquest, and the second by writers not established but who were likely related to Arana (Recinos and Goetz 1953). The dance-play *Rab'inal Achi* was purportedly first copied in 1855 by the Belgian cleric Charles É. Brasseur de Bourboug (1862) from an oral version recited to him by Bartolome Sis, an Achi Maya of Rabinal, Guatemala. Events in these three documents extend into a mythological past and may be based on Precolumbian codices. Incidents of known dates begin in the late fifteenth century (Howell 2004).

The warrior dance described in the above documents is no longer performed, and as there is no known ethnohistoric record of its origin, content, form, or decline, it likely disappeared before or during the early Colonial period. Possibly this dance, unlike sacrifice bailes such as the *Rab'inal Achi*, was regarded as a significant enough threat to fledgling Spanish hegemony to be marked early on for eradication. But if, as theorized, the K'iche' transferred some of its Precolumbian components to the *Moros* (a Spanish-introduced warrior dance), one such component could have been the requisite instrumentation for warrior dances: again, the flute and drum.

K'iche'an documents, particularly the *Título*, the *Annals*, and the *Rab'inal Achi*, sometimes include words or phrases related to flutes or drums, among which are su, *cham*, and k'ojom. Su, as established, is a flute or a chirimia; cham or *cham cham* is another term for flute (Edmonson 1976b); and k'ojom is a percussion instrument: "an instrument struck or plucked" (O'Brien-Rothe 1998:723). At present, "k'ojom" is sometimes used for the marimba, which leads Dennis Tedlock (2003:292) to propose that the word may have once referred to a slit-drum, the other Maya instrument with wooden keys, or lamellas, struck by mallets (Edmonson 1976b:101). Countering this meaning, my Guatemalan informants used "k'ojom" solely to indicate a skin drum, reserving "tun" for slit-drum. Moreover, to my untrained ear, the word sounds similar to *kai yum*, the Lacandon name for a pottery-framed skin drum also known from the Maya archaeological record. Nevertheless, "k'ojom" does have multiple meanings and is also used as a generic term for music, as in Casa K'ojom, "House of Music" (Samuel Arce's private museum near Antigua).

On the page in the *Título C'oyoi* numbered 21 by Carmack (1973:277, 295, 325) are the adjacent phrases *ixajil tun* (sacrifice dance) and *bixa subakiba* (song with bone flute).[2] Carmack (1973:21–22) determined that this section of the text included an inventory of prehispanic dances. If he is correct, the phrase *ixajil tun* . . . *bixa subakiba* suggests that tun dances, ixajil tun, like the *Rab'inal Achi*, which during the time of the *Título's* writing used a slit-drum and/or trumpet(s), should be considered separate from the su dances, or bixa subakiba, identified then as now as those using flutes. Indeed, if the words and phrases in this document are part of a dance inventory, bixa subakiba (or a portion of this phrase) may have been the K'iche' name for the Precolumbian highland Maya warrior dance, which would mean that "su," as in the case of "tun," once stood for both an instrument and the dance it accompanied. I have not located the pairing of *xajil* (dance) with *tza* (warrior)—or related spellings for these words—which would translate literally as "warrior dance" (Carmack 1973:299).

In the *Título C'oyoi* the best evidence for an association of the flute and drum with the warrior dance is found in a description of ceremonies known to have been enacted prior to the decisive battle for Guatemala, near Quezaltenango at Xelaju, between Tecum Uman and Pedro Alvarado (Carmack 1973:282–283, 302, 340). *Su uk'o* (flute-drum) is mentioned near the end of a passage detailing this event, which also lists several K'iche' warriors (identified by their titles) who "performed the song and dance with the flute(s) and drum at the stone buildings of Xelaju" (Carmack 1973:302). A full reading of this text implies that Tecum Uman joined in the pre-battle music-dance ceremony after an earlier *xajoj cham cham* (flute dance) where attending warriors danced in his honor (Carmack 1973).

In the *Annals of the Cakchiquels* (Recinos and Goetz 1953), flutes and drums were also sounded before a war during the late fifteenth century initiated by several vassal groups against their K'iche' overlords. As in the *Título C'oyoi*, use of these instruments might indicate a pre-battle warrior dance. In the *Annals* it is recounted that Kay Junahpu, a leader of the rebelling Tukuches, led a successful attack on the K'iche', and to paraphrase from that document: On 11 Ah (May 18, 1493), the morning of the attack, the sound of his flutes and drums was heard (Carmack 1973:108).

These and other writings describe highland Guatemalan battles as characterized by "war cries, the sound of flutes, the beating of drums and the shells" (Carmack 1973:103). And it is possible that flutes were part of the requisite paraphernalia of warriors. In fact, in the *Título C'oyoi*, warriors are named in association with companion objects that include *ubak cham* (bone flutes), as well as lances, deer hooves, and lion's claws (Carmack 1973:277). Although flutes and drums may have been two among several sound makers warriors carried, it is noteworthy that instruments other than the flute and drum are not listed for K'iche'an pre-battle ceremonies explicitly described (Howell 2004).

In the *Rab'inal Achi*, these two instruments are requested by a warrior for a dance independent of the commencement of war. Near the end of the baile is a scene in which the captive K'iche' warrior-prince asks his Rabinal captors to allow him to hear the sounds of flutes and drum: *yaqui zu . . . yaqui gohom . . . Queche zu . . . Queche gohom* (Brasseur 1862:106–107) (Mexican flute . . . Mexican drum . . . K'iche' flute . . . K'iche' drum). When the request is denied, the warrior "moves back and forth to and from the four corners of the court to the rhythm of flutes and drums" (Brasseur 1862:107). According to the storyline of the play, no war is in immediate preparation, but the dance occurs shortly before the K'iche' warrior engages in a ceremonial battle with the Rabinal warrior societies, ending in his death by sacrifice. Accordingly, the inclusion of the three main components of the warrior dance in the *Rab'inal Achi*, as described in the *Título C'oyoi* and the *Annals of the Cakchiquels*—the combined flute and drum, the dance, and the battle with warriors—suggests that in this scene of the baile the K'iche' prince performs the warrior dance.

As an addendum, the dancing warrior, like the one described above, may be the subject of a painting on a palace wall at the Postclassic K'iche' capital, K'umarkaj. This mural (in Mixtec-Puebla style) features a splendidly dressed K'iche' warrior in ritualized motion, his preparation for combat confirmed by his outfit of feathered leg bands, armbands, sandals, short embroidered skirt, and round shield with attached arrows held in his left hand. The extended stance of the figure and the container rattle in his right hand imply a dance, an interpretation that I share with Ruud W. van Akkeren (2000:329) and Carmack (1973:295), but if any instruments in addition to the rattle (like a flute and drum) were meant to accompany this dance, they are not included in the mural (Figure 14.1).

The *Baile de los Moros y Cristianos*: A Spanish Warrior Dance

The proposed post-conquest descendant of the K'iche' warrior dance can be traced to a type of pre-Renaissance European dance that emphasized fertility and war. During the late Middle Ages, this dance was known as a "Morris dance" or the *moriscas* (Moorish) (Kurath 1949:94, 96; Sachs 1937:87; Warman 1985 [1972]:16). Curt Sachs (1937:333) describes the moriscas as the most frequently mentioned European dance of the fifteenth century, and he discusses it as having two forms: a solo dance, derived from Moorish court performances, and a dance of two or more performers, emphasizing swordplay between Christians and Moslems (Sachs 1937:333). A version of the second form ultimately emerged in the Spanish kingdom of Valencia following the expulsion of Moors from neighboring Andalusia and was probably the dance-play exported to New Spain during the Colonial period (Bode 1961:211). I have reviewed ethnographies of the Spanish *Baile de los Moros y Cristianos* as currently performed in Alcoy, Valencia, the Spanish town with the oldest known tradition (since the 1680s) (Harris 1994; Imafuku 1986), and will summarize some of the dance-play's aspects below.

On the day before the feast of San Jorge, a troupe of masked actors in the roles of Christians arrives in Alcoy to the accompaniment of a brass band. Their captain is given the keys to a wooden castle built for the celebration in the town plaza, and later masked actors in the roles of Moors arrive to similar brass band accompaniment. The next morning, the Moors try to gain control of the castle by negotiation,

14.1. Dancing warrior at K'umarkaj (author's drawing from Carmack 1981).

but when this fails, they overrun the structure and replace the Spanish flag with their own, temporarily signifying Islamic victory.

In the afternoon of the same day the Christian captain approaches the castle and demands its surrender. Verbal exchanges again give way to battle, at the height of which a boy, personifying San Jorge, rides up on horseback and the Christians rallying behind the saint's manifestation retake the castle for good. (At the conclusion of these events, participants and observers attend a Mass given at one of the town's local cathedrals.) Points to keep in mind are the themes of battle preparation, battle, and musical instrument accompaniment, here a brass band.

MARK HOWELL

14.2. Cobán *Moros* procession showing actors and musicians on their way to a performance in front of the central church (photograph by author, August 2001).

The *Baile de los Moros y Cristianos*: Highland Guatemalan Versions

The *Baile de los Moros y Cristianos* as currently performed in highland Guatemala typically features one scene abstracted from a drama comprised of several, focusing on troop assembly, negotiations, battle, and surrender (Horspool 1982). I witnessed two such performances of the baile during the respective saint days of St. Domingo in Cobán in 2001 and St. Pablo in Rabinal in 2002. In each, short speeches were delivered by actors in masks between dances (most often representing sword fights), accompanied by flute and drum (Figure 14.2).

Although both productions were visually and aurally arresting, it was difficult to discern the storyline from the scenes presented. Luckily, in highland Guatemala there are several written scripts for this dance-play type used for rehearsal purposes, all with a somewhat similar plot (Bode 1961). One, *Original del Baile de los Moros y Cristianos*, written in Spanish by Jose Angel Octgin in 1964, tells of a Christian king who solicits soldiers to join in his effort to remove the Moors then occupying Spain. The Moorish king makes a similar solicitation of Moorish soldiers, and members of both sides give speeches directed at their compatriots as well as their adversaries. Some speeches involve negotiations to avoid war, but ultimately the negotiations fail and fighting breaks out. During the battle the Moorish king is killed, an event interpreted by both sides as symbolic of Christian victory.

Octgin's script provides no clues about the staging of its performance, although the characters either speak sequentially or those of the same "faith" speak collectively, as if in chorus. (There are more sequential than collective speeches.) Concerning musical accompaniment, of its fifty-five pages (written in longhand) ten include tambor (drum) cues, given on pages 3, 12, 19, 20, 21, 26, 34, 46, 54, and 55. The only other instrument mentioned is a flute ("pito"), called for on page 37. I suspect that the tambor cues are meant to signal both instruments for when to play. Like the *Baile de los Moros y Cristianos* performed in Alcoy, Spain, the highland Guatemalan versions incorporate the play as part of a saint-day festival and include negotiations, battles and accompanying music, in this case flute and drum (Harris 1994; Howell 2004; Kurath 1949).

The History and Distribution of Conquest Bailes in México and Central America

In 1538, a syncretic dance-play was first documented in the Americas, performed in the town of Tlaxcala, México (Hunter 1961:118). This unnamed baile featured dialogue in Nahuatl and a concluding dance performed to a Spanish song (Hunter 1961:118). The inclusion of two culturally disparate components—in this case, Mesoamerican language and Spanish music—established a tradition that was followed throughout the Colonial period.

Although there are other occasional ethnohistoric references from the sixteenth century to European or European-inspired dance-plays performed in the Americas, their major dissemination is documented as occurring between 1650 and 1700, a century or more after conquest (Brisset 1995:205; Taylor 1999:38; Warman 1985 [1972]:90). Moreover, a dance-play listed as the *Baile de los Moros y Cristianos* was not performed in the Americas until sometime during the reign of the Spanish monarch Charles III (1759–1788) (Taylor 1999:38). All the same, an unidentified baile based on a similar theme has been described as performed in México in 1680 (Taylor 1999:39), a time period that coincides with the beginning of the *Baile de los Moros y Cristianos* tradition in Spain.

In 1542, the first documented Guatemalan dance-play with a conquest theme was performed at Quezaltenango to commemorate the decisive Spanish victory over the Maya that occurred near there in 1524 (Harrison and Wauchope 1961:223;

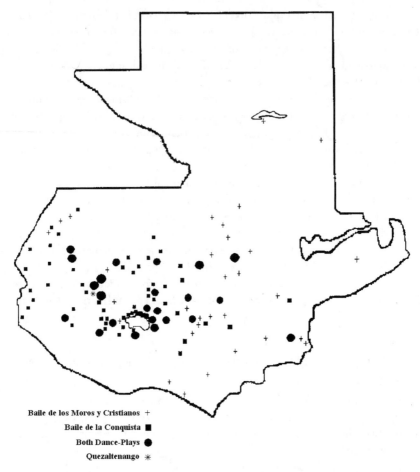

Baile de los Moros y Cristianos +
Baile de la Conquista ■
Both Dance-Plays ●
Quezaltenango ✳

14.3. Distribution of conquest dance-plays in Guatemala (map derived from Guatemala Departamento de Arte Folklorico Nacional 1971 and Rodriguez Rouanet 1992; author's computer drawing).

Mariani 1995:69, 74–75). Today, *La Conquista* (*Baile de la Conquista*) tradition remains centered in southwest Guatemala, in and around Quezaltenango, and this baile continues to be Guatemala's most widely performed, if unevenly represented, dance-play.[3] For unknown reasons, performances of the baile are rather rare in the northern, eastern, and extreme southern regions, where it appears to have been replaced by the *Moros* conquest dance. In much of the rest of the country the two bailes are often paired and are typically performed for the same saint-day celebrations (Guatemala Departamento de Arte Folklorico Nacional 1971; Rodriguez Rouanet 1992) (Figure 14.3).

Source of the Instrumentation Used for Conquest Bailes in Highland Guatemala

The only apparent exceptions to flute-drum accompaniment of the *Moros* bailes in Guatemala are versions with their unique instrumentation listed in the dance-play title, such as *Baile de los Moros Marimbita* and *Baile de los Moros Tun* (Guatemala Departamento de Arte Folklorico Nacional 1971; Rodriguez Rouanet 1992). For the *Baile de los Moros y Cristianos* in Spain, along with brass and woodwind ensembles, the choice of instruments varies among communities, but includes, in some instances, a pairing of flute and drum played by one individual, referred to as the pipe and tabor (Harris 1994:47; Horspool 1982:252).[4] Other instruments documented are assorted combinations of castanets, violin, flute, oboe, bagpipe, and accordion (Harris 1994:47; Horspool 1982:252.)

Flutes

There is a Colonial period European flute type known as the recorder that resembles the flute now used for the highland Guatemalan *Moros* that is almost always found to be made of a short length of hollow material, usually cane, with a thin sliver of similar material inserted into the mouthpiece end, producing a duct channel.

Six is the standard number of finger holes for highland Guatemalan *Moros* flutes, a number that can produce a diatonic (7-note) European-style scale of non-overblown pitches (Horspool 1982; Howell 2004).[5] In 2001 I examined a flute used for the Cobán *Moros* and found that it had a key center of Db major, but perhaps more telling was that it incorporated a component known as a "framed aperture," a feature somewhat common to archaeologically recovered Maya flutes and to my knowledge non-existent on European models. Framed aperture refers to a partition outlining all or some of the perimeter around a flute aperture (the proximal opening on the top of a flute). When a framed aperture is used, the instrument's overtones—the extra notes common to all pitches—are subtracted according to a ratio determined by the size of the aperture opening, its shape and distance from the proximal end, and its height and width in comparison to the surrounding area. Overtones are what give instruments their specific tone quality, and the incorporation of a framed aperture on a flute indicates a concern for tonal variety.[6]

Flutes recovered from Maya archaeological sites are typically duct types, and ceramic versions (the majority) are those that often have a framed aperture, mirroring the form for the contemporary Cobán *Moros* flute examined. Precolumbian Maya flutes (from both the highlands and lowlands) have been found with various numbers of finger holes, ranging from two to thirteen (and including six) (Howell 2004), but the majority typically have four, duplicating the number found on the rather common Aztec ceramic "flower-shaped" flute. Four, of course, represents

14.4. Framed aperture shown on a four-holed tubular flute. Two views of the same instrument; crosshatching on front view denotes frame (drawing by author, 2005).

the cardinal directions important throughout Mesoamerica. A morphological difference between Aztec and K'iche' four-holed flutes is that the former are usually tubular shaped whereas the latter are usually vessel shaped, a design type most often referred to as an ocarina (Figure 14.4).

The use of four finger holes on flutes from two Mesoamerican cultures suggests possible Precolumbian scale standardization, but as theorized, pitch may not have been as important a Maya cultural consideration as tone quality, at least as based on the framed apertures found on many of the highland Guatemalan models and the Maya employ of the unique-sounding goiter flute discussed shortly (Howell 2004).

A bone flute (*sub'akiba*) is the material type mentioned at least twice in the *Título C'oyoi* in the context of warrior dances (Carmack 1973:351). Bone flutes are also described in the *Popol Vuj*, where they are included among the symbols of lordship ceremonially given to three members of the dominant K'iche' lineage by the Yucatán ruler Nakxit (Tedlock 1987:328). The association of the bone flute with K'iche' royalty and their warriors may mean that bone was a preferred—or perhaps culturally essential—material for flutes used for the warrior dance.

More than 125 intentionally hollowed bones of various lengths, from birds and mammals (counting humans), have been uncovered at Maya archaeological sites (O'Brien 1983:14), including at Kaminaljuyú, Zacaleu, and Nebaj in the highlands (Borhegyi 1965; Dixon 1958:57; O'Brien 1983:map; Smith and Kidder 1943:161). In addition, writings from Colonial chroniclers in Maya lands describe musicians playing flutes and flute-like instruments made of bone (Healy 1988:27). For instance, Landa reported that the Yucatán Maya used deer-bone whistles for their dances (Stevenson 2001b:357). Even so, an intact Postclassic K'iche' bone flute has yet to be discovered, and highland Maya ceramic flutes, or flute-like instruments, such as ocarinas and whistles, are the only types that have been verified archaeologically. On top of that, the number of ceramic flutes fluctuates according to time periods, and it is only during the Late Classic period that they are found in significant quantity (Borhegyi 1965:49). It is tempting to see a drop-off in clay flutes, ocarinas, and whistles after the Classic period as resulting from a change in materials (to bone perhaps?). But it could just as easily be the result of a scaling back of instrument manufacture or bias in excavation choices.

To summarize, modern K'iche' flutes are usually tubular-shaped with six finger holes whereas archaeologically recovered ones are usually from the Classic period or earlier and are typically vessel-shaped with four finger holes. It is conceivable that warrior-dance flutes have not survived, as they often have been described as made of bone. But like many Precolumbian Maya flutes recovered, the contemporary model examined in Cobán included a framed aperture, indicating a concern for tone quality perhaps superceding that for pitch, a concern not noted in Western flutes.

Chirimias and goiter flutes

Although *La Conquista* is a dance-play of only peripheral interest to this chapter, there are aspects of its two accompanying instruments that address the issue of local versus introduced sound makers. For *La Conquista*, "su" means the European-derived double-reed instrument known in Latin America by its Spanish name, chirimia.[7] And although there are no known reed instruments ascribed to pre-conquest Amerindians, there is a Precolumbian Maya instrument with a similar "reedy sound" known as the goiter flute because of a goiter-shaped bulb attached to the tubular part of the instrument, usually near the mouthpiece end (Stevenson 2001b:357). The attached bulb is in essence an ocarina, which adds a second sound blending with that generated by the instrument's tubular component, and it is the combination of the two sounds that causes the instrument to yield what I characterize as a buzzing, nasal, or reedy tone. This goiter section is sometimes in the shape of an animal or part of an animal, such as a pelican or a bat's head.

The tone quality of the goiter flute varies according to the sizes of the two ducts, their distance from each other, and the spatial dimensions of the sound-making parts (Rawcliffe, personal communication, 2003). Although some versions have finger holes (usually one or two) and are therefore correctly called flutes (instruments sounding more than one pitch), others are restricted to a single, non-overblown pitch and are more correctly "goiter whistles." In either case, the instrument type is

14.5. Goiter flute with bat-head goiter, in the Museo de Antropología e Historia in Mérida (drawing by author, 2004).

somewhat common in the prehispanic record (Howell 2004; Martí 1998 [1971]; Rawcliffe 1992; Stevenson 2001a) (Figure 14.5).

Notwithstanding the lack of archaeological evidence for indigenous Mesoamerican reed instruments, Norman Hammond (1972b:225) reprinted accounts by Landa and Herrera describing a "five-holed reed oboe," which he suggests may have been an indigenous Maya reed instrument, although he acknowledges that there is no evidence for it in the prehispanic record. That said, it is curious that until at least the mid-1960s the Lacandon played a homemade double-reed instrument (no name given by source [Stevenson 1968]), and it is conceivable that this sound maker was a remnant version of a Precolumbian type. In any case, apparent Maya fascination with a reedy sound, whether produced on a goiter flute or a chirimia, further substantiates a Maya interest in the tone qualities of instruments, a concern that could be culturally significant and helpful in revealing the sources for instruments now used. The use of composite flute parts in one instrument (as characterize goiter flutes), like the use of framed apertures, is not known in European models.

Skin Drums

The two K'iche' skin drums, witnessed at the 2001 Cobán and at the 2002 Rabinal performances of the *Moros*, were roughly the same size, approximately sixty centimeters long and forty centimeters in diameter, and each resembled a type of mallet-struck double-headed skin drum common in Renaissance and post-Renaissance Europe (Blades 1980). Miguel Sum Meja, a drummer in Cobán specializing in the music for the two contemporary conquest bailes under discussion, uses both male and female deerskins for his drum membranes, and while demonstrating to me the music of the *Moros*, played on one side of his drum, and when demonstrating the music of *La Conquista*, played on the other. When turning his drum over, Sum Meja made a dramatic gesture with his arms and face, as if indicating that I would soon notice a difference in sound, but to my ears neither the tone quality nor pitch of his drum changed significantly from one side to the other. As duality is a major ordering principle in Maya cosmology, the change of drum heads for different dance-plays may suggest a concern with metaphysical balancing that supersedes tone or pitch differences for this instrument.

Given the tendency of the K'iche' to use indigenous versions of flutes for the *Moros*, it is somewhat surprising that the skin drum now paired with it for these bailes seems to owe more to introduced European designs than to Maya ones. Archaeological and iconographical records of Precolumbian Maya skin drums confirm only two primary types: the small vase-shaped, pottery-framed drum called *kai yum* by the Lacandon and the waist-high Mesoamerican wood-framed drum called *pax* (or *zakatan*) by the Maya and *huehuetl* by the Aztecs (Hammond 1972a; Stevenson 1968). Both of these were affixed with one skin and were played with the hands.

A third pre-conquest skin-drum type listed by Carmack (1981:61) in his translations of Colonial period Guatemalan documents may have had as much, or more, of an influence on modern highland Guatemalan drums than European models. In his description, Carmack (1981:61) writes that during prehispanic wars the K'iche' used a drum made from a gourd along with a (bone?) flute to signal the time for attack. If true, this gourd drum may be the drum described in indigenous documents that was paired with the flute for K'iche' warrior dances. Despite this intriguing possibility, because the drum was made of an organic material, artifact evidence for it does not likely exist. It therefore follows that the lack of specimens means we may never know if it had two skins and/or if it was struck with mallets. Still, as concerns the first point, the use of a gourd as a drum body implies construction in a manner similar to that used to make gourd bowls. (A large number of drums have bodies shaped like bowls.) If so, the narrow stem portion at the top of the plant would most likely have been the only part removed so that the remainder of the gourd could be covered over with a membrane. If my supposition is correct, the K'iche' gourd drum would only have had one skin. The question of how it would have been played (with or without mallets) is not answered.

There are iconographic examples of a fourth possible prehispanic drum type that differs from the pax and kai yum, as well as from the gourd drum described by Carmack. Hammond (1972a:129–130) published rubbings of this instrument ascribed to three Late Classic plaques from Lubaantún, Belize, and on them the sound maker looks something like a modern European-style bass drum. This Precolumbian drum could represent a prototype for the currently used *Moros* drum, although only two of the three rubbings are clear enough to be of use in an argument for this proposition. In both examples, the drum looks the same, a similarity that implies a drum type, not a single unique instrument, although it is possible that the same drum is being shown twice. Hammond estimates the drums shown on the plaques all at around fifty centimeters in circumference (Hammond 1972a:130), a dimension similar to the circumference of modern Guatemalan tambors. In one of the two representations, the instrument is played by a drummer who is at the rear of what appears to be a group of seated musicians, one of whom holds a container rattle aloft in his left hand. This drummer is in left profile and holds the so-called bass drum in front of his body, which is turned to the viewer, in essence positioning the instrument in the same way as modern Western bass drummers do

14.6. Drummer with other musicians on a Lubaantún plaque (drawing by author, 2004, from Hammond 1972b).

when marching. In current saint-day processions the tambor is often carried with the skins facing right and left, meaning that the drum is positioned in the same way as the one shown on the Lubaantún plaque (Figure 14.6).

This Lubaantún drummer's left hand is gripped into a fist that is placed in the middle of the drum. This position suggests that the musician is holding a mallet, but because Hammond's reprint is less than definitive, it is difficult to determine if he holds such an object or is simply gripping his fist. Because of the position of the instrument, one also cannot know if this instrument had two skins, and the assumption that it did is solely based on the similarity of this instrument to the Western bass drum rather than on the evidence presented. In Hammond's other discernable representation, the drum is shown being played by a musician who appears to be sitting on the instrument while striking it, with only his left leg visible and dangling in front of the drumskin. One must assume that the other leg dangles in front of the drum's other side, which perhaps had another skin, but as with the first picture described, there is no way to know this. In fact, this musician appears to beat the drum near his visible thigh with both hands, implying that this was the only side of the drum affixed with a skin.

It is curious that the two K'iche' drummers interviewed for this chapter, Libereia and Sum Meja (in 2001), stressed binary opposition as represented in the male and female skins of their double-headed drums—a very important aspect of their Precolumbian ancestors—but that these ancestors left such little evidence of duality in their own drum construction, the double-shafted kai yum (pottery drum) being an exception (Gates 1978a). Two significant differences in modern and recovered Precolumbian K'iche' skin drums include the numbers of skins attached to the frames (two versus one) and the methods of playing (mallets versus hands). The lack of proof for mallet-played skin drums or double-skinned single-shaft types strongly suggests that the skin drum now used by the K'iche' for the *Moros* and other conquest bailes is more closely associated with the European version of the instrument. The Maya may have adopted this European instrument precisely because it was the drum sounded by the victors at battles between the Spanish and Maya armies, or it may have been preferred over an indigenous version because it was louder, easier to play, to make, or for any of a number of other reasons not ascertained. Despite the evidence for Maya embracing Spanish tambors, Carmack's described gourd drum and Hammond's rubbings of bass drum–like instruments represent candidates for indigenous K'iche' warrior-dance drum prototypes. (As concerns the disappearance of the Precolumbian kai yum and pax from the highland Maya performance tradition after conquest, perhaps these two drum types were never used in dance-plays, or at least not in those that evolved into modern bailes.)

Summary and Conclusions

Spanish authorities probably considered it fortuitous that a dance-play tradition already existed in the Americas when they arrived and began to calculate ways to turn these performances to their advantage. Shortly after the conquest they were introducing new dance-plays, or new themes into existing ones, that dramatized the superiority of the European-Christian worldviews, implying that Amerindians who submitted to this outlook would be accommodated in the now Spanish-controlled and Christianized America. Regardless, Amerindians undoubtedly found ways to turn these performance events to their advantage. One way may have been by adding local instruments (i.e., slit-drums and flutes) or by pairing specific instruments to specific events (i.e., tun [slit drum] with sacrifice bailes and su [flute or chirimia] with conquest bailes), with the intent of keeping pre-conquest ceremonial associations alive.

Regarding the instrument-baile pairing for conquest, or warrior, dances, there is much etymological, archaeological, and ethnohistorical evidence for flutes and sundry drum types in the highlands, and the literary evidence confirms a flute-drum ensemble providing music for K'iche'an warriors in Postclassic pre-war celebrations. The Maya writers who described these instruments as played before the advent of Postclassic period hostilities may have mentioned flutes and drums only as representative examples of many sound makers used to excite participants and observers in a manner expected on such occasions. But in a passage in the *Rab'inal Achi* where the K'iche' warrior-prince asks for the music of the flute and drum there is the suggestion of a performance tradition more prescribed than random.

Possibly an association of the flute and drum with warrior themes led to instrumentation that has become standardized in post-conquest performances of the *Moros* in highland Guatemala. In fact, the flute and drum are not typical for Spanish versions of this dance-play, unless the pipe and tabor, sometimes used there, are amended to form a two-man group. It is also important to remember that the double-reed instrument, chirimia, paired with a skin drum for another conquest baile, *La Conquista*, is given the K'iche' name for flute, su, meaning that the su-tambor pairing, regardless of the type of su, characterizes the instrumentation for known conquest, or warrior, dance-plays.

The insertion of indigenous instruments into bailes introduced from Spain preserves traditions at a music level that perhaps went undetected by later colonizers, traditions like duality (preserved in the use of male and female drumskins), directionality (preserved in the number of finger holes found on flutes), and tonal preferences (preserved in flute designs featuring framed apertures and the multiple sound-making components of goiter flutes).

It is my hope that full comprehension of the reasons for instrument-baile associations may one day aid in revealing the sounds of Precolumbian Maya musics, the Holy Grail of Maya music archaeology. In the meantime these associations may inform us of K'iche' Maya conceptions of ceremonies that include music and unveil their strategies for dealing with cultural change.

Notes

1. Carmack (1973:273–286) reprints the *Título C'oyoi* in its entirety and in K'iche' in his book *Quichean Civilization*. He also includes an English translation, on pages 287–306, and notes on the translation, on pages 307–345. The original is now part of the Robert Garrett Collection of Middle American Manuscripts of the Princeton University Library (Carmack 1973:39). Recinos and Goetz (1953) translated the sixteenth-century *Annals of the Cakchiquels* from the original Kakchikel into English. Included in the footnotes is information concerning their translation choices.

2. In this section all of the K'iche' translations in parentheses without quotation marks are mine.

3. *La Conquista* is produced in some 69 of the 300 largest Guatemalan municipalities, making it the most popular traditional dance-play performed in the country (Brisset 1995; Rodriguez Rouanet 1992). Variously titled versions of the *Moros* are currently performed in approximately fifty of the larger Guatemalan towns, which rank it second (Guatemala Departamento de Arte Folklorico Nacional 1971; Rodriguez Rouanet 1992).

4. The pipe and tabor, a virtual one-man band comprising a single musician simultaneously playing a flute and a drum, is the nearest Spanish equivalent to the flute-drum duos found today for the highland Guatemala *Moros*. Ironically, it is a performance tradition that may have developed independently in both the Old and New Worlds (Boilès 1966).

5. Non-overblown pitches are those produced on a flute using only a moderate force of air. It is the standard playing style in the highlands.

6. In spring 2003, flautist and instrument builder Susan Rawcliffe demonstrated to me an amazing variety of tonal qualities on flutes that she had constructed with framed apertures duplicating those on Maya archaeological models.

7. During fieldwork in highland Guatemala (2001 and 2002) I viewed at least a dozen chirimias. All were made of cherrywood and, like the *Moros* flutes, had six finger holes.

Footpath of the Dawn, Footpath of the Sun: Maya Worldviews at Lake Atitlán

CHAPTER FIFTEEN

Robert S. Carlsen

Guatemala's Lake Atitlán is a place of extraordinary beauty. The "umbilicus of the world," as it is traditionally called by local Maya inhabitants, was praised by Aldous Huxley (1934:128) as being like Italy's Lake Como with the "additional embellishment of several immense volcanoes" and by the noted nineteenth-century traveler and writer John Lloyd Stephens (1969 [1854]:158) as being "the most magnificent spectacle we ever saw." When the Maya epic *Popol Vuj* refers to it as the "Heart of Lakes," Lake Atitlán is even elevated to a deified status (Edmonson 1971:4). This status must in some way explain the numerous pottery vessels offered to the lake by the region's ancient residents.

Although surprisingly little archaeology has been conducted in the immediate Lake Atitlán area, it is certain that the region has been inhabited for considerable time.[1] One can only speculate as to whether the lake's splendor was a primary attraction for the region's early inhabitants, but another factor was clearly of great importance: security. The natural geography of Lake Atitlán has long presented significant barriers to the interaction of different social groups. A windy lake surface prone to becoming quite treacherous without warning, towering volcanoes, and dauntingly steep cliffs certainly impeded the plans of numerous would-be invaders. These conditions have also played a role in the primary task of this chapter, which is to describe and to interpret the worldviews of the Maya inhabitants of the Lake Atitlán region at the time of the conquest.

Some fifty years ago the cultural geographer Felix McBryde (1947 [1935]:2) observed that there was probably "no region in the New

World that surpasses western Guatemala for illustrating the relationship between culture and nature. Here is one of the largest concentrations of individualistic Indian populations, preserving much of its Maya background." McBryde explains this cultural conservatism in terms of the formidable natural obstacles to the interaction between communities mentioned above. Writing about the Lake Atitlán basin, he (McBryde 1947 [1935]:2) notes that "many of the villages may be separated from their neighbors by two miles or less, and yet being isolated by physical barriers such as precipitous headlands, cliff shores, and a dangerous lake surface, they may have distinct economies, dress, and even vocabularies." Adding to the role that local geography has played in cultural continuity has been the larger region's economic peripherality. A lack of significant, readily exploitable natural resources in highland Guatemala dampened Spanish interest in the region, particularly in the more geographically isolated areas.[2]

I should note that the geographic isolation and remarkable cultural continuity observed by McBryde no longer hold true. Over the course of the last half century Lake Atitlán has gradually been transformed into a major tourist destination, with the hordes being drawn both by the magnificent lake and also the area's lingering reputation for "traditional" Maya culture. Moreover, the obstacles to social interaction once presented by precipitous headlands and a dangerous lake surface have proven to be of little challenge to modern boats and paved roads. More recently, cell phones, the Internet, and cable television have taken their tolls. Although the region's traditional Maya culture may be virtually extinct in a number of lake communities and only a receding echo in others, it is still possible to discern the cultural patterns that until recently were of central importance. Most living Maya in the Lake Atitlán area, as elsewhere throughout Guatemala, are now orthodox Catholic or evangelical Protestant, but a steadily diminishing number do retain significant knowledge of the traditional culture (*costumbre* hereafter).[3] Vincent Stanzione's recent (2003) collaboration with Miguel Dulce demonstrates the value of working with surviving *costumbristas* (followers of costumbre). Similarly, the books, dissertations, and articles written about Lake Atitlán over the past fifty years provide an invaluable corpus of work.

With a primary focus on the largest Lake Atitlán town, Tz'utujil Maya Santiago Atitlán, this chapter reconstructs dominant local post-conquest Maya cultural beliefs and paradigms. I explain that a relative lack of Spanish colonizing intensity and an adaptive indigenous culture allowed the tenaciously nativistic local Maya population to significantly influence colonial relations and hence the course and design of its own history. Of central importance to the emergent cultural patterns was transculturation, a transformative dynamic that allowed the indigenous population to purposefully conceal and to store defining elements of its pre-European way of life in imported cultural components brought by the Spanish invaders. Discernable in the resulting cultural expression is a mix of remarkable continuity and change in the worldviews of the local Maya population.

Dynamics of Cultural Concealment in Post-Conquest Highland Guatemala

More than two centuries ago Guatemalan archbishop Cortés y Larraz lamented the "invincible tenacity" girding the Maya population's refusal of its own spiritual conquest (García Añoveros 1987:72). Commenting on the archbishop's view, Spanish historian Jesús María García Añoveros (1987:157) writes that although the Maya did not accept Christianity, "they accepted and submitted to the colonial order even less." Perhaps no single aspect of post-conquest Maya culture better exemplifies this tendency than the audacious god Maximón, who is still worshipped in Santiago Atitlán (Figure 15.1). E. Michael Mendelson (1959), the preeminent scholar of the Maximón cult, has traced the god's roots both to the ancient Maya deity Mam, a name commonly still used, and to Judas Iscariot.[4] Connections with the ancient Maya notwithstanding, the deity clearly embodies an anti-Catholic dimension. By elevating Judas, an enemy of orthodox Catholicism, to a deified status the local Maya reaffirmed their separation from the dominant ethnic sector.

The Maximón/Mam cult exemplifies the manner in which the Maya have integrated foreign intrusions, in this case Judas Iscariot, successfully "Mayanizing" them using ancient symbolic conceptions. In order to better understand the significance of the Mayanization of intrusive elements, it is helpful to keep in mind that a primary characteristic of the social landscape of the Maya world over the past centuries has been what Mary Louise Pratt (1992:4) refers to as highly asymmetrical relations of power. In the colonial environment there was little that the Maya could do should the Spanish choose to import something. The Maya could only watch as the Spaniards brought in the saints, new architectural styles, and so forth. As a result of the intrusions, over time few aspects of indigenous cultural expression were left untouched by European contact. Temples were sacked, churches built in their places, and the walls of those churches lined with images of the saints. The fact is that many indigenous societies were completely subsumed into the Spanish sphere. However, reflecting cultural resilience and transformative capacity, in other generally rural areas most cultural aspects could nonetheless be traced to the pre-conquest past. As Pratt (1992:6) points out, "while subjugated peoples cannot readily control what emanates from the dominant culture, they do determine to varying extents what they absorb into their own and what they use it for." The process in which marginal groups select and invent from materials transmitted to them by a dominant metropolitan culture is called "transculturation."[5] Reflecting this process, defining aspects of Maya post-conquest culture retained an identifiably indigenous meaning, although commonly within a new European outer form.[6]

15.1. From midday Wednesday through midday Friday during Holy Week, Maximón is hung from a post adorned with willow branches. During that time the deity represents the tree at the center of the world, the axis mundi. In this image, the primary attendant to Maximón, his *telinel*, offers a prayer and liquor to the god (photograph by Paul Harbaugh).

That outer form is particularly evident in the *cofradía*, an institution that in many Maya towns has provided the primary venue for transculturation. Introduced into the Maya world within a decade of the conquest, cofradías had long existed in Spain as voluntary lay organizations whose primary purpose was the veneration of a particular saint as well as providing funerals and taking care of members' widows. The initial cofradía prototype in the Maya world matched closely its European counterpart, including the provision of social services. The Spaniards' reasons for the institution's introduction, however, had little to do with altruism. Rather, it was intended that cofradías provide for the collection of revenues and further the Maya's integration into the Church. Catholic priests, who in Guatemala were often poor, itinerant, and living in distant towns, came to be reliant on the funds paid by cofradías for the saying of Mass on saint's days. Having direct control neither over the cofradía funds nor over the amount of the stipend, it is of little surprise that the priests were forced to concede to certain Maya demands. Bluntly, the Maya utilized cofradía revenues to buy off otherwise intrusive outsiders, particularly priests, and in that way they subsidized a degree of cultural autonomy.

This "barter" aspect allowed many Maya communities to subvert the second Spanish motivation for the introduction of cofradías: the facilitation of the Maya integration into the Church. Evading the scrutiny of their pious overlords living in distant towns, the Maya used the cofradías to transfer important aspects of pre-conquest religious ritual, re-fabricating the institution in the process. Given that the cofradías were ostensibly Catholic, as long as what the Church looked upon as patently "idolatrous gear" was kept from sight, the system was on the whole at least minimally acceptable. This is certainly not to say that "idolatry" disappeared. As exemplified by Maximón, it flourished, and in important ways the cofradía system has provided the platform for that survival. Although enough of the accouterments of Catholicism were generally present in the cofradías to deflect direct intervention, at the same time the system constituted a "barrier," the occult side of which offered a venue for the celebration of characteristically Maya ritual.[7] Those rituals have often echoed the ancient past.

Lake Atitlán as Sacred Landscape

Evident in the costumbre practiced in Santiago Atitlán's cofradías is a concept of sacred center manifest locally and similarly a belief in ancestral renewal that ties together the town itself, the local Maya population, and vegetation/agriculture. Costumbristas say that Santiago Atitlán is the center of everything that is the R'muxux Ruchulew (literally, "Umbilicus of the World"). This sense of sacred centrality is often expressed in vegetal terms with the town equated to a cosmic world tree, the axis mundi. Adding to this understanding is that the leader of the cofradía, the *cabecera*, is the tree's trunk. In fact, he is sometimes called just that, "trunk." One of the most pervasive concepts of cofradía religion is that the ancestors, and hence the past, constitute the root at the base of the tree. Fundamental to costumbre is a focus on that ancestral realm at the root, which through ritual is believed to regenerate and sustain the town and its living residents. I have referred elsewhere (Carlsen 1997:47–67) to this general process as "the flowering of the dead."

Although I will say considerably more later about the pedigree of local beliefs, it is worth noting here that this type of understanding is certainly not limited to the post-conquest Maya. A major body of evidence for the ancient Maya comes from the Classic period site of Palenque, México. The central design element in most of Palenque's major monuments is the axis mundi, which takes form as either a tree or maize. In all of its representations, this axis mundi is portrayed as growing out of the head of an ancestral deity. That god has been described variously as one of "generations, ancestry, and lineages" (Schele 1976:24) and as a "seed from which a corn plant containing the Ancestors grows" (Freidel 1987:14).

Complementing the costumbrista concept of sacred center is a most important understanding of sacred periphery. The full 360-degree horizon as viewed from Santiago Atitlán is made up of towering peaks and ridges forming the basin in which the lake is located. With the town, the Umbilicus of the World, anchoring the center, those towering peaks and ridges form the periphery of a unified concept of sacred landscape. This concept, Rqan Saq, Rqan Q'iij, or "Footpath of the Dawn, Footpath of the Sun," is so important and so basic to the costumbre of Santiago Atitlán that it could almost serve as the formal name of the local religion. In its simplest terms, this concept interprets the locales on the horizon where the sun rises and sets as a counter-clockwise "footpath" along which the sun, "Our Father," walks.

Footpath of the Dawn, Footpath of the Sun forms a four-cornered construct geographically surrounding the town.[8] Two of the corners, southeast and northeast on the compass, anchor the endpoints of a line demarcated by sunrises. The other two corners, northwest and southwest, form a parallel line on the opposite side of the town demarcated by sunsets. In terms of geographical place-names, the sun rises at the southeast corner at a place called Prwa Juyu, and at the northeast corner at Rosba; at the northwest corner the sun sets at Patziapa and at the southwest corner at Chumil. Complementing the two sides formed by sunrises and sunsets are sides formed essentially by the path of the sun across the sky at the summer solstice (northeast to northwest corners) and by the path of the sun across the sky at the winter solstice (southwest to southeast corners). My qualifying word "essentially" underscores a fascinating aspect of this defining concept of the local religion. The sun rises at Rosba (the northeast corner) on June 21, the summer solstice. Yet, fully four days of sunrises and sunsets pass until on June 25 it sets over Patziapa (the northwest corner). Similarly, the sun sets over Chumil (southwest corner) on December 21, the winter solstice, but does not rise directly over Prwa Juyu (southeast corner) until December 25 (Figure 15.2). Again, there is a curious lag time of four days. Costumbristas believe that following the summer solstice, four days of cofradía ritual are required in order to transfer the Footpath of the Sun from its sun-

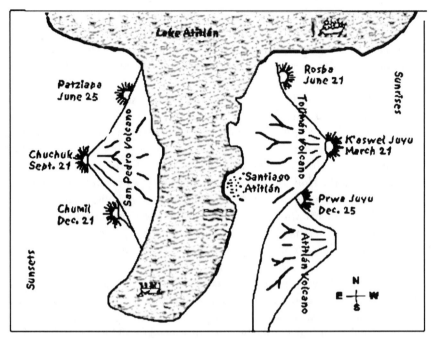

15.2. According to the worldview of costumbristas in Santiago Atitlán, their town is the center of the world, which is to say, of everything that is. The places where the sun rises and sets, as seen from the town, combine to form a four-cornered construct. That construct forms the basis of Footpath of the Sun, Footpath of the Dawn.

rise progression in the east to its sunset progression in the west. Similarly, following the winter solstice, four days of ritual are essential to its transfer from the sunset progression in the west back to its sunrise progression in the east. This ritual bearing of the sun across the sky is a primary reason that in the Tz'utujil Maya language costumbristas are called Aj'samaj Acha ("Working People").

A final aspect of Footpath of the Dawn, Footpath of the Sun brings this discussion of sacred landscape back to where it started: the concept of sacred center. The midpoint of the sun's easterly walk across the sky (sunrise) occurs on the spring equinox at a place called K'aswel Juyu. Similarly, the midpoint of the sun's walk across the sky to the west (sunset) takes place on the autumnal equinox at a place called Chuchuk. Costumbristas conceive of a line from K'aswel Juyu to Chuchuk, a line across the sky that situates Santiago Atitlán at the center of the entire Footpath of the Dawn, Footpath of the Sun configuration. The line across the middle of the sky also divides the world into halves, with the area to the north associated with life and the area to the south associated with death. Consistent with the fact that that Footpath of the Dawn, Footpath of the Sun combines a concept of space with a concept of time, the line across the sky not only divides the world into two complimentary geographical spheres but similarly divides the year into halves. Those halves correspond to the rainy season, from the spring equinox until the autumnal equinox, and the dry season, from the autumnal equinox to the spring equinox.

The primary public celebration of the middle of the year occurs at what might be considered the starting point of this configuration—if a never-ending cycle can have a starting point—in conjunction with the spring equinox.[9] Although the spring equinox is technically March 21, in Santiago Atitlán the public celebration of this event takes place at Holy Week, in particular Holy Monday through Good Friday. I should note that the Holy Week costumbre in Santiago Atitlán pays only minimal attention to the role of Jesus, who, consistent with the agricultural underpinnings of costumbre, is equated with maize. Instead, it is the god who includes Lord of the Middle (R'jawal R'k'ux Ruchiliew) in its multitude of names who takes center stage. Other names of this complex deity are Maximón and Mam, introduced earlier. The Lord of the Middle / Maximón / Mam occupies the space/time between the dead/dry half of the year and its living/rainy counterpart (Figure 15.3). Years ago Mendelson (1959:58; also see Thompson 1970:298–299) wrote about the ancient Maya association of Mam and calendrics, specifically the *wayeb'*, the five "delicate" days of the solar calendar that lie between the now-dead old year and the yet-to-be-reborn new year. Mendelson makes a strong case that the five days from Holy Monday through Good Friday constitute direct continuity of the wayeb'. If the costumbres are performed correctly during this delicate period, the old dead year gives way to the new living year, the rain comes, and the maize grows.

The Footpath of the Dawn, Footpath of the Sun complex constitutes a truly grand performance of transculturation, the process in which marginal groups select and invent from materials transmitted to them by a dominant metropolitan culture. Consistent with that process, some aspects of the complex have ancient antecedents. As I have discussed, a concept of space/time that combines an understanding of sacred center manifest on a local level with a corollary understanding of renewal in an ancestral form can be traced to the pre-conquest Maya. Similarly, the concept of a four-cornered world and cosmos was embraced throughout ancient Mesoamerica.[10] Although aspects such as these cast light on local Maya worldviews prior to the conquest, other aspects of the Footpath of the Dawn, Footpath of the Sun complex are clearly European in origin. For instance, it should be recalled that the deity variously called Maximón and Mam is also associated with Judas. However, whereas the Biblical Judas is most notable for his betrayal of Christ, the transculturated Judas and Jesus are friends who co-conspire the latter's death. Their logic is that for Jesus to be reborn he must first die. Not lost on the local population is that enduring Maya paradigms work well as scripts for Jesus's resurrection from death back into life and similarly for the transition from the dry season to the wet.

15.3. Holy Week marks the only time during the year that Maximón makes a public appearance. During that time he is guaranteed to draw a crowd wherever he goes. The ultimate goal of the Holy Week rituals is to induce the life-giving rain to come (photograph by Paul Harbaugh).

In retrospect, it is clear that the message of Judas and Jesus brought by the Spanish friars failed to convert the local Maya population to Christianity. Rather, the local Maya converted Judas and Jesus to costumbre.[11]

Maya Saints and Catholic Idols

Writing in 1648 about the failure of Guatemala's highland Maya to become truly Christian, Thomas Gage (1958:234) argued that the indigenous population accepted the Catholic saints "because they look upon them as much like unto their forefathers' idols." Although Gage's observation was at least partly on the mark, I argue that neither the saints nor idolatry had much to do with the European's inability to convert the Maya population. The real obstacle to their evangelizing agenda was a locally relevant and highly adaptive Maya cultural nexus whose arguably most important quality was its capacity to remain nearly invisible to the would-be foreign masters. "Any ideology is powerful to the extent that it hides itself in the unmarked reflexes of everyday life, and vulnerable to the extent that it becomes open to scrutiny and argument" (Comaroff and Comaroff 1991:78); defining Maya cultural paradigms, such as those underlying their conceptions of time and space, remained hidden in the collective mind of the community. This adaptive cultural nexus proved to be adept at accommodating and integrating intrusive cultural elements, and then employing those very elements to store the original indigenous paradigms.[12] For instance, soon after the introduction of Jesus into highland Guatemala, the central figure of Christianity was himself "flowering from the dead." Quite simply, what the foreigners perceived as "idolatry" was more a symptom of their own impotence than the cause of some sort of Maya "paganism."

One essential element in the highland Maya's success in resisting spiritual conquest has been remarkable creativity, a quality that has seemingly always gone hand in hand with Maya culture. Complimenting the creativity apparent in ideology and worldviews discussed above is an assemblage of material culture. In effect, the objects making up that assemblage constitute "mirrors of a worldview."[13] I find several classes of objects in Santiago Atitlán particularly revealing in this regard, perhaps none more so than textiles.

Handwoven cloth and costume arguably constitute the most salient aspect of post-conquest highland Maya culture. One particularly interesting expression of the Maya textile tradition is what is commonly referred to as the "village specific costume," a pattern in which residents wear a style of handwoven garment unique to their town or region. Although it is unlikely that this pattern has a direct pre-conquest antecedent, it nonetheless resonates with the aforementioned concept of ancestral renewal that ties together the town itself and the local Maya population. In fact, some costumbristas claim that the reason they wear the local style of dress is because "it puts them in the form of the ancestors" (Prechtel and Carlsen 1988:130; also see Warren 1989:57).[14] The symbolic content of several common garment types in Santiago Atitlán refers also to the concept of sacred center, introduced earlier. One such garment is the *nim pöt*, which is a type of blouse worn exclusively by female cofradía members. Of particular note is the embroidered collar, which features the volcanoes surrounding Santiago Atitlán. When a costumbrista puts on this garment, she situates herself symbolically in the Umbilicus of the World. It is significant that custom mandates that the nim pöt be woven using *batz'in batz'*, handspun white cotton. Batz'in batz' is associated with Maximón, but also with ancestral renewal. Upon death, it is customary for costumbristas to have their groin area bound in a ritual manner using handspun white cotton. This custom is believed to prefigure a person's rebirth, their flowering from the dead. For this reason, for males the bound area is called *awex* (sprout).

Related to cloth is another important class of objects, the bundles found in Santiago Atitlán's cofradías.[15] As evidenced by their representation on Classic period polychrome vases, rolled cloth bundles have long been important in Maya culture and ritual. In fact, the importance of bundles extended well beyond the Maya realm into other parts of Mesomerica. For instance, the Aztecs believed that the power of the *calpulteotl*, a lineage deity, was contained partly in a bundle under the control of priests (López Austin 1980). Bundles are also mentioned in both the Postclassic texts *Popol Vuj* (Tedlock 1985:198) and *El Título de Totonicapán* (Carmack and Mondloch 1983:185). The specific bundle written about in those texts was named Pizom Q'aq'al (Bundle of Flames) and, as with the Aztecs, was associated with the human lineage. Representing a remarkable example of continuity with the pre-conquest past, the bundle cult still exists in Santiago Atitlán (Figure 15.4).

Although there are several different types of bundles in the town today, including those of *aj'kuna* (shamans), the most pertinent to this discussion are those kept the town's cofradías. Cofradía bundles comprise rolled cloth, most containing secondary objects. Some bundles are occasionally opened, and others never are. Bundles are generally kept in wooden boxes placed to the side of cofradía altars and are only taken out of those boxes during times of ritual use. Consistent with ancient beliefs, Santiago Atitlán's cofradía bundles have a symbolic association with ancestry and lineage. This association is evident in bundle names, for instance, Cofradía San Juan's "Heart of the Placenta" (R'kux Alaniem). Of particular significance here is the word "heart," which refers to a belief that bundles contain the original ancestral essence of the object for which they are named. When the bundles are used to promote fertility, human or agricultural, the offspring are thought to have been regenerated in an ancestral form.[16] Other bundles that are significant in this regard include Cofradía San Felipe's "Heart of Maize" (R'kux Ixim) and Cofradía San Juan's "Heart of Food and Water" (R'kux R'way Ya).

Although the symbolic ideas informing the role of bundles in contemporary Maya ritual are of pre-European origin, it is highly unlikely that the actual cloth making up any of the cofradía bundles is ancient. The humid climate of highland Guatemala, in combination with ritual "feeding" of the bundles using copious amounts of liquor (and more recently, aftershave lotions and deodorant sprays), is simply not conducive to the preservation of cloth. However, other objects used in

15.4. The most important cofradía bundle in Santiago Atitlán is the Heart of Food and Water bundle, most commonly called simply Martín. In what probably represents direct continuity with the Precolumbian past, cofradía bundles are associated with priests, called *nabeysils*. This image shows a nabeysil dancing with the Martín bundle (photograph by Paul Harbaugh).

costumbre are nonperishable and are clearly of pre-conquest origin. One example is the pre-European stone statuary found in several of the town's cofradías. Of particular note is that although these statues are of pre-conquest manufacture, apparently none of them represent direct continuity with the ancient Maya past (Figure 15.5). A primary characteristic of the statues is that they are relatively recently "found" objects that are believed by their finders to have been purposefully placed as gifts from the deities. In this regard, the statues are similar to another category of objects, what in Tz'utujil Maya is called *q'iijb'al*.

Variously translated as "divining implement," "talisman," or "fetish," q'iijb'al can come in such forms as pottery fragments, obsidian blade cores, small ceramic figurines, as well as rock crystals and assorted other naturally occurring objects.[17] Q'iijb'al are commonly the property of aj'kuna and *ajq'iij* (shamans) and serve as primary objects in their personal bundles. The objects are also occasionally encountered on cofradía altars or on the personal altars of town residents. Like cofradía

15.5. Perhaps the most important religious object in Cofradía Ch'eep San Juan is this preconquest stone jaguar, generally simply called Tigre. The object was reportedly found near Santiago Atitlán in the early decades of the twentieth century. Note the three Maximón masks on the altar behind Tigre (photograph by author).

statuary, q'iijb'al are found items and do not represent direct continuity with the ancient Maya past. The fact that these items are discontinuities may at first seem to disqualify them as indicators of pre-European beliefs or ritual practices. However, in a fascinating article, Linda Brown (2000) writes that ancient Mesoamericans also collected formerly discarded objects virtually identical to q'iijb'al. Those objects were then seemingly curated for use in religious ritual. That the contemporary Maya practice of collecting formerly discarded objects for ritual use is actually a practice continuous with the pre-conquest past is an intriguing idea, although one that may be unprovable. In contrast, one characteristic of both the q'iijb'al and the statuary can be demonstrated: the by now-familiar theme of a focus on ancestral renewal.

It is common in Santiago Atitlán that q'iijb'al objects and pre-conquest statuary alike are described as being "pure *nawal*," meaning that they are infused with nawal essence. The quintessentially costumbrista concept nawal is manifested in diverse forms in the local culture, the common denominator being a relation to a magical ancestral past that continues to empower the present.[18] Just as the nawal essence may permeate and empower objects, it can do the same with humans. Although costumbristas contend that this still happens, they say that it now occurs in a far more anemic manner than in earlier epochs. Ancestral individuals infused with the essence are themselves called Nawales, and the few living representatives are described as being "part Nawal." Some costumbrista accounts posit the existence of twelve great ancestral male Nawales, whereas other accounts cite thirteen.[19] In an exemplary display of tranculturation, costumbrista theology folds the apostles of Christ together with pre-conquest Tz'utujil Maya "kings" into the ancestral Nawales. These great beings are also rain gods, in which form they are sometimes collectively called Achijab and are thought to still wield considerable influence over the town. The ancestral Achijab, clad in their mist capes (*suutz' moyew*) and prone to throwing lightning bolts and bringing the life-sustaining rains, sit on their thrones (*palibal*) atop the mountains ringing Santiago Atitlán, the Umbilicus of the World. This grand display of sacred geography forms the literal worldview of the costumbristas, the Working People, of Santiago Atitlán, Guatemala.

When the Saints Come Marching In: Assessing Continuity and Change in Post-Conquest Maya Worldviews

Costumbrista beliefs, such as Footpath of the Dawn, Footpath of the Sun, offer scholars a remarkable portal onto the conquest and its significance. On the one hand, some defining costumbrista beliefs are demonstrably pre-conquest. An ancient pedigree is demonstrated in the concept of sacred center manifest on a local level. Similarly, a belief that the sacred center is an axis mundi in the form of a tree is identifiably pre-European, as is the understanding of a surrounding four-cornered world and cosmos.[20] Continuity with the ancient Maya past can also be demonstrated in the costumbrista understanding that human intervention in the form of religious ritual is a requirement for the renewal and continuity of an inherently unstable cosmos (e.g., Carrasco 1990).

Although it is impossible to ignore the continuing impact of the ancient past on the costumbres, one should not discount the fundamental economic and political changes triggered by the conquest. Quite simply, all the cultural continuities have occurred within a fundamentally altered social landscape and hence may have underlying meanings other than first meet the eye. In assessing those meanings, we need to keep in mind that Maya beliefs, such as those about ancestral renewal, have always had broad social and political implications. "Communing with deceased progenitors was not a religious experience divorced from political and economic realities . . . rather, it was a practice grounded in pragmatism that drew power from the past, legitimized the current state of affairs (including all the inequities in rights and privileges), and charted a course for the future" (McAnany 1995:1). Given the monumental political and economic changes brought by the conquest, it is not surprising that the interdependent Maya cultural understandings also took on new significance.

When the Spanish arrived in highland Guatemala in 1524 and began their attempts to subdue and to control the indigenous population to "conquer" them, the Maya's cultural focus on the ancestral past assumed significant political and ethnic dimensions that had not previously existed. Although it was the foreigners' intention to impose an entirely new way of life, their plans failed to take into account potent Maya worldviews focused on the ancestral past, which is to say, on non-change. By aiding and abetting the Maya's refusal of their own spiritual conquest, the steadfast embrace of an ancestral pre-European past took on entirely new and often subversive dimensions. In that regard, the ancestors showed their mettle when it came to transforming the Spanish cofradía into an indigenous institution that was covertly, if not overtly, anti-European. Similarly, the saints of Catholicism were converted and then enlisted as soldiers in the Maya holy war.[21] That struggle would ultimately continue for much of the next 500 years, and it constitutes one of the most remarkable chapters in New World history.

Notes

1. Samuel K. Lothrop's (1933) pioneering study remains one of the better publications on Atitlán archaeology. The interested reader is also directed to Barrientos (1996), Benítez (2001), Sabom-Bruchez (1994a, 1994b, 1995a, 1995b), and Bruchez and Carlson (1994). Evident from regional artifacts is significant Mexican influence, most notably from Teotihuacán and the Mixtec area.

2. For the Spanish, the conquest was a maximizing capitalist venture, hence "being entrepreneurs, lay Spaniards were drawn to areas where environmental conditions or natural endowments would maximize material enrichment" (Lutz and Lovell 1990:36). Accordingly,

there existed a correlation between colonizing intensity and the wealth that an area possessed, with those areas lacking precious metals tending to receive scant attention. Significantly, in Guatemala only a few areas possessed known reserves of such resources, and even those were soon depleted. Throughout the Colonial period, the general trend was toward even greater peripheralization, to the point that Guatemala was eventually abandoned "by not only most commercial houses, but by the Crown itself" (Wortman 1975:251).

3. Some contemporary scholars caution against using the term "traditional," arguing that it is inherently vague and romantic. I disagree. I define the term "traditional" as "in accordance with old inherited patterns of thinking and behaving." This need be neither vague nor romantic but can be an accurate assessment. In fact, this definition might just as well be used for "costumbre," which is an indigenous term that has long been recognized by scholars as being central to the dominant earlier patterns of Maya thinking and behaving.

4. Mendelson's early 1950s work in Atitlán led to his Ph.D. dissertation from the University of Chicago (1956). He returned to Atitlán for a year of research in the late 1970s. Results of that work were ultimately published under the heteronym Nathaniel Tarn. Of particular importance is Tarn's 1998 book *Scandals in the House of Birds: Shamans and Priests on Lake Atitlán*.

5. Transculturation is a subset of syncretism, the blending of two formerly discrete religious traditions to form a new tradition. However, whereas syncretism can be subconscious and hence unintentional, transculturation always reflects purposeful action (also see Carlsen 2001).

6. Transculturation is also evident in the integration of Catholic saints and crosses into the cultural traditions of the post-conquest Yukatek Maya (see also Pugh, this volume).

7. Murdo MacLeod (1973) was the first scholar to discuss the barter and barrier functions of Mesoamerican cofradías.

8. Footpath of the Dawn, Footpath of the Sun was first discussed in the literature in a 1988 essay written by Martín Prechtel (prior to his decision to write for a New Age reader) and me. That essay mistakenly assigned the northwest corner to Sololá and the southeast corner to Xucoxom. Based on subsequent fieldwork and on Stanzione's very detailed (2003) study, the present essay corrects those errors.

9. See Prudence M. Rice (this volume) for analysis of the Maya concept of repetitive time.

10. Commonly included in that understanding is the belief that the sky is trussed by four deified corner trees. Local costumbrista cosmology is consistent with that belief.

11. Underscoring the potency of transculturation, costumbristas believe that there are four Jesuses. Two of the Jesuses are associated with the world's male space/time and two with the female space/time. In fact, the latter two Jesuses are considered to be female and are dressed as such when brought into public.

12. Adding to the integrative potency of Footpath of the Dawn, Footpath of the Sun is another indigenous paradigm called Jaloj-K'exoj. See Carlsen (1997:47–67) for a comprehensive analysis of that paradigm.

13. "Mirrors of a worldview" comes from the title of a recently published book that considers Maya worldview through the lens of textile art (see Holsbeke and Montoya 2003). My contribution to that book, a chapter titled "Subversive Threads," looks at the role of handwoven cloth in highland Maya's effort to maintain cultural autonomy.

14. I have written elsewhere of a costumbrista belief in Santiago Atitlán that cloth woven on a backstrap loom is born, or more specifically, reborn in an ancestral form (Prechtel and Carlsen 1988). It has come to my attention that some writers have adopted this concept and are claiming it for towns other than Santiago Atitlán (e.g., Froman 1992:10–11). It is my understanding, however, that this concept is unique to Santiago Atitlán.

15. The contemporary Atiteco bundle cult was first discussed by E. Michael Mendelson (1958). In Santiago Atitlán, bundles are housed in Cofradías San Antonio, San Gregorio, San Juan, San Nicolás, San Martín, and Ch'eep San Juan.

16. Evident in this understanding is a concept of reincarnation. Unlike reincarnation in a Hindu sense where a person's actual ego is reborn, the counterpart found in Santiago Atitlán posits a recycling of ancestral human and vegetal life essence. This belief has pre-conquest antecedents. In an article that discusses the centrality of ancient Mayan understandings of cyclic death and rebirth, Clemency Coggins (1989:66) states that "the poor were probably not entitled to the same afterlife [as the elites], although resurrection following an agricultural model . . . might in theory have been accessible to all." Evidence from Santiago Atitlán suggests that this was the case.

17. Vincent Stanzione (personal communication, 2005) explains that q'iijb'al are believed to be placed along a person's path by the sun (q'iij).

18. Vincent Stanzione (2003:323) defines the term *nawal* as "ancient way of being; a transforming power used to control the world; an ancient being."

19. There are male and female Nawales, the one being the consort and paired with the other. Male Nawales are sometimes called Nawal Taq Achi, and females sometimes called Nawal Taq Ixqi.

20. For instance, see Rice's (this volume) discussion of the ancient Maya concept of a quadripartite world with a world tree at its center.

21. For Santiago Atitlán, this is exemplifed by the town's patron "saint," Santiago. In native taxonomy, Santiago is categorized as a *bokunab*, an antiquated and esoteric term now used only in the cofradías. Derived from the word *bokul* (so many), the etymology of bokunab is evident. According to legend, Santiago's bokunab quality became apparent when, as a soldier, a strike from his sword created twin enemies where formerly there had been one. Fortunately for the local Maya, the god's talent was better applied in agricultural fecundity. Santiago, who is also called Q'anial Acha, "Abundance Man," joins other bokunab in the Atiteco pantheon as a fertility deity (see Stanzione 2003:145).

Maya Sacred Landscapes at Contact

CHAPTER SIXTEEN

Timothy W. Pugh

The Maya derived some of their most powerful and sacred symbols from the natural world. Plants, animals, and topographic features, such as caves, mountains, and water sources, found prominent roles in the sacred landscape. Many aspects of the built environment signified natural elements—for example, temple platforms represented hills and mountains. Furthermore, the Maya directed many rituals toward deities and ancestors who controlled elements of the natural landscape such as animal abundance, disease, land fertility, and rain. The world occupied by humans was not strongly distinguished from the realms of deities, as access points to these places were scattered across the land. Cosmogony and history occurred in the landscape and was likewise remembered through visiting sacred places. Hence, the Maya at conquest strongly wove their worldviews into the landscape. The landscape provided objectives for ritual action as well as natural metaphors, and human action and contemplation upon the landscape imbued the world with significance.

The landscape has long been a subject of interest to archaeologists but has generally been characterized as a "passive backdrop" (Knapp and Ashmore 1999:2). Static objective landscapes have been critiqued in favor of a processual landscape or landscape as praxis (Hirsh 1995:5; Jordan 2003:11–23). Peter Jordan (2003:279–283) defined the "enculturation of the landscape" as a process that produces the sacred landscape. Such meaning-producing practices occur as people create objects to place at sacred places and visit sites and make modifications to them. Hence, meaning is an unfinished project that is always under construction. The meanings of sacred places change through time as they are replicated. The significance of a place can increase or diminish, if not disappear. It might also be revitalized, contested, appropriated, defaced, or even destroyed (Bender 1998:97–130; van de Guchte 1999:155).

Landscapes are frequently represented—maps being the most common form of representation in Western societies. Such representations are foundations of social identity as they encode "the memories, meanings, and sense of belonging as well as the process of social relations and interaction" (Smith 2003:71). Landscape images also occur in forms other than maps. They can be recorded in a variety of media and emphasize qualities other than horizontal relationships. They may represent dimensions other than the material world and the world may be depicted in an idealized manner. Ritual paraphernalia can signify the otherworlds through which the shaman travels (Jordan 2001:88; Pentikäinen 1998:26–48). Some representations are small, but others are quite large and incorporate a number of buildings into a microcosm (Wheatley 1971:436–451).

Landscape studies integrate economic and symbolic approaches (Stewart and Strathern 2003:10). Given the focus of this volume, the present chapter will be skewed toward Maya ideational landscapes; however, one will note frequent references to the economic landscape. At the local level, the economic landscape included the residence, milpas, clay sources, stone sources, water sources, hunting and fishing areas, forests, and so on. These areas were not divorced from the sacred landscape as many ritual activities were directed toward ensuring good harvests, success in hunting/fishing, and offerings to animal or forest lords (Astor-Aguilera, this volume; L. Brown 2005). Furthermore, these spaces were encoded with gender and status values and, therefore, composed a significant portion of Maya worldviews (Clendinnen 1980:375–377). At the regional level, the economic landscape included long-distance trade networks, which brought in nonlocal (depending on the area) items such as obsidian, greenstone, serpentine, salt, bird feathers, copal, copper, coral, marine resources, pigments, honey, and cacao. Many of these items played critical roles in ritual activities (Brady 2005; Chuchiak, this volume). The larger economic landscape was also connected to the sacred landscape as some trading activities may have been combined with pilgrimages (Freidel and Sabloff 1984:179–192).

Maya Sacred Landscapes

Maya landscapes at contact included the earth, where people lived, as well as the heavens and the underworld (Chase and Chase, this volume). The specific form of the world—the *imago mundi*—varied immensely. From the Late Postclassic period until present, the Maya imagined the world in various shapes including circular, crocodilian, globular, house, rectangular, squash, and turtle forms (Hanks

1990:304–306; Schuman 1964:351–352; Sosa 1985:417; Taube 1988a:154–174). These forms are not mutually exclusive and one social group could utilize them all. In colonial documents, landscape representations are usually circular, often quartered. The modern Ch'orti' represent the world with five stones—four of which form a rectangle and the fifth, the center (Girard 1995:51). The Maya world is bounded. In Yucatán, the edges of the flat earth are considered a "great beach" and the salt water beyond this beach both bounds the human world and connects the earth and sky (Sosa 1985:319). The Lacandon world is also surrounded by water (Davis 1978:19–24).

The Maya world emerged from the primordial sea. *Tzuk*, "partition," refers to the primordial division of the universe (Freidel et al. 1993:140). The term also designates markers, composed of five stones, defining the boundaries of milpas (Hanks 1990:357). Larger piles of stones mark the boundaries between communities (Hanks 1990:356). During the Colonial period, stone piles rested on the edges of towns at each of the cardinal directions. These mounds played a role in New Year rites (Landa 1941:139) and may have represented mountains (Taube 1988a:287). In modern Yucatán, the edges of communities are marked by green crosses and altars also following this layout (Sosa 1985:429) and are, therefore, microcosms. Paths encircling rectangular milpas are boundaries and cleaning these paths helps maintain the boundaries and protect that which lies inside (Hanks 1990:356). Maya farmers measured the paths with cords. Similar cord paths mark ceremonial spaces as well as the edges of communities (Taube 1988a:159–160). Such enclosed spaces are known as *ak*, which include houses, temples, and villages as well as caves and cenotes (Clendinnen 1980:381). Cords were also used to create the world as a metaphorical milpa in the *Popol Vuj* (Tedlock 1985:72). The modern Maya of Santiago Atitlán imagine a rectangular road surrounding their world (Carlsen, this volume). It extends along the high mountain peaks surrounding the area and is the path around which the sun travels. Paths surrounding modern Yukatek communities are the locations of important rites protecting the town from evil winds (Sosa 1985:343). During the Colonial period, larger calendar-ending rites involved counterclockwise circuits around Yucatán (Edmonson 1986:27).

The ideal social space among the modern Yukatek is internally divided (Hanks 1990:306). Postclassic to Colonial period settlements had internal factions (Freidel and Sabloff 1984:182; Restall 1997:15–17). Space was also divided into residential groups, which at some sites were lumped together into recognizable social factions (Alexander 2005:170–173; Brown 1999:569). Although they frequently had more, the Maya often imagined their settlements and polities as having four parts, a form that also represented time (Coe 1965; Coggins 1980; Girard 1995:23–70; Pugh 2001b; Rice, this volume). Ritual events in Colonial period Yucatán suggest quadripartite divisions in settlements (Coe 1965:107–109). The cities of Mayapán and Utatlán also had four primary divisions (Edmonson 1986:81; Fox 1994:162–167).

Entire polities and larger regions were similarly partitioned (Edmonson 1986:16–58; Marcus 1993:128–153). The Itza of Contact period Petén divided their polity into four parts (Jones 1998:94–96). Quadripartite spaces also had a center forming a quincunx.

The centers of Postclassic communities included public ceremonial areas. These spaces generally incorporated plazas, temples, council houses, shrines, and "natural" features. Plazas were large flat areas, usually covered by a plaster surface representing the primordial sea (Freidel et al. 1993:139–140). They held large groups of people involved in religious, social, and economic activities. These areas also connected the buildings surrounding the plaza. Many activities in these buildings likely extended into the plazas. Temples were primarily points of interaction with deities. They were also monumental and, therefore, foundations of social identity, memory, and forgetting (Connerton 1989:43; Forty 2001:6–10; Lefebvre 1991:222–225). Council houses involved spousal exchange, marriage rites (Carmack 1981:192; Rice 1988:240–241), and divination (Pugh 2001a:549). Shrines varied in use, but many were used for ancestor veneration (Pugh 2003a:946).

Community centers frequently included natural features such as cenotes/caves and large trees. Caves played critical roles in Maya landscapes long before the Late Postclassic period and still continue to do so (Pugh 2005; Stone, this volume). Many modern Maya believe that deities and other supernatural beings occupy caves, cenotes, chultuns, and rock shelters (L. Brown 2005:137–139; Davis 1978:77; Hofling 1991:136–192; Vogt and Stuart 2005). Water inside caves is pure/sacred (Brady and Ashmore 1999:127) and liminal (Chase and Chase, this volume). Caves are strongly linked to the underworld but also contain celestial elements and are, therefore, axis mundi. Since caves exist in material form, they engraved cosmology into the landscape (Halperin 2005:73) and are/were critical pilgrimage sites (Brady and Veni 1992:163; Patel, this volume; Roys 1943:82; Stone, this volume; Turner 1973:229). Stones were sometimes removed from caves and used in above-surface rituals (Brady et al. 1997; Davis 1978:77; McGee 1998:43–45; Peterson et al. 2005). On the other hand, at Chamula, stones and sherds are thrown "into a cave as tribute" to supernatural beings (Bricker 1973:114). Buildings were often aligned with subsurface features and their presence frequently designated the center of a community (Brady 1997; Pugh 2001b:251; 2003b:416–422). Prominent buildings might be linked to the features by causeways and other features (Halperin 2005:76–80). When absent, penetrations into the earth were frequently constructed and the Maya did not distinguish between the artificial and natural "caves" (Brady and Veni 1992; Pugh 2005:63). Similarly, large temple platforms represented hills or mountains, which were also powerful symbols (see Carlsen, this volume). Together, the mountain and cave are very sacred and represent the earth, as penetrations into mountains are close to the earth's central cosmic force (Fischer 1999:482).

Like caves and mountains, trees were polyvalent symbols found throughout Mesoamerica. Large trees, especially ceibas, stand in the center of many Maya settlements and are often symbols of community (Schwartz 1990:131). Other trees such as cacao, copal, and mahogany were also important. The sacred tree that grew at the edge of Chan Santa Cruz helped unify people during the Caste War. The Mexican military discerned its efficacy and cut it down (Reed 1964:135–144). During some rites, the Maya cut trees and re-erected them in the plaza (Thompson 1930:111). Trees were frequently depicted with a reptilian head at their base representing a cave. Such "world-trees" separated and connected the earth, sky, and underworld (Taube 1988a:171). Trees also were represented by a cruciform pattern. As with caves and artificial tunnels, the Maya do not appear to have strongly differentiated between trees and crosses.

Although various Maya groups used similar buildings and natural features, they arranged them differently. Certain configurations coincide with ethnic boundaries (Pugh 2003b:410). The arrangement of buildings reflected and helped externalize communal worldviews. They were frequently arranged as microcosms (Ashmore 1991, 1992). For example, at Late Postclassic Zacpetén in Petén, Guatemala, a borrow pit and large amounts of human bone of the west side of the central plaza contrast with high temples and deity effigies on the east side; therefore, western death and eastern life associated with the solar cycle was written into the plaza (Pugh 2003b:423–426). Central architecture and natural features provided the community a foundation in time, space, and society. Residential architecture was frequently aligned with civic-ceremonial structures. For example, the Northern Lacandon oriented their residential architecture with the god house (McGee 2002:138). Domestic groups at many Late Postclassic sites in Petén were clustered around ceremonial areas (Rice 1988:236).

Like other ordered spaces, domestic groups have four corners, a center, and boundaries consecrated and cleansed with ritual performances (Hanks 1990:324–325). The four posts and hearth of the house were a commonly used imago mundi; hence, residential form was projected upon the world; Postclassic residential groups included ritual activity areas (Pugh 2002:313–319; 2004:361–365; Smith 1962:267), and residences are sometimes clustered around underground features (Brown 1999:569–570). The shape and habits of residential groups and villages also composed part of Maya worldviews at contact (Clendinnen 1980:377–378). Coresidence, production, consumption, transmission, and reproduction occur in residences (Ashmore and Wilk 1988:6). These activities are the impetus of many ritual activities in the community center. In addition to the consciously constructed perimeters, household and more inclusive identities emerge from "routine social practices" (Bourdieu 1977; Knapp and Ashmore 1999:20). Leslie Cecil (this volume) remarks that the production of material culture, from resource extraction to manufacture techniques (the technological style), is an important aspect of worldviews that contributed to the social identity of the Kowoj. These practices occurred within and were, therefore, part of the Kowoj social landscape. During New Year rites, household goods were "terminated" and replaced. They also swept their houses and placed the debris and terminated objects in special deposits located outside the community. These deposits were considered contagion and strictly avoided (Hutson and Stanton 2007:137–138; Landa 1941 [1566]:151–152). Hence, everyday objects became sacred after their use-lives and their discard embedded this significance into the landscape.

Outside of human settlements were the undivided forest and its creatures. Similar to the Siberian Khanty (Jordan 2003:280–281), the Maya made offerings to obtain permission from forest lords and animal masters before using land or wild animals (Astor-Aguilera, this volume; L. Brown 2005:137–139; Hofling 1991: 136–66). The forest could also be a dangerous place, especially when lost. As mentioned below, one might wander into another cosmic plane. The Maya term for being in the forest connotes that it is "dangerous and unpredictable" compared to bounded human spaces (Hanks 1990:306). Wandering lost in the forest was also a metaphor for displacement and migration and a frequent theme in ethnic origin myths (Edmonson 1986:59–61; Ringle, this volume).

The relationship between the human and divine worlds was reciprocal and involved travel to sacred places. Ritual movement outside the community occurred during ceremonial circuits and pilgrimages conducted during major calendrical rites. Cenotes, caves, wells, and other holes in the earth were the locations of rituals and pilgrimages (Brady and Veni 1992:163; Patel, this volume; Roys 1943:82) and appear to have been quite important during New Year and *k'atun* rites (Taube 1988a:307; Stone, this volume). Trees such as Chan Santa Cruz, ruins, and other shrines were also visited. These features were centers for the people living near them and "centers-out-there" for pilgrims (Turner 1973:229). Elites likely made ritual circuits to peripheral "centers" in order to maintain political boundaries (McAnany 1995:87–88) and reenact the primordial wanderings of mythical heroes. Pilgrims visited the shrines of Ix Chel on Cozumel to ensure fertility (Patel, this volume). Chich'en Itzá, Mayapán, and Tulum were also pilgrimage sites (Arnauld 1997; Freidel and Sabloff 1984:179–192; Landa 1941 [1566]:109). Ceremonial circuits and other pilgrimages incorporated landscape, time, and the social reality. They also connected the spaces of living humans to the underworld, while at the same time securing the boundaries between the two realms.

The Underworld

Penetrations into the earth—caves, cenotes, chultuns, tunnels, and tombs—connected the human world with the underworld. The Yukatek believe that the sun sets in a cave in the west and rises through a cave in the east—metaphorically representing death and life—and in the process passed through the underworld (Sosa 1985:414–424). The Maya strongly related death and rebirth (Astor-Aguilera, this volume; Carlsen, this volume; Miller 1982:85–98). As the world of the newly dead, the underworld had a close relationship with the living. Tombs were often reentered and some were built with "psychoducts" linking the living with the dead (Chase and Chase, this volume). Miguel Astor-Aguilera (this volume) notes that modern Yukatek use bundles of human bones to communicate with and feed ancestors. The human remains are exhumed and placed in a cloth bundle, which is then stored in a shrine or altar. Apparently, these bundles were once reburied (Astor-Aguilera, this volume). Late Postclassic evidence for such practices was found adjacent to a shrine at Zacpetén (Pugh 2001a:377).

Some Maya imagined an underworld with nine levels (Thompson 1970:195); however, its appearance varied. Among some groups in Yucatán, it has two levels. One level includes "underground rivers" and below that is a layer of fire (Hanks 1990:305–306). The latter level suggests Christian influence. The belief in a watery underworld had a long history in Mesoamerica (Chase and Chase, this volume). Many Maya believe the chthonic landscape held various trials, obstacles, and punishment for the dead (Boremanse 1998a:91–96). Primordial heroes traveled to the underworld in the final acts of creation (Boremanse 1998a:91–96; Tedlock 1985:110–160). The underworld contains water and the winds that keep water in motion. The winds that propel water emerge from the sun and some are dangerous and can cause sickness (Hanks 1990:306; Sosa 1985:445–451). Healing rites generally involve immobilizing the "out-of-place" winds and sending them into the forest or "abandoned" chultuns—again subterranean features (Hanks 1990:339–349). The underworld is also not distinct from the sky. The water that runs underground is the same water that rains from the sky and is "freed" from the underground through rituals and the Chaak rain deities (Sosa 1985:396). Celestial winds drive the water between the earth and sky (Hanks 1990:305–306).

The Sky

Many Maya imagined the sky as a landscape. The Northern Lacandon imagined stars as tree roots. They named the visible stars of the Milky Way *sak bel akyum*, or "white road of our lords" (McGee 2002:129). The Yukatek believe that the Milky Way formed a road upon which the sun/Jesus walks with the souls of humans (Sosa 1985:430). The sky also holds temples that are replicated in modern rituals in Yucatán (Hanks 1990:373–374). The sky had multiple levels differing in their composition and occupants. Sometimes it had thirteen levels (Thompson 1970:195), although the modern Yukatek note five celestial levels (Hanks 1990:304–306). The Lacandon universe is usually described as having five circular layers (Davis 1978:18; McGee 1990:61), although Didier Boremanse (1982:84) suggests seven.

In the Lacandon underworld, the newly dead were punished for sins. Above the underworld is the material world, which is surrounded by the ocean and occupied by living humans, less-righteous souls, and earth deities (Davis 1978:19–24). The celestial gods and the souls of righteous people occupy the third layer. Feathered serpent pillars separate the third layer and fourth layer, the domain of the god of the gods, K'akoch (Davis 1978:22–23). The fifth layer is the sunless and cold domain of minor deities and the first humans (McGee 1990:61) and will also be occupied by the last humans (Bruce 1979:8).

The Maya observed the movements of the sun, moon, and stars and aligned many buildings with astronomical bodies. Many constructions at Mayapán were oriented toward the solstices and equinoxes. These buildings were designed as replicas of structures at Chich'en Itzá, yet Venus orientations present in the latter were not discerned at Mayapán (Aveni et al. 2004:139–141; Milbrath and Peraza Lope, this volume). However, the cycles of Venus do appear to have concerned the occupants of Late Postclassic Tulum (Miller 1982:85–91). Many sections in the Maya codices also describe astronomical events (Vail and Aveni 2004b:5–6). Until recently, the Northern Lacandon oriented their god houses toward both Polaris, the polar star, and Yaxchilán (McGee 2002:129–138). The sun's movement defines the "sacred periphery" of Santiago Atitlán (Carlsen, this volume). The corners of the rectangular peripheral path are defined by the solstitial and equinoctial positions; hence, the yearly cycle is written into the landscape. Furthermore, Tz'utujil Maya draw a line between points aligned with the sunrise at the spring equinox and sunset at the fall equinox to divide the year in half, thereby defining and spatializing the rainy and dry seasons. Critical rituals coincide with the four annual solar points (Carlsen, this volume).

The sky was attached to the earth but was not as accessible as the underworld since humans were "bound" within the limits of the earth (Sosa 1985:423). The cosmic sea connected the earth and sky. This boundary was also marked and bridged by a "sacred green cross" (Sosa 1985:429). At night the sun, moon, and some stars passed into the underworld—the sun metaphorically "entered its house" (Sosa 1985:425). Venus was also associated with the underworld (Miller 1982:88–91). The Southern Lacandon believed that the sun and moon, which were male and female, respectively, were married and lived together in a cave (Soustelle 1961:48). Hence, although modern astronomers consider the sun, moon, and stars celestial objects, they were both sky and earth beings for many Maya groups (Sosa 1985:424–429).

Interactions between Planes

Many Maya believed humans could travel to the heavens and underworld. Some powerful shamans visited deities, and people occasionally ventured into other cosmic planes by accident (Davis 1978:27). It was also possible to be summoned by deities, especially if one broke a moral law. However, the usual conclusions of such journeys were not pleasant for the human participants (Hofling 1991:136–166; Redfield and Villa Rojas 1962 [1934]:207–208); hence, most preferred to avoid such travels. Nevertheless, all people traveled to other realms of existence after death (Davis 1978:27). Some groups believed that a part of a person—their co-essence—existed in the heavens or underworld while the individual still lived (Chase and Chase, this volume; Vogt 1993 [1976]:19).

Travel to other cosmic planes involved transformations. Not everything on the landscape was always as it seemed—many things varied depending on who observed or received them. The Northern Lacandon believe that deities see the world in its reverse form. To them, caves and stone vaults in ruins appear as wood and thatch houses, big things are small, hot things are cold, as so on. Materials offered to deities are also transformed into their reverse forms. For example, burned copal becomes tortillas (Davis 1978:24–25). One would assume that a human in the deities' worlds would also see things differently from the deities. Hence, the Maya appreciated the subjective nature of the landscape.

Since the sky was largely off limits to the Maya and human access to the underworld was limited to torch-lit journeys into caves, they employed various devices to converse with the denizens of these supernatural planes. Socially and spiritually powerful individuals interacted with deities on behalf of other people (Boremanse 1998a:31, 66–67; Chase and Chase, this volume). The Postclassic and Contact period Maya also communicated with deities through deity images. As outlined by John Chuchiak (this volume), deity images in Late Postclassic, Contact, and Colonial period Yucatán were primarily composed of wood, stone, and ceramics; however, many were composed of special materials. For example, the wooden figures were usually made of cedar, and the clay for the ceramic effigies was sometimes gathered from caves and/or tempered by the pulverized remains of former censers. At Mayapán, some statues were composed of stucco and speleothems (Proskouriakoff 1962b:136). The Maya conducted rituals in a special house to activate the vessels just as they did sacred spaces. Some deity effigy censers were activated during *wayeb'* rites during which the new effigies were paired for a short time with the images they were replacing (Coe 1965; D. Chase 1985b:119; Landa 1941 [1566]:139–140). Through these objects the Maya communicated with their deities and requested good harvests and health. Postclassic period deity-image censers, and presumably other deity representations, were primarily within ceremonial buildings (Pugh et al. 2006). Lacandon effigy censers were connected to the "residence" of the deity that they represented. This "residence" was a known cave or ruin, often distant from the community. If Late Postclassic censers did likewise, then the temple full of censers represented the sacred landscape (Pugh 2005:53).

Humans could also communicate with deities through natural imagery such as caves/tunnels and trees/crosses, which bridge the earth, sky, and underworld. The modern Maya of Santiago Atitlán imagine their community as a world tree stand-ing at the center of the universe with the *cofradía* leader standing as the tree and the ancestors as the roots (Carlsen, this volume). Gabrielle Vail (this volume) notes that world trees represented in the Maya codices bridged the earth, sky, and under-world. She further notes that the trees represented "world destruction and renewal." Many crosses, which are related to trees, are believed to be occupied by divine spirits (Astor-Aguilera, this volume; Sosa 1985:241).

Ritual spaces also facilitated interactions between cosmic planes. The Maya built and/or consecrated religious settings as liminal spaces connecting the earth with other cosmic planes (Chase and Chase, this volume). For example, temples stood between the earth and sky, and caves and tombs opened into the underworld. These places often included symbolism tying them to other cosmic planes, such as water creatures and sky serpents. As noted, ceremonial architecture was frequently oriented with both caves and celestial bodies, thereby linking the buildings with the sky and underworld. Arthur Miller (1982:96–98) suggested that the murals of Tulum depicted the boundary between the underworld and the material plane. As Elizabeth Graham (this volume) argues, the various objects and places men-tioned above were also metaphorical—they had significance in addition to their role in communication. For example, the Great Ballcourt of Chich'en Itzá may have been used as a liminal space where one could communicate with deities, but it also included imagery of creation events (Schele and Mathews 1998:206–255).

Consecration or dedication of spaces was human action intended to ensoul the landscape or objects and connect them with otherworlds. Such actions involved ritualized caching, construction, and renovation. Caching deposits special objects and/or materials into the earth or a construction. Activated spaces were "alive" and connected with the divine (Pendergast 1998:61–62; Stross 1998:35). Buildings and objects often were "terminated" at the end of a certain cycle of time. Termination "killed" the building or object through destruction or defacement and the removal of caches (Mock 1998:9–10). Terminated landscapes and objects might later be rededicated. Stratigraphy of ceremonial buildings represents generations of "death and rebirth" (Mock 1998:6–13). These generations of landscapes "lived and died" in tune with the flow of cyclical time.

Time

Human action constantly transformed the Maya landscape as settlement centers were reseated and sacred places were terminated and consecrated. These actions were generally attuned with calendrical and astronomical cycles. The sea at the world's edges was a potential danger as it could flood unless the proper ritu-als were performed at calendrical junctures (Taube 1988a:171–172; Vail, this vol-ume). Many Maya objectified time as a road circumscribing the landscape (Bruce

1979:102; Carlsen, this volume). Late Postclassic spatial representations were frequently bordered by k'atun wheels. K'atun wheels were calendars of the *may*, a cycle of approximately 256 years (Rice, this volume). Modern Yukatek note that the spatial edge of the world is equivalent to the end of time (Sosa 1985:428–429); hence, earthly boundaries corresponded with temporal boundaries. Since the boundary is a beach, it is understandable that the end of the world is often imagined as a flood. The placement of calendrical junctions and the primordial sea along the borders of representations of time/space further supports Diane Chase and Arlen Chase's (this volume) suggestion that the latter was liminal since calendrical completions are also in between states. The occupants of Santiago Atitlán imagined their community to be surrounded by a counterclockwise path traveled by the sun (Carlsen, this volume). This path pivoted the horizontal axis, placing the sky to the north and the underworld to the south (following Coggins 1980). The sun's movement across the landscape is the most basic element of Maya time; hence, time and space are inseparable.

Time is also incorporated into the landscape through architectural construction. The primary temple of Chich'en Itzá, the Castillo, was covered with temporal markings including quadripartite time/space, 364 steps representing the "computing year," and 52 niches signifying the Calendar Round. The building also casts it renowned (although contentious) serpent shadow at the spring equinox, and one of its axes faces toward sunset on the summer solstice (Aveni et al. 2004:129–130). The Castillo of Mayapán was likewise quadripartite and had 260 steps representing the *tzolk'in* cycle (Aveni et al. 2004:130).

Vail (this volume) investigates the calendrical, spatial, and ritual significance of the *Madrid Codex*. Like the k'atun turtles, a representation in this screenfold book depicts a landscape surrounded by time, but in this case the landscape is square with four parts and a center and the calendar is the 52-year Calendar Round. The Calendar Round combines the 260-day tzolk'in and the 365-day *ja'ab'* cycles. Vail also argues that ritual actions associated with the Calendar Round, such as human sacrifice and ritual circuits, are depicted in this figure. She suggests that the use of the 52-year cycle differs from most other Postclassic Maya time/space representations, which use *tun* and k'atun cycles and that this variance may indicate influence from Central México.

Music was critical to the everyday life and the sacred landscape and was connected to cyclical time. Rodney Needham (1967:611–613) suggested that percussion in rituals signaled the transition from one state of being to another and associated transformations with the emotional effect of the music. Musical instruments are found in Late Postclassic Maya ritual contexts (Pugh 2001a:530–533) and images in the Maya codices and Santa Rita murals clearly indicate that Maya rituals incorporate music. In fact, Late Postclassic k'atun rituals were associated with the rattle and the drum (Roys 1967:77–78). Percussion instruments often become emblems of the transition they help mediate (Needham 1967:611). Mark Howell (this volume) investigates both modern highland Maya dance-plays and archaeological data in order to extrapolate elements of Precolumbian music. Although the dance-plays are now Spanish/Maya hybrids, they helped the Maya remember important elements in their historical consciousness.

The Past in the Past

Ruined settlements were scattered across the Postclassic Maya landscapes. Some recent Yukatek believed that dwarves and/or giants built the ruins as well as Colonial period churches (Sosa 1985:409–410). Others specified that it was the Itza who built the ruins and still lived in caves beneath the masonry structures (Villa Rojas 1945:153). Among the Northern Lacandon, caves and archaeological ruins were considered to be the homes of deities. The deities once occupied Yaxchilán and Palenque and the Lacandon faced their god houses toward the former (Davis 1978:18–24; McGee 2002:129–138). The Northern Lacandon also incorporated several rock-art sites into their sacred landscape. Some of these carvings and paintings were composed by earlier, perhaps Late Postclassic, occupants of the region (Palka, this volume; Pugh 2001a:117).

Past constructions were critical aspects of Postclassic and Contact period sacred landscapes. Similar to the Northern Lacandon, many Postclassic Maya made pilgrimages to Classic and Preclassic period sites. Both historical accounts and artifacts in the Sacred Cenote document that Chich'en Itzá was an important pilgrimage site (Coggins and Shane 1984:111–155; Landa 1941 [1566]:180). Cerros, in northern Belize, was an important site of Late Postclassic pilgrimages from nearby Santa Rita (Walker 1990:472). The Maya did not just passively visit these places. A buried Late Classic temple at Dzibilchaltun was partially uncovered by the Late Postclassic occupants, who excavated a tunnel through the western doorway of the buried central chamber, built an altar in the inner chamber, placed a cache in front of the altar, and repainted the altar three times on k'atun- and half-k'atun-ending dates (Andrews IV and Andrews V 1980:112–116; Thompson 1980:116–117). In addition, they reconstructed the building's western stairway. These Late Postclassic occupants also excavated tunnels into and renovated stairways on other buildings at Dzibilchaltun (Andrews IV and Andrews V 1980:25). Late Postclassic offerings, caches, and burials were found in some temples at Tikal (Adams and Trik 1958:134), and Classic period monuments were moved and sometimes reset and venerated by Postclassic period occupants of various sites (Graham 1994:113, 129; Hammond and Bobo 1994:26–32; Pugh 2001a:228, 256; Satterthwaite 1958:75–76).

The Late Postclassic Maya appropriated portions of earlier structures for use in their own constructions. The Kowoj of Zacpetén incorporated Terminal Classic monuments and cut limestone masonry blocks into ceremonial buildings and elite residential architecture (Pugh 2001a, 2002). Offerings near the carved monuments indicate that they played a role in ritual events. Classic period architectural features were also incorporated into buildings at Mayapán (Milbrath and Peraza Lope, this volume; Proskouriakoff 1962b:92) and Tipu (Cecil, this volume) as well as Colonial period churches including Telchaquillo (Proskouriakoff 1962b:92) and Izamal. In addition to using the stones and monuments of earlier peoples, both the Maya and Spaniards appropriated past places by building on top of them. Modern highland Maya believe that ancient artifacts, from statuary to potsherds, are powerful divinatory objects associated with the ancestors (Brown 2000:330; Carlsen, this volume). I observed the use of ancient objects in modern rites in Chamula, Chiapas, México, and San José, Petén, Guatemala. The inhabitants of San José argue that the artifacts demonstrate the antiquity of human skulls that they use in their modern celebrations.

The past was also mimicked by Postclassic constructions. The occupants of Mayapán built the Castillo and Caracol as replicas of buildings at Chich'en Itzá (Aveni et al. 2004:130; Milbrath and Peraza Lope, this volume). The Late Postclassic Kowoj constructed replicas of Mayapán-style temple assemblages in Petén, Guatemala, in order to connect themselves with their homeland (Pugh 2003b:426). Although it is unlikely that all examples of mimicry share a common explanation, many were likely attempts to maintain continuity with the past as well as to create spiritual connections. Such architectural quotations are a form of power as they create precedence for the present in the past (Leone 1984:27–28).

Politics of Landscape

As with any form of knowledge, landscape is a contested form of power. Landscape can be considered a process that involves "controversy and conflict" (Strathern and Stewart 2003:229). Control over the landscape can be achieved in various ways—one can occupy it, walk across its surface, record it, or conduct critical rituals on it. Mapping records the landscape and social entities occupying it, but this practice is also a tool of social power (Smith 2003:84–85). Another strategy is to claim to have occupied the area first (Kopytoff 1987:52–62). Honoring the graves of ancestors buried within the landscape or the historical/sacred places upon the landscape is another manner of laying claim to a particular landscape. Even when history does not record the actions of ancestors, other strategies such as archaeology can embed the present in the past (Dietler 1994:597–599). Of course, any of these strategies might be countered by those of opposing groups.

As a critical dimension of worldviews, time was involved in politics. Many rulers used linear and cyclical time, especially the movement of the sun, to legitimate their power. Furthermore, some ethnic groups had their own calendars, and part of their political struggles was temporal (Milbrath and Peraza Lope, this volume; Rice, this volume). In Late Postclassic to Contact period Yucatán and perhaps before, the "capital" city of Maya polities shifted at the end of the may cycle of approximately 256 years. Towns within the polity also served as seats of the k'atun, which was likewise transferred cyclically according to that cycle (Rice, this volume). One can imagine the intense politics behind the selection of cycle seats.

Monuments are frequently destroyed or covered to undermine their social power (Forty 2001:10–12; Lefebvre 1991:221–225). Susan Milbrath and Carlos Peraza Lope (this volume) argue that the architecture of the ceremonial core of Mayapán became a symbolic battleground between the Xiw and Kokom during the Middle Postclassic period. When the Kokom dominated politics, they dismantled and covered Xiw constructions in the site's ceremonial core. The Kokom copied constructions from Chich'en Itzá and remodeled the city's architecture with an international style that reflected their connections with distant trading partners. After they successfully revolted, the Xiw revitalized the architecture of the city by dismantling and covering many Kokom constructions. Even buried buildings can be excavated and reinstated into the sacred landscape, as clearly seen at Dzibilchaltun, previously discussed.

Historical migration events played critical roles in the construction of Postclassic Maya landscapes. Places of origin and promised lands, whether real or imagined, help unify people and provide a basis for common identity (Malkki 1997:70–72; Smith 1992:438–452). They are often sacred, as the deeds of ancestors were considered heroic or pure. Their purity might arise from their liminality or perfection in character (Malkki 1997:67). As a symbol of social foundation, migration stories are myths that can play a part in ritual performance. A migration can be a stage of cosmogony because it is a crucial origin point that defines the composition and characteristics of the ethnic group. For example, the Aztec capital, Tenochtitlan, may have been built to resemble their mythical homeland, Aztlan (Boone 1991:122). Mayapán was likewise a powerful distant center for various Maya groups at contact. The Kowoj of Petén, Guatemala, created representations of the ceremonial spaces at Mayapán in order to advertise their connections with this city. Their most critical ritual events occurred—in a virtual sense—in the ethnic homeland. As noted, the Kowoj placed architectural elements from ruined Classic period structures, as well as carved monuments, into prominent places in their ceremonial and elite architecture to publicize that they also had historical ties in Petén. Hence, the Kowoj architecture symbolized a bifocal landscape projecting their identity as both legitimate locals and powerful foreigners.

Groups displaced by economically or militarily powerful migrant groups and denied the prestige of "first occupancy" can resist assimilation and social domination by constructing identities in their own terms. Indigenous groups throughout the Americas appropriated Spanish symbols and used them against the Spaniards as well as in internal conflicts between factions (Rappaport 1987:46–53; Silverblatt

1988:184; Whitehead 1993:297–298). William Ringle (this volume) notes that two lords of the Colonial period Pech family referred to themselves as first conquistadors. A myth common in Mesoamerica is that of the wandering creator—a quasi-historical figure responsible for making critical changes to the landscape. The Maya paralleled Spanish conquistadors with the indigenous wandering creator Quetzalcoatl. As the conquistadors reformatted the Maya landscape, the Pech family likewise paralleled their recent ancestral figures with the Spaniards (Ringle, this volume). Maya temporal systems and perceptions of history also resisted the conquest and colonialism, and elements of Spanish history and religion were incorporated into these alternative timescapes (Rice, this volume). Andrea Stone (this volume) observed that colonial symbols of power were hybridized into Maya practices and taken underground—literally—into cave rituals celebrating the k'atun. The double-headed Hapsburg eagle, "circular frontal faces," and images of horsemen were Spanish symbols appropriated by the Maya and incorporated into Maya cave ritual. Since they were used in clandestine indigenous rites, they played a role in Maya resistance to the Spaniards. The Maya also resisted Spanish efforts to end their use of deity effigy censers until the nineteenth century in Yucatán and until present among the Lacandon (Chuchiak, this volume; Palka, this volume). Ultimately, many deities were syncretized with Catholic saints, Jesus, and the cross (Redfield and Villa Rojas 1962 [1934]:97–110). The Lacandon recently stopped regularly using their censers because television revealed a much larger world than was explained by their worldviews (McGee 2002:150–152).

The situation of contact varied from place to place. Ethnic diversity resulted in differential responses from indigenous groups (Gasco 2005:95–96). The Spaniards also did not follow a unified "ideology of domination" (Rodríguez-Alegría 2005:37–39). In Santiago Atitlán, the colonial situation was one of weak dominance by the Spaniards and appropriation and resistance on the part of the Maya (Carlsen, this volume). The Maya adopted the cofradía system but utilized it to preserve their own traditions as well as to "convert" the Catholic saints to fill the roles of indigenous deities. The cofradías directly maintained certain traditions, such as the use of cloth bundles containing various objects associated with ancestors. It was not just the objects held within the bundles that evoked the ancestors but also the textiles decorated with traditional designs. These bundles brought about the renewal of the land's fertility and the ancestors' reproduction as offspring. The highland Maya also maintained some traditional musical practices when they appropriated Spanish dance-plays (Howell, this volume).

Landscape politics are often subtle as humans create boundaries through variations in cultural practices (Wiessner 1983:257). Cecil (this volume) investigates how ceramic vessels used in ritual events help to communicate the social history and identity of the Kowoj. The use of this particular form of material culture as well as temple assemblages were critical aspects of the communal and regional landscape of the Kowoj. Although ritual is a powerful form of communication, even the raw materials and undecorated ceramic colors and textures differentiated the Kowoj from the Itza. Robert Carlsen (this volume) likewise discerned that the production and wearing of community-specific textiles helped the Maya of Santiago Atitlán to recreate themselves as the ancestors. Hence, they create a landscape of ancestors by transmitting communal styles to the next generation. Mobile material culture is often distinguished from the landscape, but the forms, colors, and textures of artifacts were cues just as critical to their living users as they are to archaeologists seeking to understand ancient cultural landscapes.

Summary

No pan-Maya worldview existed at contact and worldviews changed through time, but several themes emerge in the consideration of meaning in Maya sacred landscapes. Maya landscapes included significance that was built, "naturally" occurring, and appropriated from the colonial other and the past. Inherent in these themes is the construction of meaning through various practices. The Maya often externalized the shape of the universe. Representations of the world, or imago mundi, ranged from simple quincunx motifs to larger and more complex arrangements. The world could be represented by a particular construction or buildings and features combined into assemblages. Temples were also constructed adjacent to caves to recreate the mountain/cave, a representation of the center of the Maya universe. Some representations were less overt, such as the grouping of censers inside of temples, which likely represented sacred spaces in the landscape. Time was incorporated into the imago mundi through calendars, numerology, the quincunx, counterclockwise movements, cyclical seating of capitals, dedications/terminations, and other forms.

The imago mundi is not the only topic communicated by landscape symbolism—events were also memorialized. Perhaps the most common event was the creation of the earth represented by the mountain/temple rising out of the cosmic sea/plaza. The wanderings and actions of powerful figures were memorialized in the landscape and architectural constructions. Some buildings and assemblages were built as "quotations"; they represented past constructions in order to appropriate the power of the past and/or establish historical relationships with past peoples. The arrival of the Spaniards was also memorialized in the landscape through the incorporation of their symbols. The landscape also involved forgetting. Battles of construction, defacement, burial, reconstruction, and excavation constantly transformed the meaning of the landscape. The Spaniards participated in this process through their practices of tabula rasa, which involved the destruction of indigenous sacra and its replacement by Catholic symbols (Giffords 2007:71–72; Roys 1952:143–177). The Maya likewise destroyed Spanish sacra (Jones 1998:348).

Both the Maya and Spaniards built upon sacred places of the past and incorporated past objects in order to establish legitimacy in the present.

The Maya incorporated community organization into the symbolism of sacred spaces. Buildings in Late Postclassic temple assemblages integrated a number of social categories, including deities, politics/lineage, and ancestors. Some ceremonial groups represented factions within communities (Fox 1994:169–170; Freidel and Sabloff 1984:183–184; Pugh 2003b:426). However, architectural features such as plazas and *sakbejo'ob* symbolically (and metaphorically) tie factions together (Freidel and Sabloff 1984:84; Kurjack and Andrews V 1976:322–324; Shaw 2001:267–269). Central trees and cenotes were also associated with collective identity and possibly factions at large sites such as Mayapán.

"Naturally" occurring sacra include elements that the Maya strongly attached to divine beings or contained large amounts of spiritual energy. As mentioned, some caves were believed to be the homes of gods and animal masters. The sacred was not evenly distributed across the natural landscape as some things—such as caves in mountains or phenomena ascribed enormous power, such as Chan Santa Cruz or the Sacred Cenote of Chich'en Itzá—possessed greater spiritual energy.

In the course of this chapter, I have described meaning as it "was" and I used modern ethnography and Classic period data as analogy for understanding landscape at conquest, perhaps giving the impression that meaning is static. However, meaning is neither static nor naturally embedded in constructions or the natural landscape—it is created, remembered, and contested through practices. Of course, praxis likewise occurs in a "world already defined" (Friedman 1992:837). Although Jordan (2001) described modern Khanty pastoralists in Siberia, I argue that his notion of landscape enculturation also works well with the Maya sacred landscape at contact. Most Maya lived in permanent settlements, but they constantly interacted with the natural world in their daily lives and ritual practices. Furthermore, many of their constructions were connected to elements of the natural landscape. Of course, most elements of the built environment differed from the nature landscape—the ritualized creation of bounded spaces would have distinguished them. Nevertheless, the built environment experienced re-enculturation through termination, dedication, and even excavation. This process emphasized human involvement in the construction of monumental spaces as well as the perpetuation of collective memories. As seen with mid-twentieth-century Maya perceptions of the builders of ancient ruins, people can become disassociated from their achievements. When construction is a celebrated ongoing process, people are less likely to be alienated from the work of their ancestors.

Sacred landscapes at conquest were varied and composed of numerous practices that facilitated interactions between humans and time, history, deities, and otherworlds. Such actions on the part of humans were often conducted to preserve or reconsecrate the landscape by repeating creation actions of deities. They coordinated their ritual cycles and, therefore, social realities with the rhythms of their universe in the form of daily and yearly cycles, celestial patterns, larger units of time, and the spaces of cosmogony. Rituals might also be conducted to influence deities whose actions could have a direct impact on sunlight, water, plants, and animals. Maya deities were not absolutely distanced from humans; their actions also occurred in the landscape in the form of solar paths, their former and now-ruined settlements, and living avatars. The actions of deities might be invisible to humans or may have occurred before the creation of humans, but they were remembered through ritual events. Meaning is not a template in the mind or one that is permanently retained from childhood programming. The sacred landscape and its meaning are externalized and transmitting through action. Worldviews are perpetuated and celebrated as practices and experiences in the world.

REFERENCES CITED

Adams, Richard E.W.
  1963   A Polychrome Vessel from Altar de Sacrificos, Peten, Guatemala. *Archaeology* 16(2):90–92.
  1986   Rio Azul. *National Geographic* 169(4):420–451.

Adams, Richard E.W., and Aubrey S. Trik
  1958   Temple I (Str. 5-I): Post-Constructional Activities. *Tikal Reports*, vol. 7. University Monograph No. 20, University of Pennsylvania, Philadelphia.

AGCA (Archivo General de Centro América, Guatemala City)
  1817   El Reverendo Padre Manuel de la Chica, sobre que se le auxilie para emprender la Conquista de los indios Lacandones en las Montañas de Verapas. (A1.12, Exp. 7065, Leg. 334).

AGG (Archivo General del Gobierno, Guatemala City)
  1936   Autos hechos en virtud de la Real Cédula de su Magistad, en que se
  [1754] ordena a este Superior Gobierno, que serciorado del estado en que se hallan las reducciones de Indios de la Provincia del Petén, año de 1754. *Boletin del Archivo General del Gobierno* 1(3):257–293.

AGI (Archivo General de Indias, Seville)
  1562   Testimonio del reo Gaspar Chim en los autos de idolatria. *Escribanía de Cámara*, 1009A, 4 folios.

Aimers, James J.
  2002   Cultural Change on a Temporal and Spatial Frontier: Ceramics of the Terminal Classic to Postclassic Transition in the Upper Belize River Valley. Ph.D. dissertation, Department of Anthropology. Tulane University, New Orleans.

REFERENCES CITED

Aimers, James J., and Prudence M. Rice
 2006   Astronomy, Ritual, and the Interpretation of Maya "E-Group" Architectural As-
         semblages. *Ancient Mesoamerica* 17(1):79–96.

Akkeren, Ruud W. van
 2000   *Place of the Lord's Daughter: Rab'inal, Its History, Its Dance-Drama*. Research
         School CNWS. School of Asian, African, and Amerindian Studies, Leiden, The
         Netherlands.

Alexander, Rani T.
 1998   Postclassic Settlement Patterns at Isla Cilvituk, Campeche, México. Paper pre-
         sented at the 63rd Annual Meeting of the Society for American Archaeology,
         Seattle.
 2005   Isla Cilvituk and the Difficulties of Spanish Colonization in Southwestern Cam-
         peche. In *The Postclassic to Spanish-Era Transition in Mesoamerica*, ed. Susan Kepecs
         and Rani Alexander, 161–181. University of New Mexico Press, Albuquerque.

Alvarado, Fray Francisco de
 1962   *Vocabulario en lengua mixteca por Fray Francisco de Alvarado*. Ed. Wigberto Ji-
 [1953] menez Moreno. Instituto Nacional Indigenista, México.

Alvarez, Cristina
 1980   *Diccionario etnolinguistico del idioma maya yucateco colonial*. 2 vols. CEM,
         UNAM, México.

Anders, Ferdinand
 1967   *Codex Tro-Cortesianus (Codex Madrid)*. Akademische Druck- und Verlagsan-
         stalt, Graz.

Anderson, James M.
 2002   *Daily Life during the Spanish Inquisition*. Greenwood Press, Westport, Connecticut.

Andrews, Anthony P.
 1990   The Role of Trading Ports in Maya Civilization. In *Vision and Revision in Maya
         Studies*, ed. Florence S. Clancy and Peter D. Harrison, 159–168. University of
         New Mexico, Albuquerque.

Andrews, E. Wyllys, IV
 1955–   Xcaret Journal. Manuscript on file, Middle American Research Institute. Tulane
 1956   University, New Orleans.

Andrews, E. Wyllys, IV, and E. Wyllys Andrews V
 1980   *Excavations at Dzibilchaltun, Yucatan, Mexico*. Middle American Research Insti-
         tute, Publication 48. Tulane University, New Orleans.

Antochiw, Michel
 1994   *Historia Cartogáfica de la Península de Yucatán*. Gobierno del Estado de Cam-
         peche.

Antochiw, Michel, and Alfredo C. Dachary
 1991   *Historia de Cozumel*. Consejo Nacional para la Cultura y las Artes, México City.

Arnauld, Marie-Charlotte
1997   Relaciones Interregionales en el Area Maya durante el Postclasico en Base a Datos Arquitectonicos. In *X Simposio de Arqueología Guatemalteca*, ed. Juan Pedro Laporte and Hector Escobeda, 117–131. Instituto de Antropología e Historia, Ministerio de Cultura y Deportes, y la Asociación Tikal, Guatemala City.

Arnold, Channing, and Fredrick J. Tabor Frost
1909   *American Egypt*. Hutchinson and Row, London.

Arnold, Dean E., and Bruce F. Bohor
1977   An Ancient Clay Mine at Yo'K'at, Yucatán. *American Antiquity* 42(4):575–582.

Ashmore, Wendy
1991   Site-Planning Principles and Concepts of Directionality among the Ancient Maya. *Latin American Antiquity* 2(3):199–226.
1992   Deciphering Maya Architectural Plans. In *New Theories on the Ancient Maya*, ed. Elin Danien and Robert Sharer, 173–184. The University Museum, University of Pennsylvania, Philadelphia.
2004   Classic Maya Landscapes and Settlement. In *Mesoamerican Archaeology*, ed. Julie A. Hendon and Rosemary A. Joyce, 169–191. Blackwell Publishers, Oxford.

Ashmore, Wendy, and Richard R. Wilk
1988   Household and Community in the Mesoamerican Past. In *Household and Community in the Mesoamerican Past*, ed. Richard R. Wilk and Wendy Ashmore, 1–27. University of New Mexico Press, Albuquerque.

Astor-Aguilera, Miguel
1998   Maya Rebirth and Renewal: The Talking Crosses and the Practice of Adaptation. Master's thesis, Department of Anthropology, University at Albany / State University of New York, Albany, New York.
2000   Survey of Talking Cross Shrines in Yucatán and Quintana Roo. Electronic document, http://www.famsi.org/reports/99034, accessed April 22, 2008.
2004   Unshrouding the Communicating Cross: The Iconology of a Maya Quadripartite Symbol. Ph.D. dissertation, Department of Anthropology, University at Albany / State University of New York, Albany, New York.
2008   *Quadripartite Crosses, Trees, and Stones: The Maya World of Communicating Objects*. Under University of New Mexico Press review.

Avendaño y Loyola, Fray Andrés de
1987   *Relation of Two Trips to Peten, Made for the Conversion of the Heathen Ytzaex and Cehaches*. Trans. Charles P. Bowditch and Guillermo Rivera, with notes by Frank E. Camparato. Labyrinthos, Culver City, California.

Aveni, Anthony F.
1980   *Skywatchers of Ancient Mexico*. University of Texas Press, Austin.
1992   *The Sky in Mayan Literature*. Oxford University Press, New York.
1999   Astronomy in the Mexican Codex Borgia. *Archaeoastronomy* (Supplement to *Journal for the History of Astronomy* 30) 24:S1–S20.
2001   *Skywatchers: A Revised and Updated Version of Skywatchers of Ancient Mexico*. University of Texas Press, Austin.

REFERENCES CITED

2002   *Empires of Time: Calendars, Clocks, and Cultures.* Rev. ed. University Press of Colorado, Boulder.

Aveni, Anthony F., Susan Milbrath, and Carlos Peraza Lope
2004   Chichén Itzá's Legacy in the Astronomically Oriented Architecture of Mayapán. *RES: Research in Aesthetics and Anthropology* 45:123–143.

Baer, Philip, and William R. Merrifield
1971   *Two Studies of the Lacandones of Mexico.* Summer Institute of Linguistics, University of Oklahoma, Norman.

Bailey, G. N.
1983   Concepts of Time in Quaternary Prehistory. *Annual Review of Anthropology* 12: 165–192.

Barrera Rubio, Alfredo, and Carlos Peraza Lope
1999   Los vestigios pictóricos de la cueva de Tixcuytún, Yucatán. In *Land of the Turkey and Deer: Recent Research in Yucatan*, ed. Ruth Gubler, 37–56. Labyrintos, Lancaster, California.
2001   La Pintura Mural de Mayapán. In *La Pintural Mural Prehispánica en México: Área Maya*, ed. Leticia Staines Cicero and Beatriz de la Fuentes, 419–446. Universidad Nacional Autónoma de México, Instituto de Investigaciones Antropológicas, México, D.F.

Barrera Vásquez, Alfredo
1980   *Diccionario maya Cordemex: Maya-español, español-maya.* 4th ed. Editorial Porrúa, S.A.
1984   *Documento n. 1 del deslinde de tierras en Yaxkukul, Yuc.* Colección Científica 125, Lingüistica. Instituto Nacional de Antropología e Historia, Centro Regional del Sureste, México, D.F.

Barrera Vásquez, Alfredo, and Sylvanus G. Morley
1949   The Maya Chronicles. Contributions to American Anthropology and History, no. 48. Carnegie Institution of Washington. Publication 585, Washington, D.C.

Barrientos, Tómas, and Henry Benítez
1996   Agua Azul, proyecto de arqueología subacuática, Atitlán. Paper presented at the X Symposia of Guatemala Archaeology, vol. 1. Museo Nacional de Arqueología y Etnología, IDAEH.

Barth, Fredrik (editor)
1969   *Ethnic Groups and Boundaries.* Little, Brown, Boston.

Bassie-Sweet, Karen
1996   *At the Edge of the World: Caves and Late Classic Maya World View.* University of Oklahoma Press, Norman.

Battiste, Marie, and James Youngblood Henderson
2000   *Protecting Indigenous Knowledge and Heritage.* Purich Publishing, Saskatoon.

Batun-Alpuche, Ivan
 2005   The Cozumel Bee Gardens. Paper presented at the Southeast Conference on Mesoamerican Archaeology and Ethnohistory. University of South Florida, Tampa.

Baudez, Claude-François
 2002   Venus y el Códice Grolier. *Arqueología Mexicana* 10(55):70–79.

Beattie, John
 1964   *Other Cultures: Aims, Methods, and Achievements in Social Anthropology.* The Free Press, New York.

Becker, Marshall J.
 1992   Burials as Caches, Caches as Burials: A New Interpretation of the Meaning of Ritual Deposits among the Classic Period Lowland Maya. In *New Theories on the Ancient Maya*, ed. Elin C. Danien and Robert J. Sharer, 185–196. University of Pennsylvania, Philadelphia.

Bell, Catherine
 1992   *Ritual Theory, Ritual Practice.* Oxford University Press, Oxford.

Bellah, Robert N.
 1964   Religious Evolution. *American Sociological Review* 29(3):358–374.

Bender, Barbara
 1998   *Stonehenge: Making Space.* Berg Publishers, Oxford.

Benítez, Henry Danilo
 2001   Patrimonio sumergido en Atitlán: Samabaj, implicaciones de un sitio arqueológico preclásico subacuático. Master's thesis, Departamento de Arqueología, Universidad de San Carlos de Guatemala, Guatemala City.

Bennassar, Bartolomé
 1981   *Inquisición española: Poder político y control social.* Editorial Crítica, Barcelona.

Berger, Peter L.
 1990   *The Sacred Canopy: Elements of a Sociological Theory of Religion.* Anchor Books, New York.

Berger, Peter L., and Thomas Luckmann
 1967   *The Social Construction of Reality: A Treatise in the Sociology of Knowledge.* Anchor Books, New York.

Berrin, Kathleen
 2004   Introduction. In *Courtly Art of the Ancient Maya*, ed. Mary Miller and Simon Martin, 12–15. Thames and Hudson, New York.

Berrin, Kathleen, and Thomas K. Seligman
 1978   *Art of the Huichol Indians.* Harry N. Abrams, New York.

Berry, Kimberly A., Sandra L. López Varela, Mary Lee Bartlett, Tamarra Martz, and Patricia McAnany
 2004   Pottery Vessels of K'axob. In *K'axob: Ritual, Work, and Family in an Ancient Maya Village*, ed. Patricia A. McAnany, 193–261. UCLA, Los Angeles.

REFERENCES CITED

Beyer, Hermann
    1933   Emendations of the Serpent Numbers of the Dresden Codex. *Anthropos* 28:1–7.

Bierhorst, John
    1992   *History and Mythology of the Aztecs: The Codex Chimalpopoca*. University of Arizona Press, Tucson.

Blades, James
    1980   Drum. In *The New Groves Dictionary of Music and Musicians*, vol. 5, ed. Stanley Sadie, 639–649. MacMillan, New York.

Bloch, Maurice
    1977   The Past and the Present in the Present. *Man* (n.s.) 12:278–292.

Blom, Frans F.
    1936   *The Conquest of Yucatan*. Riverside Press, Cambridge, Massachusetts.

Boas, Franz
    1896   The Limitations of the Comparative Method in Anthropology. *Science* 4:901–908.

Bode, Barbara
    1961   The Dance of the Conquest of Guatemala. In *The Native Theater in Middle America*, ed. Margaret Harrison and Robert Wauchope, 203–298. Middle American Research Institute, Publication 27. Tulane University, New Orleans.

Boilès, Charles Lafayette
    1966   The Pipe and Tabor in Mesoamerica. *Yearbook of the Inter-American Institute for Musical Research* 9:45–63.

Bolles, David
    1990   The Maya Calendar: The Solar-Agricultural Year and Correlation Questions. *Mexicon* 12(5):85–89.

Bonfil Batalla, Guillermo
    1996   *México Profundo: Reclaiming a Civilization*. Trans. Philip A. Dennis. University of Texas Press, Austin.

Boone, Elizabeth H.
    1991   Migration Histories as Ritual Performance. In *Aztec Ceremonial Landscapes*, ed. Davíd Carrasco, 42–151. University Press of Colorado, Niwot.
    1994   Introduction: Writing and Recording Knowledge. In *Writing without Words: Alternative Literacies in Mesoamerica and the Andes*, ed. Elizabeth H. Boone and Walter D. Mignolo, 3–26. Duke University Press, Durham, North Carolina.
    2000   *Stories in Red and Black: Pictorial Histories of the Aztecs and Mixtecs*. University of Texas Press, Austin.
    2003   A Web of Understanding: Pictorial Codices and the Shared Intellectual Culture of Late Postclassic Mesoamerica. In *The Postclassic Mesoamerican World*, ed. Michael E. Smith and Francis F. Berdan, 207–221. University of Utah Press, Salt Lake City.

2007   *Cycles of Time and Meaning in the Mexican Books of Fate.* University of Texas Press, Austin.

Boot, Erik
1997   Kan Ek': The Last Ruler of the Itsa. *Yumtzilob* 9(1):5–22.
2005   *Continuity and Change in Text and Image at Chichén Itzá, Yucatán, México: A Study of the Inscriptions, Iconography, and Architecture at a Late Classic to Early Postclassic Maya Site.* CNWS, Leiden, The Netherlands.

Boremanse, Didier
1982   A Comparative Study in Lacandon Maya Mythology. *Journal de la Société des Américanistes de Paris* 68:71–98.
1998a   *Hach Winik: The Lacandon Maya of Chiapas, Southern Mexico.* Institute for Mesoamerican Studies, Monograph 11. University at Albany, New York.
1998b   Representaciones Metafóricas de los Antiguos Mayas en Mitos Y Ritos Religiosos Lacandones. *Journal de la Société des Américanistes* 84(1):201–209.

Borhegyi, Stephan F. de
1965   Archaeological Synthesis of the Guatemalan Highlands. In *Handbook of Middle American Indians*, vol. 2, part 1, ed. Robert Wauchope, 3–58. University of Texas Press, Austin.

Bourdieu, Pierre
1977   *Outline of a Theory of Practice.* Cambridge University Press, Cambridge.
1995   In Other Words. In *Histories: French Constructions of the Past*, ed. Jacques Revel and Lynn Hunt, 514–520. Trans. Arthur Goldhammer. The New Press, New York.

Bowditch, Charles P., and Guillermo Rivera (translators)
1987   *Relation of Two Trips to Peten.* Labyrithos, Culver City, California.

Bowler, Peter J.
1984   *Evolution: The History of an Idea.* University of California Press, Berkeley.

Boyer, Pascal
1994   *The Naturalness of Religious Ideas.* University of California Press, Berkeley.

Bozanic, Jeffrey
1991   Cozumel Pottery Report. Unpublished report on file with the Island Caves Research Center, Inc., Melbourne, Florida.

Bradley, Richard
1991   Ritual, Time and History. *World Archaeology* 23(2):209–219.
2005   *Ritual and Domestic Life in Prehistoric Europe.* Routledge, London.

Brady, James E.
1997   Settlement Configuration and Cosmology: The Role of Caves at Dos Pilas. *American Anthropologist* 99(3):602–618.
2005   The Impact of Ritual on the Maya Economy. In *Stone Houses and Earth Lords*, ed. Keith Prufer and James Brady, 115–134. University Press of Colorado, Boulder.

REFERENCES CITED

Brady, James E., and Wendy Ashmore
1999   Mountains, Caves, Water: Ideational Landscapes of the Ancient Maya. In *Archaeologies of Landscape*, ed. Wendy Ashmore and A. Bernard Knapp, 124–145. Blackwell Publishers, Oxford.

Brady, James E., Anne Scott, Hector Neff, and Michael D. Glascock
1997   Speleothem Breakage, Movement, Removal, and Caching: An Aspect of Ancient Maya Cave Modification. *Geoarchaeology* 12(6):725–750.

Brady, James E., and George Veni
1992   Man-Made and Pseudo-Karst Caves: The Implications of Subsurface Features within Maya Centers. *Geoarchaeology* 7(2):149–167.

Brandt, Elizabeth
1996   The Fight for Dzil Nchaa Si An, Mt. Graham: Apaches and Astrophysical Development in Arizona. *Cultural Survival Quarterly* 19(4):50–57.

Brasseur de Bourbourg, Charles É.
1862   *Gramatica de la lengua Quiche suivie d'un vocabulaire et du drame de Rabinal-Achí.* Arthus Bertrand, Paris.

Braswell, Geoffrey E.
2001   Ethnogenesis, Social Structure, and Survival: The Nahuaization of K'iche'an Culture, 1450–1550. In *Maya Survivalism*, ed. Ueli Hostettler and Matthew Restall, 51–58. Acta Mesoamericana 12. Verlag Anton Saurwein, Markt Schwaben.
2003   *The Maya and Teotihuacan: Reinterpreting Early Classic Interaction.* University of Texas Press, Austin.

Braudel, Fernand
1972   *The Mediterranean and the Mediterranean World in the Age of Philip II.* Collins, London.

Brenner, Mark, David Hodell, Jason H. Curtis, Michael F. Rosenmeier, Flavio S. Anselmetti, and Daniel Ariztegui
2003   Paleolimnological Approaches for Inferring Past Climate Change in the Maya Region: Recent Advances and Methodological Limitations. In *The Lowland Maya Area: Three Millennia at the Human-Wildland Interface*, ed. Arturo Gómez-Pompa, Michael F. Allan, Scott L. Fedick and Juan Jiménez-Osornio, 45–74. Haworth Press, New York.

Breuil, Veronique
1986   Registro de las cuevas de la region Xcochcax: Informe del trabajo de la temporada 1986. Manuscript in the possession Andrea Stone, University of Wisconsin–Milwaukee.

Bricker, Harvey M., and Victoria R. Bricker
2007   When Was the Dresden Venus Table Efficacious? In *Skywatching in the Ancient World: New Perspectives in Cultural Astronomy*, ed. Clive Ruggles and Gary Urton, 95–119. University Press of Colorado, Boulder.

Bricker, Victoria R.
1973   *Ritual Humor in Highland Chiapas.* University of Texas Press, Austin.

1977   The Caste War of Yucatán: The History of a Myth and the Myth of History. In *Anthropology and History in Yucatán*, ed. Grant D. Jones, 251–258. University of Texas Press, Austin.

1981   *The Indian Christ, the Indian King: The Historical Substrate of Maya Myth and Ritual.* University of Texas Press, Austin.

1984   Las ceremonias de año Nuevo en los Monumentos Clásicos Mayas. In *Investigaciones Recientes en el Area Maya* 2:226–246. XVII Mesa Redonda del la Sociedad Mexicana de Anthropología, Saltillo, Coahuila, México.

1989   Calendrical Meaning of Ritual among the Maya. In *Ethnographic Encounters in Southern Mesoamerica: Essays in Honor of Evon Z. Vogt, Jr.*, ed. Victoria R. Bricker and Gary H. Gossen, 231–249. Institute of Mesoamerican Studies in Culture and History, vol. 3. University of New York at Albany, Albany.

1991   Faunal Offerings in the Dresden Codex. In *Sixth Palenque Round Table, 1986*, ed. Virginia M. Fields, 285–292. University of Oklahoma Press, Norman.

2001   A Method for Dating Venus Almanacs in the Borgia Codex. *Archaeoastronomy (JHA 32)* 26:S21–S44.

2009   A Comparison of Venus Instruments in the Borgia and Madrid Codices. In *Astronomers, Scribes, and Priests: Intellectual Interchange between the Northern Maya Lowlands and Highland Mexico in the Late Postclassic Period*, ed. Gabrielle Vail and Christine Hernández. Dumbarton Oaks, Washington, D.C., in press.

Bricker, Victoria R., and Harvey M. Bricker
1988   The Seasonal Table in the Dresden Codex and Related Almanacs. *Archaeoastronomy* (Supplement to *Journal for the History of Astronomy*) 12:S1–S62.

1992   A Method for Cross-Dating Almanacs with Tables in the Dresden Codex. In *The Sky in Mayan Literature*, ed. Anthony F. Aveni, 43–86. Oxford University Press, New York.

2005   Astronomical References in the Water Tables on Pages 69 to 74 of the Dresden Codex. In *Painted Books and Indigenous Knowledge in Mesoamerica: Manuscript Studies in Honor of Mary Elizabeth Smith*, ed. Elizabeth Hill Boone, 213–229. Middle American Research Institute, Publication 69. Tulane University, New Orleans.

Bricker, Victoria R., and Helga-Maria Miram
2002   *An Encounter of Two Worlds: The Book of Chilam Balam of Kaua.* Middle American Research Institute, Publication 68. Tulane University, New Orleans.

Bricker, Victoria R., and Gabrielle Vail (editors)
1997   *Papers on the Madrid Codex.* Middle American Research Institute, Publication 64. Tulane University, New Orleans.

Brinton, Daniel G.
1969   The Chronicle of Chac-Xulub-Chen. In *The Maya Chronicles*, ed. Daniel G. Brinton, 189–259. AMS Press, New York.

Brisset, Demetrio
1995   Supervivencias actuales del Baile de la Conquista en Guatemala. *Revista de Indias* 55:203–221.

REFERENCES CITED

Broda, Johanna
  2004   Los Muertos y el ciclo agrícola en la cosmovisión mesoamericana: Una perspectiva histórica y comparativa. In *Imagen de la Muerte*, ed. Nanda Leonardini, David Rodríguez Quispe, and Virgilio Freddy Cabanillas, 245–261. Universidad Nacional Mayor de San Marcos, San Marcos, Lima, Perú.

Brody, J. J.
  1997   The Rhetoric of Formalism: Interpreting Anasazi Architecture. In *Anasazi Architecture and American Design*, ed. Baker H. Morrow and V. B. Price, 5–15. University of New Mexico Press, Albuquerque.

Brotherston, Gordon
  1983   The Year 3113 BC and the Fifth Sun of Mesoamerica: An Orthodox Reading of the Tepexic Annals (Codex Vindobonensis obverse). In *Calendars in Mesoamerica and Peru: Native American Computations of Time*, ed. Anthony F. Aveni and Gordon Brotherston, 167–220. BAR International Series 174. Oxford.

Brown, Clifford T.
  1999   Mayapán Society and Ancient Social Organization. Ph.D. dissertation, Department of Anthropology, Tulane University, New Orleans.
  2005   Estudio de la geometría fractal del patrón de asentamiento. Paper presented at the Segundo Congreso Internacional de Cultura Maya. Mérida, Yucatán

Brown, Linda A.
  2000   From Discard to Divination: Demarcating the Sacred through the Collection and Curation of Discarded Objects. *Latin American Antiquity* 11:319–333.
  2005   Planting the Bones: Hunting Ceremonialism at Contemporary and Nineteenth-Century Shrines in the Guatemalan Highlands. *Latin American Antiquity* 16(2): 131–146.

Bruce, Robert D.
  1968   *Gramática del Lacandón*. Instituto Nacional de Antropología e Historia, México City.
  1974   *El Libro de Chan K'in*. Instituto Nacional de Antropología e Historia, México City.
  1979   *Lacandon Dream Symbolism*. Ediciones Euroamericanas, México.

Bruce, Robert D., Carlos Robles U., and Enriqueta Ramos Chao
  1971   *Los Lacandones: Cosmovisión Maya*. Instituto Nacional de Antropología e Historia, México City.

Bruchez, Margaret, and David L. Carlson
  1994   Proyecto de Investigación Arqueológica, Departamento de Sololá, Guatemala, C.A., Los Informes Finales. An Archaeological Investigation, Department of Solola, Guatemala, C.A. Archaeological Surveys Number 10, Archaeological Research Laboratory, College Station, Texas.

Buikstra, Jane E., and Kenneth C. Nystrom
  2003   Embodied Traditions: The Chachapoya and Inka Ancestors. In *Theory, Method, and Practice in Modern Archaeology*, ed. Robert J. Jeske and Douglas K. Charles, 29–48. Praeger Publishing, Westport, Connecticut.

Bullard, William R.
1960   Maya Settlement Patterns in Northeastern Petén, Guatemala. *American Antiquity* 25(3):355–372.
1970   Topoxté: A Postclassic Maya Site in Petén, Guatemala. In *Monographs and Papers in Maya Archaeology*, ed. William R. Bullard, 245–308. Papers of the Peabody Museum of Archaeology and Ethnology, no. 61. Harvard University, Cambridge, Massachusetts.

Bullchild, Percy
1985   *The Sun Came Down: The History of the World as My Blackfeet Elders Told It.* Harper and Row, San Francisco.

Burkhart, Louise M.
1989   *The Slippery Earth: Nahua-Christian Moral Dialogue in Sixteenth-Century Mexico.* University of Arizona Press, Tucson.

Burns, Allan F.
1983   *An Epoch of Miracles.* University of Texas Press, Austin.

Burton, James H., and Arleyn W. Simon
1993   Acid Extraction as a Simple and Inexpensive Method for Compositional Characterization of Archaeological Ceramics. *American Antiquity* 58(1):45–59.
1996   A Pot Is Not a Rock: A Reply to Neff, Glascock, Bishop, and Blackman. *American Antiquity* 61(2):405–413.

Byland, Bruce E., and John M.D. Pohl
1994   *In the Realm of 8 Deer: The Archaeology of the Mixtec Codices.* University of Oklahoma Press, Norman.

Cabrera, Ruben, Saburo Sugiyama, and George L. Cowgill
1991   The Templo de Quetzalcoatl Project at Teotihuacan: A Preliminary Report. *Ancient Mesoamerica* 2:77–92.

Calvin, Inga
1997   Where the *Wayob* Live: A Further Examination of Classic Maya Supernaturals. In *The Maya Vase Book,* vol. 5, ed. Justin Kerr, 868–883. Kerr Associates, New York.

Cancian, Frank
1965   *Economics and Prestige in a Maya Community: The Religious Cargo System in Zinacantán.* Stanford University Press, Stanford, California.

Carlsen, Robert S.
1997   *The War for the Heart and Soul of a Highland Maya Town.* University of Texas Press, Austin.
2001   Transculturation. In *Oxford Encyclopedia of Mesoamerican Cultures*, vol. 3, ed. Davíd Carrasco, 257–260. Oxford University Press, New York.

Carlsen, Robert S., and Martin Prechtel
1991   The Flowering of the Dead: An Interpretation of Highland Maya Culture. *Man* 26(1):23–42.

REFERENCES CITED

Carlson, John B.

1981   A Geomatic Model for the Interpretation of Mesoamerican Sites: An Essay in Cross-Cultural Comparison. In *Mesoamerican Sites and World-Views*, ed. Elizabeth P. Benson, 143–215. Dumbarton Oaks, Washington, D.C.

1983   The Grolier Codex: A Preliminary Report on the Content and Authenticity of a Thirteenth-Century Maya Venus Almanac. In *Calendars in Mesoamerica and Peru: Native American Computations of Time*, ed. Anthony F. Aveni and Gordon Brotherston, 27–57. BAR International Series 174, Oxford.

Carmack, Robert M.

1973   *Quichean Civilization: The Ethnohistoric, Ethnographic, and Archaeological Sources.* University of California Press, Berkeley.

1981   *The Quiché Mayas of Utatlán: The Evolution of a Highland Guatemala Kingdom.* University of Oklahoma Press, Norman.

Carmack, Robert M., Janine Gasco, and Gary H. Gossen

1996   *The Legacy of Mesoamerica: History and Culture of a Native American Civilization.* Simon and Schuster, Upper Saddle River, New Jersey.

Carmack, Robert M., and James L. Mondloch

1983   *Título de Totonicapán.* Universidad Nacional Autónoma de México, México.

Carrasco, David

1990   *Religions of Mesoamerica: Cosmovision and Ceremonial Centers.* HarperCollins, New York.

Casado López, Maria Pilar, Adriana Velázquez Morlet, and Edmundo Lopéz de la Rosa

1990   Pictografías y petrograbados. In *El arte rupestre en México*, ed. Maria Pilar Casado López and Lorena Mirambell, 569–583. INAH, México.

Caso, Alfonso

1961   Nombres calendáricos de los dioses. *El México Antiguo* 9:77–100.

Cecil, Leslie G.

1997   Pilot Study for the Identification of a Topoxté Red Production Center in the Postclassic Period. Manuscript on file, Department of Anthropology, Southern Illinois University Carbondale, Carbondale.

1999   Ceramics from Tipuj: Structures 1–6 of Complex I. Manuscript on file, Department of Anthropology, Southern Illinois University Carbondale, Carbondale.

2001   The Technological Styles of Late Postclassic Slipped Pottery Groups in the Petén Lakes Region, El Petén, Guatemala. Ph.D. dissertation, Department of Anthropology, Southern Illinois University, Carbondale, Illinois.

2002   Postclassic Decorative Motifs and Social Identity in Petén, Guatemala. Paper presented at the 67th Annual Meeting of the Society for American Archaeology, Denver.

2004   Inductively Coupled Plasma Emission Spectroscopy and Postclassic Petén Slipped Pottery: An Examination of Pottery Wares, Social Identity, and Trade. *Archaeometry* 46:385–404.

2006   Instrumental Neutron Activation Analysis (INAA) and Postclassic Maya Pottery Manufacturing. *Transactions of the American Nuclear Society* 94:489–490.

2007   Postclassic Maya Ceramic Advances: Conjoining Stylistic, Technological, and Chemical Compositional Data. In *Developments in Ceramic Materials Research*, ed. Dena Rosslere, 1–34. Nova Science Publishers, Hauppauge, New York.

2009   Technological Styles of Slipped Pottery and Kowoj Identity. In *The Kowoj: Identity, Migration, and Geopolitics in Late Postclassic Petén, Guatemala*, ed. Prudence M. Rice and Don S. Rice, 221–237. University Press of Colorado, Boulder.

Cecil, Leslie G., and Hector Neff
2006   Chemical Analysis of Petén Postclassic Slips and Decorative Paints: Associations of Socio-political Identity and Resource Procurement. *Journal of Archaeological Science* 33(10):1482–1491.

Cecil, Leslie G., and Timothy W. Pugh
2004   Kowoj Symbolism and Technology at Late Postclassic Tipuj. Paper presented at the 69th Annual Society for American Archaeology Meeting, Montreal, Canada.

Chamberlain, Robert S.
1948   *The Conquest and Colonization of Yucatan, 1517–1550*. Carnegie Institution of Washington, Publication 582, Washington, D.C.
1966   *The Conquest and Colonization of Yucatan, 1517–1550*. Octagon Books, New York.

Chance, John K.
1996   Mesoamerica's Ethnographic Past. *Ethnohistory* 43(3):379–403.

Chance, John K., and John Taylor
1985   Cofradias and Cargos: An Historical Perspective on the Mesoamerican Civil-Religious Hierarchy. *American Ethnologist* 12(1):1–26.

Chase, Arlen F., and Diane Z. Chase
1985   Postclassic Temporal and Spatial Frames from the Lowland Maya: A Background. In *The Lowland Maya Postclassic*, ed. Arlen F. Chase and Prudence M. Rice, 1–22. University of Texas Press, Austin.
1986   Caracol: Belize's National Treasure. *The New Belize* 16(12):15–16.
1987a   *Glimmers of a Forgotten Realm: Maya Archaeology at Caracol, Belize*. University of Central Florida, Orlando.
1987b   *Investigations at the Classic Maya City of Caracol, Belize: 1985–1987*. Pre-Columbian Art Research Institute Monograph 3, San Francisco.
1994   Maya Veneration of the Dead at Caracol, Belize. In *Seventh Palenque Round Table, 1989*, ed. Merle G. Robertson, 55–62. Pre-Columbian Art Research Institute, San Francisco.
2005   The Early Classic Period at Caracol: Transitions, Complexity, and Methodological Issues in Maya Archaeology. *Research Reports in Belizean Archaeology* 2:17–38.

Chase, Arlen F., Nikolai Grube, and Diane Z. Chase
1991   Three Terminal Classic Monuments from Caracol, Belize. *Research Reports on Ancient Maya Writing*, no. 36, Center for Maya Research, Washington, D.C.

REFERENCES CITED

Chase, Diane Z.

1985a   Between Earth and Sky: Idols, Images, and Postclassic Cosmology. In *Fifth Palenque Round Table, 1983,* vol. 7, ed. Merle G. Robertson, 223–233. Pre-Columbian Art Research Institute, San Francisco.

1985b   Ganned But Not Forgotten: Late Postclassic Archaeology and Ritual at Santa Rita, Corozal, Belize. In *The Lowland Maya Postclassic,* ed. Arlen Chase and Prudence M. Rice, 104–125. University of Texas Press, Austin.

1986   Social and Political Organization in the Land of Cacao and Honey: Correlating the Archaeology and Ethnohistory of the Postclassic Lowland Maya. In *Late Lowland Maya Civilization,* ed. Jeremy A. Sabloff and Anthony Andrews, 347–377. University of New Mexico Press, Albuquerque.

1988   Caches and Censerwares: Meaning from Maya Pottery. In *A Pot for All Reasons: Ceramic Ecology Revisited,* ed. Louana Lackey and Charles Kolb, 81–104. Laboratory of Anthropology, Temple University, Philadelphia.

Chase, Diane Z., and Arlen Chase

1988   *A Postclassic Perspective: Excavations at the Maya Site of Santa Rita Corozal, Belize.* Pre-Columbian Art Research Institute, Monograph 4. San Francisco.

1989   Routes of Trade and Communication and the Integration of Maya Society: The Vista from Santa Rita Corozal. In *Coastal Maya Trade and Exchange,* ed. Heather McKillop and Paul Healy, 19–32. Occasional Papers in Anthropology No. 8, Trent University, Toronto.

1998   The Architectural Context of Caches, Burials, and Other Ritual Activities for the Classic Period Maya (as Reflected at Caracol, Belize). In *Function and Meaning in Classic Maya Architecture,* ed. Stephen D. Houston, 299–332. Dumbarton Oaks, Washington, D.C.

2001   Underlying Structure in Maya Persistence: An Archaeological Perspective. *Acta Mesoamericana* 12:37–50. (special issue ed. Ueli Hostettler and Matthew Restall titled *Maya Survivalism*), Markt Schwaben, Verlag A. Saurwein, Germany.

2003   Secular, Sagrado, y Revisitado: La Profanacion, Alteracion, y Reconsagracion de los Antiguos Entierros Mayas. In *Antropología de la Eternidad: La Muere en la Cultura Maya,* ed. Andrés Cuidad Ruiz, Mario Humberto Ruz Sosa, and María Josefa Iglesias Ponce de Leon, 255–277. Publicación 7, Sociedad de los Estudios Mayas, Madrid.

2004a   Archaeological Perspectives on Classic Maya Social Organization from Caracol, Belize. *Ancient Mesoamerica* 15:111–119.

2004b   Patrones de Enterramiento y Cíclos Residenciales en Caracol, Belice. In *Culto Funerario en la Sociedad Maya: Memoria de la Cuarta Mesa Redonda de Palenque,* ed. Rafael Cobos, 203–230. INAH, México, D.F.

2005   The Early Classic Period at Santa Rita Corozal: Issues of Hierarchy, Heterarchy, and Stratification in Northern Belize. *Research Reports in Belizean Archaeology* 2:111–125.

Chidester, David

1996   *Savage Systems: Colonialism and Comparative Religion in Southern Africa.* University of Virginia Press, Charlottesville.

Christenson, Allen J.

2001   *Art and Society in a Highland Maya Community: The Altarpiece of Santiago Atitlán*. University of Texas Press, Austin.

2003   *Popol Vuh: The Sacred Book of the Maya*. O Books, New York.

2007   *Popol Vuh: The Sacred Book of the Maya*. University of Oklahoma Press, Norman.

Chuchiak, John F., IV

2000   The Indian Inquisition and the Extirpation of Idolatry: The Process of Punishment in the *Provisorato de Indios* in the Diocese of Yucatán, 1563–1821. Ph.D. dissertation, Department of Latin American Studies, Tulane University, New Orleans.

2001   Pre-Conquest Ah Kinob in a Colonial World: The Extirpation of Idolatry and the Survival of the Maya Priesthood in Colonial Yucatan. In *Maya Survivalism*, ed. Ueli Hostettler and Matthew Restall, 135–155. Acta Mesoamericana 12. Verlag Anton Saurwein, Markt Schwaben.

2002   Toward a Regional Definition of Idolatry: Reexamining Idolatry Trials in the *Relaciones de Meritos* and Their Role in Defining the Concept of Idolatria en Colonial Yucatán, 1570–1780. *Journal of Early Modern History* 6(2):1–29.

2004a   It Is Their Drinking that Hinders Them?: Balché and the Use of Ritual Intoxicants among the Colonial Yucatec Maya, 1550–1780. *Estudios de Cultura Maya* 24:1–43.

2004b   Papal Bulls, Extirpators, and the Madrid Codex: The Content and Probable Provenience of the Madrid 56 Patch. In *The Madrid Codex: New Approaches to Understanding an Ancient Maya Manuscript*, ed. Gabrielle Vail and Anthony F. Aveni, 57–88. University Press of Colorado, Boulder.

2005   *In Servitio Dei*: Fray Diego de Landa, the Franciscan Order, and the Return of the Extirpation of Idolatry in the Colonial Diocese of Yucatán, 1573–1579. *The Americas* 61(4):611–646.

Clendinnen, Inga

1980   Landscape and World View: The Survival of Yucatec Maya Culture under Spanish Conquest. *Comparative Studies in Society and History* 22:374–393.

1982   Reading the Inquisitorial Record in Yucatan: Fact or Fantasy? *The Americas* 38(3):327–345.

1987   *Ambivalent Conquests: Maya and Spaniard in Yucatan, 1517–1570*. Cambridge University Press, Cambridge.

1991a   *Aztecs*. Cambridge University Press, Cambridge.

1991b   "Fierce and Unnatural Cruelty": Cortés and the Conquest of Mexico. *Representations* 33:65–100.

Cline, Howard

1944   Lore and Deities of the Lacandon Indians, Chiapas, Mexico. *Journal of American Folklore* 57:107–115.

Closs, Michael

1989   Cognitive Aspects of Ancient Maya Eclipse Theory. In *Archaeoastronomy*, ed. Anthony F. Aveni, 389–415. Cambridge University Press, Cambridge.

REFERENCES CITED

Coe, Michael D.
1965   A Model of Ancient Community Structure in the Maya Lowlands. *Southwestern Journal of Anthropology* 21(2):97–114.
1973   *The Maya Scribe and His World*. Grolier Club, New York.
1989   The Royal Fifth: Earliest Notices of Maya Writing. In *Research Reports on Ancient Maya Writing* 28. Center for Maya Research, Washington, D.C.

Coe, Michael D., and Justin Kerr
1997   *The Art of the Maya Scribe*. Thames and Hudson, London.

Coe, Michael D., and Mark Van Stone
2001   *Reading the Maya Glyphs*. Thames and Hudson, London.
2005   *Reading the Maya Glyphs*, 2nd ed. Thames and Hudson, London.

Coe, William R., and Edwin M. Shook
1961   Tikal Report No. 6: The Carved Wooden Lintels of Tikal. In *Tikal Reports Numbers 5–10*, ed. Richard E.W. Adams, Vivian L. Broman, William R. Coe, William A. Haviland Jr., Ruben E. Reina, Linton Satterthwaite, Edwin M. Shook, and Aubrey S. Trik, 15–111. The University Museum, Philadelphia.

Coggins, Clemency C.
1975   Painting and Drawing Styles at Tikal: A Historical and Iconographic Reconstruction. Ph.D. dissertation, Department of Anthropology, Harvard University, Cambridge, Massachusetts.
1980   The Shape of Time: Some Political Implications of a Four-Part Figure. *American Antiquity* 45(4):727–739.
1989   Classic Maya Metaphors of Death and Life. *RES* 16:65–84.
1992   *Artifacts from the Cenote of Sacrifice, Chichen Itza, Yucatan*. Peabody Museum of Archaeology and Ethnology 10. Harvard University Press, Cambridge.

Coggins, Clemency C., and Orrin C. Shane
1984   *Cenote of Sacrifice: Maya Treasures from the Sacred Well at Chich'en Itza*. University of Texas Press, Austin.

Coleman, Simon
2004   The Magic of Anthropology. *Anthropology News* 45(8):8, 11.

Collingwood, R. G.
1960   *The Idea of Nature*. Oxford University Press, London.

Comaroff, Jean, and John L. Comaroff
1991   *Of Revelation and Revolution: Christianity, Colonialism, and Consciousness in South Africa*. University of Chicago Press, Chicago.
1997   *Of Revelation and Revolution: The Dialects of Modernity on a South African Frontier*, vol. 2. University of Chicago Press, Chicago.

Connerton, Paul
1989   *How Societies Remember*. Cambridge University Press, Cambridge.

Connor, Judith G.
1975 Ceramics and Artifacts. In *A Study of Changing Pre-Columbian Commercial Systems*, ed. Jeremy A. Sabloff and William L. Rathje, 114–135. Peabody Museum of Archaeology and Ethnology, Harvard University, Cambridge.
1983 The Ceramics of Cozumel, Quintana Roo, Mexico. Ph.D. dissertation, Department of Anthropology, University of Arizona, Tucson.

Córdova, Fray Juan de
1578 *Vocabulario en lengua zapoteca*. Ediciones Toledo (INAH), México.

Cortés, Hernán
1976 *Cartas de Relacíon*, 9th ed. Editorial Porrua, México.

Cortez, Constance
2002 New Dance, Old Xius: The "Xiu Family Tree" and Maya Cultural Continuity after the Conquest. In *Heart of Creation: The Mesoamerican World and the Legacy of Linda Schele*, ed. Andrea Stone, 201–215. University of Alabama Press, Tuscaloosa.

Cosgrove, Dennis
1989 Geography Is Everywhere: Culture and Symbolism in Human Landscapes. In *Horizons in Human Geography*, ed. Derek Gregory and Rex Walford, 118–135. Macmillan, London.

Craine, Eugene R., and Reginald C. Reindorp (translators and editors)
1970 *The Chronicles of Michoacan*. University of Oklahoma Press, Norman.
1979 *The Codex Pérez and the Book of Chilam Balam of Maní*. University of Oklahoma Press, Norman.

Curet, L. Antonio, Barbara L. Stark, and Sergio Vázquez Z.
1994 Postclassic Changes in Veracruz, Mexico. *Ancient Mesoamerica* 5(1):13–32.

Danforth, Marie E.D., D. Light, M. N. Cohen, and C. W. Armstrong
1985 Genetic Distance between Subgroups in the Tipu Population. Paper presented at the 1985 Northeastern Anthropological Association Meetings, Lake Placid, New York.

Davidson, William
1967 Study of Settlement Patterns, Cozumel Island, Quintana Roo, Mexico. Master of Arts, Memphis State University, Memphis, Tennessee.

Davis, Virginia D.
1978 Ritual of the Northern Lacandon Maya. Ph.D. dissertation, Department of Anthropology, Tulane University. University Microfilms, Ann Arbor.

Dawkins, Richard
2004 *The Ancestor's Tale: A Pilgrimage to the Dawn of Life*. Orion, London.

De Robina, Ricardo
1956 *Estudio preliminar de las ruinas de Hochob, municipio de Hopelchén, Campeche*. Editorial Atenae, Campeche, México.

REFERENCES CITED

De Vos, Jan

1988a   *La Paz de Dios y del Rey: La Conquista de la Selva Lacandona: 1525–1821.* Fondo de Cultura Económica, México City.

1988b   *Viajes al Desierto de la Soledad: Cuando la Selva Lacandona Aun Era Selva.* Secretaríade Educación Pública, M. A. Porrúa, México.

DeClue, Gregory

2005   *Interrogations and Disputed Confessions: A Manual for Forensic Psychological Practice.* Professional Resource Press, Sarasota, Florida.

DeCorse, Christopher R.

1998   Culture Contact and Culture Change in West Africa. In *Studies in Culture Contact: Interaction, Culture Change, and Archaeology*, ed. James G. Cusick, 358–377. Center for Archaeological Investigations, Occasional Paper No. 25, Southern Illinois University, Carbondale.

Deevey, E. S., M. Brenner, M. S. Flannery, and G. H. Yezdani

1980   Lakes Yaxhá and Sacnab, Petén, Guatemala, Limnology and Hydrology. *Archiv für Hydrobiology* 57(7):419–460.

Del Chamberlain, Von

1982   *When Stars Came Down to Earth: Cosmology of the Skidi Pawnee Indians of North America.* Ballena Press, Los Altos, California.

Delgado, James P.

1998   *Encyclopedia of Underwater and Maritime Archaeology.* Yale University Press, New Haven, Connecticut.

Delgado Kú, Pedro Candelario

2004   Estudio de la arquitectura pública del núcleo principal de Mayapán, Yucatán. Thesis profesional, Universidad Autónoma de Yucatán. Facultad de Ciencias Antropológicas.

Demarest, Arthur A.

1984   Overview: Mesoamerican Human Sacrifice in Evolutionary Perspective. In *Ritual Human Sacrifice in Mesoamerica*, ed. Elizabeth H. Boone, 227–247. Dumbarton Oaks, Washington, D.C.

1992a   Archaeology, Ideology, and Pre-Columbian Cultural Evolution: The Search for an Approach. In *Ideology and Pre-Columbian Civilizations*, ed. Arthur A. Demarest and Geoffrey W. Conrad, 1–13. School of American Research Press, Santa Fe, New Mexico.

1992b   Ideology in Ancient Maya Cultural Evolution: The Dynamics of Galactic Polities. In *Ideology and Pre-Columbian Civilizations*, ed. Arthur A. Demarest and Geoffrey W. Conrad, 135–157. School of American Research Press, Santa Fe, New Mexico.

2004   *Ancient Maya: The Rise and Fall of a Rainforest Civilization.* Cambridge University Press, Cambridge.

Demarest, Arthur A., and Geoffrey W. Conrad (editors)

1992   *Ideology and Pre-Columbian Civilizations.* School of American Research Press, Santa Fe, New Mexico.

352

Demarest, Arthur A., Prudence M. Rice, and Don S. Rice
2004   *The Terminal Classic in the Maya Lowlands: Collapse, Transition, and Transformation*. University Press of Colorado, Boulder.

Dening, Greg
1980   *Islands and Beaches: Discourse on a Silent Land, Marquesas, 1774–1880*. Melbourne University Press, Carlton.

Díaz, Gisele, and Alan Rogers
1993   *The Codex Borgia: A Full-Color Restoration of the Ancient Mexican Manuscript*. Introduction and commentary by Bruce E. Byland. Dover Publications, New York.

Díaz del Castillo, Bernal
1956   *The Discovery and Conquest of Mexico, 1517–1521*. Trans. A. P. Maudslay. Farrar,
[1632] Strauss, and Cudahy, New York.
1963   *The Conquest of New Spain*. Trans. and intro. J. M. Cohen. Penguin, Baltimore.

Dietler, Michael
1994   "Our Ancestors the Gauls": Archaeology, Ethnic Nationalism, and the Manipulation of Celtic Identity in Modern Europe. *American Anthropologist* 96(3): 584–605.

Dietler, Michael, and Ingrid Herbich
1998   Habitus, Techniques, Style: An Integrated Approach to the Social Understanding of Material Culture and Boundaries. In *The Archaeology of Social Boundaries*, ed. Miriam T. Stark, 232–263. Smithsonian Institution Press, Washington, D.C.

Dixon, Keith A.
1958   Two Masterpieces of Middle American Bone Sculpture. *American Antiquity* 24: 53–62.

Douglas, Mary
1966   *Purity and Danger*. Routledge, London.

Dowson, Thomas A.
1998   Rain in Bushman Belief, Politics, and History: The Rock-Art of Rain-Making in the South-Eastern Mountains, Southern Africa. In *The Archaeology of Rock Art*, ed. Christopher Chippindale and Paul S.C. Tacon, 73–89. Cambridge University Press, Cambridge.

Dubisch, Jill
1995   *In a Different Place: Pilgrimage, Gender, and Politics at a Greek Island Shrine*. Princeton University Press, Princeton, New Jersey.

Duby, Gertrude, and Frans Blom
1962   The Lacandon. In *Handbook of Middle American Indians,* vol. 7, ed. Robert Wauchope, 276–297. University of Texas Press, Austin.

Dumond, Don E.
1977   Independent Maya of the Late Nineteenth Century: Chiefdoms and Power Politics. In *Anthropology and History in Yucatán*, ed. Grant D. Jones, 103–138. University of Texas Press, Austin.

1985   The Talking Crosses of the Yucatan: A New Look at Their History. *Ethnohistory* 32(4):291–308.

1997   *The Machete and the Cross: Campesino Rebellion in Yucatan*. University of Nebraska Press, Lincoln.

Durán, Diego

1967   *Historia de las Indias de Nueva España e islas de la tierra firme*. Ed. Angel María Garibay K. Editorial Porrúa, México.

Durkheim, Émile

1912   *Les Formes Élémentaires de la Vie Religieuse: Le Système Totémique en Australie*. Alcan, Paris.

1933   *The Division of Labor in Society*. Trans. George Simpson. The Free Press, New York.

1965   *The Elementary Forms of the Religious Life*. Trans. J. W. Swain. The Free Press,
[1912] New York.

1982   *The Rules of Sociological Method*. Ed. Steven Lukes and trans. W. D. Halls. The Free
[1895] Press, New York.

Earle, Duncan M.

1986   The Metaphor of the Day in Quiche: Notes on the Nature of Everyday Life. In *Symbol and Meaning beyond the Closed Community: Essays in Mesoamerican Ideas*, ed. Gary H. Gossen, 155–172. Institute for Mesoamerican Studies, Studies on Culture and Society, vol. 1. State University of New York at Albany, Albany.

Edmonson, Munro S.

1971   *The Book of Counsel: The Popol Vuh of the Quiche Maya of Guatemala*. Middle American Research Institute, Publication 35. Tulane University, New Orleans.

1976a   The Maya Calendar Reform of 11.16.0.0.0. *Current Anthropology* 17:713–717.

1976b   *Quiche-English Dictionary*. Ed. Margaret A. Harrison and Robert Wauchope.
[1965] Middle American Research Institute, Publication 30. Tulane University, New Orleans.

1982   *The Ancient Future of the Itza: The Book of Chilam Balam of Tizimin*. University of Texas Press, Austin.

1985   The Baktun Ceremonial of 1618. In *Fourth Palenque Round Table, 1980*, vol. 6, ed. Merle G. Robertson and Elizabeth P. Benson, 261–265. Pre-Columbian Art Research Institute, San Francisco.

1986   (translated and annotated) *Heaven Born Merida and Its Destiny: The Book of Chilam Balam of Chumayel*. University of Texas Press, Austin.

1988   *The Book of the Year: Middle American Calendrical Systems*. University of Utah Press, Salt Lake City.

1993   The Mayan Faith. In *South and Mesoamerican Native Spirituality: From the Cult of the Feathered Serpent to the Theology of Liberation*, ed. Gary H. Gossen and Miguel Leon-Portilla, 65–85. Crossroad, New York.

Ekholm, Gordon F.

1942   Excavations at Guasave, Sinaloa, Mexico. *American Museum of Natural History Anthropological Papers* 38 (Part 2), New York.

Eliade, Mircea

1954   *The Myth of the Eternal Return: Cosmos and History.* Princeton University Press, Princeton, New Jersey.

1959   *The Sacred and the Profane: The Nature of Religion.* Trans. Willard R. Trask. Harcourt, New York.

1974   *Man and the Sacred: A Thematic Source Book of the History of Religions.* Harper and Row, New York.

1976   *Myths, Rites, Symbols: A Mircea Eliade Reader.* Ed. Wendell C. Beane and William G. Doty. Harper and Row, New York.

1990   *Symbolism, The Sacred, and The Arts.* Ed. Diane Apostolos-Cappadona. Crossroad, New York.

Escalona Ramos, Antonio

1946   Algunas Ruinas Prehistóricas en Quintana Roo. *Boletín de la Sociedad Mexicana de Geografía y Estadística* 61(3):513–628.

Escamilla Ojeda, Bárbara, Carlos Peraza Lope, and Pedro Delgado Kú

2004   La obsidiana y el pedernal de Mayapán, Yucatán. *Investigadores de la Cultura Maya* 12:234–247.

Escobedo, Héctor L.

2004   Tales from the Crypt: The Burial Place of Ruler 4, Piedras Negras. In *Courtly Art of the Ancient Maya,* ed. Mary Miller and Simon Martin, 277–279. Thames and Hudson, New York.

Eshelman, Catharine G.

2001   El ritual y la reproducción de la cultura: Ceremonias agrícolas, los muertos y la expresión estética entre los nahuas de Guerrero. In *Cosmovisión, Ritual e Identidad de los Pueblos Indígenas de México,* ed. Johanna Broda and Félix Báez-Jorge, 239–297. Fondo de Cultura Economica, México.

Evans, Susan T.

2004   *Ancient Mexico and Central America.* Thames and Hudson, London.

Evans-Pritchard, E. E.

1940   *The Nuer.* Clarendon Press, Oxford.

1961   *Anthropology and History.* Manchester University Press, Manchester. (Reprinted in *Essays in Social Anthropology* by E. E. Evans-Pritchard, 46–65. Faber and Faber, London, 1962.)

Farriss, Nancy M.

1984   *Maya Society under Colonial Rule: The Collective Enterprise of Survival.* Princeton University Press, Princeton, New Jersey.

1987   Remembering the Future, Anticipating the Past: History, Time, and Cosmology among the Maya of Yucatan. *Comparative Studies in Society and History* 29:566–593.

Feeley-Harnik, Gillian

1985   Issues in Divine Kingship. *Annual Review of Anthropology* 14:273–313.

REFERENCES CITED

Feldman, Lawrence H.
2000   *Lost Shores, Forgotten Peoples: Spanish Explorations of the South East Mayan Lowlands*. Duke University Press, Durham, North Carolina.

Fischer, Edward F.
1999   Cultural Logic and Maya Identity. *Cultural Anthropology* 40(4):473–499.

Folan, William J.
1969   Sacalum, Yucatan: A Pre-Hispanic and Contemporary Source of Attapulgite. *American Antiquity* 34(4):182–183.

Foor, Charles W.
1994   Analysis of Late Postclassic Censer Materials from Structure II, Negroman-Tipu, Belize. Master's thesis, Department of Anthropology, Southern Illinois University, Carbondale.

Förstemann, Ernst
1880   *Die Maya Handschrift der Königlichen öffentlichen Bibliotek zu Dresden*. Mit 74 Tafeln in Chromo-Lightdruck. Verlag der A. Naumannschen Lichtdruckeret, Leipzig.

Forsyth, Donald W.
2004   Reflexiones sobre la ocupación postclásica en Champotón a través de la cerámica. *Los Investigadores de la Cultura Maya* 12(1):33–37.

Forty, Adrian
2001   Introduction. In *The Art of Forgetting*, ed. Adrian Forty and Susanne Küchler, 1–18. Berg, Oxford.

Fox, James A., and John S. Juteson
1986   Classic Maya Dynastic Alliance and Succession. In *Ethnohistory, Supplement to the Handbook of Middle American Indians*, vol. 4, ed. Ronald Spores, 7–34. University of Texas Press, Austin.

Fox, John W.
1987   *Maya Postclassic State Formation: Segmentary Lineage Migration in Advancing Frontiers*. Cambridge University Press, Cambridge.
1994   Political Cosmology among the Quiché Maya. In *Factional Competition and Political Development in the New World*, ed. Elizabeth Blumfield and John W. Fox, 158–170. Cambridge University Press, New York.

Frake, Charles O.
1992   Lessons of the Mayan Sky: A Perspective from Medieval Europe. In *The Sky in Mayan Literature*, ed. Anthony F. Aveni, 274–291. Oxford University Press, New York.

Frazer, James G.
1911–   *The Golden Bough: A Study in Magic and Religion*, 12 vols. Macmillan, London.
1915

Freidel, David A.
1975   The Ix Chel Shrine and Other Temples of Talking Idols. In *A Study of Changing Pre-Columbian Commercial Systems: The 1972–1973 Seasons at Cozumel,*

Mexico, ed. Jeremy A. Sabloff and William L. Rathje, 107–113. Monographs of the Peabody Museum, no. 3. Peabody Museum of Archaeology and Ethnology, Cambridge.

1987 Children of First Father's Skull. Paper presented at the 68th Annual Meeting of the American Anthropological Association, Chicago.

Freidel, David A., and Jeremy A. Sabloff
1984 *Cozumel, Late Maya Settlement Patterns*. Academic Press, Orlando.

Freidel, David A., and Linda Schele
1988 Kingship in the Late Preclassic Lowlands: The Instruments and Places of Ritual Power. *American Anthropologist* 90(3):547–567.

Freidel, David A., Linda Schele, and Joy Parker
1993 *Maya Cosmos: Three Thousand Years on the Shaman's Path*. W. Morrow, New York.

Freud, Sigmund
1950 *Totem and Taboo: Some Points of Agreement between the Mental Lives of Savages*
[1913] *and Neurotics*. Trans. James Stachey. W. W. Norton, New York.

Friedman, Jonathan
1992 The Past in the Future: History and the Politics of Identity. *American Anthropologist* 94:837–859.

Froman, Loralie
1992 Giving Birth to Weavings. *Fiber Art* (March/April):10–11.

Frost, Elsa C.
1993 Indians and Theologians: Sixteenth-Century Spanish Theologians and Their Concept of the Indigenous Soul. In *South and Meso-American Native Spirituality: From the Cult of the Feathered Serpent to the Theology of Liberation*, ed. Gary H. Gossen, 119–139. Crossroad, New York.

Furst, Jill L.
1986 The Lords of "Place of the Ascending Serpent": Dynastic Succession on the Nuttal Obverse. In *Symbol and Meaning beyond the Closed Corporate Community: Essays in Mesoamerican Ideas*, ed. Gary H. Gossen, 57–68. Institute for Mesoamerican Studies, State University of New York, Albany.

Furst, Peter T.
1996 Myth as History, History as Myth: A New Look at Some Old Problems in Huichol Origins. In *People of the Peyote: Huichol Indian History, Religion, and Survival*, ed. Stacy B. Schaefer and Peter T. Furst, 26–60. University of New Mexico Press, Albuquerque.

Gage, Thomas
1929 *New Survey of the West Indies*. R. M. McBride, New York.
1958 *Thomas Gage's Travels in the New World*. Ed. J. Eric S. Thompson. University of Oklahoma Press, Norman.

REFERENCES CITED

Gann, Thomas W.F.
1900 *Mounds in Northern Honduras.* Nineteenth Annual Report of the Bureau of American Ethnology, 661–692. Smithsonian Institution, Washington, D.C.
1918 *The Maya Indians of Southern Yucatán and Northern British Honduras.* Smithsonian Bureau of American Ethnology, Washington, D.C.

Gann, Thomas W.F., and J. Eric S. Thompson
1931 *The History of the Maya from the Earliest Times to the Present Day.* Charles Scribner's Sons, New York.

García Añoveros, Jesús Maria
1987 *Población y estado sociorreligioso de la diocesis de Guatemala en el último tercio del siglo XVIII.* Editorial Universitaria, Guatemala.

Garciagodoy, Juanita
1998 *Digging the Days of the Dead: A Reading of Mexico's Días de Muertos.* University Press of Colorado, Niwot.

Garibay, Ángel M.
1979 *Teogonía e Historia de lost Mexicanos: Tres Opúsculos del Siglo XVI.* Editorial Porrúa, S.A., México, D.F.

Garwood, Paul, David Jennings, Robin Skeates, and Judith Toms
1991 Preface. In *Sacred and Profane: Proceedings of a Conference on Archaeology, Ritual and Religion,* ed. Paul Garwood, David Jennings, Robin Skeates, and Judith Toms, v–x. Oxford University Press, Oxford.

Garza, Mercedes de la
1983 *Relaciones histórico-geográficas de la gobernación de Yucatán: Mérida, Valladolid y Tabasco.* Instituto de Investigaciones Filológicas, Centro de Estudios Mayas, Fuentes para el Estudio de la Cultura Maya, 2 vols. Universidad Nacional Autónoma de México, México.
1996 La Religión: Los Dioses, El Mundo y el Hombre. In *Los Mayas: Su Tiempo Antiguo,* ed. Mercedes de la Garza, Ana Luisa Izquierdo, and Gerardo Bustos, 197–220. Universidad Autónoma de México, Instituto de Investigaciones Filológicas, Centro de Estudios Mayas, México.

Gasco, Janine
2005 The Consequences of Spanish Colonial Rule for the Indigenous Peoples of Chiapas, Mexico. In *The Postclassic to Spanish-Era Transition in Mesoamerica,* ed. Susan Kepecs and Rani Alexander, 77–96. University of New Mexico Press, Albuquerque.

Gates, William
1978a *An Outline Dictionary of Maya Glyphs: With a Concordance and Analysis of Their Relationships.* Dover Publications, New York.
1978b *Yucatan Before and After the Conquest.* Dover, New York.
[1937]

Geertz, Clifford
 1973   Person, Time, and Conduct in Bali. Reprinted in *The Interpretation of Culture*. Basic Books, New York.

Gell, Alfred
 1996   *The Anthropology of Time: Cultural Constructions of Temporal Maps and Images*. Berg, Oxford.

Gerola, Giuseppe
 1934   L'aquila bizantina e l'aquila imperiale a due teste. *Felix Ravenna* 43:7–36.

Gibbs, Raymond W.
 1994   *The Poetics of Mind*. Cambridge University Press, Cambridge.

Giddens, Anthony
 1981   *A Contemporary Critique of Historical Materialism*. Macmillan, London.

Giffords, Gloria F.
 2007   *Sanctuaries of Earth, Stone, and Light: The Churches of Northern New Spain, 1530–1821*. University of Arizona Press, Tucson.

Gilberti, Fray Maturino
 1962   *Diccionario de la lengua tarasca o de Michoacan*. Balsal Editores, México.
 [1559]

Gill, Richardson B.
 2000   *The Great Maya Droughts: Water, Life, and Death*. University of New Mexico Press, Albuquerque.

Gill, Sam D.
 1982   *Native American Religions: An Introduction*. Wadsworth, Belmont, CA.
 1998   *Storytracking: Texts, Stories, and Histories in Central Australia*. Oxford University Press, New York.

Gillespie, Susan D.
 2002   The Body and Soul among the Maya: Keeping Spirits in Place. In *The Space and Place of Death*, ed. Helaine Silverman and David B. Small, 67–78. American Anthropological Association, Washington, D.C.

Gingerich, Willard
 1986   Quetzalcoatl and the Agon of Time: A Literary Reading of the *Anales de Cuauhtitlan*. *New Scholar* 10:41–60.

Girard, Raphael
 1995   *People of the Chan*. Continuum Foundation, Chino Valley, Arizona.

Girard, René
 1977   *Violence and the Sacred*. Trans. Patrick Gregory. Johns Hopkins University Press, Baltimore.

Glass, John B., and Donald Robertson
 1975   A Census of Native Middle American Pictorial Manuscripts. In *Guide to Ethnohistorical Sources,* part 3, ed. Howard F. Cline, 81–252. *Handbook of Middle*

American Indians, vol. 14, Robert Wauchope, gen. ed. University of Texas Press, Austin.

Glassie, Henry H.
1975   *Folk Housing in Middle Virginia: A Structural Analysis of Historic Artifacts*. University of Tennessee Press, Knoxville.

Godelier, Maurice
1978   Economy and Religion: An Evolutionary Optical Illusion. In *The Evolution of Social Systems: Proceedings of a Meeting of the Research Seminar in Archaeology and Related Subjects*, ed. Jonathan Friedman and M. J. Rowlands, 3–11. University of Pittsburgh Press, Pittsburgh.

Goetz, Delia
1953   *Title of the Lords of Totonicapán*. Trans. Adrian Recinos. University of Oklahoma Press, Norman.

Goldenweiser, Alexander
1917   Religion and Society: A Critique of Émile Durkheim's Theory of the Origin and Nature of Religion. *The Journal of Philosophy, Psychology, and Scientific Methods* 14:113–124.

Goody, Jack
1961   Religion and Ritual: The Definitional Problem. *British Journal of Sociology* 12: 142–164.
1962   *Death, Property and the Ancestors: A Study of the Mortuary Customs of the Lodagaa of West Africa*. Stanford University Press, Stanford, California.
1977   Against "Ritual": Loosely Structured Thoughts on a Loosely Defined Topic. In *Secular Ritual*, ed. Sally F. Moore and Barbara G. Myerhoff, 25–35. Van Gorcum, Amsterdam.

Gosden, Christopher
1994   *Social Being and Time*. Blackwell, Oxford.
2004   *Archaeology and Colonialism: Cultural Contact from 5000 B.C. to the Present*. Cambridge University Pres, Cambridge.

Gose, Peter
1996   Oracles, Divine Kingship, and Political Representation in the Inka State. *Ethnohistory* 43(1):1–32.

Gosner, Kevin
1992   *Soldiers of the Virgin: The Moral Economy of a Colonial Maya Rebellion*. University of Arizona Press, Tucson.

Gossen, Gary H.
1975   Animal Souls and Human Destiny in Chamula. *Man*, N.S. 10:448–461.
1986a   The Chamula Festival of Games: Native Macroanalysis and Social Commentary in a Maya Carnival. In *Symbol and Meaning beyond the Closed Community: Essays in Mesoamerican Ideas*, ed. Gary H. Gossen, 227–254. Institute for Mesoamerican Studies, State University of New York, Albany.

1986b   Mesoamerican Ideas as a Foundation for Regional Synthesis. In *Symbol and Meaning beyond the Closed Community*, ed. Gary H. Gossen, 1–8. Institute of Mesoamerican Studies, State University of New York, Albany.

1993   Introduction. In *South and Meso-American Native Spirituality: From the Cult of the Feathered Serpent to the Theology of Liberation*, ed. Gary H. Gossen, 1–38. Crossroad, New York.

2002   *Four Creations: An Epic Story of the Chiapas Mayas*. University of Oklahoma Press, Norman.

Gossen, Gary H., and Richard M. Leventhal

1993   The Topography of Ancient Maya Religious Pluralism: A Dialogue with the Present. In *Lowland Maya Civilization in the Eighth Century A.D.*, ed. Jeremy A. Sabloff and John S. Henderson, 185–217. Dumbarton Oaks, Washington, D.C.

Graff, Donald H.

1997   Dating a Section of the Madrid Codex: Astronomical and Iconographic Evidence. In *Papers of the Madrid Codex*, ed. Victoria Bricker and Gabrielle Vail, 147–167. Middle American Research Institute, Publication 64. Tulane, New Orleans.

Graham, Elizabeth A.

1987   Resource Diversity in Belize and Its Implications for Models of Lowland Trade. *American Antiquity* 52:753–767.

1989   Brief Synthesis of Coastal Site Data from Colson Point, Placencia, and Marco Gonzalez, Belize. In *Coastal Maya Trade*, ed. Heather McKillop and Paul F. Healy, 135–154. Occasional Papers in Anthropology, no. 8. Trent University, Peterborough, Ontario.

1991   Archaeological Insights into Colonial Period Maya Life at Tipu, Belize. In *Columbian Consequences,* vol. 3: *The Spanish Borderlands in Pan-American Perspective*, ed. David H. Thomas, 319–335. Smithsonian Institution Press, Washington, D.C.

1992   Idol Speculation: The Spirit World of Pagans and Priests. Paper presented at the 25th Annual Meeting of the Society for Historical Archaeology, Kingston, Jamaica.

1994   *The Highlands of the Lowlands: Environment and Archaeology in the Stann Creek District, Belize, Central America*. Monographs in World Archaeology, no. 19. Prehistory Press, Madison, Wisconsin.

1998   Mission Archaeology. *Annual Review of Anthropology* 27:25–62.

2004   Lamanai Reloaded: Alive and Well in the Early Postclassic. In *Archaeological Investigations in the Eastern Maya Lowlands*, ed. Jaime Awe, John Morris, and Sherilyne Jones, 223–241. Research Reports in Belizean Archaeology, vol. 1. Institute of Archaeology, NICH, Belmopan, Belize.

2006a   An Ethnicity to Know. In *Maya Ethnicity: The Construction of Ethnic Identity from Preclassic to Modern Times*, ed. Frauke Sachse, 109–124. Acta Mesoamerica, vol. 19. Verlag Anton Saurwein, Markt Schwaben, Germany.

2006b   Darwin at Copan. Paper presented at the 11th European Maya Conference, Malmö University, Malmö, Sweden.

REFERENCES CITED

2007   Lamanai, Belize, from Collapse to Conquest—Radiocarbon Dates from Lamanai. Paper presented at the 106th Meeting of the American Anthropological Association, Washington, D.C.

2008   Socially Sanctioned Killing in America, Then and Now. Paper presented at the 73rd Meeting of the Society for American Archaeology, Vancouver.

2009   *Idol Rich: Spanish and Maya Christians in the Land that Became Belize.* University Press of Florida, Gainesville, in press.

Graham, Elizabeth A., Grant D. Jones, and Robert R. Kautz

1985   Archaeology and Ethnohistory of a Spanish Colonial Frontier: An Interm Report on the Macal-Tipu Project in Western Belize. In *Lowland Maya Postclassic*, ed. Arlen F. Chase and Prudence M. Rice, 206–214. University of Texas Press, Austin.

Graham, Elizabeth A., David M. Pendergast, and Grant D. Jones

1989   On the Fringes of Conquest: Maya-Spanish Contact in Colonial Belize. *Science* 246:1254–1259.

Graham, Ian

1967   *Archaeological Investigations in El Peten, Guatemala.* Middle American Research Institution, Publication 33. Tulane University, New Orleans.

1986   Looters Rob Graves and History. *National Geographic* 169(4):452–461.

Green, Miranda

1996   *Celtic Goddesses: Warriors, Virgins, and Mothers.* George Braziller, New York.

Greene, Brian

2004   *The Fabric of the Cosmos: Space, Time, and the Texture of Reality.* Knopf, New York.

Greenleaf, Richard E.

1969   *The Mexican Inquisition of the Sixteenth Century.* University of New Mexico Press, Albuquerque.

1978   The Mexican Inquisition and the Indians: Sources for the Ethnohistorian. *The Americas* 38(3):327–345.

1994   Persistence of Native Values: The Inquisition and the Indians of Colonial Mexico. *The Americas* 50(3):351–376.

Gregory, Derek

1985   Areal Differentiation and Post-Modern Human Geography. In *Social Relations and Spatial Structures*, ed. Derek Gregory and John Urry, 67–96. Macmillan, London.

Grofe, Michael J.

2007   The Serpent Series: Precession in the Maya Dresden Codex. Ph.D. dissertation, Department of Anthropology, University of California, Davis.

Grube, Nikolai

2001   Dresden Codex. In *The Oxford Encyclopedia of Mesoamerican Culture: The Civilization of Mexico and Central America*, vol. 1, ed. Davíd Carrasco, 337–339. Oxford University Press, New York.

Grube, Nikolai, and Werner Nahm
1994   A Census of Xibalba: A Complete Inventory of Way Characters on Maya Ce-
        ramics. In *The Maya Vase Book*, vol. 4, ed. Justin Kerr, 686–715. Kerr Associates,
        New York.

Guatemala Departamento de Arte Folklorico Nacional (corporate author)
1971   *Danzas folkloricas de Guatemala*. Direccion General de Cultura y Bellas Artes
        Departamento de Arte Folklorico Nacional, Guatemala City.

Hacking, Ian
2002   *Historical Ontology*. Harvard University Press, Cambridge, Massachusetts.

Haldane, J.B.S.
1956   Time in Biology. *Science Progress* 44:358–402.

Hallowell, A. Irving
1967   *Culture and Experience*. Schocken Books, New York.
1976   Ojibwa Ontology, Behavior, and World View. In *Contributions to Anthropology:*
[1960] *Selected Papers of A. Irving Hallowell*, ed. R. Fogelson, 357–390. University of
        Chicago Press, Chicago.

Hallpike, C. R.
1979   *The Foundations of Primitive Thought*. Clarendon, Oxford.

Halperin, Christina
2005   Social Power and Sacred Space at Actun Nak Beh, Belize. In *Stone Houses and
        Earth Lords*, ed. Keith Prufer and James Brady, 71–90. University Press of Colo-
        rado, Boulder.

Haly, Richard
1992   Bare Bones: Rethinking Mesoamerican Divinity. *History of Religions* 31(3):269–
        304.

Hammond, Norman
1972a   Classic Maya Music, Part 1: Maya Drums. *Archaeology* 25:125–131.
1972b   Classic Maya Music, Part II: Shakers, Rattles, Raspers. *Archaeology* 25:222–228.

Hammond, Norman, and Mathew R. Bobo
1994   Pilgrimage's Last Mile: Late Maya Monument Veneration at La Milpa, Belize.
        World Archaeology 26(1):19–34.

Hanks, William F.
1987   Discourse Genres in a Theory of Practice. *American Ethnologist* 14:668–692.
1990   *Referential Practice: Language and Lived Space among the Maya*. University of
        Chicago Press, Chicago.

Haraway, Donna J.
1991   *Simians, Cyborgs, and Women: The Reinvention of Nature*. Routledge, New York.

Harris, Max
1994   Muhammed and the Virgin: Folk Dramatizations of Battles between Moors
        and Christians in Modern Spain. *The Drama Review: The Journal of Performance
        Studies* 38(1):45–61.

REFERENCES CITED

Harrison, Margaret A.L., and Robert Wauchope (editors)
   1961   *The Native Theatre in Middle America*. Middle American Research Institute, Publication 27. Tulane University, New Orleans.

Harrison, Peter D.
   1999   *The Lords of Tikal: Rulers of an Ancient Maya City*. Thames and Hudson, New York.

Harrison-Buck, Eleanor
   2004   Nourishing the Animus of Lived Space through Ritual Caching. In *K'axob: Ritual, Work, and Family in an Ancient Maya Village*, ed. Patricia A. McAnany, 65–104. Cotsen Institute of Technology, UCLA, Los Angeles.

Hassig, Ross
   1988   *Aztec Warfare: Imperial Expansion and Political Control*. University of Oklahoma Press, Norman.
   2001   *Time, History, and Belief in Aztec and Colonial Mexico*. University of Texas Press, Austin.

Headrick, Annabeth
   1999   The Street of the Dead . . . It Really Was: Mortuary Bundles at Teotihuacan. *Ancient Mesoamerica* 10:69–85.
   2004   The Quadripartite Motif and the Centralization of Power. In *K'axob: Ritual, Work, and Family in an Ancient Maya Village*, ed. Patricia A. McAnany, 367–378. Cotsen Institute of Technology, UCLA, Los Angeles.

Healy, Paul F.
   1988   Music of the Maya. *Archaeology* 41:24–31.

Heckenberger, Michael J.
   2005   *The Ecology of Power: Culture, Place, and Personhood in the Southern Amazon, A.D. 1000–2000*. Routledge, New York.

Heidegger, Martin
   1996   *Being and Time: A Translation of Sein und Zeit*. Trans. Joan Stambaugh. SUNY Press, Albany.

Hemming, John
   1970   *The Conquest of the Incas*. Harcourt, Brace, and Jovanovich, New York.

Hermes, Bernard
   2000   Ofrendas. In *El sitio Maya de Topoxté: Investigaciones en una isla del lago Yaxhá, Petén, Guatemala,* ed. Wolfgang W. Wurster, 77–90. Verlag Philipp von Zabern, Bonn.

Hernández, Christine, and Victoria R. Bricker
   2004   The Inauguration of Planting in the Borgia and Madrid Codices. In *The Madrid Codex: New Approaches to Understanding an Ancient Maya Manuscript*, ed. Gabrielle Vail and Anthony F. Aveni, 277–320. University Press of Colorado, Boulder.

Hernández, Christine, and Gabrielle Vail

2007 Astronomical Interpretations of Maya Almanacs: A View from the Late Postclassic Maya Codices. Paper presented at the 72nd Annual Meeting of the Society for American Archaeology, Austin, Texas.

2009 A Case for Scribal Interaction: Evidence from the Madrid and Borgia Group Codices. In *Astronomers, Scribes, and Priests: Intellectual Interchange between the Northern Maya Lowlands and Highland Mexico during the Late Postclassic Period*, ed. Gabrielle Vail and Christine Hernández. Dumbarton Oaks, Washington, D.C., in press.

Herndon, Kristina S.

1994 The Children of Tipu: Gender, Health, and Social Change in a Sixteenth Century Maya Population. Master's thesis, Department of Anthropology, University of Southern Mississippi, Hattiesburg.

Hertz, Robert

1973 The Pre-Eminence of the Right Hand: A Study in Religious Polarity. In *Right and*
[1909] *Left: Essays on Dual Symbolic Classification*, ed. Rodney Needham, 3–31. University of Chicago Press, Chicago.

Heyden, Doris

1991 Dryness before the Rains: Toxcatl and Tezcatlipoca. In *To Change Place: Aztec Ceremonial Landscapes*, ed. Davíd Carrasco, 188–203. University Press of Colorado, Boulder.

Heylighen, Francis

2000 What Is a World View? In *Pricipia Cybernetica Web*, ed. F. Helighen, C. Joslyn, and V. Turchin. Principia Cybernetica, Brussels. http://pespmc1.vub.ac.be/WORLVIEW.html, accessed April 16, 2007.

Hill, Jane

1992 The Flower World of Old Uto-Aztecan. *Journal of Anthropological Research* 48: 117–144.

Hill, Jonathan D.

1996a Ethnogenesis in the Northwest Amazon: An Emerging Regional Picture. In *History, Power, and Identity: Ethnogenesis in the Americas, 1492–1992*, Jonathan D. Hill, 142–160. University of Iowa Press, Iowa City.

1996b Introduction. In *History, Power, and Identity: Ethnogenesis in the Americas, 1492–1992*, ed. Jonathan D. Hill, 1–19. University of Iowa Press, Iowa City.

Hirsh, Eric

1995 Introduction Landscape: Between Space and Place. In *The Anthropology of Landscape: Perspectives on Place and Space*, ed. Eric Hirsch and Michael O' Hanlon, 1–30. Clarendon Press, Oxford.

Hitchens, Christopher

2007 *The Portable Atheist: Essential Readings for the Nonbeliever*. Da Capo Press / Perseus Books Group, Philadelphia.

REFERENCES CITED

Hodder, Ian
1977   The Distribution of Material Culture Items in the Baringo District, Western Kenya. *Man* 12:239–269.
1982   Theoretical Archaeology: A Reactionary View. In *Symbolic and Structural Archaeology*, ed. Ian Hodder, 1–16. Cambridge University Press, Cambridge.
1995   *Theory and Practice in Archaeology*. Routledge, New York.

Hofling, Charles A.
1991   *Itzá Maya Texts with a Grammatical Overview*. University of Utah Press, Salt Lake City.

Holland, William R.
1964   Contemporary Tzotzil Cosmological Concepts as a Basis for Interpreting Prehistoric Maya Civilization. *American Antiquity* 29:301–306.

Holsbeke, Mireille, and Julia Montoya (editors)
2003   *With Their Hands and Their Eyes: Maya Textiles, Mirrors of a Worldview*. Etnografisch Museum, Antwerp.

Horspool, Glen Arvel
1982   The Music of the Quiché Maya of Momostenango in its Cultural Setting. Ph.D. dissertation, Department of Anthropology, University of California, Los Angeles.

Hosler, Dorothy
1994   *The Sounds and Colors of Power: The Sacred Metallurgical Technology of Ancient West Mexico*. MIT Press, Cambridge, Massachusetts.

Houston, Stephen D.
1996   Symbolic Sweatbaths of the Maya: Architectural Meaning in the Cross Group at Palenque, Mexico. *Latin American Antiquity* 7(2):132–151.
1998   Classic Maya Depictions of the Built Environment. In *Function and Meaning in Classic Maya Architecture*, ed. Stephen D. Houston, 333–372. Dumbarton Oaks, Washington, D.C.
2000   Into the Minds of the Ancients: Advances in Maya Glyph Studies. *Journal of World Prehistory* 14(2):121–201.
2004   The Acropolis of Piedras Negras: Portrait of a Court System. In *Courtly Art of the Ancient Maya*, ed. Mary Miller and Simon Martin, 271–276. Thames and Hudson, New York.

Houston, Stephen D., Oswaldo Chinchilla Mazariegos, and David Stuart
2001a   Epilogue. In *The Decipherment of Ancient Maya Writing*, ed. Stephen D. Houston, Oswaldo Chinchilla Mazariegos, and David Stuart, 505–506. University of Oklahoma Press, Norman.
2001b   Introduction. In *The Decipherment of Ancient Maya Writing*, ed. Stephen D. Houston, Oswaldo Chinchilla Mazariegos, and David Stuart, 3–23. University of Oklahoma Press, Norman.

Houston, Stephen D., and David Stuart
1996   Of Gods, Glyphs and Kings: Divinity and Rulership among the Classic Maya. *Antiquity* 70(268):289–312.

1998   The Ancient Maya Self: Personhood and Portraiture in the Classic Period. *RES* 33:73–101.

Houston, Stephen, David Stuart, and Karl Taube
2006   *The Memory of Bones: Body, Being, and Experience among the Classic Maya*. University of Texas Press, Austin.

Howe, Leopold E.A.
1981   The Social Determination of Knowledge: Maurice Bloch and Balinese Time. *Man* 16:220–234.

Howell, Mark Harold
2004   An Ethnoarchaeomusicological Investigation of Highland Guatemalan Dance-Plays. Ph.D. dissertation, Music Department, Graduate Center of the City University of New York, New York.

Hunt, Eva
1977   *The Transformation of the Hummingbird: Cultural Roots of a Zinacantecan Mythical Poem*. Cornell University Press, Ithaca, New York.

Hunter, William A.
1961   The Calderonian Auto Sacramental El Gran Teatro Del Mundo: An Edition and Translation of a Nahuatl Version. In *The Native Theater in Middle America*, ed. Margaret Harrison and Robert Wauchope, 105–201. Middle American Research Institute, Publication 27. Tulane University, New Orleans.

Hutson, Scott R., and Travis W. Stanton
2007   Cultural Logic and Practical Reason: The Structure of Discard in Ancient Maya Houselots. *Cambridge Archaeological Journal* 17(2):123–144.

Huxley, Aldous
1934   *Beyond the Mexique Bay*. Harper and Brothers, New York.

Imafuku, Ryuta
1986   History and Otherness: The Theme of "Moors and Cristians" and Its Variations. Master of Music Thesis, University of Texas at Austin, Austin.

Ingold, Tim
2000   *The Perception of the Environment: Essays on Livelihood, Dwelling, and Skill*. Routledge, London.

Inomata, Takeshi
2006   Politics and Theatricality in Mayan Society. In *Archaeology of Performance: Theaters of Power, Community, and Politics*, ed. Takeshi Inomata and Lawrence S. Coben, 187–221. Altamira, Lanham, Maryland.

Inomata, Takeshi, and Lawrence S. Coben
2006   Overture: An Invitation to the Archaeological Theater. In *Archaeology of Performance: Theaters of Power, Community, and Politics*, ed. Takeshi Inomata and Lawrence S. Coben, 11–44. Altamira, Lanham, Maryland.

REFERENCES CITED

Jacobi, Keith P.
  2000   *Last Rites of the Tipu Maya: Genetic Structuring in a Colonial Cemetery.* University of Alabama Press, Tuscaloosa.

John, Jennifer
  2008   Postclassic Maya Ceramic Iconography at Lamanai, Belize, Central America. Ph.D. dissertation, Institute of Archaeology, University College, London.

Johnson, Jay K.
  1985   Postclassic Maya Site Structure at Topoxté, El Petén, Guatemala. In *The Lowland Maya Postclassic,* ed. Arlen F. Chase and Prudence M. Rice, 151–165. University of Texas Press, Austin.

Johnson, Matthew
  1999   *Archaeological Theory: An Introduction.* Blackwell Publishers, Oxford.

Jones, Andy
  2005   Live in Fragments? Personhood and the European Neolithic. *Journal of Social Archaeology* 5(2):193–224.

Jones, Christopher
  1969   The Twin-Pyramid Group Pattern: A Classic Maya Architectural Assemblage at Tikal, Guatemala. Ph.D. dissertation, Department of Anthropology, University of Pennsylvania, Philadelphia.

Jones, Christopher, and Linton Satterthwaite
  1982   *The Monuments and Inscriptions of Tikal: The Carved Monuments.* Tikal Report 33A, Monograph 44, The University Museum, University of Pennsylvania, Philadelphia.

Jones, Grant D.
  1974   Revolution and Continuity in Santa Cruz Maya Society. *American Ethnologist* 1:659–683.
  1989   *Maya Resistance to Spanish Rule: Time and History on a Colonial Frontier.* University of New Mexico Press, Albuquerque.
  1992   Rebellious Prophets. In *New Theories on the Ancient Maya,* ed. Elin C. Danien and Robert J. Sharer, 197–204. University of Pennsylvania, Philadelphia.
  1998   *The Conquest of the Last Maya Kingdom.* Stanford University Press, Stanford, California.
  2005   Ethnohistorical Knowledge and Interdisciplinary Research: Rethinking Colonial "Resistance" on the Colonial Frontiers of Yucatán. In *A Catalyst for Ideas: Anthropological Archaeology and the Legacy of Douglas W. Schwartz,* ed. Vernon L. Scarborough, 289–318. School of American Research Press, Santa Fe, New Mexico.
  2009   The Kowojs of Central Petén, Guatemala, in Ethnohistoric Perspective. In *The Kowoj: Identity, Migration, and Geopolitics in Late Postclassic Petén, Guatemala,* ed. Prudence M. Rice and Don S. Rice, 55–69. University Press of Colorado, Boulder.

Jones, Grant D., Robert R. Kautz, and Elizabeth A. Graham
1986   Tipu: A Maya Town on the Spanish Colonial Frontier. *Archaeology* 39(1):40–47.

Jones, Grant D., Don S. Rice, and Prudence M. Rice
1981   The Location of Tayasal: A Reconsideration in Light of Petén Maya Ethnohistory and Archaeology. *American Antiquity* 46:530–547.

Jordan, Peter
2001   The Materiality of Shamanism as a "World-View": Praxis, Artefacts and Landscape. In *The Archaeology of Shamanism*, ed. Neil Price, 87–104. Routledge, New York.
2003   *Material Culture and the Sacred Landscape: The Anthropology of the Siberian Khanty.* Altamira Press, Walnut Creek, California.

Joyce, Rosemary A.
2000   *Gender and Power in Prehispanic Mesoamerica.* University of Texas Press, Austin.
2003   Concrete Memories: Fragments of the Past in the Classic Maya Present (500–1000 AD). In *Archaeologies of Memory*, ed. Ruth M. Van Dyke and Susan E. Alcock, 104–125. Blackwell, Oxford.

Just, Brian R.
2004   *In Extenso* Almanacs in the Madrid Codex. In *The Madrid Codex: New Approaches to Understanding an Ancient Maya Manuscript*, ed. Gabrielle Vail and Anthony F. Aveni, 255–276. University Press of Colorado, Boulder.

Kamstra, Jacques H.
1989   The Religion of Japan: Syncretism or Religious Phenomenalism. In *Dialogue and Syncretism: An Interdisciplinary Approach*, ed. Jerald D. Gort, Hendrik M. Vroom, Rein Fernhout, and Anton Wessels, 134–145. William B. Eerdmans Publishing, Grand Rapids, Michigan.

Karttunen, Frances E.
1994   *Between Worlds: Interpreters, Guides, and Survivors.* Rutgers University Press, New Brunswick, New Jersey.

Kazhdan, Alexander P. (editor)
1991   *Oxford Dictionary of Byzantium.* Oxford University Press, Oxford.

Kearney, Michael
1975   World View Theory and Study. *Annual Review of Anthropology* 4:247–270.
1984   *World View.* Chandler and Sharp Publishers, Novato, California.
1986   *The Winds of Ixtepeji: World View and Society in a Zapotec Town.* Waveland Press, Prospect Heights, Illinois.

Kehoe, Alice Beck
1989   *The Ghost Dance: Ethnohistory and Revitalization.* Holt, Rhinehart and Winston, Fort Worth, Texas.
2000   *Shamans and Religion: An Anthropological Exploration in Critical Thinking.* Waveland Press, Long Grove, Illinois.

REFERENCES CITED

Kemp, Barry J.
1989   *Ancient Egypt: Anatomy of a Civilization*. Routledge, London.

Kepecs, Susan
1998   Diachronic Ceramic Evidence and Its Social Implications in the Chikinchel Region, Northeast Yucatán, Mexico. *Ancient Mesoamerica* 9(1):121–135.

Kepecs, Susan M., and Marilyn A. Masson
2003   Political Organization in Yucatán and Belize. In *The Postclassic Mesoamerican World*, ed. Michael E. Smith and Frances F. Berdan, 40–44. University of Utah Press, Salt Lake City.

Kirch, Patrick V., and Marshall D. Sahlins
1992   *Anahulu: The Anthropology of History in the Kingdom of Hawaii*. Vols. 1 and 2. University of Chicago Press, Chicago.

Klass, Morton
1995   *Ordered Universes: Approaches to the Anthropology of Religion*. Westview Press, Boulder, Colorado.

Knab, Timothy J.
2004   *The Dialogue of Earth and Sky: Dreams, Souls, Curing, and the Modern Aztec Underworld*. University of Arizona Press, Tucson.

Knapp, A. Bernard, and Wendy Ashmore
1999   Archaeological Landscapes: Constructed, Conceptualized, Ideational. In *Archaeologies of Landscape: Contemporary Perspectives*, ed. Wendy Ashmore and A. Bernard Knapp, 1–32. Blackwell, Oxford.

Knowlton, Timothy
N.d.   *Genesis and Darkness: Words and Worlds of Classical Yucatecan Maya Creation Myths*. University Press of Colorado, Boulder. Accepted for publication.

Konrad, Herman W.
1991   Pilgrimage as Cyclical Process: The Unending Pilgrimage of the Holy Cross of the Quintana Roo Maya. In *Pilgrimage in Latin America*, ed. N. Ross Crumrine and E. Alan Morinis, 123–137. Greenwood Press, New York.

Koontz, Rex, Kathryn Reese-Taylor, and Annabeth Headrick (editors)
2001   *Landscape and Power in Ancient Mesoamerica*. Westview Press, Boulder, California.

Kopytoff, Igor
1987   The Internal African Frontier: The Making of African Political Culture. In *The African Frontier: The Reproduction of Traditional African Societies*, ed. Igor Kopytoff, 3–84. Indiana University Press, Bloomington.

Kowalski, Jeff Karl
1987   *The House of the Governor: A Maya Palace at Uxmal, Yucatan, Mexico*. University of Oklahoma Press, Norman.
2003   Collaboration and Conflict: An Interpretation of the Relationship between Uxmal and Chichén Itzá during the Terminal Classic / Early Postclassic Periods. In

Escondino en la Selva, ed. Hanns J. Prem, 235–272. Universidad de Bonn, Bonn, Germany, and Instituto Nacional de Antropología e Historia, México, D.F.

2007   What's "Toltec" at Uxmal and Chichén Itzá? Merging Maya and Mesoamerican Worldviews and World Systems in Terminal Classic to Early Postclassic Yucatán. In *Twin Tollans: Chichén Itzá, Tula, and the Epiclassic to Early Postclassic Mesoamerican World*, ed. Jeff Karl Kowalski and Cynthia Kristan-Graham, 251–314. Dumbarton Oaks Research Library and Collections, Washington, D.C.

Kristan-Graham, Cynthia
2001   A Sense of Place at Chichen Itza. In *Landscape and Power in Ancient Mesoamerica*, ed. Rex Koontz, Kathryn Reese-Taylor, and Annabeth Headrick, 317–369. Westview Press, Boulder, Colorado.

Kubler, George
1961   On the Colonial Extinction of the Motifs in Pre-Columbian Art. In *Essays in Pre-Columbian Art and Archaeology*, ed. Samuel Lothrop, 14–34. Harvard University Press, Cambridge, Massachusetts.
1969   *Studies in Classic Maya Iconography.* Connecticut Academy of Arts and Sciences, New Haven.
1985   Precolumbian Pilgrimages in Mesomerica. In *Fourth Palenque Round Table, 1980*, ed. Elizabeth P. Benson, 313–316. Precolumbian Art Research, San Francisco.

Kurath, Gertrude P.
1949   Mexican Moriscas: A Problem in Dance Acculturation. *Journal of American Folklore* 62:87–106.

Kurjack, Edward B., and E. Wyllys Andrews V
1976   Early Boundary Maintenance in Northwest Yucatan, Mexico. *American Antiquity* 41(3):318–325.

Lakoff, George, and Mark Johnson
1980   *Metaphors We Live By.* University of Chicago Press, Chicago.

Lakoff, George, and Mark Turner
1989   *More than Cool Reason: A Field Guide to Poetic Metaphor.* University of Chicago Press, Chicago.

Lampe, Frederick P.
2003   Creating a Second-Storey Woman: Introduced Delineation between Natural and Supernatural in Melanesia. *Anthropological Forum* 13(2):167–174.

Landa, Diego de
1941   *Relación de las cosas de Yucatan, a translation.* Trans. A. M. Tozzer. Peabody Museum
[1566] of American Archaeology and Ethnology, Cambridge, Massachusetts.

Las Casas, Bartolomé de
1992   *The Devastation of the Indies: A Brief Account.* Trans. Herma Briffault. Johns Hopkins University Press, Baltimore.

Lassiter, G. Daniel
2004   *Interrogations, Confessions, and Entrapment.* Springer, Berlin.

REFERENCES CITED

Latour, Bruno
1993   *We Have Never Been Modern*. Trans. Catherine Porter. Harvard University Press, Cambridge, Massachusetts.

Laudan, Larry
1996   *Beyond Positivism and Relativism: Theory, Method, and Evidence*. Westview Press, Boulder, Colorado.

Leach, Edmund R.
1966a   *Rethinking Anthropology*. Humanities, New York.
1966b   Sermons by a Man on a Ladder. *The New York Review of Books*, October 20, 1966.

Lechtman, Heather
1977   Style in Technology—Some Early Thoughts. In *Material Culture: Styles, Organization, and Dynamics of Technology*, ed. Heather Lechtman and Robert S. Merrill, 3–20. West Publishing Company, St. Paul, Minnesota.
1993   Technologies of Power—The Andean Case. In *Configurations of Power in Complex Society*, ed. Patricia J. Netherly and John S. Henderson, 244–280. Cornell University Press, Ithaca, New York.
1994   The Materials Science of Material Culture: Examples from the Andean Past. In *Archaeometry of Pre-Columbian Sites and Artifacts*, ed. David A. Scott and Pieter Meyers, 3–11. Getty Conservation Institute, Los Angeles.

Lefebvre, Henri
1991   *The Production of Space*. Trans. Donald Nicholson-Smith. Blackwell, Cambridge.

Lemonnier, Pierre
1992   *Elements for an Anthropology of Technology*. Anthropological Papers No. 88, Museum of Anthropology, University of Michigan, Ann Arbor.
1993   Introduction. In *Technological Choices*, ed. Pierre Lemonnier, 1–35. Routledge, London.

León-Portilla, Miguel
1988   *Time and Reality in the Thought of the Maya*. 2nd ed. University of Oklahoma Press, Norman.

Leone, Mark P.
1984   Interpreting Ideology in Historical Archaeology: Using the Rules of Perspective in the William Paca Garden in Annapolis, Maryland. In *Ideology, Power, and Prehistory*, ed. Daniel Miller and Christopher Tilley, 25–35. Cambridge University Press, Cambridge.

Lévi-Strauss, Claude
1969   *The Elementary Structures of Kinship*. Beacon Press, Boston.
[1949]

Liljefors Persson, Bodil
2000   *The Legacy of the Jaguar Prophet: An Exploration of Yucatec Maya Religion and Historiography*. Lund Studies in History of Religions, vol. 10. Religionshistoriska avdelningen, Lunds universitet (University of Lund), Lund.

Lindberg, David C.
1992   *The Beginnings of Western Science: The European Scientific Tradition in Philosophical, Religious, and Institutional Context, 600 B.C. to A.D. 1450.* University of Chicago Press, Chicago.

Lizana, Bernardo de
1893   *Historia de Yucatán: Devocionario de Ntra. Sra. De Izmal y conquista espiritual.*
[1633]   Museo Nacional, México.

Looper, Matthew G.
1995   The Three Stones of Maya Creation Mythology at Quirigua. *Mexicon* 17(2):24–30.
2001   Design Interpretation in Mam Textile Histories. In *Maya Survivalism*, ed. Ueli Hostettler and Matthew Restall, 281–294. Acta Mesoamericana 12. Verlag Anton Saurwein, Markt Schwaben.

López Austin, Alfredo
1980   *Cuerpo humano e ideología: Las concepciones de los antiguos nahuas.* Universidad Nacional Autónoma de México, México.
1997   *Tamoanchan, Tlalocan: Places of Mist.* University Press of Colorado, Boulder.

López de Cogolludo, Fray Diego
1867   *Historia de Yucatán.* Merída, México.
[1688]
1957   *Historia de Yucatán.* Colección de Grandes Crónicas Mexicanas, 3. Editorial Academia Literaria, México.

López de Gómara, Francisco
1964   *Cortés: The Life of the Conqueror by His Secretary.* Ed. and trans. Lesley B. Simpson. University of California Press, Berkeley.
[1881]

Lothrop, Samuel K.
1924   *Tulum: An Archaeological Study of the East Coast of Yucatan.* Carnegie Institution of Washington, Washington, D.C.
1933   *Atitlán: An Archaeological Study of Ancient Remains on the Borders of Lake Atitlan, Guatemala.* Carnegie Institution of Washington, Publication No. 44, Washington, D.C.

Love, Bruce
1989   Yucatec Sacred Breads through Time. In *Word and Image in Maya Culture: Explorations in Language, Writing, and Representation*, ed. William F. Hanks and Don S. Rice, 336–350. University of Utah Press, Salt Lake City.
1994   *The Paris Codex: Handbook for a Maya Priest.* University of Texas Press, Austin.
2004   Maya Gods of the Yucatan in the Sixteenth and Seventeenth Centuries. Paper Presented at the Olmec, Maya, Aztec Papers in Honor of H. B. Nicholson, November 13, 2004, Friends of Archaeology, Cotsen Institute of Archaeology, University of California, Los Angeles.

REFERENCES CITED

Lowe, Setha M.
  1995   Indigenous Architecture and the Spanish American Plaza in Mesoamerica and the Caribbean. *American Anthropologist* 97:748–762.

Lowie, Robert H.
  1952   *Primitive Religion*. Liveright, New York.

Lumholtz, Carl G.
  1902   *Unknown Mexico*, vol. 2. Scribner's and Sons, New York.

Luna Erreguerena, Pilar
  1989   Underwater Archaeology in Mexico. In *Underwater Archaeology Proceedings of the Society for Historical Archaeology Conference*, ed. J. Barto Arnold III, 149–151. Society for Historical Archaeology, Tucson, Arizona.

Lutz, Christopher H., and W. George Lovell
  1990   Core and Periphery in Colonial Guatemala. In *Guatemalan Indians and the State, 1540–1988*, ed. Carol A. Smith, 35–71. University of Texas Press, Austin.

Lyotard, Jean-François
  1984   *The Postmodern Condition: A Report on Knowledge*. Trans. Geoff Bennington and Brian Massumi. University of Minnesota Press, Minneapolis.

MacLeod, Murdo J.
  1973   *Spanish Central America: A Socioeconomic History, 1520–1720*. University of California Press, Berkeley.

Madsen, William
  1967   Religious Syncretism. In *Social Anthropology. Handbook of Middle American Indians*, vol. 6, ed. Manning Nash, 369–391. University of Texas Press, Austin.

Maler, Teobert
  1901   *Researches in the Central Portion of the Usumatsintla Valley*. Memoirs of the Peabody Museum of American Archaeology and Ethnology, vol. 2, no. 1. Harvard University, Cambridge, Massachusetts.

Malinowski, Bronislaw
  1922   *Argonauts of the Western Pacific*. E. P. Dutton, New York.

Malkki, Lisa H.
  1997   National Geographic: The Rooting of Peoples and the Territorialization of National Identity among Scholars and Refugees. In *Culture, Power, Place: Explorations in Critical Anthropology*, ed. A. Gupta and J. Ferguson, 52–74. Duke University Press, Durham, North Carolina.

Marcos, (Subcomandante)
  1995   *Shadows of Tender Fury: The Letters and Communiqués of Subcomandante Marcos and the Zapatista Army of National Liberation*. Monthly Review Press, New York.

Marcus, Joyce
  1978   Archaeology and Religion: A Comparison of the Zapotec and Maya. *World Archaeology* 10:172–191.

1992   *Mesoamerica Writing Systems: Propoaganda, Myth, and History of Four Ancient Civilizations*. Princeton University Press, Princeton, New Jersey.

1993   Ancient Maya Political Organization. In *Lowland Maya Civilization in the Eighth Century A.D.*, ed. Jeremy A. Sabloff and John S. Henderson, 111–183. Dumbarton Oaks Research Library and Collections, Washington, D.C.

Mariani, Evelyn Weiss

1995   Samuel Martí (1906–1975): A Mexican Ethnomusicologist; His Work, Thesis and Contributions. Ph.D. dissertation, Michigan State University, East Lansing, Michigan.

Martí, Samuel

1998   *Music before Columbus: Música precolombina*. 2nd ed. Ediciones Euroamericanas
[1971]   Klaus Thiele, México City.

Martin, Simon

2006   Cacao in Ancient Maya Religion: First Fruit from the Maize Tree and Other Tales from the Underworld. In *Chocolate in Mesoamerica: A Cultural History of Cacao*, ed. Cameron L. McNeil, 154–183. University Press of Florida, Gainesville.

Martin, Simon, and Nikolai Grube

2000   *Chronicle of the Maya Kings and Queens: Deciphering the Dynasties of the Ancient Maya*. Thames and Hudson, London.

Martínez Hernández, Juan (editor and translator)

1926   *Crónica de Yaxkukul*. Talleres de la Compañía Tipográfica Yucateca, Mérida.

1929   *Diccionario de Motul maya-español atribuido a fray Antonio de Ciudad Real y Arte de lengua maya por Fray Juan Coronel*. Compañia Tipográfica Yucateca, Mérida.

Martínez Marín, Carlos

1972   Santuarios y Peregrinaciones en el Mexico Prehispanico. In *Religion en Meso-america*, ed. Jaime Litvak King and Noemi Castillo Tejeros, 161–176. XII Mesa Redonda Sociedad Mexicana de Antropologia, México City.

Marzal, Manuel M.

1993   Transplanted Spanish Catholicism. In *South and Meso-American Native Spirituality: From the Cult of the Feathered Serpent to the Theology of Liberation*, ed. Gary H. Gossen, 140–169. Crossroad, New York.

Mason, Gregory

1927   *Silver Cities of Yucatan*. Putnam, New York.

Masson, Marilyn A.

1999   Postclassic Maya Ritual at Laguna de On, Belize. *Ancient Mesoamerica* 10:51–68.

2000   *In the Realm of Nachan Kan: Postclassic Maya Archaeology at Laguna de On, Belize*. University Press of Colorado, Boulder.

2003   The Late Postclassic Symbol Set in the Maya Area. In *The Postclassic Mesoamerican World*, ed. Michael E. Smith and Frances F. Berdan, 194–200. University of Utah Press, Salt Lake City.

REFERENCES CITED

Masson, Marilyn A., Timothy S. Hare, and Carlos Peraza Lope
    2006   Postclassic Maya Society Regenerated at Mayapán. In *The Regeneration of Complex Societies*, ed. Glenn Schwarz and John Nichols, 188–207. University of Arizona Press, Tucson.

Masson, Marilyn A., and Carlos Peraza Lope
    2007   Kukulkan/Quetzalcoatl, Death God, and Creation Mythology of Burial Shaft Temples at Mayapán. *Mexicon* 29(3):7–85.

Mathews, Jennifer P., and James F. Garber
    2004   Models of Cosmic Order: Physical Expression of Sacred Space among the Ancient Maya. *Ancient Mesoamerica* 15:49–59.

Matos Moctezuma, Eduardo
    1987   *El rostro de la muerte en el México prehispánico*. Garcia Valadés Editores, México.

Mauss, Marcel
    1967   *The Gift: Forms and Functions of Exchange in Archaic Societies*. Trans. Ian Cunnison. W. W. Norton, New York.
    [1925]

McAnany, Patricia
    1995   *Living with the Ancestors: Kinship and Kingship in Ancient Maya Society*. University of Texas Press, Austin.
    1998   Ancestors and the Classic Maya Built Environment. In *Function and Meaning in Classic Maya Architecture*, ed. Stephen D. Houston, 271–298. Dumbarton Oaks, Washington, D.C.

McBryde, Felix W.
    1947   *Cultural and Historical Geography of Southwest Guatemala*. Institute of Social Anthropology Publication No. 4. Smithsonian Institution, Washington, D.C.
    [1935]

McCafferty, Geoffrey G.
    2007   Alter Egos: Domestic Ritual and Social Identity in Postclassic Cholula, Mexico. In *Commoner Ritual and Ideology in Ancient Mesoamerica*, ed. Nancy Gonlin and Jon C. Lohse, 213–250. University Press of Colorado, Boulder.

McClintock, Walter
    1935   *The Blackfoot Beaver Bundle*. Southwest Museum, Los Angeles.

McGee, Harold F.
    1985   Playing at Knowing: *Patol* and Pueblo World View. In *Contributions to the Archaeology and Ethnohistory of Greater Mesoamerica*, ed. William J. Folan, 261–292. Southern Illinois University Press, Carbondale.

McGee, R. Jon
    1984   The Influence of Pre-Hispanic Maya Religion in Contemporary Lacandon Ritual. *Journal of Latin American Lore* 10(2):175–187.
    1990   *Life, Ritual, and Religion among the Lacandon Maya*. Wadsworth, Belmont, California.
    1998   The Lacandon Incense Burner Renewal Ceremony: Termination and Dedication Ritual among the Contemporary Maya. In *The Sowing and the Dawning: Termi-*

nation, Dedication, and Transformation in the Archaeological and Ethnographic Record of Mesoamerica, ed. Shirley B. Mock, 41–46. University of New Mexico Press, Albuquerque.

2002   *Watching Lacandon Maya Lives.* Allyn and Bacon, Boston.

2005   The Importance of Yaxchilan in the Rituals of the Non-Christian Lacandon. *Mesoamerican Voices* (December 2, 2005):63–76.

McKeever Furst, Jill Leslie
1995   *The Natural History of the Soul in Ancient Mexico.* Yale University Press, New Haven, Connecticut.

McKillop, Heather
2002   *Salt: White Gold of the Ancient Maya.* University Press of Florida, Gainesville.

Means, Philip A.
1973   *Biblioteca Andina: Essays on the Lives and Works of the Chroniclers.* Yale University Press, New Haven, Connecticut.

1974   *History of the Spanish Conquest of Yucatan and of the Itzas.* Kraus Reprint, Millwood,
[1917]   New York.

Mendelson, E. Michael
1956   Religion and World-View in Santiago Atitlan. Ph.D. dissertation, Anthropology Department, University of Chicago, Chicago.

1958   A Guatemalan Sacred Bundle. *Man* 58:121–126.

1959   Maximon: An Iconographical Introduction. *Man* 59:57–60.

Meskell, Lynn
2003   Memory's Materiality: Ancestral Presence, Commemorative Practice and Disjunctive Locales. In *Archaeologies of Memory*, ed. Ruth M. Van Dyke and Susan E. Alcock, 34–55. Blackwell, Oxford.

Meskell, Lynn M., and Rosemary A. Joyce
2003   *Embodied Lives: Figuring Ancient Maya and Egyptian Experience.* Routledge, New York.

Metcalf, Peter, and Richard Huntington
1991   *Celebrations of Death: The Anthropology of Mortuary Ritual.* 2nd ed. Cambridge University Press, Cambridge.

Meyerhoff, Barbara
1982   Rites of Passage: Process and Paradox. In *Celebration: Studies in Festivity and Ritual*, ed. Victor Turner, 109–135. Smithsonian Institution Press, Washington, D.C.

Middlestone, A. P., I. C. Freestone, and M. N. Lesse
1985   Textural Analysis of Ceramic Thin Sections: Evaluations of Grain Sampling Procedures. *Archaeometry* 27(1):64–74.

Milbrath, Susan
1999   *Star Gods of the Maya: Astronomy in Art, Folklore, and Calendars.* University of Texas Press, Austin.

REFERENCES CITED

2002   New Questions Concerning the Authenticity of the Grolier Codex. *Latin American Indian Literatures Journal* 18(1):50–83.

2004   The Maya Katun Cycle and the Retrograde Periods of Jupiter and Saturn. *Archaeoastronomy: The Journal of Astronomy in Culture* 18:81–97.

2005   Last Great Capital of the Maya. *Archaeology* 58(2):26–29.

Milbrath, Susan, and Carlos Peraza Lope

2003a   Mayapán's Scribe: A Link with Classic Maya Artists. *Mexicon* 25(5):120–123.

2003b   Revisiting Mayapán, Mexico's Last Maya Capital. *Ancient Mesoamerica* 14:1–46.

2007   Incenarios efigie de Mayapán: Inconografía, contexto y relaciones externas. Paper presented at the 7th Congreso Internacional de Mayistas. Mérida, Yucatán.

Miller, Arthur G.

1975   *The Codex Nuttall: A Picture Manuscript from Ancient Mexico.* Dover Publications, New York.

1977   The Maya and the Sea: Trade and Cult at Tancah and Tulum, Quintana Roo, Mexico. In *The Sea in the Pre-Columbian World*, ed. Elizabeth P. Benson, 97–138. Dumbarton Oaks Research Library and Collections, Washington, D.C.

1982   *On the Edge of the Sea: Mural Painting at Tancah-Tulum, Quintana Roo, Mexico.* Dumbarton Oaks, Washington, D.C.

1986   *Maya Rulers of Time / Los soberanos mayas del tiempo.* University Museum, University of Pennsylvania, Philadelphia.

Miller, Mary, and Simon Martin (editors)

2004   *Courtly Art of the Ancient Maya.* Thames and Hudson, New York.

Miller, Mary E., and Karl A. Taube

1993   *The Gods and Symbols of Ancient Mexico and the Maya: An Illustrated Dictionary of Mesoamerican Religion.* Thames and Hudson, London.

Miram, Helga-Maria

1994   A Method for Recalibrating Historical Dates in the Books of Chilam Balam. In *Hidden among the Hills: Maya Archaeology in the Northwest Yucatan Peninsula*, ed. Hanns J. Prem, 376–388. Verlag von Flemming, Möckmül.

Miram, Helga-Maria, and Victoria Bricker

1996   Relating Time to Space: The Maya Calendar Compasses. In *Palenque Round Table, 1993*, ed. Martha Macri and Jan McHargue, 393–402. Palenque Round Table Series 10. Pre-Columbian Art Research Institute, San Francisco.

Mock, Shirley B.

1998   Prelude. In *The Sowing and the Dawning: Termination, Dedication, and Transformation in the Archaeological and Ethnographic Record*, ed. Shirley B. Mock, 3–18. University of New Mexico Press, Albuquerque.

Moholy-Nagy, Hattula

2006   *The Artifacts of Tikal: Social and Ceremonial Artifacts.* Tikal Report No. 27a. University of Pennsylvania Museum of Archaeology and Anthropology, Philadelphia.

Molina, Fray Alonso de
1977   *Vocabulario en la lengua castellana y mexicana, y mexicana y castellana.* Editorial
[1571]   Porrúa, México.

Monaghan, John D.
1998   Dedication: Ritual or Production? In *The Sowing and the Dawning,* ed. Shirley B.
        Mock, 47–52. University of New Mexico Press, Albuquerque.
2000   Theology and History in the Study of Mesoamerican Religions. In *Ethnol-
        ogy: Supplement to the Handbook of Middle American Indians,* vol. 6, ed. John
        D.Monaghan, 24–49. Victoria R. Bricker, gen. ed. University of Texas Press,
        Austin.

Monastersky, Richard
2002   Recycling the Universe, New Theory Posits that Time Has No Beginning or End.
        Chronicle of Higher Education (June 7, 2002), A19–A21.

Montgomery, John
2002   *How to Read Maya Hieroglyphs.* Hippocrene Books, New York.

Morayta Mendoza, L. Miguel
1997   La tradición de los aires en una comunidad del norte del estado de Morelos:
        Ocotepec. In *Graniceros: Cosmovisión y meteorología indígenas de Mesoaméri-
        ca,* ed. Beatriz Albores and Johanna Broda, 217–232. Universidad Nacional
        Autónoma de México, México.

Morinis, E. Alan
1992   Introduction. In *Sacred Journeys: The Anthropology of Pilgrimage,* ed. E. Alan
        Morinis, 1–29. Greenwood Press, Westport, Connecticut.

Morley, Sylvanus G.
1911   The Historical Value of the Books of Chilam Balam. *Journal of the Archaeological
        Institute of America* 15(2):195–214.
1920   *The Inscriptions at Copan.* Carnegie Institution of Washington, Washington,
        D.C.

Morrison, Kenneth M.
1992   Sharing the Flower: A Non-Supernaturalistic Theory of Grace. *Religion* 22:207–
        219.
2002   *The Solidarity of Kin: Ethnohistory, Religious Studies, and the Algonkian-French
        Religious Encounter.* State University of New York Press, Albany.

Motolinía, Toribio de Benavente
1971   *Memoriales o libro de las cosas de la Nueva España y de los naturals de ella.* Ed.
        Edmundo O'Gorman. Universidad Nacional Autónoma de México, México.

Múnera Bermudez, Luis Carlos
1991   Una representacíon de bulto mortuorio. In *Teotihuacan 1980–1982: Nuevas
        Interpretaciones,* ed. Rubén Cabrera Castro, Ignacio Rodríguez García, and
        Noel Morelos García, 335–341. Instituto Nacional de Antropología e Historia,
        México.

REFERENCES CITED

Munn, Nancy D.
1992   The Cultural Anthropology of Time: A Critical Essay. *Annual Review of Anthropology* 21:93–123.

Nájera Coronado, Martha Illia
1996   La Religión: Los Rituales. In *Los Mayas: Su Tiempo Antiguo*, ed. Mercedes de la Garza, Ana Luisa Izquierdo, and Gerardo Bustos, 221–257. Universidad Autónoma de México, Instituto de Investigaciones Filológicas, Centro de Estudios Mayas, México.

Nash, June C.
1970   *In the Eyes of the Ancestors: Belief and Behavior in a Maya Community*. Yale University Press, New Haven, Connecticut.

Nations, James D.
1984   The Lacandones, Gertrude Blom, and the Selva Lacandona. In *Gertrude Blom Bearing Witness*, ed. Alex Harris and Margaret Sartor, 27–41. University of North Carolina Press, Chapel Hill.

Navarrete, Carlos
1976   Elementos arqueológicos de mexicanización en el área maya meridional durante el Posclásico tardío. *Estudios de la Cultura Náhuatl* 12:345–382.
1996   Elementos arqueológicos de mexicanización en las tierras altas mayas. In *Temas mesoamericanos*, ed. Sonia Lombardo and Enrique Nalda, 305–342. Instituto Nacional de Antropología e Historia, México City.

Needham, Rodney
1967   Percussion and Transition. *Man* 2(4):606–614.

Neff, Hector
2003   Analysis of Mesoamerican Plumbate Pottery Surfaces by Laser Ablation–Inductively Coupled Plasma–Mass Spectrometry (LA–ICP–MS). *Journal of Archaeological Science* 30(1):21–35.

Netanyahu, Benzion
2001   *The Origins of the Inquisition in Fifteenth-Century Spain*. New York Review Books, New York.

Newsome, Elizabeth A.
2001   *Trees of Paradise and Pillars of the World: The Serial Stela Cycle of "18-Rabbit–God K," King of Copan*. University of Texas Press, Austin.

Nicholson, Henry B.
1960   The Mixteca-Puebla Concept in Mesoamerican Archaeology: A Re-Examination. In *Men and Cultures: Selected Papers from the Fifth International Congress of Anthropological and Ethnological Sciences*, ed. Anthony F.C. Wallace, 612–617. University of Pennsylvania, Philadelphia.
1982   The Mixteca-Puebla Concept Revisited. In *Art and Iconography of Late Post-Classic Central México*, ed. Elizabeth H. Boone, 227–254. Dumbarton Oaks, Washington, D.C.

Nicholson, Henry B., and Eloise Quiñones Keber
    1994   *Mixteca-Puebla: Discoveries and Research in Mesoamerican Art and Archaeology.* Labyrinthos, Culver City, California.

Nielsen, Jesper, and James E. Brady
    2006   The Couple in the Cave: Origin Iconography of a Ceramic Vessel from Los Naranjos, Honduras. *Ancient Mesoamerica* 17(2):203–217.

Nielsen, Jesper, and Toke Sellner Reunert
    2008   Dante's Heritage: Questioning the Multi-Layered Model of the Mesoamerican Universe. Manuscript on file, Department of American Indian Languages and Cultures, University of Copenhagen.

Nola, Robert, and Howard Sankey (editors)
    2000   *After Popper, Kuhn and Feyerabend*: Recent Issues in Theories of Scientific Method. Kluwer Academic, Dordrecht.

Normark, Johan
    2003   Caves and Settlement in the *Ejido* of Sacalaca. In Final Report of the Cochuah Regional Survey's 2003 Field Season, ed. Justine Shaw, 70–91. Unpublished manuscript in the possession of Andrea Stone, University of Wisconsin–Milwaukee.

O'Brien, Linda
    1983   Three Maya Bone Tubes from the Crossley-Holland Collection of Musical Artifacts: A Comparative Study. In *Selected Reports in Ethnomusicology*, vol. 4: *Essays in Honor of Peter Crossley-Holland on His Sixty-fifth Birthday*, ed. Nicole Marzac-Holland and Nazir A. Jairazbhoy, 11–28. University of California Press, Los Angeles.

O'Brien-Rothe, Linda
    1998   Guatemala. In *The Garland Encyclopedia of World Music*, vol. 2: *South America, Mexico, Central America, and the Caribbean*, ed. Dale Olsen and Daniel Sheehy, 721–733. Garland, New York.

Octgin, Jose Angel
    1964   Original del Baile de los Moros y Cristianos. Manuscript courtesy of Cakchiquel Collection. Tulane University Latin American Library, New Orleans.

Orozco y Jimenez, Francisco
    1911   *Colección de documentos inéditos relativos a la Iglesia de Chiapas.* 2 vols. Imprenta de la Sociedad Católica, San Cristobal de las Casas, Chiapas, México.

Osborne, Ian, Linda Rowan, and Robert Coontz
    2002   Spacetime, Warped Branes, and Hidden Dimensions [introduction to a thematic section on spacetime]. *Science* 396:1417–1439.

Otto, Rudolf
    1958   *The Idea of the Holy: An Inquiry into the Non-Rational Factor in the Idea of the Di-*
    [1923] *vine and its Relation to the Rational.* Trans. John W. Harvey. Oxford University Press, Oxford.

REFERENCES CITED

Palka, Joel W.

1998   Lacandon Maya Culture Change and Survival in the Lowland Frontier of the Expanding Guatemalan and Mexican Republics. In *Studies in Culture Contact: Interaction, Culture Change, and Archaeology*, ed. James G. Cusick, 457–475. Center for Archaeological Investigations, Occasional Paper No. 25, Southern Illinois University, Carbondale.

2005a   Maya Rock Art and Lacandon Sacred Landscapes. *Journal of the Precolumbian Research Institute* 5(3):1–7.

2005b   *Unconquered Lancandon Maya: Ethnohistory and Archaeology of Indigenous Culture Change*. University Press of Florida, Gainesville.

Pals, Daniel L.

2006   *Eight Theories of Religion*. Oxford University Press, Oxford.

Parkes, Donn, and Nigel J. Thrift

1980   *Times, Spaces, and Places*. Wiley, Chichester, England.

Pasztory, Esther

1974   *The Iconography of the Teotihuacan Tlaloc*. Studies in Pre-Columbian Art and Archaeology, no. 15. Dumbarton Oaks, Washington, D.C.

1983   *Aztec Art*. University of Oklahoma Press, Norman.

Patch, Robert W.

1993   *Maya and Spaniard in Yucatan, 1648–1812*. Stanford University Press, Stanford, California.

2002   *Maya Revolt and Revolution in the Eighteenth Century*. M. E. Sharpe, Armonk, New York.

Patterson, Thomas C.

1985   Pachacamac: An Andean Oracle under Inca Rule. In *Recent Studies in Andean Prehistory and Protohistory*, ed. S. Peter Kvietok and Daniel H. Sanweiss, 159–176. Cornell University Press, Ithaca, New York.

Paxton, Merideth

2001   *The Cosmos of the Yucatec Maya: Cycles and Steps from the Madrid Codex*. University of New Mexico Press, Albuquerque.

Paz, Octavio

1985   *The Labyrinth of Solitude: Life and Thought in Mexico*. Grove Press, New York.

Pech, Nakuk

1882   The Chronicle of Chac Xulub Ch'en. In *The Maya Chronicles*, ed. Daniel Brinton, 189–259. Library of Aboriginal American Literature, vol. 1, Philadelphia.

Pendergast, David M.

1989   The Loving Couple: A Mystery from the Maya Past. *Royal Ontario Museum Archaeological Newsletter*, Series 2, no. 30. Royal Ontario Museum, Toronto.

1991   The Southern Maya Lowlands Contact Experience: The View from Lamanai, Belize. In *Columbian Consequences*, vol. 3: *The Spanish Borderlands in Pan-American Perspective*, ed. David H. Thomas, 337–354. Smithsonian Institution, Washington, D.C.

1998   Intercessions with the Gods: Caches and Their Significance at Altun Ha and La-
        manai. In *The Sowing and the Dawning: Termination, Dedication, and Transfor-
        mation in the Archaeological and Ethnographic Record of Mesoamerica*, ed. Shirley
        B. Mock, 55–63. University of New Mexico Press, Albuquerque.

Pendergast, David M., and Elizabeth A. Graham
1990   An Island Paradise (??): Marco Gonzalez 1990. *ROM Archaeological Newsletter*,
        Series 2, no. 41. Royal Ontario Museum, Toronto.

Peniche Rivero, Piedad
1990   *Sacerdotes y Comerciantes: El Poder de los Mayas e Itzaes de Yucatán en los siglos
        VII a XVI.* Fondo de Cultura Economica, México.

Pentikäinen, Juha
1998   *Shamanism and Culture.* Etnika, Helsinki.

Peraza Lope, Carlos
1996   Unidades Ceramicas de San Gervasio, Cozumel, Quintana Roo, Mexico. *Mexi-
        con* 18(4):67–70.
1999   Mayapán: Ciudad-Capital del Posclásico. *Arqueología Mexicana* 7(37):48–53.

Peraza Lope, Carlos, Pedro Delgado Kú, Bárbara E. Ojeda, and Mario Garrido Euán
1999   *Trabajos de mantenimiento y conservación arquitectónica en Mayapán, Yucatán:
        Informe de la segunda temporada: 1997.* Instituto Nacional de Antropología e
        Historia, Merída, Yucatán.

Peraza Lope, Carlos, Bárbara Escamilla Ojeda, and Pedro Delgado Kú
2005   *Trabajos de mantenimiento y conservación arquitectónica en Mayapán, Yucatán:
        Informe de la segunda temporada: 2004–2005.* Instituto Nacional de Antrop-
        ología e Historia, Merída, Yucatán.

Peraza Lope, Carlos, and Marilyn A. Masson
2005   Patrones espaciales del uso de efigies incensarios y esculturas en Mayapán. Se-
        gundo Congreso Internacional de la Cultural Maya, Merída.

Peraza Lope, Carlos, Marilyn Masson, Timothy H. Hare, and Pedro C. Delgado Kú
2006   The Chronology of Mayapan: New Radiocarbon Evidence. *Ancient Mesoamerica*
        17(2):153–175.

Perera, Victor, and Robert D. Bruce
1985   *The Last Lords of Palenque: The Lacandon Mayas of the Mexican Rain Forest.*
        University of California Press, Berkeley.

Perez, Joseph
2005   *The Spanish Inquisition: A History.* Trans. Janet Lloyd. Yale University Press, New
        Haven, Connecticut.

Pérez Martínez, Héctor
1936   *Historia y crónica de Chac-Xulub-Chen.* Talleres Gráficos de la Nación, Secretaría
        de Educación Pública, México.

REFERENCES CITED

Perry, Mary E., and Anne J. Cruz (editors)
    1991   *Cultural Encounters: The Impact of the Inquisition in Spain and the New World.* University of California Press, Berkeley.

Perttula, Timothy K.
    2002   Caddoan Area Protohistory and Archaeology. In *Between Contacts and Colonies: Archaeological Perspectives on the Protohistoric Southeast*, ed. Cameron B. Wesson and Mark A. Rees, 49–66. University of Alabama Press, Tuscaloosa.

Peterson, Polly A., Patricia A. McAnany, and Allan B. Cobb
    2005   De-fanging the Earth Monster: Speleothem Transport to Surface Sites in the Sibun Valley. In *Stone Houses and Earth Lords*, ed. Keith Prufer and James Brady, 225–247. University Press of Colorado, Boulder.

Pharo, Lars K.
    2007   The Concept of "Religion" in Mesoamerican Languages. *Numen* 54:28–70.

Phillips, David A.
    1979   Material Culture and Trade of the Postclassic Maya. Ph.D. dissertation, Department of Anthropology, University of Arizona, Tucson.

Pohl, John M.D.
    1994   *The Politics of Symbolism in the Mixtec Codices.* Vanderbilt University Press, Nashville, Tennessee.

Pohl, Mary
    1981   Ritual Continuity and Transformation in Mesoamerica: Reconstructing the Ancient Maya Cuch Ritual. *American Antiquity* 46(3):513–529.

Pollock, Harry E.D.
    1980   *The Puuc: An Architectural Survey of the Hill Country of Yucatan and Northern Campeche, Mexico.* Peabody Museum of Archaeology and Ethnology No. 19. Harvard University, Cambridge, Massachusetts.

Pratt, Mary Louise
    1992   *Imperial Eyes: Travel Writing and Transculturation.* Routledge, London.

Prechtel, Martin, and Robert S. Carlsen
    1988   Weaving and Cosmos amongst the Tzutujil Maya of Guatemala. *RES* 15:124–132.

Proskouriakoff, Tatiana
    1955   Mayapán: The Last Stronghold of a Civilization. *Archaeology* 7(2): 96–103.
    1962a   The Artifacts of Mayapán. In *Mayapán, Yucatan, Mexico*, ed. Harry E.D. Pollock, Ralph L. Roys, Tatiana Proskouriakoff, and A. Ledyard Smith, 321–442. Carnegie Institution of Washington Publication 619, Washington, D.C.
    1962b   Civic and Religious Structures of Mayapán. In *Mayapán, Yucatán, México*, ed. Harry Pollock, Ralph L. Roys, Tatiana Proskouriakoff, and A. Ledyard Smith, 87–164. Carnegie Institution of Washington, Washington, D.C.
    1965   Sculpture and Major Arts of the Maya Lowlands. In *Archaeology of Southern Mesoamerica, 1. Handbook of Middle American Indians*, vol. 2, ed. Gordon R. Willey, 469–497. University of Texas Press, Austin.

1978   Olmec Gods and Maya God-Glyphs. In *Codex Wauchope: A Tribute Roll*, ed. Marco Giardino, Barbara Edmonson, and Winifred Creamer, 113–117. Tulane University, New Orleans.

Proskouriakoff, Tatiana, and Charles R. Temple
1955   A Residential Quadrangle—Structures R-85 to R-90. *Current Reports* No. 29, 289–362. Carnegie Institution of Washington, Washington, D.C.

Pugh, Timothy W.
2001a   Architecture, Ritual, and Social Identity at Late Postclassic Zacpetén, Petén, Guatemala: Identification of the Kowoj. Ph.D. dissertation, Department of Anthropology, Southern Illinois University, Carbondale.
2001b   Flood Reptiles, Serpent Temples, and the Quadripartite Universe: The Imago Mundi of Late Postclassic Mayapán. *Ancient Mesoamerica* 12(2):247–258.
2002   Remembering Mayapán: Petén Kowoj Architecture as Social Metaphor and Power. In *The Dynamics of Power*, ed. Maria O'Donovan, 301–323. Center for Archaeological Investigations, Carbondale, Illinois.
2003a   A Cluster and Spatial Analysis of Ceremonial Architecture at Late Postclassic Mayapán. *Journal of Archaeological Science* 30:941–953.
2003b   The Exemplary Center of the Late Postclassic Kowoj Maya. *Latin American Antiquity* 14(4):408–430.
2004   Activity Areas, Form, and Social Inequality in Late Postclassic Domestic Groups at Zacpetén, Petén, Guatemala. *Journal of Field Archaeology* 29:351–367.
2005   Caves and Artificial Caves in Late Postclassic Maya Ceremonial Groups. In *Stone Houses and Earth Lords: Maya Religion in the Cave Context*, ed. Keith M. Prufer and James E. Brady, 47–69. University Press of Colorado, Boulder.

Pugh, Timothy W., and Prudence M. Rice
1996   Arquitectura Estilo Mayapán y evidencias de organización dual en el sitio postclásico de Zacpetén, Petén, Guatemala. In *X Simposio de Investigaciones Arqueologicas en Guatemala*, 521–532. Museo Nacional de Arqueología y Etnología, Guatemala City.

Pugh, Timothy W., Prudence M. Rice, and Don S. Rice
2006   Urban Planning in Middle Postclassic to Contact Period Petén, Guatemala. Paper presented at the 71st Annual Meeting of the Society for American Archaeology, San Juan.

Pyburn, K. Anne
2004   Introduction: Rethinking Complex Society. In *Ungendering Civilization*, ed. K. Anne Pyburn, 1–46. Routledge, New York.

Querejazu Lewis, Roy (editor)
1992   *Arte rupestre colonial y republicano de Bolivia y paises vecinos*. Contribuciones al estudio del arte rupestre sudamericano no. 3. Sociedad de Investigación del Arte Rupestre de Bolivia, La Paz.

Quirarte, Jacinto
1975   The Wall Paintings of Santa Rita, Corozal. *Belizean Studies* 3(4):5–29.

1982   The Santa Rita Murals: A Review. In *Aspects of the Mixteca-Puebla Style and Mixtec and Central Mexican Culture in Southern Mesoamerica*, ed. Jennifer S.H. Brown and W. Wyllys Andrews V, 43–59. Middle American Research Institute, Occasional Papers 4. Tulane University, New Orleans.

Radcliffe-Brown, Alfred R.
1964   *The Andaman Islanders*. The Free Press, New York.
[1922]

Rappaport, Joanne
1987   Mythic Images, Historical Thought, and Printed Texts: The Páez and the Written Word. *Journal of Anthropological Research* 43(1):43–61.

Rawcliffe, Susan
1992   Complex Acoustics in Pre-Columbian Flute Systems. In *Musical Repercussions of 1492: Encounters in Text and Performance*, ed. Carol E. Robertson, 5–15. Smithsonian Institution Press, Washington, D.C.

Read, Kay A.
1998   *Time and Sacrifice in the Aztec Cosmos*. Indiana University Press, Bloomington, Indiana.

Recinos, Adrian
1972   *Popol Vuh: The Sacred Book of the Ancient Quiche Maya*. Trans. Sylvanus G. Morley. University of Oklahoma Press, Norman.

Recinos, Adrian, and Delia Goetz
1953   *The Annals of the Cakchiquels*. University of Oklahoma Press, Norman.

Reddel, James
1977   *A Preliminary Survey of the Caves of the Yucatan Peninsula*. Speleo Press, Austin.

Redfield, Robert
1989   *The Little Community and Peasant Society and Culture*. University of Chicago Press, Chicago.

Redfield, Robert, and Alfonso Villa Rojas
1962   *Chan Kom: A Maya Village*. University of Chicago Press, Chicago.
[1934]

Reed, Nelson A.
1964   *The Caste War of Yucatan*. Stanford University Press, Stanford, California.
2001   *The Caste War of Yucatan*. Rev. ed. Stanford University Press, Stanford, California.

Reese-Taylor, Kathryn, and Rex Koontz
2001   The Cultural Poetics of Power and Space in Ancient Mesoamerica. In *Landscape and Power in Ancient Mesoamerica*, ed. Rex Koontz, Kathryn Reese-Taylor, and Annabeth Headrick, 1–27. Westview Press, Boulder, Colorado.

Reeves, Brian O.K.
1993   Iniskim: A Sacred Nitsitapii Religious Tradition. In *Kunaitupii: Coming Together on Native Sacred Sites, their Sacredness, Conservation, and Interpretation*, ed.

Brian O.K. Reeves and Margaret A. Kennedy, 194–259. Archaeological Society at Alberta, Calgary.

Renfrew, Colin

1972　*The Emergence of Civilisation: The Cyclades and the Aegean in the Third Millennium B.C.* Methuen, London.

1994　The Archaeology of Religion. In *The Ancient Mind: Elements of Cognitive Archaeology*, ed. Colin Renfrew and Ezra B.W. Zubrow, 47–54. Cambridge University Press, Cambridge.

Restall, Matthew

1997　*The Maya World: Yucatec Culture and Society, 1550–1850.* Stanford University Press, Stanford, California.

1998　*Maya Conquistador.* Beacon Press, Boston.

2001a　The Janus Face of Maya Identity in Post-Conquest Yucatan. In *Maya Survivalism*, ed. Ueli Hostettler and Matthew Restall, 15–23. Acta Mesoamericana 12. Verlag Anton Saurwein, Markt Schwaben.

2001b　The People of the Patio: Ethnohistorical Evidence of Yuactec Maya Royal Courts. In *Royal Courts of the Ancient Maya*, vol. 2: *Data and Case Studies*, ed. Takeshi Inomata and Stephen D. Houston, 335–390. Westview Press, Boulder.

Restall, Matthew, and John F. Chuchiak IV

2002　A Reevaluation of the Authenticity of Fray Diego de Landa's *Relacion de las Cosas de Yucatan. Ethnohistory* 49(3):651–669.

Rice, Don S.

1986　The Petén Postclassic: A Settlement Perspective. In *Late Lowland Maya Civilization: Classic to Postclassic*, ed. Jeremy A. Sabloff and E. Wyllys Andrews V, 310–344. University of New Mexico Press, Albuquerque.

1988　Classic to Postclassic Maya Household Transition in the Central Petén, Guatemala. In *Household and Community in the Mesoamerican Past*, ed. Richard Wilk, 227–248. University of New Mexico Press, Albuquerque.

1989　Historical Contexts and Interpretive Themes. In *Word and Image in Maya Culture*, ed. William F. Hanks and Don S. Rice, 2–7. University of Utah Press, Salt Lake City.

Rice, Don S., Prudence M. Rice, Romulo Sánchez-Polo, and Grant D. Jones

1996　*Proyecto Maya-Colonial: Geografía Política de Siglo XVII en el Centro del Petén, Guatemala.* Informe Preliminary al Instituto de Anthropología e Historia de Guatemala sobre Investigaciones del Campo en los años 1994 y 1995. Museo Nacional de Arqueología y Etnología, Guatemala City.

Rice, Prudence M.

1979　Ceramic and Nonceramic Artifacts of Lakes Yaxhá-Sacnab, El Petén, Guatemala, Part I. *Ceramica de Cultura Maya* 11:1–85.

1982　Pottery Production, Pottery Classification, and the Role of Physiochemical Analyses. In *Archaeological Ceramics*, ed. J. S. Olin and A. D. Franklin, 47–56. Smithsonian Institution Press, Washington, D.C.

REFERENCES CITED

1984   The Ceramics of Negroman-Tipu: A Preliminary Overview. Paper presented at the Northwest Anthropological Association, Hartford, Connecticut.

1985   Postclassic and Historic Pottery from Negroman-Tipuj. Paper Presented at the 50th Annual Meeting of the Society for American Archaeology, Denver, Colorado.

1987   *Macanché Island, El Petén, Guatemala.* University Press of Florida, Gainesville.

1989   Reptiles and Rulership: A Stylistic Analysis of Petén Postclassic Pottery. In *Word and Image in Maya Culture*, ed. William F. Hanks and Don S. Rice, 306–318. University of Utah Press, Salt Lake City.

1999   Rethinking Classic Lowland Maya Pottery Censers. *Ancient Mesoamerica* 10:25–50.

2004   *Maya Political Science: Time, Astronomy, and the Cosmos.* University of Texas Press, Austin.

2007   *Maya Calendar Origins: Monuments, Mythistory, and the Materialization of Time.* University of Texas Press, Austin.

Rice, Prudence M., and Leslie G. Cecil

2009   Iconography of Petén Postclassic Plates and Collared Jars and Its Association with New Year Rituals. In *The Kowoj: Identity, Migration, and Geopolitics in Late Postclassic Petén, Guatemala*, ed. Prudence M. Rice and Don S. Rice, 238–275. University Press of Colorado, Boulder.

Riese, Berthold

1982   Eine mexikanische Gottheit im Venuskapitel der Mayahandschrift Codex Dresdensis. *Société Suisse des Américanistes* 46:37–39.

Ringle, William M.

1988   *Of Mice and Monkeys: The Value and Meaning of T1016: The God C Hieroglyph.* Center for Maya Research, Washington, D.C.

2004   On the Political Organization of Chichen Itza. *Ancient Mesoamerica* 15:167–218.

Ringle, William M., and George J. Bey III

2001   Post-Classic and Terminal Classic Courts of the Northern Maya Lowlands. In *Royal Courts of the Ancient Maya*, vol. 2: *Data and Case Studies*, ed. Takeshi Inomata and Stephen D. Houston, 266–307. Westview Press, Boulder, Colorado.

Ringle, William M., Tomás G. Negrón, and George J. Bey III

1998   The Return of Quetzalcoatl: Evidence for the Spread of a World Religion during the Epiclassic Period. *Ancient Mesoamerica* 9:183–232.

Rissolo, Dominique

2003   *Ancient Maya Cave Use in the Yalahau Region, Northern Quintana Roo, Mexico.* Association for Mexican Cave Studies Bulletin 12. Association for Mexican Cave Studies, Austin, Texas.

2005   Beneath the Yalahau: Emerging Patterns of Ancient Maya Ritual Cave Use from Northern Quintana Roo. In *In the Maw of the Earth Monster,* ed. James Brady and Keith Prufer, 342–372. University of Texas Press, Austin.

Robertson, Donald

1970   The Tulum Murals: The International Style of the Late Post-Classic. In *Verhand-*

lungen del XXXVIII Internationalen Amerikanisten-Kongres, Stuttgart-München, 1968, vol. 2, 77–88. Kommissionsverlag Klaus Renner, Munich.

Robicsek, Francis, and Donald M. Hales
1981   *The Maya Book of the Dead: The Ceramic Codex*. University of Virginia Art Museum, Charlottesville.

Rodríguez-Alegría, Enrique
2005   Consumption and the Varied Ideologies of Domination in Colonial Mexico City. In *The Postclassic to Spanish-Era Transition in Mesoamerica*, ed. Susan Kepecs and Rani Alexander, 35–48. University of New Mexico Press, Albuquerque.

Rodriguez Rouanet, Francisco
1992   *Danzas folkloricas de Guatemala*. Colección Tierra Adentro 15. Subcentro Regional de Artesianias y Artes Populares, Guatemala.

Rogers, J. Daniel
1990   *Objects of Change: The Archaeology and History of Arikara Contact with Europeans*. Smithsonian Institution Press, Washington, D.C.

Rosado Iturralde, Gonzálo de Jesus
1949   *Breve Historia de Cozumel*. Club del Libro, Linotipografica Peninsular, Mérida, Yucatán.

Rosny, Léon de
1888   *Codex Peresianus: Manuscrit hiératique des anciens Indiens de l'Amérique Central, conservé à la Bibliothèque nationale de Paris*. Bureau de la Société Américaine, Paris.

Roth, Cecil
1996   *The Spanish Inquisition*. W. W. Norton, New York.

Rowe, Marvin
2001   Dating by AMS Radiocarbon Analysis. In *Handbook of Rock Art Research*, ed. David S. Whitley, 139–166. Altamira Press, Walnut Creek, California.
2004   Radiocarbon Dating of Ancient Pictograms with Accelerator Mass Spectrometry. *Rock Art Research* 21(2):145–154.

Roys, Ralph L.
1933   *The Book of Chilam Balam of Chumayel*. Carnegie Institution of Washington, Publication 438, Washington, D.C.
1935   Place Names of Yucatan. *Maya Research* 2:1–10
1943   *The Indian Background of Colonial Yucatan*. Carnegie Institution of Washington. Publication 548, Washington, D.C.
1949   *Guide to the Codex Perez*. Contributions to American Anthropology and History, no. 49. Carnegie Institution of Washington, Publication 585, Washington, D.C.
1952   *Conquest Sites and the Subsequent Destruction of Maya Architecture in the Interior of Northern Yucatan*. Carnegie Institution of Washington, Washington, D.C.

1954   *The Maya Katun Prophecies of the Books of Chilam Balam, Series I.* Contributions to American Anthropology and History, no. 57. Carnegie Institution of Washington, Publication 606, Washington, D.C.

1957   *The Political Geography of the Yucatan Maya.* Carnegie Institution of Washington, Publication 613, Washington, D.C.

1962   Literary Sources for the History of Mayapan. In *Mayapan, Yucatan, Mexico,* ed. Harry Pollock, Ralph L. Roys, Tatiana Proskouriakoff, and A. Ledyard Smith, 25–86. Carnegie Institution of Washington, Publication 619, Washington, D.C.

1967   (translated and annotated) *The Book of Chilam Balam of Chumayel.* University of Oklahoma Press, Norman.

1972   *The Indian Background of Colonial Yucatan.* University of Oklahoma Press, Norman.

Roys, Ralph L., France V. Scholes, and Eleanor B. Adams
1940   *Report and Census of the Indians of Cozumel 1570.* Carnegie Institution of Washington Publication No. 523, Contribution 30, Washington, D.C.

Rugeley, Terry
1996   *Yucatán's Maya Peasantry and the Origins of the Caste War.* University of Texas Press, Austin.

2001   *Maya Wars: Ethnographic Accounts from Nineteenth-Century Yucatán.* University of Oklahoma Press, Norman.

Ruppert, Karl, and A. L. Smith
1954   Excavations in House Mounds at Mayapan. *Current Reports of the Carnegie Institution of Washington, Department of Anthropology, 1952–1954* 1(1):45–67.

Russell, Bradley
2000   Postclassic Pottery Censers in the Maya Lowlands: A Study of Form, Function, and Symbolism. Master's thesis, Department of Anthropology, State University of New York, Albany.

Sabom-Bruchez, Margaret
1994a   Preliminary Findings. Initial Surveys Conducted on the Northern Rim of Lake Atitlán, Department of Sololá, Guatemala, C.A. Paper presented at 59th Annual Meeting, Society for American Archaeology, Anaheim, California.

1994b   Primer Informe del Proyecto de Arqueología de Sololá. VIII Simposio de Arqueología Guatemalteca. Guatemala City.

1995a   Excavations, Underwater Reconnaissance, and Paleoenvironmental Surveys, Northern Rim Lake Atitlán, Guatemala: Results of 1994 Field Season. Paper presented at 60th Annual Meeting of the Society for American Archaeology, Minneapolis, Minnesota.

1995b   Informe del Proyecto de Arqueología de Sololá. IX Simposio de Arqueología Guatemalteca. Guatemala City.

Sachs, Curt
1937   *World History of the Dance.* W. W. Norton, New York.

Sachse, Frauke (editor)

2006   *Maya Ethnicity: The Construction of Ethnic Identity from Preclassic to Modern Times*. Acta Mesoamerica, vol. 19. Verlag Anton Saurwein, Markt Schwaben, Germany.

Sahagún, Fray Bernardino de

1932   *A History of Mexico*. Trans. F. R. Bandelier I. Fisk University Press, Nashville, Tennessee.

1950–   *Florentine Codex: General History of the Things of New Spain*, 13 vols. Ed. Arthur
1982   J.O. Anderson and Charles E. Dibble. University of Utah Press, Salt Lake City.

1953   *Book 7—The Sun, Moon, and Stars, and the Binding of the Years*. Monograph 14, pt. 8 of *The Florentine Codex: General History of the Things of New Spain*, trans. and annot. by Arthur J.O. Anderson and Charles E. Dibble. Monographs of the School of American Research, Santa Fe, New Mexico.

1980   The Aztec-Spanish Dialogues of 1524. Ed. and trans. J. Jorge Klor de Alva. *Alche-*
[1564] *ringa: Ethnopoetics* 4:52–193.

Saliba, John A.

1976   *"Homo Religiosus" in Mircea Eliade*. E. J. Brill, Leiden.

Sánchez de Aguilar, Pedro

1937   *Informe contra idolorum cultores del obispado de Yucatán*. Editorial G. Triay e Hijos, Mérida.

Sanders, William T.

1960   *Prehistoric Ceramics and Settlement Patterns in Quintana Roo, Mexico*. Contributions to American Anthropology and History 12(60). Carnegie Institution of Washington, Publication 606. Washington, D.C.

Sandstrom, Alan R.

1991   *Corn Is Our Blood: Culture and Ethnic Identity in a Contemporary Aztec Indian Village*. University of Oklahoma Press, Norman.

Satterthwaite, Linton

1958   The Problem of Abnormal Stela Placements at Tikal and Elsewhere, Tikal Report No. 3. In *Tikal Reports, Numbers 1–4*, 62–83. The University Museum, Philadelphia.

Sayther, Terry, Deborah Stuart, and Allan Cobb

1998   Pictographic Rock Art in Actun Kaua, Yucatan, Mexico. *American Indian Rock Art* 22:95–102.

Scarre, Chris

1994   The Meaning of Death: Funerary Beliefs and the Prehistorian. In *The Ancient Mind: Elements of Cognitive Archaeology*, ed. Colin Renfrew and Ezra B.W. Zubrow, 75–82. Cambridge University Press, Cambridge.

Schaafsma, Polly

1980   *Indian Rock Art of the Southwest*. School of American Research, Santa Fe, New Mexico.

1999   Tlalocs, Kachinas, Sacred Bundles, and Related Symbolism in the Southwest and

Mesoamerica. In *The Casas Grandes World*, ed. Curtis F. Schaafsma and Carroll L. Riley, 164–192. University of Utah Press, Salt Lake City.

Schaefer, Stacy B., and Peter T. Furst
1996   Introduction. In *People of the Peyote: Huichol Indian History, Religion, and Survival*, ed. Stacy B. Schaefer and Peter T. Furst, 1–25. University of New Mexico Press, Albuquerque.

Schele, Linda
1976   Accession Iconography of Chan-Bahlum in the Group of the Cross at Palenque. In *The Art, Iconography and Dynastic History of Palenque, Part III*, ed. Merle Greene Robertson, 9–34. Robert Louis Stevenson School, Pre-Columbian Art Research, Pebble Beach, California.
1984   Human Sacrifice among the Classic Maya. In *Ritual Human Sacrifice in Mesoamerica*, ed. Elizabeth H. Boone, 7–48. Dumbarton Oaks, Washington, D.C.
1989   A Brief Note on the Name of a Vision Serpent. In *The Maya Vase Book: Volume 1*, ed. Justin Kerr, 146–148. Kerr Associates, New York.
1992   *Notebook for the XVIth Maya Hieroglyph Workshop*. Department of Art and Art History, University of Texas at Austin.
2002   Creation and the *Ritual of the Bacabs*. In *Heart of Creation: The Mesoamerican World and the Legacy of Linda Schele*, ed. Andrea Stone, 21–33. University of Alabama Press, Tuscaloosa.

Schele, Linda, and David A. Freidel
1990   *A Forest of Kings: The Untold Story of the Ancient Maya*. William Morrow, New York.

Schele, Linda, and Nikolai Grube
1995   *The Proceedings of the Maya Hieroglyphic Workshop: Late Classic and Terminal Classic Warfare, March 11–12, 1995*. Transcribed and ed. Phil Wanyerka. Schele and Grube, Austin, Texas.

Schele, Linda, Nikolai Grube, and Erik Boot
1998   Some Suggestions on the K'atun Prophecies in the Books of Chilam Balam in Light of Classic-period History. In *Memorias del Tercer Congreso Internacional de Mayistas (9–15 de Julio, 1995)*, 399–446. Universidad Autonoma de México, Centro de Estudios Maya, México.

Schele, Linda, and Peter Mathews
1998   *The Code of Kings: The Language of Seven Sacred Maya Temples and Tombs*. Scribner's, New York.

Schele, Linda, and Mary E. Miller
1986   *The Blood of Kings: Dynasty and Ritual in Maya Art*. George Braziller, New York.

Schellhas, Paul
1904   *Representations of Deities of the Maya Manuscripts*. Harvard University Press, Cambridge.

Schevill, Margot
1985   *Evolution in Textile Design from the Highlands of Guatemala*. Occassional Papers 1. Lowie Museum of Anthropology, University of California, Berkeley.

Scholes, France V.
1935   The First Decade of the Inquisition in New Mexico. *New Mexico Historical Review* 10:195–234.

Scholes, France V., and Eleanor B. Adams
1938   *Don Diego Quijada, Alcalde Mayor de Yuacatan 1561–1565*. Editorial Porrúa, México.
1991   *Documents Relating to the Mirones Expedition to the Interior of Yucatan, 1621–1624*. Labyrinthos, Culver City, California.

Scholes, France V., and Ralph Roys
1938   Fray Diego de Landa and the Problem of Idolatry in Yucatan. In *Cooperation in Research*, 585–620. Carnegie Institution, Washington, D.C.
1968   *The Maya Chontal Indians of Acalan-Tixchel: A Contribution to the History and Ethnography of the Yucatan Peninsula*. University of Oklahoma Press, Norman.

Scholes, France V., and Eric Thompson
1977   The Francisco Peréz Probanza of 1654–1656 and the Matrícula of Tipu (Belize). In *Anthropology and History in Yucatán*, ed. Grant D. Jones, 43–68. University of Texas Press, Austin.

Schuman, Otto
1964   El Origen del Mundo: Un Cuento Maya-Itza. *Tlalocan* 4(4):351–352.

Schutz, Alfred
1964   *Collected Papers II: Studies in Social Theory*. Ed. Arvid Brodersen. Martinus Nijhoff, The Hague.

Schwartz, Norman B.
1990   *Forest Society: A Social History of Peten, Guatemala*. University of Pennsylvania Press, Philadelphia.

Séjourné, Laurette
1966   *El lenguaje de las formas en Teotihuacán*. Siglo XXI, México.

Seler, Eduard
1898   Die Venusperiode in den Bilderschriften der Codex Borgia-Gruppe. *Zeitschrift für Ethnologie* 30:346–383.

Serra Puche, Mari Carmen
2001   The Concept of Feminine Places in Mesoamerica: The Case of Xochitecatl, Tlaxcala, Mexico. In *Gender in Pre-Hispanic America*, ed. Cecelia F. Klein, 255–283. Dumbarton Oaks, Washington, D.C.

Shanks, Michael, and Christopher Tilley
1987   *Social Theory and Archaeology*. Polity Press, Oxford.

REFERENCES CITED

Sharer, Robert J.
1994   *The Ancient Maya*, 5th ed. Stanford University Press, Stanford, California.
2006   *The Ancient Maya*, 6th ed. Stanford University Press, Stanford, California.

Sharer, Robert J., and Wendy Ashmore
1987   *Archaeology: Discovering Our Past*. Mayfield Publishing, Palo Alto, California.

Sharer, Robert J., and Loa Traxler
2003   Las tumbas reales mas tempranas de Copan: Muerte y renacimiento en un reino maya clasico. In *Antropología de la Eternidad: La Muerte en la Cultura Maya*, ed. Andrés Ciudad Ruiz, Mario Humberto Ruz Sosa, and María Josefa Iglesias Ponce de Leon, 145–159. Publicación 7, Sociedad de los Estudios Mayas, Madrid.

Shaw, Justine
2001   Maya Sacbeob: Form and Function. *Ancient Mesoamerica* 12:261–272.

Shook, Edwin M.
1954a   The Temple of Kukulkan at Mayapán. *Current Reports* No. 20, 89–108. Carnegie Institution of Washington, Washington, D.C.
1954b   Three Temples and Their Associated Structures at Mayapán. *Current Reports* No. 14, 254–291. Carnegie Institution of Washington, Washington, D.C.

Shook, Edwin M., and William N. Irving
1955   Colonnaded Buildings at Mayapán. *Current Reports* No. 22, 127–167. Carnegie Institution of Washington, Washington, D.C.

Sidrys, Raymond V.
1983   *Archaeological Excavations in Northern Belize, Central America*. Institute of Archaeology, Monograph 17, University of California, Los Angeles.

Silverblatt, Irene
1988   Political Memories and Colonizing Symbols: Santiago and the Mountain Gods of Peru. In *Rethinking History and Myth: Indigenous South American Perspectives on the Past*, ed. Jonathan D. Hill, 174–194. University of Illinois Press, Chicago.

Silverman, Lisa
2001   *Tortured Subjects: Pain, Truth, and the Body in Early Modern France*. University of Chicago Press, Chicago.

Smart, Ninian
1995   *Worldviews, Crosscultural Explorations of Human Beliefs*. Prentice Hall, Englewood Cliffs, New Jersey.

Smith, A. Ledyard
1934   Two Recent Ceramic Finds at Uaxactun. In *Contributions to American Archaeology Volume II, No. 5,* 1–25. Publication 436, Carnegie Institution of Washington, Washington, D.C.
1962   Residential and Associated Structures at Mayapán. In *Mayapán Yucatán México*, ed. Harry Pollock, Ralph L. Roys, Tatiana Proskouriakoff, and A. Ledyard Smith, 166–277. Carnegie Institution of Washington, Washington, D.C.

Smith, A. Leyard, and Alfred V. Kidder
  1943   *Explorations in the Motagua Valley, Guatemala.* Contributions to American An-
         thropology and History, no. 41, Carnegie Institution, Washington, D.C.

Smith, Angéle
  2003   Landscape Representations: Place and Identity in Nineteenth-Century Ord-
         nance Survey Maps in Ireland. In *Landscape, Memory and History*, ed. Pamela
         Stewart and Andrew Strathern, 71–88. Pluto Press, London.

Smith, Anthony D.
  1992   Chosen Peoples: Why Ethnic Groups Survive. *Ethnic and Racial Studies* 15(3):
         436–456.

Smith, Jonathan Z.
  1987   *To Take Place: Toward Theory in Ritual.* University of Chicago Press, Chicago.

Smith, Michael E.
  1986   The Role of Social Stratification in the Aztec Empire: A View from the Prov-
         inces. *American Anthropologist* 88:70–91.

Smith, Michael E., and Frances F. Berdan
  2003a Postclassic Mesoamerica. In *The Postclassic Mesoamerican World*, ed. Michael E.
         Smith and Francis F. Berdan, 3–13. University of Utah Press, Salt Lake City.
  2003b (editors) *The Postclassic Mesoamerican World.* University of Utah Press, Salt Lake
         City.

Smith, Michael E., and Cynthia M. Heath-Smith
  1980   Waves of Influence in Postclassic Mesoamerica: A Critique of the Mixteca-Pueb-
         la Concept. *Anthropology* 4(2):18–50.

Smith, Robert E.
  1971   *The Pottery of Mayapan, Including Studies of Ceramic Material from Uxmal,
         Kabah, and Chichen Itza.* Papers of the Peabody Museum of Archaeology and
         Ethnology, Harvard University, vol. 66. Peabody Museum of Archaeology and
         Ethnology, Harvard University, Cambridge.

Smith, Robert E., Gordon R. Willey, and James C. Gifford
  1960   The Type-Variety Concept as a Basis for the Analysis of Maya Pottery. *American
         Antiquity* 25(3):330–340.

Sosa, John R.
  1985   The Maya Sky, the Maya World: A Symbolic Analysis of Yucatec Maya Cosmol-
         ogy. Ph.D. dissertation, Department of Anthropology, State University of New
         York, Albany.
  1986   Maya Concepts of Astronomical Order. In *Symbol and Meaning beyond the
         Closed Community: Essays in Mesoamerican Ideas*, ed. Gary H. Gossen, 185–196.
         Institute for Mesoamerican Studies, Studies on Culture and Society, vol. 1. State
         University of New York, Albany.
  1990   Cosmological, Symbolic and Cultural Complexity among the Contemporary
         Maya of Yucatan. In *World Archaeostronomy: Selected Papers from the 2nd Oxford*

International Conference on Archaeostronomy, ed. Anthony F. Aveni, 130–142. Cambridge University Press, Cambridge.

Soukhanov, Anne H. (editor)
1992 *The American Heritage Dictionary of the English Language*. 3rd ed. Houghton Mifflin, Boston.

Soustelle, Georgette
1961 Observaciones sobre la Religion de los Lacandones del Sur de Mexico. *Guatemala Indigena* 1(1):31–105.

Soustelle, Jacques
1935 Les idees religieuses des Lacandons. *La Terre et la Vie* 4:170–178.
1937 La culture matérielle des Indiens Lacandons. *Journal de la Societé des Américanistes* 29(1):1–95.
1970 *The Four Suns*. Grossman Publishers, New York.

Spicer, Edward H.
1980 *The Yaquis: A Cultural History*. University of Arizona Press, Tucson.

Spiro, Melford E.
1971 Religion: Problems of Definition and Explanation. In *Anthropological Approaches to the Study of Religion*, ed. Michael Banton, 85–126. Tavistock, London.

Stanzione, Vincent J.
2003 *Rituals of Sacrifice: Walking the Face of the Earth on the Sacred Path of the Sun; A Journey through the Tz'utujil Maya World of Santiago Atitlán*. University of New Mexico Press, Albuquerque.

Stenzel, Werner
1972 The Sacred Bundles in Mesoamerican Religion. *Actas del XXXVIII Congreso Internacional de Americanistas* 2:347–352.

Stephens, John L.
1969   *Incidents of Travel in Central America, Chiapas and Yucatan*. Dover Publications,
[1854] New York.

Stevenson, Robert
1968 *Music in Aztec and Inca Territory*. University of California Press, Berkeley.
2001a Maya Music. Part 1. In *The New Grove Dictionary of Music and Musicians*, ed. Stanley Sadie, 168–170. MacMillan, New York.
2001b Music. In *The Oxford Encyclopedia of Mesoamerican Cultures*, ed. Davíd Carrasco, 356–358. Oxford University Press, New York.

Stewart, Charles, and Rosalind Shaw
1994 *Syncretism/Anti-Syncretism: The Politics of Religious Synthesis*. Routledge, New York.

Stewart, Pamela J., and Andrew Strathern
2003 Introduction. In *Landscape, Memory and History*, ed. Pamela Stewart and Andrew Strathern, 1–15. Pluto Press, London.

Stone, Andrea

1988   Sacrifice and Sexuality: Some Structural Relationships in Classic Maya Art. In *The Role of Gender in PreColumbian Art and Architecture*, ed. Virginia E. Miller, 75–103. University Press of America, Lanham, Maryland.

1989   Disconnection, Foreign Insignia, and Political Expansion: Teotihuacan and the Warrior Stelae of Piedras Negras. In *Mesoamerica after the Decline of Teotihihuacan, A.D. 700–900*, ed. Richard A. Diehl and Janet C. Berlo, 153–172. Dumbarton Oaks, Washington, D.C.

1995   *Images from the Underworld: Naj Tunich and the Tradition of Maya Cave Painting*. University of Texas Press, Austin.

2003   The Double-Headed Eagle: From Ancient Rome to the Caves of Yucatan. Paper presented at the Annual Meeting of the American Anthropological Association, Chicago.

Strathern, Andrew, and Pamela J. Stewart

2003   Epilogue. In *Landscape, Memory and History*, ed. Pamela Stewart and Andrew Strathern, 229–236. Pluto Press, London.

Strecker, Matthias, and Martin Künne

2003   Bibliografía anotada. In *Arte rupestre de México oriental y Centro América*, ed. Martin Künne and Matthias Strecker, 241–346. Indiana Supplement 16, Berlin.

Strecker, Matthias, and Andrea Stone

2003   Arte rupestre de Yucatán y Campeche. In *Arte rupestre de México oriental y Centro América*, ed. Martin Künne and Matthias Strecker, 53–78. Gebr under Mann Verlag, Berlin.

Stresser-Péan, Guy

1990   Pinturas rupestres del Risco de los Monos, situación del acantilado, San Antonio, Nogalar. In *El arte rupestre en México*, ed. Maria Pilar Casado López and Lorena Mirambell, 587–599. INAH, México.

Stross, Brian

1998   Seven Ingredients in Mesoamerican Ensoulment: Dedication and Termination in Tenejapa. In *The Sowing and the Dawning: Termination, Dedication, and Transformation in the Archaeological and Ethnographic Record of Mesoamerica*, ed. Shirley B. Mock, 31–39. University of New Mexico Press, Albuquerque.

Stuart, David

1996   Kings of Stone: A Consideration of Stelae in Ancient Maya Ritual and Representation. *RES* 29/30:148–171.

2005   *The Inscriptions from Temple XIX at Palenque*. The Pre-Columbian Art Research Institute, San Francisco.

Sugiyama, Saburo

1993   Worldview Materialized in Teotihuacan, Mexico. *Latin American Antiquity* 4(2): 103–129.

REFERENCES CITED

Sullivan, Paul R.
  1989   *Unfinished Conversations: Mayas and Foreigners between Two Wars*. Knopf, New York.

Sundstrom, Linnea
  2004   *Storied Stone: Indian Rock Art of the Black Hills Country*. University of Oklahoma Press, Norman.

Taboada Téllez, Freddy
  1992   El arte rupestre indígena de Chiripaca, Depto. de La Paz, Bolivia. In *Arte rupestre colonial y republicano de Bolivia y paises vecinos*, ed. R. Querejazu Lewis, 111–167. Sociedad de Investigación del Arte Rupestre de Bolivia, La Paz.

Tarn, Nathaniel
  1998   *Scandals in the House of Birds: Shamans and Priests on Lake Atitlán*. Marsilio Publishers, New York.

Taschek, Jennifer T., and Joseph W. Ball
  1999   Las Ruinas de Arenal: Preliminary Report on a Subregional Major Center in the Western Belize Valley (1991–1992 Excavations). *Ancient Mesoamerica* 10(2): 215–236.

Tate, Carolyn E.
  1992   *Yaxchilan: The Design of a Maya Ceremonial City*. University of Texas Press, Austin.

Taube, Karl A.
  1985   The Classic Maya Maize God: A Reappraisal. In *Fifth Palenque Round Table, 1983*, ed. Merle Green Robertson and Virginia M. Fields, 171–181. The Pre-Columbian Art Research Institute, San Francisco.
  1987   A Representation of the Principal Bird Deity in the Paris Codex. *Research Reports on Ancient Maya Writing* 6, 1–10.
  1988a   The Ancient Yucatec New Year Festival: The Liminal Period in Maya Ritual and Cosmology. Ph.D. dissertation, Department of Anthropology, Yale University, New Haven, Connecticut.
  1988b   A Prehispanic Maya Katun Wheel. *Journal of Anthropological Research* 44(2): 183–203.
  1989   Ritual Humor in Classic Maya Religion. In *Word and Image in Maya Culture: Explorations in Language, Writing, and Represenations*, ed. William F. Hanks and Don S. Rice, 351–382. University of Utah Press, Salt Lake City.
  1992   *The Major Gods of Ancient Yucatan*. Studies in Pre-Columbian Art and Archaeology, no. 32. Dumbarton Oaks, Washington, D.C.
  1993   *Aztec and Maya Myths*. British Museum Press, London, and University of Texas Press, Austin.
  2001   The Breath of Life: The Symbolism of Wind in Mesoamerica and the American Southwest. In *Road to Aztlan: Art from a Mythic Homeland*, ed. Virginia M. Fields and Victor Zamudio-Taylor, 102–123. LACMA, Los Angeles.
  2006   Climbing Flower Mountain: Concepts of Resurrection and the Afterlife at Teotihuacan. In *Arqueologia e Historia del Centro de Mexico: Homenaje a Eduardo*

Matos Moctezuma, ed. Leonardo López Luján, Davíd Carrasco, and Lourdes Cué, 153–170. Instituto Nacional de Antropologia e Historia, Conaculta, México.

2007   At Dawn's Edge: Tulum, Santa Rita and Floral Symbolism in the International Style of Late Postclassic Mesoamerica. Paper presented at Astronomers, Scribes, and Priests: Intellectual Interchange between the Northern Maya Lowlands and Highland Mexico in the Late Postclassic Period, Washington, D.C.

Taube, Karl A., and Bonnie L. Bade
1991   An Appearance of Xiuhtecuhtli in the Dresden Venus Pages. In *Research Reports on Ancient Maya Writing* 35. Center for Maya Research, Washington, D.C.

Taylor, Scott
1999   The Passage of Time: Highland Mayan World-Views and the "Dance of the Conquest." M.M. Thesis, Music Department, University of Texas at Austin, Austin.

Tedlock, Barbara
1992   *Time and the Highland Maya*. Rev. ed. University of New Mexico Press, Albuquerque.

Tedlock, Dennis
1982   *Time and the Highland Maya*. University of New Mexico Press, Albuquerque.
1985   *Popol Vuh: The Definitive Edition of the Mayan Book of the Dawn of Life and the Glories of Gods and Kings*. Simon and Schuster, New York.
1987   (translator) *Popol Vuh: The Mayan Book of the Dawn of Life*. Touchstone, New York.
1993   (translator) Torture in the Archives: Mayans Meet Europeans. *American Anthropologist* 95:139–152.
2003   (translator) *Rabinal Achi: A Mayan Drama of War and Sacrifice*. Oxford University Press, New York.

Teeter, Wendy G., and Arlen F. Chase
2004   Adding Flesh to Bones: Using Zooarchaeology Research to Answer Big-Picture Questions. *Archaeofauna* 13:155–172.

Thomas, Cyrus
1884   Notes on Certain Maya and Mexican Manuscripts. In *Third Annual Report of the Bureau of American Ethnology, 1881–82*, 7–65. Bureau of American Ethnology, Smithsonian Institution, Washington, D.C.

Thomas, Julian
2007   Archaeology's Humanism and the Materiality of the Body. In *The Archaeology of Identities*, ed. Timothy Insoll, 211–224. Routledge, New York.

Thompson, J. Eric S.
1930   *Ethnology of the Mayas of Southern and Central British Honduras*. Field Museum of Natural History, Chicago.
1934   *Sky Bearers, Colors, and Directions in Maya and Mexican Religion*. Contributions to American Archaeology, vol. 2, no. 10. Carnegie Institution of Washington, Publication 436. Washington, D.C.

1950 *Maya Hieroglyphic Writing: An Introduction.* Carnegie Institution of Washington, Publication 589. Carnegie Institution of Washington, Washington, D.C.

1954 *The Rise and Fall of Maya Civilization.* University of Oklahoma Press, Norman.

1957a Deities Portrayed on Censers at Mayapan. *Current Reports* No. 40, 599–632. Carnegie Institution of Washington, Washington, D.C.

1957b A Presumed Residence of the Nobility at Mayapan. *Current Reports* No. 2, 71–89. Carnegie Institution of Washington, Washington, D.C.

1960 *Maya Hieroglyphic Writing: An Introduction.* University of Oklahoma Press, Norman.

1970 *Maya History and Religion.* University of Oklahoma Press, Norman.

1971 *Maya Hieroglyphic Writing: An Introduction.* 3rd ed. University of Oklahoma Press, Norman.

1972 *A Commentary on the Dresden Codex: A Maya Hieroglyphic Book.* American Philosophical Society, Philadelphia.

1975 Introduction to the reprint edition of Henry Mercer. In *The Hill Caves of Yucatan.* University of Oklahoma Press, Norman.

1977 A Proposal for Constituting a Maya Subgroup, Cultural and Linguistic in the Petén and Adjacent Regions. In *Anthropology and History in Yucatan*, ed. Grant D. Jones, 3–42. University of Texas Press, Austin.

1980 Analysis of Decadent Period Painted Medallions in the Temple of the Seven Dolls. In *Excavations at Dzibilchaltun, Yucatan, Mexico*, ed. E. Wyllys Andrews IV and E. Wyllys Andrews V, 116–117. Middle American Research Institute, New Orleans.

1990 *Maya History and Religion.* University of Oklahoma Press, Norman.

1997 *Historía y religion de los mayas.* Siglo XXI Editores, México.

Thompson, Philip C.
1999 *Tekanto, a Maya Town in Colonial Yucatán.* Middle American Research Institute, Publication 67. Tulane University, New Orleans.

Tilley, Christopher Y.
1999 *Metaphor and Material Culture: Social Archaeology.* Blackwell, Oxford.

Tozzer, Alfred M.
1907 *A Comparative Study of the Mayas and the Lacandones.* Archaeological Institute of America, Report of the Fellow in American Archaeology, 1902–1905. Macmillan, New York.

1941 *Landa's Relación de las Cosas de Yucatan.* Papers of the Peabody Museum of American Archaeology and Ethnology, vol. 18, Harvard University Press, Cambridge.

Trigger, Bruce G.
2003 *Understanding Early Civilizations: A Comparative Study.* Cambridge University Press, Cambridge, Massachusetts.

Turner, Victor
1969 *The Ritual Process: Structure and Anti-Structure.* Aldine, Chicago.

1973 The Center out There: Pilgrim's Goal. *History of Religions* 12:191–230.

1974   *Dramas, Fields, and Metaphors: Symbolic Action in Human Society*. Cornell University Press, Ithaca.

Tylor, Edward B.
1903   *Primitive Culture: Researches into the Development of Mythology, Philosophy, Re-*
[1871] *ligion, Language, Art, and Custom*, 2 vols. John Murray, London.

Uc González, Eunice
1999   El Puuc en Yucatán. In *Cenotes y grutas de Yucatán*, ed. Luis Armando Ruíz Sosa, 132–141. Secretaría de Ecología del Estado de Yucatán, Mérida.

Upton, Dell
1996   Ethnicity, Authenticity, and Invented Traditions. *Historical Archaeology* 30(2):1–7.

Vail, Gabrielle
1996   The Gods in the Madrid Codex: An Iconographic and Glyphic Analysis. Ph.D. dissertation, Department of Anthropology, Tulane University, New Orleans.
2000   Pre-Hispanic Maya Religion: Conceptions of Divinity in the Postclassic Maya Codices. *Ancient Mesoamerica* 11:123–147.
2004   A Reinterpretation of *Tzolk'in* Almanacs in the Madrid Codex. In *The Madrid Codex: New Approaches to Understanding an Ancient Maya Manuscript*, ed. Gabrille Vail and Anthony F. Aveni, 215–252. University Press of Colorado, Boulder.
2005   Renewal Ceremonies in the Madrid Codex. In *Painted Books and Indigenous Knowledge in Mesoamerica: Manuscript Studies in Honor of Mary Elizabeth Smith*, ed. Elizabeth Hill Boone, 179–209. Middle American Research Institute, Publication 69. Tulane University, New Orleans.
2006   The Maya Codices. *Annual Review for Anthropology* 35:497–519.
2008   Cosmos and Creation among the Late Postclassic Maya. Paper prepared for the electronic symposium Celestial References in Mesoamerican Creation Stories for the 73rd Annual Meeting of the Society for American Archaeology, Vancouver.
2009   Serpents and Stones of Foundation in the Maya Codices. Submitted for publication in *Glyph Dwellers*, an online journal of the Department of Native American Studies, University of California–Davis.

Vail, Gabrielle, and Anthony Aveni
2004a   (editors) *The Madrid Codex: New Approaches to Understanding an Ancient Maya Manuscript*. University Press of Colorado, Boulder.
2004b   Research Methodologies and New Approaches to Interpreting the Madrid Codex. In *The Madrid Codex: New Approaches to Understanding and Ancient Maya Manuscript*, ed. Gabrielle Vail and Anthony Aveni, 1–32. University Press of Colorado, Boulder.

Vail, Gabrielle, and Victoria R. Bricker (compilers), Anthony F. Aveni, Harvey M. Bricker, John F. Chuchiak, Christine L. Hernández, Bryan R. Just, Martha J. Macri, and Merideth Paxton
2003   New Perspectives on the Madrid Codex. *Current Anthropology* 44(5):S105–S112.

REFERENCES CITED

Vail, Gabrielle, and Christine M. Hernández
2006   Fire Drilling, Bloodletting, and Sacrifice: Yearbearer Rituals in the Maya and Borgia Group Codices. In *Sacred Books, Sacred Languages: Two Thousand Years of Ritual and Religious Maya Literature, 8th European Maya Conference, Museo de América, Madrid, November 2003*, ed. Rogelio Valencia and Geneviève Le Fort, 65–79. Verlag Anton Saurwein, Markt Schwaben, Germany.
2009a   (editors) *Astronomers, Scribes, and Priests: Intellectual Interchange between the Northern Maya Lowlands and Highland Mexico during the Late Postclassic Period*. Dumbarton Oaks, Washington, D.C., in press.
2009b   Construction of Memory: The Use of Late Classic Divinatory Texts in a Late Postclassic Maya Codex. Submitted to Special Section of *Ancient Mesoamerica, Memory and Social Construct in Ancient Mesoamerica*, ed. Travis Stanton, in press
2009c   Cords and Crocodilians: Creation Mythology in Late Postclassic Maya Iconography and Texts. Submitted for publication in the *Proceedings of the 12th European Maya Conference, Geneva, Switzerland, 3–8 Dececmber 2007*, ed. Geneviève Le Fort, Raphaël Gardiol, and Sebastian Matteo. Verlag Anton Saurwein, Markt Schwaben, Germany, in press.

Vaillant, George C.
1940   Patterns in Middle American Archaeology. In *The Maya and Their Neighbors*, ed. Clarence L. Hay, 295–305. D. Appleton-Century, New York.

Van de Guchte, Maarten
1999   The Inca Cognition of Landscape. In *Archaeologies of Landscape*, ed. Wendy Ashmore and A. Bernard Knapp, 149–168. Blackwell, Oxford.

Van Gennep, Arnold
1960   *The Rites of Passage*. Trans. Monika Vizedom and Solon T. Kimball. University of Chicago Press, Chicago.

Velásquez Morlet, Adriana, Maria del Pilar Casado Lopez, and Edmundo Lopez de la Rosa
1988   *Zonas Arqueologicas, Yucatan*. Instituto Nacional de Anthropologia y Historia, México City.

Villacorta, Carlos A., and J. Antonio Villacorta
1976   *Códices mayas*. 2nd ed. Tipographia Nacional, Guatemala.

Villagutierre Soto-Mayor, Juan de
1983   *History of the Conquest of the Province of the Itza: Subjugation and Events of the Lacandon and Other Nations of Uncivilized Indians in the Lands from the Kingdom of Guatemala to the Provinces of Yucatan in North America*. Trans. Robert D. Wood and ed. Frank E. Comparato. Labyrinthos, Culver City, California.

Villa Rojas, Alfonso
1945   *The Maya of East Central Quintana Roo*. Carnegie Institution of Washington, Publication 559. Washington, D.C.
1978   *Los elegidos de Dios: Etnografía de los mayas de Quintana Roo*. Instituto Nacional Indigenista, México.

1985   *Estudios Etnológicos: Los Mayas*. Universidad Nacional Autónoma de México, México City.

1988   Appendix A: The Concepts of Space and Time among the Contemporary Maya. In *Time and Reality in the Thought of the Maya*, ed. Miguel León-Portilla, 113–159. University of Oklahoma Press, Norman.

1995   *Estudios Etnologicos: Los Mayas*. Universidad Nacional Autonoma de México, México.

Vogt, Evon Z.

1969   *Zinacantán: A Maya Community in the Highlands of Chiapas*. Harvard University Press, Cambridge, Massachusetts.

1993   *Tortillas for the Gods: A Symbolic Analysis of Zinacanteco Rituals*. Harvard Uni-
[1976] versity Press, Cambridge, Massachusetts.

1998   Zinacanteco Dedication and Termination Rituals. In *Sowing and the Dawning*, ed. Shirley B. Mock, 21–30. University of New Mexico Press, Albuquerque.

Vogt, Evon Z., and David Stuart

2005   Some Notes on Caves among the Ancient and Modern Maya. In *In the Maw of the Earth Monster*, ed. James Brady and Keith Prufer, 155–185. University of Texas Press, Austin.

Von Winning, Hasso

1977   Rituals Depicted on Polychrome Ceramics from Nayarit. In *Pre-Columbian Art History: Selected Readings*, ed. Alana Cordy-Collins and Jean Seren, 121–134. Peek Publications, Palo Alto, California.

Walker, Debra S.

1990   Cerros Revisited: Ceramic Implications of Terminal Classic and Postclassic Settlement and Pilgrimage in Northern Belize. Ph.D. dissertation, Anthropology Department, Southern Methodist University, Dallas, Texas. University Microfilms, Ann Arbor.

Warman, Arturo

1985   *La danza de moros y cristianos*. 2nd ed. Instituto Nacional de Antropología e His-
[1972] toria, México City.

Warren, Kay B.

1989   *The Symbolism of Subordination: Indian Identity in a Guatemalan Town*. 2nd ed. University of Texas Press, Austin.

Watanabe, John M.

1983   In the World of the Sun: A Cognitive Model of Mayan Cosmology. *Man* 18(4): 710–728.

1990   From Saints to Shibboleths: Image, Structure, and Identity in Maya Religious Syncretism. *American Ethnologist* 17(1):131–150.

1995   Maya Religion. In *The Encyclopedia of Religion*, ed. Mircea Eliade, vol. 9, 298–301. MacMillan Publishing, New York.

Weber, Donald

1995   From Limen to Border: A Meditation on the Legacy of Victor Turner for American Cultural Studies. *American Quarterly* 47(3):525–536.

REFERENCES CITED

Weber-Wilson, Eden
  1991   Classification of Postclassic Redware Pottery from Negroman-Tipu, Belize. Master's thesis, Department of Anthropology, University of Florida, Gainesville.

Webster, David A.
  1976   On Theocracies. *American Anthropologist* 78(4):812–827.
  2000   The Not So Peaceful Civilization: A Review of Maya War. *Journal of World Prehistory* 14:65–119.

Weisman, Brent R.
  1999   *Unconquered People: Florida's Seminole and Miccosukee Indians*. University Press of Florida, Gainesville.

Wheatley, Paul
  1971   *The Pivot of the Four Corners*. Aldine Publishing, Chicago.

White, Christine D.
  1996   Sutural Effects of Fronto-Occipital Cranial Modification. *American Journal of Physical Anthropology* 100:397–410.

White, Christine D., Jay Maxwell, David M. Pendergast, and Fred J. Longstaffe
  2009   Cultural Embodiment and the Enigmatic Identity of the Lovers from Lamanai. In *Bioarchaeology and Identity in the Americas*, ed. Kelly Knudson and Chris Stojonowski. University of Florida Press, Gainesville.

White, Christine D., and Henry P. Schwarcz
  1988   Ancient Maya Diet: As Inferred from Isotopic and Elemental Analysis of Bone. *Journal of Archaeological Science* 16:451–474.

White, Richard
  1991   *The Middle Ground: Indians, Empires, and Republics in the Great Lakes Region, 1650–1815*. Cambridge University Press, Cambridge.

Whitehead, Neil
  1993   Ethnic Transformation and Historical Discontinuity in Native Amazonia and Guayana, 1500–1900. *L'Homme* 33(2–4):285–305.

Whitrow, G. J.
  1988   *Time in History: Views of Time from Prehistory to the Present Day*. Oxford University Press, Oxford.

Whittaker, Gordon
  1986   The Mexican Names of Three Venus Gods in the Dresden Codex. *Mexicon* 8: 56–60.

Whittkower, Rudolph
  1938/   Eagle and Serpent: A Study in the Migration of Symbols. *Journal of Warburg*
  1939   *Institute* 29:293–325.

Wiener, Margaret J.
  2004   Making World through Religion, Science and Magic. *Anthropology News* 45(8): 10–11.

Wiessner, Polly
  1983   Style and Social Information in Kalahari San Projectile Points. *American Antiquity* 48:253–276.

Wilce, James M., and Michael Silverstein
  2004   Where Hybrid "Monsters" Dwell. *Anthropology News* 45(8):9, 11.

Winters, Howard D.
  1955a   Excavation of a Colonnaded Hall at Mayapan. *Current Reports* No. 31, 380–396. Carnegie Institution of Washington, Washington, D.C.
  1955b   Three Serpent Column Temples and Associated Platforms at Mayapán. *Current Reports* No. 32, 397–423. Carnegie Institution of Washington, Washington, D.C.
  1955c   A Vaulted Temple at Mayapán. *Current Reports* No. 30, 363–379. Carnegie Institution of Washington, Washington, D.C.

Wissler, Clark
  1912   Ceremonial Bundles of the Blackfeet Indians. *American Museum of Natural History Anthropological Papers* 7(2):65–289.
  1920   The Sacred Bundles of the Pawnee. *Natural History* 20:569–571.

Wortman, Miles
  1975   Government Revenue and Economic Trends in Central America, 1787–1819. *Hispanic America Historical Review* 55:251–286.

Wright, Rita
  1985   Technology and Style in Ancient Ceramics. In *Ancient Technology to Modern Science,* ed. W. D. Kingery, 5–25. American Ceramic Society, Columbus, Ohio.

Wrobel, Gabriel
  2002   Morphological Variation among the Historic Period Maya at Tipu, Belize FAMSI Report. Electronic document, http://www.famsi.org/reports/01081/index.html, accessed June 15, 2008.

Zimmermann, Günter
  1956   *Die Hieroglyphen der Maya-Handschriften*. Cram de Gruyter, Hamburg.

MIGUEL ASTOR-AGUILERA (Ph.D. 2004, SUNY Albany) is an assistant professor in the Department of Religious Studies at Arizona State University. He specializes in Mesoamerican cosmologies and their historical traditions, Precolumbian, colonial, and contemporary. Astor-Aguilera is an ethnographer, iconographer, and archaeologist whose current research focuses on Maya religious specialists in the Yucatán peninsula.

ROBERT CARLSEN (Ph.D. 1992, University of Colorado at Boulder) recently retired from the Department of Anthropology at the University of Colorado at Denver and is now an independent researcher. He has written on a variety of topics related to the highland Maya, including issues of human rights, cultural continuity and change, and Maya textile art. He is author of *The War for the Heart and Soul of a Highland Maya Town* (Austin: University of Texas Press, 1987).

LESLIE G. CECIL (Ph.D. 2001, Southern Illinois University Carbondale) is an assistant professor of anthropology in the Department of Sociology at Stephen F. Austin State University. Her research addresses issues of how the Postclassic Maya (ca. AD 900–1700), during times of social and political stress, used pottery to help identify themselves as part of a cohesive socio-political group. She gathers technological and stylistic data by employing an array of methods that include X-ray diffraction, scanning electron microscopy, inductively coupled plasma spectroscopy, and instrumental neutron activation analysis.

She has published articles in *Archaeometry*, *Journal of Archaeological Sciences*, and the *Transactions of the American Nuclear Society*. She has also published articles in a number of edited volumes.

ARLEN F. CHASE (Ph.D. 1983, University of Pennsylvania) is a Pegasus professor and the chair of anthropology at the University of Central Florida. His research interests focus on archaeological method and theory in the Maya area with particular emphasis on contextual, settlement, and ceramic analysis and secondary interests on urbanism, ethnicity, and epigraphic interpretation. For more than two decades, he has co-directed excavations at Caracol, Belize; before that he worked on a seven-year project at Santa Rita Corozal in the same country. He has authored more than 100 articles and book chapters as well as the books *The Lowland Maya Postclassic* (Austin: University of Texas Press, 1985; edited with P. M. Rice), *Investigations at the Classic Maya City of Caracol, Belize* (San Francisco: Pre-Columbian Art Research Institute, 1987, with D. Z. Chase), *A Postclassic Perspective* (San Francisco: Pre-Columbian Art Research Institute, 1988; with D. Z. Chase), *Mesoamerican Elites: An Archaeological Assessment* (Norman: University of Oklahoma Press, 1992 and 1994; edited with D. Z. Chase), and *Studies in the Archaeology of Caracol, Belize* (San Francisco: Pre-Columbian Art Research Institute, 1994; with D.Z. Chase). PDFs of his writings may be found at www.caracol.org.

DIANE Z. CHASE (Ph.D. 1982, University of Pennsylvania) is a Pegasus professor and the vice provost of academic affairs at the University of Central Florida. Her primary focus of research is on the ancient Maya of Central America. Her research interests focus on archaeological method and theory in the Maya area with particular emphasis on complex societies and hermeneutics, ethnohistory, and osteological and mortuary analysis. For more than two decades, she has co-directed excavations at Caracol, Belize; before that she directed a seven-year project at Santa Rita Corozal in the same country. She has authored more than 100 articles and book chapters, as well as the books *Investigations at the Classic Maya City of Caracol, Belize* (San Francisco: Pre-Columbian Art Research Institute, 1987, with A. F. Chase), *A Postclassic Perspective* (San Francisco: Pre-Columbian Art Research Institute, 1988; with A. F. Chase), *Mesoamerican Elites: An Archaeological Assessment* (Norman: University of Oklahoma Press, 1992 and 1994; edited with A. F. Chase), and *Studies in the Archaeology of Caracol, Belize* (San Francisco: Pre-Columbian Art Research Institute, 1994; with A. F. Chase). PDFs of her writings may be found at www.caracol.org.

JOHN F. CHUCHIAK IV (Ph.D. 2000, Tulane University) is currently associate professor of colonial Latin American history, the holder of the Young Honors College endowed professorship, and the director of the Latin American, Caribbean and

Hispanic Studies program at Missouri State University. He is a colonial Mexican historian and a Maya ethnohistorian with more than eighteen years of archival and field experience in studying the history of the Yucatec Maya. He is the author of *The Holy Office of the Inquisition in New Spain: A Documentary History* (Springfield, MO: Forbes Mills Press, 2009 [forthcoming]), and co-author with Walther Kirchner of *History of Western Civilization to 1500* (New York: HarperCollins Publishers, College Series, 2006), as well as co-editor with Dr. Antje Gunsenheimer and Dr. Tsubasa Okoshi of *Text and Context: Analyzing Colonial Yucatec Maya Texts and Literature in Cross-Cultural Perspective* (Bonn, Germany: Bonner Amerikanistische Studien, Institut für Altamerikanistik und Ethnologie, Universität Bonn, 2007). He was also a recent guest co-editor and contributor with Dr. Pete Sigal of a 2007 special edition of the journal *Ethnohistory: Sexual Encounters/Sexual Collisions: Alternative Sexualities in Colonial Mesoamerica* (54:1 [January 2007]). His major articles have appeared in *Iglesia y sociedad en América Latina Colonial, Saastun: Revista de Cultura Maya, Swedish Missiological Themes, Current Anthropology, Estudios de Cultura Maya*, the *Journal of Early Modern History*, the *Journal of Ethnohistory*, and *The Americas*. He is also the author of several dozen other papers and articles published in a number of edited volumes and anthologies.

ELIZABETH GRAHAM (Ph.D. 1983, Cambridge University) is a senior lecturer at the Institute of Archaeology, University College London. Her research areas include periods of transition from the Maya collapse through the Spanish colonial period, coastal adaptations, and the environmental impact of urban populations in the humid tropics. She is the author of *The Highlands of the Lowlands: Environment and Archaeology in the Stann Creek District, Belize, Central America* (Madison, WI: Prehistory Press, 1994) and an upcoming book on the Maya-Spanish encounter in Belize in the sixteenth century.

MARK HOWELL (Ph.D. 2004, Graduate Center of the City University of New York) is the director of the Winterville Mounds Park and Museum near Greenville, Mississippi. Research for his chapter involved two trips to Guatemala, in 2000 and 2001, where he observed the Baile de los Moros performed several times, in both Coban and Rabinal. Although the storyline, costumes, and even choreography seem largely derived from European models, the music seems non-Western. It was this anomaly that led him to a more in-depth research into the origins of the dance-play; in particular that of the music used in its accompaniment.

SUSAN MILBRATH (Ph.D. 1975, Columbia University) is curator of Latin American art and archaeology at the Florida Museum of Natural History and an affiliate professor of anthropology at the University of Florida. Her long-term research on the Mesoamerican worldview has demonstrated links between astronomy and seasonal ceremonies, identifying a number of important religious images related to astronomy. The results of this research are published in numerous articles and in her book *Star Gods of the Maya: Astronomy in Art, Folklore, and Calendars* (Austin: University of Texas Press, 1999). Her most recent research focuses on the archaeology and ethnohistory of Mayapan, the last Maya capital in Mexico. This site provides an ideal opportunity to study the interface between the archaeological data and the historical records of the early colonial period. She has published a number of papers on Mayapan, including "Revisiting Mayapan: Mexico's Last Maya Capital," *Ancient Mesoamerica* 14:2 (2003): 1–47 (with Carlos Peraza Lope), and "Chichen Itza's Legacy in the Astronomically Oriented Architecture of Mayapan," *RES* 45 (spring 2004): 123–143 (with Anthony F. Aveni and Carlos Peraza Lope).

JOEL PALKA (Ph.D. 1995, Vanderbilt University) is an associate professor in anthropology and Latin American studies at the University of Illinois–Chicago. His current archaeological and ethnohistoric research in remote areas of the lowland rainforests of Chiapas, Mexico, and Peten, Guatemala, focuses on indigenous agency and culture change within Maya cultures not conquered by the Spanish.

SHANKARI PATEL is a Ph.D. student at the University of California Riverside. She received her M.S. in anthropology, geography, and religious studies from California State University, Los Angeles. Her interests include pilgrimages, oracles, Maya cave archaeology, and Cozumel archaeology.

CARLOS PERAZA LOPE is an archaeologist affiliated with the Yucatán office of the Instituto Nacional de Antropolgía e Historia. He has been excavating and consolidating the major buildings in the ceremonial center of Mayapán since 1996. He has uncovered remarkable murals on several building and has found a rather shocking scatter of human bones that may date to the destruction of the site. He has published articles in journals and edited volumes with Marilyn Masson and Susan Milbrath.

TIMOTHY W. PUGH (Ph.D. 2001, Southern Illinois University Carbondale) is an associate professor of anthropology at Queens College and the Graduate Center of the City University of New York. His research focuses on reconstructing the political geography of fifteenth- to seventeenth-century central Petén, Guatemala, and his interests include the Maya, architecture, spatial analysis, ritual, social memory, and cultural contact. He has published articles in *Latin American Antiquity, Ancient Mesoamerica,* the *Journal of Field Archaeology,* and the *Journal of Archaeological Sciences.* In addition to his articles, he has published many chapters in edited volumes.

PRUDENCE M. RICE (Ph.D. 1976, Pennsylvania State University) is Distinguished Professor of Anthropology at Southern Illinois University Carbondale, where she also holds the position of associate vice chancellor for research. She has done field and laboratory research in the Petén lakes region of Guatemala since the 1970s and also carried out an investigation of the Spanish Colonial wine industry in far southern Peru in the late 1980s. Her current research interests include pottery analysis and Maya calendrical ritual.

WILLIAM RINGLE (Ph.D. 1985, Tulane University) is a professor of anthropology and department chair at Davidson College. Ringle is an archaeologist specializing in the northern Maya. He and George Bey co-directed the Ek Balam Project (1986–1999), and since 2000 they, together with Tomas Gallareta, direct the Bolonchen Regional Archaeological Project in the Puuc Hills of Yucatan.

ANDREA STONE (Ph.D. 1983, University of Texas at Austin) is professor of art history at the University of Wisconsin–Milwaukee. She is author of *Images from the Underworld: Naj Tunich and the Tradition of Maya Cave Painting* (Austin: University of Texas Press, 1995) and editor of *Heart of Creation: The Mesoamerican World and the Legacy of Linda Schele* (Tuscaloosa: University of Alabama Press, 2002) and is currently completing *Understanding Maya Art* with Marc Zender and a monograph on petroglyphs from Lake Güija, El Salvador. She has also written numerous articles on Maya art and iconography, Maya cave art, and Mesoamerican rock art.

GABRIELLE VAIL (Ph.D. 1996, Tulane University) specializes in the study of the Maya hieroglyphic codices. She is the director of the Florida Institute for Hieroglyphic Research and holds research appointments at New College of Florida in Sarasota and the Middle American Research Institute, Tulane University.

Page numbers in italics indicate illustrations

Acantunes, 150

Acculturation, and Colonial art, 130–33

Achijab, 312

Actun Hom, *5*; double-headed eagle in, *114*, 116

Actun Huachap, 112

Actun Kaua, *5*; art in, 112, 113, *125, 126,* 131

Afterlife, 163, 235–36

Agency, indigenous, 40, 263–64

Agricultural cycles, 172–73, 176, 229

Aguilar, Geronimo de, 47, 57(n12)

Aguilar, Gregorio de, 154

Ahau K'atun, 201, 204(n10)

Ah Chun Than, 153

Ah Kin Na Chi Pot, 154

Ah Muzencab, *166*

Ajaw glyphs, 117, 119, 120, *121*

Ajaw Kan Ek', 168

AjChan, 242

Akyantho', 271

Alcoy (Valencia), *Baile de los Moros y Cristianos,* 284–85

All Souls Day, 223, 236

Almanacs, 94, 109(n3); in codices, 86, 89, 90, 93

Altar 1 (Zacpetén), *233*

Altar Q (Copán), 7

Altars, 190, *233*; cofradía, 310, *311*

Alvarado, Pedro, 283

Ancestors, ancestral beings, 163, 179, 180, 242; characteristics of, 181–82; identity and, 7–8; veneration of, 164–65, 167; wind-like persons, 173–74

Annals of the Cakchiquels, 281, 282, 283, 284, 296(n1)

Arana, Hernández, 282

Archaeological sites, modern beliefs about, 328–29

Architecture, 8, 35, 242, 321, 326; Cocom-Itza, 192–93; codex depictions of, 196, 198; directionality and, 11–12; Mayapán, 189–90, 200, 201, 203–4(nn5, 9); remodeling and renewing, 328–29; Tipu, 245–48; Xiu, 183–84; Xiu-Puuc revival, 194–95

Astronomy, 26, 324; time and, 326–27

Atitlán, Lake, *5,* 299, 300; as sacred landscape, 303–7

Avendaño y Loyola, Andrés de, 242, 243

Axis mundi, *302, 303–4, 305,* 320. See *also* World trees

Aztecs, 48, 67, 106, 208, 289, 309, 330; belief system, 223, 224; in Mayapán, 77, 198, 199; New Fire ceremony, 107–8; time concepts, 63, 81(n6)

Bacabs (Bak'abs; B'akabs), 102, 106, 223, *224*

Baile de la Conquista, 280, 281, *288,* 296(n3); musical instruments used in, 291–92, 296

Baile de los Moros y Cristianos, 9, 14, 279–80; in Guatemala, 286–287, *287;* musical instruments used, 289, 292–93, 296; in Spain, 284–85

Baile del Venado, 14, 280

B'ak'tun, 67, 69, 81(n11); Colonial period celebrations of, 77–79, 81(n13)

Balché bark, 153

Balkanization, 40

Baptisms, mass, 50

Basic Ceremonial Group (Mayapán), 194

Battles, music associated with, 283

Belize, 1, 2, 35, 239. *See also various sites*

Benavides, Juan de, 151

Binary opposition, in drums, 294–95

Birds, 109(n9), 208; in cave art, 113–17, 130; planes of existence and, 230–31

Birthing places, 167

Birth shrines, 214

Blood, bloodletting, 8, 106, 107, 150, 181; as communicating object, 176–78

Blouses, cofradía, 308–9

B'olon ti' K'uh, 11, 99

Bonampak, 71

Bones, 181, 323; nonhuman beings and, 173–74

Books of Chilam Balam, 1, 7, 72, 74, 81(n7), 86, 104, *119,* 122, 130, 131, 165, 201; calendar system in, 48–49; creation stories in, 87, 110(n15); floods in, 99, 101–2; on Mayapán, 76–77; migrations in, 45–46; prophecy in, 47–48

Borgia Group, 101, *274*

Boundaries, community, 319

Bow and arrow, 198

Bowls, 176; with quadripartite-cross designs, 167, 171

Brasseur de Bourboug, Charles É., 282

Braziers. *See* Censers

Building of the Serpent (Xochitecatl), 210

Buildings. *See* Architecture; *by type*

Bundle of Flames, 309

Bundles, 178, 323; objects in, 309–11; Santiago Atitlán, 312, 315(n15); talking, 8, 171, 174

Burial 20 (Caye Coco), 148

Burials, 148, 167, 247, 277; cultural variety in, 35–36; at Lamanai, 34–35; underworld symbolism in, 227–28

Butterflies, 208

Cab, Martin, 151

Caches, caching, 11, 220, *224,* 234, 326; and planes of existence, 226–27

Calendar Round, 67, 81(n4), 86, 107, 327

Calendar systems, 13, 38(n5), 47, 50, 58(n14), 59(n22), 80, 84, 85–86, 184, 306, 327; celebrations and, 77–79; Colonial period, 48–49; Mayapán, 200–201, 202; Mesoamerican, 66–71; Postclassic and Contact period, 71–77; ritual, 14–15, 322

Calendrical cycles, 39, 334; geopolitics, 75–77; time and, 326–27

Calotmul, 152

Campeche, 111, 153; double-headed eagle in, *114,* 116

Campeche calendar, 71

Canoes, 235

Canuls, 2, 196, 198, 202, 204(n7)

Captives, *232;* sacrifice of, 32–33

Caracol (Belize), *5;* caches in, 11, 226, 236; funerary rituals in, 229–30; underworld iconography at, 225, 227–28, *228, 232*

Caracol (Chich'en Itzá), 193, 329

Cardinal directions, 75, 223, 319; in god houses, 276–77, 324; in musical instruments, 289–90; and pilgrimages, 207–8, 209, 212; Santiago Atitlán, 304–5

Caste War of Yucatán, 171, 216, 321

Castillo (Chich'en Itzá), 193, 202, 327

Castillo (Mayapán), *188,* 192, 193, 199, 202, 327, 329

Catholic Church, Catholicism, 36, 162, 219, 229, 266, 230, 303; conversion to, 236, 331; inquisition, 168–69; saints, 308, 313; syncretism with, 9, 221, 223; worship in, 29, 30, 31, 156–57(n14)

Cauac. *See* Earth monster

Caves, 13, 320, 321, 326, 328, 332; circular faces in, 117–22; on Cozumel, 212–16; crosses and ornamental motifs in, 124–26; colonial imagery in, 9, 111–12; double-headed eagles in, 113–17; European style art in, 130–33; horse and rider motif in, 122–24; idol clay from, 146, 153; Lacandon ceremonial use of, 272, 274; oracles, 211–12; ritual in, 116–17, 129–30; schematic figures in, 126–28; symbolism of, 87, 324; underworld entrances, 221, 225, 232, 322–23

Caye Coco, *5,* 148

Cedar, idols made from, 144, 157(n18), 325

Cehac, censer manufacture in, 153, 154
Cehach Maya, 267
Cehpech province, 7, 40, 189; chronicles of, 42–45, 46, 51–52
Ceiba pentandra, 75, 231–32, 321
Celestial realm. *See* Upper world
Cemeteries, 174. *See also* Burials; Funerary rituals
Cenote Ch'en Mul group (Mayapán), 184, 193, 194, 195, 200, 203
Cenote of Sacrifice (Chich'en Itzá), 184, 206, 210, 333
Cenotes, 184, 320, 322; on Cozumel, 212–15, 216; ritual importance of, 206–7
Censers, 189, 203(n3), 248, 332; effigy, 8, 136, 137, *138,* 142, 146–49, *149,* 156(n7), 190, 193, 196, 198, 203(n4), 245, 325, 331; Lacandon use of, 265, 272, 275; manufacture of, 149–51; Quetzalcoatl/Kukulcan and, 192, 203(n4); trade in, 153–54
Ceramics, 8, 221, 226, *169, 234*; Kowoj-made, 252–57; at Mayapán, 189–92, 196, 204(n6); with quadripartite-cross designs, *167,* 171; at Tipu, 240–41, 248–52
Ceremonial groups, at Tipu, 245–46
Ceremonies, 228; period-ending, 96–97, 130; world tree, 94, 95
Chaak (Chac), 8, 89, 106, 109(n11), 184, 190, 323; agricultural cycles, 172–73; cult of, 194, 195; offerings to, 135–36
Chable, Antonio, 135–36
Chacmool, 5
Chac Xulub Ch'en, 5, 42; narrative from, 40, 43, *44,* 50, 51–52
Chak'an Itza (Chakan Itza), 2, 244
Chak Chel, 99, 107
Chak Xiwitel, 105
Chalcatongo, 211–12
Champoton, 5, 48, 51, 153, 196
Chamula, 176, 329
Chancenote, 153
Chankanaab, 213
Chan Kom, 5, 180, 228
Chan Santa Cruz, 321, 322
Charles V, double-headed eagle, 115, 116
Che, Francisco, 152
Chen Mul Modeled effigy censers, 190, *191,* 203(n3)
Chen Pita, 212–13, *214*
Chi, Gaspar, 41

Chiapas, 1, 111, 329; Lacandon in, 3, 261, 265–68, 267, 272–73, 274
Chicchan Serpent, 196
Chich'en Itzá, *5,* 12, 39, 41, 42, 50, 53, 54, 58(n20), 166, 200, 210, 212, 242, 326, 327, 330, 333; Cocom from, 8, 185, 189, 190; descendants from, 2–3; feathered serpent cult at, 190, 192, 193; Kukulcan and, 45, 203(n4); and Mayapán, 201, 202, 324; pilgrimages to, 184, 206; Spanish search for, 51, 52
Chilam Balam, 47
Chilam Balam of Chumayel, 48, 50, 52, 58(n16), 74, 76, 77, 204(n9), 242; b'ak'tun celebration in, 78–79; circular faces in, 117, *119,* 120, 121; crocodilians in, 98, 101; re-creation in, 93–94
Chilam Balam of Ixil, circular faces in, 117, *119,* 120
Chilam Balam of Kana, 40
Chilam Balam of Kaua, 120, *128*
Chilam Balam of Maní, 2, 74
Chilam Balam of Tizimin, 2, 74, 76, 98, 101, 116
Chinchinicab, 43
Chirimias, 280, 281, 291, 297(n7)
Chol (Ch'ol), 221, 265, 266, 267, 268
Ch'olti-Lacandon, 267
Cholan Maya, 3
Chontal Maya, 71, 105, 203(n4), 266
Chontalpa, 196, 204(n6)
Ch'orti', 319
Christianity, 47, 48, 53, 57(n11), 162, 230, 308; concepts of creation in, 27, 28; conversion to, 36, 50, 221, 223, 331; impacts of, 219–20; Lacandon and, 270, 275; resistance to, 215, 301, 308; symbolism of, 20–21, 229
"Chronicle of Ah Naum Pech" (Martínez Hernández), 47
Chronicles, 57(n7), 58(n16), 74; evaluation of, 53–56; events portrayed in, 51–53; Pech family, 42–47, 57(n11); time in, 47–51. *See also* Books of Chilam Balam; Codices
Chu-Ha, 213
Chukuch Nok. *See* Lacandon
Chultuns, 322, 323
Chuncaan (Mérida), 53
Churches, 267, 279, 329; at Tipu, 243, 247
Cilvituk, Isla, 245
Cities, city-states, 163; geopolitical cycles, 75–77, 330

Civil war, Mayapán, 40–41

Classic period, 32, 35, 61, 80(n1), 96, 112, 236, 328; caches, 220, 226; creation stories, 86–87, 93; liminality in, 233–34; Long Count use, 69–71; planes of existence, 225, 227–28; rulership, 162–63

Clay, in idol manufacture, 144, 146, 150, 153, 325

Clemencia Cream Paste ware, 249, 251, 252–53, 254, 255, 258, 260(n4)

Cliffs, Lacandon shrines, 272–73

Cloth, in cofradía bundles, 309–10, 315(n14)

Clothing, cofradía, 308–9

Coastal settlements, Postclassic, 35

Cobán, 5; *Baile de los Moros y Cristianos* in, 286; musical instruments used in, 289, 291, 292

Cochuah zone, 113

Cocom (Kokom), 2, 8, 12, 13, 40–41, 57(n5), 330; feathered serpent cult, 185–86, 192–93; foreign influence on, 195–200; at Mayapán, 76–77, 189, 190, 202; and Xiu, 183–84, 204(n7)

Cocom-Itza (Kokom-Itza), 76–77, 192–93

Codex Bodley, 209, *211*

Codex Colombino, 209, 212

Codex Madrid, 196

Codex Nuttall, 196

Codex Pérez (Códice Pérez), 49, 57(n3), 96–97

Codex Selden, 209, 212

Codex Vindobonensis, 54, 209

Codex Zouche-Nuttal (Nuttal-Zoche) and Egerton, 209, *211*, 212

Codices, 8, 11, 84, 165, 208, 209, *211*; architecture depicted in, 196, 198; on oracular priests, 209–10; stone images shown in, 144, *145*. *See also by name*

Codices Becker I and II, 209

Cofradías, 12, 302, 313, 315(n21), 331; bundles used by, 309–12, 315(n15); clothing, 308–9; dance-plays, 279–80; Santiago Atitlán, 303–7, 326

Cogolludo, Diego López de, 46, 58(n20), 166

Coixtlahuaca group, 210

Colonial period, 1, 3, 7, 8, 68, 72, 184, 185, 214, 216, 313–14(n2), 329; autonomous religious systems, 128–30; b'ak'tun celebrations, 77–78; calendrical reform, 48–49; cave art, 111–12; circular faces in, 117–22; crosses and ornamental motifs, 124–26; dance-plays, 279–80, 287–88; double-headed eagles in,

113–17; horse and rider motif in, 122–24; idol use, 12, 135–55; imagery, 9–10; pictorial conventions, 130–33; quadripartism, 319–20; schematic figures, 126–28

Colors, and directions, 75

Communicating objects, 166, 168, 176–77, 180; bundles as, 8, 171, 174, *175*, 323

Communication, 35; with deities, 325–26; ritual, 174–75

Communities, 34, 36, 319; rituals, 129–30, 236; spatial organization of, 321–22

Complex I (Tipu), 245–46, *246*, 257–58

Concept(s), 17; of creation, 27–28; histories of, 18–19; religion as, 22–25; science as, 25–26; worldview as, 21–22; worship, 28–31

Confederacies, Mayapán, 41

Conkal, 42

Contact period, 1, 245, 325; geopolitical organization, 75–76

Continuity, 236

Contreras, Juan de, 215

Conversions, 220, 221, 223, 331

Copal, 146, 153

Copán, *5*, 7, *68*, 225

Copper bells, 196

Cords, 319

Cortés, Hernán, 48, 52, 54, 168, 242

Cosmic planes, 223–24, 322; connections among, 225–27; iconography of, 228, 230–31; interactions between, 324–26; liminality in, 229–36. *See also* Earth; Underworld; Upperworld

Cosmology, 10–11, 45, 75, 81(n8), 84, 159–60, 164, 165, 176, 223; Iberian-Catholicism and Mesoamerican, 167–68; landscape and, 318–29; pilgrimages, 207–8; regenerative, 236–37; sky in, 323–24; underworld in, 322–23

Costumbre, 9, 10, 11, 300, 314(nn3, 11); bundles used in, 309–11; pre-European beliefs, 312–13; in Santiago Atitlán, 303–7

Cotton, 309

Count of days, 67, 77, 85, 327

Covoh (Couoh). *See* Kowoj

Cozumel, *5*, 46, 151, 166, 245; cenotes on, 206–7; Ix Chel, 9, 12, 143; as pilgrimage center, 146, 205, 210, 212–15, 217; pirate raids on, 215–16

Craftsmen, idol manufacturing, *146*, 150, 154

Creation, 81(n5); in codices, 89–93; establishment of universe, 86–87; Madrid codex depictions, 105–8; Maya beliefs of, 27–28; in murals, 87–89; stories of, 83, 331; and Venus events, 99–105; of worlds, 94–99, 108

Crocodilians, crocodiles, 227, 234; earth as, 87, 98–99; in *Popol Vuj,* 88–89; symbology of, 96, 100–101, 102, 104, 110(n16), 233

Crosses, 131, 321; in cave art, 124–26; as communicating object, 176, *177*; in Mayan symbology, 165, 166, *167*, 321; talking, 8, 171

Cul cheob, 144

Cults, community ritual, 129–30. *See also* Cofradías

Cul tunichob, 142–44

Cuzcas, 153

Dance-plays, 296(nn3, 4), 328; highland Guatemalan, 279–80, 287–88; musical instruments used in, 289–95; Spanish, 284–87

Dances: calendrical ritual, 14–15; pre-Hispanic, 282–83; warrior, 283–84, 295

Day of the Dead, 223

Days, 85; counts of, 66–67

Death, 315(n16), 324; concepts of, 163, 181; and life, 182, 323; liminality of, 229–30, 235–36; rituals for, 219–20, 223. *See also* Funerary rituals

Death god, portrayals of, 89, 90; rituals for, 94, 95

Deer, as sun, 221

Deities, 8, 10, 26, 68, 105, 110(n14), 157(n15), 235, 308, 309, 320, 331; agricultural cycles, 172–73; birth of, 89–90; in caches, 226–27; calendar systems and, 38(n5), 84; communication with, 9, 325–26; concepts of, 179–80; Lacandon, 271, 275–76; at Mayapán, 190, 192, 195, 198, 199; quadripartite, 75, 81(n8); Santiago Atitlán, 306, 312, 315(n21); Spanish views of, 136–37; veneration of, 137–39; worship of, 28, 29. *See also* Idols

Descriptio Idolorum, 136, 142

Destruction, 76, 142, 326, 330, 332; by floods, 101–2; and k'atun cycles, 194–95, 199–200; Venus imagery and, 100–101; of worlds, 84, 93, 94–99, 104, 108

Díaz Cuscat, Pedro, 176

Díaz del Castillo, Bernal, 165

Directionality, directions, 11–12, 75, 223, 236, 324; iconography of, 220, 226, 227; in musical instruments, 289–90; and pilgrimages, 207–8; Santiago Atitlán, 304–5

Dishes, offertory, 153

Divination, 26, 329

Divining implements, 310–11, 315(n17)

Diving figures, 226, *235*

Domingo, Kaqchikel ritual calendar, 13–14

Domingo, Santo, 286

Dominguez de Sepúlveda, Juan Pablo, 153, 154

Doncel, Julian, 51–52

Doors, symbolic, 225

Dresden Codex, 8, 84, 86, 108, 109(nn7, 8, 9); creation stories in, 89, *90, 92,* 93; destruction and re-creation themes in, 94–95; flood imagery in, 98, *100,* 101–2; Venus depictions in, 99, 101, 104–5

Dress, symbolism of, 308–9

Droughts, 184, 203, 204(n10)

Drums, 296; double-headed, 294–95; pre-Hispanic, 293–94; skin, 281, 292–95; slit-drum, 280, 281, 282; and warrior dance, 283–84

Dualism, duality, 25, 247; in drums, 294–95

Dwarfs, 230

Dzibichen, *5,* 130; art in, 112, *114,* 116, 117, *118,* 120–22, *123,* 124, *125,* 126, *127*

Dzibilchaltun, 328, 330

Dzonotchel, stone images in, 143–44

Dzuluinicob region, 239

Eagle, double-headed, 10, 113–17, 130, 131, 132, 331

Earth (terrestrial world), 10, 11, 223, 332; as crocodile, 87, 89, 98

Earth crocodile. *See* Itzam Kab' Ayin

Earth Lords, 236

Earth monster (cauac), 87, 89, 225, *228,* 230, 235, 236; destruction of, 98–99, *100,* 100–101

East, and pilgrimages, 207–8, 209, 212, 217

Economics, 34; underground, 153–54

El Caobal, *5,* 269–70, *270*

Elites, 6, 32, 34, 117, 124, 141, 158(n29), 167, 239; burials, 227–28; genealogies, 7–8; Colonial period, 132–33; Mayapán, 40–41, 202; Pech, 41–42; pilgrimages by, 205, 209

El Mangal, god pot from, *273,* 275

Encomiendas, in Cehpech province, 44, 51–52

Epidemics, at Mayapán, 200, 204(n10)

Equinoxes, at Santiago Atitlán, 305–6

Estada, Juan de, 244

Ethnicity, 3, 331; Lacandon, 267–68; of Lamanai inhabitants, 34–35; of Tipu residents, 244–45

Faces, circular, 10, 13, 117–22, 331
Families, 132, 152, 236; Cocom and Xiu, 183–84; household idols, 141–42; Mayapán elite, 40–42; Pech, 41–43
Feathered serpent cult, 185, *187*, 190, 192–93, 199, 203–4(n5), 324; pilgrimages and, 205, 207, 208–9, 216–17
Feathers, 176, 210
Fertility, 174, 229, 231
Fetishes, 310–11, 315(n17). *See also* Idols
Figurines, figures, in caches, *224, 226. See also* Idols
Firearms, 270, 271
Fish, 235
Floods, 99; imagery of, 98, *100*, 101–4
Flores Island, 242
Flower World complex, 208, 217
Flutes, 280, 289, 296, 297(nn6, 7); bone, 290–91; and dances, 282–83; goiter, 291–92; and warrior dance, 283–84
Footpath of the Dawn, Footpath of the Sun, 12, 14; construction of, 304–5, 314(n8); and sacred center, 305–6
Formative Period, 70, 81(n9)
Franciscans, 48, 170
Fuensalida, Bartolomé de, 242, 243, 244
Fugitives, 153, 154
Funerary rituals, 247, 277; liminality of, 229–30, 235–36

Genealogies, 7–8, *44,* 242. *See also* Lineages
Geomancy, 227
Geopolitical organization, space and time in, 75–77
God houses, 275, 276–77, 324
God impersonators, 144
God L, 89, 99, *102,* 104, 109(n11)
God of sustenance. *See* K'awil
God pots, Lacandon, 137–39, 150, *273,* 275–76, *276*
Gods. *See* Deities
Gods of the Lower World, 11, 99
Gods of the Upper World, 11
Great Ballcourt (Chich'en Itzá), 326
Grolier codex, 84, 109(n2)
Guatemala, 1, 3, 115, 132, 300, 313–14(n2); *Baile de los Moros y Cristianos, 286,* 286–87; dance-plays, 279–80, 287–95; warrior dance, 283–84. *See also* Highland Guatemala; *various regions*

Haab (ja'ab) cycle, 107
Hachakyum, 271
Hach Winik. *See* Lacandon
Hall of Chac Masks (Mayapán), 184, *188*, 194, 195, 202
Hall of Sun Disks (Mayapán), 198, *199*
Hapsburgs, and double-headed eagle, 115, 116, 331
Heads, as iconic objects, 168
Heart of Food and Water bundle, 309, *310*
Heart of Maize bundle, 309
Heart of the Placenta bundle, 309
Hecelchakan, 153
Hero Twins, 89
Highland Guatemala, 3; cofradía rituals in, 12, 313; dance-plays, 279–80, *286,* 286–88, 296(n4); resistance in, 215, 301, 308
Histories, 7, 13, 84; of concepts, 18–19; native construction of, 39–40, 76; Pech family in, 42–43
Histoyre du Mechique, 98–99
Hocaba component, 189, 190, 193
Hochob, 116
Holy Trinity, 223
Holy Week, Santiago Atitlán, *302,* 306, *307*
Horse and rider motifs, 131, 331; in cave art, 122–24
Horses, 124, 131, 168
Households, 129; private worship in, 141–42, 156(n13); spatial organization and ritual of, 321–22
Houses, 87, 174
Huichol, 115, 174–75
Huipils, 115
Hunac Ceel, 210
Hybridity, 168

Iconography, 107; colonial era, 9–10, 20–21, 132; planes of existence, 225, 230–31
Identity, 8, 12, 40, 129, 132, 330; Kowoj, 257–60; Lacandon, 268–69; lineages and, 7–8; Tipu residents, 244–45, 248
Idolatry, 137, 152, 155(n3), 156(n5), 203(n4), 303; Spanish punishment of, 116–17, 151, 170; trials for, 135–36, 139–41; underground trade and, 153–54
Idols, 8, 12, 155(n3), 157(n20), 158(n29), 168, 195, 325; effigy censers as, 144–49, 156(n7), 190, 331; guarding and keeping, 151–52, 156(n13); household use of, 141–42; illicit

trade in, 153–54, 158(n31); Ix Chel, 9, 143; manufacture of, 149–51, 153–54, 157(n18); offerings to, 135–36, *147*; ritual use of, 140–41, 156(n6); Spanish accounts of, 33–34, 36; types of, 142–44; worship of, 29–30

Ilhuitl glyph, 249

Imagery, 83; colonial, 9–10, 20–21; worship and, 29–31

Incense burners, incensarios. *See* Censers

Inheritance, of idols, 152, 158(n29)

Inquisition, Spanish, 168–70

Instruments. *See* Musical instruments

Intercardinal directions, 75

International art style, 204(n8), 208–9; in murals, 196–98; and pilgrimages, 207, 210, 211–12, 216–17

Interrogation, by Spanish, 168–70

Invisibles, invisible substances, 181–82. *See also* Nonhuman beings

Itsamna (Itzamna, Itzam Na), 46, 90, 94, 95, 106, 190, 273

Itsanokuh, 273

Itsanokuh (Petha), Lake, 272

Itza, 2, 12, 52, 74, 82(n14), 153, 168, 257, 320, 328; calendar systems, 13, 79, 184; feathered serpent cult, 192–93; and Mayapán, 185–86, 201; in Petén, 3, 241, 243, 244–45

Itzaj Maya, 266, 267

Itza Kan, 239

Itzam Kab' Ayin (Itzam Cab Ain), 87, 98, 101, 102, 104, 110(n16); in *Popol Vuj,* 88–89

Itzamna (Itsamna, Itzam Na), 46, 90, 94, 95, 106, 190, 273

Ix Ahau Caan, 151–52

Ix Chel, 9, 12, 143; pilgrimage sites, 212, 214

Ixlú, 245, 252

Izamal, 210, 329

Jadeite, 226, 227, 228

Jaguar: as liminal being, 232–33; in way carving, 221, *222*

Jaguar Paddler, 87, 88

Jesus, 323; indigenous interpretation of, 308, 314(n11); and Judas, 306–7

Jorge, San, 284, 285

Judas Iscariot, 306–7; as Maximón, 9, 301

Jun Ajaw, 105

Kablikot, 10, 115

Kai yum, 293, 294–95

Kakatunal, 105

Kakchikel (Kaqchikel), 3, 13–14

Kaku Pacal, 42

Kalkoj, 115

Kan Ek' (Kan Ek), 2–3, 244

K'atuns (katuns), k'atun cycles, 69, 71, 74, 130, 184, 200, 322, 330; architectural revival and, 192, 193, 204(n9); Colonial period use, 48–49, 79; depiction of, 13, 119; at Mayapán, 186–87(table), 199–201, 202, 203(n2); music and, 327–28; prophecies, 121–22; use of, 47, 67–68; Yucatán geopolitics, 75–77, 81(n13)

K'atun wheels, 120, 327

K'awil, 94, 95, 96, 98, 101, 104, 110(n15); bundles, 171, *172*

Kay Junahpu, 283

Kehach Maya, 267

K'iche', 3, 9, 87, 98, 132; double-headed bird in, 115, 117; musical instruments, 280–81, 289–90, 291, 293, 295; narratives, 281–82; warrior dance, 279, 282–84

Kimil (death god), 94, 95

Kingdoms, independent Maya, 266

Kingship, divine, 70, 71. *See also* Rulers, rulership

K'inich ajaw, 94–95

K'inich Yax K'uk' Mo, 7

Kinship, 164, 179; Kowoj, 241–42

Knowledge: landscapes as, 329–30; religious, 23–24

K'ojom, 282

Kokom. *See* Cocom

Kokom-Itza. *See* Cocom-Itza

Kowoj (Covoh), 2, 328–29, 332; architecture, 12, 247, 322; and Mayapán, 241–42; pottery made by, 8, 248–57; at Tipu, 239, 242–43, 244, 257–60

K'oyoi lineage, 282

Kukulcan (Kukulkan). *See* Quetzalcoatl

K'umarkaj, dancing warrior mural at, 284, *285*

Lacandon, 3, 10, 261, 278, 319, 321, 328; agency, 263–64; birth of gods in, 89–90; ceremonial landscapes, 272–74; cosmology, 323–24, 325; culture contact, 262–63; ethnic origins of, 267–68; god pots, 137–39, 150, 331; historic culture of, 264–67; identity in, 268–69; musical instruments of, 292, 293; religion and ritual, 142, 275–77; trade goods, 269–71

Lacanjá, 265

Ladinos, 265, 266, 269, 278(n2)

Lady 9 Grass, 211–12

Lahun Chan, 105

La Libertad, 269

Lamanai, *5,* 21; ethnic diversity at, 34–35

Landa, Diego de, 1–2, 77, 84, 94, 141, 165, 166, 183, 192, 210, 291; on idolatry, 153–54; on Mayapán, 196, 198; *Relacion de las cosas de Yucatan,* 102, 220; on wooden idols, 144, 149–50

Landscape(s), 46; cosmology and, 10–12; as knowledge, 329–30; Lacandon ceremonial, 272–74; Lake Atitlán as sacred, 303–7; pilgrimages, 206–7; politics of, 330–32; sacred, 317–26, 332–34; of sky, 323–24; symbology of, 10–12; time and, 326–27

Late Classic period, 35, 213, 291

Late Postclassic period, 2, 71, 83, 84, 98, 108, 130, 131, 132, 236, 241, 242, 327; geopolitical organization, 75–77; remodeling and renewal, 328–29

Late Preclassic period, 85, 111; creation stories, 86–87

League of Mayapán, 2

Life, concepts of, 221, 323

Liminality, 220–21, *228,* 231, 237, 326; funerary rituals, 229–30; of symbolic creatures, 232–36

Lineages, 158(n29), 163, 309; documentation of, 55–56, 74; elite, 40–42; identity and, 7–8, 132; Kowoj, 241–42

Loltun, *5;* art at, 112, 113, *127;* idol clay from, 146, 153

Long Count, 13, 14, 68, 77, 84, 85–86, 109(n3); Classic period use, 69–71

Long-nosed merchant god, 8

Lopez, Tomas, 52

López de Gómara, Francisco, 166

Lord 8 Deer, pilgrimage of, *211*

Lord of the Middle. *See* Maximón

Lords of the K'atun, 120

Lords of the Night, 69, 224

Lot C72 (Mayapán), 190

Lubaantún, *5;* drums from, 293, *294*

Lunar cults, 210

Macanché Island, ceramics from, 251, 252, 255

Machaquila, stela from, *231*

Madrid Codex, 8, 84, 327; birth of gods in, 89–90, *91,* 93; creation events in, 105–8

Maize, 104, 231, 235

Maize god, 84

Malah, Diego, 154

Malah, Juan, 146

Mam (Maximón), 9, 75, 301, *302,* 303, 306

Manche-Ch'ol Maya, 266

Maní, *5,* 41, 48, 200

Mapas de Cuauhtinchan, 210

Marimba, 280

Martínez Hernández, "Chronicle of Ah Naum Pech," 47, 57(n7)

Masks, 144, *146;* Chac, 184–85, 194, 195

Matillas Fine Orange, 196, 204(n6)

Maximón (Mam), 9, 75, 301, *302,* 303, 306

Maxtunil, 42

Maya Blue, 196

Maya Long Count, 13

Mayanized Mexicans, 72

Mayapán, *5,* 8, 39, 45, 48, 53, 204(n10), 245, 249, 329, 330; architecture, 12, 203–4(n5), 247, 324, 327; ceramics, 189–92, 204(n6); Cocom-Itza architecture at, 192–93; Cocom and Xiu in, 183, 184, 185, 188–89; collapse of, 76–77, 81(n10); civil war in, 40–41; effigy censers, 137, 148; elite families from, 41–42; foreign influences on, 195–200; k'atun cycles and, 130, 186–87(table), 203(2); and Kowoj, 241–42; Kowoj ceramics at, 252, 254; migration from, 2, 3; murals at, 84, 196–98; revival at, 201–3; Temple of the Fishermen, 98, 99, *100,* 100–101; Xiu-Puuc architecture at, 194–95

Mayapán calendar, 77, 79, 81(nn4, 12)

Maya Santiago Atitlán, *5*

May cycles, 76, 184, 327; destruction at end of, 199–200, 330

Memories, collective, 4, 6, 7, 39

Mensabak, *5,* 265, 273

Mensabak, Lake, 273; rock art, *274*

Mérida, 53, 157(n19); b'ak'tun celebrations in, 77–79

Metaphors, Maya use of, 19–21, 231–32

Metnal, 87, 230

Mexicans (Canul), at Mayapán, 196, 198

Mexico, Valley of, famine in, 81(n10), 196; feathered serpent cult, 190, 192

Migrations, 2, 3, 8, 11, 241, 242, 267, 330; mythological role of, 45–46; narratives of, 52, 282

Milky Way, 323
Milpas, boundaries of, 319
Miramar, 5, 214; cave art at, 112, *114*, 116, 117, *118*, 122–23, *123*, 126, *127*
Miramar, Lake, 266
Missions, Lacandon, 266, 267, 269
Mixteca-Puebla art style. *See* International art style
Mixteca, 71, 72, 196, 208, 209; pilgrimages, 211–12, 217
Momostenango, 176
Monkey gods, 190
Montalvo y Vera, Joseph, 135
Monte Alban, 210
Montejo, Francisco de (Montejo the Adelanto), 44, 48, 50, 51–52, 54, 58(n20)
Montejo the Younger, 50
Moon Goddess. *See* Ix Chel
Motul, 5, 42
Mountains, sacred landscape, 320, 332
Mujeres, Isla de las, 214
Muralla de Leon, 245
Murals, 83, 84, 208, 217, 227, 326; at Mayapán, 100–101, 196–98, 200; at Santa Rita Corozal, 86, 87–89; warrior dance on, 284, *285*
Music, 279; and time, 327–28
Musical instruments: in dance-plays, 280, 289–96; K'iche', 281, 282–83; in warrior dances, 283–84
Mythology, 10; creation, 27, 86–87; roles of, 44–45

Na Ho' Ka'an, 87–88
Nahuatl (Aztec), 72, 105, 108
Najá, 5, 265, 273
Nakxit, 290
Nature, 12, 176, 300, 317, 322; religion and, 137, 179–80
Navula group ceramics, 189
Nawales, 312, 315(n19)
New Fire ceremony, 67, 81(n4), 107–8
New Year ceremonies, 8, 94, 322
Nik, 90
Nim pöt, 308–9
Nixtun Ch'ich', 252
Nobility. *See* Elites
Noh, Miguel, 140
Nojpeten (Tah Itza), 5, 168, 242
Nojpeten-Tayasal, 168

Nonhuman beings, 173, 178, 180, 181; communication with, 174–75, 179; veneration of, 175–76
Novelo, Diego Marcos, 143–44

Oaxaca, 196, 208, 210, 217
Observatories, 193
Obsidian, 196, 226
Octgin, Jose Angel, *Original del Baile de los Moros y Cristianos,* 287
Offerings, 9, 178, 228, 322, 329; to Chac, 135–36; to cofradía bundles, 309–10; to idols, 140–41, *147*, 151–52, 153
Old God N, 228, *229*
Open halls, at Tipu, 246–47
Oracles, 166, 206, 207; on Cozumel, 212–16; Mixtec and Zapotec, 211–12; at pilgrimage centers, 210–11, 217; priests and, 209–10
Oratorios, 245; at Tipu, 246–47, 258
Orbita, Juan de, 242, 243, 244
Original del Baile de los Moros y Cristianos (Octgin), 287
Ornamentation, Colonial period, 124–26
Oxkutzcab, 5, 142, 153
Oxlahuntiku (Oxlahun ti K'uh), 11, 99

Pablo, San, 286
Palenque, 5, 101, 167, 224, 225, *328*; and Lacandon, 267, 269; Temple 14 k'awil bundle, *172*; Temple XIX, 98–99
Palenque calendar, 71
Paris codex, 84, 86, 87, 102, *103*, 108, 122; period-ending ceremonies in, 96–98
Paths, as boundaries, 319
Pawahtuns, 101, 102, 106
Paxcamán ceramic group, 258
Pech, Ah Kom, 42, 43, 57(n8)
Pech, Ah Macan, 42, 43, 44, 55
Pech, Ah Naum, 42, 47
Pech, Ah Tunal, 57(n8)
Pech, Francisco, 139, 151–52
Pech, Ixkil Itzam, 42
Pech, Naum, 43
Pech, Nohcabal, 41–42
Pech, Pablo (Nakuk Pech), 7, 40, 42, 43, 44, 50–51, 52, 53, 55, 57(n8), 58(n19)
Pech, Pedro, 43
Pech family, 331; chronicles of, 41–47, 50–51, 57(n11)
Personification heads, European, 119–20

Petén, 2, 3, 12, 21, 76, 196, 259–60(n1), 320, 329; contact period, 242–43; Lacandon in, 261, 265–68, 272; territorial control in, 244–45

Petén Itza, 2, 242, 243

Petén Itza, Lake, 2, 241, 242

Petén lakes region, *240*; Kowoj in, 239, 241, 242; Kowoj pottery in, 252–57; Spanish conquest of, 244, 266

Peto, idolatry in, 152

Peto Cream ware, 189

Petrographic analysis, of Tipu ceramics, 251–52

Pigments, AMS dating of, 112

Pilgrimage centers, 8, 9, 184; Cozumel as, 12, 146, 205, 212–16; oracles at, 210–11

Pilgrimages, 209, *211*, 320, 322, 328; directions and, 207–8; International art style and, 216–17; landscape and, 206–7; role of, 205–6

Pirates, attacks on Cozumel, 215–16

Planes of existence. *See* Cosmic planes

Planets, 25, 26. *See also* Venus

Plantation owners, 236

Platforms, 189, 203(n3), 245, 272

Plazas, 320, 321

Plumeria, 89–90

Political factions, shrines and, 209–10

Politics, 12; time, timekeeping, 329–30

Popol Vuj, 98, 104, 110(n14), 165, 223, 290, 299, 309; creation stories in, 88–89; directions in, 207–8

Postclassic period, 1, 3, 8, 9, 13, 14, 32, 81(nn4, 9), 137, 190, 196, 225, 236, *240*, 249, 279, 325; caching, 220, 227; cultural changes in, 35–36; directions and, 207–8; Mayapán, 185, 201–2; pilgrimages, 217, 328; rulership, 164–65; Tipu, 239, 243, 245–47, 259

Pottery. *See* Ceramics

Ppole, 5; clay censers from, 146, 154

Portals, 225, 228, 231–32

Prayer, 30

Preclassic period, 70, 81(n9), 217, 328; caches, 226, 234

Priests: and cofradía bundles, *310*; of Mayapán, 183, 195; oracular, 209–10

Prophecy, 39, 52, 59(n22), 76, 95, 217; in chronicles, 47–48; k'atun, 121–22

Puebla, 208, 210

Putanza, Juan de Penonias de, 282

Putun, 72, 196

Pu'uc (Puuc) region, 2, 8, 71, 113, 189; and Mayapán, 194–95, 203; Xiu in, 184–85

Pyramid of Flowers (Xochitecatl), 210

Pyramids: feathered serpent cult, *188*, 192; Mayapán, 199, 202; solar alignments, 12, *188*, 193

Pyrite mirrors, 226

Q'iijb'al, 310–12, 315(n17)

Q152. *See* Round Temple

Q162. *See* Castillo (Mayapán)

Q218 temple (Mayapán), 193

Quadripartism, 75, 81(n8), *106*, 107, *167*, 168, 171, 176, 227, 228, 319–20, 327; costumbre ritual, 312–13; Santiago Atitlán, 304–6

Quebrada, Cueva, 213

Quetzalcoatl (Kukulcan), 36, 52, 54, 99, 137, 183, 203(n4), 331; architecture for, 192–93, 196; and calendar system, 48, 58(n14); and earth monster, 99, 101; at Mayapán, 190, 204(n6); and migrations, 45–46

Quetzalcoatl cult. *See* Feathered serpent cult

Quexil, Lake, 242

Quezaltenango, conquest dance-play at, 287–88

Quincunx patterns, 227, *233*

Quintana Roo, 171, 176, 180, 206; double-headed eagle symbol in, 115–16

Quirigua, Stela C, 86–87, 89

Rabinal, 5; *Baile de los Moros y Cristianos* in, 286, 292

Rab'inal Achi, 281, 282, 283–84, 295

Radiocarbon dating, AMS, 112

Rain gods, 89, 106. *See also* Chaak

Rebellions. *See* Revolts

Rebirth: cycle of, 230, 315(n16), 323, 326; symbolism of, 228, *229*, 309

Reciprocation, agricultural cycles, 172–73

Re-creations: in *Chilam Balam of Chumayel*, 93–94; of worlds, 84, 93–99

Regeneration, 223, 236–37

Relación de Cabiche, 137

Relación de Citilcum, 137

Relación de las cosas de Yucatán (Landa), 102, 220

Relación de Mérida, 141

Relación de Motul, 42

Relación de Valladolid, 146

Religion, 178–79, 235; Christian impact on, 219–20; Colonial period, 128–30, 155, 156(n5); as concept, 22–25; Lacandon,

275–77; non-Western, 160–63; polytheistic, 137–39; private worship, 141–42, 156(n13); rulership and, 162–64; and science, 25–26

Renewal, 7; architectural, 328–29

Reptiles, 21. *See also* Crocodilians; Serpents

Residential architecture, organization of, 321–22

Resistance, 244, 262, 330–31; in highland Guatemala, 301, 308; pilgrimage and oracles as, 207, 214–16

Revival, revivalism, at Mayapán, 201–3

Revolts, 40; Caste War, 171, 216, 321; Xiu, 2, 183, 199–200, 202, 204(n9)

Rio Azul, 227

Rites of passage, 220–21

Ritual, 4, 6, 12, 45, 53, 54, 65, 74, 156–57(nn6, 24), 236, 240, 320, 329; calendar system, 13–15, 334; cave, 116–17; death, 219–20; effigy censer manufacture, 149–51; household, 321–22; identity and, 8–9; idol use in, 140–41, 156(n6); Lacandon, 265, 272–74, 275–77; liminality in, 220–21; may cycles and, 76–77; public vs. private, 129–30; rain, 135–36; in space and time, 75–77; women in, 208–9, 210

Ritual specialists, 153, 173, 178; calendar, 13–14

Roads, 319; time as, 326–27

Rock art, Lacandon, 272, 273, *274*

Roman Catholic Church. *See* Catholic Church, Catholicism

Round Temple (Mayapán), 12, *189*, 192, 193, 200, 329

Ruiz de Arze, Martin, 146

Rulers, rulership, 96, 162–63, 167, 183, 221, 235; genealogies, 7–8; Postclassic, 164–65; in Yucatán, 75–76

Sacalca, 146

Sac Bahlan, 266

Sakbe system, 212

Sacpuy, Lake, 242

Sacred, sacredness, 179; Classic Maya, 162–63; communication with, 174–75; defining, 161–62; landscape, 317–29, 332–34

Sacred Cenote (Chich'en Itzá), 184, 206, 210, 333

Sacrifices, 14, 31, 79, 153, 230, 280; blood, 106, 107, 150; of captives, 32–33; to idols, 151–52

Sahagún, Bernardino de, 107, 173

Saints, 308, 315(n21), 331; cofradías, 303, 313; worship and, 31, 156–57(n14)

Saints days, dance-plays, 284, 286, 287, 288

Salazar, Gonzalo de, 144

Salpetén, Lake, 241, 255

Salt, processing of, 35

San Bartolo, 217

Sanchez de Aguilar, Pedro, 154, 157(n20)

San Gervasio, *5*, 196; oracle shrine at, 212, *213*, 214

San José, 329

San Miguel (Cozumel), 151, 216

Santa Catalina, idol use, 140–41

Santa Cruz Cave, art in, 113, *114*, 116, 122, *123*, 126, *127*, 131

Santa Maria (Cozumel), 216

Santamaria, Juan de, 138–39

Santa Rita Corozal, *5*, 221, *229*, 236; caches from, 11, *224*, 226, 227, *235*; murals, 84, 86, 87–89, 208, 225

Santiago Atitlán, 9, 11, 115, 300, 301, 315(nn14, 21), 326, 327, 331; boundaries, 319, 324; bundles, 309–12, 315(n15); sacred landscape in, 303–7; textiles in, 308–9, 332

Schematic figures, Colonial period, 126–28

Science, as concept, 25–28

Screenfold books. *See* Codices

Sculptures, ancestors in, 181–82

Sea creatures, in planes of existence, 225, 226

Seashells, 226, 227, 228

Secular, and sacred, 163

Serpent-column temples (Mayapán), 193, 203–4(n5)

Serpents, 89; celestial, 225, 230; feathered/plumed, *187*, 192, 208, 209; iconography, 21, *232*; liminality of, 234–35; at Mayapán, 185, 190, 196, 203–4(n5)

Shamans: bundles used by, 309, 310; cosmic planes and, 324–25

Shark teeth, 226, 234

Short Count, 14, 71, 74

Shrines, 31, 174, 176, 195, 217; Lacandon, 272–74; sociopolitical role of, 209–10; at Tipu, 245, 246–47

Sis, Bartolome, 282

Sital, 135

Site planning, 11–12

Skeletal remains, 173–74

Sky, landscape of, 323–24

Skybands, 102; thrones, 96–98

Slave trade, 153

Snail-Inclusion Paste ware, 249, 251, 254, 255, 257, 258

Snakes. *See* Serpents

Social space, divisions of, 319–20

Solar alignments: pyramids, 12, *188*, 193; Santiago Atitlán, 304–5

Solstices, Footpath of the Dawn, Footpath of the Sun ceremonies, 304–5

Souls, 223; communication with, 177–78

Space, 326; divisions of, 319–20; geopolitical organization, 75–77; residential, 321–22; sacred, 332–33; time and, 66, 75; worldview and, 10–12

Spanish, 48, 79, 331; in chronicles, 51–52; destruction of idols, 142, 151–52; on idolatry, 36, 116–17, 135–37, 139–41; interrogation by, 168–69; on Maya imagery, 165–66; at Tipu, 242–43; worldviews of, 33–34; in Yucatán, 47, 244

Spanish Conquest, 3, 12, 86, 165–66, 215, 266, 313–14(n2); cultural responses to, 7, 9–10; dance-plays about, 287–88; imagery recorded during, 165–66

Speaking Cross, 216

Stelae, 194; creation stories on, 86–87, 89; k'atun cycles on, 77, 200; with planes of existence, 225, *231*

Stingray paddler, 87, 88

Stingray spines, 153, 226, 228

Structures, directionality of, 11–12

Su, 280, 281, 282–83, 291, 296

Sum Meja, Miguel, 292, 294

Sun, 75, 221, 223, 227, 230, 315(n17), 323, 324, 327; circular face depictions of, 120–21

Sun god, 84

Supernatural, 179; relationship with, 180–81

Symbolism, 11, 75, 87, 107, 220; adoption of, 20–21; of textiles, 308–9; Spanish, 330–31

Syncretism, 9–10, 167–68, 220, 221, 223, 279, 331; in dance-plays, 287–88

Talismen, 310–11, 315(n17)

Talking idols/statues, 168, 171

"Talking" objects, 166, 168

Talking crosses, 8, 171

Tambor, 281, 287, 293, 294, 295, 296

Tancah, 208

Tapia, Nicolas de, 154

Tases phase, 190, 192, 195, 198, 203(n3)

Tawisikal, 105

Tecpán, 13–14

Tecum Uman, 283

Tekanto, 80

Tekit, 139

Telchaquillo, 329

Temple XIX (Palenque), 98–99

Temple of the Fishermen (Mayapán), 98, 99; mural imagery in, *100,* 100–101, 196–98

Temple of the Five Niches (Mayapán), 196

Temple 1 (Tikal), *222*

Temples, 212, 320, 323, 326, 328, 332; Mayapán, 199, 202; serpent, 190, 193; at Tipu, 245, 246, 258

Templo Mayor, 198

Tenochtitlan, 330

Teotihuacán, 210

Terminal Classic period, 32, 71, 184, 189, 196, 200, 203(n4), 328; burial customs, 35–36; in Yucatán, 76, 193

Territory, control of, 244–45

Textiles, 308–9, 332

Teya, 140

Tezcatlipoca, 99, 100

365-day calendar (ja'ab), 67, 71, 79, 327

Three-stone earth, 176

Tihoo (TiHo), *5,* 41, 53, 77; Spanish in, 47, 48, 51

Tikal, 5, 200, 224, 225; jaguar way, 221, *222*; liminal symbology at, 233–34, 235

Tikal calendar, 69, 76, 81(n4)

Time, timekeeping, 61, 65, 80, 81(n6), 306, 326; celebrations and, 77–78; in chronicles, 46–51; cyclical, 24–25, 85–86; geopolitical organization, 75–77; landscape and, 326–27; linear vs. cyclical, 62–63; Maya concepts of, 13–15, 24–25, 66–71; music and, 327–28; and politics, 329–30; as representation, 63–64; and space, 75, 319–20

Tipu, 5, 239, 259–60(nn1, 2), 329; architecture at, 245–48; ceremonial groups, 246–47; ethnicity at, 244–45; Kowoj at, 257–58; occupation of, 243–44; pottery from, 8, 248–57; pottery manufacture, 240–41; Spanish and Kowoj at, 242–43

Titulo C'oyoi, 281, 296(n1); warrior dance in, 282–83, 284, 290

Titulo de Totonicapán, El, 309

Tixcuytun, art in, 124–26, 131

Tlaloc, 273, 274

Tlaltecuhtli, 199

Tlaxcala, 208, 210, 287

Tombs, 225, 227, 235, 322, 326; rebirth symbology in, 228, *229*, 323

Topoxté Island, 5, 196, 245, 249; ceramics, 252–54, 255, 257; Kowoj at, 241, 242, 244

Toral, Francisco, 44, 50, 136

Torture, by Spanish, 168–70

Trade, 158(n32); in idols, 153–54, 158(n31); Lacandon, 269–71; Mayapán and, 189, 196, 202

Traders, 9, 34, 189, 196

Transcendency, 221

Transculturation, 306–7, 314(nn5, 6)

Transformation, 325

Trees, 171, 176, 320, 321. *See also* World trees

Trials, idolatry, 135–36, 139–41

Tribute, warfare and, 32, 33

Trumpets, valveless, 280, 281, 282

Tukuches, 283

Tula, 48

Tulum, *5*, 198, 249, 324; murals at, 196, *208*, 225, 326

Tun, tunichob, 142–44, 157(n15)

Tun dances, 14, 280, 282–83

Tunnels, 322

Turtles, 223, 227, 233

Tutul Xiu, 40, 41, 57(n5)

260-day calendar (count of days; tzolk'in), 67, 77, 85, 327

Tzeltal, 265, 268

Tzimin Chaak, 168

Tzolk'in, 67, 77, 85, 327

Tz'utujil, 9, 115, 300, 310, 312

Uaxactún, ceramics from, *234*

Uc, Marcos, 140–41

Uman, Tecum, 283

Umbilicus of the World, 309, 312; Santiago Atitlán and, 303, 304

Underworld, 10–11, 87, 219, 223, 225, 277, 322–23, 324, 326; caves as entrances to, 221, 320; liminality in, 229–30; symbology of, 226, *234*; underwater iconography, 227–28

Universe, partitions of, 319. *See also* Cosmic planes

Upperworld, 10, 11, 26, 223; levels of, 224–25

Universe: establishment of, 86–87; organization of, 10–11

Usumacinta region, 71

Uxmal, 76, 184

Valencia, *Baile de los Moros y Cristianos,* 284–85

Valladolid, 51, 116; calendar system in, 48, 49–50, 58(n16)

Valladolid calendar, 79

Veneration: of nonhuman beings, 175–76; reciprocal, 172–73; vs. worship, 28–29, 30

Venus, 84, 89, 109(n4), 324; depictions of, 99–105, 110(nn16, 17, 18), 190

Venus cults, 210

Veracruz, 199, 204(nn6, 8)

Vieja, La, 216

Virgen de Santa Rita, La, 216

Vitzil Orange-Red ware, 249, 258

Warfare, 76; dances and music associated with, 283–87, 293; Mayapán, 40–41, 57(n5); and sacrifice, 31–33

Warrior dances: K'iche', 279, 282–84, *285*, 295; Spanish, 284–87

Warriors, 32, 104, 244

Water, 219, 320; pilgrimages and, 206, 212

Way, jaguars and, 221, *222*, 233

Wayeb', 67, 85, 227, 306

West Mexico, and Lamanai, 34–35

Whistles. *See* Flutes

Wind, 173; caves and, 115–16

Wind/wind-like persons (pixano'ob), 173–74, 181

Winik. *See* Lacandon

Wixárika-Huichol, 174, 176, 179

Women: in ceremonial contexts, 208–9; as oracles, 210–12; pilgrimages of, 214, 217

World(s), 180, 319, 321; destruction and re-creation of, 84, 93–99, 104, 108

World trees, 75, 231–32, 321; dedications to, 94, 95; Maximón as, *302*; Santiago Atitlán as, 303–4, 326

Worldviews: as concept, 21–22; indigenous frameworks, 178–82; strategic values of, 36–37

Worship: concept of, 28–31; private, 141–42

Wuk Ha' Nal, 89

Xajil family, 282

Xcaret Cave Temple, *215*

Xelaju, battle at, 283

Xel-ha, 5

Xibalba (Xib'alb'a). *See* Underworld

Xipe Totec, 199

Xiu (Xiw), 2, 8, 12, 74, 330; b'ak'tun celebration of, 78–79; calendar system, 13, 81(n13); and Cocom family, 183–84, 204(n7); in Mayapán, 41, 76–77, 194–95, 199–200, 202, 204(n9), 241; Puuc region, 184–85

Xiu, Gaspar Antonio, 165, 204(n9)

Xiu Coat of Arms, 120, 131

Xiu Family Tree, 131, 132

Xiuhmolpilli, 67

Xnuc, La, 216

Xochitecatl, 210

Yalahau region, 206

Yaxcaba, 142

Yaxchilán, 5, 71, 224, 272, 324, 328

Yaxkukul, 5; chronicle from, 42, 43–44, 50, 57(n7)

Yax Pasaj, 7

Year-bearers, 68, 85; in Dresden codex, 94–95, 95, 108

Years, bundles of, 67–68

Yucatán, 1–2, 36, 40, *41,* 47, 74, 189, 196, 212, 216, 266, 267, 291; calendrical systems in, 77–80; cave art in, 111–12, *114,* 116, *118*; circular faces in, *119,* 330; geopolitical organization, 75–76, 330; horse and rider motif, 122–24; idol trade in, 153–54; idol use in, 135–55; migrations in, 45–46; pilgrimages in, 206, 207–8

Yukatek (Yucatec) Maya, 7–8, 87, 267, 327; agricultural cycles, 172–73; communicating objects, 176, *177*; histories, 84, 88; on nonhuman beings, 173–74, 179–80; planes of existence for, 224–25; sacred in, 161–62; social space, 319–20; underworld concepts, 322–23

Zacpetén, 5, 196, *233,* 244, 249, 328–29; architecture, 242, 245, 321; ceramics, 252, 254, 255, 257, 258

Zama, 154

Zapotecs, 71; pilgrimages, 211–12, 217

Zinacanteco, 176–77